AMERICAN CONSTITUTIONAL LAW

THE SUPREME COURT IN AMERICAN HISTORY—
CIVIL RIGHTS AND LIBERTIES

Volume 2

RONALD D. ROTUNDA

DOY AND DEE HENLEY CHAIR
AND DISTINGUISHED PROFESSOR OF JURISPRUDENCE
CHAPMAN UNIVERSITY
DALE E. FOWLER SCHOOL OF LAW

WEST
ACADEMIC
PUBLISHING

© 2016 LEG, Inc. d/b/a West Academic
    444 Cedar Street, Suite 700
    St. Paul, MN 55101
    1-877-888-1330

West, West Academic Publishing, and West Academic are trademarks of West Publishing Corporation, used under license.

Printed in the United States of America

ISBN: 978-1-63460-779-7

To Nicholas & Penelope

Preface

These two volumes are a compact pedagogical tool to introduce students to the role of the U.S. Supreme Court in American history. I have organized the chapters both historically and topically, focusing on the issues that are of basic historical significance as well as those areas of contemporary interest that are likely to be increasingly important in the years ahead.[1]

The high Court's rulings both reflect and mold the underlying historical, political, economic, and legal principles of American constitutional law. The U.S. Supreme Court is an unusual political institution but it is more than a political actor: it also is a court. The judges do not simply *announce* what is the law from time to time; they are supposed to (and normally do) develop the law from the precedent that earlier courts gave them.

When we see the Court in historical context, we better understand how we got to where we are now and where we are likely to go. At times, the Court has tried to veer too far from the direction of the country by writing opinions that became self-inflicted wounds. One such opinion is *Dred Scott v. Sandford*, 60 U.S. (19 How.) 393 (1857), holding that blacks, even freed black slaves, could not become citizens. Another is *Lochner v. New York*, 198 U.S. 45 (1905), holding that it was unconstitutional for New York to impose a maximum workweek of 60 hours. Whether the more recent decisions dealing with sexual autonomy and gay marriage will be more like *Lochner* or more like *Brown v. Board of Education*, 347 U.S. 483 (1954), which prohibited state enforced racial discrimination in schools, is a question the future will answer.

Unless we *see* the development of the law in historical context, we will not understand both the power of the Court has acquired and the limitations on that power. That is much more important than simply acquiring conclusory knowledge of intricate and changing rules. Only about half of what a student learns in school today will be law in a decade or so, and it is difficult now to predict which half.[2]

---

[1] Those looking for a research (as opposed to a teaching) tool and for commentary on the Constitution, see [pardon the shameless self-promotion] RONALD D. ROTUNDA & JOHN E. NOWAK, TREATISE ON CONSTITUTIONAL LAW: SUBSTANCE AND PROCEDURE (5th Ed., Westlaw Thomson Reuters 2012-2013)(with annual pocket parts)(6 volumes). See also, JOHN E. NOWAK & RONALD D. ROTUNDA, CONSTITUTIONAL LAW (West Academic, West Hornbook Series, 8th ed. 2010), and RONALD D. ROTUNDA & JOHN E. NOWAK, PRINCIPLES OF CONSTITUTIONAL LAW (West Academic, Concise Hornbook Series, 5th ed. 2016).

[2] Some imagine the law as a big book of rules, which the student must learn. There is the story of the first year student visiting his grandmother. "So, you've been studying law for two weeks. How many laws have

Consequently, understanding the basic principles and appreciating them in their historical context is of greater significance. While doing that, students will learn how the Supreme Court has evolved over the last two centuries to become the most powerful Court the world has ever known. Many nations throughout the world (particularly those newly formed with the breakup of the Soviet Union) now seek to emulate the U.S. Supreme Court, in order to protect the rights of citizens.

I seek to keep these two volumes of manageable size without sacrificing thoroughness, for it is better to know a few things well than to know many things superficially.[3] It is also important to understand the Supreme Court by reading the opinions of the Court rather than reading what the editor (in this case, me) thinks about those opinions. The Court is the most public institution of the three branches of Government. Everything that goes into a decision (the briefs and motions), the reasons for the decision (the opinion) and the result (the holding) are public. We can properly criticize the Court when its reasons are unpersuasive (or perhaps risible).

The President can always argue that his or her decisions (particularly in the area of foreign policy) rely on information that the Government cannot reveal. The Court, in contrast, cannot respond by saying, "Trust me, I know things I cannot reveal to you."

Congresspersons, in justifying their votes, often focus on the need to compromise, what they sometimes call horse-trading. The Justices do not do that. There is no evidence that a Justice will vote one way in an abortion case on the promise that another Justice will change his vote in a free speech case. Justices don't horse trade.[4]

None of that is to suggest that the Court's logic has the rigor of Euclidian Geometry. The Justices do not shed their personalities and background when the

---

you learned?" See, Arthur Sutherland, *Prologue to an Introduction* vii, vii, in AN INTRODUCTION TO LAW: SELECTED ESSAYS REPRINTED FROM THE HARVARD LAW REVIEW (1965).

   [3]   Thus, this book often omits secondary authority cited within an excerpted case. Also deleted are many internal case and statute citations within a case. Footnotes within cases are numbered as the original. There is no special indication when footnotes, case law, and other authority are deleted within a case.

   [4]   The justices confirm the historical evidence. E.g., Candid Camera with Supreme Court Justices [Justice Sandra Day O'Connor, Antonin Scalia and Stephen Breyer], NBC NEWS, April 22, 2005, ("In response to questions, the justices said they never horse-trade for votes, although at times they might seek a unanimous vote if possible in a particularly controversial case."), http://www.nbcnews.com/id/7598231/ns/politics/t/candid-camera-supreme-court-justices/#.V3wwy3obhQ4 (7/5/2016).

Adam Liptak, Compromise at the Supreme Court Veils Its Rifts, New York Times, July 1, 2014, http://www.nytimes.com/2014/07/02/us/supreme-court-term-marked-by-unanimous-decisions.html?_r=0 ("Chief Justice Roberts, who completed his ninth term, does not get his way by backslapping or horse-trading, but by writing savvy opinions, making strategic opinion assignments to the other justices and sometimes working to protect the Supreme Court from accusations that it is a political institution.")(7/5/2016).

Senate confirms them. Yet, they also serve for life, with no diminution in salary, so they are not like ordinary politicians. The issues that confront them when the President first nominated them may not be the important issues a decade or more in the future. In the course of examining the Court's work, we will see how the Justices change and how later Courts reject or follow in the paths that the earlier Justices created.

I am grateful for all the assistance from my colleagues, particularly John E. Nowak, the David C. Baum Professor Emeritus, University of Illinois College of Law, and Ms. Maria Sanchez, my faculty assistant at Chapman University, Fowler School of Law. I am particularly grateful to the excellent editors at West Academic —Greg Olson, Cathy Lundeen and Heather Sieve.

Ronald D. Rotunda

Orange, CA
July 2016

Table of Contents

Table of Cases

AMERICAN CONSTITUTIONAL LAW

THE SUPREME COURT IN AMERICAN HISTORY—
CIVIL RIGHTS AND LIBERTIES

Volume 2

CHAPTER 1

The Development of Judicial Review

1.1 INTRODUCTION

Our Constitution of 1787 is the oldest in the world, by far. The next oldest date from the 19th Century—Norway's, from 1815; Luxembourg, 1868; the Argentina's (written in 1853, but the current version is the reformed text of 1994). All the other constitutions date from the 20th or 21st Centuries.

Economists often talk about short-range and long-range planning. Short range typically means anytime within the next six months. Any effort to look at the future more than six months away is long-range planning. Measured by that standard, the Framers of the Constitution were far sighted indeed. After more than 220 years, our Constitution is still alive and well.

Many of the Framers intended that their written Constitution would endure for ages. Near the end of the Constitutional Convention, James Madison objected to a requirement that there would be one representative for every thirty thousand inhabitants. "The future increase of population if the Union should be permanent will render the number of representatives excessive." Nathaniel Gorham, a delegate from Massachusetts, replied, "It is not to be supposed that the government will last so long as to produce this effect. Can it be supposed that this vast country, including the western territory, will, one hundred and fifty years hence, remain one nation?" Madison apparently thought so. He and Sherman moved to insert the words "shall not exceed" before the words "one for every thirty thousand."[5] If the Constitution had required one representative for every 30,000 people, the House would now have about 1,000 representatives.

---

[5]   5 Debates on the Adoption of the Federal Constitution in the Convention Held at Philadelphia in 1787, at p. 392 (J. Elliott ed. 1845). The final language is at, U.S. Constitution, Art. I, § 2, clause 3.

Our Constitution has proven to be an important safeguard of human rights, because of the development of a particularly powerful legal and political body, the U.S. Supreme Court, which is now the most powerful court the world has ever known. As we shall see, the Supreme Court can override the will of the majority expressed in an act of Congress.[6] Through its apportionment decisions requiring one person, one vote, it can require the redistribution of voting power in every state of the Union and in every subdivision[7] It can forbid, or approve, racial[8] or political[5] gerrymandering. It can create a right of travel or right to abortion, and refuse to tell us where it comes from.[9] In the Watergate controversy, it forcefully reminded the President that, in this nation, all persons, even the President, are subject to the rule of law.[10]

We might more precisely say that the President is subject to the rule of the Supreme Court. As Charles Evans Hughes (who was to become Chief Justice in 1930) warned in 1907, "We are under a Constitution, but the Constitution is what the judges say it is."[11] On the other hand, Charles Warren, the great historian of the Supreme Court countered, "However the Court may interpret the provisions of the Constitution, it is still the Constitution which is the law and not the decision of the Court."[12] Or as federal district judge Charles Wyzanski, Jr. noted, "neither have I ever accepted the notion that under our system of Constitutional Law the Supreme Court is THE LAST WORD."[13]

---

[6]   *Marbury v. Madison*, 5 U.S. (1 Cranch) 137, 180, 2 L.Ed. 60 (1803) (laws repugnant to Constitution are void).

[7]   See *Hadley v. Junior College Dist.*, 397 U.S. 50, 54–56, 90 S.Ct. 791, 794–95, 25 L.Ed.2d 45 (1970) (whenever officials elected by popular vote—whether their duties are called legislative or administrative—one person, one vote applies); *Reynolds v. Sims*, 377 U.S. 533, 568, 84 S.Ct. 1362, 1385, 12 L.Ed.2d 506 (1964) (one person, one vote mandated), rehearing denied 379 U.S. 870, 85 S.Ct. 12, 13 L.Ed.2d 76 (1964).

[8]   *Gomillion v. Lightfoot*, 364 U.S. 339, 341–42, 81 S.Ct. 125, 127–28, 5 L.Ed.2d 110 (1960) (racial gerrymandering against blacks held to be unconstitutional); *United Jewish Organizations of Williamsburgh, Inc. v. Carey*, 430 U.S. 144, 155–65, 97 S.Ct. 996, 1005–09, 51 L.Ed.2d 229 (1977) (plurality opinion upholding racial gerrymandering engaged in pursuant to federal statute in order to aid black voters).

[9]   *Roe v. Wade*, 410 U.S. 113, 153, 93 S.Ct. 705, 727, 35 L.Ed.2d 147 (1973) (whether right to privacy founded in "Fourteenth Amendment's concept of personal liberty" or "Ninth Amendment's reservation of rights to the people" not important), rehearing denied 410 U.S. 959, 93 S.Ct. 1409, 35 L.Ed.2d 694 (1973); *Shapiro v. Thompson*, 394 U.S. 618, 630, 89 S.Ct. 1322, 1329, 22 L.Ed.2d 600 (1969) ("We have no occasion to ascribe the source of this right to travel interstate to a particular constitutional provision").

[10]   *United States v. Nixon*, 418 U.S. 683, 703–07, 94 S.Ct. 3090, 3105–07, 41 L.Ed.2d 1039 (1974) (no absolute presidential privilege to confidential communications).

[11]   Hughes, Speech before Elmira Chamber of Commerce, quoted in William VanAlstyne, *A Critical Guide to Marbury v. Madison*, 1969 Duke L.J. 1, 2, n. 4 (1969).

[12]   Charles Warren, 3 The Supreme Court In United States History, pp. 470–71 (Little Brown & Co. 1922).

[13]   Letter from Judge Wyzanski to Judge (now Justice) Breyer, quoted in Breyer, In Memoriam: Charles E. Wyzanski, Jr., 100 Harvard L.Rev. 707, 709 (1987).

To be sure, our written Constitution is an enduring document, and our Supreme Court is an important institution, vital to our nation's history. Yet, it was not always so. In order to achieve a better understanding of the role of the Supreme Court today and in the future, we should look at the origins of our Constitution and the origins of Judicial Review.

1.2 THE ARTICLES OF CONFEDERATION

1.2.1 Creating the Articles of Confederation

When delegates from twelve of the colonies (Georgia did not participate) met in Philadelphia in the fall of 1774, they adopted the Declaration and Resolves of the First Continental Congress. Congress addressed the Declaration of Independence to the Crown because the colonists denied that Parliament—a body in which they were not represented—had any authority to legislate over their internal affairs. For example, the fourth Resolve of 1774 stated:

> [T]he foundation of English liberty, and of all free government, is a right in the people to participate in their legislative council: and as the English colonists are not represented, and from their local and other circumstances, cannot properly be represented in the British parliament, they are entitled to a free and exclusive power of legislation in their several provincial legislatures, where their right of representation can alone be preserved, in all cases of taxation and internal policy, subject only to the negative of their sovereign.[14]

This Declaration and Resolves portended much of the Declaration of Independence, as well as the U.S. Constitution and the Bill of Rights. It proclaimed the right "to life, liberty, and property;" the "inestimable privilege of [accused persons] being tried by their peers of the vicinage; . . . a constitutional trial by jury of the vicinage;" and "a right peaceably to assemble, consider of their grievances, and petition the king." It objected to judges who "have been made dependent on the crown alone for their salaries, and [to] standing armies kept in times of peace. . . ."[15]

Shortly thereafter, the Revolution began in Massachusetts with the Battles of Lexington and Concord. The Second Continental Congress—the convention of

---

[14] Declaration and Resolves of The First Continental Congress, Oct. 14, 1774, reprinted in Documents Illustrative of The Formation of the Union of the American States, H.R.Doc. No. 398, 69th Cong., 1st Sess. 1, 3 (1927).

[15] H.R.Doc. No. 398, 69th Cong., 1st Sess. 2 to 3 (1927).

delegates from the Thirteen Colonies that started meeting in the summer of 1775, in Philadelphia—became a *de facto* government out of necessity and acquiescence. Georgia joined the twelve, and the Continental Congress became the "Thirteen United Colonies." This Second Continental Congress urged the other colonies to come to the defense of Massachusetts. It also issued bills of credit, began to organize a military force, and appointed George Washington as Commander in Chief of the Army.

On June 7, 1776, Richard Henry Lee proposed that the Continental Congress issue a Declaration of Independence.[16] On July 2, the Continental Congress passed that resolution—an event that John Adams incorrectly predicted would "be celebrated by succeeding generations as the great anniversary festival."[17] Two days later the Continental Congress adopted the Declaration of Independence, and three days after that, it officially broke the ties with Great Britain. Yet it was not until over two years later, on July 9, 1778, that the Articles of Confederation came into being.[18] Another three years would pass before all thirteen of the ex-colonies ratified the new Articles of Confederation.[18]

It is often said that the city is united when the enemy is at the gates. So it was that the pressures of the Revolutionary War created a superficial union that hid the many differences among the new states. Indeed, after the successful conclusion of the War, some observers expected that within a few years the ex-colonies would seek reunification with Great Britain. There was also serious talk of dividing the union into two, three, or more confederacies. After the Revolutionary War, the "individual state governments were proving fairly satisfactory, but the union was not."[19]

1.2.2   Life Under the Articles of Confederation

Like the Greek City States, the thirteen American colonies, during and after the Revolutionary War, had several important common purposes, many local differences and no central unifying force. Under the Articles of Confederation of 1777, the state legislatures decided how to appoint their delegates to the Congress. No less than two and no more than seven delegates represented each state, which had only one vote, regardless of population. The states could recall and replace

---

[16] Resolution Introduced in the Continental Congress by Richard Henry Lee (Va.) Proposing a Declaration of Independence, June 7, 1776, reprinted in Documents Illustrative Of The Formation of the Union of the American States, H.R.Doc. No. 398, 69th Cong., 1st Sess. 21 (1927).

[17] The Works of John Adams, vol. 2, pp. 507–09 (Charles Francis Adams ed. 1850).

[18] Articles of Confederation art. XIII, cl. 3 (1778).

[19] Max Farrand, The Framing of the Constitution of the United States 1 (1913).

one or more of their representatives at any time, just like a foreign nation cold recall its ambassador. With this arrangement, the representatives were responsive to the states *qua* states, and not to the persons within each state or to the nation as a whole, much like the United Nations ambassadors today.

The central government at that time could not exercise many essential powers (*e.g.*, to engage in a war, enter into a treaty, coin money, borrow or appropriate money, or appoint a commander in chief) unless nine of the thirteen states agreed. Regarding commercial matters, the central government had even less power. The Articles of Confederation specifically prohibited the central government from making any treaty of commerce "whereby the legislative powers of the respective states would be restrained from imposing such imports and duties on foreigners, as their own people are subjected to, or from prohibiting the exportation or importation of any species of goods or commodities whatsoever."[20] Like the United Nations, Congress also had no power of direct taxation. Congress had to rely on the individual states to levy taxes in proportion to the value of all the land within their borders.

The states' rivalries caused them to enact tariffs, and other economic barriers that Balkanized the country and obstructed commerce. The seaport states had the advantage of tariff revenues while the landlocked states had to rely on regressive property taxes and poll taxes. James Madison compared New Jersey, situated between the ports of Philadelphia and New York, "to a cask tapped at both ends," and North Carolina, placed between Virginia and South Carolina, he compared "to a patient bleeding at both arms."[21] When the inhabitants of the landlocked states purchased goods imported from abroad, they understood that they were really financing the needs of the seaport states.

Later, Justice Cardozo acknowledged in *Baldwin v. G.A.F. Seelig, Inc.* (1935),[22] one of the major incentives for a more unified nation was the need to eliminate "the mutual jealousies and aggressions of the States, taking form in customs barriers and other economic retaliation." Two centuries later, similar motivations led to the European Union. The trade wars and other mutual jealousies led the United States to establish an economic and political union. Unlike the European

---

[20]   Articles of Confederation art. IX, at cl. 6.

[21]   5 Debates on The Adoption of the Federal Constitution in the Convention Held at Philadelphia in 1787, at p. 112 (J. Elliott ed. 1845)(quoting James Madison).

[22]   294 U.S. 511, 522 (1935), citing inter alia, 2 Farrand, Records of the Federal Convention, at 308; 3 Farrand, id., at 478, 547, 548; The Federalist, No. 42.

Union, the move to a federal political union occurred at the same time as the economic union.

In foreign relations, states purported to exercise a power over foreign affairs that could be inconsistent with the central government's purpose. South Carolina's constitution empowered its government "to make war, conclude a peace, enter into treaties, lay embargoes, and provide an army and navy." Other states implicitly or explicitly purported to exercise one or more powers over foreign affairs. The eloquent Patrick Henry, who proclaimed he was not a Virginia but an American, competed with the United States in 1778, when he negotiated with Spain in 1778 for a loan and offered permission to the erect a fort on Virginia's border.[23] In short, Congress, under the Articles of Confederation, was only "a political gelding and its resolves were puissant only as the states might make them so."[24]

The Constitutional Convention was the response to these trade wars, jealousies, and discontent.

1.3 THE CONSTITUTIONAL CONVENTION OF 1787

1.3.1   Convening the Convention

In 1785, Virginia and Maryland each appointed several commissioners to settle the dispute and "great inconveniences" regarding the navigation and jurisdiction of the Chesapeake Bay, and the Potomac and Pocomoke Rivers. The meeting was successful and the delegates called for a broader meeting inviting the "states of the Union" to discuss trade policies and "to consider how far a uniform system in their commercial regulations may be necessary to their common interest." On January 21, 1786, Congress passed a Resolution calling for such a meeting in September, but it was a disappointment. Only five states sent delegates. Those delegates suggested a new meeting in May 1787, in Philadelphia. Congress passed a Resolution on February 21, 1878, calling for a meeting—

> for the *sole and express purpose of revising* the Articles of Confederation and reporting to Congress and the several legislatures such alterations . . . as shall, when agreed to in Congress and confirmed by the States render

---

[23] C.H. Van Tyne, Sovereignty in the American Revolution: An Historical Study, 12 Am. Historical Rev. 529, 540 (Oct.-July, 1906–07).

[24] Julius Goebel, Jr., The Oliver Wendell Holmes Devise History of the Supreme Court of the United States: Antecedents and Beginnings to 1801, Volume 1, p. 197 (P. Freund, ed., 1971).

the Federal Constitution adequate to the exigencies of Government and the preservation of the Union.[25]

As we shall see, the Framers went well beyond that Resolution, for their proposal called for an entirely new Constitution, and that Constitution provided, in Article VI, that it would come into effect when nine states ratified. The Articles required unanimity for any revisions.[26]

When the delegates from the states met in Philadelphia in the hot summer of 1787, many agreed that the Articles of Confederation were wanting, but they agreed on little else. As if to symbolize their disagreements, only twelve of the thirteen ex-colonies sent delegates to Philadelphia, and several of the twelve who did show up arrived late. New Hampshire's delegates did not arrive until July, weeks after the Constitutional Convention had started.

Rhode Island never did send delegates. Its House of Assembly rejected the call to the Convention. Various merchants and leaders in the state wrote the Constitutional Convention; chastised their state legislature as "composed of a licentious number of men, destitute of education, and many of them void of principle;" and promised the Constitutional Convention that they would use their influence to persuade Rhode Island to go along with the results.[27] Perhaps it was best that Rhode Island never participated. The Convention had a contagious excitement about it. The delegates that Rhode Island might have sent—those licentious men void of principle—could have impeded the Convention, just as slate in coal impedes combustion.

On May 25, 1787, when representatives of a majority of the states finally arrived, eleven days behind schedule, the delegates began their deliberations. The task of the Convention was to forge a nation out of these twelve (or thirteen) states. These states were not really "nations" but artificial constructs. They did not have the long tradition of nationhood that countries like England, France, or Spain had. In fact, of all the states in the Union even today, only one has no straight lines for any of its borders—Hawaii, a chain of islands. The task of the founding fathers was to create a nation out of states. That is a difficult task, to be sure, but not as difficult as making a nation out of separate nations.

---

[25] Report of Proceedings in Congress, February 21, 1787, reprinted in Documents Illustrative of The Formation of the Union of the American States, H.R.Doc. No. 398, 69th Cong., 1st Sess. 46 (emphasis added).

[26] Articles of Confederation art. XIII, cl. 1 (1778).

[27] 5 Debates on the Adoption of the Federal Constitution in the Convention Held at Philadelphia in 1787, at pp. 577–78 (J. Elliott ed. 1845) (reprinting letters from General John Varnum of Rhode Island to Constitutional Convention, and from various "merchants, tradesmen, and others, of this place, deeply affected with the evils of the present unhappy times").

Nonetheless, these artificial constructs had enough differences, real or imagined, to make the task of nation-building more than a little difficult. Thomas Jefferson, for example, in his library in 1783, classified the laws of the American states other than Virginia as "Foreign Laws."[28] The original thirteen states also thought of themselves as independent sovereigns. Their state constitutions so provided. It was not until after the Civil War that the typical American citizen referred to "the United States." Before that, people said, "these United States." It took nearly a century and a bloody war before the average citizen thought that the "United States" was a singular, rather than a plural, noun. Our use of language is revealing.

The delegates to the Constitutional Convention began their efforts by promptly electing George Washington as their presiding officer. They also agreed that each state should have one vote in the proceeding, with seven states constituting a quorum, and with only a simple majority needed to decide all issues. They also agreed to conduct all deliberations in secret, so the delegates could speak in complete candor. They also agreed not to call the yeas and nays by delegate name; they would only record votes by states.

1.3.2   The Virginia Plan

On May 29, only four days after the Convention began, Virginia proposed dramatic changes to the Articles. In several important aspects the Virginia Plan was the closest to the final draft. Virginia proposed that, unlike the Articles, there should be two Houses of Congress, not one. Under the Virginia Plan the people of the several states would choose the lower House, and the members of that House would choose the upper House. In a manner analogous to the English Parliament, Congress would elect a President. This plan would create a Judicial Council of Revision (composed of the Executive and members of the Judiciary) to review the constitutionality of both state and federal laws.

The Virginia Plan would establish three branches of government. The Articles of Confederation vested all the power that existed in a unicameral Congress. The Virginia Plan would give the central Government much more power, but then divide it into three branches in order to check the possible abuse of power.

Ben Franklin urged a unicameral legislature, but the delegates agreed that to a bicameral legislature. The small states were cautious of the Virginia Plan. They

---

[28]   Julius Goebel, Jr., The Oliver Wendell Holmes Devise History of the Supreme Court of the United States: Antecedents and Beginnings To 1801, vol. 1, at p. xv (1971).

objected, among other things, that the Virginia Plan proposed that election to both Houses of the national legislature be in proportion to the number of free inhabitants. That favored big states like Virginia.

1.3.3   The New Jersey Plan

In opposition to the Virginia Plan was the New Jersey Plan. It was very similar to the Articles. It proposed relatively minor, amendments and gave each state, regardless of size, one vote in the national legislature. A majority of the delegates rejected the New Jersey Plan. The small states were not happy.[29]

1.3.4   The Hamiltonian/New York Plan

The young and brilliant New York attorney Alexander Hamilton frequently absented himself from the Constitutional Convention. For the most part, he played no significant role there, except for two major incidences. First, near the end of the debate he delivered an impassioned plea for unanimous ratification of the Constitution. Second, near the beginning, he strongly opposed the New Jersey Plan. In his speech against that proposal, he spoke strongly in favor of the British system, which he called "the best in the world."

Hamilton proposed what some call the New York Plan, but we really should call it the Hamilton Plan, because his own co-delegates from New York did not embrace it. It was somewhat like the Virginia Plan but much more centralized. The people would not elect the Executive or Senators directly; rather they would elect electors who would elect these officials who would serve for life during good behavior. The Executive would have a veto power that Congress could not override. The Executive would appoint the governors of each of the states.

The states disagreed about the merits of the Virginia Plan and the New Jersey Plan. Hamilton's proposal probably helped the Virginia Plan, because he made it seem less radical. In addition, modifications of the Virginia Plan muted some major opposition. For example, in a dramatic compromise, the delegates decided that only the lower house should be based on population. This change limited the opposition of the smaller states.[30]

---

[29]   Max Farrand, The Framing of the Constitution 84–91 (1913).

[30]   Max Farrand, The Framing of the Constitution, pp. 74–76, 84, 89, 91, 96–97, 105 (1913) (this "Great Compromise" lessened the concerns of smaller states).

1.3.5   Small State-Large State Compromises

Some of the small states threatened to withdraw from the Convention notwithstanding earlier compromises. In July, the Convention sent the entire matter a Committee of Eleven to work on a compromise. One member from each state had a representative. Recall that Rhode Island did not attend the Convention and the New Hampshire delegation did not even arrive until the last week in July. The small states did not walk out, a spirit of compromise prevailed, and the Convention produced a Constitution. Let us focus on a few of the important compromises.

The delegates agreed that the people directly would elect the Representatives to the lower House, with representation in proportion to population. In the Senate, two Senators would represent each state, regardless of the state's population. The legislature in each state would elect their Senators, rather than by the people directly. In other words, the people directly elect the members of one House, with representation in proportion to the population. In the other House, the state legislatures would choose their Senators directly, with two Senators for each state, regardless of size. No bill could become a law unless a majority of both Houses (representing the people, and the states) agreed.

Another feature, also intended to mollify the interests of the smaller states, was that the people would vote for electors and those electors would choose the President. If no one received a majority of the electoral votes, then the House of Representatives would choose the President, but in this election, each state, regardless of size, would receive only one vote. This procedure, which the delegates thought (erroneously) would be a frequent occurrence, was another nod in the direction of the smaller states.[31]

1.3.6   Northern and Southern Compromises

The South was worried that the North would seek to put a tariff on the South's chief export, cotton. Thus, the Constitution, Art. I, § 9. Clause 5, forbids Congress from laying any duty or tax on articles exported from any state. But, as a nod to the North, a simple majority could enact a tariff on imports.

Then there was that peculiar institution, slavery. The issue of slavery embarrassed the Framers, as reflected by the fact that nowhere in the original text

---

[31] 5 Debates on the Adoption of the Federal Constitution in the Convention Held at Philadelphia in 1787, at pp. 519–20 (J. Elliott ed. 1845).

of the Constitution is the word "slavery" even mentioned.[32] One big question involved the importation of new slaves. The delegations from North and South Carolina and Georgia demanded that their right to import new slaves must be "untouched." Others believed in free trade, even as to slaves, and objected to any central regulation of any imports. Still others believed that slavery was a great moral evil.

The result, expressed in Section 9 of Article I, is what Gouverneur Morris of Pennsylvania called "a bargain among the Northern and Southern States."[33] This bargain prevented Congress from prohibiting the importation of slaves before the year 1808, but allowed it to impose a nonexcessive duty. The language used is quaint:

> The Migration or Importation of Such Persons as any of the States now existing shall think proper to admit, shall not be prohibited by the Congress prior to the Year one thousand eight hundred and eight, but a Tax or duty may be imposed on such Importation, not exceeding ten dollars for each Person.[34]

Charles Pinckney of South Carolina defended this clause when addressing his state legislature. It was necessary, he said, so that delegates from the eastern states would be able to show their people that there was some possibility of restraining new importation after 1808. In return, the eastern delegates would endeavor "to restrain the religious and political prejudices of our people on this subject." Under all the circumstances, concluded Pinckney, "We have made the best terms for the security of this species of property it was in our power to make." "We would have made it better if we could; but on the whole, I do not think them bad."[35] The compromise worked. The Framers apparently thought it better that the Constitution be conceived in original sin than not conceived at all.

Recall that the Virginia Plan provided that representation in the national legislature should be in proportion to the number of "free inhabitants." Virginia was a slave state. Other slave states were less happy with this proposal. They wanted to count all of their slaves in their population base for purposes of determining the number of representatives they should have. The slaves could not

---

[32] Art. I, § 2, clause 2 ("those bound for service"); § 9, clause 1 ("Such Persons").

[33] 5 Debates on the Adoption of the Federal Constitution in the Convention Held at Philadelphia in 1787, at p. 460 (J. Elliott ed. 1845). After this important compromise, the delegates agreed fugitive slave clause unanimously without debate. Max Farrand, The Framing of the Constitution 152 (1913).

[34] U.S. Const. art. I, cl. 1, § 9.

[35] Quoted in Max Farrand, The Framing of the Constitution 151 (1913).

vote, of course, but counting them would boost the number of representatives to which the slave states would be entitled in the House of Representatives.

Some people now assert, mistakenly, that the slave states thought that a black slave was worth less than a white man, and that is why the Constitution valued a slave as only three-fifths of a free man. That story is simply incorrect. It was the free states that did not want to count the slaves at all. Elbridge Gerry of Massachusetts, for example, argued, "property [is] not the rule of representation. Why, then, should the blacks, who were property in the south, be, in the rule of representation, more than the cattle and horses of the north?"[36]

The important moral compromise[37] was that, for purposes of representation, five slaves are counted as if they were three free persons. In the uncomfortable language of Article I, which refused to mention the word "slave," the Constitution says, "Representatives . . . shall be apportioned among the several States . . . by adding to the whole Number of free Persons . . . three-fifths of all other persons."

1.3.7   Judicial Review and the Council of Revision

Recall that the Virginia Plan proposed a "Council of Revision," composed of the Executive and members of the Judiciary, to review the constitutionality of both state and federal laws. The final document did not include that because many delegates objected to joining the Executive and Judiciary together in the exercise of a veto power. They did not like joining together executive and judicial powers. Others argued that under the proposed Constitution the Judiciary already would have an opportunity to pass on the constitutionality of state or federal laws.[38]

The belief that the Framers never contemplated any judicial review—that the concept sprang from Chief Justice Marshall's forehead as Pallas Athena sprang from the forehead of Zeus—is simply wrong. Indeed, Hamilton's Federalist Paper No. 78 later specifically explained that the judiciary must regard the Constitution as "fundamental law" and prefer it to any statute if "there should happen to be an irreconcilable variance between the two. . . ." The Framers could not envision how powerful the Court would become after two centuries, but their secret

---

[36]   5 Debates on the Adoption of the Federal Constitution in the Convention Held at Philadelphia in 1787, at p. 181 (J. Elliott ed. 1845).

[37]   Professor Max Farrand argues that the three-fifths rule was "certainly not" one of "the important compromises of the convention," and that slavery was not the important "moral question" that it was later to become. Max Farrand, The Framing of the Constitution of the United States, pp. 107–08 (1913). However, he admits that the delegates considered the compromise regarding the importation of slaves both a moral question and an important compromise. Farrand, pp. 149–51. He also admits that Madison, the contemporary observer, regarded the three-fifths rule as a significant compromise between North and South. Farrand, pp. 110–11.

[38]   Max Farrand, The Framing of the Constitution 156–57 (1913).

debates (as well as the public debates reflected in *The Federalist Papers*[39]) indicate that they thought the courts would have some role to play in invalidating unconstitutional law.[40]

1.3.8 The Constitution of 1787 and the Seeds of an Expanded Democracy

Given the compromises the Framers had to make, it is not too surprising that the new Constitution was not very democratic. The new charter did not abolish slavery. It did not even guarantee suffrage rights, because the states set the qualifications for voters. For example, Art. I, § 2, clause 1, provides that each states' qualifications for voting for election to the House of Representatives are the same as the qualifications set for the most numerous branch of the state legislature.

If the Constitution had stipulated the voting qualifications for federal office, it probably would have adopted the typical state rule, which imposed a requirement that the voter must own real property (a freeholder). The voter often had to be a male, and white. Because the Constitution did not freeze such requirements, it left open the way for the gradual extension of the franchise, and that extension actually occurred, often a statutory extension of the franchise and sometimes by constitutional amendment. Over time, more of the governed acquired the right to vote.

The Constitution does prohibit any religious test for any office, state or federal office,[41] a requirement very progressive for its time. The original Constitution also prohibits Congress from limiting the jury trial right in criminal cases, from restricting the right of habeas corpus, and from enacting any ex post facto law or bill of attainder.[42] The original Constitution also forbids states from enacting any bill of attainder or ex post facto law.[43] To protect reasonable expectations the Constitution forbade states from impairing the obligation of

---

[39] See *The Federalist Papers*, No. 78 (1788), excerpted in the NOTES following *Marbury v. Madison*.

[40] Max Farrand, The Framing of the Constitution 119–20 (1913). The debates bear out Farrand's conclusions. See 1 Max Farrand, The Records of the Federal Convention 97–98 (1911) (remarks of Gerry (June 4, 1787)); id. at 109 (remarks of King (June 4, 1787)); 2 M. Farrand, The Records of the Federal Convention 73 (1911) (remarks of Wilson (July 21, 1787)); id. at 74 (remarks of Madison (July 21, 1787)); id. at 76 (remarks of Martin (July 21, 1787)); id. at 78 (remarks of Mason (July 21, 1787)); id. at 92–93 (remarks of Madison (July 21, 1787)); id. at 298 (remarks of Pinckney (Aug. 15, 1787)); id. at 299 (remarks of G. Morris (Aug. 15, 1787)); id. at 373, 376 (remarks of Williamson (Aug. 22, 1787)).

[41] U.S. Constitution, Art. VI, cl. 3.

[42] U.S. Constitution, Art. III, § 2, cl. 3; Art. I, § 9, cl. 2, 3.

[43] U.S. Constitution, Art. I, cl. 2, 3; Art. III, § 2, cl. 3; Art. I, § 10, cl. 1.

contracts.[44] (In 1791, the Bill of Rights granted additional individual freedoms, though these rights did not apply to the states before the Fourteenth Amendment.[45])

1.3.9   Enumerated Powers

The Framers of the Constitution chose a federal rather than a unitary system of government but, unlike the Articles of Confederation, the Constitution explicitly delegated to the central government certain significant powers. Most of these delegated powers are in Article I, § 8 of Constitution. The Constitution gave the central government the power to act directly on individuals, instead of the states. The central government now could tax directly. The people of the states directly elected their state's members of the House of Representatives.

In addition, other clauses of the Constitution explicitly grant other powers to the President, Congress, or the federal courts. For example, Article II, section 2, clause 1, gives the President the power to grant pardons for offenses against the United States, and section 3 of that article gives the President power to receive ambassadors, from which is implied the President's power to recognize foreign governments. Article III creates federal judicial power and grants to Congress the power to establish federal courts inferior to the U.S. Supreme Court. Article IV, section 3, clause 2, grants Congress the power to dispose of and regulate the territory or other property of the United States, and section 4 of that same article provides that the United States shall guarantee to every state in the Union a republican form of government. Later, various Amendments provided that Congress should have the power to enforce those Amendments by appropriate legislation.

One of the most significant (and most litigated) enumerated powers is the commerce power (U.S. Const., Art. I, § 8, cl. 3), which we examine in Chapter 6. Another very significant power is the "necessary and proper" power (U.S. Const., Art. I, § 8, cl. 18), which is the focus of Chapter 2.

The important point to bear in mind is that the central government only has those powers that the Constitution expressly (or impliedly) delegates to it. The Tenth Amendment (as the Court now interprets it) reserves all other powers to the people. In each state, the people may choose to delegate as much of that power as they wish to the state except to the extent to which the Constitution explicitly

---

[44]   U.S. Constitution, Art. I, § 10, cl. 1.

[45]   *Barron v. Mayor and City Council of Baltimore*, 32 U.S. (7 Pet.) 243, 250, 8 L.Ed. 672 (1833) held that that the 5th, 6th, and 8th Amendments only apply to United States Government.

placed restraints on the states. Thus, the federal government has the limited powers delegated to it: it can exercise these powers—as well as implied powers necessary and proper to the exercise of those powers—unless that exercise violates a specific restraint on the federal government embodied in the Constitution.

For example, Congress has the explicit power to "define and punish Piracies and Felonies committed on the high Seas, and Offenses against the Law of Nations." Art. I, § 8, cl. 10. In the exercise of that power, Congress may also "make all Laws which shall be necessary and proper for carrying into Execution" this power. Art. I, § 8, cl. 18. This broad power is limited, however, by the fact that Congress cannot validly enact a bill of attainder or an *ex post facto* law. Art. I, § 9, cl. 3. Similarly Congress has the power to "lay and collect Taxes, Duties, Imposts and Excises." Art. I, § 8, cl. 1. Congress also has all powers "necessary and proper" to effectuate the taxing power, but this power is nonetheless limited by the requirement that "[n]o Tax or Duty shall be laid on Articles exported from any State." Art. I, § 9, cl. 5.

States may exercise all other powers if the state's constitution authorized those powers and their exercise does not violate the federal constitution. If the state can, under its own law, exercise a power—and that decision is up to the state, not to the central government—then we look to the federal Constitution to see if that power is restricted. For example, a state cannot grant, "Letters of Marque and Reprisal" or "enter into any Treaty." Art. I, § 10, cl. 1. As a result, a state law—or state constitutional provision—must fall if it is in conflict with valid federal laws or treaties because they are the "supreme Law of the Land." Art. VI, cl. 2.

The federal government then is supreme within the areas of its delegated authority, if not restricted by the federal Constitution itself. The states are supreme within all other areas of authority unless restricted by the federal Constitution or valid federal laws or treaties.

1.4 THE AMENDMENTS

1.4.1 The Bill of Rights

After the Convention, various delegates and others worked tirelessly for the unanimous adoption of the Constitution. Some of the states ratified but suggested that there should be a Bill of Rights. On June 21, 1788, nine states had ratified, so the Constitution went into effect by its own terms. Yet neither New York nor Virginia had ratified. It was important to add these large states to the roster. The new Constitution needed only nine signatories to go into effect, but it would need these large states in order to succeed. On June 25, 1788, Virginia narrowly approved the Constitution. A month and a day later, New York also approved, urging that the first Congress propose a Bill of Rights. Others made similar proposals. Politicians promised to do that and, after ratification, the politicians actually kept their promise.

When the first Congress met under the new Constitution, it proposed a Bill of Rights, on September 25, 1789. Two months later North Carolina became the twelfth state to ratify. Finally, tardy state of Rhode Island ratified on May 29, 1790, by the very close vote of thirty-four to thirty-two. In 1791, the first ten amendments became part of the Constitution.[46]

There was a question whether these new amendments to the Constitution would be incorporated into the body of the Constitution or affixed to the end of the document. Madison thought that they should be incorporated into the body of the Constitutional text, while Roger Sherman argued that they should be grouped together. Sherman's view prevailed, which is why today we have a "Bill of Rights" with all the symbolism that related to listing these fundamental rights together.

The Bill of Rights sometimes refers to the first eight amendments. The Ninth Amendment cautions us that one should not construe the enumeration of certain rights to deny or disparage or deny other rights. The Tenth Amendment, discussed in Chapter 6, says that a government of limited powers is a government of limited powers. Still, typically people refer to all ten as the Bill of Rights.

1.4.2   Subsequent Amendments

11th Amendment. The 11th Amendment places a specific limitation on the power of federal courts to hear claims that U.S. or foreign citizens bring in federal court against states. This amendment does not overturn the supremacy clause or immunize states from the applicability of federal law, but it does require that plaintiffs bring some types of suits initially in state court. The purpose of this amendment was to overturn *Chisholm v. Georgia*, 2 U.S. (2 Dall.) 419(1793). The 11th amendment, ratified in 1798, reversed this case. It is unusual that Supreme Court decisions are reversed by amendment.

---

[46]   Rhode Island was not the only tardy state. While it was the last original state to ratify the Constitution, it was not until 1939 that Connecticut, Georgia, and Massachusetts got around to ratifying the first ten amendments. These ratifications were not legally necessary, but are symbolically interesting.

12th Amendment. This amendment revised the method of choosing the President and the Vice President. It takes into account the fact that political parties formed and that the President and the Vice President were running together on a ticket.

13th, 14th, & 15th Amendments. These amendments (ratified in 1865, 1868, and 1870) were all passed in response to the Civil War. The 13th Amendment, which abolished slavery, is the only amendment that applies to private action. In other words, if you own a slave, you are violating the Constitution. In the Twentieth Century, the Supreme Court relied on this Amendment to support civil rights laws that restrict the actions of *private* individuals whether or not they are in interstate commerce. The 14th Amendment, and the equal protection clause, is the focus of Chapter 4. Finally, the 15th Amendment guarantees the right to vote without regard to race, color, or previous condition oh servitude.

> *Dred Scott v. Sandford*, 60 U.S. (19 How.) 393 (1857) held, *inter alia*, that blacks, even freed black slaves, could not become citizens. The first sentence of 1 of the 14th amendment overruled that case. It was only the second time that a constitutional amendment overruled a Supreme Court decision.

16th Amendment. This amendment authorized the income tax. It overruled *Pollock v. Farmer's Loan & Trust Co.*, 157 U.S. 429 (initial decision), 158 U.S. 601 (decision on rehearing) (1895).

17th Amendment. This amendment changed the method of selection of U.S. Senators, so that the people elect them directly rather than the members of the most numerous branch of the state legislature selecting Senators.

18th & 21st Amendments. In 1919, the 18th Amendment established prohibition. After that, the people sobered up and repealed it with the **21st Amendment**, in 1933. **The 21st Amendment** does more than repeal the **18th**; it allows states to ban the importation notwithstanding restrictions that might otherwise exist due to the Commerce Clause.

19th Amendment. This amendment guarantees that the right to vote may not be abridged because of sex.

20th Amendment. This amendment deals with the election of the President and Vice President and begins their terms of office on January 21st following the election.

22nd Amendment. This amendment establishes a term limit of two terms for the President. [This amendment is sometimes called the anti-FDR amendment.]

23rd Amendment. This amendment grants electoral votes to residents of the District of Columbia.

24th Amendment. This amendment, ratified in 1964, prohibits the poll tax for federal elections. Later, in *Harper v. Virginia State Board of Elections*, 383 U.S. 663 (1966), the Court interpreted the 14th Amendment to declare unconstitutional the poll tax in *all* elections, state as well as federal. The 21st Amendment is, consequently, a redundancy.

25th Amendment. This amendment also regulates the election of the President and Vice President, and provides for the succession in the event that the office of President or Vice President becomes vacant.

26th Amendment. This amendment prohibits states and the federal government from abridging the right to vote because of age for citizens who are at least 18 years old. This amendment, in effect, overturned part of *Oregon v. Mitchell*, 400 U.S. 112 (1970), which had held that Congress did not have the power to enfranchise 18-year-olds in *state* elections.

This amendment marked only the fourth time in our entire history that the people have overturned the Court on a matter of Constitutional law. Recall the other times included—

> • **The 11th Amendment** [*Chisholm v. Georgia*, 2 U.S. (2 Dall.) 419 (1793)],

> • **The 14th Amendment** [*Dred Scott v. Stanford*, 60 U.S. (19 How.) 393 (1857)], and

> • **The 16th Amendment** [*Pollock v. Farmer's Loan & Trust Co.*, 157 U.S. 429 (initial decision), 158 U.S. 601 (decision on rehearing) (1895)]

1.5 THEORIES OF CONSTITUTIONAL INTERPRETATION

There may be as many schools of thought on how to interpret the Constitution, as there are ways of interpreting the Bible. Different Justices use different methods and the same Justices may use different methods over time.

The various legal schools of thought give different emphasis to several factors that affect interpretation: the intent of the Framers, the relevance of history, changed circumstances, the "plain language" of the provision—there are a few that are plain, *e.g.*, Art. III, § 3, cl. 1 (no conviction of treason, if the conviction is based on a confession, unless the defendant confesses "in open Court," or there is "the Testimony of two Witnesses").[47] Court decisions, in turn, reflect the scholarly thought associated with the various schools of interpretation.

1.5.1   Formal Jurisprudence

Formal jurisprudence was popular among judges and scholars during much of our history. Many formal jurisprudents believe in natural law and that "law" existed apart from those who decreed it. They saw judges as "finding" or discovering the law, not simply announcing it. Legislators codified the law because principles of higher law beyond their control bound them. The law, in this view, was truly neutral in that it did not favor particular classes of persons. They saw the law as a set of principles that judges discovered and applied to cases before them.

> [I]n all early civilizations we find a law like that "of the Medes and the Persian that changeth not," and why all early "law-giving" consisted in efforts to record and make known a claw that was conceived as unalterably given. A "legislator" might endeavor to purge the law of supposed corruption, or to restore it to its pristine purity, but it was not thought that he could make new law. . . . The historians of law are agreed that in this respect all the famous early "law-givers," from Ur-Nammu and Hammurabi to Solon, Lykurgus and the authors of the Roman Twelve Tables, did not intend to create new law but merely to state what law was and had always been.[48]

Oliver Wendell Holmes saw judge-made law quite differently. "The common law is not a brooding omnipresence in the sky, but the articulate voice of some sovereign or quasi sovereign that can be identified; although some decisions with which I have disagreed seem to me to have forgotten the fact."[49]

In modern times, judges look to the text of the Constitution; the Framers' intent; constitutional theory (some of which can be quite abstract); precedent; and

---

[47]   The testimony must be to the "same overt Act," a requirement that is hardly as self-defining as "two Witnesses."

[48]   Friedrich A. Hayek, Law, Legislation and Liberty: Rules and Order 81 (U. Chicago Press, 1973) (footnotes omitted).

[49]   *Southern Pacific Co. v. Jensen*, 244 U.S. 205, 222 (1917) (Holmes, J., dissenting). In this case, the lower court awarded damages to the dependents of a longshoreman killed on an ocean-going steamship. The Supreme Court reversed and remanded for further proceedings.

(moral and policy values. The judge's use of any argument does not preclude the use of other arguments—either simultaneously or subsequently. The validity of any, or all, of these approaches is the subject of much debate in the literature and the caselaw.

1.5.2   Sociological Jurisprudence

Sociological jurisprudence was the first jurisprudential movement that arose in the early twentieth century, as a response to the formal jurisprudence. Roscoe Pound, Dean of Harvard Law School from 1916 to 1936, was the leading figure, if not the founder, of this movement. The sociological jurisprudents responding to Holmes' critiques of formal jurisprudence, believed that the courts could derive law from basic principles that are discoverable from moral philosophy, history, and a societal consensus that judges could observe and verify. They rejected the formal jurisprudence by admitting that judicial rulings involved judge-made rather than judicially discovered law. Sociological jurisprudents believed that judges should make law by adjusting legal principles to changing social conditions. This jurisprudential movement dovetailed nicely with the progressive movement in the early part of the twentieth century. Sociological jurisprudents believed that there was a societal consensus on social progress and that judges should help to reform social and economic conditions.

1.5.3   Legal Realists

The Legal Realists took the position that law must inevitably reflect divisions within society. Realists believed that the rulings of judges reflected only the views of individual judges with the power to decree the outcome of a case before them. They went beyond the sociological jurisprudence by claiming not only that judges made law but also that there was no law that existed apart from governmental decisionmakers. In other words, the judges not only made the law, they were the law. Legislative and executive branch officials also were the law. The law was simply what governmental officials decided to do in resolving disputes between individuals or economic forces.

Realists believed that one could "explain" a court decision, but one could not prove is right or wrong because the realists denied the existence of any set of normative principles that could be proven true. Realists invited the legal profession to explain the worth of judicial decisions in terms of which classes were benefited or harmed by judicial rulings, rather than in terms of legal principles defined by either formal or sociological jurisprudence. Legal realism was particularly popular during the 1930's.

1.5.4 Neutral Principles or Process-Oriented Jurisprudence

The Neutral Principles or Process Oriented school of thought arose in reaction to the Legal Realists. During the late 1930's a school of constitutional law scholars sought to justify Supreme Court rulings that favored judicial power to enforce civil liberties while limiting judicial power to enforce economic liberties. This school of jurisprudence is called the "neutral principles" or "process oriented" theory of constitutional law. Those who supported this theory argued that judges should identify a "neutral basis" or "neutral principle" that should not be dependent on the parties to the litigation. That is why the principle is "neutral." Adherents urged judges to use their judicial power to protect values that are based on an open political process. For example, when judges invalidate laws that restrict the right to vote, or when they strike down laws that restrict free speech, they are opening up the democratic process.

In the now famous "*Carolene Products* Footnote 4," the Court argued that a more active judicial role is justified when the Court was enforcing textual guarantees of the Constitution, defining and protecting rights of the political process, or protecting discrete and insular minorities. The *Carolene Products* approach to constitutional adjudication selects these areas for independent judicial activity that involved defenses of values that the Court should not entrust to the democratic process. The footnote says:

> There may be narrower scope for operation of the presumption of constitutionality [1] when legislation appears on its face to be within a specific prohibition of the Constitution, such as those of the first ten Amendments, which are deemed equally specific when held to be embraced within the Fourteenth. [2] It is unnecessary to consider now whether legislation which restricts those political processes which can ordinarily be expected to bring about repeal of undesirable legislation, is to be subjected to more exacting judicial scrutiny under the general prohibitions of the Fourteenth Amendment than are most other types of legislation [such as] restrictions upon the right to vote; on restraints upon the dissemination of information; on interferences with political organizations; as to prohibition of peaceable assembly. [3] Nor need we enquire whether similar considerations enter into the review of statutes

directed at particular religious, or racial minorities; whether prejudice against discrete and insular minorities may be a special condition, which tends seriously to curtail the operation of those political processes ordinarily to be relied upon to protect minorities, and which may call for a correspondingly more searching judicial inquiry.[50]

In the 1960s and 1970s, Professor Alexander Bickel, a major academic scholar of the Supreme Court, criticized the neutral principles school. Bickel argued that there is no basis for choosing majoritarian theories of government over other theories of the workings of a democracy as the basis for defining a judicial role in the governmental process. He argued that any claim that the Supreme Court enhances the democratic process by striking down legislation is "question begging."[51] In response, advocates of neutral principles and democratic process argued that they derive democratic process values from an examination of the Constitution. These values, they said, are not the arbitrary exercise of political power by judges. They are not realists because they find "law" in a jurisprudence based upon their view of the proper functioning of the Court in a democracy.

1.5.5   Textualists

Textualists focus on the words or text of the Constitution divorced from the history surrounding those words. It is more common to find textualists as an important tool to interpret statutes. Textualist judges argue that courts should not treat committee reports, debates on the House or Senate floor, or sponsors' statements as authoritative evidence of legislative intent. Instead, the courts should look at the words of the statute, not its legislative history. Justice Hugo Black, for example, was fond of saying that when the First Amendment provides that "Congress shall make no law . . . abridging the freedom of speech," it mean "no law:"

> Certainly the First Amendment's language leaves no room for inference that abridgments of speech and press can be made just because they are slight. That Amendment provides, in simple words, that "Congress shall

---

[50]   *United States v. Carolene Products Co.*, 304 U.S. 144, 152–53 n.4 (1938) (internal citations omitted). The Court, over the dissent of Justice McReynolds (who wrote on opinion), held that it is constitutional for Congress to prohibit the shipments of a compound of condensed milk and coconut oil made in imitation or semblance of condensed milk or cream. This federal law did not infringe on the due process clause of the Constitution or violate any other provision.

[51]   Alexander Bickel, The Supreme Court and the Idea of Progress 34–35, 83, 108–15, 166–67 (Yale Press ed. 1978).

make no law * * * abridging the freedom of speech, or of the press." I
read "no law * * * abridging" to mean no law abridging. The First
Amendment, which is the supreme law of the land, has thus fixed its
own value on freedom of speech and press by putting these freedoms
wholly "beyond the reach" of federal power to abridge.[52]

1.5.6   Strict Construction

Strict Construction is another theory of constitutional interpretation that
goes back to the early 19th Century. Often, proponents of strict construction
argue that the Court should interpret Constitutional narrowly. Justice Scalia has
criticized strict constructionism as "a degraded form of textualism that brings the
whole philosophy [of textualism] into disrepute." He adds, "I am not a strict
constructionist, and no one ought to be," because a "text should not be construed
strictly, and it should not be construed leniently; it should be construed
reasonably, to contain all that it fairly means."[53]

President Thomas Jefferson called himself a "strict constructionist." In 1792,
he advised President Washington that Congress did not have the power to
incorporate the Bank of United States. The Supreme Court decided to the
contrary in *McCulloch v. Maryland*, 17 U.S. (4 Wheat.) 316 (1819). When the United
States acquired the Louisiana Purchase by treaty from France in 1803, Jefferson
drafted a proposed Constitutional Amendment to authorize it, but his advisers
convinced him not to go that route because the delay might cause the deal to fail.
The treaty doubled the size of the United States, at a cost of less than 3 cents per
acre.[54]

1.5.7   Originalism

Originalism is yet another theory. Originalists often do not consider
themselves Textualists. Originalism is both an old and a modern theory of
interpretation. The modern jurisprudential competition to the neutral principles
school has come from two sides. First, there is the "Originalist" (sometimes called
the "interpretivist") school of scholars and judges who believe that courts should
apply the words of the Constitution as the drafters understood them. This school

---

[52]   *Smith v. California*, 361 U.S. 147, 157 (1959) (Black, J., concurring).

[53]   Antonin Scalia, A Matter of Interpretation (Princeton U. Press 1997).

[54]   Note that Article II, § 2, cl. 2 authorizes the President "to make Treaties, provided that two thirds of
the Senators present concur." In addition, Art. IV, § 3, cl. 1 contemplates that new states shall be added to the
union, and that Congress has the power to legislate regarding property of the United States. Art. IV, § 3, cl. 2

of thought is called "Originalism" because it focuses on the original intent of the Framers of the constitution and the amendments.

Originalists readily concede that the historical intent of the Framers or the ratifiers is often not clear. The use of Originalism theory does not require that the judge ignore the policies or history behind a law, or the costs and benefits of any given interpretation. Originalist theory is an effort to cabin the judge and to place some limits on judicial review.

Recall that the Constitutional Convention operated in secrecy. It was not until many years after the ratification of the Constitution that Congress ordered that the printing of those proceedings and fragmentary minutes in the hands of the Government.[55] The people who publicly debated and ratified the new Constitution—the generation of 1787—had no access to the Convention notes. Indeed, when President Washington, in his message to Congress of March 30, 1796, referred to the unpublished *Journal of the Constitutional Convention* in support of a particular interpretation of the Constitution, various members of Congress thought that his reference had violated the Convention's rule of secrecy.[56] Much of what we now know comes from one person, Madison, who took it upon himself to compile a more complete and unofficial record. Madison's notes, however, were not published until 1840.

Writing that did not see the light of day until over a half century after the Convention could not have influenced those who voted for an ratified the Constitution because the writings were hidden from them. That is not to say that the Convention notes are necessarily irrelevant as an aid in interpreting the written document. The secret Convention notes may help tell us what certain words *may* mean, how much one can stretch or restrict language.

Originalists look to sources such as the Federalist Papers, the historical circumstances, and the state ratifying conventions as a guide to interpreting the Constitution. For example, while James Madison opposed looking at secret,

---

[55] The Resolve of Congress of March 27, 1818 ordered printed those papers in the possession of John Quincy Adams that related to the Constitutional Convention. These papers included the minutes of the Journal of the Convention. Charles Warren, The Making of the Constitution 797–98 (Little Brown & Co. 1928). The year 1821 saw the publication of the notes of Robert Yates, a member of the Convention. Yates, however, left the Convention on July 10, 1787, over two months before the Convention adjourned. Madison's notes were not published until 1840. Warren notes: "It is a singular fact that it was not until fifty-three years after the Constitution was signed that the American people were afforded any adequate knowledge of the debates of the Federal Convention." Charles Warren, id., at 802.

[56] See 5 Annals of Cong. 775–76 (1996) (remarks of Rep. James Madison); id., at 734 (remarks of Rep. Albert Gallatin). Madison also wrote Jefferson that Washington's use of the Convention's Journal violated the Convention's rule of secrecy. Letter from James Madison to Thomas Jefferson (Apr. 4, 1796), quoted in Charles Warren, The Making of the Constitution 796 (Little Brown & Co. 1928).

"private" intent, expressed in the halls of the Philadelphia Convention, he also urged us to look "for the meaning of that instrument beyond the face of the instrument . . . not in the General Convention which proposed, but in the State Conventions which accepted and ratified it."[57] Originalists add that the early case law and constitutional authorities recognized that publicly available authorities, such as The Federalist Papers, offered a contemporary and very relevant explication of the meaning of the new Constitution.[58]

Originalists concede that we must read history in context. Sometimes it may tell us that the Framers may have intended that a particular clause to be ambiguous, perhaps to paper over differences, to provide for flexibility, or to allow for evolutionary growth in the law.[59] In addition, history will not speak with a clear voice, and reasonable people will interpret the evidence differently. However, Originalists argue that these limitations do not mean that the intent of the ratifiers is irrelevant, or that the Framers and ratifiers intended for us to ignore that intent when we can discover it. Pharaoh's dreams were not easy to interpret, but Joseph did not therefore advise Pharaoh to ignore them.

Justice Joseph Story was what we today would call an Originalist. In his *Constitutional Commentaries* he argued, "The first and fundamental rule in the interpretation of all instruments is, to construe them according to the sense of the terms and the intention of the parties." Turning to The Federalist Papers was one of Justice Story's "Rules of Interpretation."[60]

Yet, Story did not focus on abstractions. He argued further, "Upon subjects of government it has always appeared to me that metaphysical refinements are out of place. A constitution of government is addressed to the common sense of the people; and was never designed for trials of logical skill, or visionary speculation."[61] Judge Robert Bork, a well-known proponent of Originalism, argued, "For Story, Kent, Cooley, and Thayer, the source was the intent of the Framers and ratifiers, and that was to be discerned from text, history, structure,

---

[57] Quoted in Charles Warren, The Making of the Constitution 794 (1928). See also Letter from James Madison to S. H. Smith (Feb. 2, 1827); Letter from James Madison to Thomas Ritchie (Sept. 15, 1821); Letter from James Madison to M. L. Hurlbert (May 1830), all cited in Charles Watter, at 801 & n.1.

[58] See *Cohens v. Virginia*, 19 U.S. (6 Wheat.) 264, 418 (1821); *McCulloch v. Maryland*, 17 U.S. (4 Wheat.) 316, 433 (1819). In *McCulloch*, 17 U.S. (4 Wheat.) at 372, Luther Martin's argument to the Court included reading extracts from The Federalist Papers and the Virginia and New York Conventions.

[59] The authors of The Federalist Papers "sometimes exaggerated [the Constitution's] advantages, and spread over the objectionable features the gloss of plausible construction." *State v. McBride*, 24 S.C.L. (Rice) 400, 410 (1839).

[60] Ronald D. Rotunda & John E. Nowak, eds., Joseph Story's Commentaries on the Constitution of the United States, § 181, at p. 135 (1987, originally published 1833).

[61] Id at p. vi (Preface by Justice Story).

and precedent. What is important about the non-interpretivists," he contends, "is not that they added moral philosophy but that moral philosophy displaces such traditional sources as text and history and renders them unimportant."[62]

1.5.8   The Living Constitution

The Living Constitution a popular modern theory is also a reaction to Originalism. In one sense, no one argues against a "living" constitution nor anyone advocate a "dead" constitution. As Justice Holmes said in the early part of the twentieth century—

> when we are dealing with words that also are a constituent act, like the Constitution of the United States, we must realize that they have called into life a being the development of which could not have been foreseen completely by the most gifted of its begetters. It was enough for them to realize or to hope that they had created an organism; it has taken a century and has cost their successors much sweat and blood to prove that they created a nation. The case before us must be considered in the light of our whole experience and not merely in that of what was said a hundred years ago.[63]

Even Chief Justice William Rehnquist, a proponent of Originalism, supports Holmes' view of interpretation. However, Rehnquist did speak derisively of those who argue that the Court should act because other branches of government have abdicated their responsibility. He disagreed with those who argue that judges should not limit themselves to the intent of the Framers, even though it "is very difficult to determine in any event." He also rejected the argument that because the Constitution uses "general language," judges "should not hesitate to use their authority to make the Constitution relevant and useful in solving the problems of modern society."[64]

Justice Stephen Breyer, in contrast, argues that because the Constitution is a "living constitution," that means, the Court should interpret it to assist progress in an ever-changing world.[65] In *McCutcheon v. Federal Election Commission*, 134 S.Ct. 1434 (2014) the Court invalidated a restriction on political contributions because Congress cannot "restrict the political participation of some in order to enhance

---

[62] Robert Bork, Styles in Constitutional Theory, 26 South Texas Law Journal 383, 394 (1985).

[63] *Missouri v. Holland*, 252 U.S. 416, 433 (1920).

[64] William Rehnquist, The Notion of a Living Constitution, 29 Harvard Journal of Law & Policy 401, 402 (1976).

[65] Justice Breyer, Supreme Court Review (Sept. 1, 2015), http://supremecourtreview.com/default/justice/index/id/43

the relative influence of others." In dissent, Justice Breyer responded, the federal restriction "advances not only the individual's right to engage in political speech, but also the public's interest in preserving a democratic order in which collective speech *matters*."[66] Justice Breyer favors what he calls "active liberty" that a more active Court embraces.[67]

A typical commentator, supporting the Living Constitution, advocates, "a more candidly creative role" for the Court because "the highest mission of the Supreme Court . . . is not to conserve judicial credibility, but in the Constitution's own phrase, 'to form a more perfect Union.' "[68] Another argues the Court should always ask, "Are you assisting the political branches in promoting progressive constitutional values like liberty, equality and justice?"[69] Another has said, "The Framers, after all, are dead, and in the contemporary world, their views are neither relevant nor morally binding."[70] Originalists would respond that the Sherman Antitrust Act of 1890 still governs us, although the people who drafted and enacted it are all dead white men.

In addition to these basic theories, there are also other guides to Constitutional Interpretation. Courts often pronounce (though not always, follow) various rules to avoid constitutional issues. Thus, the Supreme Court will not determine the constitutionality of legislation in a friendly, nonadversary proceeding. The Court also says that it will not anticipate and decide a constitutional issue before it necessarily must reach the question; it will not formulate a constitutional rule broader than necessary to decide the facts before it; it will not decide a properly presented constitutional issue if nonconstitutional grounds exist, such as a statutory interpretation that would save the constitutionality of the statute. The Court will not hear a complaint as to the alleged constitutionality of a statute if the statute's operation does not in fact injure the plaintiff. In other words, the plaintiff must have "standing," that is, the statute must affect him adversely.

---

[66] Emphasis in original. Chief Justice Roberts, in the majority, responded, "the dissent's 'collective speech' reflected in laws is of course the will of the majority, and plainly can include laws that restrict free speech. The whole point of the First Amendment is to afford individuals protection against such infringements. The First Amendment does not protect the government, even when the government purports to act through legislation reflecting 'collective speech.' "

[67] Stephen Breyer, Active Liberty: Interpreting Our Democratic Constitution (Alfred A. Knopf, 2005).

[68] Laurence Tribe, American Constitutional Law iv (1978).

[69] Professor Jack Balkin of Yale, quoted in, Rosen, What's a Liberal Justice Now?, New York Times Magazine, May 26, 2009.

[70] Craig R. Ducat, Modes of Constitutional Interpretation 103 (West. Pub. Co. 1978) (footnote omitted).

1.6 THE COURT BEFORE MARBURY V. MADISON

In the beginning, the Supreme Court was hardly a powerful legal or political entity. It was not until September 24, 1789, that President George Washington signed the first judiciary act into law and then sent his Supreme Court nominations to the Senate for confirmation. The first Chief Justice was John Jay, then only forty-four years old. Jay had very little judicial experience prior to his appointment, and while he was Chief, he spent much of his time abroad, involved in diplomatic duties. In 1795, he would resign to become Governor of New York.

John Rutledge of South Carolina, another nominee, never attended a formal session of the Court. He resigned in 1791 so that he could become Chief Justice of the South Carolina Court of Common Pleas and Sessions. In 1795, Washington reappointed him to the U.S. Supreme Court, this time as Chief Justice. He sat as a recess appointment, but the Senate rejected his regular appointment.

Washington also nominated Robert Hanson Harrison, who rejected the honor. Some secondary sources claim that Harrison rejected the appointment solely because of his ill health. However, when he wrote Washington, on October 27, 1789, he did not rely on that excuse and remained on the General Court of Maryland. To fill that slot, in the following year Washington nominated James Iredell of North Carolina, then only thirty-eight years of age. Iredell accepted but died only nine years later, in 1799. He stopped attending Court sessions starting with the August 1799, Term of the Court.

Washington also nominated John Blair of Virginia, who had been a delegate to the Constitutional Convention. Blair attended Court sessions irregularly and resigned in 1706 because of ill health. James Wilson of Pennsylvania, another nominee, served on the Court until his death in 1798. The only Washington nominee to serve past 1800 was William Cushing of Massachusetts.

This first Court had only six members (a federal statute, not the Constitution, controls the number of Justices), and very little business. The first term lasted only about a week. All the Court did was set up house, appoint a clerk, and admit a few lawyers to practice before the Court. The second term lasted only two days. It was not until February of 1793 that the Court reached its first major decision. The beginning was inauspicious. The case was *Chisholm v. Georgia*,[71] which the Eleventh Amendment overruled.[72]

The year after *Chisolm*, Jay became a special ambassador to England, while remaining Chief Justice. Many contemporaries criticized Jay's dual appointments as a violation of the American principle of separation of powers. About a year later, Jay resigned from the Court. Jay's replacement was Senator Oliver Ellsworth—the Senate rejected Washington's first choice, and his second declined the offer. In 1799 Ellsworth became Ambassador to France; he resigned from the Court the next year.

During the last years of the eighteenth century, the Federalist Party controlled the national government. The time witnessed intense political rivalry. The Federalists used the powers of the national government for partisan purposes, exemplified by the use of the Sedition Act to punish those who spoke out against President Adams or the Federalist Congress. The political opposition reacted with animosity towards the Federalists and the Federalist judges who enforced the Sedition Act against other political parties. This set the stage for *Marbury v. Madison.*

The Supremacy Clause figures prominently in *Marbury*. The Constitution provides that the states as well as federal legislative, executive, and judicial officials would be bound by oath or affirmation (under Article VI) to support the Constitution. This Article also includes the Supremacy Clause:

> This Constitution, and the Laws of the United States which shall be made in Pursuance thereof; and all Treaties made, or which shall be made, under the Authority of the United States, shall be the supreme law of the Land; and the Judges in every State shall be bound thereby, any Thing in the constitution or Laws of any State to the Contrary notwithstanding.

---

[71] *Chisholm v. Georgia*, 2 U.S. (2 Dall.) 419 (1793), was an original action with Alexander Chisholm suing the State of Georgia in the U.S. Supreme Court for payment of a debt. Georgia never contested the debt but refused to appear, claiming that federal courts had no jurisdiction over such a suit. The Court ruled (4 to 1) that Article 3, § 2 limited the states' sovereign immunity and granted federal courts the power to hear disputes between private citizens and states.

[72] U.S. Const. Amendment 11 (1798). Congress proposed this amendment on September 5, 1794.

1.7 THE ESTABLISHMENT OF JUDICIAL REVIEW

MARBURY V. MADISON

5 U.S. (1 Cranch) 137, 2 L.Ed. 60 (1803)

[In 1800, the Jeffersonians took control of the executive and legislative branches of the government from Adams' Federalist Party. However, Adams remained President until March 4, 1801.* He responded to the Jeffersonian victory by seeking to maintain Federalist control of the judiciary through his appointment power. After Oliver Ellsworth (who was the third person to hold the position of Chief Justice) resigned that post, Adams sought to reappoint John Jay. Jay had earlier resigned as the first Chief Justice. He declined to serve again because of his ill health and the heavy duties that the Chief Justice would have "riding circuit," that is, presiding at lower court trials. Jay's letter to Adams also bemoaned the fact that the efforts "made to place the Judicial Department on a proper footing have proved fruitless." On January 20, 1801, Adams turned to John Marshall, who was then Adams' secretary of state. Marshall, who had no judicial experience, took judicial office on February 4, 1801, while continuing to serve as secretary of state.

[Adams and the Federalist lame duck Congress increased the jurisdiction of the lower federal courts and the number of circuit judgeships to sixteen by enacting the Circuit Courts Act of February 13, 1801. Adams quickly appointed these judges, whom the Senate confirmed on March 2, 1801. On February 17, Congress enacted another law, which authorized Adams to appoint, to five-year terms, justices of the peace for Washington County in the District of Columbia (on the east side of the Potomac River) and Alexandria County, which was at that time part of the District. The President could appoint the number of justices of the peace that he "shall from time to time think expedient." Adams quickly appointed forty-two justices of the peace. On March 3, 1801 (one day before President Jefferson took the reins of power), the Federalist Senate confirmed these judges. By midnight of March 3, Marshall—who was still serving as secretary of state while also sitting as Chief Justice—had not yet delivered four of these judicial commissions. The new President, Thomas Jefferson, ordered his secretary of state, James Madison, to refuse to deliver them. In response, William Marbury, Dennis Ramsay, Robert Townsend Hoe, and William Harper hired Charles Lee (who had been attorney general in Adams' administration) to sue Madison. They

---

* The terms of the President and Vice-President now end at noon on the twentieth day of January following the election. See U.S. Constitution, Amendment XX, section 1.

filed suit directly in the Supreme Court in December of 1801, and they sought a court ruling that would order Madison to deliver their commissions. This order to compel performance of an official duty is called a writ of mandamus.

[Marbury's attorney, in support of the jurisdiction of the Supreme Court, relied on section 13 of the Judiciary Act of 1789, which provided in part that "the Supreme Court shall also have appellate jurisdiction from the circuit courts and courts of the several states, in the cases hereinafter specially provided for; and shall have power to issue writs of prohibition to the district courts, when proceeding as courts of admiralty and maritime jurisdiction; and *writs of mandamus,* in cases warranted by the principles and usages of law, to any courts appointed, or persons holding office, under the authority of the United States." (Emphasis added).

[Madison did not hire counsel and did not appear. Marbury filed suit on December 21, 1801, but the Supreme Court did not hear the case until 1803 because the new Jeffersonian Congress enacted a statute that eliminated part of the Supreme Court 1802 term. The Court did not meet again for fourteen months. Congress also passed the Repeal Act, which repealed the Circuit Courts Act of February 13, 1801. (One week after the Court decided *Marbury v. Madison*, it declined an opportunity to invalidate the Repeal Act. See *Stuart v. Laird* [1803].)

[Thus, it was not until February 24, 1803, that Marshall delivered the opinion of the Court. Marshall strongly denounced Jefferson for refusing to deliver the commission to Marbury. But, said Marshall, although Marbury had a right to the commission, his remedy did not lie in the Supreme Court because section 13 of the Judiciary Act is unconstitutional to the extent that it seeks to increase the original jurisdiction of the Supreme Court. Normally one would expect that the Court would first rule on its jurisdiction to decide the case, for if it has no jurisdiction, the Court would not need to decide the rest of the case. However, that more logical order would not have allowed Marshall to engage in gratuitous criticism of the new President.

[On February 24, 1803, Chief Justice John Marshall delivered the opinion of the Court.]

CHIEF JUSTICE JOHN MARSHALL.

At the last term on the affidavits then read and filed with the clerk, a rule was granted in this case, requiring the secretary of state to show cause why a mandamus should not issue, directing him to deliver to William Marbury his commission as a justice of the peace for the county of Washington, in the District of Columbia.

No cause has been shown, and the present motion is for a mandamus. The peculiar delicacy of this case, the novelty of some of its circumstances, and the real difficulty attending the points which occur in it, require a complete exposition of the principles on which the opinion to be given by the court is founded.

These principles have been, on the side of the applicant very ably argued at the bar. In rendering the opinion of the court, there will be some departure in form, though not in substance, from the points stated in that argument.

In the order in which the court has viewed this subject, the following questions have been considered and decided.

1st. Has the applicant a right to the commission he demands?

2d. If he has a right, and that right has been violated, do the laws of his country afford him a remedy?

3d. If they do afford him a remedy, is it a mandamus issuing from this court?

The first object of inquiry is,

1st. Has the applicant a right to the commission he demands? . . .

Mr. Marbury, then, since his commission was signed by the President, and sealed by the Secretary of State, was appointed; and as the law creating the office, gave the officer a right to hold for five years, independent of the executive, the appointment was not revocable, but vested in the officer legal rights, which are protected by the laws of his country.

To withhold his commission, therefore, is an act deemed by the court not warranted by law, but violative of a vested legal right.

This brings us to the second inquiry; which is,

2d. If he has a right, and that right has been violated, do the laws of this country afford him a remedy?

The government of the United States has been emphatically termed a government of laws, and not of men. It will certainly cease to deserve this high appellation, if the laws furnish no remedy for the violation of a vested legal right. . . .

It remains to be inquired whether,

3d. He is entitled to the remedy for which he applies. . . .

With respect to the officer to whom it would be directed. The intimate political relation subsisting between the President of the United States and the heads of departments, necessarily renders any legal investigation of the acts of one of those high officers peculiarly irksome, as well as delicate; and excites some hesitation with respect to the propriety of entering into such investigation. [T]he assertion, by an individual, of his legal claims in a court of justice, to which claims it is the duty of that court to attend, should at first view be considered by some, as an attempt to intrude into the cabinet, and to intermeddle with the prerogatives of the executive.

It is scarcely necessary for the court to disclaim all pretensions to such jurisdiction. An extravagance, so absurd and excessive, could not have been entertained for a moment. The province of the court is, solely, to decide on the rights of individuals, not to inquire how the executive, or executive officers, perform duties in which they have a discretion. Questions in their nature political, or which are, by the constitution and laws, submitted to the executive, can never be made in this court.

But, if this be not such a question; if, so far from being an intrusion into the secrets of the cabinet, it respects a paper which, according to law, is upon record, and to a copy of which the law gives a right, on the payment of ten cents; if it be no intermeddling with a subject over which the executive can be considered as having exercised any control; what is there in the exalted station of the officer, which shall bar a citizen from asserting, in a court of justice, his legal rights? . . .

This, then, is a plain case for a mandamus, either to deliver the commission, or a copy of it from the record; and it only remains to be inquired,

Whether it can issue from this court.

The act to establish the judicial courts of the United States authorizes the Supreme Court "to issue writs of mandamus in cases warranted by the principles and usages of law, to any courts appointed, or persons holding office, under the authority of the United States."

The Secretary of State, being a person holding an office under the authority of the United States, is precisely within the letter of the description, and if this court is not authorized to issue a writ of mandamus to such an officer, it must be because the law is unconstitutional, and therefore absolutely incapable of conferring the authority, and assigning the duties which its words purport to confer and assign.

The constitution vests the whole judicial power of the United States in one Supreme Court, and such inferior courts as congress shall, from time to time, ordain and establish. This power is expressly extended to all cases arising under the laws of the United States; and, consequently, in some form, may be exercised over the present case; because the right claimed is given by a law of the United States.

In the distribution of this power it is declared that "the Supreme Court shall have original jurisdiction in all cases affecting ambassadors, other public ministers and consuls, and those in which a state shall be a party. In all other cases, the Supreme Court shall have appellate jurisdiction."

It has been insisted, at the bar, that as the original grant of jurisdiction, to the Supreme and inferior courts, in general, and the clause, assigning original jurisdiction to the Supreme Court, contains no negative or restrictive words, the power remains to the legislature, to assign original jurisdiction to that court in other cases than those specified in the article which has been recited; provided those cases belong to the judicial power of the United States.

If it had been intended to leave it in the discretion of the legislature to apportion the judicial power between the Supreme and inferior courts according to the will of that body, it would certainly have been useless to have proceeded further than to have defined the judicial power, and the tribunals in which it should be vested. The subsequent part of the section is mere surplusage, is entirely without meaning, if such is to be the construction. If congress remains at liberty to give this court appellate jurisdiction, where the constitution has declared their jurisdiction shall be original; and original jurisdiction where the constitution has declared it shall be appellate; the distribution of jurisdiction, made in the constitution, is form without substance.

Affirmative words are often, in their operation, negative of other objects than those affirmed; and in this case, a negative or exclusive sense must be given to them, or they have no operation at all. It cannot be presumed that any clause in the constitution is intended to be without effect; and, therefore, such a construction is inadmissible, unless the words require it. . . .

The authority, therefore, given to the Supreme Court, by the act establishing the judicial courts of the United States, to issue writs of mandamus to public officers, appears not to be warranted by the constitution; and it becomes necessary to inquire whether a jurisdiction so conferred can be exercised.

The question, whether an act, repugnant to the constitution, can become the law of the land, is a question deeply interesting to the United States; but, happily, not of an intricacy proportioned to its interest. It seems only necessary to recognize certain principles, supposed to have been long and well established, to decide it.

That the people have an original right to establish, for their future government, such principles, as, in their opinion, shall most conduce to their own happiness is the basis on which the whole American fabric has been erected. The exercise of this original right is a very great exertion; nor can it, nor ought it, to be frequently repeated. The principles, therefore, so established, are deemed fundamental. And as the authority from which they proceed is supreme, and can seldom act, they are designed to be permanent.

This original and supreme will organizes the government, and assigns to different departments their respective powers. It may either stop here, or establish certain limits not to be transcended by those departments.

The government of the United States is of the latter description. The powers of the legislature are defined and limited; and that those limits may not be mistaken, or forgotten, the constitution is written. To what purpose are powers limited, and to what purpose is that limitation committed to writing, if these limits may, at any time, be passed by those intended to be restrained? The distinction between a government with limited and unlimited powers is abolished, if those limits do not confine the persons on whom they are imposed, and if acts prohibited and acts allowed, are of equal obligation. It is a proposition too plain to be contested, that the constitution controls any legislative act repugnant to it; or, that the legislature may alter the constitution by an ordinary act.

Between these alternatives there is no middle ground. The constitution is either a superior paramount law, unchangeable by ordinary means, or it is on a level with ordinary legislative acts, and, like other acts, is alterable when the legislature shall please to alter it.

If the former part of the alternative be true, then a legislative act contrary to the constitution is not law: if the latter part be true, then written constitutions are absurd attempts, on the part of the people, to limit a power in its own nature illimitable.

Certainly all those who have framed written constitutions contemplate them as forming the fundamental and paramount law of the nation, and, consequently, the theory of every such government must be, that an act of the legislature, repugnant to the constitution, is void.

This theory is essentially attached to a written constitution, and, is consequently, to be considered, by this court, as one of the fundamental principles of our society. It is not therefore to be lost sight of in the further consideration of this subject.

If an act of the legislature, repugnant to the constitution, is void, does it, notwithstanding its invalidity, bind the courts, and oblige them to give it effect? Or, in other words, though it be not law, does it constitute a rule as operative as if it was a law? This would be to overthrow in fact what was established in theory; and would seem, at first view, an absurdity too gross to be insisted on. It shall, however, receive a more attentive consideration.

It is emphatically the province and duty of the judicial department to say what the law is. Those who apply the rule to particular cases, must of necessity expound and interpret that rule. If two laws conflict with each other, the courts must decide on the operation of each.

So if the law be in opposition to the constitution; if both the law and the constitution apply to a particular case, so that the court must either decide that case conformably to the law, disregarding the constitution; or conformably to the constitution, disregarding the law; the court must determine which of these conflicting rules governs the case. This is of the very essence of judicial duty.

If, then, the courts are to regard the constitution, and the constitution is superior to any ordinary act of the legislature, the constitution, and not such ordinary act, must govern the case to which they both apply.

Those, then, who controvert the principle that the constitution is to be considered, in court, as a paramount law, are reduced to the necessity of maintaining that courts must close their eyes on the constitution, and see only the law.

This doctrine would subvert the very foundation of all written constitutions. It would declare that an act which, according to the principles and theory of our government, is entirely void, is yet, in practice, completely obligatory. It would declare that if the legislature shall do what is expressly forbidden, such act, notwithstanding the express prohibition, is in reality effectual. It would be given to the legislature a practical and real omnipotence, with the same breath which professes to restrict their powers within narrow limits. It is prescribing limits, and declaring that those limits may be passed at pleasure.

That it thus reduces to nothing what we have deemed the greatest improvement on political institutions, a written constitution, would of itself be sufficient, in America, where written constitutions have been viewed with so much reverence, for rejecting the construction. But the peculiar expressions of the constitution of the United States furnish additional arguments in favour of its rejection.

The judicial power of the United States is extended to all cases arising under the constitution.

Could it be the intention of those who gave this power, to say that in using it the constitution should not be looked into? That a case arising under the constitution should be decided without examining the instrument under which it arises?

This is too extravagant to be maintained.

In some cases, then, the constitution must be looked into by the judges. And if they can open it at all, what part of it are they forbidden to read or to obey?

There are many other parts of the constitution which serve to illustrate this subject.

It is declared that "no tax or duty shall be laid on articles exported from any state." Suppose a duty on the export of cotton, of tobacco, or of flour; and a suit instituted to recover it. Ought judgment to be rendered in such a case? Ought the judges to close their eyes on the constitution, and only see the law?

The constitution declares "that no bill of attainder or ex post facto law shall be passed."

If, however, such a bill should be passed, and a person should be prosecuted under it; must the court condemn to death those victims whom the constitution endeavors to preserve?

"No person," says the constitution, "shall be convicted of treason unless on the testimony of two witnesses to the same overt act, or on confession in open court."

Here the language of the constitution is addressed especially to the courts. It prescribes, directly for them, a rule of evidence not to be departed from. If the legislature should change that rule, and declare one witness, or a confession out of court, sufficient for conviction, must the constitutional principle yield to the legislative act?

From these, and many other selections which might be made, it is apparent, that the Framers of the constitution contemplated that instrument as a rule for the government of courts, as well as of the legislature.

Why otherwise does it direct the judges to take an oath to support it? This oath certainly applies in an especial manner, to their conduct in their official character. How immoral to impose it on them, if they were to be used as the instruments, and the knowing instruments, for violating what they swear to support!

The oath of office, too, imposed by the legislature, is completely demonstrative of the legislative opinion on this subject. It is in these words: "I do solemnly swear that I will administer justice without respect to persons, and do equal right to the poor and to the rich; and that I will faithfully and impartially discharge all the duties incumbent on me as _____, according to the best of my abilities and understanding agreeably to the constitution and laws of the United States."

Why does a judge swear to discharge his duties agreeably to the constitution of the United States, if that constitution forms no rule for his government? If it is closed upon him, and cannot be inspected by him?

If such be the real state of things, this is worse than solemn mockery. To prescribe, or to take this oath, becomes equally a crime.

It is also not entirely unworthy of observation, that in declaring what shall be the supreme law of the land, the constitution itself is first mentioned; and not the laws of the United States generally, but those only which shall be made in pursuance of the constitution, have that rank.

Thus, the particular phraseology of the constitution of the United States confirms and strengthens the principle, supposed to be essential to all written constitutions, that a law repugnant to the constitution is void; and that courts, as well as other departments, are bound by that instrument.

The rule must be discharged.

NOTES

1. President Jefferson could not disobey Marshall's ruling, because Jefferson technically won. Still, the Supreme Court clearly assumed and exercised the power to invalidate a federal law that it found to be in violation of the Constitution. Jefferson, two decades after *Marbury*, still bristled at what

Marshall had done. In his letter to Justice William Johnson, in 1823, Jefferson complained that Marshall decided issues that not part of the case:

> This practice of Judge Marshall, of travelling out of his case to prescribe what the law would be in a moot case not before the court, is very irregular and very censurable. . . . Among the midnight appointments of Mr. Adams, were commissions to some federal justices of the peace for Alexandria. These were signed and sealed by him, but not delivered. I found them on the table of the department of State, on my entrance into office, and I forbade their delivery. Marbury, named in one of them, applied to the Supreme Court for a mandamus to the Secretary of State, (Mr. Madison) to deliver the commission intended for him. The court determined at once, that being an original process, they had no cognizance of it; and therefore the question before them was ended. But the Chief Justice went on to lay down what the law would be, had they jurisdiction of the case, to wit: that they should command the delivery. The object was clearly to instruct any other court having the jurisdiction, what they should do if Marbury should apply to them. Besides the impropriety of this gratuitous interference, could anything exceed the perversion of law? . . . Yet this case of Marbury and Madison is continually cited by bench and bar, as if it were settled law, without any animadversion on its being merely an obiter dissertation of the Chief Justice.[73]

2. The Court exercised the power to invalidate federal laws, at first, with a great deal of restraint. *Dred Scott v. Sandford* (1857) was the next major case[74] where Court invalidated federal legislation. It declared unconstitutional the Missouri Compromise, which granted freedom to slaves in certain territories. From 1787 to 1958, in only 81 instances did the Court invalidate an Act of Congress. *Trop v. Dulles*, 356 U.S. 84, 104 (1958). Since then, it's been more active.

---

[73] Letter from Thomas Jefferson to William Johnson, 12 June 1823, reprinted in Selected Letters of Thomas Jefferson 167 (Yamaguchy Incorporated, 2015).

[74] *Hodgson v. Bowerbank*, 9 U.S. (5 Cranch) 303 (1809)—a case decided after *Marbury* and before *Dred Scott*—ruled that ruled that § 11 of the Judiciary Act cannot constitutionally provide for federal jurisdiction in all suits simply because one of the parties is an alien, without regard to the citizenship of the other party. The Court rejected the argument presented that "[T]he judiciary act gives jurisdiction to the circuit courts in all suits in which an alien is a party." Chief Justice Marshall's curt response: "Turn to the article of the Constitution of the United States, for the statute cannot extend the jurisdiction beyond the limits of the Constitution."

3.   Article III of the Constitution tells us comparatively little about the third branch of government. For example, the article establishes "one supreme Court," but nowhere are we told how many Justices shall sit on the Court, or even if they must be lawyers. Article III similarly is silent on the question of "judicial review," that is, whether courts have the power to review the other branches of government to see if their acts conform to the Constitution. However, the doctrine of judicial review was in the air, so to speak, long before *Marbury.*

4.   In *Dr. Bonham's Case,* 8 Coke Rep. 118a (C.P. 1610), Lord Chief Justice Edward Coke stated: "[W]hen an Act of Parliament is against common right and reason, or repugnant, or impossible to be performed, the common law will control it and adjudge such Act to be void." Coke's dictum was only one of five points on which Coke had based his decision, but it was this statement that observers often discussed and quoted.

     The English Privy Council had the power to review acts of the colonies thought to be in violation of English law or their charters, and prior to *Marbury* some state courts purported to have the power of judicial review.

5.   In the Federalist *Papers,* No. 78 (1788), Alexander Hamilton, in discussing the proposed Constitution, argued:

     The complete independence of the courts of justice is peculiarly essential in a limited Constitution. By a limited Constitution, I understand one which contains certain specified exceptions to the legislative authority; such, for instance, as that it shall pass no bills of attainder, no *ex-post-facto* laws, and the like. Limitations of this kind can be preserved in practice no other way than through the medium of courts of justice, whose duty it must be to declare all acts contrary to the manifest tenor of the Constitution void. Without this, all the reservations of particular rights or privileges would amount to nothing.

6.   The U.S. Supreme Court, before Marshall, purported to exercise the power of judicial review, though it never invalidated any laws. A prime example is *Hayburn's Case* (1792). Several lower courts refused to implement a federal statute on the grounds of unconstitutionality. The issue went to the Supreme Court, but prior to its decision, Congress avoided a constitutional confrontation by amending the legislation. The Supreme Court then dismissed on grounds of mootness. In footnote (a) to the dismissal, the

Supreme Court reporter noted the objections of various Justices to the repealed law.

In *Hylton v. United States* (1796), the Court refused to invalidate a federal tax on carriages as unconstitutional. The Court simply assumed and did not discuss the source of this power of judicial review. In *Hollingsworth v. Virginia* (1798), the Supreme Court (in a footnote) refused to declare the Eleventh Amendment unconstitutional. Opponents of this amendment challenged it arguing that the President had not signed the resolution proposing the amendment to the states. The Court said that his signature was not necessary.

However, it was left to Marshall to actually exercise and justify the power.

7. The year after the Court decided *Marbury v. Madison,* the House of Representatives impeached Justice Samuel Chase by a vote of 73 to 42. Chase was a partisan Justice who had campaigned in 1800 for Adams in his unsuccessful attempt at reelection. For these and similar activities, Chase earned the enmity of the Jeffersonians. The complaint against Chase failed to collect the necessary two-thirds vote in the Senate, but if a broad theory of the impeachment power had been successful, it was widely thought that Marshall would be next on the impeachment list. Marshall and the other Justices had to sleep uneasily for a while, for the Chase impeachment directly threatened the independence of the judiciary. In fact, a concerned Marshall wrote to Chase during this period:

> "I think the modern doctrine of impeachment should yield to an appellate jurisdiction in the legislature. A reversal of those decisions would certainly better comport with the mildness of our character than [would] a removal of the judge who has rendered them unknowing of his fault." 3 Albert J. Beveridge, Life of Marshall 177 (1916–1919).

EAKIN V. RAUB
12 Sergent & Rawle 330, 343–56 (Pa. 1825)

[Plaintiffs claimed title to some land given to them by will. Defendants responded that the state statute of limitations barred the plaintiffs' claim. In the course of this argument, an issue was raised as to the constitutionality (under the state constitution) of the state statute of limitations. Justice John Gibson disagreed with his two colleagues on the bench as to the power of the court to review the constitutionality of the law, and his dissent is a thoughtful response to John Marshall's argument in *Marbury v. Madison*.]

GIBSON, J., dissenting.

. . . I will avail myself . . . to express an opinion which I have deliberately formed, on the abstract right of the judiciary to declare an unconstitutional act of the legislature void. It seems to me, there is a plain difference, hitherto unnoticed, between acts that are repugnant to the constitution of the particular state, and acts that are repugnant to the constitution of the United States; my opinion being, that the judiciary is bound to execute the former, but not the latter. I shall hereafter attempt to explain this difference, by pointing out the particular provisions in the constitution of the United States, on which it depends. I am aware, that a right to declare all constitutional acts void, without distinction as to either constitution, is generally held as a professional dogma; but I apprehend, rather as a matter of faith than of reason. I admit, that I once embraced the same doctrine, but without examination, and I shall, therefore, state the arguments that impelled me to abandon it, with great respect for those by whom it is still maintained. But I may premise, that it is not a little remarkable, that although the right in question has all along been claimed by the judiciary, no judge has ventured to discuss it, except Chief Justice Marshall (in *Marbury v. Madison,* 1 Cranch 176); and if the argument of a jurist so distinguished for the strength of his ratiocinative powers be found inconclusive, it may fairly be set down to the weakness of the position which he attempts to defend. . . .

The constitution of Pennsylvania contains no express grant of political powers to the judiciary. But to establish a grant by implication, the constitution is said to be a law of superior obligation; and consequently, that if it were to come into collision with an act of the legislature the latter would have to give way; this is conceded. But it is a fallacy to suppose that they can come into collision *before the judiciary*. . . . The constitution and the *right* of the legislature to pass the act, may be in collision; but is that a legitimate subject for judicial determination? If it be, the judiciary must be a peculiar organ, to revise the proceedings of the legislature, and to correct its mistakes; and in what part of the constitution are we to look for this proud preeminence? Viewing the manner in the opposite direction, what would be thought of an act of assembly in which it should be declared that the supreme court had, in a particular case, put a wrong construction on the constitution of the United States, and that the judgment should therefore be reversed? It would doubtless be thought a usurpation of judicial power. But it is by no means clear, that to declare a law void which has been enacted according to the forms prescribed in the constitution, is not a usurpation of legislative power. It is an act of sovereignty; and sovereignty and legislative power are said by Sir William Blackstone to be convertible terms. It is the business of the judiciary to interpret the laws, not scan the authority of the lawgiver; and without the latter, it cannot take cognizance of a collision between a law and the constitution. So that to affirm that the judiciary has a right to judge of the existence of such collision, is to take for granted the very thing to be proved. . . .

But the judges are sworn to support the constitution, and are they not bound by it as the law of the land? . . . The oath to support the constitution is not peculiar to the judges, but is taken indiscriminately by every officer of the government, and is designed rather as a test of the political principles of the man, than to bind the officer in the discharge of his duty; otherwise it were difficult to determine what operation it is to have in the case of a recorder of deeds, for instance, who in the execution of his office has nothing to do with the constitution. But granting it to relate to the official conduct of the judge, as well as every other officer, and not to his political principles, still it must be understood in reference to supporting the constitution, *only as far as that may be involved in his official duty;* and consequently if his official duty does not comprehend an inquiry into the authority of the legislature, neither does his oath. . . . But the oath was more probably designed to secure the powers of each of the different branches from being usurped by any of the rest; for instance, to prevent the house of representatives from erecting itself into a court of judicature, or the supreme court from attempting to control the legislature: and in this view, the oath furnishes an argument, equally plausible *against* the right of the judiciary. . . .

But do not the judges do a *positive* act in violation of the constitution when they give effect to an unconstitutional law? Not if the law has been passed according to the forms established in the constitution. The fallacy of the question is in supposing that the judiciary adopts the acts of the legislature as its own; whereas the enactment of a law and the interpretation of it are not concurrent acts, and as the judiciary is not required to concur in the enactment, neither is it in the breach of the constitution which may be the consequence of the enactment; the fault is imputable to the legislature, and on it the responsibility exclusively rests. In this respect the judges are in the predicament of jurors, who are bound to serve in capital cases although unable, under any circumstances, to reconcile it to their duty to deprive a human being of life. . . .

But it has been said that this construction would deprive the citizen of the advantages which are peculiar to a written constitution, by at once declaring the power of the legislature, in practice, to be illimitable. I ask, what are those advantages? The principles of a written constitution are more fixed and certain, and more apparent to the apprehension of the people than principles which depend on tradition and the vague comprehension of the individuals who compose the nation, . . . for, after all, there is no effectual guard against legislative usurpation, but public opinion, the force of which, in this country, is inconceivably great. Happily, this is proved by experience to be a sufficient guard against palpable *infra*ctions. . . . Once let public opinion be so corrupt as to sanction every misconstruction of the constitution, and abuse of power, which the temptation of the moment may dictate, and the party which may happen to be predominant, will laugh at the puny efforts of a dependent power to arrest it in its course.

For these reasons, I am of opinion, that it rests with the people, in whom full and absolute sovereign power resides, to correct abuses in legislation, by instructing their representatives to repeal the obnoxious act. . . . It might, perhaps, have been better to vest the power in the judiciary; as it might be expected, that its habits of deliberation, and the aid derived from the arguments of counsel, would more frequently lead to accurate conclusions. On the other hand, the judiciary is not infallible; and an error by it would admit of no remedy but a more distinct expression of the public will, through the extraordinary medium of a convention; whereas, an error by the legislature admits of a remedy by an exertion of the same will, in the ordinary exercise of the right of suffrage—a mode better calculated to attain the end, without popular excitement. It may be said, the people would probably not notice an error of their representatives. But they would as probably do so, as notice an error of the judiciary; and beside, it is a *postulate* in the theory of our government, and the very basis of the superstructure, that the people are wise, virtuous, and competent to manage their own affairs; and if they are not so, in fact, still, every question of this sort must be determined according to the principles of the constitution, as it came from the hands of its Framers, and the existence of a defect which was not foreseen, would not justify those who administer the government, in applying a corrective in practice, which can be provided only by a convention. . . .

But in regard to an act of assembly, which is found to be in collision with the constitution, laws or treaties of the United States, I take the duty of the judiciary to be exactly the reverse. By becoming parties to the federal constitution the states have agreed to several limitations of their individual sovereignty, to enforce which, it was thought to be absolutely necessary, to prevent them from giving effect to laws in violation of those limitations, through the instrumentality of their own judges. Accordingly, it is declared in the fifth article and second section of the federal constitution, that "This constitution, and the laws of the United States which shall be made in pursuance thereof, and all treaties made, or which shall be made under the authority of the United States, shall be the *supreme* law of the land; and the *judges* in every *state* shall be BOUND thereby; anything in the *laws* or *constitution* of any *state* to the contrary notwithstanding." [J]udges are to be bound by the federal constitution and laws, notwithstanding anything in the constitution or laws of the particular state *to the contrary*. If, then, a state were to declare the laws of the United States not to be obligatory on her judges, such an act would unquestionably be void; for it will not be pretended, that any member of the union can dispense with the obligation of the federal constitution; and if it cannot be done directly, and by a general declaratory law, neither can it indirectly, and by by-laws dispensing with it in particular cases. This, therefore, is an express grant of the power. . . .

NOTES

1.   Notice how Justice Gibson, both in the beginning of his dissent and at the end, drew a distinction between the power of judges to declare state laws invalid as violating the U.S. Constitution (a power that he would grant) and the power of judges to invalidate state laws as violating the state constitution (a power that he would deny). Gibson later changed his position and accepted judicial review because of what he saw as the acquiescence of the people and practical necessity. *Norris v. Clymer,* 2 Pa. 277, 281 (1845).

      What do you think of Justice Gibson's original distinction? Justice Holmes once said, "I do not think the United States would come to an end if we lost our power to declare an Act of Congress void. I do think the Union would be imperiled if we could not make that declaration as to the laws of the several States." Holmes, Collected Legal Papers 295–96 (1920). In Switzerland, for example, although Swiss courts have the power to disregard the laws of the cantons judged to conflict with the Swiss federal constitution, the courts have no power of judicial review over federal laws.

2.   Can democracy exist *without* having the courts as the final arbiters? In England, Parliament can change judicial decisions by statute. Although the French have a written constitution, French judges have no general power of judicial review over the constitutionality of legislation.

      Can democracy exist *with* the courts as final arbiters? Marshall says that our government is "a government of laws, and not of men." However, judges are just as human as legislators are. Is our government a government of judges? Charles Evans Hughes remarked in 1907, "We are under a Constitution, but the Constitution is what the judges say it is." In 1930, Hughes became Chief Justice.

Is there a danger that the institution of judicial review will encourage the other branches of government to abdicate their responsibility to follow the Constitution? In 1935, President Roosevelt wrote a letter urging a congressman to support a bill. The letter concluded: "I hope your committee will not permit doubts as to constitutionality, however reasonable, to block the suggested legislation."

MARTIN V. HUNTER'S LESSEE
14 U.S. (1 Wheat.) 304, 4 L.Ed. 97 (1816)

[The first case in which the Supreme Court held a state statute unconstitutional was *Fletcher v. Peck,* 10 U.S. (6 Cranch) 87, 3 L.Ed. 162 (1810), but the case came to the Supreme Court from the U.S. circuit court for the district of Massachusetts, not from a state court. Chief Justice Marshall wrote the opinion of the Court, which held that a state law of Georgia impaired the obligation of contracts. *Martin v. Hunter's Lessee* was the first case in which the authority of the U.S. Supreme Court to review state court decisions in matters involving federal questions was challenged by the state courts; the Supreme Court responded by squarely upholding the constitutionality of section 25 of the Judiciary Act of 1789, which gave the Supreme Court appellate review over such state court decisions. Charles Warren, in his history of the Supreme Court, concluded that *Martin's* "vital effect upon the history of the United States of this courageous maintenance of Federal supremacy and of the constitutional powers of the Federal Judiciary can hardly be over-emphasized. . . ."[75]

[The decision in *Martin* ended over a century of litigation over who had title to approximately 300,000 acres in Virginia known as Northern Neck. Before the Revolutionary War, Lord Fairfax had title to the land. In 1779, the legislature of the Commonwealth of Virginia passed a law providing for forfeiture of property belonging to British subjects, who then were enemy aliens. This law provided a procedure for forfeiture of such land, an inquest of office. In 1782 the Virginia legislature passed another law declaring that Northern Neck was probably claimed by enemy aliens and was therefore forfeited. The procedure for forfeiture of such land pursuant to the Act of 1779 was not followed. Other legislation also

---

[75] Charles Warren, 1, The Supreme Court in United States History 450–51 (Little Brown & Co. 1922).

specifically dealing with Northern Neck followed. It was pursuant to one of these laws, the Act of 1785, that David Hunter claimed his land in Northern Neck.

[Meanwhile, the Revolutionary War had ended, and the Treaty of 1783 with England had declared that there should be "no future confiscations" of land belonging to British subjects.

[David Hunter in 1791 sued in the Virginia state courts to eject Lord Fairfax's heir, Denny Martin Fairfax, to whom Lord Fairfax willed the land. Hunter lost the state trial court in 1794; in 1810, the Virginia Court of Appeals reversed the trial court. Pursuant to section 25 of the Judiciary Act of 1789, the case went to the U.S. Supreme Court. Chief Justice Marshall took no part in the case because he had personal interests in the case: he had contracted with Martin to purchase part of Northern Neck. Therefore, the task of writing the opinion fell to Justice Story.

[President Madison appointed Joseph Story to the Supreme Court in 1811, when Story was only 32 years old. He wasn't Madison's first choice, but his third.[76] Story was a state legislator. He had also been a U.S. Representative from Massachusetts, but he quit because he said he did not like the political chicanery of Washington DC. (Yes, even then there was political chicanery. Some things never change.)

[Story accepted the political appointment and gave up his private practice, even though it meant he took about a 50% cut in salary, to $3500 a year. By the time of his death at age 66, he was earning over $10,000 per year in book royalties. His salary is associate Justice had moved up to $4500 per year, plus he was also a chaired professor at Harvard Law School. His yearly income at that point was at least a $1 million a year in present day dollars. All at a time when there was no federal or state income tax! Story was a very successful lawyer.

[Madison, a Jeffersonian, appointed Story to be an intellectual counterweight to the Federalist, John Marshall. Some say that Story quickly came under Marshall's spell. Others think Story was his own man. Story held that the land had not properly passed to Hunter before the treaty came into existence; consequently, the treaty protected the alien. *Fairfax Devisee v. Hunter's Lessee,* 11 U.S. (7 Cranch) 603, 622, 3 L.Ed. 453 (1813).

[The Supreme Court then sent the case back to the Virginia Court of Appeals, which objected both to the fact that the U.S. Supreme Court reversed the Virginia Court and to the offensive tone of the Supreme Court mandate. The Virginia

---

[76] Madison nominated Levi Lincoln, who declined because of ill health, and also John Quincy Adams, who declined and decided to remain as Ambassador to Russia.

Court reprinted the mandate, which in part stated: "You therefore are commanded that such proceedings be had in said cause as according . . . to said judgment and instructions of said Supreme Court ought to be had, the said writ of error notwithstanding." *Hunter v. Martin, devisee of Fairfax,* 18 Va. (4 Munford) 1, 3 (1815).[77] The Virginia court refused to obey the mandate and held:

> The court is unanimously of opinion that the appellate power of the Supreme Court of the United States does not extend to this court under a sound construction of the constitution of the United States; that so much of the 25th section of the act of Congress, to establish the judicial courts of the United States, as extends the appellate jurisdiction of the Supreme Court to this court, is not in pursuance of the constitution of the United States. That the writ of error in this cause was improvidently allowed under the authority of that act; that the proceedings thereon in the Supreme Court were *coram non judice*[78] in relation to this court, and that obedience to its mandate be declined by the court.

[The case then went back to the U.S. Supreme Court.

[Once again, the task of writing the opinion fell to Story. His opinion, supporting a strong national judicial supremacy, is all the more remarkable when one realizes that the Federalist Chief Justice did not sit on this case and that Presidents Jefferson or Madison had appointed all but one of the other Justices.]

MR. JUSTICE STORY delivered the opinion of the court.

This is a writ of error from the Court of Appeals of Virginia, founded upon the refusal of that court to obey the mandate of this court, requiring the judgment rendered in this very cause, at February term, 1813, to be carried into due execution. . . .

The questions involved in this judgment are of great importance and delicacy. Perhaps it is not too much to affirm that, upon their right decision, rest some of the most solid principles which have hitherto been supposed to sustain and protect the constitution itself. The great respectability, too, of the court whose decisions we are called upon to review, and the entire deference which we entertain for the learning and ability of that court, add much to the difficulty of

---

[77] The tone of Supreme Court mandates has softened. Typically if the Supreme Court remands a case to *state* courts, the mandate provides for "further proceedings not inconsistent with this opinion." In contrast, as to lower federal courts the language is more assertive: such a remand provides for "further proceedings consistent with this opinion."

[78] Ed. Note: Latin for "not before a judge," meaning that the U.S. Supreme Court lacked the authority to decide this case.

the task which has so unwelcomely fallen upon us. It is, however, a source of consolation that we have had the assistance of most able and learned arguments to aid our inquiries; and that the opinion which is now to be pronounced has been weighed with every solicitude to come to a correct result, and matured after solemn deliberation.

Before proceeding to the principal questions, it may not be unfit to dispose of some preliminary considerations which have grown out of the arguments at the bar.

The constitution of the United States was ordained and established, not by the states in their sovereign capacities, but emphatically, as the preamble of the constitution declares, by "the people of the United States." [I]t is perfectly clear that the sovereign powers vested in the state governments, by their respective constitutions, remained unaltered and unimpaired, except so far as they were granted to the government of the United States. . . .

The constitution unavoidably deals in general language. It did not suit the purposes of the people, in framing this great charter of our liberties, to provide for minute specifications of its powers, or to declare the means by which those powers should be carried into execution. It was foreseen that this would be a perilous and difficult, if not an impracticable, task. The instrument was not intended to provide merely for the exigencies of a few years, but was to endure through a long lapse of ages, the events of which were locked up in the inscrutable purposes of Providence. It could not be foreseen what new changes and modifications of power might be indispensable to effectuate the general objects of the charter; and restrictions and specifications which, at the present, might seem salutary, might, in the end, prove the overthrow of the system itself. Hence its powers are expressed in general terms, leaving to the legislature, from time to time, to adopt its own means to effectuate legitimate objects, and to mold and model the exercise of its powers, as its own wisdom and the public interests should require.

With these principles in view—principles in respect to which no difference of opinion ought to be indulged—let us now proceed to the interpretation of the constitution, so far as regards the great points in controversy. . . .

This leads us to the consideration of the great question as to the nature and extent of the appellate jurisdiction of the United States. . . . The appellate power is not limited by the terms of the third article to any particular courts. The words are, "the judicial power (which includes appellate power) shall extend to all cases," etc., and "in all other cases before mentioned the Supreme Court shall have appellate jurisdiction." It is the case, then, and not the court, that gives the jurisdiction. If the judicial power extends to the case, it will be in vain to search in the letter of the constitution for any qualification as to the tribunal where it depends. It is incumbent, then, upon those who assert such a qualification to show its existence by necessary implication. If the text be clear and distinct, no restriction upon its plain and obvious import ought to be admitted, unless the inference be irresistible.

If the constitution meant to limit the appellate jurisdiction to cases pending in the courts of the United States, it would necessarily follow that the jurisdiction of these courts would, in all the cases enumerated in the constitution, be exclusive of state tribunals. How otherwise could the jurisdiction extend to all cases arising under the constitution, laws and treaties of the United States, or to all cases of admiralty and maritime jurisdiction? If some of these cases might be entertained by state tribunals, and no appellate jurisdiction as to them should exist, then the appellate power would not extend to all, but to some, cases. If state tribunals might exercise concurrent jurisdiction over all or some of the other classes of cases in the constitution without control, then the appellate jurisdiction of the United States might, as to such cases, have no real existence, contrary to the manifest intent of the constitution. Under such circumstances, to give effect to the judicial power, it must be construed to be exclusive; and this not only when the *casus faederis* should arise directly, but when it should arise, incidentally, in cases pending in state courts. This construction would abridge the jurisdiction of such courts far more than has been ever contemplated in any act of Congress.

On the other hand, if, as has been contended, a discretion be vested in Congress to establish, or not to establish, inferior courts at their own pleasure, and Congress should not establish such courts, the appellate jurisdiction of the Supreme Court would have nothing to act upon, unless it could act upon cases pending in the state courts. Under such circumstances it must be held that the appellate power would extend to state courts; for the constitution is peremptory that it shall extend to certain enumerated cases, which cases could exist in no other courts. Any other construction, upon this supposition, would involve this strange contradiction, that a discretionary power vested in Congress, and which they might rightfully omit to exercise, would defeat the absolute injunctions of the constitution in relation to the whole appellate power.

But it is plain that the Framers of the constitution did contemplate that cases within the judicial cognizance of the United States not only might but would arise in the state courts, in the exercise of their ordinary jurisdiction. With this view the sixth article declares, that "this constitution, and the laws of the United States which shall be made in pursuance thereof, and all treaties made, or which shall be made, under the authority of the United States, shall be the supreme law of the land, and the judges in every state shall be bound thereby, anything in the constitution or laws of any state to the contrary notwithstanding." It is obvious that this obligation is imperative upon the state judges in their official, and not merely in their private, capacities. From the very nature of their judicial duties they would be called upon to pronounce the law applicable to the case in judgment. They were not to decide merely according to the laws or constitution of the state, but according to the constitution, laws and treaties of the United States—"the supreme law of the land." . . .

It must, therefore, be conceded that the constitution not only contemplated, but meant to provide for cases within the scope of the judicial power of the United States, which might yet depend before state tribunals. It was foreseen that in the exercise of their ordinary jurisdiction, state courts would incidentally take cognizance of cases arising under the constitution, the laws and treaties of the United States. Yet to all these cases the judicial power, by the very terms of the constitution, is to extend. It cannot extend by original jurisdiction if that was already rightfully and exclusively attached in the state courts, which (as has been already shown) may occur; it must, therefore, extend by appellate jurisdiction, or not at all. It would seem to follow that the appellate power of the United States must, in such cases, extend to state tribunals; and if in such cases, there is no reason why it should not equally attach upon all others within the purview of the constitution. . . .

It is a mistake [to believe] that the constitution was not designed to operate upon states, in their corporate capacities. It is crowded with provisions which restrain or annul the sovereignty of the states in some of the highest branches of their prerogatives. The tenth section of the first article contains a long list of disabilities and prohibitions imposed upon the states. Surely, when such essential portions of state sovereignty are taken away, or prohibited to be exercised, it cannot be correctly asserted that the constitution does not act upon the states. The language of the constitution is also imperative upon the states as to the performance of many duties. It is imperative upon the state legislatures to make laws prescribing the time, places, and manner of holding elections for senators and representatives, and for electors of President and Vice-President. And in these, as well as some other cases, Congress have a right to revise, amend, or supersede the laws which may be passed by state legislatures. When, therefore, the states are stripped of some of the highest attributes of sovereignty, and the same are given to the United States; when the legislatures of the states are, in some respects, under the control of Congress, and in every case are, under the constitution, bound by the paramount authority of the United States; it is certainly difficult to support the argument that the appellate power over the decisions of state courts is contrary to the genius of our institutions. The courts of the United States can, without question, revise the proceedings of the executive and legislative authorities of the states, and if they are found to be contrary to the constitution, may declare them to be of no legal validity. Surely the exercise of the same right over judicial tribunals is not a higher or more dangerous act of sovereign power.

Nor can such a right be deemed to impair the independence of state judges. It is assuming the very ground in controversy to assert that they possess an absolute independence of the United States. In respect to the powers granted to the United States, they are not independent; they are expressly bound to obedience by the letter of the constitution; and if they should unintentionally transcend their authority, or misconstrue the constitution, there is no more reason for giving their judgments an absolute and irresistible force than for giving it to the acts of the other co-ordinate departments of state sovereignty. The argument urged from the possibility of the abuse of the revising power is equally unsatisfactory. It is always a doubtful course to argue against the use of existence of a power, from the possibility of its abuse. . . .

The constitution has presumed (whether rightly or wrongly we do not inquire) that state attachments, state prejudices, state jealousies, and state interests, might sometimes obstruct, or control, or be supposed to obstruct or control, the regular administration of justice. . . . This is not all. A motive of another kind, perfectly compatible, with the most sincere respect for state tribunals, might induce the grant of appellate power over their decisions. That motive is the importance, and even necessity of uniformity of decisions throughout the whole United States, upon all subjects within the purview of the constitution. Judges of equal learning and integrity, in different states, might differently interpret a statute, or a treaty of the United States, or even the constitution itself. . . .

On the whole, the court are of opinion that the appellate power of the United States does extend to cases pending in the state courts; and that the 25th section of the judiciary act, which authorizes the exercise of this jurisdiction in the specified cases, by a writ of error, is supported by the letter and spirit of the constitution. We find no clause in that instrument which limits this power; and we dare not interpose a limitation where the people have not been disposed to create one.

Strong as this conclusion stands upon the general language of the constitution, it may still derive support from other sources. It is an historical fact that this exposition of the constitution, extending its appellate power to state courts, was, previous to its adoption, uniformly and publicly avowed by its friends, and admitted by its enemies, as the basis of their respective reasonings, both in and out of the state conventions. . . . It is an historical fact that the Supreme Court of the United States have, from time to time, sustained this appellate jurisdiction in a great variety of cases, brought from the tribunals of many of the most important states in the Union, and that no state tribunal has ever breathed a judicial doubt on the subject, or declined to obey the mandate of the Supreme Court, until the present occasion. This weight of contemporaneous exposition by all parties, this acquiescence of enlightened state courts, and these judicial decisions of the Supreme Court through so long a period, do, as we think, place the doctrine upon a foundation of authority which cannot be shaken, without delivering over the subject to perpetual and irremediable doubts. . . .

It is the opinion of the whole court that the judgment of the Court of Appeals of Virginia, rendered on the mandate in this cause, be reversed, and the judgment of the District Court, held at Winchester, be, and the same is hereby affirmed.

[The opinion of JOHNSON, J., concurring in the result, is omitted.]

NOTES

1. Story relies in part on the intent of the Framers, historical practice, and the previous acquiescence of state courts. Do you find these historical arguments compelling? Federalist Papers No. 82, by Hamilton, argued: "[W]hat relation would subsist between the national and state courts in these instances of concurrent jurisdiction? I answer, an appeal would certainly lie from the latter, to the supreme court of the United States." Should Story have mentioned this fact? Note that the lengthy opinion excerpted above has a dearth of citations of authority.

2. After *Martin,* the Supreme Court held, in *Cohens v. Virginia,* 19 U.S. (6 Wheat.) 264, 5 L.Ed. 257 (1821), that it also had jurisdiction under section 25 of the Judiciary Act to review state criminal proceedings. The Court, speaking through Chief Justice Marshall, held that the Eleventh Amendment (which requires that some types of suits brought against states cannot be initiated in federal court) did not apply when suit was instituted by the state rather than by a noncitizen against a state, and that the fact that a state was a party to the

suit was no objection to the Court's exercise of its jurisdiction. Marshall decided on the merits in favor of Virginia. An arch-foe of Marshall, Spencer Roane of the Virginia Court of Appeals, reacted in a letter of December 11, 1821: "The career of this high court must be stopped or the liberties of our country are annihilated."[79]

The decisions in *Martin* and in *Cohens v. Virginia* should have settled the matter, and as a matter of legal precedent, they did. Nonetheless, in practice state courts have occasionally rejected the doctrine of federal supremacy and Supreme Court review of their decisions. "Between 1789 and 1860 the courts of seven States denied the constitutional right of the United States Court to decide cases on writs of error to State courts—Virginia, Ohio, Georgia, Kentucky, South Carolina, California, and Wisconsin. The Legislatures of all of these states (except California), and also of Pennsylvania and Maryland, formally adopted resolutions or statutes against this power of the Supreme Court. Bills were introduced in Congress on at least ten occasions to deprive the Court of its jurisdiction."[80] For example, House Report No. 43, 21st Cong., 2d Sess. (1831) concluded that "the twenty-fifth section, an act of Congress, entitled 'An act to establish the judicial courts of the United States,' passed on the 4th September, 1789, is unconstitutional, and ought to be repealed. . . . If the *nature* of the *case* be the only ground of jurisdiction, will it not authorize the Supreme Court to issue a citation or writ of error to a court of England or France, on the pretext" that "one of the questions arose under a treaty of the United States?"

3. In *Ableman v. Booth,* 62 U.S. (21 How.) 506, 16 L.Ed. 169 (1858), the Court denied the power of the Wisconsin Supreme Court to issue a writ of habeas corpus to release a prisoner who was being held in federal custody for aiding in the escape of a fugitive slave. Chief Justice Taney broadly stated, "It was felt by the statesmen who framed the Constitution, and by the people who adopted it, that it was necessary that many of the rights of sovereignty which the States then possessed should be ceded to the General Government; and that, in the sphere of action assigned to it, it should be supreme, and strong enough to execute its own laws by its own tribunals, without interruption from a State or from State authorities."

---

[79] Roane to Archibald Thweat, reprinted in 2 John P. Branch, Historical Papers of Randolph-Macon College 140–41 (1905).

[80] Warren, Legislative and Judicial Attacks on the Supreme Court of the United States: A History of the Twenty-fifth Section of the Judiciary Act, 47 Am.L.Rev. 1, 3–4 (1913).

For 80 years prior to *Booth,* state courts had often asserted "a right, through the use of habeas corpus, to take persons out of the custody of federal officials." Even after *Booth,* various state courts still granted habeas relief on the grounds that *Booth* only applied where the prisoner was held under actual federal process.

Then, in *Tarble's Case,* 80 U.S. (13 Wall.) 397 (1871), the Court clearly extended *Booth* to cases where there was no federal judicial proceeding. *Tarble's Case* prohibited state courts (again, it was in Wisconsin) from using habeas to order the release of a U.S. Army enlisted soldier under the custody of a recruiting officer. Tarble's father sued, claiming that his son was under age and had enlisted without consent. State officials, Justice Field said, could not interfere with "the execution of [the military] power of the National government."

In *Tennessee v. Davis,* 100 U.S. 257, 25 L.Ed. 648 (1880), a federal revenue officer was indicted by Tennessee for murdering some armed men when they assaulted him while he was trying to seize apparatus "used for the illicit and unlawful distillation of spirits." The Supreme Court held that he could remove his criminal trial to federal court for trial in order to present his federal defenses. The Court rejected the state's argument that it violated state sovereignty to require the state to prosecute the state case in federal court. That argument "assumes that the States are completely and in all respects sovereign."

In *Testa v. Katt,* 330 U.S. 386, 67 S.Ct. 810, 91 L.Ed. 967 (1947), the Court held Congress could compel state courts to enforce federal law. The federal Emergency Price Control Act authorized the buyer of goods to sue the seller if he or she sold for more than the ceiling price. The buyer could collect punitive damages of three times the amount overcharged plus attorney's fees. The Rhode Island Supreme Court refused; it held that it would not enforce the penal statute of a "foreign" sovereign in the "private international sense." Relying on the supremacy clause, Art. VI, § 2, Justice Black for the Court reversed the state court. Black said that it was unnecessary to decide whether the federal statute was penal "in the 'public international,' 'private international,' or any other sense." Unless Congress precludes state court jurisdiction, states cannot "deny enforcement to claims growing out of a valid federal law."

4.   In *Cooper v. Aaron,* 358 U.S. 1, 78 S.Ct. 1401, 3 L.Ed.2d 5 (1958) (August Special Term), the Court—in a dramatic opinion signed by each of the nine

Justices[81]—rejected the claim of the governor and legislature of Arkansas that they were not bound by *Brown v. Board of Education,* 347 U.S. 483, 74 S.Ct. 686, 98 L.Ed. 873 (1954), which prohibited state-enforced racial discrimination in schools. The Supreme Court heard oral argument on Sept. 11, 1958, decided the case on September 12, and issued its opinion on September 29. The Court said:

> We are urged to uphold a suspension of the Little Rock School Board's plan to do away with segregated public schools in Little Rock until state laws and efforts to upset and nullify our holding in *Brown v. Board of Education* have been further challenged and tested in the courts. We reject these contentions. . . . Article VI of the Constitution makes the Constitution the "supreme Law of the Land." [Chief Justice Marshall] declared, in the notable case of *Marbury v. Madison*, that "It is emphatically the province and duty of the judicial department to say what the law is." This decision declared the basic principle that the federal judiciary is supreme in the exposition of the law of the Constitution, and that principle has ever since been respected by this Court and the Country as a permanent and indispensable feature of our constitutional system. It follows that the interpretation of the Fourteenth Amendment enunciated by this Court in the *Brown* case is the supreme law of the land, and Art. VI of the Constitution makes it of binding effect on the States "any Thing in the Constitution or Laws of any State to the Contrary notwithstanding." Every state legislator and executive and judicial officer is solemnly committed by oath taken pursuant to Art. VI, cl. 3, "to support this Constitution," Chief Justice Taney, speaking for a unanimous Court in 1859, said that this requirement reflected the Framers' "anxiety to preserve it [the Constitution] in full force, in all its powers, and to guard against resistance to or evasion of its authority, on the part of a State." *Ableman v. Booth.*

---

[81] The opinion was too important to be designated "per curiam," *i.e.*, signed by none of the Justices. Apparently each Justice wanted to be listed, so the opinion listed them all. The first line of the opinion read, "Opinion of the Court by The CHIEF JUSTICE, MR. JUSTICE BLACK, MR. JUSTICE FRANKFURTER, MR. JUSTICE DOUGLAS, MR. JUSTICE BURTON, MR. JUSTICE CLARK, MR. JUSTICE HARLAN, MR. JUSTICE BRENNAN, and MR. JUSTICE WHITTAKER."

1.8 CONSTITUTIONAL LIMITATIONS ON JUDICIAL REVIEW

1.8.1   Advisory Opinions

Recall that in *Marbury v. Madison,* Chief Justice Marshall argued that the courts have no choice but to exercise judicial review in all cases properly brought before them. "Those who apply the rule to particular cases, must of necessity expound and interpret the rule. If two laws conflict with each other, the courts must decide on the operation of each."

Not all cases are properly before the court. *Marbury* was one example of a case that the court held was not properly before it. Article III of the Constitution places other limits on the jurisdictional power of federal courts. In general, Article III, § 2, cls. 1 and 2 authorize Congress to give federal courts jurisdiction based on either the nature of the question or the nature of the parties. Federal questions are those that arise under the Constitution, treaties, or laws of the United States (including admiralty laws). Federal courts can also have jurisdiction because of the nature of the parties—that is, if the parties are ambassadors, citizens from different states ("diversity jurisdiction), states, or the United States.

Even if the nature of the question or the nature of the parties brings a case is within Article III, another important limit, in Article III, § 2, cl. 1, is that the federal judicial power only extends to "cases" or "controversies." Federal judges may not act in a nonjudicial capacity. An early decision implementing this principle is *Hayburn's Case,* 2 U.S. (2 Dall.) 409, 1 L.Ed. 436 (1792). A statute empowered federal courts to determine the propriety and amount of pensions for disabled veterans of the Revolutionary War. The statute provided for the Secretary of War to review the court decision and transmit an opinion to Congress. If Congress agreed, it would appropriate the necessary funds. In effect, the litigant could appeal from the Court to the Secretary of War to Congress. Because the Secretary of War and Congress could reject the judicial decision, the Circuit Court for the District of Pennsylvania refused to consider William Hayburn's application for a pension under the statute. Attorney General Edmund Randolph then sought a writ of mandamus in the Supreme Court.

While this case was pending, Congress avoided a constitutional confrontation by amending the legislation to provide other relief for the pensioners. Therefore, the Supreme Court dismissed on grounds of mootness. In footnote (a) to the dismissal, however, the reporter noted some of the earliest thinking on the constitutional division between the legislative and judicial functions. This footnote quoted Chief Justice Jay and Justice Cushing, who (sitting as circuit court judges), ruled that the duties under the original Act were not judicial—they were actually administrative—so judges could not perform them in their capacity as judges. This footnote in *Hayburn's Case* also cited letters to the President from two circuit courts concerning the same statute. They concluded that no decision of any court of the United States could be liable to revision or suspension by the legislature because the Congress had no judicial power but impeachment.

Some state courts give *advisory opinions*, if their state constitutions allow that. Article III does not impose the case or controversy restriction to state courts because Article II does not apply to state courts. However, because of the "case or controversy" requirement, federal judges may not give advisory opinions. They may not simply announce their view of interesting legal questions. The leading case is *Muskrat v. United States*.

MUSKRAT V. UNITED STATES
219 U.S. 346, 31 S.Ct. 250, 55 L.Ed. 246 (1911)

[Congress enacted a statute in 1902 that transferred the ownership of Cherokee property from the tribe to individual members of the tribe. Five years later Congress enacted two other statutes that increased the number of Cherokees entitled to take ownership of the land and limited the rights of the Cherokees to sell the land. In order to answer the question whether these later acts were unconstitutional (Did they deprive the first group of Cherokees of property without due process and just compensation?), Congress also provided for jurisdiction in the court of claims and the U.S. Supreme Court, to rule on the constitutionality of these two statutes. The United States was the defendant, and if the plaintiffs were successful, the United States would pay plaintiffs' attorney fees.]

MR. JUSTICE DAY delivered the opinion of the Court.

These cases arise under an act of Congress undertaking to confer jurisdiction upon the Court of Claims, and upon this court on appeal, to determine the validity of certain acts of Congress. . . . This act is the authority for the maintenance of these two suits.

The first question in these cases, as in others, involves the jurisdiction of this court to entertain the proceeding, and that depends upon whether the jurisdiction conferred is within the power of Congress, having in view the limitations of the judicial power as established by the Constitution of the United States. . . .

It will serve to elucidate the nature and extent of the judicial power thus conferred by the Constitution to note certain instances in which this court has had occasion to examine and define the same. As early as 1792, an act of Congress, March 23, 1792, was brought to the attention of this court, which undertook to provide for the settlement of claims of widows and orphans barred by the limitations theretofore established regulating claims to invalid pensions. The act was not construed by this court, but came under consideration before the then Chief Justice and another Justice of this court and the District Judge, and their conclusions are given in the margin of the report of *Hayburn's Case*. The act undertook to devolve upon the Circuit Court of the United States the duty of examining proofs, of determining what amount of the monthly pay would be equivalent to the disability ascertained, and to certify the same to the Secretary of War, who was to place the names of the applicants on the pension list of the United States in conformity thereto, unless he had cause to suspect imposition or mistake, in which event he might withhold the name of the applicant and report the same to Congress.

In the note to the report of the case in 2 Dall, it appeared that CHIEF JUSTICE JAY, MR. JUSTICE CUSHING and District Judge Duane unanimously agreed: . . .

> That neither the legislative nor the executive branches can constitutionally assign to the judicial any duties but such as are properly judicial, and to be performed in a judicial manner.

> That the duties assigned to the Circuit Courts, by this act, are not of that description. . . .

In 1793, by direction of the President, Secretary of State Jefferson addressed to the Justices of the Supreme Court a communication soliciting their views upon the question whether their advice to the executive would be available in the solution of important questions of the construction of treaties, laws of nations and laws of the land, which the Secretary said were often presented under circumstances which *"do not give a cognizance of them to the tribunals of the country."* The answer to the question was postponed until the subsequent sitting of the Supreme Court, when Chief Justice Jay and his associates answered to President Washington that in consideration of the lines of separation drawn by the Constitution between the three departments of government, and being judges of a court of last resort, afforded strong arguments against the propriety of extra judicially deciding the questions alluded to, and expressing the view that the power given by the Constitution to the President of calling on heads of departments for opinions "seems to have been purposely, as well as expressly, united to the executive departments." Correspondence & Public Papers of John Jay, vol. 3, p. 486. . . . It is therefore apparent that from its earliest history this court has consistently declined to exercise any powers other than those which are strictly judicial in their nature.

It therefore becomes necessary to inquire what is meant by the judicial power thus conferred by the Constitution upon this court and with the aid of appropriate legislation upon the inferior courts of the United States. "Judicial power," says Mr. Justice Miller, in his work on the Constitution, "is the power of a court to decide and pronounce a judgment and carry it into effect between persons and parties who bring a case before it for decision." Miller, Const. 314. . . .

[B]y the express terms of the Constitution, the exercise of the judicial power is limited to "cases" and "controversies." Beyond this it does not extend, and unless it is asserted in a case or controversy within the meaning of the Constitution, the power to exercise it is nowhere conferred.

What, then, does the Constitution mean in conferring this judicial power with the right to determine "cases" and "controversies." A "case" was defined by Mr. Chief Justice Marshall as early as the leading case of *Marbury v. Madison* to be a suit instituted according to the regular course of judicial procedure. And what more, if anything, is meant in the use of the term "controversy?" That question was dealt with by Mr. Justice Field, at the circuit, in the case of *Re Pacific R. Commission*, 32 Fed. 241, 255. Of these terms that learned Justice said:

> "The judicial article of the Constitution mentions cases and controversies. The term 'controversies,' if distinguishable at all from 'cases,' is so in that it is less comprehensive than the latter, and includes only suits of a civil nature. . . . The term ["case"] implies the existence of present or possible adverse parties, whose contentions are submitted to the court for adjudication."

The power being thus limited to require an application of the judicial power to cases and controversies, Is the act which undertook to authorize the present suits to determine the constitutional validity of certain legislation within the constitutional authority of the court? This inquiry in the case before us includes the broader question, When may this court, in the exercise of the judicial power, pass upon the constitutional validity of an act of Congress? That question has been settled from the early history of the court, the leading case on the subject being *Marbury v. Madison*.

In that case Chief Justice Marshall, who spoke for the court, was careful to point out that the right to declare an act of Congress unconstitutional could only be exercised when a proper case between opposing parties was submitted for judicial determination; that there was no general veto power in the court upon the legislation of Congress; and that the authority to declare an act unconstitutional sprang from the requirement that the court, in administering the law and pronouncing judgment between the parties to a case, and choosing between the requirements of the fundamental law established by the people and embodied in the Constitution and an act of the agents of the people, acting under authority of the Constitution, should enforce the Constitution as the supreme law of the land. The Chief Justice demonstrated, in a manner which has been regarded as settling the question, that with the choice thus given between a constitutional requirement and a conflicting statutory enactment, the plain duty of the court was to follow and enforce the Constitution as the supreme law established by the people. And the court recognized, in *Marbury v. Madison* and subsequent cases, that the exercise of this great power could only be invoked in cases which came regularly before the courts for determination. . . .

Again, in the case of *Cohen v. Virginia,* 6 Wheat. 264, 5 L.Ed. 257 [1821] Chief Justice Marshall, amplifying and reasserting the doctrine of *Marbury v. Madison,* recognized the limitations upon the right of this court to declare an act of Congress unconstitutional, and granting that there might be instances of its violation which could not be brought within the jurisdiction of the courts, . . . said:

> "This may be very true; but by no means justifies the inference drawn from it. The article does not extend the judicial power to every violation of the Constitution which may possibly take place, but to 'a case in law or equity' in which a right under such law is asserted in a court of justice. If the question cannot be brought into a court, then there is no case in law or equity, and no jurisdiction is given by the words of the article."

See also, in this connection, *Chicago & G.T.R. Co. v. Wellman,* 143 U.S. 339, 36 L.Ed. 176, 12 Sup.Ct.Rep. 400 [1892], [which said that judicial review] "is legitimate only in the last resort, and as a necessity in the determination of real, earnest, and vital controversy between individuals. It never was the thought that, by means of a friendly suit, a party beaten in the legislature could transfer to the courts an inquiry as to the constitutionality of the legislative act."

Applying the principles thus long settled by the decisions of this court to the act of Congress undertaking to confer jurisdiction in this case, we find that [i]t is therefore evident that there is neither more nor less in this procedure than an attempt to provide for a judicial determination, final in this court, of the constitutional validity of an act of Congress. Is such a determination within the judicial power conferred by the Constitution, as the same has been interpreted and defined in the authoritative decisions to which we have referred? We think it is not. That judicial power, as we have seen, is the right to determine actual controversies arising between adverse litigants, duly instituted in courts of proper jurisdiction. The right to declare a law unconstitutional arises because an act of Congress relied upon by one or the other of such parties in determining their rights is in conflict with the fundamental law. The exercise of this, the most important and delicate duty of this court, is not given to it as a body with revisory power over the action of Congress, but because the rights of the litigants in justiciable controversies require the court to choose between the fundamental law and a law purporting to be enacted within constitutional authority, but in fact beyond the power delegated to the legislative branch of the Government. This attempt to obtain a judicial declaration of the validity of the act of Congress is not presented in a "case" or "controversy" to which, under the Constitution of the United States, the judicial power alone extends. It is true the United States is made a defendant to this action, but it has no interest adverse to the claimants. The object is not to assert a property right as against the Government, or to demand compensation for alleged wrongs because of action upon its part. The whole purpose of the law is to determine the constitutional validity of this class of legislation, in a suit not arising between parties concerning a property right necessarily involved in the decision in question, but in a proceeding against the Government in its sovereign capacity, and concerning which the only judgment required is to settle the doubtful character of the legislation in question. Such judgment will not conclude private parties, when actual litigation brings to the court the question of the constitutionality of such legislation. In a legal sense the judgment could not be executed, and amounts in fact to no more than an expression of opinion upon the validity of the acts in question. Confining the jurisdiction of this court within the limitations conferred by the Constitution, which the court has hitherto been careful to observe, and whose boundaries it has refused to transcend, we think the Congress, in the act of March 1, 1907, exceeded the limitations of legislative authority, so far as it required of this court action not judicial in its nature within the meaning of the Constitution. . . .

The questions involved in this proceeding as to the validity of the legislation may arise in suits between individuals, and when they do and are properly brought before this court for consideration they, of course, must be determined in the exercise of its judicial functions. For the reasons we have stated, we are constrained to hold that these actions present no justiciable controversy within the authority of the court, acting within the limitations of the Constitution under which it was created. . . . The judgments will be reversed and the cases remanded to the Court of Claims, with directions to dismiss the petition for want of jurisdiction.

NOTES

1. In *United States v. Johnson,* 319 U.S. 302, 63 S.Ct. 1075, 87 L.Ed. 1413 (1943) (per curiam), a tenant protected by federal rent control sued the landlord, who won in the lower court by arguing that the rent control law and the regulations were unconstitutional. On appeal to the Supreme Court, the Government intervened and submitted plaintiff-tenant's affidavit. It showed that the plaintiff did not employ, pay, or even meet his attorney, had no knowledge of who paid the $15 filing fee, was assured by the defendant-landlord that the tenant would incur no expenses by bringing the suit, never read the complaint, and had no knowledge of the amount of judgment asked for until he read about it in the newspapers. The landlord's affidavit did not deny any of these allegations, and plaintiff-tenant did not even file a brief in the trial court. The parties submitted no false or fictitious facts to the lower court or Supreme Court. So, why should the Court refuse to decide it? The Supreme Court held that the suit was a collusive and friendly one. "Even in a litigation where only private rights are involved, the judgment will not be allowed to stand where one of the parties has dominated the conduct of the suit by payment of fees of both." The problem was not that one party paid the other side's attorney's fees (the Government routinely pays the fees of the public defender in criminal cases), but that the landlord used these fees to control both sides of the litigation—landlord and tenant.

2. *Moore v. Charlotte-Mecklenburg Board of Education,* 402 U.S. 47, 91 S.Ct. 1292, 28 L.Ed.2d 590 (1971) (per curiam), held: "At the hearing both parties argued to the three-judge court that the [state] anti-busing law was constitutional and urged that the order of the District Court adopting the Finger plan should be set aside. We are thus confronted with the anomaly that both litigants desire precisely the same result, namely a holding that the antibusing plan is constitutional. There is, therefore, no case or controversy within the meaning of Art. III of the Constitution. *Muskrat v. United States.*"

3. However, the fact that the Government confesses error in a criminal case does not require the Court to reverse the conviction. The public interest in

reaching the proper result in a criminal case is entrusted not just to the prosecutors but to the Court; also: "[O]ur judgments are precedents, and the proper administration of the criminal law cannot be left merely to the stipulation of the parties." *Young v. United States,* 315 U S. 257, 62 S.Ct. 510, 86 L.Ed. 832 (1942).

1.8.2   Political Questions

Recall that in *Marbury v. Madison* Chief Justice Marshall said: "The province of the court is, solely, to decide on the rights of individuals, not to inquire how the executive, or executive officers, perform duties in which they have a discretion. Questions in their nature political, or which are, by the constitution and laws, submitted to the executive, can never be made in this court." Marshall went on to say that the question raised by *Marbury* was not political. But what are the political questions? Marshall's successor, Chief Justice Taney, write the first major decision on this question.

LUTHER V. BORDEN
48 U.S. (7 How.) 1, 12 L.Ed. 581 (1849)

[In 1663 the colony of Rhode Island accepted a charter from Charles II as its fundamental law. After the Revolution, Rhode Island, unlike the other states, never adopted a new state constitution. Even after Rhode Island ratified the U.S. Constitution, the state government kept the colonial charter and made no successful effort to change legislation that limited the right to vote to property owners.

[After peaceful efforts at legislative reform failed, a group led by Thomas W. Dorr called for a constitutional convention, which drafted a new constitution in October 1841. In December 1841, the voters (including many of those not eligible to vote under the charter government) ratified the new constitution in a referendum. The charter government did not recognize the Dorr government, and Dorr and his friends responded by trying (unsuccessfully) to seize the Providence arsenal. The charter government declared martial law, and Governor King asked President Tyler for aid in putting down Dorr's rebellion. Tyler sided with the charter government, but thought that the introduction of federal troops before an actual insurrection was premature.

[Meanwhile, these activities generated bad publicity for the charter government, and in 1842 Rhode Island finally adopted a new constitution that increased the suffrage and accepted some other reforms. The rebellion was soon put down, and Dorr was captured, tried for treason for attempting to overthrow the charter, convicted, and sentenced to life imprisonment. The Supreme Court denied a writ of habeas corpus for jurisdictional reasons. *Ex parte Dorr,* 44 U.S. (3 Howard) 103, 11 L.Ed. 514 (1844). The next month, Dorr filed a new petition before the Supreme Court. However, six months later the Rhode Island legislature granted Dorr amnesty. The petition before the U.S. Supreme Court was not withdrawn, but it never came to oral argument. Eventually, in December of 1849, the Supreme Court dismissed it.

[Dorr's supporters were determined to vindicate the lawfulness of their revolt; Martin Luther, a supporter of Dorr, sued Luther Borden and others for trespass. Borden, on behalf of the charter government, had entered Luther's house in an effort to arrest Luther. Luther argued that Borden had no right to enter the house because he represented no lawful government. A majority of the people of Rhode Island favored the Dorr group, and, said Luther's lawyer, government is instituted "for the benefit, protection, and security of the people, nation, or community. And that when any government shall be found inadequate or contrary to these purposes, a majority of the community hath an indisputable, inalienable, and indefeasible right to reform, alter, or abolish the same."]

MR. CHIEF JUSTICE TANEY delivered the opinion of the court.

This case has arisen out of the unfortunate political differences which agitated the people of Rhode Island in 1841 and 1842.

[T]he Constitution of the United States, as far as it has provided for an emergency of this kind, and authorized the general government to interfere in the domestic concerns of a State, has treated the subject as political in its nature, and placed the power in the hands of that department. The fourth section of the fourth article of the Constitution of the United States provides that the United States shall guarantee to every State in the Union a republican form of government, and shall protect each of them against invasion; and on the application of the Legislature or of the executive (when the Legislature cannot be convened) against domestic violence.

Under this article of the Constitution it rests with Congress to decide what government is the established one in a State. For as the United States guarantee to each State a republican government, Congress must necessarily decide what government is established in the State before it can determine whether it is republican or not. And when the senators and representatives of a State are admitted into the councils of the Union, the authority of the government under which they are appointed, as well as its republican character, is recognized by the proper constitutional authority. And its decision is binding on every other department of the government, and could not be questioned in a judicial tribunal. It is true that the contest in this case did not last long enough to bring the matter to this issue; and as no senators or representatives were elected under the authority of the government of which Mr. Dorr was the head, Congress was not called upon to decide the controversy. Yet the right to decide is placed there, and not in the courts.

So, too, as relates to the clause in the above mentioned article of the Constitution, providing for cases of domestic violence. It rested with Congress, too, to determine upon the means proper to be adopted to fulfill this guarantee. They might, if they had deemed it most advisable to do so, have placed it in the power of a court to decide when a contingency had happened which required the federal government to interfere. But Congress thought otherwise, and no doubt wisely; and by the Act of February 28, 1795, provided, that, "in case of an insurrection in any State against the government thereof it shall be lawful for the President of the United States, on application of the Legislature of such State or of the executive (when the Legislature cannot be convened), to call forth such number of the militia of any other State or States, as may be applied for, as he may judge sufficient to suppress such insurrection."

By this act, the power of deciding whether the exigency had arisen upon which the government of the United States is bound to interfere, is given to the President. He is to act upon the application of the Legislature or of the executive, and consequently he must determine what body of men constitute the Legislature, and who is the governor, before he can act. The fact that both parties claim the right to the government cannot alter the case, for both cannot be entitled to it. If there is an armed conflict, like the one of which we are speaking, it is a case of domestic violence, and one of the parties must be in insurrection against the lawful government. And the President must, of necessity, decide which is the government, and which party is unlawfully arrayed against it, before he can perform the duty imposed upon him by the act of Congress.

After the President has acted and called out the militia, is a circuit court of the United States authorized to inquire whether his decision was right? Could the court, while the parties were actually contending in arms for the possession of the government, call witnesses before it and inquire which party represented a majority of the people? If it could, then it would become the duty of the court (provided it came to the conclusion that the President had decided incorrectly) to discharge those who were arrested or detained by the troops in the service of the

United States or the government, which the President was endeavoring to maintain. If the judicial power extends so far, the guarantee contained in the Constitution of the United States is a guarantee of anarchy, and not of order. Yet if this right does not reside in the courts when the conflict is raging, if the judicial power is at that time bound to follow the decision of the political, it must be equally bound when the contest is over. It cannot, when peace is restored, punish as offenses and crimes the acts which it before recognized, and was bound to recognize, as lawful.

It is true that in this case the militia were not called out by the President. But upon the application of the governor under the charter government, the President recognized him as the executive power of the State, and took measures to call out the militia to support his authority if it should be found necessary for the general government to interfere; and it is admitted in the argument, that it was the knowledge of this decision that put an end to the armed opposition to the charter government, and prevented any further efforts to establish by force the proposed constitution. The interference of the President, therefore, by announcing his determination, was as effectual as if the militia had been assembled under his orders. And it should be equally authoritative. For certainly no court of the United States, with a knowledge of this decision, would have been justified in recognizing the opposing party as the lawful government; or in treating as wrong-doers or insurgents the officers of the government which the President had recognized, and was prepared to support by an armed force. In the case of foreign nations, the government acknowledged by the President is always recognized in the courts of justice. And this principle has been applied by the act of Congress to the sovereign States of the Union.

It is said that this power in the President is dangerous to liberty, and may be abused. All power may be abused if placed in unworthy hands. But it would be difficult, we think, to point out any other hands in which this power would be more safe, and at the same time equally effectual. When citizens of the same State are in arms against each other, and the constituted authorities unable to execute the laws, the interposition of the United States must be prompt, or it is of little value. The ordinary course of proceedings in courts of justice would be utterly unfit for the crisis. And the elevated office of the President, chosen as he is by the people of the United States, and the high responsibility he could not fail to feel when acting in a case of so much moment, appear to furnish as strong safeguards against a willful abuse of power as human prudence and foresight could well provide. At all events, it is conferred upon him by the Constitution and laws of the United States, and must therefore be respected and enforced in its judicial tribunals. . . . Undoubtedly, if the President in exercising this power shall fall into error, or invade the rights of the people of the State, it would be in the power of Congress to apply the proper remedy. But the courts must administer the law as they find it. . . .

The high power has been conferred on this court of passing judgment upon the acts of the State sovereignties, and of the legislative and executive branches of the federal government, and of determining whether they are beyond the limits of power marked out for them respectively by the Constitution of the United States. This tribunal, therefore, should be the last to overstep the boundaries which limit its own jurisdiction. And while it should always be ready to meet any question confided to it by the Constitution, it is equally its duty not to pass beyond its appropriate sphere of action, and to take care not to involve itself in discussions which properly belong to other forums. No one, we believe, has ever doubted the proposition, that, according to the institutions of this country, the sovereignty in every State resides in the people of the State, and that they may alter and change their form of government at their own pleasure. But whether they have changed it or not by abolishing an old government, and establishing a new one in its place, is a question to be settled by the political power. And when that power has decided, the courts are bound to take notice of its decision, and to follow it.

The judgment of the Circuit Court must therefore be affirmed.

[The opinion of WOODBURY, J., dissenting, is omitted.]

COLEMAN V. MILLER
307 U.S. 433, 59 S.Ct. 972, 83 L.Ed. 1385 (1939)

[The principal case applying the political question doctrine to issues relating to amendments to the Constitution is *Coleman v. Miller*. Plaintiffs in that case included members of the Kansas Senate, whose votes against ratification of a constitutional amendment had been overridden. The amendment in question was the child labor amendment, proposed in 1924, thirteen years before the Kansas legislature ratified it. The purpose of this amendment was to overturn Supreme Court decisions forbidding Congress to regulate child labor. The child labor amendment never passed (one of many unsuccessful attempts to overturn Supreme Court decisions). After 1936, the Supreme Court changed its definition of interstate commerce and allowed Congress to prohibit child labor. See Chapter 6.

[The disgruntled Kansas legislators sued in state court to restrain the Kansas secretary of state from authenticating the ratifying resolution. They presented three claims: (1) that the lieutenant governor could not cast the deciding vote in the senate because he was not part of the legislature within the meaning of Article V of the United States Constitution; (2) that Kansas could not ratify the amendment because it had previously rejected it; and (3) that the amendment could not be ratified because it was no longer "viable," not having been ratified within a reasonable time.

[Chief Justice Hughes's opinion for the Court held that the complaining senators had *standing* to sue, that is, that allegedly invalid ratification adversely affected them so they could bring the case; Justices Frankfurter, Roberts, Black, and Douglas dissented on this point. The Court said that it was "equally divided" on the issue of whether the lieutenant governor could cast the deciding vote on ratification, with the same four Justices arguing that this issue was non justiciable. Thus, the case focused on the last two issues.]

CHIEF JUSTICE HUGHES delivered the opinion of the Court. . . .

1. The state court adopted the view expressed by text-writers that a state legislature which has rejected an amendment proposed by the Congress may later ratify. The argument in support of that view is that Article 5 says nothing of rejection but speaks only of ratification and provides that a proposed amendment shall be valid as part of the Constitution when ratified by three-fourths of the States; that the power to ratify is thus conferred upon the State by the Constitution and, as a ratifying power, persists despite a previous rejection. The opposing view proceeds on an assumption that if ratification by "Conventions" were prescribed by the Congress, a convention could not reject and, having adjourned sine die, be reassembled and ratify. It is also premised, in accordance with views expressed by text-writers, that ratification if once given cannot afterwards be rescinded and the amendment rejected, and it is urged that the same effect in the exhaustion of the State's power to act should be ascribed to rejection; that a State can act "but once, either by convention or through its legislature."

Historic instances are cited. In [December 18] 1865, the Thirteenth Amendment was rejected by the legislature of New Jersey which subsequently ratified it, but the question did not become important as ratification by the requisite number of States had already been proclaimed. The question did arise in connection with the adoption of the Fourteenth Amendment. The legislatures of Georgia, North Carolina and South Carolina had rejected the amendment in November and December, 1866. New governments were erected in those States (and in others) under the direction of Congress. The new legislatures ratified the amendment, that of North Carolina on July 4, 1868, that of South Carolina on

July 9, 1868, and that of Georgia on July 21, 1868. Ohio and New Jersey first ratified and then passed resolutions withdrawing their consent. As there were then thirty-seven States, twenty-eight were needed to constitute the requisite three-fourths. On July 9, 1868, the Congress adopted a resolution requesting the Secretary of State to communicate "a list of the States of the Union whose legislatures have ratified the fourteenth article of amendment," and in Secretary Seward's report attention was called to the action of Ohio and New Jersey. On July 20th Secretary Seward issued a proclamation reciting the ratification by twenty-eight States, including North Carolina, South Carolina, Ohio and New Jersey, and stating that it appeared that Ohio and New Jersey had since passed resolutions withdrawing their consent and that "it is deemed a matter of doubt and uncertainty whether such resolutions are not irregular, invalid and therefore ineffectual." The Secretary certified that if the ratifying resolutions of Ohio and New Jersey were still in full force and effect, notwithstanding the attempted withdrawal, the amendment had become a part of the Constitution. On the following day the Congress adopted a concurrent resolution which, reciting that three-fourths of the States having ratified (the list including North Carolina, South Carolina, Ohio and New Jersey), declared the Fourteenth Amendment to be a part of the Constitution and that it should be duly promulgated as such by the Secretary of State. Accordingly, Secretary Seward, on July 28th, issued his proclamation embracing the States mentioned in the congressional resolution and adding Georgia.

Thus the political departments of the Government dealt with the effect both of previous rejection and of attempted withdrawal and determined that both were ineffectual in the presence of an actual ratification. While there were special circumstances, because of the action of the Congress in relation to the governments of the rejecting States (North Carolina, South Carolina and Georgia), these circumstances were not recited in proclaiming ratification and the previous action taken in these States was set forth in the proclamation as actual previous rejections by the respective legislatures. This decision by the political departments of the Government as to the validity of the adoption of the Fourteenth Amendment has been accepted.

We think that in accordance with this historic precedent the question of the efficacy of ratifications by state legislatures, in the light of previous rejection or attempted withdrawal, should be regarded as a political question pertaining to the political departments, with the ultimate authority in the Congress in the exercise of its control over the promulgation of the adoption of the amendment.

The precise question as now raised is whether, when the legislature of the State, as we have found, has actually ratified the proposed amendment, the Court should restrain the state officers from certifying the ratification to the Secretary of State, because of an earlier rejection, and thus prevent the question from coming before the political departments. We find no basis in either Constitution or statute for such judicial action. Article 5, speaking solely of ratification, contains no provision as to rejection. Nor has the Congress enacted a statute relating to rejections. The statutory provision with respect to constitutional amendments is as follows:

> "Whenever official notice is received at the Department of State that any amendment proposed to the Constitution of the United States has been adopted, according to the provisions of the Constitution, the Secretary of State shall forthwith cause the amendment to be published, with his certificate, specifying the States by which the same may have been adopted, and that the same has become valid, to all intents and purposes, as a part of the Constitution of the United States."

The statute presupposes official notice to the Secretary of State when a state legislature has adopted a resolution of ratification. We see no warrant for judicial interference with the performance of that duty.

2.   The more serious question is whether the proposal by the Congress of the amendment had lost its vitality through lapse of time and hence it could not be ratified by the Kansas legislature in 1937. The argument of petitioners stresses the fact that nearly thirteen years elapsed between the proposal in 1924 and the ratification in question. It is said that when the amendment was proposed there was a definitely adverse popular sentiment and that at the end of 1925 there had been rejection by both houses of the legislatures of sixteen States and ratification by only four States, and that it was not until about 1933 that an aggressive campaign was started in favor of the amendment. In reply, it is urged that Congress did not fix a limit of time for ratification and that an unreasonably long time had not elapsed since the submission; that the conditions which gave rise to the amendment had not been eliminated; that the prevalence of child labor, the diversity of state laws and the disparity in their administration, with the resulting competitive inequalities, continued to exist. Reference is also made to the fact that a number of the States have treated the amendment as still pending and that in the proceedings of the national government there have been indications of the same view. It is said that there were fourteen ratifications in 1933, four in 1935, one in 1936, and three in 1937.

We have held that the Congress in proposing an amendment may fix a reasonable time for ratification. *Dillon v. Gloss,* 256 U. S. 368, 65 L. ed. 994, 41 S.Ct. 510. There we sustained the action of the Congress in providing in the proposed Eighteenth Amendment that it should be inoperative unless ratified within seven years. No limitation of time for ratification is provided in the instant case either in the proposed amendment or in the resolution of submission. But petitioners contend that, in the absence of a limitation by the Congress, the Court can and should decide what is a reasonable period within which ratification may be had. We are unable to agree with that contention.

It is true that in *Dillon v. Gloss* the Court said that nothing was found in Article 5 which suggested that an amendment once proposed was to be open to ratification for all time, or that ratification in some States might be separated from that in others by many years and yet be effective; that there was a strong suggestion to the contrary in that proposal and ratification were but succeeding steps in a single endeavor; that as amendments were deemed to be prompted by necessity, they should be considered and disposed of presently; and that there is a fair implication that ratification must be sufficiently contemporaneous in the required number of States to reflect the will of the people in all sections at relatively the same period; and hence that ratification must be within some reasonable time after the proposal. These considerations were cogent reasons for the decision in *Dillon v. Gloss,* that the Congress had the power to fix a reasonable time for ratification. But it does not follow that, whenever Congress has not exercised that power, the Court should take upon itself the responsibility of deciding what constitutes a reasonable time and determine accordingly the validity of ratifications. That question was not involved in *Dillon v. Gloss* and, in accordance with familiar principle, what was there said must be read in the light of the point decided.

Where are to be found the criteria for such a judicial determination? None are to be found in Constitution or statute. In their endeavor to answer this question petitioners' counsel have suggested that at least two years should be allowed; that six years would not seem to be unreasonably long; that seven years had been used by the Congress as a reasonable period; that one year, six months and thirteen days was the average time used in passing upon amendments which have been ratified since the first ten amendments; that three years, six months and twenty-five days has been the longest time used in ratifying. To this list of variables, counsel add that "the nature and extent of publicity and the activity of the public and of the legislatures of the several States in relation to any particular proposal should be taken into consideration." That statement is pertinent, but there are additional matters to be examined and weighed. When a proposed amendment springs from a conception of economic needs, it would be necessary, in determining whether a reasonable time had elapsed since its submission, to consider the economic conditions prevailing in the country, whether these had so far changed since the submission as to make the proposal no longer responsive to the conception which inspired it or whether conditions were such as to intensify the feeling of need and the appropriateness of the proposed remedial action. In short, the question of a reasonable time in many cases would involve, as in this case it does involve, an appraisal of a great variety of relevant conditions, political, social and economic, which can hardly be said to be within the appropriate range of evidence receivable in a court of justice and as to which it would be an extravagant extension of judicial authority to assert judicial notice as the basis of deciding a controversy with respect to the validity of an amendment actually ratified. On the other hand, these conditions are appropriate for the consideration of the political departments of the Government. The questions they involve are essentially political and not justiciable. They can be decided by the Congress with the full knowledge and appreciation ascribed to the national legislature of the political, social and economic conditions which have prevailed during the period since the submission of the amendment.

Our decision that the Congress has the power under Article 5 to fix a reasonable limit of time for ratification in proposing an amendment proceeds upon the assumption that the question, what is a reasonable time, lies within the congressional province. If it be deemed that such a question is an open one when the limit has not been fixed in advance, we think that it should also be regarded as an open one for the consideration of the Congress when, in the presence of certified ratifications by three-fourths of the States, the time arrives for the promulgation of the adoption of the amendment. The decision by the Congress, in its control of the action of the Secretary of State, of the question whether the amendment had been adopted within a reasonable time would not be subject to review by the courts. . . . The state officials should not be restrained from certifying to the Secretary of State the adoption by the legislature of Kansas of the resolution of ratification.

As we find no reason for disturbing the decision of the Supreme Court of Kansas in denying the mandamus sought by petitioners, its judgment is affirmed but upon the grounds stated in this opinion.

Affirmed.

Concurring opinion by JUSTICE BLACK, in which JUSTICE ROBERTS, JUSTICE FRANKFURTER and JUSTICE DOUGLAS join.

The Court here treats the amending process of the Constitution in some respects as subject to judicial construction, in others as subject to the final authority of the Congress. There is no disapproval of the conclusion arrived at in *Dillon v. Gloss,* that the Constitution impliedly requires that a properly submitted amendment must die unless ratified within a "reasonable time." Nor does the Court now disapprove its prior assumption of power to make such a pronouncement. And it is not made clear that only Congress has constitutional power to determine if there is any such implication in Article 5 of the Constitution. On the other hand, the Court's opinion declares that Congress has the exclusive power to decide the "political questions" of whether a State whose legislature has once acted upon a proposed amendment may subsequently reverse its position, and whether, in the circumstances of such a case as this, an amendment is dead because an "unreasonable" time has elapsed. No such division between the political and judicial branches of the government is made by Article 5 which grants power over the amending of the Constitution to Congress alone. Undivided control of that process has been given by the Article exclusively and completely to Congress. The process itself is "political" in its entirety, from submission until an amendment becomes part of the Constitution, and is not subject to judicial guidance, control or interference at any point.

Since Congress has sole and complete control over the amending process, subject to no judicial review, the views of any court upon this process cannot be binding upon Congress, and in so far as *Dillon v. Gloss* attempts judicially to impose a limitation upon the right of Congress to determine final adoption of an amendment, it should be disapproved. If Congressional determination that an amendment has been completed and become a part of the Constitution is final and removed from examination by the courts, as the Court's present opinion recognizes, surely the steps leading to that condition must be subject to the scrutiny, control and appraisal of none save the Congress, the body having exclusive power to make that final determination.

Congress, possessing exclusive power over the amending process, cannot be bound by and is under no duty to accept the pronouncements upon that exclusive power by this Court or by the Kansas courts. Neither State nor Federal courts can review that power. Therefore, any judicial expression amounting to more than mere acknowledgment of exclusive Congressional power over the political process of amendment is a mere admonition to the Congress in the nature of an advisory opinion, given wholly without constitutional authority.

JUSTICE BUTLER, dissenting.

In *Dillon v. Gloss*. . . . one imprisoned for transportation of intoxicating liquor in violation of § 3 of the National Prohibition Act . . . instituted habeas corpus proceedings to obtain his release on the ground that the Eighteenth Amendment was invalid because the resolution proposing it declared that it should not be operative unless ratified within seven years. The Amendment was ratified in less than a year and a half. We definitely held that Article 5 impliedly requires amendments submitted to be ratified within a reasonable time after proposal; that Congress may fix a reasonable time for ratification, and that the period of seven years fixed by the Congress was reasonable. . . .

Upon the reasoning of our opinion in that case, I would hold that more than a reasonable time had elapsed and that the judgment of the Kansas supreme court should be reversed.

The point, that the question—whether more than a reasonable time had elapsed—is not justiciable but one for Congress after attempted ratification by the requisite number of States, was not raised by the parties or by the United States appearing as amicus curiae; it was not suggested by us when ordering reargument. As the Court, in the Dillon *Case,* did directly decide upon the reasonableness of the seven years fixed by the Congress, it ought not now, without hearing argument upon the point, hold itself to lack power to decide whether more than 13 years between proposal by Congress and attempted ratification by Kansas is reasonable.

MR. JUSTICE MCREYNOLDS joins in this opinion.

[The separate opinion of FRANKFURTER, J., joined by ROBERTS, BLACK, & DOUGLAS, JJ., is omitted.]

NOTES

1.   In various cases prior to *Coleman,* the Court had ruled on the constitutionality of amendments. In *Hollingsworth v. Virginia,* 3 U.S. (3 Dall.) 378, 381 & n. 1, 1 L.Ed. 644, 646 & n. 1 (1798) (Eleventh Amendment), the Court ruled that the fact that Congress had never sent the amendment to the President for his signature before it was sent to states for ratification did not invalidate the amendment. The Presidential signature requirement only applies to ordinary legislation.

In *Hawke v. Smith, No. 1,* 253 U.S. 221, 40 S.Ct. 495, 64 L.Ed. 871 (1920) (Eighteenth Amendment), the Court invalidated a provision of the state constitution that required submission of the state's ratification to a referendum of the state's voters; the "plain" language of Article V limits ratification to state "legislatures." See also, *Hawke v. Smith, No. 2,* 253 U.S. 231, 40 S.Ct. 498, 64 L.Ed. 877 (1920) (Nineteenth Amendment).

In the *National Prohibition Cases, (Rhode Island v. Palmer* and related cases) 253 U.S. 350, 40 S.Ct. 486, 64 L.Ed. 946 (1920) (Eighteenth Amendment), the Court, with no majority opinion, upheld and interpreted the Eighteenth Amendment and the National Prohibition Law, better known as the Volstead Act, when various challenges were raised. The Court agreed that the two-thirds vote requirement in each House of Congress means two-thirds of the members present, assuming the presence of a quorum, and does not require two-thirds vote of the entire membership, present and absent.

Dillon v. Gloss, 256 U.S. 368, 41 S.Ct. 510, 65 L.Ed. 994 (1921) (Eighteenth Amendment), upheld the power of Congress to set a reasonable time for ratification.

In *Leser v. Garnett,* 258 U.S. 130, 42 S.Ct. 217, 66 L.Ed. 505 (1922) (Nineteenth Amendment), the unanimous Court rejected the argument that the Nineteenth Amendment, prohibiting abridgment of the vote because of sex, was "so great an addition to the electorate" that it could not be applied to a state without its consent. The Court also rejected the argument that a state constitution could forbid the state from ratifying an amendment. Relying on and extending the holding in *Hawke v. Smith,* the Court ruled that the function of ratification is a federal function that "transcends any limitations sought to be imposed by the people of a state." Finally the Court turned to the question whether two states adopted their ratifying resolutions in violation of those states' legislative procedures. The two other states later ratified, assuring passage of the amendment, but the Court that it wanted to give a "broader" answer: When a state gives duly authenticated official notice to the U.S. Secretary of State that it has adopted the resolution of ratification, that notice is "conclusive upon him, and, being certified to by his proclamation, is conclusive upon the courts."

When Congress proposed the Equal Rights Amendment in March 1972, it set no time limit for ratification in the amendment itself, unlike the procedure it had used in several other amendments. See, *e.g.,* Eighteenth Amendment, § 3; Twentieth Amendment, § 6; and Twenty-first Amendment, § 3. However, the resolution accompanying the proposed E.R.A. set a time limit of seven years. When the requisite number of states failed to ratify by that date, Congress by a simple majority passed a new Resolution extending the time to ratify until June 30, 1982. The President signed this Resolution. In 1981 a federal district court ruled that this extension was unconstitutional. The Supreme Court, on appeal, denied the motions to expedite plenary consideration and stayed the judgment of the district court pending the sending down of the judgment. Approximately ten months later, after the new time limit of the E.R.A. extension had passed and the proposed E.R.A. had died for lack of ratification by the required number of states, the Supreme Court dismissed the case on grounds of mootness and vacated the judgment of the trial court. *Idaho v. Freeman,* 529 F.Supp. 1107 (D. Idaho 1981), judgment stayed sub nom., *National Organization for Women v. Idaho,* 455 U.S. 918, 102 S.Ct. 1272, 1273, 71 L.Ed. 458 (1982), dismissed as moot, 459 U.S. 809, 103 S.Ct. 22, 74 L.Ed.2d 39 (1982).[82]

In 1984 the California Supreme Court prohibited placing on the ballot a proposed "balanced federal budget statutory initiative" that would have required the state legislature to request Congress to call a constitutional convention to amend the U.S. Constitution to require a balanced federal budget. The parties asked Justice Rehnquist, sitting as a single Justice (a circuit court judge), to stay the state court's order, but he refused and said that he doubted that Justice Black's concurring opinion in *Coleman v. Miller*— which expansively read the political question doctrine as applied to the amendment process—would command a majority of the present Supreme Court. *Uhler v. AFL-CIO,* 468 U.S. 1310, 105 S.Ct. 5, 82 L.Ed.2d 896 (1984).

As the proposed child labor amendment illustrates, it is much easier to persuade the Supreme Court to overrule itself than it is to persuade Congress and the States to overrule the Supreme Court. In only a handful of cases has the cumbersome amendment process been successful: the Eleventh Amendment, overruling *Chisholm v. Georgia,* 2 U.S. (2 Dall.) 419, 1 L.Ed. 440 (1793); Fourteenth Amendment, § 1, overruling *Dred Scott v. Sandford,* 60 U.S. (19 How.) 393, 15 L.Ed. 691 (1857); Sixteenth Amendment, overruling *Pollock v. Farmers' Loan & Trust Co.,* 157 U.S. 429, 15 S.Ct. 673, 39 L.Ed. 759 (1895); and the Twenty-sixth Amendment, overruling part of *Oregon v. Mitchell,* 400 U.S. 112, 91 S.Ct. 260, 27 L.Ed.2d 272 (1970).

2.   Opponents of child labor proposed the unsuccessful child labor amendment because earlier Supreme Court decisions prohibited Congress from

---

[82]   See, Rotunda, Running Out of Time: Can the E.R.A. Be Saved, 64 American Bar Association Journal 1507 (1978).

regulating child labor. Would the Court be in a conflict of interest position if it not only prevented Congress from regulating child labor but also prevented Congress from using the amendment process to overrule that decision?

BAKER V. CARR

369 U.S. 186, 82 S.Ct. 691, 7 L.Ed.2d 663 (1962)

[While all of the voters in a state may vote for governor, typically voters are divided into districts when they vote for other officers, such as state representative, state senator, or U.S. representative. If a state has three U.S. representatives and has a population of 300,000 people, apportionment is made on a one-person, one-vote principle when each of the districts has 100,000 people. If district *A* has only 10,000 people and still elects one representative, while districts *B* and *C* each have 145,000 people, the voters of district *A* have more political power. It is said that the districts are malapportioned, and that a vote in district *A* is worth more (14½ times more) than a vote in district *B*.

[This malapportionment of districts gives greater political power to certain geographic regions and the people within them. The malapportioned districts may still be compact and natural in shape. However, the districts are sometimes divided into unusual shapes in order to accomplish an ulterior purpose, for example, to favor certain political candidates or to fence out certain racial groups. When Elbridge Gerry was governor of Massachusetts in 1812, he pioneered this type of districting, which came to be called gerrymandering because one of the irregularly shaped districts in northeastern Massachusetts looked a little like a salamander.

[Thus, districts may be malapportioned on the basis of population and yet be compact and natural in shape. Or, the population of the district may be apportioned equally, and yet they may be gerrymandered. Or, the districts may be both malapportioned and gerrymandered.

[The first major case to reach the Supreme Court claiming that Congressional election districts for the House of Representatives were malapportioned because they lacked compactness of territory and approximate equality of population was *Colegrove v. Green*, 328 U.S. 549, 66 S.Ct. 1198, 90 L.Ed. 1432 (1946). Only seven Justices participated in this case. Although a majority of the voting justices dismissed the suit, no majority favored treating reapportionment as a political question. Justice Frankfurter, in an opinion concurred in by only Justices Reed and Burton, argued that "due regard for the effective working of our Government revealed this issue to be of a peculiarly political nature and therefore not meet for judicial determination. [The] Courts ought not to enter this political thicket."

[Justice Rutledge, in a separate opinion, assumed jurisdiction but declined to exercise it. He concurred with the decision not to intervene because, among other things, only a short time remained before the election. Justices Black, Douglas, and Murphy dissented, and Jackson took no part in the decision.

[The next major case to reach the Supreme Court was *Gomillion v. Lightfoot*, 364 U.S. 339, 81 S.Ct. 125, 5 L.Ed.2d 110 (1960). Here the Court acted, but purportedly on a narrow ground. Justice Frankfurter wrote the majority opinion. In this case, black voters who had been residents of the City of Tuskegee sued after the Alabama legislature enacted a statute redefining the city of Tuskegee by altering its shape from a square to a strangely shaped twenty-eight-sided figure. Plaintiffs relied on the equal protection guarantees of the Fourteenth Amendment and the right to vote under the Fifteenth Amendment. They claimed that the gerrymandered boundaries were created solely for the purpose of fencing out black voters from the town in order to deprive them of their preexisting right to vote in the municipal election. The Court agreed that the claim was justiciable, relying only on the Fifteenth Amendment. By placing the case on such grounds, Frankfurter perhaps hoped to prevent it from becoming a more general precedent.

[Justice Whittaker's concurrence was analytically more satisfying, he relied on equal protection. The black voters still had the right to vote, but they could not vote in Tuskegee. Their valid complaint was that they were treated differently by their separation into different districts:

> It seems to me that the "right . . . to vote" that is guaranteed by the Fifteenth Amendment is but the same right to vote as is enjoyed by all others within the same . . . political division. . . . "[F]encing Negro citizens out of" Division A and into Division B is an unlawful segregation of races of citizens, in violation of the Equal Protection Clause of the Fourteenth Amendment.

[Then came *Baker v. Carr.*

[In spite of a state constitutional requirement for decennial reapportionment, the Tennessee legislature had not enacted any reapportionment of the state legislative districts since 1901. Because of population growth and shifts, plaintiffs sued Joseph Cordell Carr, the Tennessee secretary of state, and other officials. Plaintiffs claimed that they and others similarly situated were denied the equal protection of the laws accorded them by the Fourteenth Amendment by virtue of the debasement of their votes, a claim that was dismissed by a three-judge federal court. Only 37 percent of the Tennessee voters elected 20 of the 33 Senators, and

40 percent of the voters elected 63 of the 99 members of the House. A single vote in Moore County, for example, was worth 19 votes in Hamilton County.]

JUSTICE BRENNAN delivered the opinion of the Court.

[The Supreme Court held (1) that the federal district court had subject matter jurisdiction of the controversy; (2) that plaintiffs had standing to sue the state's Secretary of State, members of the State Board of Elections, and similar individuals; and (3) that it would not be necessary at this time for the Court to consider what remedy would be most appropriate if appellants prevail at the trial. The Court then turned to the question of whether the subject matter of the suit was justiciable, *i.e.*, did it involve a political question.]

JUSTICIABILITY

In holding that the subject matter of this suit was not justiciable, the District Court relied on *Colegrove v. Green,* . . . and subsequent per curiam cases. . . . We understand the District Court to have read the cited cases as compelling the conclusion that since the appellants sought to have a legislative apportionment held unconstitutional, their suit presented a "political question" and was therefore non justiciable. We hold that this challenge to an apportionment presents no non-justiciable "political question." The cited cases do not hold the contrary.

Of course the mere fact that the suit seeks protection of a political right does not mean it presents a political question. Such an objection "is little more than a play upon words." . . . Rather, it is argued that apportionment cases, whatever the actual wording of the complaint, can involve no federal constitutional right except one resting on the guaranty of a republican form of government, and that complaints based on that clause have been held to present political questions which are nonjusticiable.

We hold that the claim pleaded here neither rests upon nor implicates the Guaranty Clause and that its justiciability is therefore not foreclosed by our decisions of cases involving that clause. The District Court misinterpreted *Colegrove v. Green* and other decisions of this Court on which it relied. Appellants' claim that they are being denied equal protection is justiciable, and if "discrimination is sufficiently shown, the right to relief under the equal protection clause is not diminished by the fact that the discrimination relates to political rights." . . . To show why we reject the argument based on the Guaranty Clause, we must examine the authorities under it. But because there appears to be some uncertainty as to why those cases did present political questions, and specifically as to whether this apportionment case is like those cases, we deem it necessary first to consider the contours of the "political question" doctrine. . . . That review reveals that in the Guaranty Clause cases and in the other "political question" cases, it is the relationship between the judiciary and the coordinate branches of the Federal Government, and not the federal judiciary's relationship to the States, which gives rise to the "political question."

We have said that "In determining whether a question falls within [the political question] category, the appropriateness under our system of government of attributing finality to the action of the political departments and also the lack of satisfactory criteria for a judicial determination are dominant considerations." Coleman v Miller. . . . The nonjusticiability of a political question is primarily a function of the separation of powers. Much confusion results from the capacity of the "political question" label to obscure the need for case-by-case inquiry. Deciding whether a matter has in any measure been committed by the Constitution to another branch of government, or whether the action of that branch exceeds whatever authority has been committed, is itself a delicate exercise in constitutional interpretation, and is a responsibility of this Court as ultimate interpreter of the Constitution. To demonstrate this requires no less than to analyze representative cases and to infer from them the analytical threads that make up the political question doctrine. We shall then show that none of those threads catches this case.

Foreign Relations. There are sweeping statements to the effect that all questions touching foreign relations are political questions. Not only does resolution of such issues frequently turn on standards that defy judicial application, or involve the exercise of a discretion demonstrably committed to the executive or legislature; but many such questions uniquely demand single-voiced statement of the Government's views. Yet it is error to suppose that every case or controversy which touches foreign relations lies beyond judicial cognizance. . . .

While recognition of foreign governments so strongly defies judicial treatment that without executive recognition a foreign state has been called "a republic of whose existence we know nothing," and the judiciary ordinarily follows the executive as to which nation has sovereignty over disputed territory, once sovereignty over an area is politically determined and declared, courts may examine the resulting status and decide independently whether a statute applies to that area. . . .

Dates of Duration of Hostilities. Though it has been stated broadly that "The power which declared the necessity is the power to declare its cessation, and what the cessation requires," here too analysis reveals isolable reasons for the presence of political questions, underlying this Court's refusal to review the political departments' determination of when or whether a war has ended. Dominant is the need for finality in the political determination, for emergency's nature demands "A prompt and unhesitating obedience," *Martin v. Mott,* 12 Wheat. 19, 30, 6 L.Ed. 537 (calling up of militia). . . . But deference rests on reason, not habit. The question in a particular case may not seriously implicate considerations of finality—*e.g.,* a public program of importance (rent control) yet not central to the emergency effort. Further, clearly definable criteria for decision may be available. In such case the political question barrier falls away. . . .

It is apparent that several formulations which vary slightly according to the settings in which the questions arise may describe a political question, although each has one or more elements which identify it as essentially a function of the separation of powers. Prominent on the surface of any case held to involve a political question is found a textually demonstrable constitutional commitment of the issue to a coordinate political department; or a lack of judicially discoverable and manageable standards for resolving it; or the impossibility of deciding without an initial policy determination of a kind clearly for nonjudicial discretion; or the impossibility of a court's undertaking independent resolution without expressing lack of the respect due coordinate branches of government; or an unusual need for unquestioning adherence to a political decision already made; or the potentiality of embarrassment from multifarious pronouncements by various departments on one question.

Unless one of these formulations is inextricable from the case at bar, there should be no dismissal for nonjusticiability on the ground of a political question's presence. The doctrine of which we treat is one of "political questions," not one of "political cases." The courts cannot reject as "no law suit" a bona fide controversy as to whether some action denominated "political" exceeds constitutional authority. The cases we have reviewed show the necessity for discriminating inquiry into the precise facts and posture of the particular case, and the impossibility of resolution by any semantic cataloguing.

But it is argued that this case shares the characteristics of decisions that constitute a category not yet considered, cases concerning the Constitution's guaranty, in Art. IV, § 4, of a republican form of government. A conclusion as to whether the case at bar does present a political question cannot be confidently reached until we have considered those cases with special care. We shall discover that Guaranty Clause claims involve those elements which define a "political question," and for that reason and no other, they are nonjusticiable. In particular, we shall discover that the nonjusticiability of such claims has nothing to do with their touching upon matters of state governmental organization.

Republican Form of Government. [T]he only significance that *Luther [v. Borden]* could have for our immediate purposes is in its holding that the Guaranty Clause is not a repository of judicially manageable standards which a court could utilize independently in order to identify a State's lawful government. The Court has since refused to resort to the Guaranty Clause—which alone had been invoked for the purpose—as the source of a constitutional standard for invalidating state action. . . .

Just as the Court has consistently held that a challenge to state action based on the Guaranty Clause presents no justiciable question so has it held, and for the same reasons, that challenges to congressional action on the ground of inconsistency with that clause present no justiciable question. In *Georgia v. Stanton,* 6 Wall. 50, 18 L.Ed. 721, the State sought by an original bill to enjoin execution of the Reconstruction Acts . . . Congress had clearly refused to recognize the republican character of the government of the suing State. It seemed to the Court that the only constitutional claim that could be presented was under the Guaranty Clause, and Congress having determined that the effects of the recent hostilities required extraordinary measures to restore governments of a republican form, this Court refused to interfere with Congress' action at the behest of a claimant relying on that very guaranty. . . .

We come, finally, to the ultimate inquiry whether our precedents as to what constitutes a nonjusticiable "political question" bring the case before us under the umbrella of that doctrine. A natural beginning is to note whether any of the common characteristics which we have been able to identify and label descriptively are present. We find none: The question here is the consistency of state action with the Federal Constitution. We have no question decided, or to be decided, by a political branch of government coequal with this Court. Nor do we risk embarrassment of our government abroad, or grave disturbance at home if we take issue with Tennessee as to the constitutionality of her action here challenged. Nor need the appellants, in order to succeed in this action, ask the Court to enter upon policy determinations for which judicially manageable standards are lacking. Judicial standards under the Equal Protection Clause are well developed and familiar, and it has been open to courts since the enactment of the Fourteenth Amendment to determine, if on the particular facts they must, that a discrimination reflects *no* policy, but simply arbitrary and capricious action.

This case does, in one sense, involve the allocation of political power within a State, and the appellants might conceivably have added a claim under the Guaranty Clause. Of course, as we have seen, any reliance on that clause would be futile. But because any reliance on the Guaranty Clause could not have succeeded it does not follow that appellants may not be heard on the equal protection claim which in fact they tender. True, it must be clear that the Fourteenth Amendment claim is not so enmeshed with those political question elements which render Guaranty Clause claims nonjusticiable as actually to present a political question itself. But we have found that not to be the case here. . . .

We conclude that the complaint's allegations of a denial of equal protection present a justiciable constitutional cause of action upon which appellants are entitled to a trial and a decision. The right asserted is within the reach of judicial protection under the Fourteenth Amendment.

The judgment of the District Court is reversed and the cause is remanded for further proceedings consistent with this opinion.

Reversed and remanded.

MR. JUSTICE WHITTAKER did not participate in the decision of this case.

MR. JUSTICE FRANKFURTER, whom MR. JUSTICE HARLAN, joins, dissenting.

Disregard of inherent limits in the effective exercise of the Court's "judicial Power" not only presages the futility of judicial intervention in the essentially political conflict of forces by which the relation between population and representation has time out of mind been and now is determined. It may well impair the Court's position as the ultimate organ of "the supreme Law of the Land" in that vast range of legal problems, often strongly entangled in popular feeling, on which this Court must pronounce. The Court's authority—possessed of neither the purse nor the sword—ultimately rests on sustained public confidence in its moral sanction. Such feeling must be nourished by the Court's complete detachment, in fact and in appearance, from political entanglements and by abstention from injecting itself into the clash of political forces in political settlements.

A hypothetical claim resting on abstract assumptions is now for the first time made the basis for affording illusory relief for a particular evil. . . . The claim is hypothetical and the assumptions are abstract because the Court does not vouchsafe the lower courts—state and federal—guidelines for formulating specific, definite, wholly unprecedented remedies for the inevitable litigations that today's umbrageous disposition is bound to stimulate in connection with politically motivated reapportionments in so many States. . . .

[Concurring opinions of DOUGLAS, CLARK, and STEWART, JJ., and the dissenting opinion of HARLAN, J., joined by FRANKFURTER, J., are omitted.]

NOTES

1. Recall that Chief Justice Marshall stated in *Marbury v. Madison:* "The province of the court is, solely, to decide on the rights of individuals, not to inquire how the executive, or executive officers, perform duties in which they have a discretion. Questions in their nature political, or which are, by the constitution and laws, submitted to the executive, can never be made in this court."

2. *Baker v. Carr* created this test to determine when a question is political, that is, nonjusticiable:

    > Prominent on the surface of any case held to involve a political question is found a textually demonstrable constitutional commitment of the issue to a coordinate political department; or a lack of judicially discoverable and manageable standards for resolving it; or the impossibility of deciding without an initial policy determination of a kind clearly for nonjudicial discretion; or the impossibility of a court's undertaking independent resolution without expressing lack of the respect due coordinate branches of government; or an unusual need for unquestioning adherence to a political decision already made; or the potentiality of embarrassment from multifarious pronouncements by various departments on one question.

3. *Baker v. Carr* finds that there is an injury but does not tell us what the remedy might be. Justice Clark, in his concurring opinion, stated, ironically: "No one . . . contends that mathematical equality among voters is required by the Equal Protection Clause." 369 U.S. at 258, Ultimately the Court mandated "one person, one vote." See Chapter 5, § 5.6.1.

4. In *Powell v. McCormack,* 395 U.S. 486, 89 S.Ct. 1944, 23 L.Ed.2d 491 (1969), the 90th Congress refused to seat Adam Clayton Powell, who had been elected to Congress in November 1966. Congress "excluded" him, that is, Congress did not allow him to take his seat and his oath of office. See U.S. Const., Art. I, § 5, cl. 1. Powell sued for a declaratory judgment that his

exclusion was unconstitutional and for back pay. The Court held that the political question doctrine did not bar this suit. The House could not exclude a member, duly elected, who met all the requirements of age, residence, and citizenship required in Art. I, § 2, cl. 2. The respondents argued that the House could expel a member for any reason whatsoever, an issue that the Court did not reach because Powell had not been "expelled." One is expelled *after* one takes one's seat. Expulsion is governed by the more open-ended standard of Art. I, § 5, cl. 2.

5. In *Gilligan v. Morgan,* 413 U.S. 1, 93 S.Ct. 2440, 37 L.Ed.2d 407 (1973), students at Kent State University sued for prospective injunctive relief against the Ohio National Guard. Plaintiffs wanted, *inter alia,* "a judicial evaluation of the 'training, weaponry and orders' of the Ohio National Guard." Because plaintiffs sought "a broad call on judicial power to assume continuing regulatory jurisdiction over the activities of the Ohio National Guard" rather than a claim for damages for past injuries or an order "against some specified and imminently threatened unlawful action," the majority found the case nonjusticiable. Chief Justice Burger for the Court found that Art. I, § 8, cl. 16, vests in Congress the responsibility to prescribe discipline of the militia, and that Congress has authorized the President to issue appropriate regulations. The majority quoted with approval the dissent in the circuit court; that dissent argued that the requested relief "would necessarily draw the courts into a nonjusticiable political question over which we have no jurisdiction."

6. In *Scheuer v. Rhodes,* 416 U.S. 232, 94 S.Ct. 1683, 40 L.Ed.2d 90 (1974), Chief Justice Burger, for a unanimous Court, allowed the estates of three students to sue to collect damages against the Ohio National Guard, the governor, and others for allegedly violating the students' civil rights. The Court specifically noted that *Gilligan* did not mandate a contrary result.

7. Should the question whether American involvement in an undeclared war is constitutional be justiciable? What about an allegation that a war violated a treaty that the United States has ratified? Litigants challenged the constitutionality of the Vietnam War in numerous cases, but the Supreme Court never decided the issue. See, *e.g., Mora v. McNamara,* 389 U.S. 934, 88 S.Ct. 282, 19 L.Ed.2d 287 (1967) (Justices Stewart and Douglas, dissenting to denial of certiorari of case in which draftees sought to enjoin their shipment to Vietnam as unconstitutional).

NIXON V. UNITED STATES

506 U.S. 224, 113 S.Ct. 732, 122 L.Ed.2d 1 (1993).

CHIEF JUSTICE REHNQUIST delivered the opinion of the Court.

Petitioner Walter L. Nixon, Jr., asks this court to decide whether Senate Rule XI, which allows a committee of Senators to hear evidence against an individual who has been impeached and to report that evidence to the full Senate, violates the Impeachment Trial Clause, Art. I, § 3, cl. 6. That Clause provides that the "Senate shall have the sole Power to try all Impeachments." But before we reach the merits of such a claim, we must decide whether it is "justiciable," that is, whether it is a claim that may be resolved by the courts. We conclude that it is not.

Nixon, a former Chief Judge of the United States District Court for the Southern District of Mississippi, was convicted by a jury of two counts of making false statements before a federal grand jury and sentenced to prison. The grand jury investigation stemmed from reports that Nixon had accepted a gratuity from a Mississippi businessman in exchange for asking a local district attorney [a state official] to halt the prosecution of the businessman's son. Because Nixon refused to resign from his office as a United States District Judge, he continued to collect his judicial salary while serving out his prison sentence. On May 10, 1989, the House of Representatives adopted three articles of impeachment for high crimes and misdemeanors. The first two articles charged Nixon with giving false testimony before the grand jury and the third article charged him with bringing disrepute on the Federal Judiciary.

After the House presented the articles to the Senate, the Senate voted to invoke its own Impeachment Rule XI, under which the presiding officer appoints a committee of Senators to "receive evidence and take testimony." Senate Impeachment Rule XI.[1] The Senate committee held four days of hearings, during

---

[1]   Specifically, Rule XI provides:

"[I]n the trial of any impeachment the Presiding Officer of the Senate, if the Senate so orders, shall appoint a committee of Senators to receive evidence and take testimony at such times and places as the committee may determine, and for such purpose the committee so appointed and the chairman thereof, to be elected by the committee, shall (unless otherwise ordered by the Senate) exercise all the powers and functions conferred upon the Senate and the Presiding Officer of the Senate, respectively, under the rules of procedure and practice in the Senate when sitting on impeachment trials.

"Unless otherwise ordered by the Senate, the rules of procedure and practice in the Senate when sitting on impeachment trials shall govern the procedure and practice of the committee so appointed. The committee so appointed shall report to the Senate in writing a certified copy of the transcript of the proceedings and testimony had and given before such committee, and such report shall be received by the Senate and the evidence so received and the testimony so taken shall be considered

which 10 witnesses, including Nixon, testified. Pursuant to Rule XI, the committee presented the full Senate with a complete transcript of the proceeding and a report stating the uncontested facts and summarizing the evidence on the contested facts. Nixon and the House impeachment managers submitted extensive final briefs to the full Senate and delivered arguments from the Senate floor during the three hours set aside for oral argument in front of that body. Nixon himself gave a personal appeal, and several Senators posed questions directly to both parties. The Senate voted by more than the constitutionally required two-thirds majority to convict Nixon on the first two articles. The presiding officer then entered judgment removing Nixon from his office as United States District Judge.

Nixon thereafter commenced the present suit, arguing that Senate Rule XI violates the constitutional grant of authority to the Senate to "try" all impeachments because it prohibits the whole Senate from taking part in the evidentiary hearings. Nixon sought a declaratory judgment that his impeachment conviction was void and that his judicial salary and privileges should be reinstated. The District Court held that his claim was nonjusticiable, and the Court of Appeals for the District of Columbia Circuit agreed.

[T]he concept of a textual commitment to a coordinate political department is not completely separate from the concept of a lack of judicially discoverable and manageable standards for resolving it; the lack of judicially manageable standards may strengthen the conclusion that there is a textually demonstrable commitment to a coordinate branch.

In this case, we must examine Art. I, § 3, cl. 6, to determine the scope of authority conferred upon the Senate by the Framers regarding impeachment. . . . The language and structure of this Clause are revealing. The first sentence is a grant of authority to the Senate, and the word "sole" indicates that this authority is reposed in the Senate and nowhere else. The next two sentences specify requirements to which the Senate proceedings shall conform: the Senate shall be on oath or affirmation, a two-thirds vote is required to convict, and when the President is tried the Chief Justice shall preside.

Petitioner argues that the word "try" in the first sentence imposes by implication an additional requirement on the Senate in that the proceedings must

---

to all intents and purposes, subject to the right of the Senate to determine competency, relevancy, and materiality, as having been received and taken before the Senate, but nothing herein shall prevent the Senate from sending for any witness and hearing his testimony in open Senate, or by order of the Senate having the entire trial in open Senate."

be in the nature of a judicial trial. From there petitioner goes on to argue that this limitation precludes the Senate from delegating to a select committee the task of hearing the testimony of witnesses, as was done pursuant to Senate Rule XI. " '[T]ry' means more than simply 'vote on' or 'review' or 'judge.' In 1787 and today, trying a case means hearing the evidence, not scanning a cold record." Brief for Petitioner 25. Petitioner concludes from this that courts may review whether or not the Senate "tried" him before convicting him.

There are several difficulties with this position which lead us ultimately to reject it. The word "try," both in 1787 and later, has considerably broader meanings than those to which petitioner would limit it. Older dictionaries define try as "[t]o examine" or "[t]o examine as a judge." See 2 S. Johnson, A Dictionary of the English Language (1785). . . .

The conclusion that the use of the word "try" in the first sentence of the Impeachment Trial Clause lacks sufficient precision to afford any judicially manageable standard of review of the Senate's actions is fortified by the existence of the three very specific requirements that the Constitution does impose on the Senate when trying impeachments: the members must be under oath, a two-thirds vote is required to convict, and the Chief Justice presides when the President is tried. These limitations are quite precise, and their nature suggests that the Framers did not intend to impose additional limitations on the form of the Senate proceedings by the use of the word "try" in the first sentence.

Petitioner devotes only two pages in his brief to negating the significance of the word "sole" in the first sentence of Clause 6. . . . We think that the word "sole" is of considerable significance. Indeed, the word "sole" appears only one other time in the Constitution—with respect to the House of Representatives' "*sole* Power of Impeachment." Art. I, § 2, cl. 5 (emphasis added). The common sense meaning of the word "sole" is that the Senate alone shall have authority to determine whether an individual should be acquitted or convicted. The dictionary definition bears this out. . . .

Petitioner finally argues that even if significance be attributed to the word "sole" in the first sentence of the clause, the authority granted is to the Senate, and this means that "the Senate—not the courts, not a lay jury, not a Senate Committee—shall try impeachments." It would be possible to read the first sentence of the Clause this way, but it is not a natural reading. Petitioner's interpretation would bring into judicial purview not merely the sort of claim made by petitioner, but other similar claims based on the conclusion that the word "Senate" has imposed by implication limitations on procedures which the Senate might adopt. Such limitations would be inconsistent with the construction of the Clause as a whole, which, as we have noted, sets out three express limitations in separate sentences.

The history and contemporary understanding of the impeachment provisions support our reading of the constitutional language. The parties do not offer evidence of a single word in the history of the Constitutional Convention or in contemporary commentary that even alludes to the possibility of judicial review in the context of the impeachment powers. This silence is quite meaningful in light of the several explicit references to the availability of judicial review as a check on the Legislature's power with respect to bills of attainder, *ex post facto* laws, and statutes. See The Federalist No. 78, p. 524 (J. Cooke ed. 1961) ("Limitations . . . can be preserved in practice no other way than through the medium of the courts of justice").

The Framers labored over the question of where the impeachment power should lie. Significantly, in at least two considered scenarios the power was placed with the Federal Judiciary. Indeed, Madison and the Committee of Detail proposed that the Supreme Court should have the power to determine impeachments. Despite these proposals, the Convention ultimately decided that the Senate would have "the sole Power to Try all Impeachments." According to Alexander Hamilton, the Senate was the "most fit depositary of this important trust" because its members are representatives of the people. See The Federalist No. 65. The Supreme Court was not the proper body because the Framers "doubted whether the members of that tribunal would, at all times, be endowed with so eminent a portion of fortitude as would be called for in the execution of so difficult a task" or whether the Court "would possess the degree of credit and authority" to carry out its judgment if it conflicted with the accusation brought by the Legislature—the people's representative. In addition, the Framers believed the Court was too small in number: "The awful discretion, which a court of impeachments must necessarily have, to doom to honor or to infamy the most confidential and the most distinguished characters of the community, forbids the commitment of the trust to a small number of persons."

There are two additional reasons why the Judiciary, and the Supreme Court in particular, were not chosen to have any role in impeachments. First, the Framers recognized that most likely there would be two sets of proceedings for individuals who commit impeachable offenses—the impeachment trial and a separate criminal trial. In fact, the Constitution explicitly provides for two separate proceedings. See Art. I, § 3, cl. 7. The Framers deliberately separated the two forums to avoid raising the specter of bias and to ensure independent judgments. . . . Certainly judicial review of the Senate's "trial" would introduce the same risk of bias as would participation in the trial itself.

Second, judicial review would be inconsistent with the Framers' insistence that our system be one of checks and balances. In our constitutional system, impeachment was designed to be the *only* check on the Judicial Branch by the Legislature. On the topic of judicial accountability, Hamilton wrote:

"The precautions for their responsibility are comprised in the article respecting impeachments. They are liable to be impeached for mal-conduct by the house of representatives, and tried by the senate, and if convicted, may be dismissed from office and disqualified for holding any other. *This is the only provision on the point, which is consistent with the necessary independence of the judicial character, and is the only one which we find in our own constitution in respect to our own judges.*" Id., No. 79 (emphasis added).

Judicial involvement in impeachment proceedings, even if only for purposes of judicial review, is counterintuitive because it would eviscerate the "important constitutional check" [by placing] final reviewing authority with respect to impeachments in the hands of the same body that the impeachment process is meant to regulate.

. . . Nixon fears that if the Senate is given unreviewable authority to interpret the Impeachment Trial Clause, there is a grave risk that the Senate will usurp judicial power. The Framers anticipated this objection and created two constitutional safeguards to keep the Senate in check. The first safeguard is that the whole of the impeachment power is divided between the two legislative bodies, with the House given the right to accuse and the Senate given the right to judge. . . . The second safeguard is the two-thirds supermajority vote requirement. [Moreover,] the lack of finality and the difficulty of fashioning relief counsel against justiciability. [O]pening the door of judicial review to the procedures used by the Senate in trying impeachments would "expose the political life of the country to months, or perhaps years, of chaos." This lack of finality would manifest itself most dramatically if the President were impeached. The legitimacy of any successor, and hence his effectiveness, would be impaired severely, not merely while the judicial process was running its course, but during any retrial that a differently constituted Senate might conduct if its first judgment of conviction were invalidated. Equally uncertain is the question of what relief a court may give other than simply setting aside the judgment of conviction. Could it order the reinstatement of a convicted federal judge, or order Congress to create an additional judgeship if the seat had been filled in the interim?

Petitioner finally contends that a holding of nonjusticiability cannot be reconciled with our opinion in *Powell v. McCormack*. Our conclusion in *Powell* was based on the fixed meaning of "[q]ualifications" set forth in Art. I, § 2. The claim by the House that its power to "be the Judge of the Elections, Returns and Qualifications of its own Members" was a textual commitment of unreviewable authority was defeated by the existence of this separate provision specifying the only qualifications which might be imposed for House membership. The decision as to whether a member satisfied these qualifications *was* placed with the House, but the decision as to what these qualifications consisted of was not.

[W]e conclude, after exercising that delicate responsibility, that the word "try" in the Impeachment Clause does not provide an identifiable textual limit on the authority which is committed to the Senate.

For the foregoing reasons, the judgment of the Court of Appeals is

Affirmed.

JUSTICE WHITE, with whom JUSTICE BLACKMUN joins, concurring in the judgment.

[I would] reach the merits of the claim. I concur in the judgment because the Senate fulfilled its constitutional obligation to "try" petitioner. It should be said at the outset that, as a practical matter, it will likely make little difference whether the Court's view or my view controls in this case.

. . . When asked at oral argument whether that direction would be satisfied if, after a House vote to impeach, the Senate, without any procedure whatsoever, unanimously found the accused guilty of being "a bad guy," counsel for the United States answered that the Government's theory "leads me to answer that question yes." . . .

[T]he term "try" is hardly so elusive as the majority would have it. Were the Senate, for example, to adopt the practice of automatically entering a judgment of conviction whenever articles of impeachment were delivered from the House, it is quite clear that the Senate will have failed to "try" impeachments. Indeed in this respect, "try" presents no greater, and perhaps fewer, interpretive difficulties than some other constitutional standards that have been found amenable to familiar techniques of judicial construction, including, for example, "Commerce . . . among the several States," Art. I, § 8, cl. 3, and "due process of law." . . .

Petitioner bears the rather substantial burden of demonstrating that, simply by employing the word "try," the Constitution prohibits the Senate from relying on a factfinding committee. . . . The fact that Art. III, § 2, cl. 3 specifically exempts impeachment trials from the jury requirement provides some evidence that the Framers were anxious not to have additional specific procedural requirements read into the term "try." Contemporaneous commentary further supports this view. Hamilton, for example, stressed that . . . the proceedings not "be tied down to . . . strict rules, either in the delineation of the offence by the prosecutors, or in the construction of it by the Judges. . . ." The Federalist No. 65. [T]he delegation of fact-finding by judicial and quasi-judicial bodies was hardly unknown to the Framers. Jefferson, at least, was aware that the House of Lords sometimes delegated fact-finding in impeachment trials to committees and recommended use of the same to the Senate. . . .

In short, textual and historical evidence reveals that the Impeachment Trial Clause was not meant to bind the hands of the Senate beyond establishing a set of minimal procedures. Without identifying the exact contours of these procedures, it is sufficient to say that the Senate's use of a factfinding committee under Rule XI is entirely compatible with the Constitution's command that the Senate "try all impeachments." Petitioner's challenge to his conviction must therefore fail.[4] . . .

JUSTICE SOUTER, concurring in the judgment.

. . . If the Senate were to act in a manner seriously threatening the integrity of its results, convicting, say, upon a coin-toss, or upon a summary determination that an officer of the United States was simply " 'a bad guy,' " judicial interference might well be appropriate. In such circumstances, the Senate's action might be so far beyond the scope of its constitutional authority, and the consequent impact on the Republic so great, as to merit a judicial response despite the prudential concerns that would ordinarily counsel silence. . . .

[The concurring opinion of STEVENS, J., is omitted.]

NOTES

1. Does a presidential impeachment by the House and removal by the Senate raise justiciable issues? If the President, contesting his impeachment, claims

---

[4] . . . Justice Souter states that the Court ought not to entertain petitioner's constitutional claim because "[i]t seems fair to conclude," that the Senate tried him. . . . At best, this approach offers only the illusion of deference and respect by substituting impressionistic assessment for constitutional analysis.

that the allegations against him do not constitute "high crimes and misdemeanors, is that issue subject to judicial review?" What if the President claims that the actions of the House or Senate were procedurally defective— *e.g.*, the Senate treated his pleading of the Fifth Amendment as evidence of guilt; or biased Senators did not recuse themselves; or other Senators only heard parts of the trial?

2.   What if the President claims that, in the middle of the lengthy impeachment process, there was an intervening federal election, and the two Houses should begin the process anew after the election? There was an intervening election between the House's impeachment of President Clinton and his trial and acquittal by the Senate. The President ultimately raised no legal motion based on this fact. In several instances, the Senate has removed federal judges whom the House, selected by the prior election, had impeached.

1.8.3   The Eleventh Amendment

The Eleventh Amendment places some constitutional limitations on the exercise of judicial review by the federal courts. The people ratified it in reaction to *Chisholm v. Georgia,* 2 U.S. (2 Dall.) 419, 1 L.Ed. 440 (1793). *Chisholm* held that noncitizens of a State could initiate a suit in federal court against that State for damages. The Eleventh Amendment does not immunize the states from the restrictions of federal law (it does not overturn the Supremacy Clause) but it does require that litigants bring some types of suits against states in state court rather than federal court.[83]

The Eleventh Amendment is sometimes called the "lawyer's amendment," because careful lawyers can avoid many of the hurdles it creates. That does not mean that the Eleventh Amendment is unimportant, for it reflects the fact that the states in the union are more than dotted lines on a map. However, the Eleventh Amendment neither overturns the Supremacy Clause nor excuses states from the operation of federal law. It does affect what cases plaintiffs can initiate in federal court if they sue for retroactive damage relief.

Ex parte Young, 209 U.S. 123, 28 S.Ct. 441, 52 L.Ed. 714 (1908) held the Eleventh Amendment did not bar an action in the federal courts seeking to enjoin *an agent* of a State (*e.g.*, the State Attorney General) from allegedly violating the

---

[83]   The language of the Eleventh Amendment does not explicitly apply to suits against a State brought by its own citizens, but the Court interprets it that way. *Hans v. Louisiana,* 134 U.S. 1, 10 S.Ct. 504, 33 L.Ed. 842 (1890). The Amendment does not apply to the political subdivisions of the State (such as cities and school boards) because it only applies to a "State." In addition, States may explicitly waive their Eleventh Amendment immunity.

Fourteenth Amendment. When a state officer's actions conflict the Constitution "he is in that case stripped of his official or representative capacity and is subject in his person to the consequences of his individual conduct." Thus the offending officer is not the "State" for Eleventh Amendment purposes; still, because he is acting under color of law, there is "state action," for purposes of the Fourteenth Amendment ("nor shall any State deprive . . ."). Because a State can act only through its flesh and blood agents, *Ex parte Young* is a significant limitation of the Eleventh Amendment.

Hence, the federal court can order damages against individual defendants even though they hold public office. *Scheuer v. Rhodes,* 416 U.S. 232, 94 S.Ct. 1683, 40 L.Ed.2d 90 (1974). In this case, personal representatives of the estates of students killed on the campus of a state-controlled university, Kent State, sued for damages. Defendants included the governor and members of the Ohio National Guard.

On the other hand, if the suit in essence seeks *retroactive* money damages from the State treasury rather than the State official, the Amendment applies even though the State is not a named party. Thus, *Edelman v. Jordan,* 415 U.S. 651, 94 S.Ct. 1347, 39 L.Ed.2d 662 (1974) held that a federal court cannot order State officials to release welfare benefits wrongfully withheld by the State because the Eleventh Amendment barred this retroactive monetary relief.

The Eleventh Amendment also permits a plaintiff to initiate a suit in federal court for *prospective* injunctive relief to prevent future Constitutional violations even though that order will require states to spend more in the future. *Milliken v. Bradley,* 433 U.S. 267, 97 S.Ct. 2749, 53 L.Ed.2d 745 (1977), affirmed the federal trial court's school desegregation order that required the state to spend money. *Milliken* reaffirmed that "the Eleventh Amendment bars an ordinary suit for money damages against the State without its consent," but added that the district court acted properly in approving a remedial reading education plan that required the State to pay one-half the costs. (The Detroit School Board paid the other half.) That some programs are "also 'compensatory' in nature does not change the fact that they are part of a plan that operates prospectively to bring about the delayed benefits of a unitary school system. We therefore hold that such prospective relief is not barred by the Eleventh Amendment."

In addition, sometimes Congress can override the Eleventh Amendment by statute. Section 5 of the Fourteenth Amendment authorizes Congress to enforce Section 1. The Fourteenth Amendment necessarily amends the state of the law before its ratification. Congress may create causes of action against the State even for retroactive damages when Congress enacts the statute pursuant to its power under § 5 of the Fourteenth Amendment. *Fitzpatrick v. Bitzer,* 427 U.S. 445, 96 S.Ct. 2666, 49 L.Ed.2d 614 (1976). In this case, present and retired male state employees sued alleging that the state's statutory retirement benefit plan discriminated against them because of their sex. The Supreme Court, speaking through Justice Rehnquist, held that the enforcement provisions of the Fourteenth Amendment and the principle of state sovereignty that it embodies necessarily limit the Eleventh Amendment. Hence, Congress may authorize back pay under the Civil Rights Act. There were no dissents. One of the purposes of the Fourteenth Amendment was to give Congress more power over the States.

However, Congress cannot constitutionally use the Commerce Clause to create private rights of action against the States and abrogate their Eleventh Amendment[84] immunity. The Eleventh Amendment prevents Congress from using the Commerce Clause to authorize private parties to file suits in federal court against unconsenting States, whether the relief sought is prospective injunctive relief or retroactive monetary relief. The Commerce Clause does not restrict the reach of the subsequently enacted Eleventh Amendment.

Alden v. Maine, 527 U.S. 706, 119 S.Ct. 2240, 144 L.Ed.2d 636 (1999) held (5 to 4) that Congress cannot use its authority under Article I to abrogate a State's immunity in that State's own courts. Plaintiffs sued Maine in Maine State Court claiming that it had violated the overtime provisions of the federal Fair Labor Standards Act. *Alden* went beyond the Eleventh Amendment: the "sovereign immunity of the States neither derives from nor is limited by the terms of the Eleventh Amendment." Instead, the Court said that it is inherent in the structure of the original constitution, and Congress does not have power under Article I to abrogate it.

A state's constitutional privilege to assert its sovereign immunity in its own courts does not give a state the right to disregard the Constitution or a valid federal law. FIRST, states may consent to suit in their own courts, just as the Federal

---

[84] *Seminole Tribe v. Florida,* 517 U.S. 44, 116 S.Ct. 1114, 134 L.Ed.2d 252 (1996) overruling *Pennsylvania v. Union Gas Co.,* 491 U.S. 1, 109 S.Ct. 2273, 105 L.Ed.2d 1 (1989).

However, *Central Virginia Community College v. Katz,* 546 U.S. 356, 126 S.Ct. 990, 163 L.Ed.2d 945 (2006) held that sovereign immunity does not bar a bankruptcy trustee's proceeding to set aside the debtor's preferential transfers to state agencies. Stevens, J., for the Court (5 to 4), reasoned that the history of the Bankruptcy Clause (Art. I, § 8, cl. 4) demonstrates that the framers intended it not only as a grant of legislative authority to Congress, but also as authorization for a limited subordination of the state sovereign immunity in the bankruptcy area. "[T]he Bankruptcy Clause of Article I, the source of Congress' authority to effect this intrusion upon state sovereignty, simply did not contravene the norms this Court has understood the Eleventh Amendment to exemplify." Thomas, J., filed a dissenting opinion joined by Roberts, C.J., and Scalia & Kennedy, JJ.

Government often does. SECOND, this immunity belongs to the states, not to lesser entities such as municipalities. THIRD, plaintiffs can seek relief against state officers under *Ex parte Young* for injunctive or declaratory relief or for money damages when sued in their individual capacities. FOURTH, the Federal Government itself could sue the States to enforce federal law. The Eleventh Amendment, by its own terms, does not apply to lawsuit that the Federal Government initiates. Under the Constitution, "the States consented to suits brought by other States or by the Federal Government." FIFTH, Congress may also authorize private suits against nonconsenting States pursuant to its § 5 enforcement power.

1.9 LEGISLATIVE RESTRICTIONS ON JUDICIAL REVIEW

Marbury v. Madison established that Congress cannot extend the original jurisdiction of the Supreme Court. Congress has always provided for the original jurisdiction of the Supreme Court by statute, although the Court has often said in dictum that its original jurisdiction exists directly by virtue of Article III and needs no enabling legislation. See, *e.g., Kentucky v. Dennison,* 65 U.S. (24 How.) 66, 98, 16 L.Ed. 717 (1861).

However, what power does Congress have to limit the original jurisdiction of the lower federal courts, or to limit the appellate jurisdiction of the Supreme Court?

The language in Article III provides that the "judicial power of the United States *shall be vested* in one supreme Court and in such inferior Courts as the Congress *may* from time to time ordain and establish." § 1 (emphasis added). Article III outlines the Supreme Court's original jurisdiction, and then provides that in all other cases within federal jurisdiction, "the Supreme Court *shall have* appellate Jurisdiction, both as to Law and Fact, and with *such Exceptions,* and under such Regulations as the Congress shall make." § 2, cl. 2 (emphasis added). May Congress simply refuse to create all lower federal courts? If it creates them, may it limit their jurisdiction? What are the limitations, if any, on Congress' right to restrict Supreme Court appellate jurisdiction?

We have no definitive answer to the first question because Congress, from the very beginning, created federal courts. A decision not to create lower federal courts may or may not have been constitutional, but it would not have been very practical. As Professor Herbert Wechsler has noted, "government cannot be run without the use of courts for the enforcement of coercive sanctions and within large areas it will be thought that federal tribunals are essential to administer federal law. Within that area, the opportunity for litigating constitutional defenses is built in and cannot be foreclosed."

If federal statute gives the lower federal courts jurisdiction but denies appellate review in the Supreme Court, the various lower federal courts will reach contrary results because there will be no Supreme Court ruling to decide the conflicts in the lower courts. If lower federal courts also do not have jurisdiction, resolution of legal issues "is perforce left to the courts of fifty states, with even greater probability of contrariety in their decisions." This inconsistency of results—some decisions expanding constitutional rights and others narrowing them—may prove to be intolerable to federal officials. And, if there is no review of these cases in the U.S. Supreme Court, that Court cannot reverse or modify the offending caselaw. Thus, rarely is congressional control over jurisdiction "exerted as a method of expressing dissidence to constitutional decisions, even when such dissidence has won the sympathy of Congress." Wechsler, The Courts and the Constitution, 65 Columbia L. Review 1001, 1006–07 (1965).

Yet this rarity does occur, and the leading decision is the case that follows:

Ex Parte McCardle
74 U.S. (7 Wall.) 506, 19 L.Ed. 264 (1869)

[During the Civil War, Lambdin P. Milligan, a Southern sympathizer and resident of Indiana, planned to release some imprisoned confederate soldiers in Indianapolis and other places and to incite insurrection. A U.S. military tribunal tried and sentenced him to death. In *Ex parte Milligan*, 71 U.S. (4 Wall.) 2, 18 L.Ed. 281 (1866), the Supreme Court held that the military commission had no jurisdiction to try to sentence him because military trial cannot replace trial by jury for civilians when the civil courts are open.

[After the war, Congress enacted various laws to reconstruct the South. The Reconstruction Acts divided the former Confederacy into various military districts. The military commanders of these districts could try offending civilians by military courts. The military commander of the Fourth District, General Ord, ordered the arrest of William McCardle, a newspaper editor, on November 8, 1867, because of various editorials that McCardle had published. His November 6 editorial, for example, described Ord and other military commanders as "infamous, cowardly, and abandoned villains who, instead of wearing shoulder straps and ruling millions of people, should have their heads shaved, their ears cropped, their foreheads branded, and their precious persons lodged in a penitentiary."

[McCardle applied to the federal circuit court for release on habeas corpus arguing that his arrest and detention were unconstitutional. Given the earlier decision in *Ex parte Milligan,* McCardle's claim presented the Court with an easy opportunity to declare the Reconstruction Acts unconstitutional, and opportunity that the Reconstruction Congress feared.

[McCardle lost the case before Judge Hill, who denied the writ of habeas corpus, but did release him on bail. Hill wrote, "I am gratified that the [new] law [of February 5, 1867] has provided a direct appeal to the Supreme Court, which meets in the Capitol on Monday next, where any error I may have committed can be corrected. . . ."

[The Supreme Court heard argument for four days in early March of 1868. It gave each side six hours of oral argument, triple the normal amount. In the middle of oral argument, Chief Justice Chase announced that he would soon have to leave to preside over the impeachment trial of President Andrew Johnson. After the end of oral argument on March 9, the Supreme Court took the case under advisement; on March 27 Congress—worried about a decision that would invalidate the Reconstruction Acts—enacted a new law that repealed the law giving McCardle appellate review in the Supreme Court. On March 30 the impeachment trial began.

[The Supreme Court heard reargument on April 12, 1869, and announced its unanimous decision, delivered by Chief Justice Chase.]

CHIEF JUSTICE CHASE delivered the opinion of the court.

The first question necessarily is that of jurisdiction; for, if the act of March 1868, takes away the jurisdiction defined by the act of February, 1867, it is useless, if not improper, to enter into any discussion of other questions.

It is quite true, as was argued by the counsel for the petitioner, that the appellate jurisdiction of this court is not derived from acts of Congress. It is, strictly speaking, conferred by the Constitution. But it is conferred "with such exceptions and under such regulations as Congress shall make."

It is unnecessary to consider whether, if Congress had made no exceptions and no regulations, this court might not have exercised general appellate jurisdiction under rules prescribed by itself. For among the earliest acts of the first Congress, at its first session, was the act of September 24th, 1789, to establish the judicial courts of the United States. That act provided for the organization of this court, and prescribed regulations for the exercise of its jurisdiction. . . .

The principle that the affirmation of appellate jurisdiction implies the negation of all such jurisdiction not affirmed having been thus established, it was an almost necessary consequence that acts of Congress, providing for the exercise of jurisdiction, should come to be spoken of as acts granting jurisdiction, and not as acts making exceptions to the constitutional grant of it.

The exception to appellate jurisdiction in the case before us, however, is not an inference from the affirmation of other appellate jurisdiction. It is made in terms. The provision of the act of 1867, affirming the appellate jurisdiction of this court in cases of *habeas corpus* is expressly repealed. It is hardly possible to imagine a plainer instance of positive exception.

We are not at liberty to inquire into the motives of the legislature. We can only examine into its power under the Constitution; and the power to make exceptions to the appellate jurisdiction of this court is given by express words.

What, then, is the effect of the repealing act upon the case before us? We cannot doubt as to this. Without jurisdiction the court cannot proceed at all in any cause. Jurisdiction is power to declare the law, and when it ceases to exist, the only function remaining to the court is that of announcing the fact and dismissing the cause. . . .

On the other hand, the general rule, supported by the best elementary writers, is, that "when an act of the legislature is repealed, it must be considered, except as to transactions past and closed, as if it never existed." [N]o judgment could be rendered in a suit after the repeal of the act under which it was brought and prosecuted.

It is quite clear, therefore, that this court cannot proceed to pronounce judgment in this case, for it has no longer jurisdiction of the appeal; and judicial duty is not less fitly performed by declining ungranted jurisdiction than in exercising firmly that which the Constitution and the laws confer.

Counsel seem to have supposed, if effect be given to the repealing act in question, that the whole appellate power of the court, in cases of *habeas corpus,* is denied. But this is an error. The act of 1868 does not except from that jurisdiction any cases but appeals from Circuit Courts under the act of 1867. It does not affect the jurisdiction which was previously exercised. The appeal of the petitioner in this case must be dismissed for want of jurisdiction.

NOTES

1. Shortly after this decision, Chief Justice Chase wrote to Judge Hill (the district judge who had decided McCardle's application for a writ of habeas corpus); at the end of his letter, dated May 1, 1869, Chase confided, "P.S. I may say to you that had the merits of the McCardle Case been decided the Court would doubtless have held that his imprisonment for trial before a military commission was illegal." Charles Fairman, 6 History of the Supreme Court of the United States: Reconstruction and Reunion 1864–88, Part One (1971), at p. 494.

    Later that year the Court held, in *Ex parte Yerger,* 75 U.S. (8 Wall.) 85, 19 L.Ed. 332 (1869), that the statute of 1868, at issue in McCardle, did not prevent Yerger's review because he used the certiorari route, not affected by the 1868 repeal legislation. The Court concluded that the writs of habeas corpus and certiorari could revise the decision of the circuit court and free the prisoner from unlawful restraint. The Court never reached a decision on the merits challenging the Reconstruction Acts, because the case was mooted when the military authorities responded by releasing Yerger from custody.

2. *United States v. Klein,* 80 U.S. (13 Wall.) 128, 20 L.Ed. 519 (1871). Klein sued in the court of claims under an 1863 statute that allowed the recovery of land captured or abandoned during the Civil War if the claimant could prove that he had not aided the rebellion. Relying on an earlier Supreme Court decision holding that a pardon proved conclusively that he had not assisted the rebellion, Klein won in the lower court. While the appeal was pending, Congress passed a statute providing that (1) a presidential pardon would not support a claim for captured property, (2) acceptance without disclaimer of a pardon for participation in the rebellion was conclusive evidence that the claimant had aided the enemy, and (3) when the court of claims based its judgment in favor of the claimant on such pardon, then the Supreme Court lacked jurisdiction on appeal.

    The Supreme Court invalidated the statute and the jurisdictional limitation. Chief Justice Chase wrote for the Court:

    > If [the statute] simply denied the right of appeal in a particular class of cases, there could be no doubt that it must be regarded as an exercise of the power of Congress to make "such exceptions from the appellate jurisdiction" as should seem to it expedient.

But the language of the proviso shows plainly that it does not intend to withhold appellate jurisdiction except as a means to an end. Its great and controlling purpose is to deny pardons granted by the President the effect which this court had adjudged them to have. . . .

It seems to us that this is not an exercise of the acknowledged power of Congress to make exceptions and prescribe regulations to the appellate power.

We must think that Congress has inadvertently passed the limit which separates the legislative from the judicial power.

Klein, which the Court decided only two years after *McCardle*, should make clear that Congress cannot impose a jurisdictional limitation that violates the Constitution. For example, Congress should not be able to provide that the Supreme Court has no appeal in cases where the plaintiff is a Southern Baptist, because that would discriminate against a particular religion in violation of the First Amendment.

3. *Lauf v. E. G. Shinner & Co.*, 303 U.S. 323, 58 S.Ct. 578, 82 L.Ed. 872 (1938), upheld the constitutionality of section 7 of the Norris LaGuardia Act. That section provides that no federal court has jurisdiction to issue an injunction "in any case involving or growing out of a labor dispute" unless the court finds that (1) the injunction is necessary to prevent irreparable injury to the complainant, (2) the complainant will be hurt more than the defendants, (3) adequate remedy at law exists, and (4) the police are unwilling or unable to provide adequate protection to the complainants' property. Congress enacted section 7 because it was upset that federal courts were too frequently siding with management and enjoining workers from striking. In *Lauf* the Court said, "There can be no question of the power of Congress thus to define and limit the jurisdiction of the inferior courts of the United States."

Yet, one should not read *Lauf* too broadly. The section did provide exclude cases where the injunction was not necessary to provide irreparable injury, the police refuse to protect the party seeking the injunction, and there was no "adequate remedy at law" (that is, no remedy of money damages). The Court did not rule that Congress could exclude the remedy of injunction if that remedy were the only way to protect a constitutional right.[85]

---

[85] In *Battaglia v. General Motors Corp.*, 169 F.2d 254 (2d Cir.), cert. denied 335 U.S. 887, 69 S.Ct. 236, 93 L.Ed. 425 (1948), the Second Circuit upheld a federal statute that removed jurisdiction from federal courts to

4. On June 20, 1991, *Lampf, Pleva, Lipkind, Prupis & Petigrow v. Gilbertson,* 501 U.S. 350 (1991), rejected many lower court cases, and held that litigation based on § 10(b) of the Securities Exchange Act and SEC Rule 10b–5 must begin within one year after discovery of the facts constituting the violation and within three years after the violation. This ruling shortened the statute of limitations. Following *Lampf,* the trial court dismissed petitioners' claims as untimely, and the judgment became final. In December 1991, the President signed a law (§ 27) providing that, if a court dismissed any § 10(b) suit as time barred after June 19, 1991—the day before *Lampf* was decided—and the case would have been timely but for *Lampf,* then the court should reinstate the case if plaintiff made the appropriate motion no later than 60 days after December 19, 1991. After § 27A was enacted, plaintiff in *Plaut v. Spendthrift Farm, Inc.,* 514 U.S. 211 (1995), filed a motion to reinstate their action. Justice Scalia, for the Court, held that § 27 violated the separation of powers because it retroactively commanded federal courts to reopen *final* judgments, in violation of *Marbury v. Madison.* In no previous instance, said the Court, has Congress enacted retroactive legislation requiring an Article III court to set aside a *final* judgment. Article III gives federal courts "the power, not merely to rule on cases, but to *decide* them." (Emphasis in original). "When a new law makes clear that it is retroactive, an appellate court must apply that law in reviewing judgments still on appeal that were rendered before the law was enacted, and must alter the outcome accordingly." However, there is a distinction between judgments that are final versus judgments that are on appeal or are subject to being appealed. Section 27A is not like a law that applies "to proceedings pending at the time, or brought after, the decision [in a particular case]." That law would not reopen final judgments.

5. In *Glidden v. Zdanok,* 370 U.S. 538, 82 S.Ct. 1459, 8 L.Ed.2d 671 (1962), Justice Douglas, dissenting, joined by Justice Black, said: "There is a serious question whether the *McCardle* Case could command a majority view today."

---

give back pay in certain cases (where the plaintiff, in pending cases, was relying on a statute that Congress had appealed). The Second Circuit said:

> "A few of the district court decisions sustaining section 2 of the Portal-to-Portal Act have done so on the ground that since jurisdiction of federal courts other than the Supreme Court is conferred by Congress, it may at the will of Congress be taken away in whole or in part. We think, however, that the exercise by Congress of its control over jurisdiction is subject to compliance with at least the requirements of the Fifth Amendment. [W]hile Congress has the undoubted power to give, withhold, and restrict the jurisdiction of courts other than the Supreme Court, it must not so exercise that power as to deprive any person of life, liberty, or property without due process of law or to take private property without just compensation."

6. Periodically, factions in Congress have introduced legislation designed to control substantive results by limiting the jurisdiction of the federal courts. See, *e.g.*, H.R. 11926, 88th Cong., 2d Sess. (1964), bill to prevent federal courts from accepting jurisdiction in reapportionment cases; S. 2646, 85th Cong., 1st Sess. (1957), bill to remove Supreme Court's appellate jurisdiction in matters relating to state laws regulating subversive activities; H.R. 13916, 92d Cong., 2d Sess. (1972), bill providing for stays of all new court orders mandating busing of students for desegregation purposes.[86]

1.10 STANDING AND TAXPAYER SUITS

Muskrat v. United States, discussed above, § 1.8.1, demonstrated that federal courts may not decide mere abstract questions of law. A "case or controversy" must exist. If such a case or controversy is present, the federal court still will not decide the issue unless the plaintiff has "standing" to sue. Has plaintiff been "injured in fact, economic or otherwise"? And, does the Court find any "fairly traceable causal connection between the claimed injury and the challenged conduct"? In general, the plaintiff must be hurt in some way by some action, the proof being that if the action stops, then the alleged harm will stop. For example, in *Barlow v. Collins,* 397 U.S. 159 (1970), the Court held that tenant farmers who were eligible for payments under a cotton program enacted as part of the Food and Agriculture Act had standing to challenge the validity of an amended regulation that would increase the rights of landlords. The farmers had a personal stake in the amended regulation, which caused them injury in fact. The farmers showed a causal connection between the action (the regulation) and the harm (losing subsidies).

Sierra Club v. Morton, 405 U.S. 727 (1972), held that the Sierra Club did not have standing to contest a proposed development in the Mineral King Valley. The majority agreed that the Sierra Club alleged an injury in fact—that the proposed road through the National Park "would destroy or otherwise adversely affect the scenery, natural and historic objects and wildlife in the park and impair the enjoyment of the park for future generations." However, the Sierra Club did not allege that the proposed development would affect it or its members in any of their aesthetic or environmental activities. In a footnote, the Court said that the Sierra Club could amend its complaint on remand. In fact, it later amended its complaint to make the necessary allegations. (Justice Douglas, in dissent, argued

---

[86] Rotunda, Congressional Power to Restrict the Jurisdiction of the Lower Federal Courts and the Problem of School Busing, 64 Georgetown U. Law Journal 839 (1976).

that trees should have standing: the Court should allow "environmental issues to be litigated before federal agencies or federal courts in the name of the inanimate object about to be despoiled ... and where injury is the subject of public outrage.")

In *Baker v. Carr*, the Court said that the "gist of the question of standing" is whether the plaintiff has "alleged such a personal stake in the outcome as to assure that concrete adverseness which sharpens the presentation of issues." Sometimes there is no standing because of Article III. At other times, the Court's own sense of self-restraint (not the Constitutional requirement of a case or controversy) leads it to find no standing. This self-restraint is part of the general judicial duty to avoid unnecessary decisions on constitutional questions. In general it may be said that if the plaintiff is protesting a claimed invasion of a generalized constitutional injury, the Court appears to be more reluctant to find standing (which would create the need to dispose of a constitutional claim) than in cases in which the plaintiff demonstrates that a federal statute grants standing. If Congress speaks, either explicitly or implicitly, the Court will accept the congressional decision to confer standing to litigate constitutional or statutory claims (assuming the Article III requirements are also met). If Congress is silent, the litigant must overcome the Article III hurdle and the hurdle that says that the Court will use standing as a tool of self-restraint. As the constitutional issues become more complex, the Court may make the standing barrier higher, in order to avoid a difficult constitutional decision and in order to assure that judicial review does not take place gratuitously.

What if the plaintiff is a taxpayer upset with the use of federal expenditures? Does a taxpayer have standing merely because he or she is a taxpayer? Sometimes there is an earmarked tax, such as a tariff on foreign beef. If plaintiff claims that paying the tariff is unconstitutional, we know that if plaintiff wins that argument, he or she does not pay the tariff. That is often not the case with federal income taxes. One set of laws provide for federal expenditures while another set imposes federal income taxes. A court injunction prohibiting the former does not affect the latter. If plaintiff claims that a particular federal expenditure (money appropriated to build a bridge) is somehow unconstitutional, a victory on that issue does not affect the rate of federal income tax. For example, let us assume that a court enjoins the Department of Defense from buying missiles costing $10 billion. The DOD will not be spending the money, but that will not affect the taxes than any of us pay. At some point, Congress may enact a law that reduces the income tax rate, but that would not be part of any remedy a court orders. Federal income taxes and federal expenditures are normally not connected.

The first important case raising this issue follows.

MASSACHUSETTS V. MELLON
FROTHINGHAM V. MELLON
262 U.S. 447, 43 S.Ct. 597, 67 L.Ed. 1078 (1923)

JUSTICE SUTHERLAND delivered the opinion of the Court.

These cases were argued and will be considered and disposed of together. . . . Both cases challenge the constitutionality of the Act of November 23, 1921, commonly called the Maternity Act. Briefly, it provides for an initial appropriation and thereafter annual appropriations for a period of five years, to be apportioned among such of the several States as shall accept and comply with its provisions, for the purpose of cooperating with them to reduce maternal and infant mortality and protect the health of mothers and infants. It creates a bureau to administer the act in cooperation with state agencies, which are required to make such reports concerning their operations and expenditures as may be prescribed by the federal bureau. Whenever that bureau shall determine that funds have not been properly expended in respect of any State, payments may be withheld.

It is asserted that these appropriations are for purposes not national, but local to the States, and together with numerous similar appropriations constitute an effective means of inducing the States to yield a portion of their sovereign rights. . . . In the *Massachusetts* case it is alleged that the plaintiff's rights and powers as a sovereign State and the rights of its citizens have been invaded and usurped by these expenditures and acts; and that, although the State has not accepted the act, its constitutional rights are infringed by the passage thereof and the imposition upon the State of an illegal and unconstitutional option either to yield to the Federal Government a part of its reserved rights or lose the share which it would otherwise be entitled to receive of the moneys appropriated. In the *Frothingham* case plaintiff alleges that the effect of the statute will be to take her property, under the guise of taxation, without due process of law.

We have reached the conclusion that the cases must be disposed of for want of jurisdiction without considering the merits of the constitutional questions. . . .

First. The State of Massachusetts in its own behalf, in effect, complains that the act in question invades the local concerns of the State, and is a usurpation of power, viz: the power of local self government reserved to the States.

Probably, it would be sufficient to point out that the powers of the State are not invaded, since the statute imposes no obligation but simply extends an option which the State is free to accept or reject. But we do not rest here. Under Article III, § 2, of the Constitution, the judicial power of this Court extends "to controversies . . . between a State and citizens of another State" and the Court has original jurisdiction "in all cases . . . in which a State shall be party." The effect of this is not to confer jurisdiction upon the Court merely because a State is a party, but only where it is a party to a proceeding of judicial cognizance. Proceedings not of a justiciable character are outside the contemplation of the constitutional grant. . . .

What, then, is the nature of the right of the State here asserted and how is it affected by this statute? [W]hat burden is imposed upon the States, unequally or otherwise? Certainly there is none, unless it be the burden of taxation, and that falls upon their inhabitants, who are within the taxing power of Congress as well as that of the States where they reside. Nor does the statute require the States to do or to yield anything. If Congress enacted it with the ulterior purpose of tempting them to yield, that purpose may be effectively frustrated by the simple expedient of not yielding.

In the last analysis, the complaint of the plaintiff State is brought to the naked contention that Congress has usurped the reserved powers of the several States by the mere enactment of the statute, though nothing has been done and nothing is to be done without their consent; and it is plain that that question, as it is thus presented, is political and not judicial in character, and therefore is not a matter which admits of the exercise of the judicial power. . . .

It follows that in so far as the case depends upon the assertion of a right on the part of the State to sue in its own behalf we are without jurisdiction. In that aspect of the case we are called upon to adjudicate, not rights of person or property, not rights of dominion over physical domain, not quasi-sovereign rights actually invaded or threatened, but abstract questions of political power, of sovereignty, of government. . . .

We come next to consider whether the suit may be maintained by the State as the representative of its citizens. To this the answer is not doubtful. We need not go so far as to say that a State may never intervene by suit to protect its citizens against any form of enforcement of unconstitutional acts of Congress; but we are clear that the right to do so does not arise here. . . . It cannot be conceded that a State, as *parens patriae,* may institute judicial proceedings to protect citizens of the United States from the operation of the statutes thereof. [I]t is the United States, and not the State, which represents them as *parens patriae,* when such representation becomes appropriate; and to the former, and not to the latter, they must look for such protective measures as flow from that status.

Second. The attack upon the statute in the *Frothingham* case is, generally, the same, but this plaintiff alleges in addition that she is a taxpayer of the United States; and her contention, though not clear, seems to be that the effect of the appropriations complained of will be to increase the burden of future taxation and thereby take her property without due process of law. The right of a taxpayer to enjoin the execution of a federal appropriation act, on the ground that it is invalid and will result in taxation for illegal purposes, has never been passed upon by this Court. . . . The interest of a taxpayer . . . in the moneys of the Treasury—partly realized from taxation and partly from other sources—is shared with millions of others; is comparatively minute and indeterminable; and the effect upon future taxation, of any payment out of the funds, so remote, fluctuating and uncertain, that no basis is afforded for an appeal to the preventive powers of a court of equity.

The administration of any statute, likely to produce additional taxation to be imposed upon a vast number of taxpayers, the extent of whose several liability is indefinite and constantly changing, is essentially a matter of public and not of individual concern. If one taxpayer may champion and litigate such a cause, then every other taxpayer may do the same, not only in respect of the statute here under review but also in respect of every other appropriation act and statute whose administration requires the outlay of public money, and whose validity may be questioned. The bare suggestion of such a result, with its attendant inconveniences, goes far to sustain the conclusion which we have reached, that a suit of this character cannot be maintained. It is of much significance that no precedent sustaining the right to maintain suits like this has been called to our attention, although, since the formation of the government, as an examination of the acts of Congress will disclose, a large number of statutes appropriating or involving the expenditure of moneys for non-federal purposes have been enacted and carried into effect. . . . Looking through forms of words to the substance of their complaint, it is merely that officials of the executive department of the government are executing and will execute an act of Congress asserted to be unconstitutional; and this we are asked to prevent. To do so would be not to decide a judicial controversy, but to assume a position of authority over the governmental acts of another and co-equal department, an authority which plainly we do not possess.

No. 24, Original, dismissed.

No. 962 affirmed.

NOTES

1. Does Article III require the conclusions in *Massachusetts* and *Frothingham* or are these decisions simply a product of judicial self-restraint? How would you develop arguments to support either view?

2. If Congress enacted a law providing funds to build a church and the Executive Branch proceeded to implement that law, who might have standing under *Frothingham* to claim a violation of the establishment of religion clause of the First Amendment?

3. Cases before and after *Massachusetts* have allowed the state to sue as *parens patriae* when the defendant was not the United States. See, *e.g., Missouri v. Illinois,* 180 U.S. 208, 21 S.Ct. 331, 45 L.Ed. 497 (1901), permitting Missouri, on behalf of its citizens, to sue Illinois and a Chicago sanitation district to enjoin the discharge of sewage into the Mississippi River. A state may also sue as *parens patriae* to enjoin antitrust violations but cannot sue for damages for its citizens because there would be duplicative recoveries by the actually injured citizens and by the state as well. *Hawaii v. Standard Oil Co.,* 405 U.S. 251, 92 S.Ct. 885, 31 L.Ed.2d 184 (1972). A state, however, may sue for damages to its proprietary interests. See, *e.g., Georgia v. Evans,* 316 U.S. 159, 62 S.Ct. 972, 86 L.Ed. 1346 (1942), holding that a state is a "person" for purposes of section 7 of the Sherman Act and therefore is entitled to sue for treble damages when, as a purchaser of asphalt, it is injured by antitrust violations. In *Wyoming v. Oklahoma,* 502 U.S. 437, 112 S.Ct. 789, 117 L.Ed.2d 1 (1992), the Court held that Wyoming had standing to challenge Oklahoma legislation that required Oklahoma coal-fired electric generating plants (including privately owned plants) producing power for sale in Oklahoma to run a mixture of coal containing at least 10% Oklahoma-mined coal. Wyoming argued the Oklahoma rule violated the dormant Commerce Clause. Although Wyoming did not itself sell coal, it imposed severance taxes on the extraction of coal within its boundaries. An Oklahoma law deprived Wyoming of tax revenues by causing a decline in the amount of coal mined in Wyoming. Wyoming does not claim merely a loss in general tax revenues; rather it has lost specific tax revenues, which are directly traceable to the Oklahoma law. The Court then found that the Oklahoma law violated the dormant Commerce Clause.

In actions by states against the United States, consider these two cases. First, in *Missouri v. Holland,* 252 U.S. 416, 40 S.Ct. 382, 64 L.Ed. 641 (1920), the Court allowed the state of Missouri to sue to enjoin a U.S. game warden from attempting to enforce the Migratory Bird Treaty Act of 1918 and accompanying regulations. The state alleged, *inter alia,* that the acts of the defendant contravened state law. The Court said that the state's bill in equity "is a reasonable and proper means to assert the alleged quasi-sovereign rights of a State" to regulate the taking of wild game within its borders. The state's complaint was about dominion over its physical domain.

Second, in *Oklahoma v. United States Civil Service Commission,* 330 U.S. 127, 67 S.Ct. 544, 91 L.Ed. 794 (1947), the Court heard a challenge to the constitutionality of the Hatch Act by Oklahoma. The U.S. Civil Service Commission notified Oklahoma that one of its employees in the state highway department had engaged in improper political activities in violation of § 12 of the federal Hatch Act. The Commission ordered the removal of the offending employee or the appropriate federal agency would withhold highway grants to Oklahoma equal to two years' compensation. Oklahoma sought review of the federal administrative order. The federal government relied in part on *Massachusetts v. Mellon* to argue that the state suffered no injury that it may legally protect from withdrawal by the United States of a grant-in-aid. The Court held:

> The issue is whether Oklahoma can challenge the constitutionality of § 12 on statutory review of a Commission order. Subsection (c) gives to any party aggrieved a judicial review of the Commission order. The review is on the entire record and extends to questions of fact and questions of law. . . . We think the challenge can be made in these review proceedings to the constitutionality of the law upon which the order under review is predicated.

The Court then upheld the constitutionality of the Commission's order. Note that Congress, by statute, explicitly provided for judicial review.

FLAST V. COHEN
392 U.S. 83, 88 S.Ct. 1942, 20 L.Ed.2d 947 (1968)

CHIEF JUSTICE WARREN delivered the opinion of the Court.

In this case, we must decide whether the *Frothingham* barrier should be lowered when a taxpayer attacks a federal statute on the ground that it violates the Establishment and Free Exercise Clauses of the First Amendment.

Appellants [sued] to enjoin the allegedly unconstitutional expenditure of federal funds under Titles I and II of the Elementary and Secondary Education Act of 1965. [They argued for] standing to maintain the action solely on their status as federal taxpayers. [Appellants claim] that federal funds appropriated under the Act were being used to finance instruction in reading, arithmetic, and other subjects in religious schools, and to purchase textbooks and other instructional materials for use in such schools. Such expenditures were alleged to be in contravention of the Establishment and Free Exercise Clauses of the First Amendment. . . .

Although the barrier *Frothingham* erected against federal taxpayer suits has never been breached, the decision has been the source of some confusion and the object of considerable criticism. The confusion has developed as commentators have tried to determine whether *Frothingham* establishes a constitutional bar to taxpayer suits or whether the Court was simply imposing a rule of self-restraint which was not constitutionally compelled. . . . The opinion delivered in *Frothingham* can be read to support either position.

. . . In terms relevant to the question for decision in this case, the judicial power of federal courts is constitutionally restricted to "cases" and "controversies," As is so often the situation in constitutional adjudication, those two words have an iceberg quality, containing beneath their surface simplicity submerged complexities which go to the very heart of our constitutional form of government. Embodied in the words "cases" and "controversies" are two complementary but somewhat different limitations. In part those words limit the business of federal courts to questions presented in an adversary context and in a form historically viewed as capable of resolution through the judicial process. And in part those words define the role assigned to the judiciary in a tripartite allocation of power to assure that the federal courts will not intrude into areas committed to the other branches of government. Justiciability is the term of art employed to give expression to this dual limitation placed upon federal courts by the case-and-controversy doctrine. . . .

Part of the difficulty in giving precise meaning and form to the concept of justiciability stems from the uncertain historical antecedents of the case-and-controversy doctrine. For example, Mr. Justice Frankfurter twice suggested that historical meaning could be imparted to the concepts of justiciability and case and controversy by reference to the practices of the courts of Westminster when the Constitution was adopted. *Joint Anti-Fascist Committee v. McGrath,* 341 U.S. 123, 150, 71 S.Ct. 624, 95 L.Ed. 817 (1951) (concurring opinion); *Coleman v. Miller,* 307

U.S. 433, 460, 59 S.Ct. 972, 985, 83 L.Ed. 1385 (1939) (separate opinion). However, the power of English judges to deliver advisory opinions was well established at the time the Constitution was drafted. . . .

Additional uncertainty exists in the doctrine of justiciability because that doctrine has become a blend of constitutional requirements and policy considerations. And a policy limitation is "not always clearly distinguished from the constitutional limitation." . . .

. . . The Government views [taxpayer] suits as involving no more than the mere disagreement by the taxpayer "with the uses to which tax money is put." According to the Government, the resolution of such disagreements is committed to other branches of the Federal Government and not to the judiciary. Consequently, the Government contends that, under no circumstances, should standing be conferred on federal taxpayers to challenge a federal taxing or spending program. An analysis of the function served by standing limitations compels a rejection of the Government's position. . . .

[I]n terms of Article III limitations on federal court jurisdiction, the question of standing is related only to whether the dispute sought to be adjudicated will be presented in an adversary context and in a form historically viewed as capable of judicial resolution. A taxpayer may or may not have the requisite personal stake in the outcome, depending upon the circumstances of the particular case. Therefore, we find no absolute bar in Article III to suits by federal taxpayers challenging allegedly unconstitutional federal taxing and spending programs. There remains, however, the problem of determining the circumstances under which a federal taxpayer will be deemed to have the personal stake and interest that impart the necessary concrete adverseness to such litigation so that standing can be conferred on the taxpayer *qua* taxpayer consistent with the constitutional limitations of Article III.

[I]n ruling on standing, it is both appropriate and necessary to look to the substantive issues . . . to determine whether there is a logical nexus between the status asserted and the claim sought to be adjudicated. . . .

The nexus demanded of federal taxpayers has two aspects to it. First, the taxpayer must establish a logical link between that status and the type of legislative enactment attacked. Thus, a taxpayer will be a proper party to allege the unconstitutionality only of exercises of congressional power under the taxing and spending clause of Art. I, § 8, of the Constitution. It will not be sufficient to allege an incidental expenditure of tax funds in the administration of an essentially regulatory statute. This requirement is consistent with the limitation imposed upon state-taxpayer standing in federal courts in *Doremus v. Board of Education,* 342 U.S. 429, 72 S.Ct, 394, 96 L.Ed. 475 (1952). Secondly, the taxpayer must establish a nexus between that status and the precise nature of the constitutional infringement alleged. Under this requirement, the taxpayer must show that the challenged enactment exceeds specific constitutional limitations imposed upon the exercise of the congressional taxing and spending power and not simply that the enactment is generally beyond the powers delegated to Congress by Art. I, § 8. When both nexuses are established, the litigant will have shown a taxpayer's stake in the outcome of the controversy and will be a proper and appropriate party to invoke a federal court's jurisdiction.

The taxpayer-appellants in this case have satisfied both nexuses to support their claim of standing under the test we announce today. Their constitutional challenge is made to an exercise by Congress of its power under Art. I, § 8, to spend for the general welfare, and the challenged program involves a substantial expenditure of federal tax funds.[23] In addition, appellants have alleged that the challenged expenditures violate the Establishment and Free Exercise Clauses of the First Amendment. Our history vividly illustrates that one of the specific evils feared by those who drafted the Establishment Clause and fought for its adoption was that the taxing and spending power would be used to favor one religion over another or to support religion in general. James Madison, who is generally recognized as the leading architect of the religion clauses of the First Amendment, observed in his famous Memorial and Remonstrance Against Religious Assessments that "the same authority which can force a citizen to contribute three pence only of his property for the support of any one establishment, may force him to conform to any other establishment in all cases whatsoever." The concern of Madison and his supporters was quite clearly that religious liberty ultimately would be the victim if government could employ its taxing and spending powers to aid one religion over another or to aid religion in general. The Establishment Clause was designed as a specific bulwark against such potential abuses of governmental power, and that clause of the First Amendment[25] operates as a

---

[23] Almost $1,000,000,000 was appropriated to implement the Elementary and Secondary Education Act in 1965.

[25] Appellants have also alleged that the Elementary and Secondary Education Act of 1965 violates the Free Exercise Clause of the First Amendment. This Court has recognized that the taxing power can be used to infringe the free exercise of religion. *Murdock v. Commonwealth of Pennsylvania,* 319 U.S. 105, 63 S.Ct. 870, 87 L.Ed. 1292 (1943). Since we hold that appellants' Establishment Clause claim is sufficient to establish the nexus between their status and the precise nature of the constitutional infringement alleged, we need not decide whether the Free Exercise claim, standing alone, would be adequate to confer standing in this case. We do note, however, that the challenged tax in *Murdock* operated upon a particular class of taxpayers. When such

specific constitutional limitation upon the exercise by Congress of the taxing and spending power conferred by Art. I, § 8.

The allegations of the taxpayer in *Frothingham v. Mellon, supra,* were quite different from those made in this case, and the result in *Frothingham* is consistent with the test of taxpayer standing announced today. The taxpayer in *Frothingham* attacked a federal spending program and she, therefore, established the first nexus required. However, she lacked standing because her constitutional attack was not based on an allegation that Congress, in enacting the Maternity Act of 1921, had breached a specific limitation upon its taxing and spending power. [T]he Due Process Clause of the Fifth Amendment does not protect taxpayers against increases in tax liability, and the taxpayer in *Frothingham* failed to make any additional claim that the harm she alleged resulted from a breach by Congress of the specific constitutional limitations imposed upon an exercise of the taxing and spending power. In essence, Mrs. Frothingham was attempting to assert the States' interest in their legislative prerogatives and not a federal taxpayer's interest in being free of taxing and spending in contravention of specific constitutional limitations imposed upon Congress' taxing and spending power.

We have noted that the Establishment Clause of the First Amendment does specifically limit the taxing and spending power conferred by Art. I, § 8. Whether the Constitution contains other specific limitations can be determined only in the context of future cases. However, whenever such specific limitations are found, we believe a taxpayer will have a dear stake as a taxpayer in assuring that they are not breached by Congress. Consequently, we hold that a taxpayer will have standing consistent with Article III to invoke federal judicial power when he alleges that congressional action under the taxing and spending clause is in derogation of those constitutional provisions which operate to restrict the exercise of the taxing and spending power. The taxpayer's allegation in such cases would be that his tax money is being extracted and spent in violation of specific constitutional protections against such abuses of legislative power. Such an injury is appropriate for judicial redress, and the taxpayer has established the necessary nexus between his status and the nature of the allegedly unconstitutional action to support his claim of standing to secure judicial review. . . .

While we express no view at all on the merits of appellants' claims in this case, their complaint contains sufficient allegations under the criteria we have

---

exercises of the taxing power are challenged, the proper party emphasis in the federal standing doctrine would require that standing be limited to the taxpayers within the affected class.

outlined to give them standing to invoke a federal court's jurisdiction for an adjudication on the merits.

Reversed.

JUSTICE DOUGLAS, concurring:

While I have joined the opinion of the Court, I do not think that the test it lays down is a durable one for the reasons stated by my Brother Harlan. I think, therefore, that it will suffer erosion and in time result in the demise of *Frothingham v. Mellon,* 262 U.S. 447, 43 S.Ct. 597, 67 L.Ed. 1078. It would therefore be the part of wisdom, as I see the problem, to be rid of *Frothingham* here and now. . . .

There has long been a school of thought here that the less the judiciary does, the better [because] the effect of a participation by the judiciary in these processes is "to dwarf the political capacity of the people, and to deaden its sense of moral responsibility." J. Thayer, John Marshall 106, 107 (1901).

The late Edmond Cahn, who opposed that view, stated my philosophy. He emphasized the importance of the role that the federal judiciary was designed to play in guarding basic rights against majoritarian control. He chided the view expressed by my Brother Harlan: "we are entitled to reproach the majoritarian justices of the Supreme Court . . . with straining to be reasonable when they ought to be adamant." . . .

JUSTICE FORTAS, concurring:

The status of taxpayer should not be accepted as a launching pad for an attack upon any target other than legislation affecting the Establishment Clause.

JUSTICE HARLAN, dissenting:

The problems presented by this case are narrow and relatively abstract, but the principles by which they must be resolved involve nothing less than the proper functioning of the federal courts, and so run to the roots of our constitutional system. The nub of my view is that the end result of *Frothingham v. Mellon,* was correct, even though, like others, I do not subscribe to all of its reasoning and premises. . . . An action brought to contest the validity of tax liabilities assessed to the plaintiff is designed to vindicate interests that are personal and proprietary. . . . I take it that the Court, although it does not pause to examine the question, believes that the interests of those who as taxpayers challenge the constitutionality of public expenditures may, at least in certain circumstances, be similar. Yet this assumption is surely mistaken.

The complaint in this case, unlike that in *Frothingham,* contains no allegation that the contested expenditures will in any fashion affect the amount of these taxpayers' own existing or foreseeable tax obligations.... Nor are taxpayers' interests in the expenditure of public funds differentiated from those of the general public by any special rights retained by them in their tax payments. The simple fact is that no such rights can sensibly be said to exist. Taxes are ordinarily levied by the United States without limitations of purpose; absent such a limitation, payments received by the Treasury in satisfaction of tax obligations lawfully created become part of the Government's general funds. The national legislature is required by the Constitution to exercise its spending powers to "provide for the common Defence and general Welfare." Art. I, § 8, cl. 1. Whatever other implications there may be to that sweeping phrase, it surely means that the United States holds its general funds, not as stakeholder or trustee for those who have paid its imposts, but as surrogate for the population at large....

Surely it is plain that the rights and interests of taxpayers who contest the constitutionality of public expenditures are markedly different from those of "Hohfeldian" plaintiffs,[5] including those taxpayer-plaintiffs who challenge the validity of their own tax liabilities. We must recognize that these non-Hohfeldian plaintiffs complain, just as the petitioner in *Frothingham* sought to complain, not as taxpayers, but as "private attorneys-general." The interests they represent, and the rights they espouse, are bereft of any personal or proprietary coloration. They are, as litigants, indistinguishable from any group selected at random from among the general population, taxpayers and nontaxpayers alike. These are and must be, to adopt Professor Jaffe's useful phrase, "public actions" brought to vindicate public rights.

[N]on-Hohfeldian plaintiffs as such are not *constitutionally* excluded from the federal courts. The problem ultimately presented by this case is, in my view, therefore to determine in what circumstances, consonant with the character and proper functioning of the federal courts, such suits should be permitted. With this preface, I shall examine the position adopted by the Court....

The Court's analysis consists principally of the observation that the requirements of standing are met if a taxpayer has the "requisite personal stake in

---

[5] The phrase is Professor Jaffe's, adopted, of course, from W. Hohfeld, Fundamental Legal Conceptions (1923). I have here employed the phrases "Hohfeldian" and "non-Hohfeldian" plaintiffs to mark the distinction between the personal and proprietary interests of the traditional plaintiff, and the representative and public interests of the plaintiff in a public action. I am aware that we are confronted here by a spectrum of interests of varying intensities, but the distinction is sufficiently accurate, and convenient, to warrant its use at least for purposes of discussion.

the outcome" of his suit. This does not, of course, resolve the standing problem; it merely restates it. The Court implements this standard with the declaration that taxpayers will be "deemed" to have the necessary personal interest if their suits satisfy two criteria: *first,* the challenged expenditure must form part of a federal spending program, and not merely be "incidental" to a regulatory program; and *second,* the constitutional provision under which the plaintiff claims must be a "specific limitation" upon Congress' spending powers. The difficulties with these criteria are many and severe, but it is enough for the moment to emphasize that they are not in any sense a measurement of any plaintiff's interest in the outcome of any suit. . . .

It is surely clear that a plaintiff's interest in the outcome of a suit in which he challenges the constitutionality of a federal expenditure is not made greater or smaller by the unconnected fact that the expenditure is, or is not, "incidental" to an "essentially regulatory" program. . . . His interest as taxpayer arises, if at all, from the fact of an unlawful expenditure, and not as a consequence of the expenditure's form. Apparently the Court has repudiated the emphasis in *Frothingham* upon the amount of the plaintiff's tax bill, only to substitute an equally irrelevant emphasis upon the form of the challenged expenditure.

The Court's second criterion is similarly unrelated to its standard for the determination of standing. The intensity of a plaintiff's interest in a suit is not measured, even obliquely, by the fact that the constitutional provision under which he claims is, or is not, a "specific limitation" upon Congress' spending powers. Thus, among the claims in *Frothingham* was the assertion that the Maternity Act deprived the petitioner of property without due process of law. The Court has evidently concluded that this claim did not confer standing because the Due Process Clause of the Fifth Amendment is not a specific limitation upon the spending powers.[11] Disregarding for the moment the formidable obscurity of the Court's categories, how can it be said that Mrs. Frothingham's interests in her suit were, as a consequence of her choice of a constitutional claim, necessarily less intense than those, for example, of the present appellants?

. . . If this case involved a tax specifically designed for the support of religion, as was the Virginia tax opposed by Madison in his Memorial and Remonstrance, I would agree that taxpayers have rights under the religious clauses of the First Amendment that would permit them standing to challenge the tax's validity in the

---

[11] It should be emphasized that the Court finds it unnecessary to examine the history of the Due Process Clause to determine whether it was intended as a "specific limitation" upon Congress' spending and taxing powers. Nor does the Court pause to examine the purposes of the Tenth Amendment, another of the premises of the constitutional claims in *Frothingham*.

federal courts. But this is not such a case, and appellants challenge an expenditure, not a tax. . . .

It seems to me clear that public actions, whatever the constitutional provisions on which they are premised, may involve important hazards for the continued effectiveness of the federal judiciary. Although I believe such actions to be within the jurisdiction conferred upon the federal courts by Article III of the Constitution, there surely can be little doubt that they strain the judicial function and press to the limit judicial authority. There is every reason to fear that unrestricted public actions might well alter the allocation of authority among the three branches of the Federal Government. It is not, I submit, enough to say that the present members of the Court would not seize these opportunities for abuse, for such actions would, even without conscious abuse, go far toward the final transformation of this Court into the Council of Revision which, despite Madison's support, was rejected by the Constitutional Convention. I do not doubt that there must be "some effectual power in the government to restrain or correct the *infra*ctions"[20] of the Constitution's several commands, but neither can I suppose that such power resides only in the federal courts.

[T]here is available a resolution of this problem that entirely satisfies the demands of the principle of separation of powers. This Court has previously held that individual litigants have standing to represent the public interest, despite their lack of economic or other personal interests, if Congress has appropriately authorized such suits. I would adhere to that principle. Any hazards to the proper allocation of authority among the three branches of the Government would be substantially diminished if public actions had been pertinently authorized by Congress and the President. . . .

[The concurring opinion of STEWART, J., is omitted.]

NOTES

1. What does *Frothingham* mean after *Flast?* Is it fair to say that all of the Justices in *Flast* agreed that Article III did not bar the plaintiffs from bringing their taxpayer suit? If so, what is the real nature of the disagreement between Douglas on the one hand and Fortas on the other? Between Harlan and the other Justices?

2. Are there any constitutional limits to the extent to which Congress by statute can either expand or contract standing? After *Flast,* could Congress provide

---

[20] The Federalist No. 80 (Hamilton).

by law that standing in such circumstances does not exist? Before *Flast,* could Congress provide that *Flast-type* standing does exist?

3.   If plaintiffs win their suit on the merits, will it result in any reduction in their tax burden, even an infinitesimal reduction? Assume that Congress enacts a tax earmarked for religious purposes, *e.g.,* a .01 percent payroll tax to finance the building of a church. If plaintiffs win their suit on the merits, will it result in a reduction of their taxes?

     In taxpayer suits such as in *Frothingham* or *Flast,* the plaintiff is really trying to challenge the spending power, not the taxing power. As Justice Harlan's dissent pointed out, such taxpayers do not object to the taxes levied but to the uses to which they apply. If Flast wins, the success does not result in any reduction of the plaintiff's tax liabilities (even minutely) or of any change in a particular level of taxation. Prohibiting an expenditure does not prohibit or affect the level of income tax.

     To be distinguished from this type of case are taxes that are *earmarked* for a certain purpose. Litigants can challenge earmarked taxes in a variety of ways even under the *Frothingham* rule. Taxpayers, as taxpayers, may contest the assessment of their tax liability by a suit for refund, in defense of a civil suit brought by the government, or in defense of a prosecution—on the grounds, for example, that the money taxed cannot constitutionally be taxed under the income tax amendment, or that reporting the income to be taxed violates the self-incrimination clause of the fifth amendment, or that the tax is really an unconstitutional penalty in the guise of a tax, or simply that the tax liability was incorrectly assessed under the applicable statutory provisions.

4.   What is the test to establish standing offered by the *Flast* majority? In footnote 23, the majority makes the point that Congress appropriated nearly $1 billion to implement the challenged law. Would plaintiffs have standing if Congress had only appropriated "three pence?"

     Assume that the U.S. Post Office plans to issue a special postage stamp to celebrate Easter. Assume further that the Post Office is not completely self-supporting and still relies on tax dollars to make up its budget deficit. Would a taxpayer have standing to challenge, as a violation of the establishment clause, the decision to issue an Easter stamp?

5.   As the Court indicated in note 25, it found taxpayer standing under the establishment clause but reserved the question of such standing under the

free exercise clause. Is there any meaningful way to distinguish between these two clauses under the *Flast* test?

6. In *Doremus v. Board of Education,* 342 U.S. 429, 72 S.Ct. 394, 96 L.Ed. 475 (1952), plaintiffs sought a declaratory judgment in state court that a state statute was unconstitutional. That statute required that public school teachers read, without comment, five verses of the Old Testament at the opening of each public school day. The state supreme court held that the law was constitutional. On appeal to the U.S. Supreme Court, the majority noted that there were two types of plaintiffs. One appellant was the parent of a 17-year-old daughter in a high school that followed the state law on Bible reading. The complaint did not allege that she was injured or offended in any way by the Bible reading. Moreover, during oral argument, plaintiff agreed, "that this child had graduated from the public schools before this appeal was taken to this Court." As to parties suing in their capacity as taxpayers, there was no allegation that the Bible reading in the public schools "is supported by any separate tax or paid for from any particular appropriation or that it adds any sum whatever to the cost of conducting the school." Nor was there any allegation that the Bible reading "increases any tax they do pay or that as taxpayers they are, will, or possibly can be out of pocket because of it."

    The Supreme Court found no standing and dismissed the appeal without reaching the merits. *Flast* cited *Doremus* with approval.

7. Since *Flast*, the Court has not found that any other clause of the Constitution meets the *Flast* test. Thus, in *United States v. Richardson,* 418 U.S. 166, 94 S.Ct. 2940, 41 L.Ed.2d 678 (1974), the Court, in a 5 to 4 opinion, held that a federal taxpayer has no standing to bring an action alleging that certain provisions concerning public reporting of expenditures under the Central Intelligence Agency Act violates Art. I, § 9, cl. 7, requiring the public reporting of public moneys. The plaintiff "asks the courts to compel the Government to give him information on precisely how the CIA spends its funds. Thus there is no logical nexus' between the asserted status of taxpayer and the claimed failure of the Congress to require the Executive to supply a more detailed report of the expenditures of that agency."

    Schlesinger v. Reservists Committee to Stop the War, 418 U.S. 208, 94 S.Ct. 2925, 41 L.Ed.2d 706 (1974) held (6 to 3) that a federal taxpayer has no standing to bring an action alleging that Article I, § 6, cl. 2—requiring that no Senator or Representative may hold any other office under the United States—made Congressmen ineligible to hold simultaneously a commission in the Armed Forces Reserve. The majority also denied standing to those who sued in their capacity as "citizens," because generalized citizen interest is not a sufficient basis for standing.

Valley Forge Christian College v. Americans United for Separation of Church and State, Inc., 454 U.S. 464, 102 S.Ct. 752, 70 L.Ed.2d 700 (1982) held (5 to 4) held that a taxpayers' organization dedicated to the separation of Church and State had no standing to challenge a transfer of surplus United States property to a religious education institution. As part of an effort to reduce the numbers of military installations, the Secretary of Defense closed a military hospital. Then, the General Services Administration, pursuant to statute, declared it "surplus property." The Department of Health, Education, and Welfare then conveyed this 77-acre tract to the Valley Forge Christian College. The property had an appraised value of $577,500, but the Secretary of HEW discounted that value to zero because of the Secretary's computation of a 100% public benefit allowance. The Valley Forge Christian College is a nonprofit educational school under the supervision of the Assemblies of God. Its self-described purpose is to train men and women for Christian service as either ministers or lay people. Faculty members must be "baptized in the Holy Spirit and be living consistent Christian lives." The plaintiffs (an organization of approximately 90,000 taxpayers) sued claiming that the transfer of property violated the Establishment Clause. The Supreme Court held that there was no standing as taxpayers:

> [T]he source of their complaint is not a congressional action, but a decision by HEW to transfer a parcel of federal property. *Flast* limited taxpayer standing to challenges directed "only [at] exercises of congressional power." Second, and perhaps redundantly, the property transfer about which respondents complain was not an exercise of authority conferred by the Taxing and Spending Clause of Art. I, § 8. The authorizing legislation, the Federal Property and Administrative Services Act of 1949, was an evident exercise of Congress' power under Art. IV, § 3, cl. 2.

The Court found no other basis for standing and explicitly added, "the assumption that if respondents have no standing to sue, no one would have standing, is not a reason to find standing."

Justice Brennan, joined by Marshall and Blackmun, dissented, and said that the majority opinion "utterly fails, except by the sheerest form of *ipse dixit*, to explain why this case is unlike *Flast*. . . ." Justice Stevens also wrote a dissenting opinion, arguing that the majority opinion "rests on the premise that the difference between a disposition of funds pursuant to the Spending Clause and a disposition of realty pursuant to the Property Clause is of fundamental jurisprudential significance."

In *Arizona Christian School Tuition Organization v. Winn*, 563 U.S. 125, 131 S.Ct. 1436, 179 L.Ed.2d 523 (2011), taxpayers sued alleging that Arizona's tuition tax credit violated the Establishment Clause. It allowed Arizona income taxpayers who voluntarily contributed money to a "student tuition organization" to receive a dollar-for-dollar *tax credit* up to $500 of their annual tax liability. Justice Kennedy, for the Court (5 to 4) held that the taxpayers have no standing under *Flast*. Arizona merely declined to impose a tax, rather than make an expenditure. The tax credit might save the state money by facilitating the operation of both religious and secular private schools. Private action (not state intervention) implemented the tax credit system. "Like contributions that lead to charitable tax deductions," tax credits "are not owed to the State and, in fact, pass directly from taxpayers to private organizations." The complaining taxpayers assume "that income should be treated as if it were government property even if it has not come into the tax collector's hands." However, private bank accounts "cannot be equated with the Arizona State Treasury."

CHAPTER 2

Substantive Due Process

2.1 THE EARLY CASES

BARRON V. MAYOR AND COUNCIL OF BALTIMORE

32 U.S. (7 Pet.) 243, 8 L.Ed. 672 (1833)

[John Barron sued the city of Baltimore in order to recover damages for injury to his wharf property. These damages occurred when the city installed new street grades, paving, and embankments that diverted the flow of streams. The new waterways deposited earth in front of Barron's wharf, ruining its value as a deep-water wharf. Barron claimed that the city's actions deprived him of a vested property right and that he was therefore entitled to just compensation under the Fifth Amendment. The state trial court found that the city owed Barron $4,500, but the appellate court reversed. Barron then appealed to the Supreme Court.]

CHIEF JUSTICE MARSHALL delivered the opinion of the Court.

The plaintiff in error contends that [his case] comes within that clause in the fifth amendment to the Constitution which inhibits the taking of private property for public use without just compensation. He insists that this amendment, being in favor of the liberty of the citizen, ought to be so construed as to restrain the legislative power of a State, as well as that of the United States. If this proposition be untrue, the court can take no jurisdiction of the cause.

The question thus presented is, we think, of great importance, but not of much difficulty.

The Constitution was ordained and established by the people of the United States for themselves, for their own government, and not for the government of the individual States. Each State established a constitution for itself, and in that constitution provided such limitations and restrictions on the powers of its particular government as its judgment dictated. The people of the United States framed such a government for the United States as they supposed best adapted to their situation, and best calculated to promote their interests. The powers they conferred on this government were to be exercised by itself; and the limitations on power, if expressed in general terms, are naturally, and, we think, necessarily applicable to the government created by the instrument. They are limitations of power granted in the instrument itself; not of distinct governments, framed by different persons and for different purposes.

If these propositions be correct, the fifth amendment must be understood as restraining the power of the general government, not as applicable to the States. In their several constitutions they have imposed such restrictions on their respective governments as their own wisdom suggested; such as they deemed most proper for themselves. It is a subject on which they judge exclusively, and with which others interfere no farther than they are supposed to have a common interest.

The counsel for the plaintiff in error insists that the Constitution was intended to secure the people of the several States against the undue exercise of power by their respective State governments; as well as against that which might be attempted by their general government. In support of this argument he relies on the inhibitions contained in the tenth section of the first article.

We think that section affords a strong if not a conclusive argument in support of the opinion already indicated by the court. . . .

If the original Constitution, in the ninth and tenth sections of the first article, draws this plain and marked line of discrimination between the limitations it imposes on the powers of the general government and on those of the States; if in every inhibition intended to act on State power, words are employed which directly express that intent, some strong reason must be assigned for departing from this safe and judicious course in framing the amendments, before that departure can be assumed.

We search in vain for that reason.

Had the people of the several States, or any of them, required changes in their constitutions; had they required additional safeguards to liberty from the apprehended encroachments of their particular governments, the remedy was in their own hands, and would have been applied by themselves. . . . Had the Framers of these amendments [the Bill of Rights] intended them to be limitations on the powers of the State governments they would have imitated the Framers of the original Constitution, and have expressed that intention. Had Congress engaged in the extraordinary occupation of improving the constitutions of the several States by affording the people additional protection from the exercise of power by their own governments in matters which concerned themselves alone, they would have declared this purpose in plain and intelligible language.

But it is universally understood, it is a part of the history of the day, that the great revolution which established the Constitution of the United States was not effected without immense opposition. Serious fears were extensively entertained that those powers which the patriot statesmen who then watched over the interests of our country, deemed essential to union, and to the attainment of those invaluable objects for which union was sought, might be exercised in a manner dangerous to liberty. In almost every convention by which the Constitution was adopted, amendments to guard against the abuse of power were recommended. These amendments demanded security against the apprehended encroachments of the general government—not against those of the local governments.

In compliance with a sentiment thus generally expressed, to quiet fears thus extensively entertained, amendments were proposed by the required majority in Congress, and adopted by the States. These amendments contain no expression indicating an intention to apply them to the State governments. This court cannot so apply them.

We are of opinion that the provision in the fifth amendment to the Constitution, declaring that private property shall not be taken for public use without just compensation, is intended solely as a limitation on the exercise of power by the government of the United States, and is not applicable to the legislation of the States. We are therefore of opinion that there is no repugnancy between the several acts of the General Assembly of Maryland, given in evidence by the defendants at the trial of this cause in the court of that State, and the Constitution of the United States.

NOTES

1. The first Congress proposed twelve amendments to the Constitution on September 25, 1789. Ten of the amendments were declared ratified in 1791. The first eight are known as the Bill of Rights.

    The legislatures of the several states did not ratify two of the proposed amendments of 1791. The first regulated the number of representatives so that no less than two hundred representatives in all nor less than one representative for every 50,000 people should serve in Congress. (In a population of 200 million, that would mean 4,000 representatives.) The second proposed amendment provided that no law varying the compensation of senators and representatives could be enacted until an election of representatives shall have intervened. Enough states—belatedly—ratified this amendment in 1992; it is now the 27th Amendment to the Constitution.

2. As Marshall acknowledged, the first ten amendments were, in effect, the price of ratification. The people wanted specific guarantees against abuse of power, even though many argued against such amendments. Hamilton, in Federalist Papers No. 84, argued that "bills of rights, in the sense and to the extent in which they are contended for, are not only unnecessary in the proposed Constitution, but would even be dangerous." Hamilton argued that the amendments were unnecessary because the Constitution grants to the central government only enumerated powers. "[W]hy declare that things shall not be done which there is no power to do?" The amendments were dangerous because a Bill of Rights "would contain various exceptions to powers not granted; and, on this very account, would afford a colorable pretext to claim more than were granted." For example, "should it be said that the liberty of the press shall not be restrained, when no power is given by which restrictions may be imposed? I will not contend that such a provision would confer a regulating power; but it is evident that it would furnish, to men disposed to usurp, a plausible pretense for claiming that power."

3. In 1865, the Thirteenth Amendment became part of the Constitution. The states ratified the Fourteenth Amendment in 1868 and the Fifteenth Amendment in 1870. All three specifically apply to the states. In particular, section one of the Fourteenth Amendment protected "the privileges or immunities of citizens of the United States." That section also guaranteed to all "persons" equal protection of the laws, and provided that no state may deprive any person of "life, liberty, or property, without due process."

The first major test of the meaning and application of these guarantees came in the following case.

SLAUGHTER-HOUSE CASES (BUTCHERS' BENEVOLENT ASSOCIATION V. CRESCENT CITY LIVE-STOCK LANDING AND SLAUGHTER-HOUSE COMPANY)

83 U.S. (16 Wall.) 36, 21 L.Ed. 394 (1873)

[Louisiana enacted a statute in 1869 that made it illegal to slaughter animals in New Orleans except "that the "Crescent City Stock Landing and Slaughter-House Company' may establish *themselves* at any point or place" as provided in the act. Other butchers sued to enjoin the state-created monopoly, lost in the state courts, and appealed to the Supreme Court. Under the Act, butchers could still slaughter, but they had to do it at the Slaughter-House Co. and pay it reasonable compensation for such use of the slaughterhouse.]

JUSTICE MILLER delivered the opinion of the Court.

Unless, . . . the exclusive privilege granted by this charter to the corporation, is beyond the power of the legislature of Louisiana, there can be no just exception to the validity of the statute. . . . The plaintiffs in error accepting this issue, allege that the statute is a violation of the Constitution of the United States in these several particulars:

That it creates an involuntary servitude forbidden by the thirteenth article of amendment;

That it abridges the privileges and immunities of citizens of the United States;

That it denies to the plaintiffs the equal protection of the laws; and,

That it deprives them of their property without due process of law; contrary to the provisions of the first section of the fourteenth article of amendment.

This court is thus called upon for the first time to give construction to these articles.

[In light of] events, almost too recent to be called history, but which are familiar to us all; and on the most casual examination of the language of [the 13th, 14th, and 15th] amendments, no one can fail to be impressed with the one pervading purpose found in them all, lying at the foundation of each, and without which none of them would have been even suggested; we mean the freedom of the slave race, the security and firm establishment of that freedom, and the protection of the newly-made freeman and citizen from the oppressions of those who had formerly exercised unlimited dominion over him. It is true that only the fifteenth amendment, in terms, mentions the negro by speaking of his color and his slavery. But it is just as true that each of the other articles was addressed to the grievances of that race, and designed to remedy them as the fifteenth.

We do not say that no one else but the negro can share in this protection. Both the language and spirit of these articles are to have their fair and just weight in any question of construction. Undoubtedly while negro slavery alone was in the mind of the Congress which proposed the thirteenth article, it forbids any other kind of slavery, now or hereafter. If Mexican peonage or the Chinese coolie labor system shall develop slavery of the Mexican or Chinese race within our territory, this amendment may safely be trusted to make it void. And so if other rights are assailed by the States which properly and necessarily fall within the protection of these articles, that protection will apply, though the party interested may not be of African descent. . . .

The first section of the fourteenth article, to which our attention is more specially invited, opens with a definition of citizenship—not only citizenship of the United States, but citizenship of the States. No such definition was previously found in the Constitution. [In the first sentence of the first section of the Fourteenth Amendment] the distinction between citizenship of the United States and citizenship of a State is clearly recognized and established. Not only may a man be a citizen of the United States without being a citizen of a State, but an important element is necessary to convert the former into the latter. He must reside within the State to make him a citizen of it, but it is only necessary that he should be born or naturalized in the United States to be a citizen of the Union.

It is quite clear, then, that there is a citizenship of the United States, and a citizenship of a State, which are distinct from each other, and which depend upon different characteristics or circumstances in the individual. We think this distinction and its explicit recognition in this amendment of great weight in this argument, because the next paragraph of this same section, which is the one mainly relied on by the plaintiffs in error, speaks only of privileges and immunities of citizens of the United States, and does not speak of those of citizens of the several States. The argument, however, in favor of the plaintiffs rests wholly on the assumption that the citizenship is the same, and the privileges and immunities guaranteed by the clause are the same.

The language is, "No State shall make or enforce any law which shall abridge the privileges or immunities of citizens of *the United States*." It is a little remarkable, if this clause was intended as a protection to the citizen of a State against the legislative power of his own State, that the word citizen of the State should be left out when it is so carefully used, and used in contradistinction to citizens of the

United States, in the very sentence which precedes it. It is too clear for argument that the change in phraseology was adopted understandingly and with a purpose.

Of the privileges and immunities of the citizen of the United States, and of the privileges and immunities of the citizen of the State, . . . it is only the former which are placed by this clause under the protection of the Federal Constitution, and that the latter, whatever they may be, are not intended to have any additional protection by this paragraph of the amendment. . . .

In the Constitution of the United States, . . . is found in section two of the fourth article, in the following words: "The citizens of each State shall be entitled to all the privileges and immunities of citizens of the several States." . . . Fortunately we are not without judicial construction of this clause of the Constitution. The first and the leading case on the subject is that of *Corfield v. Coryell,* decided by Mr. Justice Washington in the Circuit Court for the District of Pennsylvania in 1823.

"The inquiry," he says, "is, what are the privileges and immunities of citizens of the several States? We feel no hesitation in confining these expressions to those privileges and immunities which are *fundamental;* which belong of right to the citizens of all free governments, and which have at all times been enjoyed by citizens of the several States which compose this Union, from the time of their becoming free, independent, and sovereign. What these fundamental principles are, it would be more tedious than difficult to enumerate. They may all, however, be comprehended under the following general heads: protection by the government, with the right to acquire and possess property of every kind, and to pursue and obtain happiness and safety, subject, nevertheless, to such restraints as the government may prescribe for the general good of the whole."

[Article 4, section 2, of the Constitution] did not create those rights, which it called privileges and immunities of citizens of the States. It threw around them in that clause no security for the citizen of the State in which they were claimed or exercise. Nor did it profess to control the power of the State governments over the rights of its own citizens. Its sole purpose was to declare to the several States, that whatever those rights, as you grant or establish them to your own citizens, or as you limit or qualify, or impose restrictions on their exercise, the same, neither more nor less, shall be the measure of the rights of citizens of other States within your jurisdiction.

It would be the vainest show of learning to attempt to prove by citations of authority, that up to the adoption of the recent amendments, no claim or pretense was set up that those rights depended on the Federal government for their existence or protection, beyond the very few express limitations which the Federal Constitution imposed upon the States—such, for instance, as the prohibition against ex post facto laws, bills of attainder, and laws impairing the obligation of contracts. But with the exception of these and a few other restrictions, the entire domain of the privileges and immunities of citizens of the States, as above defined, lay within the constitutional and legislative power of the States, and without that of the Federal government. Was it the purpose of the fourteenth amendment, by the simple declaration that no State should make or enforce any law which shall abridge the privileges and immunities of *citizens of the United States,* to transfer the security and protection of all the civil rights which we have mentioned, from the States to the Federal government? And where it is declared that Congress shall have the power to enforce that article, was it intended to bring within the power of Congress the entire domain of civil rights heretofore belonging exclusively to the States?

All this and more must follow, if the proposition of the plaintiffs in error be sound. For not only are these rights subject to the control of Congress whenever in its discretion any of them are supposed to be abridged by State legislation, but that body may also pass laws in advance, limiting and restricting the exercise of legislative power by the States, in their most ordinary and usual functions, as in its judgment it may think proper on all such subjects. [S]uch a construction followed by the reversal of the judgments of the Supreme Court of Louisiana in these cases, would constitute this court a perpetual censor upon all legislation of the States, on the civil rights of their own citizens, with authority to nullify such as it did not approve as consistent with those rights, as they existed at the time of the adoption of this amendment. . . .

Having shown that the privileges and immunities relied on in the argument are those which belong to citizens of the States as such, and that they are left to the State governments for security and protection, and not by this article placed under the special care of the Federal government, we may hold ourselves excused from defining the privileges and immunities of citizens of the United States which no State can abridge, until some case involving those privileges may make it necessary to do so. But lest it should be said that no such privileges and immunities are to be found if those we have been considering are excluded, we venture to suggest some which owe their existence to the Federal government, its National character, its Constitution, or its laws.

One of these is well described in the case of *Crandall v. Nevada,* [73 U.S. (6 Wall.) 35, 18 L.Ed. 744 (1867)]. It is said to be the right of the citizen of this great country, protected by implied guarantees of its Constitution, "to come to the seat of government to assert any claim he may have upon that government, to transact any business he may have with it, to seek its protection, to share its offices, to engage in administering its functions. He has the right of free access to its seaports, through which all operations of foreign commerce are conducted, to the sub-treasuries, land offices, and courts of justice in the several States." Another privilege of a citizen of the United States is to demand the care and protection of the Federal government over his life, liberty, and property when on the high seas or within the jurisdiction of a foreign government. Of this there can be no doubt, nor that the right depends upon his character as a citizen of the United States. The right to peaceably assemble and petition for redress of grievances, the privilege of the writ of *habeas corpus,* are rights of the citizen guaranteed by the Federal Constitution. The right to use the navigable waters of the United States, however they may penetrate the territory of the several States, all rights secured to our citizens by treaties with foreign nations are dependent upon citizenship of the United States, and not citizenship of a State. . . .

The argument has not been much pressed in these cases that the defendant's charter deprives the plaintiffs of their property without due process of law, or that it denies to them the equal protection of the law. [U]nder no construction of [the due process clause] that we have ever seen, or any that we deem admissible, can the restraint imposed by the State of Louisiana upon the exercise of their trade by the butchers of New Orleans be held to be a deprivation of property within the meaning of that provision. . . . The existence of laws in the States where the newly emancipated negroes resided, which discriminated with gross injustice and hardship against them as a class, was the evil to be remedied by [the equal protection] clause, and by it such laws are forbidden.

If, however, the States did not conform their laws to its requirements, then by the fifth section of the article of amendment Congress was authorized to enforce it by suitable legislation. We doubt very much whether any action of a State not directed by way of discrimination against the negroes as a class, or on account of their race, will ever be held to come within the purview of this provision. It is so clearly a provision for that race and that emergency, that a strong case would be necessary for its application to any other. But as it is a State that is to be dealt with, and not alone the validity of its laws, we may safely leave that matter until Congress shall have exercised its power, or some case of State oppression, by denial of equal justice in its courts, shall have claimed a decision at our hands. We find no such case in the one before us, and do not deem it necessary to go over the argument again, as it may have relation to this particular clause of the amendment.

The judgments of the Supreme Court of Louisiana in these cases are

Affirmed.

JUSTICE FIELD, dissenting.

[If the Fourteenth Amendment] only refers, as held by the majority of the court in their opinion, to such privileges and immunities as were before its adoption specially designated in the Constitution or necessarily implied as belonging to citizens of the United States, it was a vain and idle enactment, which accomplished nothing, and most unnecessarily excited Congress and the people on its passage. . . . But if the amendment refers to the natural and inalienable rights which belong to all citizens, the inhibition has a profound significance and consequence.

What, then, are the privileges and immunities which are secured against abridgment by State legislation? In the first section of the Civil Rights Act Congress has given its interpretation to these terms, or at least has stated some of the rights which, in its judgment, these terms include; it has there declared that they include the right "to make and enforce contracts, to sue, be parties and give evidence, to inherit, purchase, lease, sell, hold, and convey real and personal property, and to full and equal benefit of all laws and proceedings for the security of person and property." That act, it is true was passed before the fourteenth amendment, but the amendment was adopted . . . to obviate objections to legislation of a similar character, extending the protection of the National government over the common rights of all citizens of the United States. Accordingly, after its ratification, Congress re-enacted the act under the belief that whatever doubts may have previously existed of its validity, they were removed by the amendment.

. . . The privileges and immunities designated are those *which of right belong to the citizens of all free governments*. Clearly among these must be placed the right to pursue a lawful employment in a lawful manner, without other restraint than such as equally affects all persons. In the discussions in Congress upon the passage of the Civil Rights Act repeated reference was made to this language of Mr. Justice Washington. It was cited by Senator Trumbull with the observation that it enumerated the very rights belonging to a citizen of the United States set forth in the first section of the act. [G]rants of exclusive privileges, such as is made by the act in question, are opposed to the whole theory of free government, and it requires no aid from any bill of rights to render them void. That only is a free government, in the American sense of the term, under which the inalienable right of every citizen to pursue his happiness is unrestrained, except by just, equal, and impartial laws.

I am authorized by THE CHIEF JUSTICE [CHASE], MR. JUSTICE SWAYNE, and MR. JUSTICE BRADLEY, to state that they concur with me in this dissenting opinion.

JUSTICE BRADLEY, also dissenting.

[Granting] monopolies, or exclusive privileges to individuals or corporations, is an invasion of the right of others to choose a lawful calling, and an infringement of personal liberty. It was so felt by the English nation as far back as the reigns of Elizabeth and James. [A] law which prohibits a large class of citizens from adopting a lawful employment, or from following a lawful employment previously adopted, does deprive them of liberty as well as property, without due process of law. Their right of choice is a portion of their liberty; their occupation is their property. Such a law also deprives those citizens of the equal protection of the laws, contrary to the last clause of the section.

[The dissenting opinion of SWAYNE, J., is omitted.]

NOTES

1. Until 1999, the Supreme Court used the privileges or immunities clause of the Fourteenth Amendment only once, in a majority opinion to invalidate state legislation. That case was *Colgate v. Harvey*, 296 U.S. 404, 56 S.Ct. 252, 80 L.Ed. 299 (1935), which the Court overruled in, *Madden v. Kentucky*, 309 U.S. 83, 60 S.Ct. 406, 84 L.Ed. 590 (1940): "We think it quite clear that the right to carry out an incident to a trade, business or calling such as the deposit of money in banks is not a privilege of national citizenship. . . . *Colgate v. Harvey* must be and is overruled." The Court then upheld a Kentucky ad valorem tax. Note that the Court decided *Madden*, unlike *Colgate*, after the Court Packing Plan, discussed in § 6–2.

   Given *Slaughter-House*'s definition of "privileges or immunities," it is no surprise that the clause has been infrequently used.

2. Then came *Saenz v. Roe*, 526 U.S. 489, 119 S.Ct. 1518, 143 L.Ed.2d 689 (1999). California limited the maximum welfare benefits to newly arrived residents (those who resided in California for less than 12 months) to the amount that

would have been paid by the state of the family's prior residence. Stevens, J., for the Court (7 to 2), invalidated the law, relying on the privileges and immunities clause of the Fourteenth Amendment. The right of the newly arrived citizen to the same privileges and immunities enjoyed by other citizens of the same State—"is protected not only by the new arrival's status as a state citizen, but also by her status as a citizen of the United States. That additional source of protection is plainly identified in the opening words of the Fourteenth Amendment. . . ." (footnote omitted).

Thomas, J., joined by Rehnquist, C.J., also a dissented. They "would be open to reevaluating [the Privileges or Immunities Clause's] meaning in an appropriate case. Before invoking the Clause, however, we should endeavor to understand what the Framers of the Fourteenth Amendment thought that it meant."

3. *Munn v. Illinois,* 94 U.S. 113, 24 L.Ed. 77 (1877), upheld an Illinois law that fixed the maximum charges for the storage of grain at warehouses in Chicago and certain other places where the grain was sold in bulk. The Court reasoned that the due process clause protects private property, but "when private property is 'affected with a public interest, it ceases to be *juris privati only.*' . . . When, therefore, one devotes his property to a use in which the public has an interest, he, in effect, grants to the public an interest in that use, and must submit to be controlled by the public for the common good, to the extent of the interest he has thus created." The negative implication of this reasoning was perhaps made clearer when the Court added by way of dictum: "[T]he legislature has no control over [a private] contract." Justice Field again dissented.

    Santa Clara County v. Southern Pacific Railway, 118 U.S. 394, 6 S.Ct. 1132, 30 L.Ed. 118 (1886), then held that corporations are "persons" within the meaning of the Fourteenth Amendment.

4. *Mugler v. Kansas,* 123 U.S. 623, 8 S.Ct. 273, 31 L.Ed. 205 (1887), sustained the validity of a state law prohibiting the manufacture and sale of alcohol. By way of dictum the Court said: "There are, of necessity, limits beyond which legislation cannot rightfully go. . . . If, therefore, a statute purporting to have been enacted to protect the public health, the public morals, or the public safety, has no real or substantial relation to those objects, or is a palpable invasion of rights secured by the fundamental law, it is the duty of the courts to so adjudge, and thereby give effect to the Constitution."

In *Chicago, Milwaukee & St. Paul Railway Co. v. Minnesota,* 134 U.S. 418, 10 S.Ct. 462, 33 L.Ed. 970 (1890), a statute empowered a state commission to set "equal and reasonable" rates for rail transport of property. However, the statute, as interpreted by the state court, made these rates conclusive and foreclosed any judicial inquiry even though the statute did not provide for any summons or notice to, or hearing for, the railroad before the commission set the rates. Because of this procedural defect, the Court invalidated the law: "It deprives the company of its right to a judicial investigation by due process of law, under the forms and with the machinery provided by the wisdom of successive ages for the investigation judicially of the truth of a matter in controversy, and substitutes therefore, as an absolute finality, the action of a railroad commission." The dissent complained that the majority's decision "practically overrules *Munn v. Illinois.*"

Allgeyer v. Louisiana, 165 U.S. 578, 17 S.Ct. 427, 41 L.Ed. 832 (1897), invalidated a statute prohibiting anyone in the state from dealing with marine insurance companies that had not complied in all respects with Louisiana law. The Court readily agreed that a state could "prohibit foreign insurance companies from doing business within its limits." But in this case no business was done in the state. The contract was made and would be performed outside the state's jurisdiction. The fact that the defendant who wished insurance mailed a letter to the out-of-state company was insufficient to support Louisiana's assertion of extraterritorial jurisdiction. The Court, per Justice Peckham, added by way of dictum: "The liberty mentioned in [the fourteenth] amendment [embraces] the right to the citizen to be free in the enjoyment of all his faculties; to be free to use them in all lawful ways; to live and work where he will; to earn his livelihood by any lawful calling; to pursue any livelihood or avocation, and for that purpose to enter into all contracts which may be proper, necessary and essential to carrying out to a successful conclusion the purposes above mentioned."

In *Holden v. Hardy,* 169 U.S. 366, 18 S.Ct. 383, 42 L.Ed. 780 (1898), the Court upheld a state law prohibiting workers in underground mines and smelters from working more than eight hours a day except in cases of emergency. The Court justified the law in light of the special health problems of such workers.

2.2 DUE PROCESS AND THE ECONOMY

LOCHNER V. NEW YORK

198 U.S. 45, 25 S.Ct. 539, 49 L.Ed. 937 (1905)

JUSTICE PECKHAM delivered the opinion of the Court.

The indictment, it will be seen, charges that the plaintiff in error violated . . . the labor law of the State of New York, in that he wrongfully and unlawfully required and permitted an employee working for him to work more than sixty hours in one week. . . .

The statute necessarily interferes with the right of contract between the employer and employees, concerning the number of hours in which the latter may labor in the bakery of the employer. The general right to make a contract in relation to his business is part of the liberty of the individual protected by the Fourteenth Amendment of the Federal Constitution. *Allgeyer v. Louisiana.* Under that provision no State can deprive any person of life, liberty or property without due process of law. The right to purchase or to sell labor is part of the liberty protected by this amendment, unless there are circumstances which exclude the right. There are, however, certain powers, existing in the sovereignty of each State in the Union, somewhat vaguely termed police powers, the exact description and limitation of which have not been attempted by the courts. Those powers, broadly stated and without, at present, any attempt at a more specific limitation, relate to the safety, health, morals and general welfare of the public. Both property and liberty are held on such reasonable conditions as may be imposed by the governing power of the State in the exercise of those powers, and with such conditions the Fourteenth Amendment was not designed to interfere. *Mugler v. Kansas.* . . .

This court has recognized the existence and upheld the exercise of the police powers of the States in many cases which might fairly be considered as border ones, and it has, in the course of its determination of questions regarding the asserted invalidity of such statutes, on the ground of their violation of the rights secured by the Federal Constitution, been guided by rules of a very liberal nature, the application of which has resulted, in numerous instances, in upholding the validity of state statutes thus assailed. Among the later cases where the state law has been upheld by this court is that of *Holden v. Hardy*. . . . It was held that the kind of employment, mining, smelting, etc., and the character of the employees in such kinds of labor, were such as to make it reasonable and proper for the State to [limit the workers to eight hours per day]. . . .

It will be observed that, even with regard to that class of labor, the Utah statute provided for cases of emergency wherein the provisions of the statute would not apply. The statute now before this court has no emergency clause in it, and, if the statute is valid, there are no circumstances and no emergencies under which the slightest violation of the provisions of the act would be innocent. There is nothing in *Holden v. Hardy* which covers the case now before us. . . .

It must, of course, be conceded that there is a limit to the valid exercise of the police power by the State. There is no dispute concerning this general proposition. Otherwise the Fourteenth Amendment would have no efficacy and the legislatures of the States would have unbounded power, and it would be enough to say that any piece of legislation was enacted to conserve the morals, the health or the safety of the people; such legislation would be valid, no matter how absolutely without foundation the claim might be. The claim of the police power would be a mere pretext—become another and delusive name for the supreme sovereignty of the State to be exercised free from constitutional restraint. This is not contended for. In every case that comes before this court, therefore, where legislation of this character is concerned and where the protection of the Federal Constitution is sought, the question necessarily arises: Is this a fair, reasonable and appropriate exercise of the police power of the State, or is it an unreasonable, unnecessary and arbitrary interference with the right of the individual to his personal liberty or to enter into those contracts in relation to labor which may seem to him appropriate or necessary for the support of himself and his family? Of course the liberty of contract relating to labor includes both parties to it. The one has as much right to purchase as the other to sell labor.

This is not a question of substituting the judgment of the court for that of the legislature. If the act be within the power of the State it is valid, although the judgment of the court might be totally opposed to the enactment of such a law. But the question would still remain: Is it within the police power of the State? and that question must be answered by the court.

The question whether this act is valid as a labor law, pure and simple, may be dismissed in a few words. There is no reasonable ground for interfering with the liberty of person or the right of free contract, by determining the hours of labor, in the occupation of a baker. There is no contention that bakers as a class are not equal in intelligence and capacity to men in other trades or manual occupations, or that they are not able to assert their rights and care for themselves without the protecting arm of the State, interfering with their independence of judgment and of action. They are in no sense wards of the State. Viewed in the light of a purely labor law, with no reference whatever to the question of health, we think that a law like the one before us involves neither the safety, the morals nor the welfare of the public, and that the interest of the public is not in the slightest degree affected by such an act. The law must be upheld, if at all, as a law pertaining to the health of the individual engaged in the occupation of a baker. It does not affect any other portion of the public than those who are engaged in that occupation. Clean and wholesome bread does not depend upon whether the baker works but ten hours per day or only sixty hours a week. The limitation of the hours of labor does not come within the police power on that ground. . . .

We think the limit of the police power has been reached and passed in this case. There is, in our judgment, no reasonable foundation for holding this is to be necessary or appropriate as a health law to safeguard the public health or the health of the individuals who are following the trade of a baker. If this statute be valid, and if, therefore, a proper case is made out in which to deny the right of an individual, *sui juris,* as employer or employee, to make contracts for the labor of the latter under the protection of the provisions of the Federal Constitution, there would seem to be no length to which legislation of this nature might not go. The case differs widely, as we have already stated, from the expressions of this court in regard to laws of this nature, as stated in *Holden v. Hardy.*

We think that there can be no fair doubt that the trade of a baker, in and of itself, is not an unhealthy one to that degree which would authorize the legislature to interfere with the right to labor, and with the right of free contract on the part of the individual, either as employer or employee. In looking through statistics regarding all trades and occupations, it may be true that the trade of a baker does not appear to be as healthy as some other trades, and is also vastly more healthy than still others. To the common understanding the trade of a baker has never been regarded as an unhealthy one. Very likely physicians would not recommend the exercise of that or of any other trade as a remedy for ill health. Some occupations are more healthy than others but we think there are none which might not come under the power of the legislature to supervise and control the hours of working therein, if the mere fact that the occupation is not absolutely and perfectly healthy is to confer that right upon the legislative department of the Government. It might be safely affirmed that almost all occupations more or less affect the health. There must be more than the mere fact of the possible existence of some small amount of unhealthiness to warrant legislative interference with liberty. It is unfortunately true that labor, even in any department, may possibly carry with it the seeds of unhealthiness. But are we all, on that account, at the mercy of legislative majorities? A printer, a tinsmith, a locksmith, a carpenter, a cabinetmaker, a dry goods clerk, a bank's, a lawyer's or a physician's clerk, or a clerk in almost any kind of business, would all come under the power of the legislature, on this assumption. No trade, no occupation, no mode of earning one's living, could escape this all-pervading power, and the acts of the legislature in limiting the hours of labor in all employments would be valid, although such limitation might seriously cripple the ability of the laborer to support himself and his family. . . .

[The State argues] that it is to the interest of the State that its population should be strong and robust, and therefore any legislation which may be said to tend to make people healthy must be valid as health laws, enacted under the police power. If this be a valid argument and a justification for this kind of legislation, it follows that the protection of the Federal Constitution from undue interference with liberty of person and freedom of contract is visionary, wherever the law is sought to be justified as a valid exercise of the police power. Scarcely any law but might find shelter under such assumptions, and conduct, properly so called, as well as contract, would come under the restrictive sway of the legislature. Not only the hours of employees, but the hours of employers, could be regulated and doctors, lawyers, scientists, all professional men, as well as athletes and artisans, could be forbidden to fatigue their brains and bodies by prolonged hours of exercise, lest the fighting strength of the State be impaired. We mention these extreme cases because the contention is extreme. We do not believe in the soundness of the views which uphold this law. On the contrary, [t]he act is not, within any fair meaning of the term, a health law, but is an illegal interference with the rights of individuals, both employers and employees, to make contracts regarding labor upon such terms as they may think best, or which they may agree upon with the other parties to such contracts. Statutes of the nature of that under review, limiting the hours in which grown and intelligent men may labor to earn their living, are mere meddle-some interferences with the rights of the individual. . . .

[M]any of the laws of this character, while passed under what is claimed to be the police power for the purpose of protecting the public health or welfare, are, in reality, passed from other motives. We are justified in saying so when, from the character of the law and the subject upon which it legislates, it is apparent that the public health or welfare bears but the most remote relation to the law. . . . It seems to us that the real object and purpose were simply to regulate the hours of labor between the master and his employees (all being men, *sui juris*), in a private business, not dangerous in any degree to morals or in any real and substantial degree, to the health of the employees. Under such circumstances the freedom of master and employee to contract with each other in relation to their employment, and in defining the same, cannot be prohibited or interfered with, without violating the Federal Constitution. . . .

Reversed.

JUSTICE HARLAN, with whom JUSTICE WHITE and JUSTICE DAY concurred, dissenting.

[T]he question is one about which there is room for debate and for an honest difference of opinion. [A]ll things considered, more than ten hours' steady work each day, from week to week, in a bakery or confectionery establishment, may endanger the health, and shorten the lives of the workmen, thereby diminishing their physical and mental capacity to serve the State, and to provide for those dependent upon them. If such reasons exist that ought to be the end of this case. . . .

JUSTICE HOLMES, dissenting.

This case is decided upon an economic theory which a large part of the country does not entertain. [M]y agreement or disagreement has nothing to do with the right of a majority to embody their opinions in law. It is settled by various decisions of this court that state constitutions and state laws may regulate life in many ways which we as legislators might think as injudicious or if you like as tyrannical as this, and which equally with this interfere with the liberty to contract. Sunday laws and usury laws are ancient examples. A more modern one is the prohibition of lotteries. The liberty of the citizen to do as he likes so long as he does not interfere with the liberty of others to do the same, which has been a shibboleth for some well-known writers, is interfered with by school laws, by the Post Office, by every state or municipal institution which takes his money for purposes thought desirable, whether he likes it or not. The Fourteenth Amendment does not enact Mr. Herbert Spencer's Social Statics. The other day we sustained the Massachusetts vaccination law. *Jacobson v. Massachusetts,* 197 U.S. 11, 25 Sup.Ct. Rep. 358, 49 L.Ed. 643. United States and state statutes and decisions cutting down the liberty to contract by way of combination are familiar to this court. *Northern Securities Co. v. United States,* 193 U.S. 197, 48 L.Ed. 679, 24 Sup.Ct.Rep. 436. [A] constitution is not intended to embody a particular economic theory, whether of paternalism and the organic relation of the citizen to the State or of *laissez faire*. It is made for people of fundamentally differing views, and the accident of our finding certain opinions natural and familiar or novel and even shocking ought not to conclude our judgment upon the question whether statutes embodying them conflict with the Constitution of the United States.

[T]he word liberty in the Fourteenth Amendment is perverted when it is held to prevent the natural outcome of a dominant opinion, unless it can be said that a rational and fair man necessarily would admit that the statute proposed would infringe fundamental principles as they have been understood by the traditions of our people and our law. It does not need research to show that no such sweeping condemnation can be passed upon the statute before us. A reasonable man might think it a proper measure on the score of health. Men whom I certainly could not pronounce unreasonable would uphold it as a first installment of a general regulation of the hours of work. Whether in the latter aspect it would be open to the charge of inequality I think it unnecessary to discuss.

NOTES

1. In the first part of Justice Peckham's opinion, he says, "This is not a question of substituting the judgment of the court for that of the legislature." Near the end, he says, "We do not believe in the soundness of the views which uphold this law." These two statements do not appear consistent. His opinion is truer to his second statement than to his first.

2. **THE BRANDEIS BRIEF.** If the Justices are going to look at the wisdom of a law, we should expect them to look at the kinds of things that legislators consider, which is what they did *Muller v. Oregon,* 208 U.S. 412, 28 S.Ct. 324, 52 L.Ed. 551 (1908). Oregon law forbade females employed in any mechanical establishment, factory, or laundry from working more than ten hours a day. Oregon convicted Muller of violating the statute. Relying on *Lochner,* he argued to the Supreme Court that the statute violated the Fourteenth Amendment. Justice Brewer, for a unanimous Court, upheld the law and the conviction, based on the following reasoning:

    > In patent cases counsel are apt to open the argument with a discussion of the state of the art. It may not be amiss, in the present case, before examining the constitutional question, to notice the course of legislation as well as expressions of opinion from other than judicial sources. In the brief filed by Mr. Louis D. Brandeis, for the defendant in error, is a very copious collection of all these matters, an epitome of which is found in the margin.† . . .

---

† The following legislation of the States impose restrictions in some form or another upon the hours of labor that may be required of women: Massachusetts: chap. 221, 1874, Rev.Laws 1902, chap. 106, § 24; Rhode Island: 1885, Acts and Resolves 1902, chap. 994, p. 73; Louisiana: § 4, Act 43, p. 55, Laws of 1886, Rev.Laws 1904, vol. 1, p. 989; Connecticut: 1887, Gen.Stat. revision 1902, § 4691; Maine: chap. 139, 1887, Rev.Stat.1903,

The legislation and opinions referred to in the margin may not be, technically speaking, authorities, and in them is little or no discussion of the constitutional question presented to us for determination, yet they are significant of a widespread belief that woman's physical structure, and the functions she performs in consequence thereof, justify special legislation restricting or qualifying the conditions under which she should be permitted to toil. Constitutional questions, it is true, are not settled by even a consensus of present public opinion, for it is the peculiar value of a written constitution that it places in unchanging form limitations upon legislative action, and thus gives a permanence and stability to popular government which otherwise would be lacking. At the same time, when a question of fact is debated and debatable, and the extent to which a special constitutional limitation goes is affected by the truth in respect to that fact, a widespread and long continued belief concerning it is worthy of consideration. We take judicial cognizance of all matters of general knowledge. . . .

That woman's physical structure and the performance of maternal functions place her at a disadvantage in the struggle for subsistence is obvious. This is especially true when the burdens of

---

chap. 40, § 48, p. 401; New Hampshire: 1887, Laws 1907, chap. 94, p. 95; Maryland: chap. 455, 1888, Pub.Gen. Laws 1903, art. 100, § 1; Virginia: p. 150, 1889–1890, Code 1904, tit. 51A, chap. 178A, § 3657b; Pennsylvania: No. 26, p. 30, 1897, Laws 1905, No. 226, p. 352; New York: Laws 1899, § 1, chap. 560, p. 752, Laws 1907, chap. 507, § 77, subdiv. 3, p. 1078; Nebraska: 1899, Comp.Stat.1905, § 7955, p. 1986; Washington: Stat.1901, chap. 68, § 1, p. 118: Colorado: Acts 1903, chap. 138, § 3, p. 310; New Jersey: 1892, Gen.Stat.1895, p. 2350, §§ 66, 67; Oklahoma: 1890, Rev.Stat.1903, chap. 25, art. 58, § 729; North Dakota: 1877, Rev. Code 1905, § 9440; South Dakota: 1877, Rev.Code (Penal Code, § 764), p. 1185; Wisconsin: § 1, chap. 83, Laws of 1867, Code 1898, § 1728; South Carolina: Acts 1907, No. 233, p. 487.

In foreign legislation Mr. Brandeis calls attention to these statutes: Great Britain: Factories Act of 1844, chap. 15, pp. 161, 171; Factory and Workshop Act of 1901, chap. 22, pp. 60, 71; and see 1 Edw. VII, chap. 22. France, 1848; Act Nov. 2, 1892, and March 30, 1900. Switzerland, Canton of Glarus, 1848; Federal Law 1877, art. 2, § 1. Austria, 1855; Acts 1897, art. 96a, §§ 1–3. Holland, 1899; art. 5, § 1. Italy, June 19, 1902, art. 7. Germany, Laws 1891.

Then follow extracts from over ninety reports of committees, bureaus of statistics, commissioners of hygiene, inspectors of factories, both in this country and in Europe, to the effect that long hours of labor are dangerous for women, primarily because of their special physical organization. The matter is discussed in these reports in different aspects, but all agree as to the danger. It would of course take too much space to give these reports in detail. Following them are extracts from similar reports discussing the general benefits of short hours from an economic aspect of the question. In many of these reports individual instances are given tending to support the general conclusion. Perhaps the general scope and character of all these reports may be summed up in what an inspector for Hanover says: The reasons for the reduction of the working day to ten hours—(a) the physical organization of women, (b) her maternal functions, (c) the rearing and education of the children, (d) the maintenance of the home—are all so important and so far reaching that the need for such reduction need hardly be discussed.

motherhood are upon her. [A]s healthy mothers are essential to vigorous offspring, the physical wellbeing of woman becomes an object of public interest and care in order to preserve the strength and vigor of the race. . . .

For these reasons, and without questioning in any respect the decision in *Lochner v. New York,* we are of the opinion that it cannot be adjudged that the act in question is in conflict with the Federal Constitution, so far as it respects the work of a female in a laundry, and the judgment of the Supreme Court of Oregon is Affirmed.

3. In *Bunting v. Oregon,* 243 U.S. 426, 37 S.Ct. 435, 61 L.Ed. 830 (1917), petitioner was convicted of violating an Oregon statute prohibiting the employment of anyone in a mill, factory, or manufacturing establishment more than ten hours in one day except for watchmen and employees when engaged in making necessary repairs or in case of emergency. The employee, however, could work up to thirteen hours a day if the employer paid time and a-half for the extra hours. Justice McKenna, for the Court, upheld the law, finding that the legislature had sufficiently justified the law in its view:

> There is a contention made that the law, even regarded as regulating hours of service, is not either necessary or useful "for preservation of the health of employees in mills, factories and manufacturing establishments". The record contains no facts to support the contention, and against it is the judgment of the legislature and the Supreme Court, which said: "In view of the well-known fact that the custom in our industries does not sanction a longer service than 10 hours per day, it cannot be held, as a matter of law, that the legislative requirement is unreasonable or arbitrary as to hours of labor. Statistics show that the average daily working time among working-men in different countries is, in Australia, 8 hours; in Great Britain, 9; in the United States, $9\frac{3}{4}$; in Denmark, $9\frac{3}{4}$; in Norway, 10; Sweden, France, and Switzerland, $10\frac{1}{2}$; Germany, $10\frac{1}{4}$; Belgium, Italy, and Austria, 11; and in Russia, 12 hours."

Chief Justice White and Justices Van Devanter and McReynolds dissented without opinion. Justice Brandeis, appointed to the Court in 1916, took no part in the consideration and decision of the case.

4. *Adkins v. Children's Hospital,* 261 U.S. 525, 43 S.Ct. 394, 67 L.Ed. 785 (1923). A congressional statute enacted in 1918 provided for the fixing of minimum wages for women and children in Washington, D.C. A hospital and a woman

hotel worker sued to enjoin the act. The lower courts enjoined the act, and
the Supreme Court, per Justice Sutherland, affirmed:

> There is, of course, no such thing as absolute freedom of contract.
> It is subject to a great variety of restraints. But freedom of contract
> is, nevertheless, the general rule and restraint the exception; and the
> exercise of legislative authority to abridge it can be justified only by
> the existence of exceptional circumstances. . . . A law forbidding
> work to continue beyond a given number of hours leaves the
> parties free to contract about wages and thereby equalize whatever
> additional burdens may be imposed upon the employer as a result
> of the restrictions as to hours, by an adjustment in respect of the
> amount of wages. . . .
>
> If now, in the light furnished by the foregoing exceptions to
> the general rule forbidding legislative interference with freedom of
> contract, we examine and analyze the statute in question, we shall
> see that it differs from them in every material respect. It is not a
> law dealing with any business charged with a public interest or with
> public work, or to meet and tide over a temporary emergency. It
> has nothing to do with the character, methods or periods of wage
> payments. It does not prescribe hours of labor or conditions under
> which labor is to be done. It is not for the protection of persons
> under legal disability or for the prevention of fraud. It is simply and
> exclusively a price-fixing law, confined to adult women (for we are
> not now considering the provisions relating to minors), who are
> legally as capable of contracting for themselves as men. . . .
>
> We are asked, upon the one hand, to consider the fact that
> several States have adopted similar statutes, and we are invited,
> upon the other hand, to give weight to the fact that three times as
> many States, presumably as well informed and as anxious to
> promote the health and morals of their people, have refrained from
> enacting such legislation. We have also been furnished with a large
> number of printed opinions approving the policy of the minimum
> wage, and our own reading has disclosed a large number to the
> contrary. These are all proper enough for the consideration of the
> lawmaking bodies, . . . but they reflect no legitimate light upon the
> question of its validity, and that is what we are called upon to

decide. The elucidation of that question cannot be aided by counting heads.

Justice Brandeis took no part in the consideration or decision, but Chief Justice Taft, joined by Justice Sanford, dissented:

> [T]he opinion herein does not overrule the *Bunting Case* in express terms, and therefore I assume that the conclusion in this case rests on the distinction between a minimum of wages and a maximum of hours in the limiting of liberty to contract. I regret to be at variance with the Court as to the substance of this distinction. [A] restriction as to one is not any greater in essence than the other, and is of the same kind. One is the multiplier and the other the multiplicand.

Justice Holmes also dissented:

> Liberty of Contract. Contract is not specially mentioned in the text that we have to construe. It is merely an example of doing what you want to do, embodied in the word liberty. But pretty much all law consists in forbidding men to do some things that they want to do, and contract is no more exempt from law than other acts.

NEBBIA V. NEW YORK

291 U.S. 502, 54 S.Ct. 505, 78 L.Ed. 940 (1934)

JUSTICE ROBERTS delivered the opinion of the Court.

The Legislature of New York established, by Chapter 158 of the Laws of 1933, a Milk Control Board with power, among other things, to "fix minimum and maximum . . . retail prices to be charged by . . . stores to consumers for consumption off the premises where sold." The Board fixed nine cents as the price to be charged by a store for a quart of milk. Nebbia, the proprietor of a grocery store in Rochester, sold two quarts and a five cent loaf of bread for eighteen cents; and was convicted for violating the Board's order. At his trial he asserted the statute and order contravene the equal protection clause and the due process clause of the Fourteenth Amendment, and renewed the contention in successive appeals to the county court and the Court of Appeals. Both overruled his claim and affirmed the conviction.

The question for decision is whether the Federal Constitution prohibits a state from so fixing the selling price of milk. We first inquire as to the occasion for the legislation and its history. During 1932 the prices received by farmers for milk were much below the cost of production. The decline in prices during 1931 and 1932 was much greater than that of prices generally. The situation of the families of dairy producers had become desperate and called for state aid similar to that afforded the unemployed, if conditions should not improve.

[A state legislative committee concluded that the] fluid milk industry is affected by factors of instability peculiar to itself which call for special methods of control. Under the best practicable adjustment of supply to demand the industry must carry a surplus of about 20 per cent., because milk, an essential food, must be available as demanded by consumers every day in the year, and demand and supply vary from day to day and according to the season; but milk is perishable and cannot be stored. Close adjustment of supply to demand is hindered by several factors difficult to control. Thus surplus milk presents a serious problem, as the prices which can be realized for it for other uses are much less than those obtainable for milk sold for consumption in fluid form or as cream. . . . The fact that the larger distributors find it necessary to carry large quantities of surplus milk, while the smaller distributors do not, leads to price-cutting and other forms of destructive competition. Smaller distributors, who take no responsibility for the surplus, by purchasing their milk at the blended prices (*i.e.*, an average between the price paid the producer for milk for sale as fluid milk, and the lower surplus milk price paid by the larger organizations) can undersell the larger distributors. Indulgence in this price-cutting often compels the larger dealer to cut the price, to his own and the producer's detriment. . . .

[A] serious question is whether, in the light of the conditions disclosed, the enforcement of § 312(e) denied the appellant the due process secured to him by the Fourteenth Amendment. . . .

The Fifth Amendment, in the field of federal activity, and the Fourteenth, as respects state action, do not prohibit governmental regulation for the public welfare. They merely condition the exertion of the admitted power, by securing that the end shall be accomplished by methods consistent with due process. And the guaranty of due process, as has often been held, demands only that the law shall not be unreasonable, arbitrary or capricious, and that the means selected shall have a real and substantial relation to the object sought to be attained. It results that a regulation valid for one sort of business, or in given circumstances, may be invalid for another sort, or for the same business under other circumstances, because the reasonableness of each regulation depends upon the relevant facts.

The milk industry in New York has been the subject of long-standing and drastic regulation in the public interest. The legislative investigation of 1932 was persuasive of the fact that for this and other reasons unrestricted competition aggravated existing evils, and the normal law of supply and demand was insufficient to correct maladjustments detrimental to the community. [T]he Milk Control Board fixed a price of ten cents per quart for sales by a distributor to a consumer, and nine cents by a store to a consumer, thus recognizing the lower costs of the store, and endeavoring to establish a differential which would be just to both. In the light of the facts the order appears not to be unreasonable or arbitrary, or without relation to the purpose to prevent ruthless competition from destroying the wholesale price structure on which the farmer depends for his livelihood, and the community for an assured supply of milk.

But we are told that ... the public control of rates or prices is *per se* unreasonable and unconstitutional, save as applied to business affected with a public interest; that a business so affected is one in which property is devoted to an enterprise of a sort which the public itself might appropriately undertake, or one whose owner relies on a public grant or franchise for the right to conduct the business, or in which he is bound to serve all who apply; in short, such as is commonly called a public utility; or a business in its nature a monopoly. The milk industry, it is said, possesses none of these characteristics, and, therefore, not being affected with a public interest, its charges may not be controlled by the state. Upon the soundness of this contention the appellant's case against the statute depends.

We may as well say at once that the dairy industry is not, in the accepted sense of the phrase, a public utility. [T]here is no closed class or category of businesses affected with a public interest, and the function of courts in the application of the Fifth and Fourteenth Amendments is to determine in each case whether circumstances vindicate the challenged regulation as a reasonable exertion of governmental authority or condemn it as arbitrary or discriminatory. The phrase "affected with a public interest" can, in the nature of things, mean no more than that an industry, for adequate reason, is subject to control for the public good. . . . So far as the requirement of due process is concerned, and in the absence of other constitutional restriction, a state is free to adopt whatever economic policy may reasonably be deemed to promote public welfare, and to enforce that policy by legislation adapted to its purpose. The courts are without authority either to declare such policy, or, when it is declared by the legislature, to override it. If the laws passed are seen to have a reasonable relation to a proper legislative purpose, and are neither arbitrary nor discriminatory, the requirements of due process are satisfied, and judicial determination to that effect renders a court *functus officio*. "Whether the free operation of the normal laws of competition is a wise and wholesome rule for trade and commerce is an economic question which this court need not consider or determine." . . . Price control, like any other form of regulation, is unconstitutional only if arbitrary, discriminatory, or demonstrably irrelevant to the policy the legislature is free to adopt, and hence an unnecessary and unwarranted interference with individual liberty. Tested by these considerations we find no basis in the due process clause of the Fourteenth Amendment for condemning the provisions of the Agriculture and Markets Law here drawn into question.

The judgment is Affirmed.

Separate opinion of JUSTICE REYNOLDS.

[T]he Court of Appeals says— . . . "With the wisdom of the legislature we have naught to do." . . . But plainly, I think, this Court must have regard to the wisdom of enactment. . . . The judgment of the court below should be reversed. Mr. Justice Van Devanter, Mr. Justice Sutherland, and Mr. Justice Butler authorize me to say that they concur in this opinion.

NOTES

1. *West Coast Hotel v. Parrish*, 300 U.S. 379, 57 S.Ct. 578, 81 L.Ed. 703 (1937), contested the minimum wage law for women and minors established by the state of Washington. The state supreme court, reversing the trial court, sustained the constitutionality of the statute, and appellant sought relief on the authority of Adkins v. Children's Hospital, *supra*. Chief Justice Hughes, for the Court, upheld the statute:

    In each case the violation alleged by those attacking minimum wage regulation for women is deprivation of freedom of contract. What is this freedom? The Constitution does not speak of freedom of contract. It speaks of liberty and prohibits the deprivation of liberty without due process of law. In prohibiting that deprivation the Constitution does not recognize an absolute and uncontrollable liberty. [R]egulation which is reasonable in relation to its subject and is adopted in the interests of the community is due process. . . .

    There is an additional and compelling consideration which recent economic experience has brought into a strong light. The exploitation of a class or workers who are in an unequal position with respect to bargaining power and are thus relatively defenceless against the denial of a living wage is not only detrimental to their health and well-being but casts a direct burden for their support upon the community. . . . While in the instant case no factual brief has been presented, there is no reason to doubt that the State of Washington has encountered the same social problem that is present elsewhere. [T]he case of *Adkins v. Children's Hospital, supra,* should be, and it is, overruled. . . .

Justice Sutherland, joined by Justices Van Devanter, McReynolds, & Butler, dissented.

Note that *Parrish* was a post-Court Packing Plan decision.

2. In *United States v. Darby,* 312 U.S. 100, 125, 61 S.Ct. 451, 462, 85 L.Ed. 609 (1941), excerpted more fully in § 6.2, the Court validated a federal law fixing the minimum wage and maximum hours of workers in interstate commerce. The due process discussion took only about one-half page in the U.S. Reports. "Since our decision on *West Coast Hotel v. Parrish,* it is no longer open to question that the fixing of a minimum wage is within the legislative power and that the base fact of its exercise is not a denial of due process under the Fifth more than under the Fourteenth Amendment. Nor is it any longer open to question that it is within the legislative power to fix maximum hours. Similarly the statute is not objectionable because applied alike to both men and women."

3. In *Ferguson v. Skrupa,* 372 U.S. 726, 83 S.Ct. 1028, 10 L.Ed.2d 93 (1963), a federal district court enjoined, as violating due process, a Kansas statute making it a misdemeanor to engage "in the business of debt adjusting" except as incident to the practice of law. Justice Black, for the Court, reversed:

> The doctrine that prevailed in *Lochner* and like cases—that due process authorizes courts to hold laws unconstitutional when they believe the legislature has acted unwisely—has long since been discarded. We have returned to the original constitutional proposition that courts do not substitute their social and economic beliefs for the judgment of legislative bodies, who are elected to pass laws. . . . Whether the legislature takes for its textbook Adam Smith, Herbert Spencer, Lord Keynes, or some other is no concern of ours. The Kansas debt adjusting statute may be wise or unwise. But relief, if any be needed, lies not with us but with the body constituted to pass laws for the State of Kansas.

No Justices dissented. Justice Harlan, concurred in the judgment "on the grounds that this state measure bears a rational relation to a constitutionally permissible objective."

4.   An often quoted test to judge the validity of economic regulation is found in *United States v. Carolene Products Co.,* 304 U.S. 144, 58 S.Ct. 778, 82 L.Ed. 1234 (1938):

> [T]he existence of facts supporting the legislative judgment is to be presumed, for regulatory legislation affecting ordinary commercial transactions is not to be pronounced unconstitutional unless in the light of the facts made known or generally assumed it is of such a character as to preclude the assumption that it rests upon some rational basis within the knowledge and experience of the legislators.

2.3 THE INCORPORATION OF THE BILL OF RIGHTS

Chief Justice Marshall held in 1833 that the Bill of Rights did not apply to the states. *Barron v. Baltimore,* 32 U.S. (7 Pet.) 243, 8 L.Ed. 672 (1833). Only a few substantive limitations in the body of the Constitution applied to the states. See, Chapter 9, on the prohibitions against bills of attainder, *ex post facto* laws, and impairments of contracts. Art. I, § 10, cl. 1. As far as federal legislation was concerned, the Court did not then exercise active review.

After the Civil War and its aftermath, the Court's attention shifted; the Fourteenth Amendment was now part of the Constitution. It contained due process language virtually identical to the Fifth's, except that it applied to the states. In addition to "process" or procedure, the Court also gave it a substantive component. We have already seen the rise and fall of substantive economic due process from the *Slaughter House Cases* to *Lochner* to *Nebbia.* The due process clause has also been used in what has become known as the selective incorporation of the substantive limitations of the Bill of Rights. We discuss this issue more thoroughly in Chapter 4. Although the due process clause has had little impact over purely economic regulation of business since 1937, some Justices and commentators have accused the Court of using that clause to return to *Lochner*-type reasoning in its treatment of due process in civil rights cases. Justice White, dissenting in *Moore v. East Cleveland,* 431 U.S. 494, 97 S.Ct. 1932, 52 L.Ed.2d 531 (1977), has succinctly summarized the development:

The emphasis of the Due Process Clause is on "process." As Mr. Justice Harlan once observed, it has been "ably and insistently argued in response to what were felt to be abuses by this Court of its reviewing power," that the Due Process Clause should be limited "to a guarantee of procedural fairness." *Poe v. Ullman,* 367 U.S. 497, 540, 81 S.Ct. 1752, 1775, 6 L.Ed.2d 989 (1961) (dissenting opinion). These arguments had seemed "persuasive" to Justices Brandeis and Holmes, *Whitney v. California,* 274 U.S. 357, 373, 47 S.Ct. 641, 647, 71 L.Ed. 1095 (1927), but they recognized that the Due Process Clause, by virtue of case-to-case "judicial inclusion and exclusion," *Davidson v. New Orleans,* 96 U.S. 97, 104, 24 L.Ed. 616 (1878), had been construed to proscribe matters of substance, as well as inadequate procedures, and to protect from invasion by the States "all fundamental rights comprised within the term liberty." *Whitney v. California, supra,* 274 U.S., at 373, 47 S.Ct., at 647.

Mr. Justice Black also recognized that the Fourteenth Amendment had substantive as well as procedural content. But believing that its reach should not extend beyond the specific provisions of the Bill of Rights, see *Adamson v. California,* 332 U.S. 46, 68, 67 S.Ct. 1672, 1683, 91 L.Ed. 1903 (1947) (dissenting opinion), he never embraced the idea that the Due Process Clause empowered the courts to strike down merely unreasonable or arbitrary legislation, nor did he accept Mr. Justice Harlan's consistent view. See *Griswold v. Connecticut,* 381 U.S. 479, 507, 85 S.Ct. 1678, 1694, 14 L.Ed.2d 510 (1965) (Black, J., dissenting), and id., at 499, 85 S.Ct., at 1689 (Harlan, J., concurring in judgment). Writing at length in dissent in *Poe v. Ullman, supra,* at 543, Mr. Justice Harlan stated the essence of his position as follows:

> This 'liberty' is not a series of isolated points pricked out in terms of the taking of property; the freedom of speech, press, and religion; the right to keep and bear arms; the freedom from unreasonable searches and seizures; and so on. It is a rational continuum which, broadly speaking, includes a freedom from all substantial arbitrary impositions and purposeless restraints, see *Allgeyer v. State of Louisiana,* 165 U.S. 578, 17 S.Ct. 427, 41 L.Ed. 832; *Holden v. Hardy,* 169 U.S. 366, 18 S.Ct. 383, 42 L.Ed. 780; *Booth v. Illinois,* 184 U.S. 425, 22 S.Ct. 425, 46 L.Ed. 623; *Nebbia v. New York,* 291 U.S. 502, 54 S.Ct. 505, 78 L.Ed. 940; *Skinner v. Oklahoma,* 316 U.S. 535, 544, 62 S.Ct. 1110, 1114, 86 L.Ed. 1655 (concurring opinion); *Schware v. Board of Bar Examiners,* 353 U.S. 232, 77 S.Ct.

752, 1 L.Ed.2d 796, and which also recognizes, what a reasonable and sensitive judgment must, that certain interests require particularly careful scrutiny of the state needs asserted to justify their abridgment. Cf. *Skinner v. Oklahoma, supra; Bolling v. Sharpe* [347 U.S. 497 (1954)].

This construction was far too open ended for Mr. Justice Black. For him, *Meyer v. Nebraska,* 262 U.S. 390, 43 S.Ct. 625, 67 L.Ed. 1042 (1923);[1] and *Pierce v. Society of Sisters,* 268 U.S. 510, 45 S.Ct. 571, 69 L.Ed. 1070 (1925);[2] as substantive due process cases, were as suspect as *Lochner v. New York,* 198 U.S. 45, 25 S.Ct. 539, 49 L.Ed. 937 (1905), *Coppage v. Kansas,* 236 U.S. 1, 35 S.Ct. 240, 59 L.Ed. 441 (1915), and *Adkins v. Children's Hospital,* 261 U.S. 525, 43 S.Ct. 394, 67 L.Ed. 785 (1923). In his view, *Ferguson v. Skrupa,* 372 U.S. 726, 83 S.Ct. 1028, 10 L.Ed.2d 93 (1963), should have finally disposed of them all. But neither *Meyer* nor *Pierce* has been overruled, and recently there have been decisions of the same genre—*Roe v. Wade,* 410 U.S. 113, 93 S.Ct. 705, 35 L.Ed.2d 147 (1973);[3] *Loving v. Virginia,* 388 U.S. 1, 87 S.Ct. 1817, 18 L.Ed.2d 1010 (1967);[4] *Griswold v. Connecticut,*[5] *supra;* and *Eisenstadt v. Baird*[6] 405 U.S. 438, 92 S.Ct. 1029, 31 L.Ed.2d 319 (1972). Not all of these decisions purport to rest on substantive due process grounds, compare *Roe v. Wade, supra,* 410 U.S., at 152–153, 93 S.Ct., at 726–727, with *Eisenstadt v. Baird, supra,* 410 U.S., at 453–454, 92 S.Ct., at 1038–1039, but all represented substantial reinterpretations of the Constitution.

The Court has used the due process cause to fashion nontextual rights, most notably what is often called a right to "privacy." It has also used the clause to incorporate some, but not all, of the substantive limitations of the Bill of Rights, and to apply those limitations to the state by virtue of the due process clause of

---

[1] *Meyer* declared unconstitutional, under the due process clause, a state law prohibiting the teaching of any subject to any person in any language other than English, in public and private schools. The statute also forbade teaching foreign languages in grade school. Meyer had been convicted of teaching the subject of reading in the German language, Justice McReynolds delivered the opinion for the Court. See § 10.4.1.

[2] In *Pierce,* the Court (again through Justice McReynolds) invalidated a state law that prohibited private or parochial schools and required normal children between 8 and 16 who have not completed the eighth grade to attend public schools. The Court found that the statute unreasonably interfered with the "liberty" of parents and the "property" of the schools.

[3] *Roe* invalidated many laws restricting abortion. See § 10.4.3.

[4] *Loving* invalidated a state antimiscegenation law.

[5] *Griswold* invalidated a state law prohibiting the use of contraceptives by married couples. See § 10.4.2.

[6] *Eisenstadt* invalidated a state statute that prohibited distribution of contraceptives to unmarried persons.

the Fourteenth Amendment. The modern test to determine whether a guarantee extended by the Bill of Rights also applies to the states is whether the clause in question is "fundamental to the American scheme of justice." *Duncan v. Louisiana,* 391 U.S. 145, 149, 88 S.Ct. 1444, 20 L.Ed.2d 491 (1968). And under the modern view, once a right is incorporated, it is applied to limit the states in the same way that it is applied to limit the federal government, *e.g., Malloy v. Hogan,* 378 U.S. 1, 84 S.Ct. 1489, 12 L.Ed.2d 653 (1964), though a minority of Justices have argued, on occasion, that the incorporated rights should be applied less strictly against the states. E.g., *Roth v. United States,* 354 U.S. 476, 496, 77 S.Ct. 1304, 1315, 1 L.Ed.2d 1498 (1957) (Harlan, J., concurring and dissenting); *Johnson v. Louisiana,* 406 U.S. 356, 366, 92 S.Ct. 1620, 1635, 32 L.Ed. 2d 152 (1972) (Powell, J., concurring).

The incorporated rights are as follows:

The Court has incorporated all of the FIRST AMENDMENT, *Cantwell v. Connecticut,* 310 U.S. 296, 60 S.Ct. 900, 84 L.Ed. 1213 (1940) (free exercise); *Everson v. Board of Education,* 330 U.S. 1, 67 S.Ct. 504, 91 L.Ed. 711 (1947) (establishment); *Gitlow v. New York,* 268 U.S. 652, 666, 45 S.Ct. 625, 630, 69 L.Ed. 1138 (1925) (speech and press); *De Jonge v. Oregon,* 299 U.S. 353, 57 S.Ct. 255, 81 L.Ed. 278 (1937) (assembly and petition).

The SECOND AMENDMENT is applicable to the states, in *McDonald v. City of Chicago,* 561 U.S. 742, 130 S.Ct. 3020, 177 L.Ed.2d 894 (2010), The Third Amendment has not been the subject of any litigation in the Supreme Court.

The FOURTH AMENDMENT also is incorporated, *Wolf v. Colorado,* 338 U.S. 25, 69 S.Ct. 1359, 93 L.Ed. 1782 (1949).

The FIFTH AMENDMENT's guarantee of a grand jury has not been applied to the states, *Hurtado v. California,* 110 U.S. 516, 4 S.Ct. 292, 28 L.Ed. 232 (1884), but the other guarantees of that Amendment are incorporated, *Benton v. Maryland,* 395 U.S. 784, 89 S.Ct. 2056, 23 L.Ed.2d 707 (1969) (double jeopardy); *Malloy v. Hogan,* 378 U.S. 1, 84 S.Ct. 1489, 12 L.Ed.2d 653 (1964) (self-incrimination); *Chicago, Burlington & Quincy Railway Co. v. Chicago,* 166 U.S. 226, 17 S.Ct. 581, 41 L.Ed. 979 (1897) (just compensation).

The SIXTH AMENDMENT protections are also applied to the states, *Klopfer v. North Carolina,* 386 U.S. 213, 87 S.Ct. 988, 18 L.Ed.2d 1 (1907) (speedy trial); *In re Oliver,* 333 U.S. 257, 68 S.Ct. 499, 92 L.Ed. 682 (1948) (public trial and notice of charges); *Irvin v. Dowd,* 366 U.S. 717, 81 S.Ct. 1639, 6 L.Ed.2d 751 (1961) (impartial jury); *Duncan v. Louisiana,* 391 U.S. 145, 88 S.Ct. 1444, 20 L.Ed.2d 491 (1968) (jury trial); *Pointer v. Texas,* 380 U.S. 400, 85 S.Ct. 1065, 13 L.Ed.2d 923 (1965) (confrontation); *Washington v. Texas,* 388 U.S. 14, 87 S.Ct. 1920, 18 L.Ed.2d 1019 (1967) (compulsory process); *Gideon v. Wainwright,* 372 U.S. 335, 83 S.Ct. 792, 9 L.Ed.2d 799 (1963) (counsel).

The SEVENTH AMENDMENT right to a jury trial in suits at common law with over $20 in controversy is not applicable to the states. *Minneapolis & St. Louis Railway Co. v. Bombolis,* 241 U.S. 211, 36 S.Ct. 595, 60 L.Ed. 961 (1916).

Most, and perhaps all, of the EIGHTH AMENDMENT is incorporated. *Robinson v. California,* 370 U.S. 660, 82 S.Ct. 1417, 8 L.Ed.2d 758 (1962) (cruel and unusual punishment); Cf. *Schilb v. Kuebel,* 404 U.S. 357, 365, 92 S.Ct. 479, 484, 30 L.Ed.2d 502 (1971) ("the Eighth Amendment's proscription of excessive bail has been assumed to have application to the States through the Fourteenth Amendment"). No cases directly address the excessive fine guarantee. Cf. *Tate v. Short,* 401 U.S. 395, 91 S.Ct. 668, 28 L.Ed.2d 130 (1971) (equal protection clause of Fourteenth Amendment used to protect indigents subject to fine).

The Court has not held the NINTH AMENDMENT applicable to the states, cf. *Griswold v. Connecticut,* 381 U.S. 479, 492, 85 S.Ct. 1678, 1686, 14 L.Ed.2d 510 (1965) (Justice Goldberg, joined by Chief Justice Warren, and Justice Brennan, concurring: "I do not mean to imply that the Ninth Amendment is applied against the States by the Fourteenth.)

The TENTH AMENDMENT does not apply to the states by its own language.

2.4 SUBSTANTIVE DUE PROCESS AND PRIVACY

2.4.1   Interference with Parental Rights

MEYER V. NEBRASKA
262 U.S. 390, 43 S.Ct. 625, 67 L.Ed. 1042 (1923)

JUSTICE MCREYNOLDS delivered the opinion of the Court.

Plaintiff in error was tried and convicted in the district court for Hamilton county, Nebraska, under an information which charged that on May 25, 1920, while an instructor in Zion Parochial School he unlawfully taught the subject of reading in the German language to Raymond Parpart, a child of 10 years, who had not attained and successfully passed the eighth grade. The information is based upon "An act relating to the teaching of foreign languages in the state of Nebraska," approved April 9, 1919. . . .[7]

The problem for our determination is whether the statute as construed and applied unreasonably infringes the liberty guaranteed to the plaintiff in error by the Fourteenth Amendment:

> No state . . . shall deprive any person of life, liberty or property without
> due process of law.

While this court has not attempted to define with exactness the liberty thus guaranteed, the term has received much consideration and some of the included things have been definitely stated. Without doubt, it denotes not merely freedom from bodily restraint but also the right of the individual to contract, to engage in any of the common occupations of life, to acquire useful knowledge, to marry, establish a home and bring up children, to worship God according to the dictates of his own conscience, and generally to enjoy those privileges long recognized at common law as essential to the orderly pursuit of happiness by free men. *Slaughterhouse Cases;* . . . *Lochner v. New York, Adkins v. Children's Hospital,*. . . . The established doctrine is that this liberty may not be interfered with, under the guise of protecting the public interest, by legislative action which is arbitrary or without reasonable relation to some purpose within the competency of the state to effect. Determination by the Legislature of what constitutes proper exercise of police power is not final or conclusive but is subject to supervision by the courts. . . . Plaintiff in error taught this language in school as part of his occupation. His right thus to teach and the right of parents to engage him so to instruct their children, we think, are within the liberty of the amendment.

The challenged statute forbids the teaching in school of any subject except in English; also the teaching of any other language until the pupil has attained and successfully passed the eighth grade, which is not usually accomplished before the age of twelve. The Supreme Court of the state has held that "the so-called ancient

---

[7]   [Footnote by the editor.] The statute provided:

Section 1. No person, individually or as a teacher, shall, in any private, denominational, parochial or public school, teach any subject to any person in any language other than the English language.

Sec. 2.   Languages, other than the English language, may be taught as languages only after a pupil shall have attained and successfully passed the eighth grade as evidenced by a certificate of graduation issued by the county superintendent of the county in which the child resides.

Sec. 3.   Any person who violates any of the provisions of this act shall be deemed guilty of a misdemeanor and upon conviction, shall be subject to a fine of not less than twenty-five dollars ($25), nor more than one hundred dollars ($100), or be confined in the county jail for any period not exceeding thirty days for each offense.

Sec. 4.   Whereas, an emergency exists, this act shall be in force from and after its passage and approval.

or dead languages" are not "within the spirit or the purpose of the act." *Nebraska District of Evangelical Lutheran Synod, etc., v. McKelvie et al.* (Neb.) 187 N.W. 927 (April 19, 1922). Latin, Greek, Hebrew are not proscribed; but German, French, Spanish, Italian, and every other alien speech are within the ban. Evidently the Legislature has attempted materially to interfere with the calling of modern language teachers, with the opportunities of pupils to acquire knowledge, and with the power of parents to control the education of their own.

It is said the purpose of the legislation was to promote civic development by inhibiting training and education of the immature in foreign tongues and ideals before they could learn English and acquire American ideals, and "that the English language should be and become the mother tongue of all children reared in this state." It is also affirmed that the foreign born population is very large, that certain communities commonly use foreign words, follow foreign leaders, move in a foreign atmosphere, and that the children are thereby hindered from becoming citizens of the most useful type and the public safety is imperiled.

That the state may do much, go very far, indeed, in order to improve the quality of its citizens, physically, mentally and morally, is clear; but the individual has certain fundamental rights which must be respected. The protection of the Constitution extends to all, to those who speak other languages as well as to those born with English on the tongue. Perhaps it would be highly advantageous if all had ready understanding of our ordinary speech, but this cannot be coerced by methods which conflict with the Constitution—a desirable end cannot be promoted by prohibited means. . . .

The desire of the Legislature to foster a homogeneous people with American ideals prepared readily to understand current discussions of civic matters is easy to appreciate. . . . But the means adopted, we think, exceed the limitations upon the power of the state and conflict with rights assured to plaintiff in error. The interference is plain enough and no adequate reason therefor in time of peace and domestic tranquility has been shown.

The power of the state to compel attendance at some school and to make reasonable regulations for all schools, including a requirement that they shall give instructions in English, is not questioned. Nor has challenge been made of the state's power to prescribe a curriculum for institutions which it supports. Those matters are not within the present controversy. Our concern is with the prohibition approved by the [state] Supreme Court. . . . No emergency has arisen which renders knowledge by a child of some language other than English so clearly harmful as to justify its inhibition with the consequent infringement of rights long freely enjoyed. [T]he statute as applied is arbitrary and without reasonable relation to any end within the competency of the state.

As the statute undertakes to interfere only with teaching which involves a modern language, leaving complete freedom as to other matters, there seems no adequate foundation for the suggestion that the purpose was to protect the child's health by limiting his mental activities. It is well known that proficiency in a foreign language seldom comes to one not instructed at an early age, and experience shows that this is not injurious to the health, morals or understanding of the ordinary child.

The judgment of the court below must be reversed and the cause remanded for further proceedings not inconsistent with this opinion.

Reversed.

MR. JUSTICE HOLMES and MR. JUSTICE SUTHERLAND, dissent.

NOTES

1. In *Troxel v. Granville*, 530 U.S. 57, 120 S.Ct. 2054, 147 L.Ed.2d 49 (2000) a fragmented Court found a substantive due process right of parents to raise their children. *Troxel* invalidated a state law that permitted "any person" to petition for visitation rights "at any time," whenever visitation may serve a child's best interest. The Troxels petitioned for the right to visit their deceased son's daughters. Granville, the girls' mother, did not oppose all visitation, but the Superior Court ordered more visitation than Granville desired, and she appealed. The State Supreme Court held that the state law unconstitutionally infringed on parents' fundamental right to rear their children. It ruled that the U.S. Constitution permits a State to interfere with this right only to prevent harm or potential harm to the child, and that the state law did not require a threshold showing of harm.

2. O'Connor, J., joined by Rehnquist, C.J., Ginsburg, J. and Breyer, J., agreed that, as applied to Granville and her family, the statute violated her due process rights: "[T]he visitation order in this case was an unconstitutional infringement on Granville's fundamental right to make decisions concerning the care, custody, and control of her two daughters. The Washington Superior Court failed to accord the determination of Granville, a fit custodial parent, any material weight." The "Due Process Clause does not permit a State to infringe on the fundamental right of parents to make childrearing decisions simply because a state judge believes a 'better' decision could be

made." Because O'Connor's opinion was based "on the sweeping breadth" of the statute, she did not consider "whether the Due Process Clause requires all nonparental visitation statutes to include a showing of harm or potential harm to the child as a condition precedent to granting visitation." Thus, this opinion does not consider the constitutionality of other nonparental visitation statutes (all 50 states have them).

3.   Souter, J., concurred in the judgment, agreed that the Court should not turn any "fresh furrows in the 'treacherous field' of substantive due process," but nonetheless concluded that, under *Meyer v. Nebraska* (1923), the "right of upbringing would be a sham if it failed to encompass the right to be free of judicially compelled visitation by 'any party' at 'any time' a judge believed he 'could make a "better" decision' than the objecting parent had done." Thomas, J., also concurring in the judgment, read *Pierce v. Society of Sisters* (1925) to hold that "parents have a fundamental constitutional right to rear their children, including the right to determine who shall educate and socialize them." He would apply strict scrutiny to infringements of this constitutional right.

4.   Stevens, J., dissented and would defer to the states on this issue. Scalia, J., also dissenting, argued that the parents' right to direct the upbringing of their children is among the "unalienable Rights" proclaimed in the Declaration of Independence, but that does not confer "upon me as a judge" the right to "deny legal effect to laws that (in my view) infringe upon what is (in my view) that unenumerated right." Kennedy, J., also dissenting, argued that the case should be remanded for further proceedings.

2.4.2   Contraception

GRISWOLD V. CONNECTICUT
381 U.S. 479, 85 S.Ct. 1678, 14 L.Ed.2d 510 (1965)

JUSTICE DOUGLAS delivered the opinion of the Court.

Appellant Griswold is Executive Director of the Planned Parenthood League of Connecticut. Appellant Buxton is a licensed physician and a professor at the Yale Medical School who served as Medical Director for the League at its Center in New Haven—a center open and operating from November 1 to November 10, 1961, when appellants were arrested.

They gave information, instruction, and medical advice to *married persons* as to the means of preventing conception. They examined the wife and prescribed the best contraceptive device or material for her use. Fees were usually charged, although some couples were serviced free. [A Connecticut statute provides that it is a crime, punishable by a fine and imprisonment of up to one year, to use "any drug, medicinal article or instrument for the purpose of preventing conception;" another statute punishes an accessory as though he were a principal. Appellants were found guilty as accessories and fined $100 each.]

[W]e are met with a wide range of questions that implicate the Due Process Clause of the Fourteenth Amendment. Overtones of some arguments suggest that *Lochner v. New York* should be our guide. But we decline that invitation. . . . We do not sit as a super-legislature to determine the wisdom, need, and propriety of laws that touch economic problems, business affairs, or social conditions. This law, however, operates directly on an intimate relation of husband and wife and their physician's role in one aspect of that relation. . . .

By *Pierce v. Society of Sisters* [268 U.S. 510, 45 S.Ct. 571, 69 L.Ed. 1070 (1925)], the right to educate one's children as one chooses is made applicable to the States by the force of the First and Fourteenth Amendments. By *Meyer v. Nebraska,* the same dignity is given the right to study the German language in a private school. In other words, the State may not, consistently with the spirit of the First Amendment, contract the spectrum of available knowledge. . . . Without those peripheral rights the specific rights would be less secure. And so we reaffirm the principle of the *Pierce* and the *Meyer* cases. In *NAACP v. Alabama,* 357 U.S. 449, 462, 78 S.Ct. 1163, 1172, we protected the "freedom to associate and privacy in one's associations," noting that freedom of association was a peripheral First Amendment right. Disclosure of membership lists of a constitutionally valid association, we held, was invalid "as entailing the likelihood of a substantial restraint upon the exercise by petitioner's members of their right to freedom of association." In other words, the First Amendment has a penumbra where privacy is protected from governmental intrusion. . . .

The foregoing cases suggest that specific guarantees in the Bill of Rights have penumbras, formed by emanations from those guarantees that help give them life and substance. Various guarantees create zones of privacy. The right of association contained in the penumbra of the First Amendment is one, as we have seen. The Third Amendment in its prohibition against the quartering of soldiers "in any house" in time of peace without the consent of the owner is another facet of that privacy. The Fourth Amendment explicitly affirms the "right of the people to be secure in their persons, houses, papers, and effects, against unreasonable searches and seizures." The Fifth Amendment in its Self-Incrimination Clause enables the citizen to create a zone of privacy which government may not force him to surrender to his detriment. The Ninth Amendment provides: "The enumeration in the Constitution, of certain rights, shall not be construed to deny or disparage others retained by the people." . . . We have had many controversies over these penumbral rights of "privacy and repose." These cases bear witness that the right of privacy which presses for recognition here is a legitimate one.

The present case, then, concerns a relationship lying within the zone of privacy created by several fundamental constitutional guarantees. And it concerns a law which, in forbidding the *use* of contraceptives rather than regulating their manufacture or sale, seeks to achieve its goals by means having a maximum destructive impact upon that relationship. Such a law cannot stand in light of the familiar principle, so often applied by this Court, that a "governmental purpose to control or prevent activities constitutionally subject to state regulation may not be achieved by means which sweep unnecessarily broadly and thereby invade the area of protected freedoms." *NAACP v. Alabama.* Would we allow the police to search the sacred precincts of marital bedrooms for telltale signs of the use of contraceptives? The very idea is repulsive to the notions of privacy surrounding the marriage relationship.

We deal with a right of privacy older than the Bill of Rights—older than our political parties, older than our school system. Marriage is a coming together for better or for worse, hopefully enduring, and intimate to the degree of being sacred. It is an association that promotes a way of life, not causes; a harmony in living, not political faiths; a bilateral loyalty, not commercial or social projects. Yet it is an association for as noble a purpose as any involved in our prior decisions.

Reversed.

JUSTICE GOLDBERG, whom CHIEF JUSTICE WARREN and JUSTICE BRENNAN join, concurring.

[T]he Court refers to the Ninth Amendment. I add these words to emphasize the relevance of that Amendment to the Court's holding. . . . The language and history of the Ninth Amendment reveal that the Framers of the Constitution believed that there are additional fundamental rights, protected from governmental infringement, which exist alongside those fundamental rights specifically mentioned in the first eight constitutional amendments. . . . It was proffered to quiet expressed fears that a bill of specifically enumerated rights could not be sufficiently broad to cover all essential rights and that the specific mention of certain rights would be interpreted as a denial that others were protected. . . .

While this Court has had little occasion to interpret the Ninth Amendment, "[i]t cannot be presumed that any clause in the constitution is intended to be without effect." *Marbury v. Madison.* [S]ince 1791 it has been a basic part of the Constitution which we are sworn to uphold. To hold that a right so basic and fundamental and so deep-rooted in our society as the right of privacy in marriage may be infringed because that right is not guaranteed in so many words by the first eight amendments to the Constitution is to ignore the Ninth Amendment and to give it no effect whatsoever. [I]t specifically states that "[t]he enumeration in the Constitution, of certain rights, shall not be *construed* to deny or disparage others retained by the people." (Emphasis added.)

A dissenting opinion suggests that my interpretation of the Ninth Amendment somehow "broaden[s] the powers of this Court." [But] I do not mean to imply that the Ninth Amendment is applied against the States by the Fourteenth. Nor do I mean to state that the Ninth Amendment constitutes an independent source of rights protected from infringement by either the States or the Federal Government. Rather, the Ninth Amendment shows a belief of the Constitution's authors that fundamental rights exist that are not expressly enumerated in the first eight amendments and an intent that the list of rights included there not be deemed exhaustive. [T]he Ninth Amendment simply lends strong support to the view that the "liberty" protected by the Fifth and Fourteenth Amendments from infringement by the Federal Government or the States is not restricted to rights specifically mentioned in the first eight amendments.

In determining which rights are fundamental, judges are not left at large to decide cases in light of their personal and private notions. Rather, they must look to the "traditions and [collective] conscience of our people" to determine whether a principle is "so rooted [there] . . . as to be ranked as fundamental." . . . "Liberty" also "gains content from the emanations of . . . specific [constitutional] guarantees" and "from experience with the requirements of a free society." *Poe v. Ullman,* 367 U.S. 497, 517, 81 S.Ct. 1752, 1763, 6 L.Ed.2d 989 (dissenting opinion of Mr. Justice Douglas).[8]

[T]he right of privacy is a fundamental personal right, emanating "from the totality of the constitutional scheme under which we live." Id. . . . The Connecticut statutes here involved deal with a particularly important and sensitive area of privacy—that of the marital relation and the marital home. This Court recognized in *Meyer v. Nebraska, supra,* that the right "to marry, establish a home

---

[8]   In light of the tests enunciated in these cases it cannot be said that a judge's responsibility to determine whether a right is basic and fundamental in this sense vests him with unrestricted personal discretion. . . .

and bring up children" was an essential part of the liberty guaranteed by the Fourteenth Amendment. . . .

The logic of the dissents would sanction federal or state legislation that seems to me even more plainly unconstitutional than the statute before us. Surely the Government, absent a showing of a compelling subordinating state interest, could not decree that all husbands and wives must be sterilized after two children have been born to them. Yet by their reasoning such an invasion of marital privacy would not be subject to constitutional challenge because, while it might be "silly," no provision of the Constitution specifically prevents the Government from curtailing the marital right to bear children and raise a family. While it may shock some of my Brethren that the Court today holds that the Constitution protects the right of marital privacy, in my view it is far more shocking to believe that the personal liberty guaranteed by the Constitution does not include protection against such totalitarian limitation of family size, which is at complete variance with our constitutional concepts. Yet, if upon a showing of a slender basis of rationality, a law outlawing voluntary birth control by married persons is valid, then, by the same reasoning, a law requiring compulsory birth control also would seem to be valid. In my view, however, both types of law would unjustifiably intrude upon rights of marital privacy which are constitutionally protected. . . .

Although the Connecticut birth-control law obviously encroaches upon a fundamental personal liberty, the State does not show that the law serves any "subordinating [state] interest which is compelling" or that it is "necessary . . . to the accomplishment of a permissible state policy." The State, at most, argues that there is some rational relation between this statute and what is admittedly a legitimate subject of state concern—the discouraging of extra-marital relations. It says that preventing the use of birth-control devices by married persons helps prevent the indulgence by some in such extra-marital relations. The rationality of this justification is dubious, particularly in light of the admitted widespread availability to all persons in the State of Connecticut, unmarried as well as married, of birth-control devices for the prevention of disease, as distinguished from the prevention of conception. [T]he state interest in safeguarding marital fidelity can be served by a more discriminately tailored statute, which does not, like the present one, sweep unnecessarily broadly, reaching far beyond the evil sought to be dealt with and intruding upon the privacy of all married couples. . . . Connecticut does have statutes, the constitutionality of which is beyond doubt, which prohibit adultery and fornication. These statutes demonstrate that means for achieving the same basic purpose of protecting marital fidelity are available to Connecticut without the need to "invade the area of protected freedoms."

[The Court] in no way interferes with a State's proper regulation of sexual promiscuity or misconduct. As my Brother Harlan so well stated in his dissenting opinion in *Poe v. Ullman, supra,* 367 U.S. at 553, 81 S.Ct. at 1782:

> Adultery, homosexuality and the like are sexual intimacies which the State forbids . . . but the intimacy of husband and wife is necessarily an essential and accepted feature of the institution of marriage, an institution which the State not only must allow, but which always and in every age it has fostered and protected. It is one thing when the State exerts its power either to forbid extra-marital sexuality . . . or to say who may marry, but it is quite another when, having acknowledged a marriage and the intimacies inherent in it, it undertakes to regulate by means of the criminal law the details of that intimacy. . . .

JUSTICE HARLAN, concurring in the judgment.

In my view, the proper constitutional inquiry in this case is whether this Connecticut statute infringes the Due Process Clause of the Fourteenth Amendment because the enactment violates basic values "implicit in the concept of ordered liberty," *Palko v. Connecticut,* 302 U.S. 319, 325, 58 S.Ct. 149, 152, 82 L.Ed. 288. For reasons stated at length in my dissenting opinion in *Poe v. Ullman,* I believe that it does. While the relevant inquiry may be aided by resort to one or more of the provisions of the Bill of Rights, it is not dependent on them or any of their radiations. The Due Process Clause of the Fourteenth Amendment stands, in my opinion, on its own bottom. . . .

While I could not more heartily agree that judicial "self restraint" is an indispensable ingredient of sound constitutional adjudication, I do submit that the formula suggested [by the dissent] for achieving it is more hollow than real. "Specific" provisions of the Constitution, no less than "due process," lend themselves as readily to "personal" interpretations by judges whose constitutional outlook is simply to keep the Constitution in supposed "tune with the times." . . . Judicial self-restraint . . . will be achieved in this area, as in other constitutional areas, only by continual insistence upon respect for the teachings of history, solid recognition of the basic values that underlie our society, and wise appreciation of the great roles that the doctrines of federalism and separation of powers have played in establishing and preserving American freedoms. . . .

JUSTICE BLACK, with whom JUSTICE STEWART joins, dissenting.

The Court talks about a constitutional "right of privacy" as though there is some constitutional provision or provisions forbidding any law ever to be passed which might abridge the "privacy" of individuals. But there is not. There are, of course, guarantees in certain specific constitutional provisions which are designed in part to protect privacy at certain times and places with respect to certain activities. Such, for example, is the Fourth Amendment's guarantee against "unreasonable searches and seizures." But I think it belittles that Amendment to talk about it as though it protects nothing but "privacy." To treat it that way is to give it a niggardly interpretation, not the kind of liberal reading I think any Bill of Rights provision should be given. The average man would very likely not have his feelings soothed any more by having his property seized openly than by having it seized privately and by stealth. He simply wants his property left alone. And a person can be just as much, if not more, irritated, annoyed and injured by an unceremonious public arrest by a policeman as he is by a seizure in the privacy of his office or home.

One of the most effective ways of diluting or expanding a constitutionally guaranteed right is to substitute for the crucial word or words of a constitutional guarantee another word or words, more or less flexible and more or less restricted in meaning. This fact is well illustrated by the use of the term "right of privacy" as a comprehensive substitute for the Fourth Amendment's guarantee against "unreasonable searches and seizures." . . . I like my privacy as well as the next one, but I am nevertheless compelled to admit that government has a right to invade it unless prohibited by some specific constitutional provision. For these reasons I cannot agree with the Court's judgment and the reasons it gives for holding this Connecticut law unconstitutional. . . .

Of the cases on which my Brothers White and Goldberg rely so heavily, undoubtedly the reasoning of two of them supports their result here—as would that of a number of others which they do not bother to name, *e.g., Lochner v. New York.* . . . The two they do cite and quote from, *Meyer v. Nebraska,* and *Pierce v. Society of Sisters,* were both decided in opinions by Mr. Justice McReynolds which elaborated the same natural law due process philosophy found in *Lochner v. New York,* one of the cases on which he relied in *Meyer,* along with such other long-discredited decisions as, *e.g., Adkins v. Children's Hospital.* . . .[7]

[The Ninth] Amendment was passed, not to broaden the powers of this Court or any other department of "the General Government," but, as every student of history knows, to assure the people that the Constitution in all its

---

[7]   In *Meyer,* in the very same sentence quoted in part by my Brethren in which he asserted that the Due Process Clause gave an abstract and inviolable right "to marry, establish a home and bring up children," Mr. Justice McReynolds also asserted the heretofore discredited doctrine that the Due Process Clause prevented States from interfering with "the right of the individual to contract."

provisions was intended to limit the Federal Government to the powers granted expressly or by necessary implication. [F]or a period of a century and a half no serious suggestion was ever made that the Ninth Amendment, enacted to protect state powers against federal invasion, could be used as a weapon of federal power to prevent state legislatures from passing laws they consider appropriate to govern local affairs. . . .

JUSTICE STEWART, whom JUSTICE BLACK joins, dissenting.

Since 1879 Connecticut has had on its books a law which forbids the use of contraceptives by anyone. I think this is an uncommonly silly law. [W]e are not asked in this case to say whether we think this law is unwise, or even asinine. We are asked to hold that it violates the United States Constitution. And that I cannot do. . . .[9]

[The opinion of WHITE, J., concurring in the judgment, is omitted.]

NOTES

1. *Eisenstadt v. Baird,* 405 U.S. 438, 92 S.Ct. 1029, 31 L.Ed.2d 349 (1972), invalidated a Massachusetts law that made it a crime to sell or distribute any contraceptive drug or device *except* that physicians could administer or prescribe contraceptives for *married* persons and pharmacists could fill prescriptions for contraceptives for *married* persons. Single persons could not, under the statutory scheme, obtain contraceptives from anyone to prevent pregnancy; married or single persons could obtain contraceptives from anyone to prevent, not pregnancy, but the spread of disease. Justice Brennan, for the Court, invalidated the statute:

   > If under *Griswold* the distribution of contraceptives to married persons cannot be prohibited, a ban on distribution to unmarried persons would be equally impermissible. It is true that in *Griswold* the right of privacy in question inhered in the marital relationship. Yet the marital couple is not an independent entity with a mind and heart of its own, but an association of two individuals each with a separate intellectual and emotional makeup. If the right of privacy means anything, it is the right of the *individual,* married or single, to be free from unwarranted governmental intrusion into matters so

---

[9] The Connecticut House of Representatives recently passed a bill (House Bill No. 2462) repealing the birth control law. The State Senate has apparently not yet acted on the measure, and today is relieved of that responsibility by the Court.

fundamentally affecting a person as the decision whether to bear or beget a child. On the other hand, if *Griswold* is no bar to a prohibition on the distribution of contraceptives, the State could not, consistently with the Equal Protection Clause, outlaw distribution to unmarried but not to married persons. In each case the evil, as perceived by the State, would be identical, and the underinclusion would be invidious. . . . We hold that by providing dissimilar treatment for married and unmarried persons who are similarly situated, Massachusetts General Laws Ann., c. 272, §§ 21 and 21A, violate the Equal Protection Clause.

2. *Carey v. Population Services Int'l,* 431 U.S. 678, 97 S.Ct. 2010, 52 L.Ed.2d 675 (1977), invalidated, insofar as it applied to nonprescription contraceptives, a New York law making it a crime (1) for any person to sell or distribute any contraceptive to a minor under the age of 16, (2) for anyone other than a licensed pharmacist to distribute contraceptives to persons 16 or older, and (3) for anyone, including licensed pharmacists, to advertise or display contraceptives. Relying on *Griswold* and *Eisenstadt,* the Court (with no majority opinion) invalidated the prohibition on the distribution of nonprescription contraceptives to adults except through licensed physicians. It also invalidated the restrictions on advertising as a violation of free speech.

    Brennan, J., joined by Stewart, Marshall, & Blackmun, JJ., argued that the state may not affect the privacy interests even of minors unless the restrictions serve significant state interests. White, J. concurred because the state did not demonstrate that the state law would measurably deter early sexual activity. Powell, J., agreed to invalidate the law because it infringed on the privacy interests of married females between 14 and 16 (a 14-year-old female may marry in New York with the consent of her parents and a family court judge), and it interfered with the parents' authority over their children (the law prohibited even parents from distributing contraceptives to their children). Stevens, J., argued that the statute violated due process by forcing minors who engage in sexual activities to bear children. Burger, C.J., and Rehnquist, J., dissented.

3. **MARRIAGE AS A FUNDAMENTAL RIGHT**. *Loving v. Virginia,* 388 U.S. 1, 87 S.Ct. 1817, 18 L.Ed.2d 1010 (1967) invalidated a Virginia law that made it a crime for whites to marry nonwhites. (The Virginia statute made an exception for the "descendants of John Rolfe and Pocahontas.") Warren, C.J., for the Court, held that this antimiscegenation law violated Equal Protection. "There

can be no doubt that restricting the freedom to marry solely because of racial classifications violates the central meaning of the Equal Protection Clause." Warren went on to hold that this law also violated Due Process. "The freedom to marry has long been recognized as one of the vital personal rights essential to the orderly pursuit of happiness by free men. Marriage is one of the 'basic civil rights of man,' fundamental to our very existence and survival. To deny this fundamental freedom on so unsupportable a basis as the racial classifications embodied in these statutes, classifications so directly subversive of the principle of equality at the heart of the Fourteenth Amendment, is surely to deprive all the State's citizens of liberty without due process of law." Stewart, J. concurred in the judgment because, "it is simply not possible for a state law to be valid under our Constitution which makes the criminality of an act depend upon the race of the actor."

2.4.3 Abortion

ROE V. WADE
410 U.S. 113, 93 S.Ct. 705, 35 L.Ed.2d 147 (1973)

JUSTICE BLACKMUN delivered the opinion of the Court.

This Texas federal appeal and its Georgia companion, *Doe v. Bolton* [410 U.S. 179, 93 S.Ct. 739, 35 L.Ed,2d 201], present constitutional challenges to state criminal abortion legislation. The Texas statutes under attack here are typical of those that have been in effect in many States for approximately a century. . . .

We forthwith acknowledge our awareness of the sensitive and emotional nature of the abortion controversy, of the vigorous opposing views, even among physicians, and of the deep and seemingly absolute convictions that the subject inspires. [P]opulation growth, pollution, poverty, and racial overtones tend to complicate and not to simplify the problem. . . .

The Texas statutes that concern us here are Arts. 1191–1194 and 1196 of the State's Penal Code. These make it a crime to "procure an abortion," as therein defined, or to attempt one, except with respect to "an abortion procured or attempted by medical advice for the purpose of saving the life of the mother." Similar statutes are in existence in a majority of the States. . . .

Jane Roe. Despite the use of the pseudonym, no suggestion is made that Roe is a fictitious person. For purposes of her case, we accept as true, and as established, her existence; her pregnant state, as of the inception of her suit in

March 1970 and as late as May 21 of that year when she filed an alias affidavit with the District Court; and her inability to obtain a legal abortion in Texas. . . .

The principal thrust of appellant's attack on the Texas statutes is that they improperly invade a right, said to be possessed by the pregnant woman, to choose to terminate her pregnancy. Appellant would discover this right in the concept of personal "liberty" embodied in the Fourteenth Amendment's Due Process Clause; or in personal, marital, familial, and sexual privacy said to be protected by the Bill of Rights or its penumbras, see *Griswold v. Connecticut,* or among those rights reserved to the people by the Ninth Amendment, *Griswold v. Connecticut,* (Goldberg, J., concurring). Before addressing this claim, we feel it desirable briefly to survey, in several aspects, the history of abortion, for such insight as that history may afford us, and then to examine the state purposes and interests behind the criminal abortion laws.

It perhaps is not generally appreciated that the restrictive criminal abortion laws in effect in a majority of States today are of relatively recent vintage. [In a lengthy historical section, the Court noted that at the time of the Persian Empire criminal abortions were severely punished, but "abortion was practiced in Greek times as well as in the Roman Era, and that "it was resorted to without scruple,' " notwithstanding the Hippocratic Oath forbidding abortions. At common law "abortion performed *before* 'quickening'—the first recognizable movement of the fetus *in utero,* appearing usually from the 16th to the 18th week of pregnancy— was not an indictable offense." After quickening, abortion was either a felony or a lesser crime.]

Three reasons have been advanced to explain historically the enactment of criminal abortion laws in the 19th century and to justify their continued existence. It has been argued occasionally that these laws were the product of a Victorian social concern to discourage illicit sexual conduct. Texas, however, does not advance this justification in the present case, and it appears that no court or commentator has taken the argument seriously. . . .

A second reason is concerned with abortion as a medical procedure. When most criminal abortion laws were first enacted, the procedure was a hazardous one for the woman. [Now,] abortion in early pregnancy, that is, prior to the end of the first trimester, although not without its risk, is now relatively safe. [Hence,] any interest of the State in protecting the woman from an inherently hazardous procedure, except when it would be equally dangerous for her to forgo it, has largely disappeared. Of course, important state interests in the areas of health and medical standards do remain. The State has a legitimate interest in seeing to it that abortion, like any other medical procedure, is performed under circumstances that insure maximum safety for the patient. This interest obviously extends at least to the performing physician and his staff, to the facilities involved, to the availability of after-care, and to adequate provision for any complication or emergency that might arise. The prevalence of high mortality rates at illegal "abortion mills" strengthens, rather than weakens, the State's interest in regulating the conditions under which abortions are performed. Moreover, the risk to the woman increases as her pregnancy continues. Thus, the State retains a definite interest in protecting the woman's own health and safety when an abortion is proposed at a late stage of pregnancy.

The third reason is the State's interest—some phrase it in terms of duty—in protecting prenatal life. Some of the argument for this justification rests on the theory that a new human life is present from the moment of conception. The State's interest and general obligation to protect life then extends, it is argued, to prenatal life. Only when the life of the pregnant mother herself is at stake, balanced against the life she carries within her, should the interest of the embryo or fetus not prevail. Logically, of course, a legitimate state interest in this area need not stand or fall on acceptance of the belief that life begins at conception or at some other point prior to live birth. In assessing the State's interest, recognition may be given to the less rigid claim that as long as at least *potential* life is involved, the State may assert interests beyond the protection of the pregnant woman alone. . . .

The Constitution does not explicitly mention any right of privacy. [A] line of decisions, however, . . . make it clear that only personal rights that can be deemed "fundamental" or "implicit in the concept of ordered liberty," *Palko v. Connecticut,* 302 U.S. 319, 325, 58 S.Ct. 149, 152, 82 L.Ed. 288 (1937), are included in this guarantee of personal privacy. They also make it clear that the right has some extension to activities relating to marriage, *Loving v. Virginia,* procreation; contraception; family relationships; and child rearing and education, *Pierce v. Society of Sisters; Meyer v. Nebraska.*

This right of privacy, whether it be founded in the Fourteenth Amendment's concept of personal liberty and restrictions upon state action, as we feel it is, or, as the District Court determined, in the Ninth Amendment's reservation of rights to the people, is broad enough to encompass a woman's decision whether or not to terminate her pregnancy. The detriment that the State would impose upon the pregnant woman by denying this choice altogether is apparent. Specific and direct harm medically diagnosable even in early pregnancy may be involved. Maternity, or additional offspring, may force upon the woman a distressful life and future. Psychological harm may be imminent. Mental and physical health may be taxed by child care. There is also the distress, for all concerned, associated with the unwanted child, and there is the problem of bringing a child into a family already unable, psychologically and otherwise, to care for it. In other cases, as in this one, the additional difficulties and continuing stigma of unwed motherhood may be involved. All these are factors the woman and her responsible physician necessarily will consider in consultation.

On the basis of elements such as these, appellant and some *amici* argue that the woman's right is absolute and that she is entitled to terminate her pregnancy at whatever time, in whatever way, and for whatever reason she alone chooses. With this we do not agree. [A] State may properly assert important interests in safeguarding health, in maintaining medical standards, and in protecting potential life. At some point in pregnancy, these respective interests become sufficiently compelling to sustain regulation of the factors that govern the abortion decision. The privacy right involved, therefore, cannot be said to be absolute. In fact, it is not clear to us that the claim asserted by some *amici* that one has an unlimited right to do with one's body as one pleases bears a close relationship to the right of privacy previously articulated in the Court's decisions. The Court has refused to recognize an unlimited right of this kind in the past. *Jacobson v. Massachusetts*, 197 U.S. 11, 25 S.Ct. 358, 49 L.Ed. 643 (1905) (vaccination); *Buck v. Bell,* 274 U.S. 200, 47 S.Ct. 584, 71 L.Ed. 1000 (1927) (sterilization). We, therefore, conclude that the right of personal privacy includes the abortion decision, but that this right is not unqualified and must be considered against important state interests in regulation. . . .

Where certain "fundamental rights" are involved, the Court has held that regulation limiting these rights may be justified only by a "compelling state interest," and that legislative enactments must be narrowly drawn to express only the legitimate state interests at stake. *Griswold v. Connecticut.* . . .

The appellee and certain *amici* argue that the fetus is a "person" within the language and meaning of the Fourteenth Amendment. In support of this, they outline at length and in detail the well-known facts of fetal development. If this suggestion of personhood is established, the appellant's case, of course, collapses, for the fetus' right to life would then be guaranteed specifically by the Amendment. The appellant conceded as much on reargument. On the other hand, the appellee conceded on reargument that no case could be cited that holds that a fetus is a person within the meaning of the Fourteenth Amendment.

The Constitution does not define "person" in so many words. Section 1 of the Fourteenth Amendment contains three references to "person." The first, in defining "citizens," speaks of "persons born or naturalized in the United States." The word also appears both in the Due Process Clause and in the Equal Protection Clause. "Person" is used in other places in the Constitution: in the listing of qualifications for Representatives and Senators, Art. I, § 2, cl. 2, and § 3, cl. 3; in the Apportionment Clause, Art. I, § 2, cl. 3;[53] in the Migration and Importation provision, Art. I, § 9, cl. 1; in the Emolument Clause, Art. I, § 9, cl. 8; in the Electors provisions, Art. II, § 1, cl. 2, and the superseded cl. 3; in the provision outlining qualifications for the office of President, Art. II, § 1, cl. 5; in the Extradition provisions, Art. IV, § 2, cl. 2, and the superseded Fugitive Slave Clause 3; and in the Fifth, Twelfth, and Twenty-second Amendments, as well as in §§ 2 and 3 of the Fourteenth Amendment. But in nearly all these instances, the use of the word is such that it has application only postnatally. None indicates, with any assurance, that it has any possible pre-natal application.

All this, together with our observation, that throughout the major portion of the 19th century prevailing legal abortion practices were far freer than they are today, persuades us that the word "person," as used in the Fourteenth Amendment, does not include the unborn. . . .

The pregnant woman cannot be isolated in her privacy. She carries an embryo and, later, a fetus, if one accepts the medical definitions of the developing young in the human uterus. The situation therefore is inherently different from marital intimacy. . . .

Texas urges that, apart from the Fourteenth Amendment, life begins at conception and is present throughout pregnancy, and that, therefore, the State has a compelling interest in protecting that life from and after conception. We need not resolve the difficult question of when life begins. When those trained in the respective disciplines of medicine, philosophy, and theology are unable to arrive at any consensus, the judiciary, at this point in the development of man's knowledge, is not in a position to speculate as to the answer.

It should be sufficient to note briefly the wide divergence of thinking on this most sensitive and difficult question. There has always been strong support for the view that life does not begin until live birth. This was the belief of the Stoics. [The] common law found greater significance in quickening. Physicians and their scientific colleagues have regarded that event with less interest and have tended

---

[53] We are not aware that in the taking of any census under this clause, a fetus has ever been counted.

to focus either upon conception, upon live birth, or upon the interim point at which the fetus becomes "viable," that is, potentially able to live outside the mother's womb, albeit with artificial aid. Viability is usually placed at about seven months (28 weeks) but may occur earlier, even at 24 weeks. . . .

In view of all this, we do not agree that, by adopting one theory of life, Texas may override the rights of the pregnant woman that are at stake. We repeat, however, that the State does have an important and legitimate interest in preserving and protecting the health of the pregnant woman, whether she be a resident of the State or a nonresident who seeks medical consultation and treatment there, and that it has still *another* important and legitimate interest in protecting the potentiality of human life. These interests are separate and distinct. Each grows in substantiality as the woman approaches term and, at a point during pregnancy, each becomes "compelling."

With respect to the State's important and legitimate interest in the health of the mother, the "compelling" point, in the light of present medical knowledge, is at approximately the end of the first trimester. This is so because of the now-established medical fact that until the end of the first trimester mortality in abortion may be less than mortality in normal childbirth. It follows that, from and after this point, a State may regulate the abortion procedure to the extent that the regulation reasonably relates to the preservation and protection of maternal health. Examples of permissible state regulation in this area are requirements as to the qualifications of the person who is to perform the abortion; as to the licensure of that person; as to the facility in which the procedure is to be performed, that is, whether it must be a hospital or may be a clinic or some other place of less-than-hospital status; as to the licensing of the facility; and the like.

This means, on the other hand, that, for the period of pregnancy prior to this "compelling" point, the attending physician, in consultation with his patient, is free to determine, without regulation by the State, that, in his medical judgment, the patient's pregnancy should be terminated. If that decision is reached, the judgment may be effectuated by an abortion free of interference by the State.

With respect to the State's important and legitimate interest in potential life, the "compelling" point is at viability. This is so because the fetus then presumably has the capability of meaningful life outside the mother's womb. State regulation protective of fetal life after viability thus has both logical and biological justifications. If the State is interested in protecting fetal life after viability, it may go so far as to proscribe abortion during that period, except when it is necessary to preserve the life or health of the mother.

Measured against these standards, Art. 1196 of the Texas Penal Code, in restricting legal abortions to those "procured or attempted by medical advice for the purpose of saving the life of the mother," sweeps too broadly. The statute makes no distinction between abortions performed early in pregnancy and those performed later, and it limits to a single reason, "saving" the mother's life, the legal justification for the procedure. The statute, therefore, cannot survive the constitutional attack made upon it here. . . .

CHIEF JUSTICE BURGER, concurring. . . .

I do not read the Court's holdings today as having the sweeping consequences attributed to them by the dissenting Justices; the dissenting views discount the reality that the vast majority of physicians observe the standards of their profession, and act only on the basis of carefully deliberated medical judgments relating to life and health. Plainly, the Court today rejects any claim that the Constitution requires abortions on demand.

JUSTICE REHNQUIST, dissenting.

. . . A transaction resulting in an operation such as this is not "private" in the ordinary usage of that word. Nor is the "privacy" that the Court finds here even a distant relative of the freedom from searches and seizures protected by the Fourth Amendment to the Constitution, which the Court has referred to as embodying a right to privacy.

If the Court means by the term "privacy" no more than that the claim of a person to be free from unwanted state regulation of consensual transactions may be a form of "liberty" protected by the Fourteenth Amendment, there is no doubt that similar claims have been upheld in our earlier decisions on the basis of that liberty. [T]hat liberty is not guaranteed absolutely against deprivation, only against deprivation without due process of law. The test traditionally applied in the area of social and economic legislation is whether or not a law such as that challenged has a rational relation to a valid state objective. *Williamson v. Lee Optical Co.,* 348 U.S. 483, 491, 75 S.Ct. 461, 466, 99 L.Ed. 563 (1955). The Due Process Clause of the Fourteenth Amendment undoubtedly does place a limit, albeit a broad one, on legislative power to enact laws such as this. If the Texas statute were to prohibit an abortion even where the mother's life is in jeopardy, I have little doubt that such a statute would lack a rational relation to a valid state objective under the test stated in *Williamson.*

[Also] the Court adds a new wrinkle to [the "compelling state interest"] test by transposing it from the legal considerations associated with the Equal

Protection Clause of the Fourteenth Amendment to this case arising under the Due Process Clause of the Fourteenth Amendment. Unless I misapprehend the consequences of this transplanting of the "compelling state interest test," the Court's opinion will accomplish the seemingly impossible feat of leaving this area of the law more confused than it found it.

. . . The decision here to break pregnancy into three distinct terms and to outline the permissible restrictions the State may impose in each one, for example, partakes more of judicial legislation than it does of a determination of the intent of the drafters of the Fourteenth Amendment. . . .

JUSTICE WHITE, with whom JUSTICE REHNQUIST joins, dissenting.

. . . In a sensitive area such as this, involving as it does issues over which reasonable men may easily and heatedly differ, [t]his issue, for the most part, should be left with the people and to the political processes the people have devised to govern their affairs. . . .

[The concurring opinions of DOUGLAS and STEWART, JJ., are omitted.]

NOTES

1. In 2004, Norma McCorvey (her identity then protected as "Jane Roe," the appellant in *Roe*) filed a motion to have the district court revisit the 1973 Supreme Court decision in *Roe v. Wade*. She had become an anti-abortion activist. The Fifth Circuit held that her motion was moot because Texas had repealed the anti-abortion statutes by implication. *McCorvey v. Hill*, 385 F.3d 846 (5th Cir. 2004), cert. denied, 543 U.S. 1154, 125 S.Ct. 1387, 161 L.Ed.2d 119 (2005). Her certiorari petition, which the Court denied, argued that since *Roe*, the evidence of changed factual circumstance includes "the testimony of women harmed by abortion; medical studies documenting abortion injuries; an explosion of knowledge since 1973 concerning the effects of abortion on women; and, the fact that abortion clinics do not provide the normal doctor-patient relationship anticipated by Roe." 2005 WL 123452.

2. Notice that the Court rejects the argument that "one has an unlimited right to do with one's body as one pleases." Justice Blackmun cited, with approval, *Jacobson v. Massachusetts* (1905), which upheld compulsory vaccination, and *Buck v Bell* (1926), which upheld the constitutionality of a Virginia statute that provided for the forced sterilization of "mental defectives" in state institutions after a finding by a hearing board that the mental defective "is the probable potential parent of socially inadequate offspring, likewise

afflicted, that she may be sexually sterilized without detriment to her general health and that her welfare and that of society will be promoted by her sterilization." Justice Holmes, speaking for the Court in *Buck*, said (it was not his finest hour):

> We have seen more than once that the public welfare may call upon the best citizens for their lives. It would be strange if it could not call upon those who already sap the strength of the State for these lesser sacrifices, often not felt to be such by those concerned, in order to prevent our being swamped with incompetence. It is better for all the world, if instead of waiting to execute degenerate offspring for crime, or to let them starve for their imbecility, society can prevent those who are manifestly unfit from continuing their kind. The principle that sustains compulsory vaccination is broad enough to cover cutting the Fallopian tubes. *Jacobson v. Massachusetts*, 197 U.S. 11, 25 S.Ct. 358, 49 L.Ed. 643 (1905). Three generations of imbeciles are enough.

Justice Butler filed, without opinion, the only dissent. The Virginia Colony for Epileptics and Feeble-Minded paroled Carrie Buck, the plaintiff in *Buck v. Bell*, shortly after the state sterilized her. Over time, reporters and others visited her and reported that she appeared to have normal intelligence. She died in 1983 and was buried near her only child, Vivian, who was born before Carrie's sterilization. Vivian's grades tended to be B's and C's. She died at age 8 from an intestinal disease.[10]

3.   Two years after *Roe*, the Court unanimously upheld a state requirement that permitted only licenses physicians to perform abortions, even if the abortion occurred in the first trimester. *Connecticut v. Menillo,* 423 U.S. 9, 96 S.Ct. 170, 46 L.Ed.2d 152 (1975) (per curiam). The Court said that *Roe* only referred to the woman's right to have an abortion "performed by a competent, licensed physician, under safe clinical conditions." Thus, a prosecution of a nonphysician for performing an abortion infringes "upon no realm of personal privacy secured by the Constitution against state interference." It was irrelevant that a trained nonphysician could perform first trimester abortions safely.

Recall that *Roe* said, "prior to this 'compelling' point, the *attending physician,* in consultation with his patient, is free to determine, without

---

[10]   Stephen Jay Gould, *Carrie Buck's Daughter*, 93 NATURAL HISTORY, July-August, 2002 (originally appearing in the 1984 issue).

regulation by the State, that, in his medical judgment, the patient's pregnancy should be terminated." (Emphasis added.) Justice Blackmun assumes the medical doctor is male and that the right to abortion is the right of "the *attending physician*, in consultation with his patient." Is *Roe v. Wade* a woman's rights case, or a doctor's rights case?

4.   *Maher v. Roe,* 432 U.S. 464, 97 S.Ct. 2376, 53 L.Ed.2d 484 (1977), held that the Constitution does not require the state nor federal government to pay for abortions for indigent women when those abortions were not medically necessary. *Harris v. McRae,* 448 U.S. 297, 100 S.Ct. 2671, 65 L.Ed.2d 784 (1980), extended that holding and upheld the power of the federal government to refuse to fund certain medically necessary abortions for indigent women. The Court upheld the most restrictive version of the Hyde Amendment (no federal funding for abortions except where the "life of the mother would be endangered if the fetus were carried to term"). While "government may not place obstacles in the path of a woman's exercise of her freedom of choice, it need not remove those not of its own creation. Indigency falls in the latter category." Brennan, Marshall, Blackmun, & Stevens, JJ., dissented. Brennan's dissent, joined by Marshall & Blackmun, argued, "abortion and childbirth, when stripped of the sensitive moral arguments surrounding the abortion controversy, are simply two alternative medical methods of dealing with pregnancy. . . . By funding all of the expenses associated with childbirth and none of the expenses incurred in terminating pregnancy, the government literally makes an offer that the indigent woman cannot afford to refuse. It matters not that in this instance the government has used the carrot rather than the stick."

5.   Justice Ruth Ginsburg, in a 2009 interview, said that *Harris v. McRae* "surprised me. Frankly I had thought that at the time *Roe* was decided, there was concern about population growth and particularly growth in populations that we don't want to have too many of."[11]

6.   *Thornburgh v. American College of Obstetricians and Gynecologists*, 476 U.S. 747, 106 S.Ct. 2169, 90 L.Ed.2d 779 (1986) invalidated a Pennsylvania law that imposed various requirements on abortion, such as a requirement that the physician advise the woman that the father is responsible for financial assistance to support the child ("poorly disguised elements of discouragement for the abortion decision"). Burger, C.J., dissented: "[E]very member of the Roe Court rejected the idea of abortion on demand." A

---

[11]   Emily Bazelon, *The Place of Women on the Court*, N.Y. TIMES MAGAZINE, July 7, 2009.

separate dissent by O'Connor, J. (joined by Rehnquist, J.) argued: "This Court's abortion decisions have already worked a major distortion in the Court's constitutional jurisprudence," but because "Pennsylvania has not asked the Court to reconsider or overrule *Roe v. Wade*, I do not address that question." That led to the next case.

PLANNED PARENTHOOD OF SOUTHEASTERN PENNSYLVANIA V. CASEY

505 U.S. 833, 112 S.Ct. 2791, 120 L.Ed.2d 674 (1992)

[Ed. Note: The opinions in this case totaled 177 pages. Only a small portion is excerpted here. This case split three ways. O'Connor, Kennedy, & Justice Souter, JJ., all signed their separate opinion. Parts I, II, & III are an Opinion of the Court, with O'Connor, Kennedy, & Souter, JJ., joined by Blackmun & Stevens, JJ.

[The issue was the constitutionality of five provisions of the Pennsylvania Abortion Control Act of 1982: (1) § 3205 requires that a woman seeking an abortion give her informed consent prior to the procedure, and that she be provided with certain information at least 24 hours before the abortion; (2) § 3206 mandates the informed consent of one parent for a minor to obtain an abortion, but provides a judicial bypass procedure;[12] (3) § 3209 commands that, unless certain exceptions apply, a married woman seeking an abortion must sign a statement indicating that she has notified her husband; (4) § 3203 defines a "medical emergency" that will excuse compliance with the foregoing requirements; and (5) §§ 3207(b), 3214(a), and 3214(f) impose certain reporting requirements on facilities providing abortion services. A majority of the Justices concluded that (1), (2), (4), and (5) are constitutional, but (3), spousal notification, is unconstitutional.

[The reasoning the Justices and their view of the importance of precedent, are what this excerpt focuses on. Note that O'Connor, Kennedy, & Souter, JJ., in their plurality, state, "We reject the trimester framework, which we do not consider to be part of the essential holding of *Roe*." They also create a new test,

---

[12] Under the Pennsylvania judicial bypass option, a minor can obtain an abortion and bypass parental notification if a state court finds that she given her informed consent, or determines that an abortion is in her best interests. The records of these court proceedings are confidential. The state trial court must render a decision within three days of the woman's application, and the entire procedure, including appeal to Pennsylvania Superior Court, is no longer than eight business days. The parental consent requirement does not apply in the case of a medical emergency.

"the undue burden standard" to determine if a restriction of abortion is constitutional.]

JUSTICE O'CONNOR, JUSTICE KENNEDY, and JUSTICE SOUTER announced the judgment of the Court and delivered the opinion of the Court with respect to Parts I, II, III, V-A, V-C, and VI, an opinion with respect to Part V-E, in which JUSTICE STEVENS joins, and an opinion with respect to Parts IV, V-B, and V-D.

I. Liberty finds no refuge in a jurisprudence of doubt. . . . At issue in these cases are five provisions of the Pennsylvania Abortion Control Act of 1982 as amended in 1988 and 1989. . . . After considering the fundamental constitutional questions resolved by *Roe,* principles of institutional integrity, and the rule of *stare decisis,* we are led to conclude this: the essential holding of *Roe v. Wade* should be retained and once again reaffirmed.

It must be stated at the outset and with clarity that *Roe*'s essential holding, the holding we reaffirm, has three parts. First is a recognition of the right of the woman to choose to have an abortion before viability and to obtain it without undue interference from the State. Before viability, the State's interests are not strong enough to support a prohibition of abortion or the imposition of a substantial obstacle to the woman's effective right to elect the procedure. Second is a confirmation of the State's power to restrict abortions after fetal viability, if the law contains exceptions for pregnancies which endanger a woman's life or health. And third is the principle that the State has legitimate interests from the outset of the pregnancy in protecting the health of the woman and the life of the fetus that may become a child. These principles do not contradict one another; and we adhere to each.

II. Constitutional protection of the woman's decision to terminate her pregnancy derives from the Due Process Clause of the Fourteenth Amendment. It declares that no State shall "deprive any person of life, liberty, or property, without due process of law." The controlling word in the case before us is "liberty." . . . At the heart of liberty is the right to define one's own concept of existence, of meaning, of the universe, and of the mystery of human life. Beliefs about these matters could not define the attributes of personhood were they formed under compulsion of the State.

. . . Abortion is a unique act. It is an act fraught with consequences for others: for the woman who must live with the implications of her decision; for the persons who perform and assist in the procedure; for the spouse, family, and society which must confront the knowledge that these procedures exist, procedures some deem nothing short of an act of violence against innocent human life; and, depending on one's beliefs, for the life or potential life that is aborted. Though abortion is conduct, it does not follow that the State is entitled to proscribe it in all instances. That is because the liberty of the woman is at stake in a sense unique to the human condition and so unique to the law. The mother who carries a child to full term is subject to anxieties, to physical constraints, to pain that only she must bear. [T]he reservations any of us may have in reaffirming the central holding of *Roe* are outweighed by the explication of individual liberty we have given combined with the force of *stare decisis*. We turn now to that doctrine.

III. . . . Although *Roe* has engendered opposition, it has in no sense proven "unworkable," representing as it does a simple limitation beyond which a state law is unenforceable. [F]or two decades of economic and social developments, people have organized intimate relationships and made choices that define their views of themselves and their places in society, in reliance on the availability of abortion in the event that contraception should fail. [W]hile the effect of reliance on *Roe* cannot be exactly measured, neither can the certain cost of overruling *Roe* for people who have ordered their thinking and living around that case be dismissed. . . .

Nor will courts building upon *Roe* be likely to hand down erroneous decisions as a consequence. Even on the assumption that the central holding of *Roe* was in error, that error would go only to the strength of the state interest in fetal protection, not to the recognition afforded by the Constitution to the woman's liberty. . . . If indeed the woman's interest in deciding whether to bear and beget a child had not been recognized as in *Roe,* the State might as readily restrict a woman's right to choose to carry a pregnancy to term as to terminate it, to further asserted state interests in population control, or eugenics, for example. [A]ny error in *Roe* is unlikely to have serious ramifications in future cases.

We have seen how time has overtaken some of *Roe*'s factual assumptions: advances in maternal health care allow for abortions safe to the mother later in pregnancy than was true in 1973, and advances in neonatal care have advanced viability to a point somewhat earlier. But these facts go only to the scheme of time limits on the realization of competing interests, and the divergences from the factual premises of 1973 have no bearing on the validity of *Roe*'s central holding, that viability marks the earliest point at which the State's interest in fetal life is constitutionally adequate to justify a legislative ban on nontherapeutic abortions. The soundness or unsoundness of that constitutional judgment in no sense turns on whether viability occurs at approximately 28 weeks, as was usual at the time of

Roe, at 23 to 24 weeks, as it sometimes does today, or at some moment even slightly earlier in pregnancy, as it may if fetal respiratory capacity can somehow be enhanced in the future.

[T]he sustained and widespread debate *Roe* has provoked calls for some comparison between that case and others of comparable dimension that have responded to national controversies. . . .

The first example is that line of cases identified with *Lochner v. New York,* (1905), which imposed substantive limitations on legislation limiting economic autonomy in favor of health and welfare regulation, adopting, in Justice Holmes' view, the theory of *laissez-faire.* . . . *West Coast Hotel Co. v. Parrish,* (1937), signaled the demise of *Lochner* by overruling *Adkins.* In the meantime, the Depression had come and, with it, the lesson that seemed unmistakable to most people by 1937, that the interpretation of contractual freedom protected in *Adkins* rested on fundamentally false factual assumptions about the capacity of a relatively unregulated market to satisfy minimal levels of human welfare. . . .

The second comparison that 20th century history invites is with the cases employing the separate-but-equal rule for applying the Fourteenth Amendment's equal protection guarantee. They began with *Plessy v. Ferguson* (1896), holding that legislatively mandated racial segregation in public transportation works no denial of equal protection, rejecting the argument that racial separation enforced by the legal machinery of American society treats the black race as inferior. [T]his understanding of the facts and the rule it was stated to justify were repudiated in *Brown v. Board of Education,* (1954). [T]he *Plessy* Court's explanation for its decision was so clearly at odds with the facts apparent to the Court in 1954 that the decision to reexamine *Plessy* was on this ground alone not only justified but required.

[N]either the factual underpinnings of *Roe*'s central holding nor our understanding of it has changed (and because no other indication of weakened precedent has been shown) the Court could not pretend to be reexamining the prior law with any justification beyond a present doctrinal disposition to come out differently from the Court of 1973. To overrule prior law for no other reason than that would run counter to the view repeated in our cases, that a decision to overrule should rest on some special reason over and above the belief that a prior case was wrongly decided.

[A decision to overrule] is usually perceived (and perceived correctly) as, at the least, a statement that a prior decision was wrong. There is a limit to the amount of error that can plausibly be imputed to prior courts. . . . The legitimacy of the Court would fade with the frequency of its vacillation.

[T]he Court's interpretation of the Constitution calls the contending sides of a national controversy to end their national division by accepting a common mandate rooted in the Constitution. [T]o overrule under fire in the absence of the most compelling reason to reexamine a watershed decision would subvert the Court's legitimacy beyond any serious question. . . .

IV. . . . Liberty must not be extinguished for want of a line that is clear. . . . We conclude the line should be drawn at viability, so that before that time the woman has a right to choose to terminate her pregnancy. We adhere to this principle for two reasons. First, as we have said, is the doctrine of *stare decisis*. . . . The second reason is that the concept of viability, as we noted in *Roe,* is the time at which there is a realistic possibility of maintaining and nourishing a life outside the womb, so that the independent existence of the second life can in reason and all fairness be the object of state protection that now overrides the rights of the woman. . . .

On the other side of the equation is the interest of the State in the protection of potential life. . . . That portion of the decision in *Roe* has been given too little acknowledgement and implementation by the Court in its subsequent cases. . . . *Roe* established a trimester framework to govern abortion regulations. . . . A framework of this rigidity was unnecessary and in its later interpretation sometimes contradicted the State's permissible exercise of its powers.

Though the woman has a right to choose to terminate or continue her pregnancy before viability, it does not at all follow that the State is prohibited from taking steps to ensure that this choice is thoughtful and informed. Even in the earliest stages of pregnancy, the State may enact rules and regulations designed to encourage her to know that there are philosophic and social arguments of great weight that can be brought to bear in favor of continuing the pregnancy to full term and that there are procedures and institutions to allow adoption of unwanted children as well as a certain degree of state assistance if the mother chooses to raise the child herself. " '[T]he Constitution does not forbid a State or city, pursuant to democratic processes, from expressing a preference for normal childbirth.' " It follows that States are free to enact laws to provide a reasonable framework for a woman to make a decision that has such profound and lasting meaning. This, too [is] the inevitable consequence of our holding that the State has an interest in protecting the life of the unborn.

We reject the trimester framework, which we do not consider to be part of the essential holding of *Roe.*

[Many] forms of state regulation might have the incidental effect of increasing the cost or decreasing the availability of medical care, whether for abortion or any other medical procedure. The fact that a law which serves a valid purpose, one not designed to strike at the right itself, has the incidental effect of making it more difficult or more expensive to procure an abortion cannot be enough to invalidate it. Only where state regulation imposes an undue burden on a woman's ability to make this decision does the power of the State reach into the heart of the liberty protected by the Due Process Clause. . . .

The very notion that the State has a substantial interest in potential life leads to the conclusion that [n]ot all burdens on the right to decide whether to terminate a pregnancy will be undue. In our view, the undue burden standard is the appropriate means of reconciling the State's interest with the woman's constitutionally protected liberty. . . . A finding of an undue burden is a shorthand for the conclusion that a state regulation has the purpose or effect of placing a substantial obstacle in the path of a woman seeking an abortion of a nonviable fetus. . . . Unless it has that effect on her right of choice, a state measure designed to persuade her to choose childbirth over abortion will be upheld if reasonably related to that goal. Regulations designed to foster the health of a woman seeking an abortion are valid if they do not constitute an undue burden. . . . We give this summary:

(a)   To protect the central right recognized by *Roe v. Wade* while at the same time accommodating the State's profound interest in potential life, we will employ the undue burden analysis as explained in this opinion. An undue burden exists, and therefore a provision of law is invalid, if its purpose or effect is to place a substantial obstacle in the path of a woman seeking an abortion before the fetus attains viability.

(b)   We reject the rigid trimester framework of *Roe v. Wade*. To promote the State's profound interest in potential life, throughout pregnancy the State may take measures to ensure that the woman's choice is informed, and measures designed to advance this interest will not be invalidated as long as their purpose is to persuade the woman to choose childbirth over abortion. These measures must not be an undue burden on the right.

(c)   As with any medical procedure, the State may enact regulations to further the health or safety of a woman seeking an abortion. Unnecessary health regulations that have the purpose or effect of presenting a substantial obstacle to a woman seeking an abortion impose an undue burden on the right.

(d)   Our adoption of the undue burden analysis does not disturb the central holding of *Roe v. Wade,* and we reaffirm that holding. Regardless of whether exceptions are made for particular circumstances, a State may not prohibit any woman from making the ultimate decision to terminate her pregnancy before viability.

(e)   We also reaffirm *Roe*'s holding that "subsequent to viability, the State in promoting its interest in the potentiality of human life may, if it chooses, regulate, and even proscribe, abortion except where it is necessary, in appropriate medical judgment, for the preservation of the life or health of the mother."

These principles control our assessment of the Pennsylvania statute, and we now turn to the issue of the validity of its challenged provisions. [Omitted and summarized above.]

JUSTICE STEVENS, concurring in part and dissenting in part. . . .

In my opinion, [sections] 3205(a)(2)(i)–(iii) of the Pennsylvania statute are unconstitutional. Those sections require a physician or counselor to provide the woman with a range of materials clearly designed to persuade her to choose not to undergo the abortion. . . .

JUSTICE BLACKMUN, concurring in part, concurring in the judgment in part, and dissenting in part. . . .

In one sense, the Court's approach is worlds apart from that of The Chief Justice and Justice Scalia. And yet, in another sense, the distance between the two approaches is short—the distance is but a single vote. I am 83 years old. I cannot remain on this Court forever, and when I do step down, the confirmation process for my successor well may focus on the issue before us today. That, I regret, may be exactly where the choice between the two worlds will be made.

CHIEF JUSTICE REHNQUIST, with whom JUSTICE WHITE, JUSTICE SCALIA, and JUSTICE THOMAS join, concurring in the judgment in part and dissenting in part.

The joint opinion, following its newly-minted variation on *stare decisis,* retains the outer shell of *Roe v. Wade,* but beats a wholesale retreat from the substance of that case. We believe that *Roe* was wrongly decided, and that it can and should be overruled consistently with our traditional approach to *stare decisis* in constitutional cases. We [sh]ould uphold the challenged provisions of the Pennsylvania statute in their entirety. . . . Unlike marriage, procreation and contraception, abortion "involves the purposeful termination of potential life." *Harris v. McRae,* (1980). . . .

The joint opinion of Justices O'Connor, Kennedy, and Souter cannot bring itself to say that *Roe* was correct as an original matter, but the authors are of the view that "the immediate question is not the soundness of *Roe's* resolution of the issue, but the precedential force that must be accorded to its holding." Instead of claiming that *Roe* was correct as a matter of original constitutional interpretation, the opinion therefore contains an elaborate discussion of *stare decisis*. This discussion of the principle of *stare decisis* appears to be almost entirely dicta, because the joint opinion does not apply that principle in dealing with *Roe*. *Roe* decided that a woman had a fundamental right to an abortion. The joint opinion rejects that view. *Roe* decided that abortion regulations were to be subjected to "strict scrutiny" and could be justified only in the light of "compelling state interests." The joint opinion rejects that view. *Roe* analyzed abortion regulation under a rigid trimester framework, a framework which has guided this Court's decisionmaking for 19 years. The joint opinion rejects that framework. . . .

The joint opinion discusses several *stare decisis* factors which, it asserts, point toward retaining a portion of *Roe*. Two of these factors are that the main "factual underpinning" of *Roe* has remained the same, and that its doctrinal foundation is no weaker now than it was in 1973. [S]urely there is no requirement, in considering whether to depart from *stare decisis* in a constitutional case, that a decision be more wrong now than it was at the time it was rendered. If that were true, the most outlandish constitutional decision could survive forever, based simply on the fact that it was no more outlandish later than it was when originally rendered. . . .

The joint opinion also points to the reliance interests involved in this context in its effort to explain why precedent must be followed for precedent's sake. . . . The Court today cuts back on the protection afforded by *Roe,* and no one claims that this action defeats any reliance interest in the disavowed trimester framework. . . .

Apparently realizing that conventional *stare decisis* principles do not support its position, the joint opinion advances a belief that retaining a portion of *Roe* is necessary to protect the "legitimacy" of this Court. . . . Under this principle, when the Court has ruled on a divisive issue, it is apparently prevented from overruling that decision for the sole reason that it was incorrect, *unless opposition to the original decision has died away.* [B]ecause the Court's duty is to ignore public opinion and criticism on issues that come before it, its members are in perhaps the worst position to judge whether a decision divides the Nation deeply enough to justify such uncommon protection. . . .

The joint opinion also agrees that the Court acted properly in rejecting the doctrine of "separate but equal" in *Brown*. [A]dherence to *Roe* today under the guise of "legitimacy" would seem to resemble more closely adherence to *Plessy* on the same ground. . . . *Brown* simply recognized, as Justice Harlan had recognized beforehand, that the Fourteenth Amendment does not permit racial segregation. . . .

[We] think [a] woman's interest in having an abortion is a form of liberty protected by the Due Process Clause, but States may regulate abortion procedures in ways rationally related to a legitimate state interest. . . .

JUSTICE SCALIA, with whom THE CHIEF JUSTICE, JUSTICE WHITE, and JUSTICE THOMAS join, concurring in the judgment in part and dissenting in part.

. . . States may, if they wish, permit abortion-on-demand, but the Constitution does not *require* them to do so. The permissibility of abortion, and the limitations upon it, are to be resolved like most important questions in our democracy: by citizens trying to persuade one another and then voting. . . . A State's choice between two positions on which reasonable people can disagree is constitutional even when (as is often the case) it intrudes upon a "liberty" in the absolute sense. Laws against bigamy, for example—which entire societies of reasonable people disagree with—intrude upon men and women's liberty to marry and live with one another. But bigamy happens not to be a liberty specially "protected" by the Constitution.

That is, quite simply, the issue in this case: not whether the power of a woman to abort her unborn child is a "liberty" in the absolute sense; or even whether it is a liberty of great importance to many women. Of course it is both. The issue is whether it is a liberty protected by the Constitution of the United States. I am sure it is not. I reach that conclusion not because of anything so exalted as my views concerning the "concept of existence, of meaning, of the universe, and of the mystery of human life." Rather, I reach it for the same reason I reach the conclusion that bigamy is not constitutionally protected—because of two simple facts: (1) the Constitution says absolutely nothing about it, and (2) the longstanding traditions of American society have permitted it to be legally proscribed.[1] . . .

---

[1]   The Court's suggestion that adherence to tradition would require us to uphold laws against interracial marriage is entirely wrong. Any tradition in that case was contradicted *by a text*—an Equal Protection Clause that explicitly establishes racial equality as a constitutional value. See *Loving v. Virginia* (1967). . . . The enterprise launched in *Roe v. Wade*, by contrast, sought to establish—in the teeth of a clear, contrary tradition—a value found nowhere in the constitutional text.

[The] argument of abortion opponents is that what the Court calls the fetus and what others call the unborn child *is a human life*. Thus, whatever answer *Roe* came up with after conducting its "balancing" is bound to be wrong, unless it is correct that the human fetus is in some critical sense merely potentially human. There is of course no way to determine that as a legal matter; it is in fact a value judgment. Some societies have considered newborn children not yet human, or the incompetent elderly no longer so. [T]he best the Court can do to explain how it is that the word "liberty" *must* be thought to include the right to destroy human fetuses is to rattle off a collection of adjectives that simply decorate a value judgment and conceal a political choice. . . .

"Liberty finds no refuge in a jurisprudence of doubt."

One might have feared to encounter this august and sonorous phrase in an opinion defending the real *Roe v. Wade*, rather than the revised version fabricated today by the authors of the joint opinion. [T]o come across this phrase in the joint opinion—which calls upon federal district judges to apply an "undue burden" standard as doubtful in application as it is unprincipled in origin—is really more than one should have to bear. . . . Reason finds no refuge in this jurisprudence of confusion.

". . . the reservations any of us may have in reaffirming the central holding of *Roe* are outweighed by the explication of individual liberty we have given combined with the force of *stare decisis*."

The [Court] insists upon the necessity of adhering not to all of *Roe,* but only to what it calls the "central holding." It seems to me that *stare decisis* ought to be applied even to the doctrine of *stare decisis,* and I confess never to have heard of this new, keep-what-you-want-and-throw-away-the-rest version. . . .

"Where, in the performance of its judicial duties, the Court decides a case in such a way as to resolve the sort of intensely divisive controversy reflected in *Roe* . . ., its decision has a dimension that the resolution of the normal case does not carry. It is the dimension present whenever the Court's interpretation of the Constitution calls the contending sides of a

---

There is, of course, no comparable tradition barring recognition of a "liberty interest" in carrying one's child to term free from state efforts to kill it. For that reason, it does not follow that the Constitution does not protect childbirth simply because it does not protect abortion. The Court's contention, that the only way to protect childbirth is to protect abortion shows the utter bankruptcy of constitutional analysis deprived of tradition as a validating factor. It drives one to say that the only way to protect the right to eat is to acknowledge the constitutional right to starve oneself to death.

national controversy to end their national division by accepting a common mandate rooted in the Constitution.”

The Court's description of the place of *Roe* in the social history of the United States is unrecognizable. [*Roe* did not] *resolve* the deeply divisive issue of abortion; it did more than anything else to nourish it, by elevating it to the national level where it is infinitely more difficult to resolve. National politics were not plagued by abortion protests, national abortion lobbying, or abortion marches on Congress, before *Roe v. Wade* was decided. . . . *Roe*'s mandate for abortion-on-demand destroyed the compromises of the past, rendered compromise impossible for the future, and required the entire issue to be resolved uniformly, at the national level. . . .

“[T]o overrule under fire . . . would subvert the Court's legitimacy. . . .” . . .

. . . I am appalled by, the Court's suggestion that the decision whether to stand by an erroneous constitutional decision must be strongly influenced—*against* overruling, no less—by the substantial and continuing public opposition the decision has generated. [T]he Court was covered with dishonor and deprived of legitimacy by *Dred Scott v. Sandford* (1857), an erroneous (and widely opposed) opinion that it did not abandon [until *Brown*]. [W]e have been subjected to what the Court calls “political pressure” by *both* sides of this issue. Maybe today's decision *not* to overrule *Roe* will be seen as buckling to pressure from *that* direction. . . .

What makes all this relevant to the bothersome application of “political pressure” against the Court are the twin facts that the American people love democracy and the American people are not fools. As long as this Court thought (and the people thought) that we Justices were doing essentially lawyers' work up here—reading text and discerning our society's traditional understanding of that text—the public pretty much left us alone. [I]f in reality our process of constitutional adjudication consists primarily of making *value judgments* . . . then a free and intelligent people's attitude towards us can be expected to be (*ought* to be) quite different. The people know that their value judgments are quite as good as those taught in any law school—maybe better. [If] our Constitution has somehow accidentally committed [value judgments] to the Supreme Court, at least we can have a sort of plebiscite each time a new nominee to that body is put forward. Justice Blackmun not only regards this prospect with equanimity, he solicits it. . . .

NOTES

1.   Some state courts are allowing wrongful death actions brought by non-viable fetuses. (Some fetuses as young as 20 weeks are now viable.) In the typical case, the pregnant woman suffers a miscarriage because of an accident (*e.g.*, tainted food) and then sues for wrongful death on behalf of the fetus. Some abortion rights groups oppose this trend in the law: "Recognition of the [nonviable] fetus as an individual person is a back-door way to undermine the rights guaranteed" by *Roe v. Wade*, said Kathryn Kolbert, of the Center for Reproductive Law & Policy, a group advocating abortion rights. Charlotte Snead, of West Virginians for Life, replied that the women-plaintiffs in these cases "were robbed of their choice." Without the injury, "there would've been a normal child."[13] What do you think?

2.   **PARTIAL BIRTH ABORTION.** *Gonzales v. Carhart*, 550 U.S. 124, 127 S.Ct. 1610, 167 L.Ed.2d 480 (2007). Congress passed the Partial-Birth Abortion Ban Act of 2003 (Act). The Act defined "partial-birth abortion" as occurring when the doctor "(A) deliberately and intentionally vaginally delivers a living fetus until, in the case of a head-first presentation, the entire fetal head is outside the [mother's] body . . ., or, in the case of breech presentation, any part of the fetal trunk past the navel is outside the [mother's] body . . ., for the purpose of performing an overt act that the person knows will kill the partially delivered living fetus"; and "(B) performs the overt act, other than completion of delivery, that kills the fetus." The Act governs any physician who is "in or affecting interstate or foreign commerce."[14] The Act thus defines Partial-Birth Abortion to prohibit what is called "intact D & E." It "does not prohibit the D & E procedure in which the fetus is removed in parts."

Kennedy, J., speaking for the Court (joined by Roberts, C. J., & Scalia, Thomas, & Alito, JJ.), upheld the law. The Court applied *Planned Parenthood v. Casey*, although it "did not find support from all those who join the instant opinion." A "premise central" to *Casey*'s "conclusion—that the government has a legitimate and substantial interest in preserving and promoting fetal life—would

---

[13]   Frances A. McMorris, *Courts are Giving New Rights to Fetuses*, Wall St. Jrl., Sept. 4, 1996, at B1, col. 4, 5 & B2 at col. 4.

[14]   Thomas, J., filed a concurring opinion, in which Scalia, J., joined. Because no litigant raised the issue, "whether the Act constitutes a permissible exercise of Congress' power under the Commerce Clause is not before the Court."

be repudiated were the Court now to affirm the judgments of the Courts of Appeals."

First, this Act does not "impose an undue burden, as a facial matter," because its restrictions on second-trimester abortions are not "too broad." Congress was moved by testimony such as a nurse's description of an "intact D & E" abortion on a 26½-week fetus:

> "Dr. Haskell went in with forceps and grabbed the baby's legs and pulled them down into the birth canal. Then he delivered the baby's body and the arms—everything but the head. The doctor kept the head right inside the uterus. . . . The baby's little fingers were clasping and unclasping, and his little feet were kicking. Then the doctor stuck the scissors in the back of his head, and the baby's arms jerked out . . . The doctor . . . stuck a high-powered suction tube into the opening, and sucked the baby's brains out. Now the baby went completely limp. . . . He cut the umbilical cord and delivered the placenta. He threw the baby in a pan, along with the placenta and the instruments he had just used.

Carhart said that it does not interpret *Casey's* requirement of a health exception to be "tantamount to allowing a doctor to choose the abortion method he or she might prefer. Where it has a rational basis to act, and it does not impose an undue burden, the State may use its regulatory power to bar certain procedures and substitute others, all in furtherance of its legitimate interests in regulating the medical profession in order to promote respect for life, including life of the unborn." Congress found this method of abortion "had a 'disturbing similarity to the killing of a newborn infant,' Congressional Findings (14)(L)." It is reasonable to infer that "a necessary effect of the regulation and the knowledge it conveys will be to encourage some women to carry the infant to full term, thus reducing the absolute number of late-term abortions."

The *Carhart* dissent argued that the standard D & E is "as brutal, if not more, than intact D & E, so that the legislation accomplishes little." The Court responded that it would be ironic if we were "first to conclude a ban on both D & E and intact D &

E was overbroad and then to say it is irrational to ban only intact D & E because that does not proscribe both procedures."

On the health question, the Court said, "The prohibition in the Act would be unconstitutional, under precedents we here assume to be controlling, if it 'subject[ed] [women] to significant health risks.' " Respondents presented "evidence that intact D & E may be the safest method of abortion," but other doctors contradicted this evidence and "considered D & E always to be a safe alternative." Given this "medical disagreement," the "Act can stand when this medical uncertainty exists." "The law need not give abortion doctors unfettered choice in the course of their medical practice, nor should it elevate their status above other physicians in the medical community." Another reason the facial attack fails is that there are alternative procedures, such as D & E.

The Court did not "place dispositive weight on Congress' findings." Some findings were inaccurate (*e.g.*, that no medical schools teach "intact D & E"). On the other hand, the Court also rejected respondents' argument that the statute must contain a health exception if "substantial medical authority supports the proposition that banning a particular procedure could endanger women's health." It is incorrect to interpret *Stenberg* "to leave no margin of error for legislatures to act in the face of medical uncertainty."

Finally, the lower courts should not have entertained these attacks on the law "on its face." The proper method to consider exceptions is by an as-applied challenge. This is the proper manner to protect the woman's health, "if it can be shown that in discrete and well-defined instances a particular condition has or is likely to occur in which the procedure prohibited by the Act must be used."

Ginsburg, J., filed a dissenting opinion, that Stevens, Souter, and Breyer, JJ., joined. "Today's decision is alarming. [F]or the first time since *Roe*, the Court blesses a prohibition with no exception safeguarding a woman's health." The Act "saves not a single fetus from destruction, for it targets only a method of performing abortion." The law does not ban non-intact D & E, but "why not," since that procedure "could equally be characterized as 'brutal,' " because it involves " 'tear[ing] [a fetus] apart' and 'ripp[ing] off' its limbs."

2.4.4   Sexual Orientation

In *Baker v. Nelson*, 291 Minn. 310, 191 N.W.2d 185 (1971), the Supreme Court of Minnesota held that state law did not allow persons of the same sex to marry and that this law did not violate the U.S. Constitution. The plaintiffs (a gay couple who applied for a marriage license) appealed to the U.S. Supreme Court, on the grounds that the Minnesota statute limiting marriage to people of the opposite sex violated their fundamental right to marry under the Due Process Clause, discriminated on the sex, in violation of Equal Protection, and violated their privacy rights under the Ninth Amendment. The U.S. Supreme Court, without oral argument, dismissed plaintiffs' claim. The entire opinion is one sentence: "The appeal is dismissed for want of a substantial federal question." *Baker v. Nelson*, 409 U.S. 810, 93 S. Ct. 37, 34 L. Ed. 2d 65 (1972).[15]

Bowers v. Hardwick, ___ U.S. ___, 106 S.Ct. 2841, 92 L.Ed.2d 140 (1986) (5 to 4) upheld the constitutionality of a Georgia sodomy law as applied to homosexuals. Justice White, for the Court, said: "The Court is most vulnerable and comes nearest to illegitimacy when it deal with judge-made constitutional law having little or no cognizable roots in the language or design of the Constitution. That this is so was painfully demonstrated by the face-off between the Executive and the Court in the 1930's. . . ." Justice Blackmun, dissenting (joined by Brennan, Marshall, & Stevens, JJ., quoted Justice Brandeis and concluded: "this case is about the most comprehensive of rights and the right most valued by civilized men, namely, the right to be let alone." Depriving "individuals of the right to choose for themselves how to conduct their intimate relationships poses a far greater threat to the values most deeply rooted in our Nation's history than tolerance of nonconformity could ever do."

Romer v. Evans, 517 U.S. 620, 116 S.Ct. 1620, 134 L.Ed.2d 855 (1996), involved an amendment to the state constitution. After several various Colorado municipalities passed ordinances banning discrimination based on sexual orientation in housing, employment, education, public accommodations, health

---

[15]   Later, *Obergefell v. Hodges*, 576 U.S. ___, 135 S. Ct. 2584, 2598, 192 L. Ed. 2d 609 (2015), in the course of holding that there is a constitutional right to same sex marriage, briefly referred to this decision, overruled it, and said, "It cannot be denied that this Court's cases describing the right to marry presumed a relationship involving opposite-sex partners. The Court, like many institutions, has made assumptions defined by the world and time of which it is a part. This was evident in *Baker v. Nelson*, a one-line summary decision issued in 1972, holding the exclusion of same-sex couples from marriage did not present a substantial federal question."

and welfare services, and other transactions and activities, Colorado voters adopted an Amendment to the State Constitution, which precluded all legislative, executive, or judicial action at any level of state or local government designed to protect the status of persons based on their "homosexual, lesbian or bisexual orientation, conduct, practices or relationships." The Supreme Court, speaking through Justice Kennedy, held (6 to 3) that this state amendment violated the U.S. Constitution. The dissent (Scalia, J., joined by Rehnquist, C.J. & Thomas, J.) cited *Bowers*, but the majority did not. The majority said the Colorado amendment's "sheer breadth" "seems inexplicable by anything but animus toward the class that it affects; it lacks a rational relationship to legitimate state interests."

Justice Kennedy, for the Court in, *Lawrence v. Texas*, 539 U.S. 558, 123 S.Ct. 2472, 156 L.Ed.2d 508 (2003), held (6 to 3) overruled *Bowers v. Hardwick*. Kennedy relied on *Planned Parenthood of Southeaster Pa. v. Casey* (1992), and in particular quoted this language, "At the heart of liberty is the right to define one's own concept of existence, of meaning, of the universe, and of the mystery of human life. Beliefs about these matters could not define the attributes of personhood were they formed under compulsion of the State." Kennedy also relied on *Roemer v. Evans*. O'Connor, J., concurring in the judgment, relied on equal protection (the statute only applied to gays), and added that this decision does not uphold gay marriage: "Texas cannot assert any legitimate state interest here, such as national security or preserving the traditional institution of marriage. Unlike the moral disapproval of same-sex relations—the asserted state interest in this case—other reasons exist to promote the institution of marriage beyond mere moral disapproval of an excluded group."

Scalia, J., joined by Rehnquist, C.J. & Thomas, J., dissented, "nowhere does the Court's opinion declare that homosexual sodomy is a 'fundamental right' under the Due Process Clause; nor does it subject the Texas Law to the standard of review that would be appropriate (strict scrutiny) if homosexual sodomy *were* a 'fundamental right.' " Thomas, J., in his separate dissent, said that the Texas law is "uncommonly silly," and, "If I were a member of the Texas Legislature, I would vote to repeal it."

In *United States v. Windsor*, 570 U.S. ___, 133 S.Ct. 2675, 186 L.Ed.2d 808 (2013), a taxpayer (the surviving spouse of same-sex couple) sued because federal tax laws did not give her the benefit of a marital deduction due to definition of "marriage" and "spouse," in the Defense of Marriage Act (DOMA). She sued for a refund of federal estate taxes ($363,053) and for a declaration that this particular provision of DOMA violated the Fifth Amendment. Kennedy, J., for the Court

(5 to 4) agreed. The federal law, which defined "marriage" as a legal union between a man and a woman and "spouse" as a person of the opposite sex deprived Windsor her "liberty" under the Fifth Amendment. DOMA deviated from the "usual tradition of recognizing and accepting state definitions of marriage," which "deprive same-sex couples of the benefits and responsibilities that come with the federal recognition of their marriages."

Roberts, C.J., dissented, as well as Alito, J., joined by Thomas, J. In Scalia, J., joined by Thomas, J., and Roberts, J., in part, dissented and said, "today's prohibition of laws excluding same-sex marriage is confined to the Federal Government (leaving the second, state-law shoe to be dropped later, maybe next Term). But I am only guessing." The guess was correct, because the next term the Court held that the Constitution guarantees same sex marriage.

OBERGEFELL V. HODGES
576 U.S. ___, 135 S.Ct. 2584, 192 L.Ed.2d 609 (2015)

JUSTICE KENNEDY delivered the opinion of the Court.

The Constitution promises liberty to all within its reach, a liberty that includes certain specific rights that allow persons, within a lawful realm, to define and express their identity. The petitioners in these cases seek to find that liberty by marrying someone of the same sex and having their marriages deemed lawful on the same terms and conditions as marriages between persons of the opposite sex.

These cases come from Michigan, Kentucky, Ohio, and Tennessee, States that define marriage as a union between one man and one woman. . . . The Court of Appeals held that a State has no constitutional obligation to license same-sex marriages or to recognize same-sex marriages performed out of State. . . . This Court granted review, limited to two questions. The first, presented by the cases from Michigan and Kentucky, is whether the Fourteenth Amendment requires a State to license a marriage between two people of the same sex. The second, presented by the cases from Ohio, Tennessee, and, again, Kentucky, is whether the Fourteenth Amendment requires a State to recognize a same-sex marriage licensed and performed in a State which does grant that right. . . .

From their beginning to their most recent page, the annals of human history reveal the transcendent importance of marriage. The lifelong union of a man and a woman always has promised nobility and dignity to all persons, without regard to their station in life. Marriage is sacred to those who live by their religions and offers unique fulfillment to those who find meaning in the secular realm. . . .

The centrality of marriage to the human condition makes it unsurprising that the institution has existed for millennia and across civilizations. Since the dawn of history, marriage has transformed strangers into relatives, binding families and societies together. Confucius taught that marriage lies at the foundation of government. This wisdom was echoed centuries later and half a world away by Cicero, who wrote, "The first bond of society is marriage; next, children; and then the family." There are untold references to the beauty of marriage in religious and philosophical texts spanning time, cultures, and faiths, as well as in art and literature in all their forms. It is fair and necessary to say these references were based on the understanding that marriage is a union between two persons of the opposite sex.

[Respondents say] it would demean a timeless institution if the concept and lawful status of marriage were extended to two persons of the same sex. Marriage, in their view, is by its nature a gender-differentiated union of man and woman. This view long has been held—and continues to be held—in good faith by reasonable and sincere people here and throughout the world.

The petitioners acknowledge this history but contend that these cases cannot end there. . . . Far from seeking to devalue marriage, the petitioners seek it for themselves because of their respect—and need—for its privileges and responsibilities. And their immutable nature dictates that same-sex marriage is their only real path to this profound commitment. . . .

The ancient origins of marriage confirm its centrality, but it has not stood in isolation from developments in law and society. The history of marriage is one of both continuity and change. That institution—even as confined to opposite-sex relations—has evolved over time. . . .

This Court first gave detailed consideration to the legal status of homosexuals in *Bowers* v. *Hardwick*, 478 U. S. 186 (1986). There it upheld the constitutionality of a Georgia law deemed to criminalize certain homosexual acts. Ten years later, in *Romer* v. *Evans*, 517 U. S. 620 (1996), the Court invalidated an amendment to Colorado's Constitution that sought to foreclose any branch or political subdivision of the State from protecting persons against discrimination based on sexual orientation. Then, in 2003, the Court overruled *Bowers*, holding that laws making same-sex intimacy a crime "demea[n] the lives of homosexual persons." *Lawrence* v. *Texas*, 539 U. S. 558, 575. . . .

The nature of injustice is that we may not always see it in our own times. The generations that wrote and ratified the Bill of Rights and the Fourteenth Amendment did not presume to know the extent of freedom in all of its dimensions, and so they entrusted to future generations a charter protecting the right of all persons to enjoy liberty as we learn its meaning. When new insight reveals discord between the Constitution's central protections and a received legal stricture, a claim to liberty must be addressed.

[T]he Court has long held the right to marry is protected by the Constitution. In *Loving* v. *Virginia*, 388 U. S. 1, 12 (1967), which invalidated bans on interracial unions, a unanimous Court held marriage is "one of the vital personal rights essential to the orderly pursuit of happiness by free men." The Court reaffirmed that holding in *Zablocki* v. *Redhail*, 434 U. S. 374, 384 (1978), which held the right to marry was burdened by a law prohibiting fathers who were behind on child support from marrying. The Court again applied this principle in *Turner* v. *Safley*, 482 U. S. 78, 95 (1987), which held the right to marry was abridged by regulations limiting the privilege of prison inmates to marry. Over time and in other contexts, the Court has reiterated that the right to marry is fundamental under the Due Process Clause. *Griswold, supra, Skinner* v. *Oklahoma ex rel. Williamson*, 316 U. S. 535, 541 (1942).

[T]his Court's cases describing the right to marry presumed a relationship involving opposite-sex partners. The Court, like many institutions, has made assumptions defined by the world and time of which it is a part. This was evident in *Baker* v. *Nelson*, 409 U. S. 810, a one-line summary decision issued in 1972, holding the exclusion of same-sex couples from marriage did not present a substantial federal question.

[I]n assessing whether the force and rationale of its cases apply to same-sex couples, the Court must respect the basic reasons why the right to marry has been long protected. This analysis compels the conclusion that same-sex couples may exercise the right to marry. The four principles and traditions to be discussed demonstrate that the reasons marriage is fundamental under the Constitution apply with equal force to same-sex couples.

A first premise of the Court's relevant precedents is that the right to personal choice regarding marriage is inherent in the concept of individual autonomy. This abiding connection between marriage and liberty is why *Loving* invalidated interracial marriage bans under the Due Process Clause. . . . The nature of marriage is that, through its enduring bond, two persons together can find other freedoms, such as expression, intimacy, and spirituality. . . .

A second principle in this Court's jurisprudence is that the right to marry is fundamental because it supports a two-person union unlike any other in its importance to the committed individuals. This point was central to *Griswold* v.

Connecticut, which held the Constitution protects the right of married couples to use contraception. . . .

A third basis for protecting the right to marry is that it safeguards children and families and thus draws meaning from related rights of childrearing, procreation, and education. [M]any same-sex couples provide loving and nurturing homes to their children, whether biological or adopted. . . . Excluding same-sex couples from marriage thus conflicts with a central premise of the right to marry. Without the recognition, stability, and predictability marriage offers, their children suffer the stigma of knowing their families are somehow lesser. They also suffer the significant material costs of being raised by unmarried parents, relegated through no fault of their own to a more difficult and uncertain family life. The marriage laws at issue here thus harm and humiliate the children of same-sex couples.

That is not to say the right to marry is less meaningful for those who do not or cannot have children. An ability, desire, or promise to procreate is not and has not been a prerequisite for a valid marriage in any State. In light of precedent protecting the right of a married couple not to procreate, it cannot be said the Court or the States have conditioned the right to marry on the capacity or commitment to procreate. The constitutional marriage right has many aspects, of which childbearing is only one.

Fourth and finally, this Court's cases and the Nation's traditions make clear that marriage is a keystone of our social order. [J]ust as a couple vows to support each other, so does society pledge to support the couple, offering symbolic recognition and material benefits to protect and nourish the union. Indeed, while the States are in general free to vary the benefits they confer on all married couples, they have throughout our history made marriage the basis for an expanding list of governmental rights, benefits, and responsibilities. These aspects of marital status include: taxation; inheritance and property rights; rules of intestate succession; spousal privilege in the law of evidence; hospital access; medical decisionmaking authority; adoption rights; the rights and benefits of survivors; birth and death certificates; professional ethics rules; campaign finance restrictions; workers' compensation benefits; health insurance; and child custody, support, and visitation rules. [B]y virtue of their exclusion from that institution, same-sex couples are denied the constellation of benefits that the States have linked to marriage. This harm results in more than just material burdens. . . . It demeans gays and lesbians for the State to lock them out of a central institution of the Nation's society. Same-sex couples, too, may aspire to the transcendent purposes of marriage and seek fulfillment in its highest meaning.

The limitation of marriage to opposite-sex couples may long have seemed natural and just, but its inconsistency with the central meaning of the fundamental right to marry is now manifest. With that knowledge must come the recognition that laws excluding same-sex couples from the marriage right impose stigma and injury of the kind prohibited by our basic charter.

. . . Many who deem same-sex marriage to be wrong reach that conclusion based on decent and honorable religious or philosophical premises, and neither they nor their beliefs are disparaged here. But when that sincere, personal opposition becomes enacted law and public policy, the necessary consequence is to put the imprimatur of the State itself on an exclusion that soon demeans or stigmatizes those whose own liberty is then denied. Under the Constitution, same-sex couples seek in marriage the same legal treatment as opposite-sex couples, and it would disparage their choices and diminish their personhood to deny them this right.

The right of same-sex couples to marry that is part of the liberty promised by the Fourteenth Amendment is derived, too, from that Amendment's guarantee of the equal protection of the laws. The Due Process Clause and the Equal Protection Clause are connected in a profound way, though they set forth independent principles. Rights implicit in liberty and rights secured by equal protection may rest on different precepts and are not always co-extensive, yet in some instances each may be instructive as to the meaning and reach of the other. [T]he right to marry is a fundamental right inherent in the liberty of the person, and under the Due Process and Equal Protection Clauses of the Fourteenth Amendment couples of the same-sex may not be deprived of that right and that liberty. The Court now holds that same-sex couples may exercise the fundamental right to marry. No longer may this liberty be denied to them. *Baker* v. *Nelson* must be and now is overruled, and the State laws challenged by Petitioners in these cases are now held invalid to the extent they exclude same-sex couples from civil marriage on the same terms and conditions as opposite-sex couples.

There may be an initial inclination in these cases to proceed with caution—to await further legislation, litigation, and debate. [T]he Constitution contemplates that democracy is the appropriate process for change, so long as that process does not abridge fundamental rights. [However, the] dynamic of our constitutional system is that individuals need not await legislative action before asserting a fundamental right. The Nation's courts are open to injured individuals who come to them to vindicate their own direct, personal stake in our basic charter. An individual can invoke a right to constitutional protection when he or she is harmed, even if the broader public disagrees and even if the legislature refuses to act. . . .

Finally, it must be emphasized that religions, and those who adhere to religious doctrines, may continue to advocate with utmost, sincere conviction that, by divine precepts, same-sex marriage should not be condoned. The First Amendment ensures that religious organizations and persons are given proper protection as they seek to teach the principles that are so fulfilling and so central to their lives and faiths, and to their own deep aspirations to continue the family structure they have long revered. The same is true of those who oppose same-sex marriage for other reasons. In turn, those who believe allowing same-sex marriage is proper or indeed essential, whether as a matter of religious conviction or secular belief, may engage those who disagree with their view in an open and searching debate. The Constitution, however, does not permit the State to bar same-sex couples from marriage on the same terms as accorded to couples of the opposite sex.

. . . Leaving the current state of affairs in place would maintain and promote instability and uncertainty. For some couples, even an ordinary drive into a neighboring State to visit family or friends risks causing severe hardship in the event of a spouse's hospitalization while across state lines. In light of the fact that many States already allow same-sex marriage—and hundreds of thousands of these marriages already have occurred—the disruption caused by the recognition bans is significant and ever-growing. . . . The Court, in this decision, holds same-sex couples may exercise the fundamental right to marry in all States. It follows that the Court also must hold—and it now does hold—that there is no lawful basis for a State to refuse to recognize a lawful same-sex marriage performed in another State on the ground of its same-sex character. . . . The judgment of the Court of Appeals for the Sixth Circuit is reversed. It is so ordered.

CHIEF JUSTICE ROBERTS, with whom JUSTICE SCALIA and JUSTICE THOMAS join, dissenting.

[T]his Court is not a legislature. Whether same-sex marriage is a good idea should be of no concern to us. Under the Constitution, judges have power to say what the law is, not what it should be. The people who ratified the Constitution authorized courts to exercise "neither force nor will but merely judgment." The Federalist No. 78.

Although the policy arguments for extending marriage to same-sex couples may be compelling, the legal arguments for requiring such an extension are not. The fundamental right to marry does not include a right to make a State change its definition of marriage. And a State's decision to maintain the meaning of marriage that has persisted in every culture throughout human history can hardly be called irrational. In short, our Constitution does not enact any one theory of marriage. The people of a State are free to expand marriage to include same-sex couples, or to retain the historic definition.

Today, however, the Court takes the extraordinary step of ordering every State to license and recognize same-sex marriage. Many people will rejoice at this decision, and I begrudge none their celebration. But for those who believe in a government of laws, not of men, the majority's approach is deeply disheartening. Supporters of same-sex marriage have achieved considerable success persuading their fellow citizens—through the democratic process—to adopt their view. That ends today. Five lawyers have closed the debate and enacted their own vision of marriage as a matter of constitutional law. Stealing this issue from the people will for many cast a cloud over same-sex marriage, making a dramatic social change that much more difficult to accept.

[T]he Court invalidates the marriage laws of more than half the States and orders the transformation of a social institution that has formed the basis of human society for millennia, for the Kalahari Bushmen and the Han Chinese, the Carthaginians and the Aztecs. Just who do we think we are? . . .

[U]nder our precedents, the Constitution protects a right to marry and requires States to apply their marriage laws equally. The real question in these cases is what constitutes "marriage," or—more precisely—*who decides* what constitutes "marriage"? [T]he majority acknowledges, marriage "has existed for millennia and across civilizations." For all those millennia, across all those civilizations, "marriage" referred to only one relationship: the union of a man and a woman. Tr. of Oral Arg. (petitioners conceding that they are not aware of any society that permitted same-sex marriage before 2001). . . . Marriage did not come about as a result of a political movement, discovery, disease, war, religious doctrine, or any other moving force of world history—and certainly not as a result of a prehistoric decision to exclude gays and lesbians. It arose in the nature of things to meet a vital need: ensuring that children are conceived by a mother and father committed to raising them in the stable conditions of a lifelong relationship. [F]or the good of children and society, sexual relations that can lead to procreation should occur only between a man and a woman committed to a lasting bond. Society has recognized that bond as marriage. And by bestowing a respected status and material benefits on married couples, society encourages men and women to conduct sexual relations within marriage rather than without. As one prominent scholar put it, "Marriage is a socially arranged solution for the problem of getting people to stay together and care for children that the mere desire for children, and the sex that makes children possible, does not solve." J. Q. Wilson, The Marriage Problem 41 (2002).

This singular understanding of marriage has prevailed in the United States throughout our history. . . . The Constitution itself says nothing about marriage, and the Framers thereby entrusted the States with "[t]he whole subject of the domestic relations of husband and wife." *Windsor*. There is no dispute that every State at the founding—and every State throughout our history until a dozen years ago—defined marriage in the traditional, biologically rooted way. . . .

Petitioners first contend that the marriage laws of their States violate the Due Process Clause. The Solicitor General of the United States, appearing in support of petitioners, expressly disowned that position before this Court. The majority nevertheless resolves these cases for petitioners based almost entirely on the Due Process Clause.

. . . Stripped of its shiny rhetorical gloss, the majority's argument is that the Due Process Clause gives same-sex couples a fundamental right to marry because it will be good for them and for society. If I were a legislator, I would certainly consider that view as a matter of social policy. But as a judge, I find the majority's position indefensible as a matter of constitutional law.

Petitioners' "fundamental right" claim falls into the most sensitive category of constitutional adjudication. Petitioners do not contend that their States' marriage laws violate an *enumerated* constitutional right, such as the freedom of speech protected by the First Amendment. There is, after all, no "Companionship and Understanding" or "Nobility and Dignity" Clause in the Constitution. They argue instead that the laws violate a right *implied* by the Fourteenth Amendment's requirement that "liberty" may not be deprived without "due process of law." [The theory of "substantive" due process] is that some liberties are "so rooted in the traditions and conscience of our people as to be ranked as fundamental," and therefore cannot be deprived without compelling justification.

Allowing unelected federal judges to select which unenumerated rights rank as "fundamental"—and to strike down state laws on the basis of that determination—raises obvious concerns about the judicial role. . . . One immediate question invited by the majority's position is whether States may retain the definition of marriage as a union of two people. Cf. *Brown* v. *Buhman*, 947 F. Supp. 2d 1170 (Utah 2013), appeal pending, No. 14–4117 (CA10). Although the majority randomly inserts the adjective "two" in various places, it offers no reason at all why the two-person element of the core definition of marriage may be preserved while the man-woman element may not. Indeed, from the standpoint of history and tradition, a leap from opposite-sex marriage to same-sex marriage is much greater than one from a two-person union to plural unions, which have deep roots in some cultures around the world. If the majority is willing to take the big leap, it is hard to see how it can say no to the shorter one.

It is striking how much of the majority's reasoning would apply with equal force to the claim of a fundamental right to plural marriage. If "[t]here is dignity in the bond between two men or two women who seek to marry and in their autonomy to make such profound choices," why would there be any less dignity in the bond between three people who, in exercising their autonomy, seek to make the profound choice to marry? . . . See Bennett, Polyamory: The Next Sexual Revolution? Newsweek, July 28, 2009 (estimating 500,000 polyamorous families in the United States); Li, Married Lesbian "Throuple" Expecting First Child, N. Y. Post, Apr. 23, 2014; Otter, Three May Not Be a Crowd: The Case for a Constitutional Right to Plural Marriage, 64 Emory L. J. 1977 (2015).

Nowhere is the majority's extravagant conception of judicial supremacy more evident than in its description—and dismissal—of the public debate regarding same-sex marriage . . . Those who founded our country would not recognize the majority's conception of the judicial role. They after all risked their lives and fortunes for the precious right to govern themselves. [P]eople are in the midst of a serious and thoughtful public debate on the issue of same-sex marriage. They see voters carefully considering same-sex marriage, casting ballots in favor or opposed, and sometimes changing their minds. They see political leaders similarly reexamining their positions, and either reversing course or explaining adherence to old convictions confirmed anew. . . .

Respect for sincere religious conviction has led voters and legislators in every State that has adopted same-sex marriage democratically to include accommodations for religious practice. The majority's decision imposing same-sex marriage cannot, of course, create any such accommodations. The majority graciously suggests that religious believers may continue to "advocate" and "teach" their views of marriage. The First Amendment guarantees, however, the freedom to "*exercise*" religion. Ominously, that is not a word the majority uses. . . .

JUSTICE SCALIA, with whom JUSTICE THOMAS joins, dissenting.

. . . . Today's decree says that my Ruler, and the Ruler of 320 million Americans coast-to-coast, is a majority of the nine lawyers on the Supreme Court. The opinion in these cases is the furthest extension in fact—and the furthest extension one can even imagine—of the Court's claimed power to create "liberties" that the Constitution and its Amendments neglect to mention. This practice of constitutional revision by an unelected committee of nine, always accompanied (as it is today) by extravagant praise of liberty, robs the People of the most important liberty they asserted in the Declaration of Independence and won in the Revolution of 1776: the freedom to govern themselves. [E]lectorates of 11 States, either directly or through their representatives, chose to expand the traditional definition of marriage. Many more decided not to. Win or lose, advocates for both sides continued pressing their cases, secure in the knowledge that an electoral loss can be negated by a later electoral win. That is exactly how our system of government is supposed to work. . . .

Judges are selected precisely for their skill as lawyers; whether they reflect the policy views of a particular constituency is not (or should not be) relevant. Not surprisingly then, the Federal Judiciary is hardly a cross-section of America. Take, for example, this Court, which consists of only nine men and women, all of them successful lawyers who studied at Harvard or Yale Law School. Four of the nine are natives of New York City. Eight of them grew up in east-and west-coast States. Only one hails from the vast expanse in-between. Not a single Southwesterner or even, to tell the truth, a genuine Westerner (California does not count). Not a single evangelical Christian (a group that comprises about one quarter of Americans), or even a Protestant of any denomination. [T]o allow the policy question of same-sex marriage to be considered and resolved by a select, patrician, highly unrepresentative panel of nine is to violate a principle even more fundamental than no taxation without representation: no social transformation without representation. [W]hat really astounds is the hubris reflected in today's judicial Putsch. The five Justices who compose today's majority are entirely comfortable concluding that every State violated the Constitution for all of the 135 years between the Fourteenth Amendment's ratification and Massachusetts' permitting of same-sex marriages in 2003.

[The Court's] opinion is couched in a style that is as pretentious as its content is egotistic. It is one thing for separate concurring or dissenting opinions to contain extravagances, even silly extravagances, of thought and expression; it is something else for the official opinion of the Court to do so.[22] Of course the

---

[22] If, even as the price to be paid for a fifth vote, I ever joined an opinion for the Court that began: "The Constitution promises liberty to all within its reach, a liberty that includes certain specific rights that allow

opinion's showy profundities are often profoundly incoherent. "The nature of marriage is that, through its enduring bond, two persons together can find other freedoms, such as expression, intimacy, and spirituality." (Really? Who ever thought that intimacy and spirituality [whatever that means] were freedoms? And if intimacy is, one would think Freedom of Intimacy is abridged rather than expanded by marriage. Ask the nearest hippie. Expression, sure enough, *is* a freedom, but anyone in a long-lasting marriage will attest that that happy state constricts, rather than expands, what one can prudently say.) . . .

JUSTICE THOMAS, with whom JUSTICE SCALIA joins, dissenting. . . .

Numerous *amici*—even some not supporting the States—have cautioned the Court that its decision here will "have unavoidable and wide-ranging implications for religious liberty." In our society, marriage is not simply a governmental institution; it is a religious institution as well. Today's decision might change the former, but it cannot change the latter. [T]he two will come into conflict, particularly as individuals and churches are confronted with demands to participate in and endorse civil marriages between same-sex couples.

The majority appears unmoved by that inevitability. It makes only a weak gesture toward religious liberty in a single paragraph. And even that gesture indicates a misunderstanding of religious liberty in our Nation's tradition. Religious liberty is about more than just the protection for "religious organizations and persons . . . as they seek to teach the principles that are so fulfilling and so central to their lives and faiths." Religious liberty is about freedom of action in matters of religion generally, and the scope of that liberty is directly correlated to the civil restraints placed upon religious practice. . . .

JUSTICE ALITO, with whom JUSTICE SCALIA and JUSTICE THOMAS join, dissenting. . . .

Today's decision usurps the constitutional right of the people to decide whether to keep or alter the traditional understanding of marriage. [It also] will be used to vilify Americans who are unwilling to assent to the new orthodoxy. [T]he majority attempts, toward the end of its opinion, to reassure those who oppose same-sex marriage that their rights of conscience will be protected. [T]hose who cling to old beliefs will be able to whisper their thoughts in the recesses of their homes, but if they repeat those views in public, they will risk being labeled as bigots and treated as such by governments, employers, and schools. . . . Recalling

---

persons, within a lawful realm, to define and express their identity," I would hide my head in a bag. The Supreme Court of the United States has descended from the disciplined legal reasoning of John Marshall and Joseph Story to the mystical aphorisms of the fortune cookie.

the harsh treatment of gays and lesbians in the past, some may think that turnabout is fair play. But if that sentiment prevails, the Nation will experience bitter and lasting wounds. . . . Most Americans—understandably—will cheer or lament today's decision [b]ut all Americans, whatever their thinking on that issue, should worry about what the majority's claim of power portends.

NOTES

1. The majority never says that sexual orientation is a suspect class, subject to strict scrutiny. Does that affect the power of the state to prohibit private discrimination against gay marriage?

2. One of the major issues that *Obergefell* raises are the rights of those people who do not believe in gay marriage on religious grounds. To what extent can the state make them participate (or do what they view as participation) in same sex marriage. *Runyon v. McCrary*, 427 U.S. 160 (1976) held that a federal law, 42 U.S.C.A § 1981, forbids racial discrimination in making private contracts. The Court specifically said that it was not interpreting that statute to apply to private schools "that practice racial exclusion on religious grounds." *Heart of Atlanta Motel, Inc. v. United States*, 379 U.S. 241 (1964) [§ 6.3], upheld federal commerce power to prohibit racial discrimination in places of public accommodation, but that law exempted landlords who lived in the building and offered "not more than five rooms for rent." This statutory exemption exists to this day. In *Hurley v. Irish-American Gay, Lesbian and Bisexual Group of Boston*, 515 U.S. 557 (1995), gay, lesbian, and bisexual descendants of Irish immigrants sought to march as a group in the St. Patrick's Day parade. The parade's private organizers refused and the state supreme court held that this exclusion violated Massachusetts' public accommodation law, which prohibits discrimination on account of sexual orientation in places of public accommodation. Souter, J, for a unanimous Court, held that Massachusetts violated the First Amendment by requiring the defendants to alter the expressive content of their parade. If a KKK member asks a baker to create a cake saying, "black lives do not matter," can the state force the baker to do that? Even if the baker is the local head of the NAACP? Can the state, under its nondiscrimination laws, force a bakery owns by gays to create a cake that says, "Gay marriage is wrong"? Or, are these examples distinguishable?

3. Do these cases apply to individuals who (on free speech or free exercise grounds) do not want to participate in gay marriages? For example, the state

could provide that the baker cannot refuse to sell a cupcake to a customer because the customer is gay. [The parade organizers did not exclude gays as individuals; they did exclude a gay pride float.] However, the baker may argue that creating a wedding cake (unlike selling a cupcake) is expressive action, part of free speech. Is participating (or refusing to participate) in a wedding part of free expression, like a parade that excludes a gay pride float? Consider wedding photographers. Taking a passport photo is not a work of art but wedding photographers argue that taking a portfolio of wedding photos is (and they charge accordingly. Assume the wedding photographer says, "I will not participate in your wedding by taking photographs because I do not believe in gay weddings"? Is that any different than saying, "I will not participate in your wedding by taking photographs because you cuckolded me and now you are marrying my ex-wife"? Or, "I will not participate in your wedding by taking photographs because you ran over my neighbor's dog 10 years ago"? Does it matter, in deciding these issues, whether or not *Obergefell* held that sexual orientation is a suspect class?

4. North Carolina, shortly after *Obergefell* enacted a law allowing certain state officials to refuse to perform gay marriage duties if they cite a "sincerely held religious objection." In that same time-frame, the Texas Attorney General issued an opinion that justices of the peace, judges, county clerks and their employees have a constitutional right of their own to refuse to facilitate gay marriages, when there may be other county employees and judges willing to do the job. Is it constitutional for the legislature to allow state officials to bow out of gay marriage when the couple seeking the license merely secures it from another? If the law does not carve out an exception, is the state improperly creating a religious test for office, in violation of the First Amendment?

5. Justice Ginsburg, while on the D.C. Circuit, wrote a law review article arguing that *Roe v. Wade*, 410 U.S. 113 (1973), would have been more acceptable if it had not gone beyond a narrow ruling on the statute in the case., "The political process was moving . . ., not swiftly enough for advocates of quick, complete change, but majoritarian institutions were listening and acting. Heavy-handed judicial intervention was difficult to justify and appears to have provoked, not resolved, conflict." Ginsburg, *Some Thoughts on Autonomy and Equality in Relation to Roe v. Wade*, 63 N. C. L. Rev. 375, 385–86 (1985) (footnote omitted). Does that apply to this case?

6. Chief Justice Roberts' dissent cites *Brown v. Buhman*, 947 F. Supp. 2d 1170 (Utah 2013), appeal pending, No. 14–4117 (10th Cir.). In that case, a polygamist family challenged the constitutionality of Utah's bigamy statute. The district court ruled that the cohabitation prong of the Statute was "unconstitutional on numerous grounds and strikes it." The court allowed the statute "to remain in force as prohibiting bigamy in the literal sense—the fraudulent or otherwise impermissible possession of two purportedly valid marriage licenses for the purpose of entering into more than one purportedly legal marriage." The plaintiffs in this case are polygamous patriarch Kody Brown and matriarchs Meri Brown, Janelle Brown, Christine Brown, and Robyn Sullivan. The TV reality series, *Sister Wives*, featured the plaintiffs, Kody Brown, his four wives, and 17 children.

CHAPTER 3

The Second Amendment

3.1 THE SECOND AMENDMENT APPLIED TO THE FEDERAL GOVERNMENT

DISTRICT OF COLUMBIA V. HELLER

554 U.S. 570, 128 S.Ct. 2783, 171 L.Ed.2d 637 (2008)

JUSTICE SCALIA delivered the opinion of the Court.

We consider whether a District of Columbia prohibition on the possession of usable handguns in the home violates the Second Amendment to the Constitution.

I. The District of Columbia generally prohibits the possession of handguns. It is a crime to carry an unregistered firearm, and the registration of handguns is prohibited. See D.C.Code §§ 7–2501.01(12), 7–2502.01(a), 7–2502.02(a)(4) (2001). . . . District of Columbia law also requires residents to keep their lawfully owned firearms, such as registered long guns, "unloaded and dissembled or bound by a trigger lock or similar device" unless they are located in a place of business or are being used for lawful recreational activities.

Respondent Dick Heller is a D.C. special police officer authorized to carry a handgun while on duty at the Federal Judicial Center. He applied for a registration certificate for a handgun that he wished to keep at home, but the District refused. He [sued], on Second Amendment grounds, to enjoin the city from enforcing the bar on the registration of handguns, the licensing requirement insofar as it prohibits the carrying of a firearm in the home without a license, and the trigger-lock requirement insofar as it prohibits the use of "functional firearms within the home." The [D.C. Circuit,] construing his complaint as seeking the right to render a firearm operable and carry it about his home in that condition only when necessary for self-defense,[2] reversed. It held that the Second Amendment protects an individual right to possess firearms and that the city's total ban on handguns, as well as its requirement that firearms in the home be kept nonfunctional even when necessary for self-defense, violated that right. . . .

II. We turn first to the meaning of the Second Amendment. The Second Amendment provides: "A well regulated Militia, being necessary to the security of a free State, the right of the people to keep and bear Arms, shall not be infringed." . . . Normal meaning may of course include an idiomatic meaning, but it excludes secret or technical meanings that would not have been known to ordinary citizens in the founding generation.

The two sides in this case have set out very different interpretations of the Amendment. Petitioners and today's dissenting Justices believe that it protects only the right to possess and carry a firearm in connection with militia service. Respondent argues that it protects an individual right to possess a firearm unconnected with service in a militia, and to use that arm for traditionally lawful purposes, such as self-defense within the home.

The Second Amendment is naturally divided into two parts: its prefatory clause and its operative clause. The former does not limit the latter grammatically, but rather announces a purpose. [A]part from that clarifying function, a prefatory clause does not limit or expand the scope of the operative clause.[3] [W]hile we will begin our textual analysis with the operative clause, we will return to the prefatory clause to ensure that our reading of the operative clause is consistent with the announced purpose.

1.   **Operative Clause.**

a.   **"Right of the People."** The first salient feature of the operative clause is that it codifies a "right of the people." The unamended Constitution and the Bill of Rights use the phrase "right of the people" two other times, in the First Amendment's Assembly-and-Petition Clause and in the Fourth Amendment's Search-and-Seizure Clause. The Ninth Amendment uses very similar terminology. All three of these instances unambiguously refer to individual rights, not "collective" rights, or rights that may be exercised only through participation in

---

[2]   That construction has not been challenged here.

[3]   [T]he key 18th-century English case on the effect of preambles, *Copeman v. Gallant,* 1 P. Wms. 314, 24 Eng. Rep. 404 (1716), stated that "the preamble could not be used to restrict the effect of the words of the purview." [W]here the text of a clause itself indicates that it does not have operative effect, such as "whereas" clauses in federal legislation or the Constitution's preamble, a court has no license to make it do what it was not designed to do. Or to put the point differently, operative provisions should be given effect as operative provisions, and prologues as prologues.

some corporate body.[5] . . . This contrasts markedly with the phrase "the militia" in the prefatory clause. [T]he "militia" in colonial America consisted of a subset of "the people"—those who were male, able bodied, and within a certain age range. Reading the Second Amendment as protecting only the right to "keep and bear Arms" in an organized militia therefore fits poorly with the operative clause's description of the holder of that right as "the people."

We start therefore with a strong presumption that the Second Amendment right is exercised individually and belongs to all Americans.

b. "Keep and Bear Arms." . . . Before addressing the verbs "keep" and "bear," we interpret their object: "Arms." The 18th-century meaning is no different from the meaning today. The 1773 edition of Samuel Johnson's dictionary defined "arms" as "weapons of offence, or armour of defence." Timothy Cunningham's important 1771 legal dictionary defined "arms" as "any thing that a man wears for his defence, or takes into his hands, or useth in wrath to cast at or strike another." . . . The term was applied, then as now, to weapons that were not specifically designed for military use and were not employed in a military capacity. . . .

We turn to the phrases "keep arms" and "bear arms." Johnson defined "keep" as, most relevantly, "[t]o retain; not to lose," and "[t]o have in custody." Johnson 1095. Webster defined it as "[t]o hold; to retain in one's power or possession." No party has apprised us of an idiomatic meaning of "keep Arms." Thus, the most natural reading of "keep Arms" in the Second Amendment is to "have weapons." . . . "Keep arms" was simply a common way of referring to possessing arms, for militiamen *and everyone else.*

At the time of the founding, as now, to "bear" meant to "carry." See Johnson 161; Webster; T. Sheridan, A Complete Dictionary of the English Language (1796). When used with "arms," however, the term has a meaning that refers to carrying for a particular purpose—confrontation. In *Muscarello v. United States,* 524 U.S. 125, 118 S.Ct. 1911, 141 L.Ed.2d 111 (1998), in the course of analyzing the meaning of "carries a firearm" in a federal criminal statute, Justice Ginsburg wrote that "[s]urely a most familiar meaning is, as the Constitution's Second Amendment . . . indicate[s]: 'wear, bear, or carry . . . upon the person or in the clothing or in a pocket, for the purpose . . . of being armed and ready for offensive

---

[5] Justice Stevens is of course correct, that the right to assemble cannot be exercised alone, but it is still an individual right, and not one conditioned upon membership in some defined "assembly," as he contends the right to bear arms is conditioned upon membership in a defined militia. And Justice Stevens is dead wrong to think that the right to petition is "primarily collective in nature."

or defensive action in a case of conflict with another person.' " (dissenting opinion) (quoting Black's Law Dictionary). We think that Justice Ginsburg accurately captured the natural meaning of "bear arms." Although the phrase implies that the carrying of the weapon is for the purpose of "offensive or defensive action," it in no way connotes participation in a structured military organization.

From our review of founding-era sources, we conclude that this natural meaning was also the meaning that "bear arms" had in the 18th century. In numerous instances, "bear arms" was unambiguously used to refer to the carrying of weapons outside of an organized militia. The most prominent examples are those most relevant to the Second Amendment: Nine state constitutional provisions written in the 18th century or the first two decades of the 19th, which enshrined a right of citizens to "bear arms in defense of themselves and the state" or "bear arms in defense of himself and the state." It is clear from those formulations that "bear arms" did not refer only to carrying a weapon in an organized military unit. Justice James Wilson interpreted the Pennsylvania Constitution's arms-bearing right, for example, as a recognition of the natural right of defense "of one's person or house"—what he called the law of "self preservation." That was also the interpretation of those state constitutional provisions adopted by pre-Civil War state courts. These provisions demonstrate—again, in the most analogous linguistic context—that "bear arms" was not limited to the carrying of arms in a militia. . . .

c. **Meaning of the Operative Clause.** Putting all of these textual elements together, we find that they guarantee the individual right to possess and carry weapons in case of confrontation. This meaning is strongly confirmed by the historical background of the Second Amendment. [I]t has always been widely understood that the Second Amendment, like the First and Fourth Amendments, codified a *pre-existing* right. The very text of the Second Amendment implicitly recognizes the pre-existence of the right and declares only that it "shall not be infringed." As we said in *United States v. Cruikshank,* 92 U.S. 542, 553, 23 L.Ed. 588 (1876), "[t]his is not a right granted by the Constitution. Neither is it in any manner dependent upon that instrument for its existence. The Second amendment declares that it shall not be infringed. . . ."

Between the Restoration and the Glorious Revolution, the Stuart Kings Charles II and James II succeeded in using select militias loyal to them to suppress political dissidents, in part by disarming their opponents. Under the auspices of the 1671 Game Act, for example, the Catholic James II had ordered general disarmaments of regions home to his Protestant enemies. These experiences caused Englishmen to be extremely wary of concentrated military forces run by the state and to be jealous of their arms. They accordingly obtained an assurance from William and Mary, in the Declaration of Right (which was codified as the English Bill of Rights), that Protestants would never be disarmed . . . This right has long been understood to be the predecessor to our Second Amendment. It was clearly an individual right, having nothing whatever to do with service in a militia. . . .

[W]hat the Stuarts had tried to do to their political enemies, George III had tried to do to the colonists. . . . That provoked polemical reactions by Americans invoking their rights as Englishmen to keep arms. A New York article of April 1769 said that "[i]t is a natural right which the people have reserved to themselves, confirmed by the Bill of Rights, to keep arms for their own defence." . . .

There seems to us no doubt, on the basis of both text and history, that the Second Amendment conferred an individual right to keep and bear arms. Of course the right was not unlimited, just as the First Amendment's right of free speech was not. Thus, we do not read the Second Amendment to protect the right of citizens to carry arms for *any sort* of confrontation, just as we do not read the First Amendment to protect the right of citizens to speak for *any purpose*. Before turning to limitations upon the individual right, however, we must determine whether the prefatory clause of the Second Amendment comports with our interpretation of the operative clause.

2. Prefatory Clause.

The prefatory clause reads: "A well regulated Militia, being necessary to the security of a free State. . . ."

a. "Well-Regulated Militia." In *United States v. Miller,* 307 U.S. 174, 179, 59 S.Ct. 816, 83 L.Ed. 1206 (1939), we explained that "the Militia comprised all males physically capable of acting in concert for the common defense." That definition comports with founding-era sources. [T]he adjective "well-regulated" implies nothing more than the imposition of proper discipline and training.

b. "Security of a Free State." . . . There are many reasons why the militia was thought to be "necessary to the security of a free state." See 3 Story § 1890. [W]hen the able-bodied men of a nation are trained in arms and organized, they are better able to resist tyranny.

3.   Relationship Between Prefatory Clause and Operative Clause

We reach the question, then: Does the preface fit with an operative clause that creates an individual right to keep and bear arms? It fits perfectly, once one knows the history that the founding generation knew and that we have described above. That history showed that the way tyrants had eliminated a militia consisting of all the able-bodied men was not by banning the militia but simply by taking away the people's arms, enabling a select militia or standing army to suppress political opponents. This is what had occurred in England that prompted codification of the right to have arms in the English Bill of Rights.

The debate with respect to the right to keep and bear arms, as with other guarantees in the Bill of Rights, was not over whether it was desirable (all agreed that it was) but over whether it needed to be codified in the Constitution. [T]he threat that the new Federal Government would destroy the citizens' militia by taking away their arms was the reason that right—unlike some other English rights—was codified in a written Constitution. . . .

[P]etitioners' interpretation does not even achieve the narrower purpose that prompted codification of the right. If, as they believe, the Second Amendment right is no more than the right to keep and use weapons as a member of an organized militia—if, that is, the *organized* militia is the sole institutional beneficiary of the Second Amendment's guarantee—it does not assure the existence of a "citizens' militia" as a safeguard against tyranny . . .

Our interpretation is confirmed by analogous arms-bearing rights in state constitutions that preceded and immediately followed adoption of the Second Amendment. [A lengthy historical discussion of analogous state constitutional provisions, post-Second Amendment commentary, pre-Civil War and post-Civil War legislation, post-Civil War commentators is omitted.]

Justice Stevens places overwhelming reliance upon this Court's decision in *United States v. Miller,* 307 U.S. 174, 59 S.Ct. 816, 83 L.Ed. 1206 (1939). [T]hat] case upheld against a Second Amendment challenge two men's federal convictions for transporting an unregistered short-barreled shotgun in interstate commerce, in violation of the National Firearms Act, 48 Stat. 1236. [T]he Court's basis for saying that the Second Amendment did not apply was . . . that the *type of weapon at issue* was not eligible for Second Amendment protection: "In the absence of any evidence tending to show that the possession or use of a [short-barreled shotgun] at this time has some reasonable relationship to the preservation or efficiency of a well regulated militia, we cannot say that the Second Amendment guarantees the right to keep and bear *such an instrument*." (emphasis added). "Certainly," the Court continued, [T]his weapon is any part of the ordinary military equipment or that its use could contribute to the common defense." Beyond that, the opinion provided no explanation of the content of the right.

This holding is not only consistent with, but positively suggests, that the Second Amendment confers an individual right to keep and bear arms (though only arms that "have some reasonable relationship to the preservation or efficiency of a well regulated militia"). Had the Court believed that the Second Amendment protects only those serving in the militia, it would have been odd to examine the character of the weapon rather than simply note that the two crooks were not militiamen. [We] read *Miller* to say only that the Second Amendment does not protect those weapons not typically possessed by law-abiding citizens for lawful purposes, such as short-barreled shotguns. That accords with the historical understanding of the scope of the right.

[N]othing in our precedents forecloses our adoption of the original understanding of the Second Amendment. It should be unsurprising that such a significant matter has been for so long judicially unresolved. For most of our history, the Bill of Rights was not thought applicable to the States, and the Federal Government did not significantly regulate the possession of firearms by law-abiding citizens. . . . This Court first held a law to violate the First Amendment's guarantee of freedom of speech in 1931, almost 150 years after the Amendment was ratified, see *Near v. Minnesota ex rel. Olson,* 283 U.S. 697, 51 S.Ct. 625, 75 L.Ed. 1357 (1931), and it was not until after World War II that we held a law invalid under the Establishment Clause, see *Illinois ex rel. McCollum v. Board of Ed. of School Dist. No. 71, Champaign Cty.,* 333 U.S. 203, 68 S.Ct. 461, 92 L.Ed. 649 (1948). Even a question as basic as the scope of proscribable libel was not addressed by this Court until 1964, nearly two centuries after the founding. See *New York Times Co. v. Sullivan,* 376 U.S. 254, 84 S.Ct. 710, 11 L.Ed.2d 686 (1964). . . .

III. Like most rights, the right secured by the Second Amendment is not unlimited. From Blackstone through the 19th-century cases, commentators and courts routinely explained that the right was not a right to keep and carry any weapon whatsoever in any manner whatsoever and for whatever purpose. For example, the majority of the 19th-century courts to consider the question held that prohibitions on carrying concealed weapons were lawful under the Second Amendment or state analogues. Although we do not undertake an exhaustive historical analysis today of the full scope of the Second Amendment, nothing in our opinion should be taken to cast doubt on longstanding prohibitions on the possession of firearms by felons and the mentally ill, or laws forbidding the carrying of firearms in sensitive places such as schools and government buildings, or laws imposing conditions and qualifications on the commercial sale of arms.[26]

We also recognize another important limitation on the right to keep and carry arms. *Miller* said, as we have explained, that the sorts of weapons protected were those "in common use at the time." We think that limitation is fairly supported by the historical tradition of prohibiting the carrying of "dangerous and unusual weapons." See 4 Blackstone 148–149 (1769).

It may be objected that if weapons that are most useful in military service—M-16 rifles and the like—may be banned, then the Second Amendment right is completely detached from the prefatory clause. But as we have said, the conception of the militia at the time of the Second Amendment's ratification was the body of all citizens capable of military service, who would bring the sorts of lawful weapons that they possessed at home to militia duty. It may well be true today that a militia, to be as effective as militias in the 18th century, would require sophisticated arms that are highly unusual in society at large. Indeed, it may be true that no amount of small arms could be useful against modern-day bombers and tanks. But the fact that modern developments have limited the degree of fit between the prefatory clause and the protected right cannot change our interpretation of the right.

IV. We turn finally to the law at issue here. [T]he law totally bans handgun possession in the home. It also requires that any lawful firearm in the home be disassembled or bound by a trigger lock at all times, rendering it inoperable.

[T]he inherent right of self-defense has been central to the Second Amendment right. The handgun ban amounts to a prohibition of an entire class of "arms" that is overwhelmingly chosen by American society for that lawful purpose. The prohibition extends, moreover, to the home, where the need for defense of self, family, and property is most acute. Under any of the standards of scrutiny that we have applied to enumerated constitutional rights,[27] banning from

---

[26] We identify these presumptively lawful regulatory measures only as examples; our list does not purport to be exhaustive.

[27] Justice Breyer correctly notes that this law, like almost all laws, would pass rational-basis scrutiny. But rational-basis scrutiny is a mode of analysis we have used when evaluating laws under constitutional commands that are themselves prohibitions on irrational laws. In those cases, "rational basis" is not just the standard of scrutiny, but the very substance of the constitutional guarantee. Obviously, the same test could not be used to evaluate the extent to which a legislature may regulate a specific, enumerated right, be it the freedom of speech, the guarantee against double jeopardy, the right to counsel, or the right to keep and bear arms. See *United States v. Carolene Products Co.,* 304 U.S. 144, 152, n. 4, 58 S.Ct. 778, 82 L.Ed. 1234 (1938) ("There may be narrower scope for operation of the presumption of constitutionality [*i.e.,* narrower than that provided by rational-basis review] when legislation appears on its face to be within a specific prohibition of the Constitution, such as those of the first ten amendments . . ."). If all that was required to overcome the right to keep and bear arms

the home "the most preferred firearm in the nation to 'keep' and use for protection of one's home and family," would fail constitutional muster.

Few laws in the history of our Nation have come close to the severe restriction of the District's handgun ban. And some of those few have been struck down [by various state courts].

It is no answer to say, as petitioners do, that it is permissible to ban the possession of handguns so long as the possession of other firearms (*i.e.,* long guns) is allowed. It is enough to note, as we have observed, that the American people have considered the handgun to be the quintessential self-defense weapon. . . . It is easier to store in a location that is readily accessible in an emergency; it cannot easily be redirected or wrestled away by an attacker; it is easier to use for those without the upper-body strength to lift and aim a long gun; it can be pointed at a burglar with one hand while the other hand dials the police. [H]andguns are the most popular weapon chosen by Americans for self-defense in the home, and a complete prohibition of their use is invalid. [The District requires] that firearms in the home be rendered and kept inoperable at all times. This makes it impossible for citizens to use them for the core lawful purpose of self-defense and is hence unconstitutional. . . .

Justice Breyer . . . criticizes us for declining to establish a level of scrutiny for evaluating Second Amendment restrictions. He proposes, . . . a judge-empowering "interest-balancing inquiry". . . . We know of no other enumerated constitutional right whose core protection has been subjected to a freestanding "interest-balancing" approach. The very enumeration of the right takes out of the hands of government—even the Third Branch of Government—the power to decide on a case-by-case basis whether the right is *really worth* insisting upon. A constitutional guarantee subject to future judges' assessments of its usefulness is no constitutional guarantee at all. Constitutional rights are enshrined with the scope they were understood to have when the people adopted them, whether or not future legislatures or (yes) even future judges think that scope too broad. We would not apply an "interest-balancing" approach to the prohibition of a peaceful neo-Nazi march through Skokie. See *National Socialist Party of America v. Skokie,* 432 U.S. 43, 97 S.Ct. 2205, 53 L.Ed.2d 96 (1977) *(per curiam)*. The First Amendment contains the freedom-of-speech guarantee that the people ratified, which included exceptions for obscenity, libel, and disclosure of state secrets, but not for the expression of extremely unpopular and wrong-headed views. The

---

was a rational basis, the Second Amendment would be redundant with the separate constitutional prohibitions on irrational laws, and would have no effect.

Second Amendment is no different. Like the First, it is the very *product* of an interest-balancing by the people—which Justice Breyer would now conduct for them anew. And whatever else it leaves to future evaluation, it surely elevates above all other interests the right of law-abiding, responsible citizens to use arms in defense of hearth and home.

Justice Breyer chides us for leaving so many applications of the right to keep and bear arms in doubt, and for not providing extensive historical justification for those regulations of the right that we describe as permissible. But since this case represents this Court's first in-depth examination of the Second Amendment, one should not expect it to clarify the entire field, any more than *Reynolds v. United States,* 98 U.S. 145, 25 L.Ed. 244 (1879), our first in-depth Free Exercise Clause case, left that area in a state of utter certainty. [Thus], we hold that the District's ban on handgun possession in the home violates the Second Amendment, as does its prohibition against rendering any lawful firearm in the home operable for the purpose of immediate self-defense. Assuming that Heller is not disqualified from the exercise of Second Amendment rights, the District must permit him to register his handgun and must issue him a license to carry it in the home.

* * *

We are aware of the problem of handgun violence in this country, and we take seriously the concerns raised by the many *amici* who believe that prohibition of handgun ownership is a solution. The Constitution leaves the District of Columbia a variety of tools for combating that problem, including some measures regulating handguns. But the enshrinement of constitutional rights necessarily takes certain policy choices off the table. These include the absolute prohibition of handguns held and used for self-defense in the home. . . . We affirm the judgment of the Court of Appeals.

It is so ordered.

JUSTICE STEVENS, with whom JUSTICE SOUTER, JUSTICE GINSBURG, and JUSTICE BREYER join, dissenting.

The question presented by this case is not whether the Second Amendment protects a "collective right" or an "individual right." Surely it protects a right that can be enforced by individuals. But a conclusion that the Second Amendment protects an individual right does not tell us anything about the scope of that right. . . . The Second Amendment was adopted to protect the right of the people of each of the several States to maintain a well-regulated militia. [T]here is no indication that the Framers of the Amendment intended to enshrine the common-law right of self-defense in the Constitution. . . .

[A]lthough the act of petitioning the Government is a right that can be exercised by individuals, it is primarily collective in nature. For if they are to be effective, petitions must involve groups of individuals acting in concert. Similarly, the words "the people" in the Second Amendment refer back to the object announced in the Amendment's preamble. They remind us that it is the collective action of individuals having a duty to serve in the militia that the text directly protects and, perhaps more importantly, that the ultimate purpose of the Amendment was to protect the States' share of the divided sovereignty created by the Constitution.

[T]he Fourth Amendment ["The right of the people to be secure in their persons . . ."] refers to a right to protect a purely individual interest. As used in the Second Amendment, the words "the people" do not enlarge the right to keep and bear arms to encompass use or ownership of weapons outside the context of service in a well-regulated militia.

[The Second Amendment] protects only one right, rather than two. It does not describe a right "to keep arms" and a separate right "to bear arms." Rather, the single right that it does describe is both a duty and a right to have arms available and ready for military service, and to use them for military purposes when necessary. Different language surely would have been used to protect nonmilitary use and possession of weapons from regulation if such an intent had played any role in the drafting of the Amendment. [N]ot a word in the constitutional text even arguably supports the Court's overwrought and novel description of the Second Amendment as "elevat[ing] above all other interests" "the right of law-abiding, responsible citizens to use arms in defense of hearth and home." . . .

JUSTICE BREYER, with whom JUSTICE STEVENS, JUSTICE SOUTER, and JUSTICE GINSBURG join, dissenting.

[T]he District's law is consistent with the Second Amendment even if that Amendment is interpreted as protecting a wholly separate interest in individual self-defense [because it] focuses upon the presence of handguns in high-crime urban areas, represents a permissible legislative response to a serious, indeed life-threatening, problem.

. . . I take as a starting point the following four propositions, based on our precedent and today's opinions, to which I believe the entire Court subscribes:

(1)   The Amendment protects an "individual" right—*i.e.,* one that is separately possessed, and may be separately enforced, by each person on whom it is conferred.

(2)   As evidenced by its preamble, the Amendment was adopted "[w]ith obvious purpose to assure the continuation and render possible the effectiveness of [militia] forces."

(3)   The Amendment "must be interpreted and applied with that end in view."

(4)   The right protected by the Second Amendment is not absolute, but instead is subject to government regulation.

My approach to this case, while involving the first three points, primarily concerns the fourth. [T]he Court normally defers to a legislature's empirical judgment in matters where a legislature is likely to have greater expertise and greater institutional factfinding capacity. . . . The ultimate question is whether the statute imposes burdens that, when viewed in light of the statute's legitimate objectives, are disproportionate.

. . . Respondent and his many *amici* . . . do disagree strongly with the District's *predictive judgment* that a ban on handguns will help solve the crime and accident problems that those figures disclose. In particular, they disagree with the District Council's assessment that "freezing the pistol . . . population within the District," will reduce crime, accidents, and deaths related to guns. And they provide facts and figures designed to show that it has not done so in the past, and hence will not do so in the future.

First, they point out that, since the ban took effect, violent crime in the District has increased, not decreased. Indeed, a comparison with 49 other major cities reveals that the District's homicide rate is actually substantially *higher* relative to these other cities than it was before the handgun restriction went into effect. [But] the District's decision represents the kind of empirically based judgment that legislatures, not courts, are best suited to make. . . . For these reasons, I conclude that the District's statute properly seeks to further the sort of life-preserving and public-safety interests that the Court has called "compelling."

[It is not] clear to me how the majority decides *which* loaded "arms" a homeowner may keep. The majority says that that Amendment protects those weapons "typically possessed by law-abiding citizens for lawful purposes." This definition conveniently excludes machineguns, but permits handguns, which the majority describes as "the most popular weapon chosen by Americans for self-defense in the home." But what sense does this approach make? According to the majority's reasoning, if Congress and the States lift restrictions on the possession and use of machineguns, and people buy machineguns to protect their homes, the Court will have to reverse course and find that the Second Amendment *does*, in fact, protect the individual self-defense-related right to possess a machinegun. On the majority's reasoning, if tomorrow someone invents a particularly useful, highly dangerous self-defense weapon, Congress and the States had better ban it immediately, for once it becomes popular Congress will no longer possess the constitutional authority to do so. In essence, the majority determines what regulations are permissible by looking to see what existing regulations permit. There is no basis for believing that the Framers intended such circular reasoning. . . .

NOTES

1. Does this case prohibit the Federal Government from banning private ownership of machine guns? Tanks? Does it allow laws that prohibit felons, minors, or the mentally ill from keeping guns? What about registration of handguns?

2. Does the dissent's position allow the government to ban self-defense? Justice Stevens says, "There is no indication that the Framers of the Amendment intended to enshrine the common-law right of self-defense in the Constitution."

3. After *Heller*, the D.C. city council enacted the Firearms Registration Amendment Act of 2008. Would-be gun owners now must go through a process requiring fingerprints, photographs and detailing of some job history. They must take a 20-question test on the District's gun laws and regulations. There is also a five-hour class, with at least one hour at a gun range. They must find trainers from a list that police have approved. Then, the applicant must take the gun to the police, who fire it for a ballistic identification. Since the *Heller* decision through April 2010, the city registered 1,071 guns, including 756 handguns and 315 "long" guns, such as rifles, about 181 guns per 100,000 residents. Before *Heller*, the rate of registered guns in Washington was close to zero. In 2009, the first full year this law was in effect, homicides

in the city from 186 in 2008 to 143 in 2009. This 2009 total was the lowest since 1966. By 2012, the murder rate in the District dropped to 88.[1]

3.2 THE SECOND AMENDMENT APPLIED TO THE STATE GOVERNMENTS

McDonald v. City of Chicago

561 U.S. 742, 130 S.Ct. 3020, 177 L.Ed.2d 894 (2010)

Justice Alito announced the judgment of the Court and delivered the opinion of the Court with respect to Parts I, II-A, II-B, II-D, III-A, and III-B, in which The Chief Justice, Justice Scalia, Justice Kennedy, and Justice Thomas join, and an opinion with respect to Parts II-C, IV, and V, in which The Chief Justice, Justice Scalia, and Justice Kennedy join.

Two years ago, in *District of Columbia* v. *Heller* (2008), we held that the Second Amendment protects the right to keep and bear arms for the purpose of self-defense, and we struck down a District of Columbia law that banned the possession of handguns in the home. The city of Chicago (City) and the village of Oak Park, a Chicago suburb, have laws that are similar to the District of Columbia's, but Chicago and Oak Park argue that their laws are constitutional because the Second Amendment has no application to the States. We have previously held that most of the provisions of the Bill of Rights apply with full force to both the Federal Government and the States. Applying the standard that is well established in our case law, we hold that the Second Amendment right is fully applicable to the States.

I.   . . . Chicago enacted its handgun ban to protect its residents "from the loss of property and injury or death from firearms." The Chicago petitioners and their *amici*, however, argue that the handgun ban has left them vulnerable to criminals. Chicago Police Department statistics, we are told, reveal that the City's handgun murder rate has actually increased since the ban was enacted and that Chicago residents now face one of the highest murder rates in the country and rates of other violent crimes that exceed the average in comparable cities.

[The Seventh Circuit rejected plaintiffs' arguments] relying on three 19th-century cases—*United States* v. *Cruikshank*, 92 U.S. 542 (1876), *Presser* v. *Illinois*, 116 U.S. 252 (1886), and *Miller* v. *Texas*, 153 U.S. 535 (1894)—that were decided in

---

[1]   Gary Fields, *New Washington Gun Rules Shift Constitutional Debate*, WALL ST. JRL., May 17, 2010, at pp. A1, A18. Jeffrey Scott Shapiro [former criminal prosecutor for DC, from 2007–09], *A Gun Ban that Misfired*, WALL ST. JRL., Jan 16, 2013, at p. A11.

the wake of this Court's interpretation of the Privileges or Immunities Clause of the Fourteenth Amendment in the *Slaughter-House Cases* (1873) [§ 6–1]. The Seventh Circuit described the rationale of those cases as "defunct" [but] observed that it was obligated to follow Supreme Court precedents that have "direct application". . . .

II. A. Petitioners argue that the Chicago and Oak Park laws violate the right to keep and bear arms for two reasons. Petitioners' primary submission is that this right is among the "privileges or immunities of citizens of the United States" and [they also] contend that the Fourteenth Amendment's Due Process Clause "incorporates" the Second Amendment right.

Chicago and Oak Park (municipal respondents) maintain that a right set out in the Bill of Rights applies to the States only if that right is an indispensable attribute of *any* "civilized" legal system. [S]ince there are civilized countries that ban or strictly regulate the private possession of handguns, the municipal respondents maintain that due process does not preclude such measures. . . .

B. [M]any legal scholars dispute the correctness of the narrow *Slaughter-House* interpretation. . . . Three years after the decision in the *Slaughter-House Cases,* the Court decided *Cruikshank* [which] reviewed convictions stemming from the infamous Colfax Massacre in Louisiana on Easter Sunday 1873. Dozens of blacks, many unarmed, were slaughtered by a rival band of armed white men. Cruikshank himself allegedly marched unarmed African-American prisoners through the streets and then had them summarily executed. Ninety-seven men were indicted for participating in the massacre, but only nine went to trial. Six of the nine were acquitted of all charges; the remaining three were acquitted of murder but convicted under the Enforcement Act of 1870, 16 Stat. 140, for banding and conspiring together to deprive their victims of various constitutional rights, including the right to bear arms.

The Court reversed all of the convictions, including those relating to the deprivation of the victims' right to bear arms. *Cruikshank*. The Court wrote [that the Second Amendment,] "means no more than that it shall not be infringed by Congress." "Our later decisions in *Presser* v. *Illinois,* 116 U.S. 252, 265 (1886), and *Miller* v. *Texas,* 153 U.S. 535, 538 (1894), reaffirmed that the Second Amendment applies only to the Federal Government."

C. . . . For many decades, the question of the rights protected by the Fourteenth Amendment against state infringement has been analyzed under the Due Process Clause of that Amendment and not under the Privileges or Immunities Clause. We therefore decline to disturb the *Slaughter-House* holding.

[However,] *Cruikshank*, *Presser*, and *Miller* do not preclude us from considering whether the Due Process Clause of the Fourteenth Amendment makes the Second Amendment right binding on the States. None of those cases "engage[d] in the sort of Fourteenth Amendment inquiry required by our later cases." . . .

D.   . . . As Justice Black noted, the chief congressional proponents of the Fourteenth Amendment espoused the view that the Amendment made the Bill of Rights applicable to the States and, in so doing, overruled this Court's decision in *Barron*.[9] Nonetheless, the Court never has embraced Justice Black's "total incorporation" theory.

While Justice Black's theory was never adopted, the Court eventually moved in that direction by initiating what has been called a process of "selective incorporation," *i.e.*, the Court began to hold that the Due Process Clause fully incorporates particular rights contained in the first eight Amendments. [T]he governing standard is not whether *any* "civilized system [can] be imagined that would not accord the particular protection." *Duncan v. Louisiana* (1968) [§ 12–5]. Instead, the Court inquired whether a particular Bill of Rights guarantee is fundamental to *our* scheme of ordered liberty and system of justice. *Id.* . . . Only a handful of the Bill of Rights protections remain unincorporated.

Finally, the Court abandoned "the notion that the Fourteenth Amendment applies to the States only a watered-down, subjective version of the individual guarantees of the Bill of Rights," stating that it would be "incongruous" to apply different standards "depending on whether the claim was asserted in a state or federal court." . . .

---

[9]   Senator Jacob Howard, who spoke on behalf of the Joint Committee on Reconstruction and sponsored the Amendment in the Senate, stated that the Amendment protected all of "the personal rights guaranteed and secured by the first eight amendments of the Constitution." Cong. Globe, 39th Cong., 1st Sess., 2765 (1866). Representative John Bingham, the principal author of the text of § 1, said that the Amendment would "arm the Congress . . . with the power to enforce the bill of rights as it stands in the Constitution today." *Id.* After ratification of the Amendment, Bingham maintained the view that the rights guaranteed by § 1 of the Fourteenth Amendment "are chiefly defined in the first eight amendments to the Constitution of the United States." Cong. Globe, 42d Cong., 1st Sess., App. 84 (1871). Finally, Representative Thaddeus Stevens, the political leader of the House and acting chairman of the Joint Committee on Reconstruction, stated during the debates on the Amendment that "the Constitution limits only the action of Congress, and is not a limitation on the States. This amendment supplies that defect, and allows Congress to correct the unjust legislation of the States." 39th Cong. Globe 2459; see also M. Curtis, No State Shall Abridge: The Fourteenth Amendment and the Bill of Rights 112 (1986) (counting at least 30 statements during the debates in Congress interpreting § 1 to incorporate the Bill of Rights); Brief for Constitutional Law Professors as *Amici Curiae* 20 (collecting authorities and stating that "[n]ot a single senator or representative disputed [the incorporationist] understanding" of the Fourteenth Amendment).

III. With this framework in mind, we now turn directly to the question whether the Second Amendment right to keep and bear arms is incorporated in the concept of due process. . . .

A. Our decision in *Heller* points unmistakably to the answer. Self-defense is a basic right, recognized by many legal systems from ancient times to the present day, and in *Heller,* we held that individual self-defense is "the *central component*" of the Second Amendment right, see also *id.* (stating that the "inherent right of self-defense has been central to the Second Amendment right"). . . . 3 J. Story, Commentaries on the Constitution of the United States § 1890, p. 746 (1833) ("The right of the citizens to keep and bear arms has justly been considered, as the palladium of the liberties of a republic; since it offers a strong moral check against the usurpation and arbitrary power of rulers; and will generally, even if these are successful in the first instance, enable the people to resist and triumph over them").

B. . . . After the Civil War, many of the over 180,000 African Americans who served in the Union Army returned to the States of the old Confederacy, where systematic efforts were made to disarm them and other blacks. The laws of some States formally prohibited African Americans from possessing firearms. For example, a Mississippi law provided that "no freedman, free negro or mulatto, not in the military service of the United States government, and not licensed so to do by the board of police of his or her county, shall keep or carry fire-arms of any kind, or any ammunition, dirk or bowie knife." . . .

Union Army commanders took steps to secure the right of all citizens to keep and bear arms, but the 39th Congress concluded that legislative action was necessary. . . . The most explicit evidence of Congress' aim appears in § 14 of the Freedmen's Bureau Act of 1866, which provided that "the right . . . to have full and equal benefit of all laws and proceedings concerning personal liberty, personal security, and the acquisition, enjoyment, and disposition of estate, real and personal, *including the constitutional right to bear arms*, shall be secured to and enjoyed by all the citizens . . . without respect to race or color, or previous condition of slavery." 14 Stat. 176–177 (emphasis added). Section 14 thus explicitly guaranteed that "all the citizens," black and white, would have "the constitutional right to bear arms." [T]he Civil Rights Act, like the Freedmen's Bureau Act, aimed to protect "the constitutional right to bear arms" and not simply to prohibit discrimination. . . . Southern resistance, Presidential vetoes, and this Court's pre-Civil-War precedent persuaded Congress that a constitutional amendment was necessary to provide full protection for the rights of blacks.[24] Today, it is generally accepted that the Fourteenth Amendment was understood to provide a constitutional basis for protecting the rights set out in the Civil Rights Act of 1866. . . .

IV. . . . According to municipal respondents, if it is possible to imagine *any* civilized legal system that does not recognize a particular right, then the Due Process Clause does not make that right binding on the States. Therefore, the municipal respondents continue, because such countries as England, Canada, Australia, Japan, Denmark, Finland, Luxembourg, and New Zealand either ban or severely limit handgun ownership, it must follow that no right to possess such weapons is protected by the Fourteenth Amendment.

[T]he implications of municipal respondents' argument are stunning. For example, many of the rights that our Bill of Rights provides for persons accused of criminal offenses are virtually unique to this country. [S]everal of the countries that municipal respondents recognize as civilized have established state churches. If we were to adopt municipal respondents' theory, all of this Court's Establishment Clause precedents involving actions taken by state and local governments would go by the boards. . . .

V. . . . Justice Breyer is incorrect that incorporation will require judges to assess the costs and benefits of firearms restrictions and thus to make difficult empirical judgments in an area in which they lack expertise. [W]hile his opinion in *Heller* recommended an interest-balancing test, the Court specifically rejected that suggestion. [T]he Due Process Clause of the Fourteenth Amendment incorporates the Second Amendment right recognized in *Heller*. The judgment of the Court of Appeals is reversed, and the case is remanded for further proceedings.

It is so ordered.

JUSTICE THOMAS, concurring in part and concurring in the judgment.

. . . I believe there is a more straightforward path to this conclusion, one that is more faithful to the Fourteenth Amendment's text and history. [T]he right to keep and bear arms is a privilege of American citizenship that applies to the States through the Fourteenth Amendment's Privileges or Immunities Clause. . . .

---

[24] For example, at least one southern court had held the Civil Rights Act to be unconstitutional. That court did so, moreover, in the course of upholding the conviction of an African-American man for violating Mississippi's law against firearm possession by freedmen. See Decision of Chief Justice Handy, Declaring the Civil Rights Bill Unconstitutional, N. Y. Times, Oct. 26, 1866, p. 2, col. 3.

JUSTICE BREYER, with whom JUSTICE GINSBURG and JUSTICE SOTOMAYOR join, dissenting.

. . . I can find nothing in the Second Amendment's text, history, or underlying rationale that could warrant characterizing it as "fundamental" insofar as it seeks to protect the keeping and bearing of arms for private self-defense purposes. [D]etermining the constitutionality of a particular state gun law requires finding answers to complex empirically based questions of a kind that legislatures are better able than courts to make. . . .

[The opinion of SCALIA, J., concurring, and STEVENS, J., dissenting, are omitted.]

NOTES

1. What difference does it make if the right to keep and bear arms is a privilege of American citizenship that applies to the States through the Fourteenth Amendment's Privileges or Immunities Clause, or a right incorporated through the due process clause? Note that the Privileges and Immunities Clause applies only to "citizens," while "due process" applies to "persons," thereby including aliens.

2. Senator Leahy asked Justice Sonia Sotomayor, at her confirmation hearing, "Is it safe to say that you accept the Supreme Court's decision as establishing that the Second Amendment right is an individual right? Is that correct?" She said, "Yes, sir." She added: "I understand how important the right to bear arms is to many, many Americans. In fact, one of my godchildren is a member of the NRA. And I have friends who hunt. I understand the individual right fully that the Supreme Court recognized in Heller." She also joined Justice Breyer's *McDonald*'s dissent. Supporters of Second Amendment incorporation cited this dissent as proof she contradicted her confirmation testimony. What do you think?

CHAPTER 4

The Criminal Process

4.1 NATIONALIZING THE CRIMINAL PROCESS

Section 2.3 of Chapter 2 briefly summarized the process by which the Court selectively incorporated the Bill of Rights into the Fourteenth Amendment. The efforts of some Justices (never totaling more than four Justices at any one time) argued that the Court should incorporate the entire Bill of Rights. This dispute raged for years. Often the focus of the debate was the question of to what extent federal rights should limit state criminal procedure.

The facts of *Hurtado* illustrate and introduce the debate regarding how much, if any, of the Bill of Rights is incorporated within the Fourteenth Amendment and how much discretion should the Justices have to decide what constitutes due process. A provision of the California Constitution of 1879 allowed criminal prosecutions to begin after either an indictment, voted on by a grand jury, or an information, which district attorney drafted. In this case, the district attorney filed an information against Hurtado, charging him with murder. At trial, the jury found Hurtado guilty, and the trial court sentenced him to death. Hurtado sought to reverse his conviction.

HURTADO V. CALIFORNIA
110 U.S. 516, 4 S.Ct. 111, 28 L.Ed. 232 (1884)

JUSTICE MATTHEWS gave the opinion of the Court.

It is claimed on behalf of the prisoner that the conviction and sentence are void, on the ground that they are repugnant to that clause of the fourteenth article of amendment to the constitution of the United States, which is in these words: "Nor shall any state deprive any person of life, liberty, or property without due process of law." The proposition of law we are asked to affirm is that an indictment or presentment by a grand jury, as known to the common law of

227

England, is essential to that "due process of law," when applied to prosecutions for felonies, which is secured and guaranteed by this provision of the constitution of the United States, and which accordingly it is forbidden to the states, respectively, to dispense with in the administration of criminal law. The question is one of grave and serious import, affecting both private and public rights and interests of great magnitude, and involves a consideration of what additional restrictions upon the legislative policy of the states has been imposed by the fourteenth amendment to the constitution of the United States. . . .

[I]t is maintained on behalf of the plaintiff in error that the phrase "due process of law" is equivalent to "law of the land," as found in the twenty-ninth chapter of *Magna Charta;* that by immemorial usage it has acquired a fixed, definite, and technical meaning; that it refers to and includes, not only the general principles of public liberty and private right, which lie at the foundation of all free government, but the very institutions which, venerable by time and custom, have been tried by experience and found fit and necessary for the preservation of those principles, and which, having been the birthright and inheritance of every English subject, crossed the Atlantic with the colonists and were transplanted and established in the fundamental laws of the state; that, having been originally introduced into the constitution of the United States as a limitation upon the powers of the government, brought into being by that instrument, it has now been added as an additional security to the individual against oppression by the states themselves; that one of these institutions is that of the grand jury, an indictment or presentment by which against the accused in cases of alleged felonies is an essential part of due process of law, in order that he may not be harassed and destroyed by prosecutions founded only upon private malice or popular fury.

[Hurtado argues that his claim] is supported by the decision of this court in *Murray's Lessee v. Hoboken Land & Imp. Co.* 18 How. 272 [1855]. There, Mr. Justice Curtis, delivering the opinion of the court, after showing that due process of law must mean something more than the actual existing law of the land, for otherwise it would be no restraint upon legislative power, proceeds as follows: "To what principle, then, are we to resort to ascertain whether this process, enacted by congress, is due process? To this the answer must be twofold. We must examine the constitution itself to see whether this process be in conflict with any of its provisions. If not found to be so, we must look to those settled usages and modes of proceeding existing in the common and statute law of England before the emigration of our ancestors, and which are shown not to have been unsuited to their civil and political condition by having been acted on by them after the settlement of this country." This, it is argued, furnishes an indispensable test of what constitutes "due process of law;" that any proceeding otherwise authorized by law, which is not thus sanctioned by usage, or which supersedes and displaces one that is, cannot be regarded as due process of law. But this inference is unwarranted. The real syllabus of the passage quoted is that a process of law, which is not otherwise forbidden, must be taken to be due process of law, if it can show the sanction of settled usage both in England and in this country; but it by no means follows, that nothing else can be due process of law. The point in the case cited arose in reference to a summary proceeding, questioned on that account as not due process of law. The answer was, however exceptional it may be, as tested by definitions and principles of ordinary procedure, nevertheless, this, in substance, has been immemorially the actual law of the land, and, therefore, is due process of law. But to hold that such a characteristic is essential to due process of law, would be to deny every quality of the law but its age, and to render it incapable of progress or improvement. It would be to stamp upon our jurisprudence the unchangeableness attributed to the laws of the Medes and Persians.

[O]wing to the progressive development of legal ideas and institutions in England, the words of *Magna Charta* stood for very different things at the time of the separation of the American colonies from what they represented originally. . . .

The constitution of the United States was ordained, it is true, by descendants of Englishmen, who inherited the traditions of the English law and history; but it was made for an undefined and expanding future, and for a people gathered, and to be gathered, from many nations and of many tongues; and while we take just pride in the principles and institutions of the common law, we are not to forget that in lands where other systems of jurisprudence prevail, the ideas and processes of civil justice are also not unknown. [W]ritten constitutions were deemed essential to protect the rights and liberties of the people against the encroachments of power delegated to their governments, and the provisions of *Magna Charta* were incorporated into bills of rights. They were limitations upon all the powers of government, legislative as well as executive and judicial. It necessarily happened, therefore, that as these broad and general maxims of liberty and justice held in our system a different place and performed a different function from their position and office in English constitutional history and law, they would receive and justify a corresponding and more comprehensive interpretation. Applied in England only as guards against executive usurpation and tyranny, here they have become bulwarks also against arbitrary legislation; but in that application, as it would be incongruous to measure and restrict them by the ancient customary English law, they must be held to guaranty, not particular forms of procedure, but the very substance of individual rights to life, liberty, and property. Restraints that could be fastened upon executive authority with precision and detail, might prove obstructive and injurious when imposed on the just and necessary discretion of legislative power. . . .

We are to construe this phrase in the fourteenth amendment by the *usus loquendi* of the constitution itself. The same words are contained in the fifth amendment. That article makes specific and express provision for perpetuating the institution of the grand jury, so far as relates to prosecutions for the more aggravated crimes under the laws of the United States. . . . It then immediately adds: "nor be deprived of life, liberty, or property without due process of law." According to a recognized canon of interpretation, especially applicable to formal and solemn instruments of constitutional law, we are forbidden to assume, without clear reason to the contrary, that any part of this most important amendment is superfluous. The natural and obvious inference is that, in the sense of the constitution, "due process of law" was not meant or intended to include, *ex vi termini,* the institution and procedure of a grand jury in any case. The conclusion is equally irresistible, that when the same phrase was employed in the fourteenth amendment to restrain the action of the states, it was used in the same sense and with no greater extent; and that if in the adoption of that amendment it had been part of its purpose to perpetuate the institution of the grand jury in all the states, it would have embodied, as did the fifth amendment, express declarations to that effect. Due process of law in the latter refers to that law of the land which derives its authority from the legislative powers conferred upon congress by the constitution of the United States, exercised within the limits therein prescribed, and interpreted according to the principles of the common law. In the fourteenth amendment, by parity of reason, it refers to that law of the land in each state which derives its authority from the inherent and reserved powers of the state, exerted within the limits of those fundamental principles of liberty and justice which lie at the base of all our civil and political institutions, and the greatest security for which resides in the right of the people to make their own laws, and alter them at their pleasure. . . .

. . . . Arbitrary power, enforcing its edicts to the injury of the persons and property of its subjects, is not law, whether manifested as the decree of a personal monarch or of an impersonal multitude. [A]ny legal proceeding enforced by public authority, whether sanctioned by age and custom, or newly devised in the discretion of the legislative power in furtherance of the general public good, which regards and preserves these principles of liberty and justice, must be held to be due process of law. . . .

Tried by these principles, we are unable to say that the substitution for a presentment or indictment by a grand jury of the proceeding by information after examination and commitment by a magistrate, certifying to the probable guilt of the defendant, with the right on his part to the aid of counsel, and to the cross-examination of the witnesses produced for the prosecution, is not due process of law. It is, as we have seen, an ancient proceeding at common law, which might include every case of an offense of less grade than a felony, except misprision of treason; and in every circumstance of its administration, as authorized by the statute of California, it carefully considers and guards the substantial interest of the prisoner. It is merely a preliminary proceeding, and can result in no final judgment, except as the consequence of a regular judicial trial, conducted precisely as in cases of indictments. . . .

For these reasons, finding no error therein, the judgment of the supreme court of California is affirmed.

JUSTICE HARLAN, dissenting.

[The] language [of the due process clause of the Fifth Amendment] is similar to that of the clause of the 14th Amendment now under examination. That similarity was not accidental, but evinces a purpose to impose upon the States the same restrictions, in respect of proceedings involving life, liberty and property, which had been imposed upon the General Government.

"Due process of law," within the meaning of the National Constitution, does not import one thing with reference to the powers of the States, and another with reference to the powers of the General Government. If particular proceedings conducted under the authority of the General Government, and involving life, are prohibited, because not constituting that due process of law required by the 5th Amendment of the Constitution of the United States, similar proceedings, conducted under the authority of a State, must be deemed illegal as not being due process of law within the meaning of the 14th Amendment. What, then, is the meaning of the words "due process of law" in the latter Amendment?

In seeking that meaning we are, fortunately, not left without authoritative directions as to the source, and the only source, from which the necessary information is to be obtained. In *Murray v. Land & I. Co.,* 18 How., 272, 276, 277, it was said:

> To what principles are we to resort to ascertain whether this process enacted by Congress is due process? To this the answer must be twofold. We must examine the Constitution itself to see whether this

process be in conflict with any of its provisions. If not found to be so, we must look *to those settled usages and modes of proceeding existing in the common and statute law of England before the emigration of our ancestors, and which are shown not to have been unsuited to their civil and political condition by having been acted on by them after the settlement of this country.*

[Clearly,] according to the settled usages and modes of proceeding existing under the common and statute law of England at the settlement of this country, information in capital cases was not consistent with the "law of the land," or with "due process of law." Such was the understanding of the patriotic men who established free institutions upon this continent. Almost the identical words of *Magna Charta* were incorporated into most of the State Constitutions before the adoption of our National Constitution. When they declared, in substance, that no person should be deprived of life, liberty or property, except by the judgment of his peers or the law of the land, they intended to assert his right to the same guaranties that were given in the mother country by the great charter and the laws passed in furtherance of its fundamental principles.

. . . If the presence in the 5th Amendment of a specific provision for grand juries in capital cases, alongside the provision for due process of law in proceedings involving life, liberty or property, is held to prove that due process of law did not, in the judgment of the Framers of the Constitution, necessarily require a grand jury in capital cases, inexorable logic would require it to be, likewise, held that the right not to be put twice in jeopardy of life and limb for the same offense, nor compelled in a criminal case to testify against one's self (rights and immunities also specifically recognized in the 5th Amendment) were not protected by that due process of law required by the settled usages and proceedings existing under the common and statute law of England at the settlement of this country. More than that, other Amendments of the Constitution proposed at the same time, expressly recognize the right of persons to just compensation for private property taken for public use; their right, when accused of crime, to be informed of the nature and cause of the accusation against them, and to a speedy and public trial, by an impartial jury of the State and district wherein the crime was committed; to be confronted by the witnesses against them; and to have compulsory process for obtaining witnesses in their favor. Will it be claimed that these rights were not secured by the "law of the land" or by "due process of law," as declared and established at the foundation of our government? Are they to be excluded from the enumeration of the fundamental principles of liberty and justice and, therefore, not embraced by "due process of law?" If the argument of my brethren be sound, those rights (although universally recognized at the establishment of our institutions as secured by that due process of law which for centuries had been the foundation of Anglo-Saxon liberty) were not deemed by our fathers as essential in the due process of law prescribed by our Constitution. . . .

It seems to me that too much stress is put upon the fact that the Framers of the Constitution made express provision for the security of those rights which at common law were protected by the requirement of due process of law and, in addition, declared, generally, that no person shall "be deprived of life, liberty or property without due process of law." The rights, for the security of which these express provisions were made, were of a character so essential to the safety of the people that it was deemed wise to avoid the possibility that Congress, in regulating the processes of law, would impair or destroy them. Hence their specific enumeration in the earlier Amendments of the Constitution, in connection with the general requirement of due process of law, the latter itself being broad enough to cover every right of life, liberty or property secured by the settled usages and modes of proceeding existing under the common and statute law of England at the time our government was founded. . . .

MR. JUSTICE FIELD did not take part in the decision of this case.

NOTES

1. In *Twining v. New Jersey,* 211 U.S. 78, 29 S.Ct. 14, 53 L.Ed. 97 (1908), the Court again rejected the incorporation theory of the Fourteenth Amendment. The Court refused to incorporate the Fifth Amendment privilege against self-incrimination into Fourteenth Amendment due process. In that case, the state trial judge noted to the jurors that the defendants had refused to testify and instructed the jurors that they may wish "to take that into consideration." Only Justice Harlan dissented.

2. Years later, *Malloy v. Hogan,* 378 U.S. 1, 84 S.Ct. 1489, 12 L.Ed.2d 653 (1964),—although it did not adopt the total-incorporation theory—did undercut *Twining* when it held that the self-incrimination privilege was applicable to the states by virtue of the due process clause. The following year, *Griffin v. California,* 380 U.S. 609, 85 S.Ct. 1229, 14 L.Ed.2d 106 (1965), specifically held that for the court or the prosecutor to comment to the jury on the defendant's exercise of his constitutional right to remain silent, or to suggest that such silence is evidence of guilt, violates due process. The Court applied to the states the federal rule that originated in an 1893 decision (in which the Court relied on a federal statute). The purpose of such comment

is an improper effort to make the assertion of a constitutional right more costly. According to the opinion, what the jurors may notice on their own is one thing. "What they may infer when the court solemnizes the silence of the accused into evidence against him is quite another." However, the Court still did not accept any total-incorporation theory. At the time that the Court decided *Griffin,* the courts or legislatures of forty-four states already forbade comment on the defendant's failure to testify.

POWELL V. ALABAMA
287 U.S. 45, 53 S.Ct. 55, 77 L.Ed. 158 (1932)

[Defendants in this case were nine blacks charged with raping two white girls on March 25, 1931. The defendants became known as the Scottsboro Boys. All the defendants were found guilty except for Roy Wright, for whom a mistrial was declared because of his extreme youth. In 1932, the state supreme court reversed the convictions of Eugene Williams because he was a minor and could not be tried until after a hearing in the juvenile court. In 1937, the state announced that it was finally releasing these two—after they had been in prison six and one-half years— because they were too young to have committed any rape. One was 12 years of age and the other was 13 at the time of the alleged rape. The state released them "on the condition that they leave the state and never return." The state also dropped charges against two others in 1937, on the grounds that they were too sick at the time of the alleged rape to have been involved at all. The other five remained in prison, and some were eventually pardoned. The Supreme Court issued it opinion in *Powell* after the first round of trials, in March 1931.

[At the request of the state, the defendants were divided into three separate groups. Each of the three trials was completed in a single day. The juries sentenced the seven defendants to death, and the state supreme court affirmed, with state Chief Justice Anderson strongly dissenting. Defendants objected to the systematic exclusion of blacks from the jury—a claim subsequently accepted in *Norris v. Alabama,* 294 U.S. 587, 55 S.Ct. 579, 79 L.Ed. 1074 (1935). In *Powell,* however, the Court found it necessary only to address the claim that "They were denied the right of counsel, with the accustomed incidents of consultation and opportunity of preparation for trial."

[The nine Scottsboro defendants were eventually tried four times. Some were sentenced to death three times. At the various trials in 1931 (the state eventually went through eleven trials), the two white girls who claimed rape testified for the prosecution. On January 5, 1933, Ruby Bates, one of the alleged victims, wrote a letter to a friend denying that the black youths had attacked her. At the retrial on April 7 of that year, Bates testified for the defense that no rape had occurred, either of her or the other girl, Victoria Price. Price kept to her original story, which had internal conflicts and was now uncorroborated. Two days later, the all-white jury convicted the defendants again.

[The Scottsboro case led to protest marches around the country and abroad, and became a cause célèbre. On October 25, 1976, Governor George Wallace of Alabama gave a "full and unconditional pardon" to the last survivor of the Scottsboro boys—Clarence Norris.[1]]

JUSTICE SUTHERLAND delivered the opinion of the Court.

The record shows that on the day when the offense is said to have been committed, these defendants, together with a number of other negroes, were upon a freight train on its way through Alabama. On the same train were seven white boys and the two white girls. A fight took place between the negroes and the white boys, in the course of which the white boys, with the exception of one named Gilley, were thrown off the train. A message was sent ahead, reporting the fight and asking that every negro be gotten off the train. The participants in the fight, and the two girls, were in an open gondola car. The two girls testified that each of them was assaulted by six different negroes in turn, and they identified the seven defendants as having been among the number. None of the white boys was called to testify, with the exception of Gilley, who was called in rebuttal.

Before the train reached Scottsboro, Ala., a sheriff's posse seized the defendants and two other negroes. Both girls and the negroes then were taken to Scottsboro, the county seat. Word of their coming and of the alleged assault had preceded them, and they were met at Scottsboro by a large crowd. It does not sufficiently appear that the defendants were seriously threatened with, or that they were actually in danger of, mob violence; but it does appear that the attitude of the community was one of great hostility. The sheriff thought it necessary to call for the militia to assist in safeguarding the prisoners. Chief Justice Anderson pointed out in his opinion that every step taken from the arrest and arraignment to the sentence was accompanied by the military. Soldiers took the defendants to Gadsden for safe-keeping, brought them back to Scottsboro for arraignment, returned them to Gadsden for safe-keeping while awaiting trial, escorted them to Scottsboro for trial a few days later, and guarded the courthouse and grounds at every stage of the proceedings. It is perfectly apparent that the proceedings, from

---

1   Haywood Patterson and Earl Conrad, Scottsboro Boy (1950); Dan Carter, Scottsboro: A Tragedy of the American South (Rev.ed.1979).

beginning to end, took place in an atmosphere of tense, hostile, and excited public sentiment. During the entire time, the defendants were closely confined or were under military guard. The record does not disclose their ages, except that one of them was nineteen; but the record clearly indicates that most, if not all, of them were youthful, and they are constantly referred to as "the boys." They were ignorant and illiterate. All of them were residents of other states, where alone members of their families or friends resided.

However guilty defendants, upon due inquiry, might prove to have been, they were, until convicted, presumed to be innocent. It was the duty of the court having their cases in charge to see that they were denied no necessary incident of a fair trial. With any error of the state court involving alleged contravention of the state statutes or [state] Constitution we, of course, have nothing to do. The sole inquiry which we are permitted to make is whether the federal Constitution was contravened; and as to that, we confine ourselves, as already suggested, to the inquiry whether the defendants were in substance denied the right of counsel, and if so, whether such denial infringes the due process clause of the Fourteenth Amendment.

First. The record shows that immediately upon the return of the indictment defendants were arraigned and pleaded not guilty. Apparently they were not asked whether they had, or were able to employ, counsel, or wished to have counsel appointed; or whether they had friends or relatives who might assist in that regard if communicated with. That it would not have been an idle ceremony to have given the defendants reasonable opportunity to communicate with their families and endeavor to obtain counsel is demonstrated by the fact that very soon after conviction, able counsel appeared in their behalf. . . .

It is hardly necessary to say that the right to counsel being conceded, a defendant should be afforded a fair opportunity to secure counsel for his own choice. Not only was that not done here, but such designation of counsel as was attempted was either so indefinite or so close upon the trial as to amount to a denial of effective and substantial aid in that regard. This will be amply demonstrated by a brief review of the record.

April 6, six days after indictment, the trials began. When the first case was called, the court inquired whether the parties were ready for trial. The state's attorney replied that he was ready to proceed. No one answered for the defendants or appeared to represent or defend them. Mr. Roddy, a Tennessee lawyer not a member of the local bar, addressed the court, saying that he had not been employed, but that people who were interested had spoken to him about the case.

He was asked by the court whether he intended to appear for the defendants, and answered that he would like to appear along with counsel that the court might appoint.

[U]ntil the very morning of the trial no lawyer had been named or definitely designated to represent the defendants. Prior to that time, the trial judge had "appointed all the members of the bar" for the limited "purpose of arraigning the defendants." Whether they would represent the defendants thereafter, if no counsel appeared in their behalf, was a matter of speculation only, or, as the judge indicated, of mere anticipation on the part of the court. . . . That this action of the trial judge in respect of appointment of counsel was little more than an expansive gesture, imposing no substantial or definite obligation upon any one, is borne out by the fact that prior to the calling of the case for trial on April 6, a leading member of the local bar accepted employment on the side of the prosecution and actively participated in the trial. [T]he circumstance lends emphasis to the conclusion that during perhaps the most critical period of the proceedings against these defendants, that is to say, from the time of their arraignment until the beginning of their trial. When consultation, thorough-going investigation and preparation were vitally important, the defendants did not have the aid of counsel in any real sense, although they were as much entitled to such aid during that period as at the trial itself. . . .

[On the morning of trial,] Mr. Roddy stated to the court that he did not appear as counsel, but that he would like to appear along with counsel that the court might appoint; that he had not been given an opportunity to prepare the case; that he was not familiar with the procedure in Alabama, but merely came down as a friend of the people who were interested; that he thought the boys would be better off if he should step entirely out of the case. Mr. Moody, a member of the local bar, expressed a willingness to help Mr. Roddy in anything he could do under the circumstances. To this the court responded: "All right, all the lawyers that will; of course I would not require a lawyer to appear if—." And Mr. Moody continued: "I am willing to do that for him as a member of the bar; I will go ahead and help do anything I can do." With this dubious understanding, the trials immediately proceeded.

The defendants, young, ignorant, illiterate, surrounded by hostile sentiment, haled back and forth under guard of soldiers, charged with an atrocious crime regarded with especial horror in the community where they were to be tried, were thus put in peril of their lives within a few moments after counsel for the first time charged with any degree of responsibility began to represent them.

. . . No attempt was made to investigate. No opportunity to do so was given. Defendants were immediately hurried to trial. . . . Under the circumstances disclosed, we hold that defendants were not accorded the right of counsel in any substantial sense. To decide otherwise, would simply be to ignore actualities. This conclusion finds ample support in the reasoning of an overwhelming array of state decisions. . . .

[Second. We must decide] whether the denial of the assistance of counsel contravenes the due process clause of the Fourteenth Amendment to the Federal Constitution. . . . An affirmation of the right to the aid of counsel in petty offenses, and its denial in the case of crimes of the gravest character, where such aid is most needed, is so outrageous and so obviously a perversion of all sense of proportion that the rule was constantly, vigorously and sometimes passionately assailed by English statesmen and lawyers. . . .

One test which has been applied to determine whether due process of law has been accorded in given instances is to ascertain what were the settled usages and modes of proceeding under the common and statute law of England before the Declaration of Independence, subject, however, to the qualification that they be shown not to have been unsuited to the civil and political conditions of our ancestors by having been followed in this country after it became a nation. Plainly, as appears from the foregoing, this test, as thus qualified, has not been met in the present case.

We do not overlook the case of *Hurtado v. California.* . . . In the face of the reasoning of the *Hurtado* Case, if it stood alone, it would be difficult to justify the conclusion that the right to counsel, being thus specifically granted by the Sixth Amendment, was also within the intendment of the due process of law clause. But the *Hurtado* Case does not stand alone. In the later case of *Chicago, Burlington & Q.R. Co. v. Chicago,* 166 U.S. 226, 241, 17 S.Ct. 581, 41 L.Ed. 979, this court held that a judgment of a state court, even though authorized by statute, by which private property was taken for public use without just compensation, was in violation of the due process of law required by the Fourteenth Amendment, notwithstanding that the Fifth Amendment explicitly declares that private property shall not be taken for public use without just compensation. Likewise, this court has considered that freedom of speech and of the press are rights protected by the due process clause of the Fourteenth Amendment, although in the First Amendment, Congress is prohibited in specific terms from abridging the right. *Gitlow v. People of State of New York,* 268 U.S. 652, 666, 45 S.Ct. 625, 69 L.Ed. 1138.

These later cases establish that notwithstanding the sweeping character of the language in the *Hurtado* Case, the rule laid down is not without exceptions. The rule is an aid to construction, and in some instances may be conclusive; but it must yield to more compelling considerations whenever such considerations exist. The fact that the right involved is of such a character that it cannot be denied without violating those "fundamental principles of liberty and justice which lie at the base of all our civil and political institutions" is obviously one of those compelling considerations which must prevail in determining whether it is embraced within the due process clause of the Fourteenth Amendment, although it be specifically dealt with in another part of the Federal Constitution. Evidently this court, in the later cases enumerated, regarded the rights there under consideration as of this fundamental character. That some such distinction must be observed is foreshadowed in *Twining v. New Jersey,* where Mr. Justice Moody, speaking for the court, said that: "It is possible that some of the personal rights safeguarded by the first eight Amendments against national action may also be safeguarded against state action, because a denial of them would be a denial of due process of law. If this is so, it is not because those rights are enumerated in the first eight Amendments, but because they are of such a nature that they are included in the conception of due process of law." [T]he right to the aid of counsel is of this fundamental character.

It never has been doubted by this court, or any other so far as we know, that notice and hearing are preliminary steps essential to the passing of an enforceable judgment, and that they, together with a legally competent tribunal having jurisdiction of the case, constitute basic elements of the constitutional requirement of due process of law. . . .

What, then, does a hearing include? Historically and in practice, in our own country at least, it has always included the right to the aid of counsel when desired and provided by the party asserting the right. The right to be heard would be, in many cases, of little avail if it did not comprehend the right to be heard by counsel. Even the intelligent and educated layman has small and sometimes no skill in the science of law. If charged with crime, he is incapable, generally, of determining for himself whether the indictment is good or bad. He is unfamiliar with the rules of evidence. Left without the aid of counsel he may be put on trial without a proper charge, and convicted upon incompetent evidence, or evidence irrelevant to the issue or otherwise inadmissible. He lacks both the skill and knowledge adequately to prepare his defense, even though he have a perfect one. He requires the guiding hand of counsel at every step in the proceedings against him. Without it, though he be not guilty, he faces the danger of conviction because he does not know how to establish his innocence. If that be true of men of intelligence, how much more true is it of the ignorant and illiterate, or those of feeble intellect. If in any case, civil or criminal, a state or federal court were arbitrarily to refuse to hear a party by counsel, employed by and appearing for him, it reasonably may not be doubted that such a refusal would be a denial of a hearing, and, therefore, of due process in the constitutional sense. . . .

In the light of the facts outlined in the forepart of this opinion—the ignorance and illiteracy of the defendants, their youth, the circumstances of public hostility, the imprisonment and the close surveillance of the defendants by the military forces, the fact that their friends and families were all in other states and communication with them necessarily difficult, and above all that they stood in deadly peril of their lives—we think the failure of the trial court to give them reasonable time and opportunity to secure counsel was a clear denial of due process.

[U]nder the circumstances just stated, the necessity of counsel was so vital and imperative that the failure of the trial court to make an effective appointment of counsel was likewise a denial of due process within the meaning of the Fourteenth Amendment. Whether this would be so in other criminal prosecutions, or under other circumstances, we need not determine. All that it is necessary now to decide, as we do decide, is that in a capital case, where the defendant is unable to employ counsel, and is incapable adequately of making his own defense because of ignorance, feeblemindedness, illiteracy, or the like, it is the duty of the court, whether requested or not, to assign counsel for him as a necessary requisite of due process of law; and that duty is not discharged by an assignment at such a time or under such circumstances as to preclude the giving of effective aid in the preparation and trial of the case. To hold otherwise would be to ignore the fundamental postulate, already adverted to, "that there are certain immutable principles of justice which inhere in the very idea of free government which no member of the Union may disregard." . . .

Judgments reversed.

[The dissenting opinion of BUTLER, J., joined by MCREYNOLDS, J., is omitted.]

PALKO V. CONNECTICUT

302 U.S. 319, 58 S.Ct. 149, 82 L.Ed. 288 (1937)

[Palko was indicted for murder in the first degree. The jury found him guilty of murder in the second degree, and he was sentenced to life imprisonment. The state, with the permission of the trial judge, appealed (pursuant to a state statute that allowed it to do so), and the state supreme court ordered a new trial because it found errors that prejudiced the state (*e.g.*, improper exclusion of testimony as to a confession by the defendant). At the second trial, the jury found him guilty of murder in the first degree, and the court sentenced Palko to death. He claimed that his second trial put him in jeopardy twice for the same offense, in violation of the Fourteenth Amendment. *Benton v. Maryland*, 395 U.S. 784, 89 S.Ct. 2056, 23 L.Ed.2d 707 (1969), later held that the double-jeopardy clause of the Fifth Amendment was applicable to the states through the due process clause of the Fourteenth Amendment. Benton said, "we today find that the double jeopardy prohibition of the Fifth Amendment represents a fundamental ideal in our constitutional heritage, and that it should apply to the States through the Fourteenth Amendment. Insofar as it is inconsistent with this holding, *Palko v. Connecticut* is overruled."]

JUSTICE CARDOZO delivered the opinion of the Court.

[I]n appellant's view the Fourteenth Amendment is to be taken as embodying the prohibitions of the Fifth. His thesis is even broader. Whatever would be a violation of the original bill of rights (Amendments 1 to 8) if done by the federal government is now equally unlawful by force of the Fourteenth Amendment if done by a state. There is no such general rule.

The Fifth Amendment provides, among other things, that no person shall be held to answer for a capital or otherwise infamous crime unless on presentment or indictment of a grand jury. This court has held that, in prosecutions by a state, presentment or indictment by a grand jury may give way to informations at the instance of a public officer. *Hurtado v. California*. [The Fifth Amendment provides also] that no person shall be compelled in any criminal case to be a witness against himself. This court has said that, in prosecutions by a state, the exemption will fail if the state elects to end it. *Twining v. New Jersey*. . . .

On the other hand, the due process clause of the Fourteenth Amendment may make it unlawful for a state to abridge by its statutes the freedom of speech which the First Amendment safeguards against encroachment by the Congress (*De Jonge v. Oregon*, 299 U.S. 353, 364, 57 S.Ct. 255, 260, 81 L.Ed. 278), or the like freedom of the press (*Near v. Minnesota*, 283 U.S. 697, 707, 51 S.Ct. 625, 627, 75 L.Ed. 1357), or the free exercise of religion (*Pierce v. Society of Sisters*, 268 U.S. 510, 45 S.Ct. 571, 69 L.Ed. 1070, 39 A.L.R. 468), or the right of peaceable assembly, without which speech would be unduly trammeled (*De Jonge v. Oregon*), or the right of one accused of crime to the benefit of counsel (*Powell v. Alabama*). In these and other situations, immunities that are valid as against the federal government by force of the specific pledges of particular amendments have been found to be implicit in the concept of ordered liberty, and thus, through the Fourteenth Amendment, become valid as against the states.

The line of division may seem to be wavering and broken if there is a hasty catalogue of the cases on the one side and the other. Reflection and analysis will induce a different view. There emerges the perception of a rationalizing principle which gives to discrete instances a proper order and coherence. The right to trial by jury and the immunity from prosecution except as the result of an indictment may have value and importance. Even so, they are not of the very essence of a scheme of ordered liberty. To abolish them is not to violate a "principle of justice so rooted in the traditions and conscience of our people as to be ranked as fundamental." Few would be so narrow or provincial as to maintain that a fair and enlightened system of justice would be impossible without them. What is true of jury trials and indictments is true also, as the cases show, of the immunity from compulsory self-incrimination. *Twining v. New Jersey, supra.* This too might be lost, and justice still be done. . . . No doubt there would remain the need to give protection against torture, physical or mental. Justice, however, would not perish if the accused were subject to a duty to respond to orderly inquiry. . . .

We reach a different plane of social and moral values when we pass to the privileges and immunities that have been taken over from the earlier articles of the Federal Bill of Rights and brought within the Fourteenth Amendment by a process of absorption. These in their origin were effective against the federal government alone. If the Fourteenth Amendment has absorbed them, the process of absorption has had its source in the belief that neither liberty nor justice would exist if they were sacrificed. This is true, for illustration, of freedom of thought and speech. Of that freedom one may say that it is the matrix, the indispensable condition, of nearly every other form of freedom.

. . . Is that kind of double jeopardy to which the statute has subjected him a hardship so acute and shocking that our policy will not endure it? Does it violate those "fundamental principles of liberty and justice which lie at the base of all our civil and political institutions"? The answer surely must be "no." What the answer would have to be if the state were permitted after a trial free from error to try the accused over again or to bring another case against him, we have no occasion to consider. We deal with the statute before us and no other. The state is not attempting to wear the accused out by a multitude of cases with accumulated trials. It asks no more than this, that the case against him shall go on until there shall be a trial free from the corrosion of substantial legal error. This is not cruelty at all, nor even vexation in any immoderate degree. If the trial had been infected with error adverse to the accused, there might have been review at his instance, and as often as necessary to purge the vicious taint. A reciprocal privilege, subject at all times to the discretion of the presiding judge, has now been granted to the state. There is here no seismic innovation. The edifice of justice stands, its symmetry, to many, greater than before. . . .

The judgment is affirmed.

MR. JUSTICE BUTLER dissents.

NOTES

1. The Court held that the California police violated due process in *Rochin v. California,* 342 U.S. 165, 72 S.Ct. 205, 96 L.Ed. 183 (1952). After the police learned that Rochin might be selling narcotics, they illegally entered his residence and found him sitting on his bed partially clothed. The police saw two pills, which Rochin quickly swallowed. The police then struggled to open his mouth. They were unsuccessful, so they took him to a hospital and had his stomach pumped. They recovered and analyzed the pills, which proved to be morphine. Rochin was convicted, and Justice Frankfurter reversed. The conviction violated due process because it "shocks the conscience." The police did not merely combat crime "too energetically." Their methods were "too close to the rack and the screw to permit of constitutional differentiation." Justice Black concurred, but did not accept Frankfurter's reasoning. Justice Frankfurter protested that the "vague contours of the Due Process Clause do not leave judges at large;" due process did not "resort to a revival of 'natural law';" and that "due process of law [is not] a matter of judicial caprice" even though it "may be indefinite and vague."

2. The modern Court has incorporated most, but not all, of the Bill of Rights, using the test of whether the clause in question "is fundamental to the American scheme of justice." *Duncan v. Louisiana,* § 4.5. Section 2.3 above summarizes the present state of the law of incorporation. The debate over the true meaning of due process and its application to nontextual rights is far from over.

4.2 THE RIGHT TO COUNSEL

In *Powell v. Alabama,* § 4.1, *supra,* the Court held that due process in that case required a right to counsel. The Court there never explicitly stated that it was creating an absolute right to counsel in all cases; it only said that in the circumstances of the case before it, a right to the effective assistance of counsel clearly existed. Subsequently, in *Betts v. Brady,* 316 U.S. 455, 62 S.Ct. 1252, 86 L.Ed. 1595 (1942), Justice Roberts for the Court held: "while want of counsel in a particular case may result in a conviction lacking in . . . fundamental fairness, we cannot say that the [Fourteenth] Amendment embodies an inexorable command that no trial for any offense, or in any court, can be fairly conducted and justice accorded a defendant who is not represented by counsel." The Court must look to "the totality of facts in a given case" to see if counsel should be appointed. What may be "shocking to the universal sense of justice" in one case may "fall short" of a denial of "fundamental fairness" in "light of other considerations." Justice Black, joined by Justices Douglas and Murphy, dissented. In the next case, the Court overruled *Betts.*

GIDEON V. WAINWRIGHT
372 U.S. 335, 83 S.Ct. 792, 9 L.Ed.2d 799 (1963)

JUSTICE BLACK delivered the opinion of the Court.

Petitioner was charged in a Florida state court with having broken and entered a poolroom with intent to commit a misdemeanor. This offense is a felony under Florida law. Appearing in court without funds and without a lawyer, petitioner asked the court to appoint counsel for him, whereupon the following colloquy took place:

> The Court: Mr. Gideon, I am sorry, but I cannot appoint Counsel to represent you in this case. Under the laws of the State of Florida, the only time the Court can appoint Counsel to represent a Defendant is when that person is charged with a capital offense. I am sorry, but I will have to deny your request to appoint Counsel to defend you in this case.

> The Defendant: The United States Supreme Court says I am entitled to be represented by Counsel.

Put to trial before a jury, Gideon conducted his defense about as well as could be expected from a layman. He made an opening statement to the jury, cross-examined the State's witnesses, presented witnesses in his own defense, declined to testify himself, and made a short argument "emphasizing his innocence to the charge contained in the Information filed in this case." The jury returned a verdict of guilty, and petitioner was sentenced to serve five years in the state prison. Later, petitioner filed in the Florida Supreme Court this habeas corpus petition attacking his conviction and sentence on the ground that the trial court's refusal to appoint counsel for him denied him rights "guaranteed by the Constitution and the Bill of Rights by the United States Government." Treating the petition for habeas corpus as properly before it, the State Supreme Court, "upon consideration thereof" but without an opinion, denied all relief. Since 1942, when *Betts v. Brady* was decided by a divided Court, the problem of a defendant's federal constitutional right to counsel in a state court has been a continuing source of controversy and litigation in both state and federal courts. To give this problem another review here, we granted certiorari. Since Gideon was proceeding *in forma pauperis,* we appointed counsel to represent him. . . . Since the facts and circumstances of the two cases are so nearly indistinguishable, we think the *Betts v. Brady* holding if left standing would require us to reject Gideon's claim that the Constitution guarantees him the assistance of counsel. Upon full reconsideration we conclude that *Betts v. Brady* should be overruled.

The Sixth Amendment provides, "In all criminal prosecutions, the accused shall enjoy the right . . . to have the Assistance of Counsel for his defence." We have construed this to mean that in federal courts counsel must be provided for defendants unable to employ counsel unless the right is competently and intelligently waived.[3] . . .

We accept *Betts v. Brady's* assumption, based as it was on our prior cases, that a provision of the Bill of Rights which is "fundamental and essential to a fair trial" is made obligatory upon the States by the Fourteenth Amendment. We think the Court in *Betts* was wrong, however, in concluding that the Sixth Amendment's guarantee of counsel is not one of these fundamental rights. Ten years before *Betts v. Brady,* this Court, after full consideration of all the historical data examined in *Betts,* had unequivocally declared that "the right to the aid of counsel is of this fundamental character." *Powell v. Alabama.* While the Court at the close of its *Powell* opinion did by its language, as this Court frequently does, limit its holding to the particular facts and circumstances of that case, its conclusions about the fundamental nature of the right to counsel are unmistakable.

[I]t is not surprising that the *Betts* Court, when faced with the contention that "one charged with crime, who is unable to obtain counsel, must be furnished counsel by the state," conceded that "[expressions in the opinions of this court

---

3   *Johnson v. Zerbst,* 304 U.S. 458, 58 S.Ct. 1019, 82 L.Ed. 1461 (1938).

lend color to the argument. . . ." The fact is that in deciding as it did—that "appointment of counsel is not a fundamental right, essential to a fair trial"—the Court in *Betts v. Brady* made an abrupt break with its own well-considered precedents. In returning to these old precedents, sounder we believe than the new, we but restore constitutional principles established to achieve a fair system of justice. Not only these precedents but also reason and reflection require us to recognize that in our adversary system of criminal justice, any person haled into court, who is too poor to hire a lawyer, cannot be assured a fair trial unless counsel is provided for him. This seems to us to be an obvious truth. Governments, both state and federal, quite properly spend vast sums of money to establish machinery to try defendants accused of crime. Lawyers to prosecute are everywhere deemed essential to protect the public's interest in an orderly society. Similarly, there are few defendants charged with crime, few indeed, who fail to hire the best lawyers they can get to prepare and present their defenses. That government hires lawyers to prosecute and defendants who have the money hire lawyers to defend are the strongest indications of the widespread belief that lawyers in criminal courts are necessities, not luxuries. The right of one charged with crime to counsel may not be deemed fundamental and essential to fair trials in some countries, but it is in ours. From the very beginning, our state and national constitutions and laws have laid great emphasis on procedural and substantive safeguards designed to assure fair trials before impartial tribunals in which every defendant stands equal before the law. This noble ideal cannot be realized if the poor man charged with crime has to face his accusers without a lawyer to assist him. A defendant's need for a lawyer is nowhere better stated than in the moving words of Mr. Justice Sutherland in *Powell v. Alabama:*

> The right to be heard would be, in many cases, of little avail if it did not comprehend the right to be heard by counsel. Even the intelligent and educated layman has small and sometimes no skill in the science of law.

The Court in *Betts v. Brady* departed from the sound wisdom upon which the Court's holding in *Powell v. Alabama* rested. Florida, supported by two other States, has asked that *Betts v. Brady* be left intact. Twenty-two States, as friends of the Court, argue that *Betts* was "an anachronism when handed down" and that it should now be overruled. We agree. . . .

JUSTICE DOUGLAS, concurring.

While I join the opinion of the Court, a brief historical resume of the relation between the Bill of Rights and the first section of the Fourteenth Amendment seems pertinent. Since the adoption of that Amendment, ten Justices have felt that it protects from infringement by the States the privileges, protections, and safeguards granted by the Bill of Rights.

. . . Unfortunately [this view] has never commanded a Court. Yet, happily, all constitutional questions are always open. And what we do today does not foreclose the matter.

My Brother Harlan is of the view that a guarantee of the Bill of Rights that is made applicable to the States by reason of the Fourteenth Amendment is a lesser version of that same guarantee as applied to the Federal Government. Mr. Justice Jackson shared that view. But that view has not prevailed and rights protected against state invasion by the Due Process Clause of the Fourteenth Amendment are not watered-down versions of what the Bill of Rights guarantees.

JUSTICE HARLAN, concurring . . .

I cannot subscribe to the view that *Betts v. Brady* represented "an abrupt break with its own well-considered precedents." . . . It is evident that [in *Powell v. Alabama,* the] limiting facts were not added to the opinion as an afterthought; they were repeatedly emphasized, and were clearly regarded as important to the result. . . . In what is done today I do not understand the Court to depart from the principles laid down in *Palko v. Connecticut,* or to embrace the concept that the Fourteenth Amendment "incorporates" the Sixth Amendment as such. On these premises I join in the judgment of the Court.

The opinion of CLARK, J., concurring in the result, is omitted.]

NOTES

1. The court appointed counsel for Gideon, who was retried and acquitted.

2. Subsequently, *Argensinger v. Hamlin,* 407 U.S. 25, 92 S.Ct. 2006, 32 L.Ed. 2d 530 (1972), invalidated a Florida rule that required the court to appoint counsel only for offenses punishable by more than six months of imprisonment. Unless the accused knowingly and intelligently waives a lawyer, the judge may not impose any imprisonment unless the accused is represented by counsel. See also *Scott v. Illinois,* 440 U.S. 367, 99 S.Ct. 1158, 59 L.Ed.2d 383 (1979) (*Gideon* applies whenever the accused in fact is sentenced to imprisonment; the right to appointed counsel does not apply if the statute merely authorizes imprisonment, if that punishment is not actually imposed).

3. In *Griffin v. Illinois*, 351 U.S. 12, 76 S.Ct. 585, 100 L.Ed. 891 (1956), a divided Court, with no majority opinion, relying on the due process and equal protection clauses, held that if the state grants an appeal in criminal cases, the state must furnish free transcripts to indigents or provide other means of adequate and effective appellate review to indigent defendants.

Douglas v. California, 372 U.S. 353, 83 S.Ct. 814, 9 L.Ed.2d 811 (1963), decided the same day as *Gideon,* held that when the state grants the first appeal in a criminal case (the Court was not considering discretionary appeals or appeals after the first appeal), under the equal protection clause the state must supply counsel to the indigent. "For there can be no equal justice where the kind of an appeal a man enjoys 'depends on the amount of money he has.' "

4. The Court has used the *Douglas-Griffin* equal protection analysis to find other rights for indigent defendants. For example, the state must waive transcript fees for appeal even if the case does not involve the incarceration of the defendant. *Mayer v. Chicago,* 404 U.S. 189, 92 S.Ct. 410, 30 L.Ed.2d 372 (1971); neither may the state require indigents to pay filing fees to have access to appellate courts, *Burns v. Ohio,* 360 U.S. 252, 79 S.Ct. 1164, 3 L.Ed.2d 1209 (1959), or to post conviction proceedings following appeals, *Smith v. Bennett,* 365 U.S. 708, 81 S.Ct. 895, 6 L.Ed.2d 39 (1961). *Smith v. Bennett,* 365 U.S. 708, 81 S.Ct. 895, 6 L.Ed.2d 39 (1961). If an indigent defendant makes a preliminary showing that his sanity at the time of the crime is likely to be a significant factor at trial, due process requires the State to provide a psychiatrist's assistance. *Ake v. Oklahoma,* 470 U.S. 68, 105 S.Ct. 1087, 84 L.Ed.2d 53 (1985). The state need not provide counsel to indigent defendants in discretionary appeals or collateral attack proceedings after their first appeal as of right. *Ross v. Moffitt,* 417 U.S. 600, 94 S.Ct. 2437, 41 L.Ed.2d 341 (1974).

The state may not imprison an indigent beyond the maximum term specified by statute because of his failure to pay the monetary provisions of his sentence. *Williams v. Illinois,* 399 U.S. 235, 90 S.Ct. 2018, 26 L.Ed.2d 586 (1970) (trial court, pursuant to statute, directed the defendant to serve the maximum term of one year and then work off, at the rate of $5 per day, the $500 of fine and $5 of costs levied against him; held, violation of equal protection). If the state provides only for fines for certain offenses, it cannot imprison indigents who are unable to pay. *Tate v. Short*, 401 U.S. 395, 91 S.Ct. 668, 28 L.Ed.2d 130 (1971) (trial court had ordered, pursuant to statute, that defendant with accumulated traffic fines of $425 be imprisoned to work off the fine at a rate of $5 per day; held, violation of equal protection). *Bearden v.*

Georgia, 461 U.S. 660, 103 S.Ct. 2064, 76 L.Ed.2d 221 (1983) (under Fourteenth Amendment court may not automatically revoke probation because defendant could not pay his fine, without first determining that defendant had not made sufficient bona fide efforts to pay, or that there did not exist adequate alternative forms of punishment, such as extending the time for making payments, reducing the fine, or directing the performance of some form of labor or public service in lieu of the fine).

Johnson v. Avery, 393 U.S. 483, 89 S.Ct. 747, 21 L.Ed.2d 718 (1969), invalidated a regulation prohibiting prisoners from assisting each other in filing habeas corpus applications and other legal actions. See also *Wolff v. McDonnell,* 418 U.S. 539, 94 S.Ct. 2963, 41 L.Ed.2d 935 (1974) (extending *Avery* to civil rights actions).

Bounds v. Smith, 430 U.S. 817, 97 S.Ct. 1491, 52 L.Ed.2d 72 (1977), relying on these cases and the *Griffin-Douglas* reasoning, held that states "must protect the rights of prisoners to access to the courts by providing them with law libraries or alternative sources of legal knowledge." Dissenting in *Bounds,* Chief Justice Burger argued that the Court "leaves us unenlightened as to the source of the 'right of access to the courts' which it perceives or of the requirement that States 'foot the bill' for assuring such access for prisoners who want to act as legal researchers and brief writers."

4.3 SELF-INCRIMINATION

In *Escobedo v. Illinois,* 378 U.S. 478, 84 S.Ct. 1758, 12 L.Ed.2d 977 (1964), the Court held that for the police to refuse to honor a suspect's request to consult with his lawyer during the course of an interrogation is a "denial of 'the Assistance of Counsel' in violation of the Sixth Amendment to the Constitution as made obligatory upon the states by the Fourteenth Amendment." This violation "renders inadmissible in a state criminal trial any incriminating statement elicited by the police during the interrogation." The Court referred to *Gideon v. Wainwright* and reasoned that if the right to use counsel at the interrogation were denied, the right to use counsel at trial would be a hollow right, no more than an appeal of the interrogation. Escobedo had requested to see his lawyer.

What if he had made no such request? What if he did not know that he had a right to counsel? Does the state have an obligation to inform a suspect of his or constitutional rights? The next case discusses that issue, and unlike *Escobedo,* it focuses on the Fifth Amendment self-incrimination clause, not the Sixth Amendment right to counsel.

MIRANDA V. ARIZONA

384 U.S. 436, 86 S.Ct. 1602, 16 L.Ed.2d 694 (1966)

CHIEF JUSTICE WARREN delivered the opinion of the Court.

The cases before us raise questions which go to the roots of our concepts of American criminal jurisprudence: the restraints society must observe consistent with the Federal Constitution in prosecuting individuals for crime. More specifically, we deal with the admissibility of statements obtained from an individual who is subjected to custodial police interrogation and the necessity for procedures which assure that the individual is accorded his privilege under the Fifth Amendment to the Constitution not to be compelled to incriminate himself. . . .

Our holding will be spelled out with some specificity in the pages which follow but briefly stated it is this: the prosecution may not use statements, whether exculpatory or inculpatory, stemming from custodial interrogation of the defendant unless it demonstrates the use of procedural safeguards effective to secure the privilege against self-incrimination. By custodial interrogation, we mean questioning initiated by law enforcement officers after a person has been taken into custody or otherwise deprived of his freedom of action in any significant way. As for the procedural safeguards to be employed, unless other fully effective means are devised to inform accused persons of their right of silence and to assure a continuous opportunity to exercise it, the following measures are required. Prior to any questioning, the person must be warned that he has a right to remain silent, that any statement he does make may be used as evidence against him, and that he has a right to the presence of an attorney, either retained or appointed. The defendant may waive effectuation of these rights, provided the waiver is made voluntarily, knowingly and intelligently. If, however, he indicates in any manner and at any stage of the process that he wishes to consult with an attorney before speaking there can be no questioning. Likewise, if the individual is alone and indicates in any manner that he does not wish to be interrogated, the police may not question him. The mere fact that he may have answered some questions or volunteered some statements on his own does not deprive him of the right to refrain from answering any further inquiries until he has consulted with an attorney and thereafter consents to be questioned.

The constitutional issue we decide in each of these cases is the admissibility of statements obtained from a defendant questioned while in custody or otherwise deprived of his freedom of action in any significant way. In each, the defendant was questioned by police officers, detectives, or a prosecuting attorney in a room in which he was cut off from the outside world. In none of these cases was the defendant given a full and effective warning of his rights at the outset of the interrogation process. In all the cases, the questioning elicited oral admissions, and in three of them, signed statements as well which were admitted at their trials. They all thus share salient features—incommunicado interrogation of individuals in a police-dominated atmosphere, resulting in self-incriminating statements without full warnings of constitutional rights.

An understanding of the nature and setting of this in-custody interrogation is essential to our decisions today. The difficulty in depicting what transpires at such interrogations stems from the fact that in this country they have largely taken place incommunicado. From extensive factual studies undertaken in the early 1930s, including the famous Wickersham Report to Congress by a Presidential Commission, it is clear that police violence and the "third degree" flourished at that time. . . .

The examples given above are undoubtedly the exception now, but they are sufficiently widespread to be the object of concern. Unless a proper limitation upon custodial interrogation is achieved—such as these decisions will advance—there can be no assurance that practices of this nature will be eradicated in the foreseeable future.

[W]e stress that the modern practice of in-custody interrogation is psychologically rather than physically oriented. . . . Interrogation still takes place in privacy. Privacy results in secrecy and this in turn results in a gap in our knowledge as to what in fact goes on in the interrogation rooms. A valuable source of information about present police practices, however, may be found in various police manuals and texts which document procedures employed with success in the past, and which recommend various other effective tactics. These texts are used by law enforcement agencies themselves as guides. . . .

The officers are told by the manuals that the "principal psychological factor contributing to a successful interrogation is privacy—being alone with the person under interrogation." [T]he manuals instruct the police to display an air of confidence in the suspect's guilt and from outward appearance to maintain only an interest in confirming certain details.

The texts thus stress that the major qualities an interrogator should possess are patience and perseverance. One writer describes the efficacy of these characteristics in this manner:

In the preceding paragraphs emphasis has been placed on kindness and stratagems. The investigator will, however, encounter many situations where the sheer weight of his personality will be the deciding factor. Where emotional appeals and tricks are employed to no avail, he must rely on an oppressive atmosphere of dogged persistence. He must interrogate steadily and without relent, leaving the subject no prospect of surcease. He must dominate his subject and overwhelm him with his inexorable will to obtain the truth. He should interrogate for a spell of several hours pausing only for the subject's necessities in acknowledgement of the need to avoid a charge of duress that can be technically substantiated. In a serious case, the interrogation may continue for days, with the required intervals for food and sleep, but with no respite from the atmosphere of domination. It is possible in this way to induce the subject to talk without resorting to duress or coercion. The method should be used only when the guilt of the subject appears highly probable.

The interrogators sometimes are instructed to induce a confession out of trickery. The technique here is quite effective in crimes which require identification or which run in series. In the identification situation, the interrogator may take a break in his questioning to place the subject among a group of men in a line-up. "The witness or complainant (previously coached, if necessary) studies the line-up and confidently points out the subject as the guilty party." Then the questioning resumes "as though there were now no doubt about the guilt of the subject." . . .

From these representative samples of interrogation techniques, the setting prescribed by the manuals and observed in practice becomes clear. In essence, it is this: To be alone with the subject is essential to prevent distraction and to deprive him of any outside support. The aura of confidence in his guilt undermines his will to resist. He merely confirms the preconceived story the police seek to have him describe. [The police] persuade, trick, or cajole him out of exercising his constitutional rights.

Even without employing brutality, the "third degree" or the specific stratagems described above, the very fact of custodial interrogation exacts a heavy toll on individual liberty and trades on the weakness of individuals. . . . In each of the cases, the defendant was thrust into an unfamiliar atmosphere and run through menacing police interrogation procedures. The potentiality for compulsion is forcefully apparent, for example, in *Miranda,* where the indigent Mexican defendant was a seriously disturbed individual with pronounced sexual fantasies. . . .

The question in these cases is whether the privilege is fully applicable during a period of custodial interrogation. . . . We are satisfied that all the principles embodied in the privilege apply to informal compulsion exerted by law-enforcement officers during in-custody questioning. An individual swept from familiar surroundings into police custody, surrounded by antagonistic forces, and subjected to the techniques of persuasion described above cannot be otherwise than under compulsion to speak. As a practical matter, the compulsion to speak in the isolated setting of the police station may well be greater than in courts or other official investigations, where there are often impartial observers to guard against intimidation or trickery. [W]ithout proper safeguards the process of in-custody interrogation of persons suspected or accused of crime contains inherently compelling pressures which work to undermine the individual's will to resist and to compel him to speak where he would not otherwise do so freely. In order to combat these pressures and to permit a full opportunity to exercise the privilege against self-incrimination, the accused must be adequately and effectively apprised of his rights and the exercise of those rights must be fully honored.

It is impossible for us to foresee the potential alternatives for protecting the privilege which might be devised by Congress or the States in the exercise of their creative rule-making capacities. Therefore we cannot say that the Constitution necessarily requires adherence to any particular solution for the inherent compulsions of the interrogation process as it is presently conducted. Our decision in no way creates a constitutional straitjacket which will handicap sound efforts at reform, nor is it intended to have this effect. We encourage Congress and the States to continue their laudable search for increasingly effective ways of protecting the rights of the individual while promoting efficient enforcement of our criminal laws. . . .

The circumstances surrounding in-custody interrogation can operate very quickly to overbear the will of one merely made aware of his privilege by his interrogators. Therefore, the right to have counsel present at the interrogation is indispensable to the protection of the Fifth Amendment privilege under the system we delineate today. . . .

An individual need not make a pre-interrogation request for a lawyer. While such request affirmatively secures his right to have one, his failure to ask for a lawyer does not constitute a waiver. No effective waiver of the right to counsel during interrogation can be recognized unless specifically made after the warnings we here delineate have been given. The accused who does not know his rights and therefore does not make a request may be the person who most needs counsel. . . . Accordingly we hold that an individual held for interrogation must be clearly informed that he has the right to consult with a lawyer and to have the lawyer with him during interrogation under the system for protecting the privilege we delineate today. As with the warnings of the right to remain silent and that anything stated can be used in evidence against him, this warning is an absolute prerequisite to interrogation. No amount of circumstantial evidence that the person may have been aware of this right will suffice to stand in its stead. Only through such a warning is there ascertainable assurance that the accused was aware of this right.

If an individual indicates that he wishes the assistance of counsel before any interrogation occurs, the authorities cannot rationally ignore or deny his request on the basis that the individual does not have or cannot afford a retained attorney. The financial ability of the individual has no relationship to the scope of the rights involved here. . . .

Once warnings have been given, the subsequent procedure is clear. If the individual indicates in any manner, at any time prior to or during questioning, that he wishes to remain silent, the interrogation must cease. At this point he has shown that he intends to exercise his Fifth Amendment privilege; any statement taken after the person invokes his privilege cannot be other than the product of compulsion, subtle or otherwise. . . .

This does not mean, as some have suggested, that each police station must have a "station house lawyer" present at all times to advise prisoners. It does mean, however, that if police propose to interrogate a person they must make known to him that he is entitled to a lawyer and that if he cannot afford one, a lawyer will be provided for him prior to any interrogation. If authorities conclude that they will not provide counsel during a reasonable period of time in which investigation in the field is carried out, they may refrain from doing so without violating the person's Fifth Amendment privilege so long as they do not question him during that time.

If the interrogation continues without the presence of an attorney and a statement is taken, a heavy burden rests on the government to demonstrate that the defendant knowingly and intelligently waived his privilege against self-incrimination and his right to retained or appointed counsel. . . . An express statement that the individual is willing to make a statement and does not want an attorney followed closely by a statement could constitute a waiver. But a valid waiver will not be presumed simply from the silence of the accused after warnings are given or simply from the fact that a confession was in fact eventually obtained. . . .

The principles announced today deal with the protection which must be given to the privilege against self-incrimination when the individual is first subjected to police interrogation while in custody at the station or otherwise deprived of his freedom of action in any significant way. It is at this point that our adversary system of criminal proceedings commences, distinguishing itself at the outset from the inquisitorial system recognized in some countries. . . .

Our decision is not intended to hamper the traditional function of police officers in investigating crime. When an individual is in custody on probable cause, the police may, of course, seek out evidence in the field to be used at trial against him. Such investigation may include inquiry of persons not under restraint. General on-the-scene questioning as to facts surrounding a crime or other general questioning of citizens in the fact-finding process is not affected by our holding. It is an act of responsible citizenship for individuals to give whatever information they may have to aid in law enforcement. In such situations the compelling atmosphere inherent in the process of in-custody interrogation is not necessarily present. . . . There is no requirement that police stop a person who enters a police station and states that he wishes to confess to a crime, or a person who calls the police to offer a confession or any other statement he desires to make. Volunteered statements of any kind are not barred by the Fifth Amendment and their admissibility is not affected by our holding today.

To summarize, we hold that when an individual is taken into custody or otherwise deprived of his freedom by the authorities in any significant way and is subjected to questioning, the privilege against self-incrimination is jeopardized. Procedural safeguards must be employed to protect the privilege and unless other fully effective means are adopted to notify the person of his right of silence and to assure that the exercise of the right will be scrupulously honored, the following measures are required. He must be warned prior to any questioning that he has the right to remain silent, that anything he says can be used against him in a court of law, that he has the right to the presence of an attorney, and that if he cannot afford an attorney one will be appointed for him prior to any questioning if he so desires. Opportunity to exercise these rights must be afforded to him throughout the interrogation. After such warnings have been given, and such opportunity afforded him, the individual may knowingly and intelligently waive these rights and agree to answer questions or make a statement. But unless and until such warnings and waiver are demonstrated by the prosecution at trial, no evidence obtained as a result of interrogation can be used against him. . . .

JUSTICE HARLAN, whom JUSTICE STEWART and JUSTICE WHITE join, dissenting:

. . . The new rules are not designed to guard against police brutality or other unmistakably banned forms of coercion. Those who use third-degree tactics and deny them in court are equally able and destined to lie as skillfully about warnings and waivers. Rather, the thrust of the new rules is to negate all pressures, to reinforce the nervous or ignorant suspect, and ultimately to discourage any confession at all. The aim in short is toward "voluntariness" in a utopian sense, or to view it from a different angle, voluntariness with a vengeance. . . .

On March 3, 1963, an 18-year-old girl was kidnapped and forcibly raped near Phoenix, Arizona. Ten days later, on the morning of March 13, petitioner Miranda was arrested and taken to the police station. At this time Miranda was 23 years old, indigent, and educated to the extent of completing half the ninth grade. He had "an emotional illness" of the schizophrenic type, according to the doctor who eventually examined him; the doctor's report also stated that Miranda was "alert and oriented as to time, place, and person," intelligent within normal limits, competent to stand trial, and sane within the legal definition. At the police station, the victim picked Miranda out of a line-up, and two officers then took him into a separate room to interrogate him, starting about 11:30 a.m. Though at first denying his guilt, within a short time Miranda gave a detailed oral confession and then wrote out in his own hand and signed a brief statement admitting and describing the crime. All this was accomplished in two hours or less without any force, threats or promises and—I will assume this though the record is uncertain—without any effective warnings at all.

Miranda's oral and written confessions are now held inadmissible under the Court's new rules. One is entitled to feel astonished that the Constitution can be read to produce this result. These confessions were obtained during brief, daytime questioning conducted by two officers and unmarked by any of the traditional indicia of coercion. [T]he resulting confessions, and the responsible course of police practice they represent, are to be sacrificed to the Court's own finespun conception of fairness which I seriously doubt is shared by many thinking citizens in this country.

[The opinion of CLARK, J., dissenting in three of the cases and concurring in the result in one of them, and the dissenting opinion of WHITE, J., joined by HARLAN and STEWART, JJ., are omitted.]

NOTES

1. The number of cases in this area is mind-boggling. The cases here merely serve to introduce you to this area and give you some sense of the issues. In *United States v. Wade*, 388 U.S. 218, 87 S.Ct. 1926, 18 L.Ed.2d 1149 (1967), the Court held that the judge must exclude courtroom identifications of an accused at trial if the accused was exhibited to the witnesses before trial at a post-identification line-up without notice to, and in the absence of, his counsel. The Court relied on *Powell v. Alabama* to support its conclusion that the Court must scrutinize "*any* pretrial confrontation of the accused to determine whether the presence of his counsel is necessary to preserve the defendant's basic right to a fair trial as affected by his right meaningfully to cross-examine the witnesses against him and to have effective assistance of counsel at the trial itself." (emphasis in original). *Gilbert v. California,* 388 U.S. 263, 87 S.Ct. 1951, 18 L.Ed.2d 1178 (1967), applied this rule to the states as well. Later, *Kirby v. Illinois*, 406 U.S. 682, 92 S.Ct. 1877, 32 L.Ed.2d 411 (1972), made clear that *Wade-Gilbert* only applied to those identifications occurring "at or after the initiation of adversary judicial proceedings—whether by way of formal charge, preliminary hearing, indictment, information, or arraignment."

2. *Brewer v. Williams,* 430 U.S. 387, 97 S.Ct. 1232, 51 L.Ed.2d 424 (1977), *excluded* a confession of a defendant who was represented by counsel who advised him to remain silent. The Court relied on the Sixth Amendment right to counsel. Defendant, after asserting his right to silence, started talking while the police were moving him from Davenport to Des Moines. The detective urged the defendant to tell him where to find the victim's body because bad weather would make it difficult to locate it, and "the parents of this little girl should be entitled to a Christian burial. . . ."

    On the other hand, *Rhode Island v. Innis*, 446 U.S. 291, 100 S.Ct. 1682, 64 L.Ed.2d 297 (1980), *admitted* as evidence a weapon of the defendant. He was informed of his *Miranda* rights three times, and he said he wanted to speak to a lawyer. But he had no lawyer. While he was with the police in the police car, the officers engaged in "off-hand remarks" in the defendant's presence. For example, they said: "A lot of handicapped children [are] running around this area," and "God forbid [that] one of them might find a weapon with shells, and they might hurt themselves." Defendant interrupted the conversation and offered to show the officers where the gun was located.

For the fourth time, the police gave defendant the *Miranda* warnings, and then let him lead them to the weapon.

Brewer and *Innis* relate to different constitutional rights. *Brewer* is a Sixth Amendment right to counsel case. The *Brewer* defendant had a lawyer and was entitled to the assistance of his counsel at the time he made incriminating statements. The defendant in *Innis* had no lawyer. *Innis* is a Fifth Amendment case—an application of *Miranda*. *Innis* explained that *Miranda* requirements "come into play whenever a person in custody is subjected to either express questioning or its functional equivalent." A "practice that the police should know is reasonably likely to evoke an incriminating response from a suspect thus amounts to interrogation." But in *Innis* the Court concluded that no functional equivalent of questioning occurred: The police only engaged in a dialogue between themselves that invited no response from defendant. The Court found no reason to believe that the police knew that the defendant would be susceptible to an appeal to his conscience.

3. In *Michigan v. Mosley,* 423 U.S. 96, 96 S.Ct. 321, 4 L.Ed.2d 313 (1976), the police arrested defendant for various robberies. In the police station the police gave defendant his *Miranda* warnings. The suspect chose to remain silent. Two hours later another policeman in a different part of the station wanted to question defendant about a murder unrelated to the robberies. This policeman gave defendant a new set of *Miranda* warnings, and defendant this time gave an incriminating statement. The Court held that "the admissibility of statements obtained after the person in custody has decided to remain silent depends under *Miranda* on whether his 'right to cut off questioning' was 'scrupulously honored.' " This incriminating testimony was admissible because "the police here immediately ceased the interrogation, resumed questioning only after the passage of a significant period of time and the provision of a fresh set of warnings and restricted the second interrogation to a crime that had not been a subject of the earlier interrogation."

With *Mosley* contrast *Edwards v. Arizona,* 451 U.S. 477, 101 S.Ct. 1880, 68 L.Ed.2d 378 (1981). After the police arrested Edwards for robbery, burglary, and first-degree murder, they gave him his *Miranda* warnings, he said that he wanted an attorney, and so the questioning stopped. The next morning, the police came to his cell and gave him his *Miranda* warnings again. This time defendant talked and implicated himself. The Court held the confession was inadmissible. In *Mosley* the defendant only invoked a right to silence, but in *Edwards* the defendant had also invoked a right to counsel. "[W]hen an accused has invoked his right to have counsel present during custodial interrogation, a valid waiver of that right cannot be established by showing only that he responded to further police-initiated custodial interrogation even if he has been advised of his rights." There can be no further interrogation "unless the accused himself initiated further communication, exchanges, or conversations with the police."

4. Recall that *Miranda* said:

> It is impossible for us to foresee the potential alternatives for protecting the privilege which might be devised by Congress or the States in the exercise of their creative rule-making capacities. Therefore we cannot say that the Constitution necessarily requires adherence to any particular solution for the inherent compulsions of the interrogation process as it is presently conducted. Our decision in no way creates a constitutional straitjacket which will handicap sound efforts at reform, nor is it intended to have this effect. We encourage Congress and the States to continue their laudable search for increasingly effective ways of protecting the rights of the individual while promoting efficient enforcement of our criminal laws

Just two years after *Miranda*, the Crime Control Act of 1968 purported to repeal *Miranda*. The law said that a confession "shall be admissible in evidence if it is voluntarily given." The law authorized the court to take into account various factors, such as "whether or not such defendant was advised or knew that he was not required to make any statement and that any such statement could be used against him." The statute also provided, "The presence or absence of any of the above-mentioned factors to be taken into consideration by the judge need not be conclusive on the issue of voluntariness of the confession." The statute lay dormant, unused and untested, until nearly a third of a century later. The Fourth Circuit admitted a confession that did not comply with Miranda and the U.S. Supreme Court reversed (7 to 2). Chief Justice Rehnquist spoke for the Court. *Dickerson v. United States*, 530 U.S. 428, 120 S. Ct. 2326, 147 L. Ed. 2d 405 (2000).

Dickerson "concede[d] that there is language in some of our opinions that supports the view" that *Miranda* is a "prophylactic" rule that is not constitutionally required, but then it held that *Miranda* was constitutionally based and the Court there did not merely exercise its supervisory authority to regulate evidence in federal courts in the absence of congressional direction. "Whether or not we would agree with *Miranda*'s reasoning and its resulting rule, were we addressing the issue in the first instance, the principles of *stare decisis* weigh heavily against overruling it now" *Miranda* invited the legislature to create a rule equally as effective in preventing coerced confessions. However, Congress merely reinstated the totality of circumstances test, and *Miranda* rejected that. "*Miranda* has become embedded in routine police practice to the point where the warnings have become part of our national culture." Justice Scalia, joined by Justice Thomas, dissented.

5. *Missouri v. Seibert*, 542 U.S. 600, 124 S.Ct. 2601, 159 L.Ed.2d 643 (2004) (5 to 4, no majority opinion), the majority ruled that *Miranda* warnings, which the police gave mid-interrogation, after defendant gave unwarned confession, were ineffective, and thus the confession repeated after defendant received *Miranda* warnings was inadmissible. In contrast, *United States v. Patane*, 542 U.S. 630, 124 S.Ct. 2620, 159 L.Ed.2d 667 (2004) (5 to 4, with no majority opinion), concluded that failure to give the suspect *Miranda* warnings did not require suppression of the weapon at firearms trial, because the weapon was recovered based on defendant's voluntary statement that he possessed it. The weapon was the physical fruits of suspect's unwarned but voluntary statements.

6. In their treatise on criminal procedure, Professors Wayne LaFave, Jerold Israel, Orin S. Kerr, & Nancy J. King discuss the effects of *Miranda*:

> [W]e lack sufficient reliable empirical data on *Miranda*'s impact and [thus], existing evidence is amenable to differing interpretations. Take, for example, the ultimate question of the "cost" of *Miranda* in terms of lost convictions. One commentator has concluded that "the existing empirical data supports the tentative estimate that *Miranda* has led to lost cases against almost four percent [3.8%] of all criminal suspects in this country who are questioned," which he extrapolates to an annual loss regarding roughly 28,000 violent crimes and 79,000 property crimes. But another commentator, working with the same data, has concluded that "the properly adjusted attrition rate is ... at most only 0.78%," a percentage which would be even lower if it were possible to factor out the amount of attrition which is instead attributable to "organizational failure and general chaos in the criminal justice system."

The situation is similar with respect to the basic question of how the post-*Miranda* confession rate compares with that which existed prior to the *Miranda* decision. One view is that suspects now confess or give incriminating statements in only about a third "of all cases presented by police for prosecution," a confession rate well below the average rate before *Miranda*. But that conclusion, it has been objected, "results from a good deal of unjustified juggling of the numbers," and it has been contended that if proper adjustments are made in the data it supports the conclusion that "the rate of confessions is roughly the same" in the pre- and post-*Miranda* eras. This situation is further complicated because of speculation by some that any loss in the number of confessions may well be offset by real benefits to law enforcement, such as that *Miranda* warnings prompt those suspects who do talk to provide more complete statements and confessions which "are virtually guaranteed to be admitted into evidence."

To what extent has *Miranda* "solved" pre-existing problems concerning police interrogation practices in this country? [T]here exists considerable difference of opinion. . . . On the plus side, . . . "*Miranda* undoubtedly serves important symbolic functions," such as "correcting the appearance that the poor and the unsophisticated were particularly vulnerable to police exploitation." Moreover, even "if the defendant already understands his rights, the very fact that the police must recite them may help to dispel the sense of total isolation and powerlessness that otherwise pervades much custodial interrogation." *Miranda* also has served "educational purposes" by causing police to be told and frequently reminded of the rights of the people with whom they deal. [Also], *Miranda* simplified to some extent judicial review of police interrogation practices; "the new questions about whether 'custodial interrogation' had occurred and whether proper warnings had been given were much more focused than the voluntariness inquiry and did not invite a balancing of subjective attitudes about the need for vigorous enforcement."[2]

---

[2] Wayne R. LaFave, Jerold H. Israel, Orin S. Kerr, & Nancy J. King, Treatise on Criminal Procedure, vol. 2, § 6.5(c),(d) (Thomson Reuters West, 2014)(footnotes omitted).

4.4 THE FOURTH AMENDMENT AND THE EXCLUSIONARY RULE

In 1886, *Boyd v. United States,* 116 U.S. 616, 6 S.Ct. 524, 29 L.Ed. 746 (1886), first created the exclusionary rule. The federal government forced defendant to turn over various papers and invoices and then introduced them into trial. The case involved fraud charges to avoid the U.S. customs revenue laws. The defendant's alternative to producing the papers was to admit to truth of the allegations. The defendant claimed that the admission of this evidence violated the Fourth and Fifth Amendments. The Court said that the two amendments are very related; they "run almost into each other." The Court found that the search violated the Fourth Amendment, and, just as the Fifth Amendment commands that compulsory self-incrimination is inadmissible in evidence, so also "we have been unable to perceive that the seizure of a man's private books and papers to be used in evidence against him is substantially different from compelling him to be a witness against himself." The Court excluded the evidence. The Court made clear that the exclusionary rule applies to all federal searches in *Weeks v. United States*, 232 U.S. 383, 34 S.Ct. 341, 58 L.Ed. 652 (1914). The Court, however, did not at first apply this rule to the states, as the following case indicates.

WOLF V. COLORADO
338 U.S. 25, 69 S.Ct. 1359, 93 L.Ed. 1782 (1949)

JUSTICE FRANKFURTER delivered the opinion of the Court.

The precise question for consideration is this: Does a conviction by a State court for a State offense deny the "due process of law" required by the Fourteenth Amendment, solely because evidence that was admitted at the trial was obtained under circumstances which would have rendered it inadmissible in a prosecution for violation of a federal law in a court of the United States because there deemed to be an *infra*ction of the Fourth Amendment as applied in *Weeks v. United States*, 232 U.S. 383, 34 S.Ct. 341, 58 L.Ed. 652 (1914). The Supreme Court of Colorado has sustained convictions in which such evidence was admitted, and we brought the cases here.

Unlike the specific requirements and restrictions placed by the Bill of Rights, Amendments I to VIII, upon the administration of criminal justice by federal authority, the Fourteenth Amendment did not subject criminal justice in the States to specific limitations. The notion that the "due process of law" guaranteed by the Fourteenth Amendment is shorthand for the first eight amendments of the Constitution and thereby incorporates them has been rejected by this Court again and again, after impressive consideration. See, *e.g., Hurtado v. California; Palko v. Connecticut.* Only the other day the Court reaffirmed this rejection after through reexamination of the scope and function of the Due Process Clause of the Fourteenth Amendment. *Adamson v. California.* The issue is closed.

. . . The security of one's privacy against arbitrary intrusion by the police—which is at the core of the Fourth Amendment—is basic to a free society. It is therefore implicit in "the concept of ordered liberty" and as such enforceable against the States through the Due Process Clause. The knock at the door, whether by day or by night, as a prelude to a search, without authority of law but solely on the authority of the police, did not need the commentary of recent history to be condemned as inconsistent with the conception of human rights enshrined in the history and the basic constitutional documents of English-speaking peoples.

Accordingly, we have no hesitation in saying that were a State affirmatively to sanction such police incursion into privacy it would run counter to the guaranty of the Fourteenth Amendment. But the ways of enforcing such a basic right raise questions of a different order. How such arbitrary conduct should be checked, what remedies against it should be afforded, the means by which the right should be made effective, are all questions that are not to be so dogmatically answered as to preclude the varying solutions which spring from an allowable range of judgment on issues not susceptible of quantitative solution.

In *Weeks v. United States,* this Court held that in a federal prosecution the Fourth Amendment barred the use of evidence secured through an illegal search and seizure. This ruling . . . was not derived from the explicit requirements of the Fourth Amendment; it was not based on legislation expressing Congressional policy in the enforcement of the Constitution. The decision was a matter of judicial implication. [M]ost of the English-speaking world does not regard as vital to such protection the exclusion of evidence thus obtained . . . As of today 30 States reject the *Weeks* doctrine, 17 States are in agreement with it. . . . Of 10 jurisdictions within the United Kingdom and the British Commonwealth of Nations which have passed on the question, none has held evidence obtained by illegal search and seizure inadmissible.

The jurisdictions which have rejected the *Weeks* doctrine have not left the right to privacy without other means of protection[1] Indeed, the exclusion of

---

[1] The common law provides actions for damages against the searching officer, against one who procures the issuance of a warrant maliciously and without probable cause. . . . Statutory sanctions in the main provide

evidence is a remedy which directly serves only to protect those upon whose person or premises something incriminating has been found. We cannot, therefore, regard it as a departure from basic standards to remand such persons, together with those who emerge scatheless from a search, to the remedies of private action and such protection as the internal discipline of the police, under the eyes of an alert public opinion, may afford. Granting that in practice the exclusion of evidence may be an effective way of deterring unreasonable searches, it is not for this Court to condemn as falling below the minimal standards assured by the Due Process Clause a State's reliance upon other methods which, if consistently enforced, would be equally effective . . . . .

We hold, therefore, that in a prosecution in a State court for a State crime the Fourteenth Amendment does not forbid the admission of evidence obtained by an unreasonable search and seizure. And though we have interpreted the Fourth Amendment to forbid the admission of such evidence, a different question would be presented if Congress under its legislative powers were to pass a statute purporting to negate the *Weeks* doctrine. We would then be faced with the problem of the respect to be accorded the legislative judgment on an issue as to which, in default of that judgment, we have been forced to depend upon our own. Problems of a converse character, also not before us, would be presented should Congress under § 5 of the Fourteenth Amendment undertake to enforce the rights there guaranteed by attempting to make the *Weeks* doctrine binding upon the States.

Affirmed.

JUSTICE BLACK, concurring.

I agree with the conclusion of the Court that the Fourth Amendment's prohibition of "unreasonable searches and seizures" is enforceable against the states. [Also,] I agree with what appears to be a plain implication of the Court's opinion that the federal exclusionary rule is not a command of the Fourth Amendment but is a judicially created rule of evidence which Congress might negate. This leads me to concur in the Court's judgment of affirmance.

JUSTICE RUTLEDGE, dissenting.

[I] reject any intimation that Congress could validly enact legislation permitting the introduction in federal courts of evidence seized in violation of the Fourth Amendment . . .

---

for the punishment of one maliciously procuring a search warrant or willfully exceeding his authority in exercising it. . . .

JUSTICE MURPHY joins in this opinion.

JUSTICE MURPHY, with whom JUSTICE RUTLEDGE joins, dissenting. . . .

If proof of the efficacy of the federal rule were needed, there is testimony in abundance in the recruit training programs and in-service courses provided the police in states which follow the federal rule. St. Louis, for example, demands extensive training in the rules of search and seizure, with emphasis upon the ease with which a case may collapse if it depends upon evidence obtained unlawfully. Current court decisions are digested and read at roll calls. [I]n New York City, we are informed simply that "copies of the State Penal Law and Code of Criminal Procedure" are given to officers, and that they are "kept advised" that illegally obtained evidence may be admitted in New York courts.

[The dissenting opinion of DOUGLAS J., is omitted.]

MAPP V. OHIO

367 U.S. 643, 81 S.Ct. 1684, 6 L.Ed. 1081 (1961)

JUSTICE CLARK delivered the opinion of the Court.

Appellant stands convicted of knowingly having had in her possession and under her control certain lewd and lascivious books, pictures, and photographs in violation of § 2905.34 of Ohio's Revised Code. [T]he Supreme Court of Ohio found that her conviction was valid though "based primarily upon the introduction in evidence of lewd and lascivious books and pictures unlawfully seized during an unlawful search of defendant's home. . . ."

On May 23, 1957, three Cleveland police officers arrived at appellant's residence in that city pursuant to information that "a person [was] hiding out in the home, who was wanted for questioning in connection with a recent bombing, and that there was a large amount of policy paraphernalia being hidden in the home." Miss Mapp and her daughter by a former marriage lived on the top floor of the two-family dwelling. Upon their arrival at that house, the officers knocked on the door and demanded entrance but appellant, after telephoning her attorney, refused to admit them without a search warrant. They advised their headquarters of the situation and undertook a surveillance of the house.

The officers again sought entrance some three hours later when four or more additional officers arrived on the scene. When Miss Mapp did not come to the door immediately, at least one of the several doors to the house was forcibly opened and the policemen gained admittance. Meanwhile Miss Mapp's attorney arrived, but the officers, having secured their own entry, and continuing in their defiance of the law, would permit him neither to see Miss Mapp nor to enter the house. It appears that Miss Mapp was halfway down the stairs from the upper floor to the front door when the officers, in this highhanded manner, broke into the hall. She demanded to see the search warrant. A paper, claimed to be a warrant, was held up by one of the officers. She grabbed the "warrant" and placed it in her bosom. A struggle ensued in which the officers recovered the piece of paper and as a result of which they handcuffed appellant because she had been "belligerent" in resisting their official rescue of the "warrant" from her person. Running roughshod over appellant, a policeman "grabbed" her, "twisted [her] hand," and she "yelled [and] pleaded with him" because "it was hurting." Appellant, in handcuffs, was then forcibly taken upstairs to her bedroom where the officers searched a dresser, a chest of drawers, a closet and some suitcases. They also looked into a photo album and through personal papers belonging to the appellant. The search spread to the rest of the second floor including the child's bedroom, the living room, the kitchen and a dinette. The basement of the building and a trunk found therein were also searched. The obscene materials for possession of which she was ultimately convicted were discovered in the course of that widespread search.

At the trial no search warrant was produced by the prosecution, nor was the failure to produce one explained or accounted for. At best, "There is, in the record, considerable doubt as to whether there ever was any warrant for the search of defendant's home."

[I]n 1949, prior to the *Wolf* case, almost two-thirds of the States were opposed to the use of the exclusionary rule, now, despite the *Wolf* case, more than half of those since passing upon it, by their own legislative or judicial decision, have wholly or partly adopted or adhered to the *Weeks* rule. [T]he second basis elaborated in *Wolf* in support of its failure to enforce the exclusionary doctrine against the States was that "other means of protection" have been afforded "the right to privacy." The experience of California that such other remedies have been worthless and futile is buttressed by the experience of other States. [T]he factual considerations supporting the failure of the *Wolf* Court to include the *Weeks* exclusionary rule when it recognized the enforceability of the right to privacy against the States in 1949, while not basically relevant to the constitutional consideration, could not, in any analysis, now be deemed controlling.

[W]e once again examine *Wolf's* constitutional documentation of the right to privacy free from unreasonable state intrusion, and, after its dozen years on our books, are led by it to close the only courtroom door remaining open to evidence secured by official lawlessness in flagrant abuse of that basic right, reserved to all persons as a specific guarantee against that very same unlawful conduct. We hold that all evidence obtained by searches and seizures in violation of the Constitution is, by that same authority, inadmissible in a state court.

Since the Fourth Amendment's right of privacy has been declared enforceable against the States through the Due Process Clause of the Fourteenth, it is enforceable against them by the same sanction of exclusion as is used against the Federal Government. Were it otherwise, then just as without the *Weeks* rule the assurance against unreasonable federal searches and seizures would be "a form of words," valueless and undeserving of mention in a perpetual charter of inestimable human liberties. . . .

. . . This Court has not hesitated to enforce as strictly against the States as it does against the Federal Government the rights of free speech and of a free press, the rights to notice and to a fair, public trial, including, as it does, the right not to be convicted by use of a coerced confession, however, logically relevant it be, and without regard to its reliability. And nothing could be more certain than that when a coerced confession is involved, "the relevant rules of evidence" are overridden without regard to "the incidence of such conduct by the police," slight or frequent. Why should not the same rule apply to what is tantamount to coerced testimony by way of unconstitutional seizure of goods, papers, effects, documents, etc.? We find that, as to the Federal Government, the Fourth and Fifth Amendments and, as to the States, the freedom from unconscionable invasions of privacy and the freedom from convictions based upon coerced confessions do enjoy an "intimate relation" in their perpetuation of "principles of humanity and civil liberty [secured] . . . only after years of struggle." They express "supplementing phases of the same constitutional purpose—to maintain inviolate large areas of personal privacy." The philosophy of each Amendment and of each freedom is complementary to, although not dependent upon, that of the other in its sphere of influence—the very least that together they assure in either sphere is that no man is to be convicted on unconstitutional evidence. Cf. *Rochin v. People of State of California,* 1952, 342 U.S. 165, 173, 72 S.Ct. 205, 210, 96 L.Ed. 183.

Moreover, our holding that the exclusionary rule is an essential part of both the Fourth and Fourteenth Amendments is not only the logical dictate of prior cases, but it also makes very good sense. There is no war between the Constitution and common sense. Presently, a federal prosecutor may make no use of evidence illegally seized, but a State's attorney across the street may, although he supposedly is operating under the enforceable prohibitions of the same Amendment. Thus the State, by admitting evidence unlawfully seized, serves to encourage disobedience to the Federal Constitution which it is bound to uphold. [I]n *Wilson v. Schnettler,* 1961, 365 U.S. 381, 81 S.Ct. 632, 5 L.Ed.2d 620, [we refused] to restrain a federal officer from testifying in a state court as to evidence unconstitutionally seized by him in the performance of his duties. [Because of this double standard, in] non-exclusionary States, federal officers, being human, were by it invited to and did, as our cases indicate, step across the street to the State's attorney with their unconstitutionally seized evidence. Prosecution on the basis of that evidence was then had in a state court in utter disregard of the enforceable Fourth Amendment. If the fruits of an unconstitutional search had been inadmissible in both state and federal courts, this inducement to evasion would have been sooner eliminated. . . .

There are those who say, as did Justice (then Judge) Cardozo, that under our constitutional exclusionary doctrine "[t]he criminal is to go free because the constable has blundered." *People v. Defore,* 242 N.Y. at page 21, 150 N.E. at page 587. In some cases this will undoubtedly be the result. But, . . . "there is another consideration—the imperative of judicial integrity." The criminal goes free, if he must, but it is the law that sets him free. Nothing can destroy a government more quickly than its failure to observe its own laws, or worse, its disregard of the charter of its own existence. As Mr. Justice Brandeis, dissenting, said in *Olmstead v. United States,* 1928, 277 U.S. 438, 485, 48 S.Ct. 564, 575, 72 L.Ed. 944: "Our government is the potent, the omnipresent teacher. For good or for ill, it teaches the whole people by its example. . . . If the government becomes a lawbreaker, it breeds contempt for law; it invites every man to become a law unto himself; it invites anarchy." . . .

The judgment of the Supreme Court of Ohio is reversed and the cause remanded for further proceedings not inconsistent with this opinion.

Reversed and remanded.

JUSTICE BLACK, concurring.

Reflection on the problem . . . in the light of cases coming before the Court since *Wolf,* has led me to conclude that when the Fourth Amendment's ban against unreasonable searches and seizures is considered together with the Fifth Amendment's ban against compelled self-incrimination, a constitutional basis emerges which not only justifies but actually requires the exclusionary rule. . . .

JUSTICE HARLAN, whom JUSTICE FRANKFURTER and JUSTICE WHITTAKER join, dissenting.

In overruling the *Wolf* case the Court, in my opinion, has forgotten the sense
. . . Since there is not the slightest suggestion that Ohio's policy is "affirmatively
to sanction . . . police incursion into privacy," what the Court is now doing is to
impose upon the States not only federal substantive standards of "search and
seizure" but also the basic federal remedy for violation of those standards. For I
think it entirely clear that the *Weeks* exclusionary rule is but a remedy which, by
penalizing past official misconduct, is aimed at deterring such conduct in the
future. I would not impose upon the States this federal exclusionary remedy. . . .

[The concurring opinion of DOUGLAS, J., and the memorandum of STEWART,
J., are omitted.]

UNITED STATES V. LEON
468 U.S. 897, 104 S.Ct. 3405, 82 L.Ed.2d 677 (1984)

[A Burbank police officer learned from a confidential informant that two
persons were selling large quantities of cocaine and methaqualone. The informant
said that he had witnessed a sale of methaqualone at the residence of one of these
individuals five months earlier, when he also saw a shoebox containing a large
amount of cash. Based on this information and some police surveillance, the
police obtained a warrant from a state superior court judge. The search produced
large quantities of drugs, and Leon and others were indicted and convicted in
federal court. The district court suppressed the evidence seized from the warrant
because it concluded that the affidavit was insufficient. (The informant was of
unproven reliability, and the police surveillance showed events "as consistent with
innocence as . . . with guilt.") The court of appeals agreed.]

JUSTICE WHITE delivered the opinion of the Court.

This case presents the question whether the Fourth Amendment
exclusionary rule should be modified so as not to bar the use in the prosecution's
case-in-chief of evidence obtained by officers acting in reasonable reliance on a
search warrant issued by a detached and neutral magistrate but ultimately found
to be unsupported by probable cause. To resolve this question, we must consider
once again the tension between the sometimes competing goals of, on the one
hand, deterring official misconduct and removing inducements to unreasonable
invasions of privacy and, on the other, establishing procedures under which
criminal defendants are "acquitted or convicted on the basis of all the evidence
which exposes the truth." . . .

The Fourth Amendment contains no provision expressly precluding the use
of evidence obtained in violation of its commands, and an examination of its

origin and purposes makes clear that the use of fruits of a past unlawful search or seizure "work[s] no new Fourth Amendment wrong." *United States v. Calandra,* 414 U.S. 338, 354, 94 S.Ct. 613, 623, 38 L.Ed.2d 561 (1974). The wrong condemned by the Amendment is "fully accomplished" by the unlawful search or seizure itself, and the exclusionary rule is neither intended nor able to "cure the invasion of the defendant's rights which he has already suffered." *Stone v. Powell,* 428 U.S., at 540, 96 S.Ct., at 3073 (White, J., dissenting). The rule thus operates as "a judicially created remedy designed to safeguard Fourth Amendment rights generally through its deterrent effect, rather than a personal constitutional right of the person aggrieved." . . .

The substantial social costs exacted by the exclusionary rule for the vindication of Fourth Amendment rights have long been a source of concern. "Our cases have consistently recognized that unbending application of the exclusionary sanction to enforce ideals of governmental rectitude would impede unacceptably the truth-finding functions of judge and jury." An objectionable collateral consequence of this interference with the criminal justice system's truth-finding function is that some guilty defendants may go free or receive reduced sentences as a result of favorable plea bargains.[6] Particularly when law enforcement officers have acted in objective good faith or their transgressions have been minor, the magnitude of the benefit conferred on such guilty defendants offends basic concepts of the criminal justice system. . . .

In *Stone v. Powell, supra,* the Court emphasized the costs of the exclusionary rule, expressed its view that limiting the circumstances under which Fourth

---

[6] Researchers have only recently begun to study extensively the effects of the exclusionary rule on the disposition of felony arrests. One study suggests that the rule results in the nonprosecution or nonconviction of between 0.6% and 2.35% of individuals arrested for felonies. Davies, A Hard Look at What We Know (and Still Need to Learn) About the "Costs" of the Exclusionary Rule: The NIJ Study and Other Studies of "Lost" Arrests, 1983 A.B.F.Res.J. 611, 621. The estimates are higher for particular crimes the prosecution of which depends heavily on physical evidence. Thus, the cumulative loss due to nonprosecution or nonconviction of individuals arrested on felony drug charges is probably in the range of 2.8% to 7.1%. Davies' analysis of California data suggests that screening by police and prosecutors results in the release because of illegal searches or seizures of as many as 1.4% of all felony arrestees, that 0.9% of felony arrestees are released because of illegal searches or seizures at the preliminary hearing or after trial, and that roughly 0.05% of all felony arrestees benefit from reversals on appeal because of illegal searches. . . .

Many of these researchers have concluded that the impact of the exclusionary rule is insubstantial, but the small percentages with which they deal mask a large absolute number of felons who are released because the cases against them were based in part on illegal searches or seizures. "[A]ny rule of evidence that denies the jury access to clearly probative and reliable evidence must bear a heavy burden of justification, and must be carefully limited to the circumstances in which it will pay its way by deterring official lawlessness." *Illinois v. Gates,* 462 U.S., at 257–8, 103 S.Ct., at 2342 (White, J., concurring in the judgment). Because we find that the rule can have no substantial deterrent effect in the sorts of situations under consideration in this case, we conclude that it cannot pay its way in those situations.

Amendment claims could be raised in federal habeas corpus proceedings would not reduce the rule's deterrent effect, and held that a state prisoner who has been afforded a full and fair opportunity to litigate a Fourth Amendment claim may not obtain federal habeas relief on the ground that unlawfully obtained evidence had been introduced at his trial. Proposed extensions of the exclusionary rule to proceedings other than the criminal trial itself have been evaluated and rejected under the same analytic approach. In *United States v. Calandra, supra,* for example, we declined to allow grand jury witnesses to refuse to answer questions based on evidence obtained from an unlawful search or seizure since "[a]ny incremental deterrent effect which might be achieved by extending the rule to grand jury proceedings is uncertain at best." Similarly, in *United States v. Janis,* [428 U.S. 433, 96 S.Ct. 3021, 49 L.Ed.2d 1046 (1976),] we permitted the use in federal civil proceedings of evidence illegally seized by state officials since the likelihood of deterring police misconduct through such an extension of the exclusionary rule was insufficient to outweigh its substantial social costs. . . . Evidence obtained in violation of the Fourth Amendment and inadmissible in the prosecution's case-in-chief may be used to impeach a defendant's direct testimony. *Walder v. United States,* 347 U.S. 62, 74 S.Ct. 354, 98 L.Ed. 503 (1954). A similar assessment of the "incremental furthering" of the ends of the exclusionary rule led us to conclude in *United States v. Havens,* 446 U.S. 620, 627, 100 S.Ct. 1912,1916, 64 L.Ed. 2d 559 (1980), that evidence inadmissible in the prosecution's case-in-chief or otherwise as substantive evidence of guilt may be used to impeach statements made by a defendant in response to "proper cross-examination reasonably suggested by the defendant's direct examination."

[W]e have not recognized any form of good-faith exception to the Fourth Amendment exclusionary rule. But the balancing approach that has evolved during the years of experience with the rule provides strong support for the modification currently urged upon us. As we discuss below, our evaluation of the costs and benefits of suppressing reliable physical evidence seized by officers reasonably relying on a warrant issued by a detached and neutral magistrate leads to the conclusion that such evidence should be admissible in the prosecution's case-in-chief.

. . . First, the exclusionary rule is designed to deter police misconduct rather than to punish the errors of judges and magistrates. Second, there exists no evidence suggesting that judges and magistrates are inclined to ignore or subvert the Fourth Amendment or that lawlessness among these actors requires application of the extreme sanction of exclusion.

Third, and most important, we discern no basis, and are offered none, for believing that exclusion of evidence seized pursuant to a warrant will have a significant deterrent effect on the issuing judge or magistrate. . . . Judges and magistrates are not adjuncts to the law enforcement team; as neutral judicial officers, they have no stake in the outcome of particular criminal prosecutions. The threat of exclusion thus cannot be expected significantly to deter them. Imposition of the exclusionary sanction is not necessary meaningfully to inform judicial officers of their errors, and we cannot conclude that admitting evidence obtained pursuant to a warrant while at the same time declaring that the warrant was somehow defective will in any way reduce judicial officers' professional incentives to comply with the Fourth Amendment, encourage them to repeat their mistakes, or lead to the granting of all colorable warrant requests.

If exclusion of evidence obtained pursuant to a subsequently invalidated warrant is to have any deterrent effect, therefore, it must alter the behavior of individual law enforcement officers or the policies of their departments. One could argue that applying the exclusionary rule in cases where the police failed to demonstrate probable cause in the warrant application deters future inadequate presentations or "magistrate shopping" and thus promotes the ends of the Fourth Amendment. Suppressing evidence obtained pursuant to a technically defective warrant supported by probable cause also might encourage officers to scrutinize more closely the form of the warrant and to point out suspected judicial errors. We find such arguments speculative and conclude that suppression of evidence obtained pursuant to a warrant should be ordered only on a case-by-case basis and only in those unusual cases in which exclusion will further the purposes of the exclusionary rule.

We have frequently questioned whether the exclusionary rule can have any deterrent effect when the offending officers acted in the objectively reasonable belief that their conduct did not violate the Fourth Amendment. . . . This is particularly true, we believe, when an officer acting with objective good faith has obtained a search warrant from a judge or magistrate and acted within its scope. In most such cases, there is no police illegality and thus nothing to deter. It is the magistrate's responsibility to determine whether the officer's allegations establish probable cause and, if so, to issue a warrant comporting in form with the requirements of the Fourth Amendment. In the ordinary case, an officer cannot be expected to question the magistrate's probable-cause determination or his judgment that the form of the warrant is technically sufficient. "[O]nce the warrant issues, there is literally nothing more the policeman can do in seeking to comply with the law." Penalizing the officer for the magistrate's error, rather than his own, cannot logically contribute to the deterrence of Fourth Amendment violations.

We conclude that the marginal or nonexistent benefits produced by suppressing evidence obtained in objectively reasonable reliance on a subsequently invalidated search warrant cannot justify the substantial costs of exclusion. We do not suggest, however, that exclusion is always inappropriate in cases where an officer has obtained a warrant and abided by its terms. . . .

In the absence of an allegation that the magistrate abandoned his detached and neutral role, suppression is appropriate only if the officers were dishonest or reckless in preparing their affidavit or could not have harbored an objectively reasonable belief in the existence of probable cause. Only respondent Leon has contended that no reasonably well-trained police officer could have believed that there existed probable cause to search his house; significantly, the other respondents advance no comparable argument. Officer Rombach's application for a warrant clearly was supported by much more than a "bare bones" affidavit. The affidavit related the results of an extensive investigation and, as the opinions of the divided panel of the Court of Appeals make clear, provided evidence sufficient to create disagreement among thoughtful and competent judges as to the existence of probable cause. Under these circumstances, the officers' reliance on the magistrate's determination of probable cause was objectively reasonable, and application of the extreme sanction of exclusion is inappropriate.

Accordingly, the judgment of the Court of Appeals is

Reversed.

JUSTICE BLACKMUN, concurring:

[T]he scope of the exclusionary rule is subject to change in light of changing judicial understanding about the effects of the rule outside the confines of the courtroom. It is incumbent on the Nation's law enforcement officers, who must continue to observe the Fourth Amendment in the wake of today's decisions, to recognize the double-edged nature of that principle.

JUSTICE BRENNAN, with whom JUSTICE MARSHALL joins, dissenting:

Ten years ago in *United States v. Calandra,* I expressed the fear that the Court's decision "may signal that a majority of my colleagues have positioned themselves to reopen the door [to evidence secured by official lawlessness] still further and abandon altogether the exclusionary rule in search-and-seizure cases." Since then, in case after case, I have witnessed the Court's gradual but determined strangulation of the rule. It now appears that the Court's victory over the Fourth

Amendment is complete. That today's decision represents the *piece de resistance* of the Court's past efforts cannot be doubted, for today the Court sanctions the use in the prosecution's case-in-chief of illegally obtained evidence against the individual whose rights have been violated—a result that had previously been thought to be foreclosed.

The Court seeks to justify this result on the ground that the "costs" of adhering to the exclusionary rule in cases like those before us exceed the "benefits." But the language of deterrence and of cost/benefit analysis, if used indiscriminately, can have a narcotic effect. It creates an illusion of technical precision and ineluctability. It suggests that not only constitutional principle but also empirical data supports the majority's result. When the Court's analysis is examined carefully, however, it is clear that we have not been treated to an honest assessment of the merits of the exclusionary rule, but have instead been drawn into a curious world where the "costs" of excluding illegally obtained evidence loom to exaggerated heights and where the "benefits" of such exclusion are made to disappear with a mere wave of the hand. [T]he task of combatting crime and convicting the guilty will in every era seem of such critical and pressing concern that we may be lured by the temptations of expediency into forsaking our commitment to protecting individual liberty and privacy. It was for that very reason that the Framers of the Bill of Rights insisted that law enforcement efforts be permanently and unambiguously restricted in order to preserve personal freedoms.

. . . To the extent empirical data is available regarding the general costs and benefits of the exclusionary rule, it has shown, on the one hand, as the Court acknowledges today, that the costs are not as substantial as critics have asserted in the past, and, on the other hand, that while the exclusionary rule may well have certain deterrent effects, it is extremely difficult to determine with any degree of precision whether the incidence of unlawful conduct by police is now lower than it was prior to *Mapp*. . . .

[The dissenting opinion of STEVENS, J., is omitted.]

NOTES

1.   The same day that the Court decided *Leon*, it decided *Massachusetts v. Sheppard*, 468 U.S. 981, 104 S.Ct. 3424, 82 L.Ed.2d 737 (1984), which stated the *Leon* rule more broadly. "[T]he exclusionary rule should not be applied when the officer conducting the search acted in objectively reasonable reliance on a

warrant issued by a detached and neutral magistrate that subsequently is determined to be invalid." In *Sheppard*, the defendant was convicted of murder. On appeal, the State Supreme Court, relying on the Fourth Amendment, excluded incriminating evidence the police found in defendant's residence. The U.S. Supreme Court (7 to 2), reversed: "An error of constitutional dimensions may have been committed with respect to the issuance of the warrant, but it was the judge, not the police officers, who made the critical mistake." The courts should not suppress evidence when "the judge failed to make all the necessary clerical corrections despite his assurances that such changes would be made" because that "will not serve the deterrent function that the exclusionary rule was designed to achieve."

2. In *Stringer v. State of Mississippi,* 491 So.2d 837 (Mississippi 1986), Justice Robertson, joined by Justices Prather and Sullivan, concurred specially and specifically refused to follow *Leon,* as a matter of state constitutional law: "We are not convinced that the public interest requires—or that our [state] constitution permits—our abandonment of our long-standing exclusionary rule which dates back at least to 1922."[3] Under Mississippi law, the "exclusionary rule has not been treated as a mere rule of evidence. . . ." Then Justice Robertson said:

> The fundamental flaw in *Leon* is its failure to perceive that its new "insight"—that in the type of cases we are concerned with, it is the issuing magistrate who violates the accused's Fourth Amendment rights, not the public officer—suggests a *greater* need for the exclusionary rule, not a lesser one.
>
> The citizen, *vis-a-vis* the searching law enforcement officer, has at least the theoretical possibility of a remedy in the form of a civil action for damages, although this remedy is as ineffective as a deterrent to police misconduct as it is inefficacious to protect and compensate the citizen. Against the issuing magistrate—be he or

---

[3] Wayne R. LaFave, Search and Seizure: A Treatise on the Fourth Amendment (Thomson-Reuters West, 5th ed. 2012), vol. 1, § 1.3(c), analyzes the empirical evidence we have on the cost of the exclusionary rule:

> The most careful and balanced assessment conducted to date of all available empirical data shows "that the general level of the rule's effects on criminal prosecutions is marginal at most." Specifically, the cumulative loss in felony cases because of prosecutor screening, police releases and court dismissals attributable to the acquisition of evidence in violation of the Fourth Amendment is from 0.6% to 2.35% (from 0.3% to 0.7% if drug and weapon cases are excluded). This same study points out that the available evidence does not show that defendants gain favorable plea bargains because of the exclusionary rule.

she a justice court judge, a municipal court judge or whatever—the citizen has *no remedy*. For unlike the law enforcement officers, judicial officers enjoy an absolute immunity to suit for damages, *Pulliam v. Allen,* 466 U.S. 522, 104 S.Ct. 1970, 1973, 80 L.Ed.2d 565, 571 (1984). [W]e perceive no vehicle for protecting these rights of our citizens and assuring that issuing magistrates take seriously their responsibilities *other than continued enforcement of this state's exclusionary rule. . . .*

[W]e call attention to the rather startling footnote 6 in *Leon. . . .* The footnote goes on in an attempt to minimize the devastating impact the facts have on *Leon* s logic. Suffice it to say that the data there discussed establishes conclusively what is implicit throughout *Leon:* That the adoption of the new federal modified exclusionary rule more reflects a shift in judicial/political ideology than a judicial response to demonstrable and felt societal needs. If it ain't broke, why fix it?

Several other state courts have also rejected *Leon.* E.g., *State v. Guzman,* 122 Idaho 981, 842 P.2d 660 (1992), *State v. Novembrino,* 105 N.J. 95, 519 A.2d 820, (N.J. 1987).

3. The cases interpreting and applying the Fourth Amendment and the exclusionary rule are legion. In 1978, Professor Wayne LaFave, the foremost expert on the Fourth Amendment, published a *three*-volume treatise on the Fourth Amendment. The fifth edition expanded to *six* volumes. *Search and Seizure: A Treatise on the Fourth Amendment* (Thomson-Reuters West, 5th ed. 2012). Every year there is a new supplement updating the law. We will not, therefore, canvass the case law. However, reading the three following cases will be useful in understanding the problems raised. The first, *Katz v. United States,* deals with electronic surveillance, although the rule it embraces sets out a basic test to determine generally when the Fourth Amendment should be applicable. The following year, *Terry v. Ohio* considered for the first time the question of when police have the right to stop and question a suspect although they do not have enough information to effectuate an arrest. The third case, *United States v. Jones,* deals with installing a Global-Positioning-System (GPS) tracking device on a jeep, without a warrant.

KATZ V. UNITED STATES

389 U.S. 347, 88 S.Ct. 507, 19 L.Ed.2d 576 (1967)

JUSTICE STEWART delivered the opinion of the Court.

The petitioner was convicted in the District Court for the Southern District of California under an eight-count indictment charging him with transmitting wagering information by telephone from Los Angeles to Miami and Boston in violation of a federal statute. At trial the Government was permitted, over the petitioner's objection, to introduce evidence of the petitioner's end of telephone conversations, overheard by FBI agents who had attached an electronic listening and recording device to the outside of the public telephone booth from which he had placed his calls. In affirming his conviction, the Court of Appeals rejected the contention that the recordings had been obtained in violation of the Fourth Amendment, because "[t]here was no physical entrance into the area occupied by [the petitioner]." . . .

The petitioner [has asked]:

A. Whether a public telephone booth is a constitutionally protected area so that evidence obtained by attaching an electronic listening recording device to the top of such a booth is obtained in violation of the right to privacy of the user of the booth.

B. Whether physical penetration of a constitutionally protected area is necessary before a search and seizure can be said to be violative of the Fourth Amendment to the United States Constitution.

We decline to adopt this formulation of the issues. In the first place the correct solution of Fourth Amendment problems is not necessarily promoted by incantation of the phrase "constitutionally protected area." Secondly, the Fourth Amendment cannot be translated into a general constitutional "right to privacy." That Amendment protects individual privacy against certain kinds of governmental intrusion, but its protections go further, and often have nothing to do with privacy at all. Other provisions of the Constitution protect personal privacy from other forms of governmental invasion. But the protection of a person's *general* right to privacy—his right to be let alone by other people—is, like the protection of his property and of his very life, left largely to the law of the individual States.

Because of the misleading way the issues have been formulated, the parties have attached great significance to the characterization of the telephone booth from which the petitioner placed his calls. The petitioner has strenuously argued that the booth was a "constitutionally protected area." The Government has maintained with equal vigor that it was not. But this effort to decide whether or not a given "area," viewed in the abstract, is "constitutionally protected" deflects attention from the problem presented by this case. For the Fourth Amendment protects people, not places. What a person knowingly exposes to the public, even in his own home or office, is not a subject of Fourth Amendment protection. But what he seeks to preserve as private, even in an area accessible to the public, may be constitutionally protected.

The Government stresses the fact that the telephone booth from which the petitioner made his calls was constructed partly of glass, so that he was as visible after he entered it as he would have been if he had remained outside. But what he sought to exclude when he entered the booth was not the intruding eye—it was the uninvited ear. He did not shed his right to do so simply because he made his calls from a place where he might be seen. No less than an individual in a business office, in a friend's apartment, or in a taxicab, a person in a telephone booth may rely upon the protection of the Fourth Amendment. One who occupies it, shuts the door behind him, and pays the toll that permits him to place a call is surely entitled to assume that the words he utters into the mouthpiece will not be broadcast to the world. To read the Constitution more narrowly is to ignore the vital role that the public telephone has come to play in private communication.

The Government contends, however, that the activities of its agents in this case should not be tested by Fourth Amendment requirements, for the surveillance technique they employed involved no physical penetration of the telephone booth from which the petitioner placed his calls. It is true that the absence of such penetration was at one time thought to foreclose further Fourth Amendment inquiry, *Olmstead v. United States*, 277 U.S. 438, 457, 464, 466, 48 S.Ct. 564, 565, 567, 568, 72 L.Ed. 944, *Goldman v. United States,* 316 U.S. 129, 134–136, 62 S.Ct. 993, 995–997, 86 L.Ed. 1322, for that Amendment was thought to limit only searches and seizures of tangible property. But "[t]he premise that property interests control the right of the Government to search and seize has been discredited." Thus, although a closely divided Court supposed in *Olmstead* that surveillance without any trespass and without the seizure of any material object fell outside the ambit of the Constitution, we have since departed from the narrow view on which that decision rested. Indeed, we have expressly held that the Fourth Amendment governs not only the seizure of tangible items, but extends as well to the recording of oral statements overheard without any "technical trespass under . . . local property law." Once this much is acknowledged, and once it is recognized that the Fourth Amendment protects people—and not simply "areas"—against unreasonable searches and seizures it becomes clear that the reach of that Amendment cannot turn upon the presence or absence of a physical intrusion into any given enclosure.

We conclude that the underpinnings of *Olmstead* and *Goldman* have been so eroded by our subsequent decisions that the "trespass" doctrine there enunciated can no longer be regarded as controlling. The Government's activities in electronically listening to and recording the petitioner's words violated the privacy upon which he justifiably relied while using the telephone booth and thus constituted a "search and seizure" within the meaning of the Fourth Amendment. The fact that the electronic device employed to achieve that end did not happen to penetrate the wall of the booth can have no constitutional significance.

The question remaining for decision, then, is whether the search and seizure conducted in this case complied with constitutional standards. In that regard, the Government's position is that its agents acted in an entirely defensible manner: They did not begin their electronic surveillance until investigation of the petitioner's activities had established a strong probability that he was using the telephone in question to transmit gambling information to persons in other States, in violation of federal law. Moreover, the surveillance was limited, both in scope and in duration, to the specific purpose of establishing the contents of the petitioner's unlawful telephonic communications. The agents confined their surveillance to the brief periods during which he used the telephone booth, and they took great care to overhear only the conversations of the petitioner himself.

Accepting this account of the Government's actions as accurate, it is clear that this surveillance was so narrowly circumscribed that a duly authorized magistrate, properly notified of the need for such investigation, specifically informed of the basis on which it was to proceed, and clearly apprised of the precise intrusion it would entail, could constitutionally have authorized, with appropriate safeguards, the very limited search and seizure that the Government asserts in fact took place. [A] judicial order could have accommodated "the legitimate needs of law enforcement" by authorizing the carefully limited use of electronic surveillance.

The Government urges that, because its agents relied upon the decisions in *Olmstead* and *Goldman,* and because they did no more here than they might properly have done with prior judicial sanction, we should retroactively validate their conduct. That we cannot do. It is apparent that the agents in this case acted with restraint. Yet the inescapable fact is that this restraint was imposed by the agents themselves, not by a judicial officer. They were not required, before commencing the search, to present their estimate of probable cause for detached scrutiny by a neutral magistrate. They were not compelled, during the conduct of the search itself, to observe precise limits established in advance by a specific court order. Nor were they directed, after the search had been completed, to notify the authorizing magistrate in detail of all that had been seized. In the absence of such safeguards, this Court has never sustained a search upon the sole ground that officers reasonably expected to find evidence of a particular crime and voluntarily confined their activities to the least intrusive means consistent with that end. Searches conducted without warrants have been held unlawful "notwithstanding facts unquestionably showing probable cause," for the Constitution requires "that the deliberate, impartial judgment of a judicial officer . . . be interposed between the citizen and the police. . . ." "Over and again this Court has emphasized that the mandate of the [Fourth] Amendment requires adherence to judicial processes," and that searches conducted outside the judicial process, without prior approval by judge or magistrate, are *per se* unreasonable under the Fourth Amendment—subject only to a few specifically established and well-delineated exceptions.

It is difficult to imagine how any of those exceptions could ever apply to the sort of search and seizure involved in this case. Even electronic surveillance substantially contemporaneous with an individual's arrest could hardly be deemed an "incident" of that arrest. Nor could the use of electronic surveillance without prior authorization be justified on grounds of "hot pursuit." And, of course, the very nature of electronic surveillance precludes its use pursuant to the suspect's consent.

The Government does not question these basic principles. Rather, it urges the creation of a new exception to cover this case.[23] It argues that surveillance of a telephone booth should be exempted from the usual requirement of advance authorization by a magistrate upon a showing of probable cause. We cannot agree. Omission of such authorization

> bypasses the safeguards provided by an objective predetermination of probable cause, and substitutes instead the far less reliable procedure of an after-the-event justification for the . . . search, too likely to be subtly influenced by the familiar shortcomings of hindsight judgment.

---

[23] Whether safeguards other than prior authorization by a magistrate would satisfy the Fourth Amendment in a situation involving the national security is a question not presented by this case.

[B]ypassing a neutral predetermination of the *scope* of a search leaves individuals secure from Fourth Amendment violations "only in the discretion of the police."

These considerations do not vanish when the search in question is transferred from the setting of a home, an office, or a hotel room to that of a telephone booth. Wherever a man may be, he is entitled to know that he will remain free from unreasonable searches and seizures. The government agents here ignored "the procedure of antecedent justification . . . that is central to the Fourth Amendment," a procedure that we hold to be a constitutional precondition of the kind of electronic surveillance involved in this case. Because the surveillance here failed to meet that condition, and because it led to the petitioner's conviction, the judgment must be reversed.

It is so ordered.

Judgment reversed.

MR. JUSTICE MARSHALL took no part in the consideration or decision of this case.

JUSTICE WHITE, concurring.

In joining the Court's opinion, I note the Court's acknowledgment that there are circumstances in which it is reasonable to search without a warrant. In this connection, in footnote 23 the Court points out that today's decision does not reach national security cases. Wiretapping to protect the security of the Nation has been authorized by successive Presidents. The present Administration would apparently save national security cases from restrictions against wiretapping. We should not require the warrant procedure and the magistrate's judgment if the President of the United States or his chief legal officer, the Attorney General, has considered the requirements of national security and authorized electronic surveillance as reasonable.

JUSTICE DOUGLAS, with whom JUSTICE BRENNAN joins, concurring.

Neither the President nor the Attorney General is a magistrate. In matters where they believe national security may be involved they are not detached, disinterested, and neutral as a court or magistrate must be. [T]he Executive Branch is not supposed to be neutral and disinterested. Rather it should vigorously investigate and prevent breaches of national security and prosecute those who violate the pertinent federal laws. The President and Attorney General . . . may even be the intended victims of subversive action. Since spies and saboteurs are as entitled to the protection of the Fourth Amendment as suspected gamblers like petitioner, I cannot agree that where spies and saboteurs are involved adequate protection of Fourth Amendment rights is assured when the President and Attorney General assume both the position of adversary-and-prosecutor and disinterested, neutral magistrate. . . .

JUSTICE BLACK, dissenting.

My basic objection is twofold: (1) I do not believe that the words of the Amendment will bear the meaning given them by today's decision, and (2) I do not believe that it is the proper role of this Court to rewrite the Amendment in order "to bring it into harmony with the times" and thus reach a result that many people believe to be desirable.

[The opinion of HARLAN, J., concurring, is omitted.]

NOTES

1. *United States v. United States District Court,* 407 U.S. 297, 92 S.Ct. 2125, 32 L.Ed.2d 752 (1972), rejected the notion that the government may engage in warrantless surveillance of a *domestic* radical group free of the restrictions of the Fourth Amendment. Indeed, "Fourth amendment protections become the more necessary when the targets of official surveillance may be those suspected of unorthodoxy in their political beliefs." The concerns of the Fourth Amendment converge with First Amendment values. The Court specifically noted that it did not address the Executive's power to engage in warrantless surveillance of "foreign powers or their agents." Surveillance in this case was of a domestic radical group, which the Court, in a footnote, defined to mean "a group or organization (whether formally or informally constituted) composed of citizens of the United States and which has no significant connection with a foreign power, its agent or agencies."

2. Subsequently, Congress enacted the Foreign Intelligence Surveillance Act of 1978 (FISA), which created the Foreign Intelligence Surveillance Court (FISC). The Chief Justice appoints eleven judges to serve seven-year terms. This court handles cases where the government seeks a search warrant. Proceedings before the FISC court are *ex parte* (there is no party opposing the warrant) and in secret. The government can appeal a denial of a warrant to the Foreign Intelligence Surveillance Court of Review. In 2002, the FISC appellate court held that (1) FISA does not require the government to demonstrate to the FISC court that its primary purpose in conducting electronic surveillance was not criminal prosecution, and (2) the Patriot Act's amendment to FISA, which permit the government to conduct surveillance

of agent of foreign power if foreign intelligence is a "significant purpose" of such surveillance, did not violate Fourth Amendment. In the course of its opinion, it noted that "all" the courts that "have decided the issue," have "held that the President did have inherent authority to conduct warrantless searches to obtain foreign intelligence information." It added, "We take for granted that the President does have that authority and, assuming that is so, FISA could not encroach on the President's constitutional power." *In re Sealed Case*, 310 F.3d 717, 742 (Foreign Intelligence Surveillance Court of Review 2002).

TERRY V. OHIO
392 U.S. 1, 88 S.Ct. 1868, 20 L.Ed.2d 889 (1968)

MR. CHIEF JUSTICE WARREN delivered the opinion of the Court.

This case presents serious questions concerning the role of the Fourth Amendment in the confrontation on the street between the citizen and the policeman investigating suspicious circumstances.

Petitioner Terry was convicted of carrying a concealed weapon and sentenced to the statutorily prescribed term of one to three years in the penitentiary. Following the denial of a pretrial motion to suppress, the prosecution introduced in evidence two revolvers and a number of bullets seized from Terry and a codefendant, Richard Chilton, by Cleveland Police Detective Martin McFadden, [who] . . . testified that while he was patrolling in plain clothes in downtown Cleveland at approximately 2:30 in the afternoon of October 31, 1963, his attention was attracted by two men, Chilton and Terry, standing on the corner of Huron Road and Euclid Avenue. He had never seen the two men before, and he was unable to say precisely what first drew his eye to them. However, he testified that he had been a policeman for 39 years and a detective for 35 and that he had been assigned to patrol this vicinity of downtown Cleveland for shoplifters and pickpockets for 30 years. He explained that he had developed routine habits of observation over the years and that he would "stand and watch people or walk and watch people at many intervals of the day." He added: "Now, in this case when I looked over they didn't look right to me at the time."

His interest aroused, Officer McFadden took up a post of observation in the entrance to a store 300 to 400 feet away from the two men. "I get more purpose to watch them when I seen their movements," he testified. He saw one of the men leave the other one and walk southwest on Huron Road, past some stores. The man paused for a moment and looked in a store window, then walked on a short distance, turned around and walked back toward the corner, pausing once again to look in the same store window. He rejoined his companion at the corner, and the two conferred briefly. Then the second man went through the same series of motions, strolling down Huron Road, looking in the same window, walking on a short distance, turning back, peering in the store window again, and returning to confer with the first man at the corner. The two men repeated this ritual alternately between five and six times apiece—in all, roughly a dozen trips. At one point, while the two were standing together on the corner, a third man approached them and engaged them briefly in conversation. This man then left the two others and walked west on Euclid Avenue. Chilton and Terry resumed their measured pacing, peering and conferring. After this had gone on for 10 to 12 minutes, the two men walked off together, heading west on Euclid Avenue, following the path taken earlier by the third man.

By this time Officer McFadden had become thoroughly suspicious. He testified that after observing their elaborately casual and oft-repeated reconnaissance of the store window on Huron Road, he suspected the two men of "casing a job, a stick-up," and that he considered it his duty as a police officer to investigate further. He added that he feared "they may have a gun." Thus, Officer McFadden followed Chilton and Terry and saw them stop in front of Zucker's store to talk to the same man who had conferred with them earlier on the street corner. Deciding that the situation was ripe for direct action, Officer McFadden approached the three men, identified himself as a police officer and asked for their names. At this point his knowledge was confined to what he had observed. He was not acquainted with any of the three men by name or by sight, and he had received no information concerning them from any other source. When the men "mumbled something" in response to his inquiries, Officer McFadden grabbed petitioner Terry, spun him around so that they were facing the other two, with Terry between McFadden and the others, and patted down the outside of his clothing. In the left breast pocket of Terry's overcoat Officer McFadden felt a pistol. He reached inside the overcoat pocket, but was unable to remove the gun. At this point, keeping Terry between himself and the others, the officer ordered all three men to enter Zucker's store. As they went in, he removed Terry's overcoat completely, removed a .38-caliber revolver from the pocket and ordered all three men to face the wall with their hands raised. Officer McFadden proceeded to pat down the outer clothing of Chilton and the third man, Katz. He discovered another revolver in the outer pocket of Chilton's overcoat, but no weapons were found to Katz. The officer testified that he only patted the men down to see whether they had weapons, and that he did not put his hands beneath the outer garments of either Terry or Chilton until he felt their guns. So far as appears from the record, he never placed his hands beneath Katz' outer garments. Officer McFadden seized Chilton's gun, asked the proprietor of the store to call a police wagon, and took all three men to the station, where Chilton and Terry were formally charged with carrying concealed weapons.

On the motion to suppress the guns the prosecution took the position that they had been seized following a search incident to a lawful arrest. The trial court rejected this theory, stating that it "would be stretching the facts beyond reasonable comprehension" to find that Officer McFadden had had probable cause to arrest the men before he patted them down for weapons. However, the court denied the defendants' motion on the ground that Officer McFadden, on the basis of his experience, "had reasonable cause to believe . . . that the defendants were conducting themselves suspiciously, and some interrogation should be made of their action." Purely for his own protection, the court held, the officer had the right to pat down the outer clothing of these men, who he had reasonable cause to believe might be armed.

"[T]he Fourth Amendment protects people, not places," *Katz v. United States,* and wherever an individual may harbor a reasonable "expectation of privacy," he is entitled to be free from unreasonable governmental intrusion. Of course, the specific content and incidents of this right must be shaped by the context in which it is asserted. For "what the Constitution forbids is not all searches and seizures, but unreasonable searches and seizures." Unquestionably petitioner was entitled to the protection of the Fourth Amendment as he walked down the street in Cleveland. The question is whether in all the circumstances of this on-the-street encounter, his right to personal security was violated by an unreasonable search and seizure. . . .

Our first task is to establish at what point in this encounter the Fourth Amendment becomes relevant. That is, we must decide whether and when Officer McFadden "seized" Terry and whether and when he conducted a "search." There is some suggestion in the use of such terms as "stop" and "frisk" that such police conduct is outside the purview of the Fourth Amendment because neither action rises to the level of a "search" or "seizure" within the meaning of the Constitution. We emphatically reject this notion. It is quite plain that the Fourth Amendment governs "seizures" of the person which do not eventuate in a trip to the station house and prosecution for crime—"arrests" in traditional terminology. It must be recognized that whenever a police officer accosts an individual and restrains his freedom to walk away, he has "seized" that person. And it is nothing less than sheer torture of the English language to suggest that a careful exploration of the outer surfaces of a person's clothing all over his or her body in an attempt to find weapons is not a "search." Moreover, it is simply fantastic to urge that such a procedure performed in public by a policeman while the citizen stands helpless, perhaps facing a wall with his hands raised, is a "petty indignity." It is a serious intrusion upon the sanctity of the person, which may inflict great indignity and arouse strong resentment, and it is not to be undertaken lightly. . . . In this case there can be no question, then, that Officer McFadden "seized" petitioner and subjected him to a "search" when he took hold of him and patted down the outer surfaces of his clothing. We must decide whether at that point it was reasonable for Officer McFadden to have interfered with petitioner's personal security as he did.[16] And in determining whether the seizure and search were "unreasonable" our inquiry is a dual one—whether the officer's action was justified at its inception, and whether it was reasonably related in scope to the circumstances which justified the interference in the first place.

If this case involved police conduct subject to the Warrant Clause of the Fourth Amendment, we would have to ascertain whether "probable cause" existed to justify the search and seizure which took place. However, that is not the case. We do not retreat from our holdings that the police must, whenever practicable, obtain advance judicial approval of searches and seizures through the warrant procedure, see *e.g., Katz v. United States,* or that in most instances failure to comply with the warrant requirement can only be excused by exigent circumstances, see, *e.g., Warden v. Hayden,* 387 U.S. 294, 87 S.Ct. 1642, 18 L.Ed.2d 782 (1967) (hot pursuit). But we deal here with an entire rubric of police conduct—necessarily swift action predicated upon the on-the-spot observations of the officer on the beat—which historically has not been, and as a practical matter could not be, subjected to the warrant procedure. Instead, the conduct involved in this case must be tested by the Fourth Amendment's general proscription against unreasonable searches and seizures.

Nonetheless, the notions which underlie both the warrant procedure and the requirement of probable cause remain fully relevant in this context. In order to

---

[16] We thus decide nothing today concerning the constitutional propriety of an investigative "seizure" upon less than probable cause for purposes of "detention" and/or interrogation. Obviously, not all personal intercourse between policemen and citizens involves "seizures" of persons. Only when the officer, by means of physical force or show of authority, has in some way restrained the liberty of a citizen may we conclude that a "seizure" has occurred. We cannot tell with any certainty upon this record whether any such "seizure" took place here prior to Officer McFadden's initiation of physical contact for purposes of searching Terry for weapons, and we thus may assume that up to that point no intrusion upon constitutionally protected rights had occurred.

assess the reasonableness of Officer McFadden's conduct as a general proposition, it is necessary "first to focus upon the governmental interest which allegedly justifies official intrusion upon the constitutionally protected interests of the private citizen," for there is "no ready test for determining reasonableness other than by balancing the need to search [or seize] against the invasion which the search [or seizure] entails." And in justifying the particular intrusion the police officer must be able to point to specific and articulable facts which, taken together with rational inferences from those facts, reasonably warrant that intrusion.[18] The scheme of the Fourth Amendment becomes meaningful only when it is assured that at some point the conduct of those charged with enforcing the laws can be subjected to the more detached, neutral scrutiny of a judge who must evaluate the reasonableness of a particular search or seizure in light of the particular circumstances. And in making that assessment it is imperative that the facts be judgment against an objective standard: would the facts available to the officer at the moment of the seizure or the search "warrant a man of reasonable caution in the belief" that the action taken was appropriate? Anything less would invite intrusions upon constitutionally guaranteed rights based on nothing more substantial than inarticulate hunches, a result this Court has consistently refused to sanction. And simple " 'good faith on the part of the arresting officer is not enough.' . . . If subjective good faith alone were the test, the protections of the Fourth Amendment would evaporate, and the people would be 'secure in their persons, houses, papers and effects,' only in the discretion of the police."

Applying these principles to this case, we consider first the nature and extent of the governmental interests involved. One general interest is of course that of effective crime prevention and detection; it is this interest which underlies the recognition that a police officer may in appropriate circumstances and in an appropriate manner approach a person for purposes of investigating possibly criminal behavior even though there is no probable cause to make an arrest. It was this legitimate investigative function Officer McFadden was discharging when he decided to approach petitioner and his companions. . . .

The crux of this case, however, is not the propriety of Officer McFadden's taking steps to investigate petitioner's suspicious behavior, but rather, whether there was justification for McFadden's invasion of Terry's personal security by searching him for weapons in the course of that investigation. We are now concerned with more than the governmental interest in investigating crime; in

---

[18] This demand for specificity in the information upon which police action is predicated is the central teaching of this Court's Fourth Amendment jurisprudence.

addition, there is the more immediate interest of the police officer in taking steps to assure himself that the person with whom he is dealing is not armed with a weapon that could unexpectedly and fatally be used against him. Certainly it would be unreasonable to require that police officers take unnecessary risks in the performance of their duties. . . .

Petitioner does not argue that a police officer should refrain from making any investigation of suspicious circumstances until such time as he has probable cause to make an arrest; nor does he deny that police officers in properly discharging their investigative function may find themselves confronting persons who might well be armed and dangerous. Moreover, he does not say that an officer is always unjustified in searching a suspect to discover weapons. Rather, he says it is unreasonable for the policeman to take that step until such time as the situation evolves to a point where there is probable cause to make an arrest. When that point has been reached, petitioner would concede the officer's right to conduct a search of the suspect for weapons, fruits or instrumentalities of the crime, or "mere" evidence, incident to the arrest.

There are two weaknesses in this line of reasoning however. First, it fails to take account of traditional limitations upon the scope of searches, and thus recognizes no distinction in purpose, character, and extent between a search incident to an arrest and a limited search for weapons. The former, although justified in part by the acknowledged necessity to protect the arresting officer from assault with a concealed weapon, is also justified on other grounds, and can therefore involve a relatively extensive exploration of the person. A search for weapons in the absence of probable cause to arrest, however, must, like any other search, be strictly circumscribed by the exigencies which justify its initiation. Thus it must be limited to that which is necessary for the discovery of weapons which might be used to harm the officer or others nearby, and may realistically be characterized as something less than a "full" search, even though it remains a serious intrusion.

A second, and related, objection to petitioner's argument is that it assumes that the law of arrest has already worked out the balance between the particular interests involved here—the neutralization of danger to the policeman in the investigative circumstance and the sanctity of the individual. But this is not so. An arrest is a wholly different kind of intrusion upon individual freedom from a limited search for weapons, and the interests each is designed to serve are likewise quite different. An arrest is the initial stage of a criminal prosecution. It is intended to vindicate society's interest in having its laws obeyed, and it is inevitably accompanied by future interference with the individual's freedom of movement, whether or not trial or conviction ultimately follows. The protective search for weapons, on the other hand, constitutes a brief, though far from inconsiderable, intrusion upon the sanctity of the person. It does not follow that because an officer may lawfully arrest a person only when he is apprised of facts sufficient to warrant a belief that the person has committed or is committing a crime, the officer is equally unjustified, absent that kind of evidence, in making any intrusions short of an arrest. Moreover, a perfectly reasonable apprehension of danger may arise long before the officer is possessed of adequate information to justify taking a person into custody for the purpose of prosecuting him for a crime. Petitioner's reliance on cases which have worked out standards of reasonableness with regard to "seizures" constituting arrests and searches incident thereto is thus misplaced. . . .

[T]here must be a narrowly drawn authority to permit a reasonable search for weapons for the protection of the police officer, where he has reason to believe that he is dealing with an armed and dangerous individual, regardless of whether he has probable cause to arrest the individual for a crime. The officer need not be absolutely certain that the individual is armed; the issue is whether a reasonably prudent man in the circumstances would be warranted in the belief that his safety or that of others was in danger. And in determining whether the officer acted reasonably in such circumstances, due weight must be given, not to his inchoate and unparticularized suspicion or "hunch," but to the specific reasonable inferences which he is entitled to draw from the facts in light of his experience.

[Officer McFadden] observed Terry, together with Chilton and another man, acting in a manner he took to be preface to a "stick-up." We think on the facts and circumstances Officer McFadden detailed before the trial judge a reasonably prudent man would have been warranted in believing petitioner was armed and thus presented a threat to the officer's safety while he was investigating his suspicious behavior. The actions of Terry and Chilton were consistent with McFadden's hypothesis that these men were contemplating a daylight robbery—which, it is reasonable to assume, would be likely to involve the use of weapons—and nothing in their conduct from the time he first noticed them until the time he confronted them and identified himself as a police officer gave him sufficient reason to negate that hypothesis.

[The protective seizure and search for weapons] unlike a search without a warrant incident to a lawful arrest, is not justified by any need to prevent the disappearance or destruction of evidence of crime. The sole justification of the search in the present situation is the protection of the police officer and others nearby, and it must therefore be confined in scope to an intrusion reasonably designed to discover guns, knives, clubs, or other hidden instruments for the assault of the police officer.

The scope of the search in this case presents no serious problem in light of these standards. Officer McFadden patted down the outer clothing of petitioner and his two companions. He did not place his hands in their pockets or under the outer surface of their garments until he had felt weapons, and then he merely reached for and removed the guns. . . .

We conclude that the revolver seized from Terry was properly admitted in evidence against him. . . . Each case of this sort will, of course, have to be decided on its own facts. We merely hold today that where a police officer observes unusual conduct which leads him reasonably to conclude in light of his experience that criminal activity may be afoot and that the persons with whom he is dealing may be armed and presently dangerous, where in the course of investigating this behavior he identifies himself as a policeman and makes reasonable inquiries, and where nothing in the initial stages of the encounter serves to dispel his reasonable fear for his own or others' safety, he is entitled for the protection of himself and others in the area to conduct a carefully limited search of the outer clothing of such persons in an attempt to discover weapons which might be used to assault him.

Such a search is a reasonable search under the Fourth Amendment, and any weapons seized may properly be introduced in evidence against the person from whom they were taken.

Affirmed.

JUSTICE DOUGLAS, dissenting.

I agree that petitioner was "seized" within the meaning of the Fourth Amendment. I also agree that frisking petitioner and his companions for guns was a "search." But it is a mystery how that "search" and that "seizure" can be constitutional by Fourth Amendment standards, unless there was "probable cause"[1] to believe that (1) a crime had been committed or (2) a crime was in the process of being committed or (3) a crime was about to be committed.

The opinion of the Court disclaims the existence of "probable cause." [T]he crime here is carrying concealed weapons; and there is no basis for concluding hat

---

[1]   The meaning of "probable cause" has been developed in cases where an officer has reasonable grounds to believe that a crime has been or is being committed. . . .

the officer had "probable cause" for believing that that crime was being committed. Had a warrant been sought, a magistrate would, therefore, have been unauthorized to issue one, for he can act only if there is a showing of "probable cause." We hold today that the police have greater authority to make a "seizure" and conduct a "search" than a judge has to authorize such action. We have said precisely the opposite over and over again. . . . To give the police greater power than a magistrate is to take a long step down the totalitarian path. . . .

[The concurring opinions of WHITE & HARLAN, JJ., are omitted.]

UNITED STATES V. JONES
565 U.S. ___, 132 S.Ct. 945, 181 L.Ed.2d 911 (2012)

[The Government obtained a search warrant permitting it to install a Global-Positioning-System (GPS) tracking device on a vehicle (a jeep) registered to the wife of defendant Jones. The warrant authorized installation in the District of Columbia and within 10 days. Agents installed the GPS on the undercarriage of the Jeep while it was parked in a public parking lot. However, they installed it on the 11th day and in Maryland. The Government then tracked the vehicle's movements for 28 days. The Government prosecuted Jones and others on conspiracy to distribute and to possess with intent to distribute five kilograms or more of cocaine and 50 grams or more of cocaine base. The trial court suppressed the GPS data obtained while the jeep was parked at Jones's residence, but admitted the remaining data arguing that Jones had no reasonable expectation of privacy when the jeep was on the public streets. The locational data connected Jones to the alleged conspirators' stash house, which contained $850,000 in cash, 97 kilograms of cocaine, and 1 kilogram of cocaine base.

[The Supreme Court, with no dissents, reversed Jones' conviction and held that the Government's attachment of the GPS device to the vehicle, and its use of it to monitor the vehicle's movements, constitutes a search under the Fourth Amendment. Justice Scalia spoke for the Court. Sotomayor, J., filed a concurring opinion, and Alito, J. filed opinion concurring in the judgment, joined by Ginsburg, Breyer, & Kagan, JJ.]

JUSTICE SCALIA delivered the opinion of the Court.

We decide whether the attachment of a Global-Positioning-System (GPS) tracking device to an individual's vehicle, and subsequent use of that device to monitor the vehicle's movements on public streets, constitutes a search or seizure within the meaning of the Fourth Amendment. [The] vehicle is an "effect" as that term is used in the [Fourth] Amendment. We hold that the Government's installation of a GPS device on a target's vehicle, and its use of that device to monitor the vehicle's movements, constitutes a "search."

It is important to be clear about what occurred in this case: The Government physically occupied private property for the purpose of obtaining information. We have no doubt that such a physical intrusion would have been considered a "search" within the meaning of the Fourth Amendment when it was adopted. *Entick v. Carrington,* 95 Eng. Rep. 807 (C.P. 1765), is a "case we have described as a 'monument of English freedom' 'undoubtedly familiar' to 'every American statesman' at the time the Constitution was adopted, and considered to be 'the true and ultimate expression of constitutional law' " with regard to search and seizure. In that case, Lord Camden expressed in plain terms the significance of property rights in search-and-seizure analysis:

> "[O]ur law holds the property of every man so sacred, that no man can set his foot upon his neighbour's close without his leave; if he does he is a trespasser, though he does no damage at all; if he will tread upon his neighbour's ground, he must justify it by law."

The text of the Fourth Amendment reflects its close connection to property, since otherwise it would have referred simply to "the right of the people to be secure against unreasonable searches and seizures"; the phrase "in their persons, houses, papers, and effects" would have been superfluous.

Consistent with this understanding, our Fourth Amendment jurisprudence was tied to common-law trespass, at least until the latter half of the 20th century. [L]ater cases, of course, have deviated from that exclusively property-based approach. In *Katz v. United States,* 389 U.S. 347, 351, 88 S.Ct. 507, 19 L.Ed.2d 576 (1967), we said that "the Fourth Amendment protects people, not places," and found a violation in attachment of an eavesdropping device to a public telephone booth. Our later cases have applied the analysis of Justice Harlan's concurrence in that case, which said that a violation occurs when government officers violate a person's "reasonable expectation of privacy."

The Government contends that the Harlan standard shows that no search occurred here, since Jones had no "reasonable expectation of privacy" in the area of the Jeep accessed by Government agents (its underbody) and in the locations of the Jeep on the public roads, which were visible to all. But we need not address the Government's contentions, because Jones's Fourth Amendment rights do not rise or fall with the *Katz* formulation. At bottom, we must "assur[e] preservation of that degree of privacy against government that existed when the Fourth Amendment was adopted." [F]or most of our history the Fourth Amendment was understood to embody a particular concern for government trespass upon the areas ("persons, houses, papers, and effects") it enumerates.[3] *Katz* did not repudiate that understanding. . . .

The Government [relies on] cases in which we rejected Fourth Amendment challenges to "beepers," electronic tracking devices that represent another form of electronic monitoring. The first case, *United States v. Knotts*, 460 U.S. 276, 103 S.Ct. 1081, 75 L.Ed.2d 55 (1983), upheld against Fourth Amendment challenge the use of a "beeper" that had been placed in a container of chloroform, allowing law enforcement to monitor the location of the container. We said that there had been no infringement of Knotts' reasonable expectation of privacy since the information obtained—the location of the automobile carrying the container on public roads, and the location of the off-loaded container in open fields near Knotts' cabin—had been voluntarily conveyed to the public. But as we have discussed, the *Katz* reasonable-expectation-of-privacy test has been *added to,* not *substituted for,* the common-law trespassory test. The holding in *Knotts* addressed only the former, since the latter was not at issue. The beeper had been placed in the container before it came into Knotts' possession, with the consent of the then-owner.

[In the] second "beeper" case, *United States v. Karo,* 468 U.S. 705, 104 S.Ct. 3296, 82 L.Ed.2d 530 (1984), [the issue was] whether the installation of a beeper in a container amounted to a search or seizure. [T]he specific question we considered was whether the installation "*with the consent of the original owner* constitute[d] a search or seizure . . . when the container is delivered to a buyer having no knowledge of the presence of the beeper." (emphasis added). We held not. The Government, we said, came into physical contact with the container only before it belonged to the defendant Karo; and the transfer of the container with the unmonitored beeper inside did not convey any information and thus did not invade Karo's privacy. That conclusion is perfectly consistent with the one we reach here. Karo accepted the container as it came to him, beeper and all, and was

---

[3]   Justice Alito's concurrence (hereinafter concurrence) doubts the wisdom of our approach because "it is almost impossible to think of late-18th-century situations that are analogous to what took place in this case." (opinion concurring in judgment). But in fact it posits a situation that is not far afield—a constable's concealing himself in the target's coach in order to track its movements. There is no doubt that the information gained by that trespassory activity would be the product of an unlawful search—whether that information consisted of the conversations occurring in the coach, or of the destinations to which the coach traveled.

In any case, it is quite irrelevant whether there was an 18th-century analog. Whatever new methods of investigation may be devised, our task, *at a minimum,* is to decide whether the action in question would have constituted a "search" within the original meaning of the Fourth Amendment. Where, as here, the Government obtains information by physically intruding on a constitutionally protected area, such a search has undoubtedly occurred.

therefore not entitled to object to the beeper's presence, even though it was used to monitor the container's location. Jones, who possessed the Jeep at the time the Government trespassorily inserted the information-gathering device, is on much different footing.

The Government also points to our exposition in *New York v. Class,* 475 U.S. 106, 106 S.Ct. 960, 89 L.Ed.2d 81 (1986), that "[t]he exterior of a car . . . is thrust into the public eye, and thus to examine it does not constitute a 'search.' " That statement is of marginal relevance here since, as the Government acknowledges, "the officers in this case did *more* than conduct a visual inspection of respondent's vehicle," Brief for United States 41 (emphasis added). By attaching the device to the Jeep, officers encroached on a protected area. In *Class* itself we suggested that this would make a difference, for we concluded that an officer's momentary reaching into the interior of a vehicle did constitute a search.

Finally, the Government's position gains little support from our conclusion in *Oliver v. United States,* 466 U.S. 170, 104 S.Ct. 1735, 80 L.Ed.2d 214 (1984), that officers' information-gathering intrusion on an "open field" did not constitute a Fourth Amendment search even though it was a trespass at common law. Quite simply, an open field, unlike the curtilage of a home, is not one of those protected areas enumerated in the Fourth Amendment. The Government's physical intrusion on such an area—unlike its intrusion on the "effect" at issue here—is of no Fourth Amendment significance.

The concurrence begins by accusing us of applying "18th-century tort law." That is a distortion. What we apply is an 18th-century guarantee against unreasonable searches, which we believe must provide *at a minimum* the degree of protection it afforded when it was adopted. The concurrence does not share that belief. It would apply *exclusively Katz*'s reasonable-expectation-of-privacy test, even when that eliminates rights that previously existed.

The concurrence faults our approach for "present[ing] particularly vexing problems" in cases that do not involve physical contact, such as those that involve the transmission of electronic signals. We entirely fail to understand that point. For unlike the concurrence, which would make *Katz* the *exclusive* test, we do not make trespass the exclusive test. Situations involving merely the transmission of electronic signals without trespass would *remain* subject to *Katz* analysis.

In fact, it is the concurrence's insistence on the exclusivity of the *Katz* test that needlessly leads us into "particularly vexing problems" in the present case. This Court has to date not deviated from the understanding that mere visual observation does not constitute a search. We accordingly held in *Knotts* that "[a] person traveling in an automobile on public thoroughfares has no reasonable expectation of privacy in his movements from one place to another." Thus, even assuming that the concurrence is correct to say that "[t]raditional surveillance" of Jones for a 4-week period "would have required a large team of agents, multiple vehicles, and perhaps aerial assistance,", our cases suggest that such visual observation is constitutionally permissible. It may be that achieving the same result through electronic means, without an accompanying trespass, is an unconstitutional invasion of privacy, but the present case does not require us to answer that question.

And answering it affirmatively leads us needlessly into additional thorny problems. The concurrence posits that "relatively short-term monitoring of a person's movements on public streets" is okay, but that "the use of longer term GPS monitoring in investigations *of most offenses*" is no good. (emphasis added). That introduces yet another novelty into our jurisprudence. There is no precedent for the proposition that whether a search has occurred depends on the nature of the crime being investigated. And even accepting that novelty, it remains unexplained why a 4-week investigation is "surely" too long and why a drug-trafficking conspiracy involving substantial amounts of cash and narcotics is not an "extraordinary offens[e]" which may permit longer observation. What of a 2-day monitoring of a suspected purveyor of stolen electronics? Or of a 6-month monitoring of a suspected terrorist? We may have to grapple with these "vexing problems" in some future case where a classic trespassory search is not involved and resort must be had to *Katz* analysis; but there is no reason for rushing forward to resolve them here.

The Government argues in the alternative that even if the attachment and use of the device was a search, it was reasonable—and thus lawful—under the Fourth Amendment because "officers had reasonable suspicion, and indeed probable cause, to believe that [Jones] was a leader in a large-scale cocaine distribution conspiracy." We have no occasion to consider this argument. The Government did not raise it below, and the D.C. Circuit therefore did not address it. We consider the argument forfeited.

The judgment of the Court of Appeals for the D.C. Circuit is affirmed. *It is so ordered.*

JUSTICE ALITO, with whom JUSTICE GINSBURG, JUSTICE BREYER, and JUSTICE KAGAN join, concurring in the judgment. . . .

This holding, in my judgment, is unwise. It strains the language of the Fourth Amendment; it has little if any support in current Fourth Amendment case law;

and it is highly artificial. I would analyze the question presented in this case by asking whether respondent's reasonable expectations of privacy were violated by the long-term monitoring of the movements of the vehicle he drove. . . .

The Court argues—and I agree—that "we must 'assur[e] preservation of that degree of privacy against government that existed when the Fourth Amendment was adopted.'" But it is almost impossible to think of late-18th-century situations that are analogous to what took place in this case. (Is it possible to imagine a case in which a constable secreted himself somewhere in a coach and remained there for a period of time in order to monitor the movements of the coach's owner?)

[T]he Court's reasoning largely disregards what is really important (the *use* of a GPS for the purpose of long-term tracking) and instead attaches great significance to something that most would view as relatively minor (attaching to the bottom of a car a small, light object that does not interfere in any way with the car's operation). . . . By contrast, if long-term monitoring can be accomplished without committing a technical trespass—suppose, for example, that the Federal Government required or persuaded auto manufacturers to include a GPS tracking device in every car—the Court's theory would provide no protection.

[T]he Court's approach leads to incongruous results. If the police attach a GPS device to a car and use the device to follow the car for even a brief time, under the Court's theory, the Fourth Amendment applies. But if the police follow the same car for a much longer period using unmarked cars and aerial assistance, this tracking is not subject to any Fourth Amendment constraints.

[T]he Court's reliance on the law of trespass will present particularly vexing problems in cases involving surveillance that is carried out by making electronic, as opposed to physical, contact with the item to be tracked. For example, suppose that the officers in the present case had followed respondent by surreptitiously activating a stolen vehicle detection system that came with the car when it was purchased. Would the sending of a radio signal to activate this system constitute a trespass to chattels? . . .

The *Katz* expectation-of-privacy test avoids the problems and complications noted above, but it is not without its own difficulties. It involves a degree of circularity, and judges are apt to confuse their own expectations of privacy with those of the hypothetical reasonable person to which the *Katz* test looks. In addition, the *Katz* test rests on the assumption that this hypothetical reasonable person has a well-developed and stable set of privacy expectations. But technology can change those expectations. Dramatic technological change may lead to periods in which popular expectations are in flux and may ultimately produce significant changes in popular attitudes. New technology may provide increased convenience or security at the expense of privacy, and many people may find the tradeoff worthwhile [or] eventually reconcile themselves to this development as inevitable.

On the other hand, concern about new intrusions on privacy may spur the enactment of legislation to protect against these intrusions. This is what ultimately happened with respect to wiretapping. After *Katz*, Congress did not leave it to the courts to develop a body of Fourth Amendment case law governing that complex subject. Instead, Congress promptly enacted a comprehensive statute, and since that time, the regulation of wiretapping has been governed primarily by statute and not by case law. In an ironic sense, although *Katz* overruled *Olmstead*, Chief Justice Taft's suggestion in the latter case that the regulation of wiretapping was a matter better left for Congress, has been borne out.

Recent years have seen the emergence of many new devices that permit the monitoring of a person's movements. In some locales, closed-circuit television video monitoring is becoming ubiquitous. On toll roads, automatic toll collection systems create a precise record of the movements of motorists who choose to make use of that convenience. Many motorists purchase cars that are equipped with devices that permit a central station to ascertain the car's location at any time so that roadside assistance may be provided if needed and the car may be found if it is stolen.

Perhaps most significant, cell phones and other wireless devices now permit wireless carriers to track and record the location of users—and as of June 2011, it has been reported, there were more than 322 million wireless devices in use in the United States. [P]hone-location-tracking services are offered as "social" tools, allowing consumers to find (or to avoid) others who enroll in these services. . . .

In the pre-computer age, the greatest protections of privacy were neither constitutional nor statutory, but practical. Traditional surveillance for any extended period of time was difficult and costly and therefore rarely undertaken. The surveillance at issue in this case—constant monitoring of the location of a vehicle for four weeks—would have required a large team of agents, multiple vehicles, and perhaps aerial assistance. Only an investigation of unusual importance could have justified such an expenditure of law enforcement resources. Devices like the one used in the present case, however, make long-term monitoring relatively easy and cheap. In circumstances involving dramatic technological change, the best solution to privacy concerns may be legislative. [H]owever, Congress and most States have not enacted statutes regulating the use of GPS tracking technology for law enforcement purposes. The best that we can do in this case is to apply existing Fourth Amendment doctrine and to ask whether the use of GPS tracking in a particular case involved a degree of intrusion that a reasonable person would not have anticipated.

Under this approach, relatively short-term monitoring of a person's movements on public streets accords with expectations of privacy that our society has recognized as reasonable. But the use of longer term GPS monitoring in investigations of most offenses impinges on expectations of privacy. For such offenses, society's expectation has been that law enforcement agents and others would not—and indeed, in the main, simply could not—secretly monitor and catalogue every single movement of an individual's car for a very long period. In this case, for four weeks, law enforcement agents tracked every movement that respondent made in the vehicle he was driving. We need not identify with precision the point at which the tracking of this vehicle became a search, for the line was surely crossed before the 4-week mark. Other cases may present more difficult questions. . . . We also need not consider whether prolonged GPS monitoring in the context of investigations involving extraordinary offenses would similarly intrude on a constitutionally protected sphere of privacy. In such cases, long-term tracking might have been mounted using previously available techniques. For these reasons, I conclude that the lengthy monitoring that occurred in this case constituted a search under the Fourth Amendment. I therefore agree with the majority that the decision of the Court of Appeals must be affirmed.

[The concurring opinion of SOTOMAYOR, J., is omitted.]

4.5 TRIAL BY JURY

DUNCAN V. LOUISIANA
391 U.S. 145, 88 S.Ct. 1444, 20 L.Ed.2d 491 (1968)

JUSTICE WHITE delivered the opinion of the Court.

Appellant, Gary Duncan, [a 19-year-old black] was convicted of simple battery in the Twenty-fifth Judicial District Court of Louisiana. [White witnesses testified that Duncan slapped a white youth on the elbow; black witnesses testified that Duncan did not slap, but merely touched, the youth.] Under Louisiana law simple battery is a misdemeanor, punishable by a maximum of two years' imprisonment and a $300 fine. Appellant sought trial by jury, but because the Louisiana Constitution grants jury trials only in cases in which capital punishment or imprisonment at hard labor may be imposed, the trial judge denied the request. Appellant was convicted and sentenced to serve 60 days in the parish prison and pay a fine of $150. [Appellant alleges] that the Sixth and Fourteenth Amendments to the United States Constitution secure the right to jury trial in state criminal prosecutions where a sentence as long as two years may be imposed. . . . The Fourteenth Amendment denies the States the power to "deprive any person of life, liberty, or property, without due process of law." In resolving conflicting claims concerning the meaning of this spacious language, the Court has looked increasingly to the Bill of Rights for guidance; many of the rights guaranteed by the first eight Amendments to the Constitution have been held to be protected against state action by the Due Process Clause of the Fourteenth Amendment. . . .

The test for determining whether a right extended by the Fifth and Sixth Amendments with respect to federal criminal proceedings is also protected against state action by the Fourteenth Amendment has been phrased in a variety of ways in the opinions of this Court. The question has been asked whether a right is among those " 'fundamental principles of liberty and justice which lie at the base of all our civil and political institutions,' " *Powell v. State of Alabama;* whether it is "basic in our system of jurisprudence," *In re Oliver,* 333 U.S. 257, 273, 68 S.Ct. 499, 507, 92 L.Ed. 682 (1948); and whether it is "a fundamental right, essential to a fair trial," *Gideon v. Wainwright.* The claim before us is that the right to trial by jury guaranteed by the Sixth Amendment meets these tests. The position of Louisiana, on the other hand, is that the Constitution imposes upon the States no duty to give a jury trial in any criminal case, regardless of the seriousness of the crime or the size of the punishment which may be imposed. Because we believe that trial by jury in criminal cases is fundamental to the American scheme of justice, we hold that the Fourteenth Amendment guarantees a right of jury trial in all criminal cases which—were they to be tried in a federal court—would come within the Sixth Amendment's guarantee. Since we consider the appeal before us to be such a case, we hold that the Constitution was violated when appellant's demand for jury trial was refused.

The history of trial by jury in criminal cases has been frequently told. It is sufficient for present purposes to say that by the time our Constitution was written, jury trial in criminal cases had been in existence in England for several centuries and carried impressive credentials traced by many to Magna Carta. Its preservation and proper operation as a protection against arbitrary rule were among the major objectives of the revolutionary settlement which was expressed in the Declaration and Bill of Rights of 1689. . . .

Jury trial came to America with English colonists, and received strong support from them. Royal interference with the jury trial was deeply resented. Among the resolutions adopted by the First Congress of the American Colonies (the Stamp Act Congress) on October 19, 1765—resolutions deemed by their authors to state "the most essential rights and liberties of the colonists"—was the declaration:

> That trial by jury is the inherent and invaluable right of every British subject in these colonies.

The First Continental Congress, in the resolve of October 14, 1774, objected to trials before judges dependent upon the Crown alone for their salaries and to trials in England for alleged crimes committed in the colonies; the Congress therefore declared:

> That the respective colonies are entitled to the common law of England, and more especially to the great and inestimable privilege of being tried by their peers of the vicinage, according to the course of that law.

The Declaration of Independence stated solemn objections to the King's making "judges dependent on his will alone, for the tenure of their offices, and the amount and payment of their salaries," to his "depriving us in many cases, of the benefits of Trial by Jury," and to his "transporting us beyond Seas to be tried for pretended offenses." The Constitution itself, in Art. III, § 2, commanded:

> The Trial of all Crimes, except in Cases of Impeachment, shall be by Jury; and such Trial shall be held in the State where the said Crimes shall have been committed.

. . . The constitutions adopted by the original States guaranteed jury trial. Also, the constitution of every State entering the Union thereafter in one form or another protected the right to jury trial in criminal cases.

[There are not] prior cases in this Court in which the prevailing opinion contains statements contrary to our holding today that the right to jury trial in serious criminal cases is a fundamental right and hence must be recognized by the States as part of their obligation to extend due process of law to all persons within their jurisdiction. Louisiana relies especially on *Maxwell v. Dow,* 176 U.S. 581, 20 S.Ct. 448, 44 L.Ed. 597 (1900); *Palko v. State of Connecticut,* 302 U.S. 319, 58 S.Ct. 149, 82 L.Ed. 288 (1937); and *Snyder v. Commonwealth of Massachusetts,* 291 U.S. 97, 54 S.Ct. 330, 78 L.Ed. 674 (1934). None of these cases, however, dealt with a State which had purported to dispense entirely with a jury trial in serious criminal cases. *Maxwell* held that no provision of the Bill of Rights applied to the States—a position long since repudiated—and that the Due Process Clause of the Fourteenth Amendment did not prevent a State from trying a defendant for a noncapital offense with fewer than 12 men on the jury. It did not deal with a case in which no jury at all had been provided. In neither *Palko* nor *Snyder* was jury trial actually at issue, although both cases contain important dicta asserting that the right to jury trial is not essential to ordered liberty and may be dispensed with by the States regardless of the Sixth and Fourteenth Amendments. These observations, though weighty and respectable, are nevertheless dicta, unsupported by holdings in this Court. [This Court has] rejected *Palko's* discussion of the self-incrimination clause. Respectfully, we reject the prior dicta regarding jury trial in criminal cases.

The guarantees of jury trial in the Federal and State Constitutions reflect a profound judgment about the way in which law should be enforced and justice administered. A right to jury trial is granted to criminal defendants in order to prevent oppression by the Government. Those who wrote our constitutions knew from history and experience that it was necessary to protect against unfounded criminal charges brought to eliminate enemies and against judges too responsive to the voice of higher authority. The Framers of the constitutions strove to create an independent judiciary but insisted upon further protection against arbitrary action. Providing an accused with the right to be tried by a jury of his peers gave him an inestimable safeguard against the corrupt or overzealous prosecutor and against the compliant, biased, or eccentric judge. [T]he jury trial provisions in the Federal and State Constitutions reflect a fundamental decision about the exercise of official power—a reluctance to entrust plenary powers over the life and liberty of the citizen to one judge or to a group of judges . . . . . The deep commitment of the Nation to the right of jury trial in serious criminal cases as a defense against arbitrary law enforcement qualifies for protection under the Due Process Clause of the Fourteenth Amendment, and must therefore be respected by the States.

Of course jury trial has "its weaknesses and the potential for misuse." We are aware of the long debate, especially in this century, among those who write about the administration of justice, as to the wisdom of permitting untrained laymen to determine the facts in civil and criminal proceedings. Although the debate has been intense, with powerful voices on either side, most of the controversy has centered on the jury in civil cases. Indeed, some of the severest critics of civil juries acknowledge that the arguments for criminal juries are much stronger. In addition, at the heart of the dispute have been express or implicit assertions that juries are incapable of adequately understanding evidence or determining issues of fact, and that they are unpredictable, quixotic, and little better than a roll of dice. Yet, the most recent and exhaustive study of the jury in criminal cases [H. Kalven, Jr., and H. Zeisel, The American Jury (1966)] concluded that juries do understand the evidence and come to sound conclusions in most of the cases presented to them and that when juries differ with the result at which the judge would have arrived, it is usually because they are serving some of the very purposes for which they were created and for which they are now employed.

The State of Louisiana urges that holding that the Fourteenth Amendment assures a right to jury trial will cast doubt on the integrity of every trial conducted without a jury. Plainly, this is not the import of our holding. Our conclusion is that in the American States, as in the federal judicial system, a general grant of jury trial for serious offenses is a fundamental right, essential for preventing miscarriages of justice and for assuring that fair trials are provided for all defendants. [W]e hold no constitutional doubts about the practices, common in both federal and state courts, of accepting waivers of jury trial and prosecuting petty crimes without extending a right to jury trial. However, the fact is that in most places more trials for serious crimes are to juries than to a court alone; a great many defendants prefer the judgment of a jury to that of a court. Even where defendants are satisfied with bench trials, the right to a jury trial very likely serves its intended purpose of making judicial or prosecutorial unfairness less likely.

Louisiana's final contention is that even if it must grant jury trials in serious criminal cases, the conviction before us is valid and constitutional because here the petitioner was tried for simple battery and was sentenced to only 60 days in the parish prison. We are not persuaded. It is doubtless true that there is a category of petty crimes or offenses which is not subject to the Sixth Amendment jury trial provision and should not be subject to the Fourteenth Amendment jury trial requirement here applied to the States. Crimes carrying possible penalties up to six months do not require a jury trial if they otherwise qualify as petty offenses, *Cheff v. Schnackenberg*, 384 U.S. 373, 86 S.Ct. 1523, 16 L.Ed.2d 629 (1966). But the penalty authorized for a particular crime is of major relevance in determining whether it is serious or not and may in itself, if severe enough, subject the trial to the mandates of the Sixth Amendment. *District of Columbia v. Clawans*, 300 U.S. 617, 57 S.Ct. 660, 81 L.Ed. 843 (1937). The penalty authorized by the law of the locality may be taken "as a gauge of its social and ethical judgments" of the crime in question. In the case before us the Legislature of Louisiana has made simple battery a criminal offense punishable by imprisonment for up to two years and a fine. The question, then, is whether a crime carrying such a penalty is an offense which Louisiana may insist on trying without a jury. We think not.

. . . We need not, however, settle in this case the exact location of the line between petty offenses and serious crimes. It is sufficient for our purposes to hold that a crime punishable by two years in prison is, based on past and contemporary standards in this country, a serious crime and not a petty offense. Consequently, appellant was entitled to a jury trial and it was error to deny it.

The judgment below is reversed and the case is remanded for proceedings not inconsistent with this opinion.

Reversed and remanded.

JUSTICE BLACK, with whom JUSTICE DOUGLAS joins, concurring:

[T]he dissent states that "the great words of the four clauses of the first section of the Fourteenth Amendment would have been an exceedingly peculiar way to say that 'The rights heretofore guaranteed against federal intrusion by the first eight Amendments are henceforth guaranteed against state intrusion as well.'" In response to this I can say only that the words "No State shall make or enforce any law which shall abridge the privileges or immunities of citizens of the United States" seem to me an eminently reasonable way of expressing the idea that henceforth the Bill of Rights shall apply to the States. What more precious "privilege" of American citizenship could there be than that privilege to claim the protections of our great Bill of Rights? I suggest that any reading of "privileges or immunities of citizens of the United States" which excludes the Bill of Rights' safeguards renders the words of this section of the Fourteenth Amendment meaningless. . . .

. . . I have been willing to support the selective incorporation doctrine, however, as an alternative, although perhaps less historically supportable than complete incorporation. The selective incorporation process, if used properly, does limit the Supreme Court in the Fourteenth Amendment field to specific Bill of Rights' protections only and keeps judges from roaming at will in their own notions of what policies outside the Bill of Rights are desirable and what are not. And, most importantly for me, the selective incorporation process has the virtue of having already worked to make most of the Bill of Rights' protections applicable to the States.

JUSTICE HARLAN, whom JUSTICE STEWART joins, dissenting:

[T]he Congressmen and state legislators who wrote, debated, and ratified the Fourteenth Amendment did not think they were "incorporating" the Bill of

Rights[9] and the very breadth and generality of the Amendment's provisions suggest that its authors did not suppose that the Nation would always be limited to mid-19th century conceptions of "liberty" and "due process of law" but that the increasing experience and evolving conscience of the American people would add new "intermediate premises." In short, neither history, nor sense, supports using the Fourteenth Amendment to put the States in a constitutional straitjacket with respect to their own development in the administration of criminal or civil law. . . .

The jury is of course not without virtues. It affords ordinary citizens a valuable opportunity to participate in a process of government, an experience fostering, one hopes, a respect for law. It eases the burden on judges by enabling them to share a part of their sometimes awesome responsibility. A jury may, at times, afford a higher justice by refusing to enforce harsh laws (although it necessarily does so haphazardly, raising the questions whether arbitrary enforcement of harsh laws is better than total enforcement, and whether the jury system is to be defended on the ground that jurors sometimes disobey their oaths). And the jury may, or may not, contribute desirably to the willingness of the general public to accept criminal judgments as just. . . .

The jury system can also be said to have some inherent defects, which are multiplied by the emergence of the criminal law from the relative simplicity that existed when the jury system was devised. It is a cumbersome process [that contributes] to delay in the machinery of justice. Untrained jurors are presumably less adept at reaching accurate conclusions of fact than judges, particularly if the issues are many or complex. And it is argued by some that trial by jury, far from increasing public respect for law, impairs it: the average man, it is said, reacts favorably neither to the notion that matters he knows to be complex are being decided by other average men, nor to the way the jury system distorts the process of adjudication.

[The concurring opinion of FORTAS, J., is omitted.]

---

[9] Fairman, Does the Fourteenth Amendment Incorporate the Bill of Rights? The Original Understanding, 2 Stan.L.Rev. 5 (1949). Professor Fairman was not content to rest upon the overwhelming fact that the great words of the four clauses of the first section of the Fourteenth Amendment would have been an exceedingly peculiar way to say that "The rights heretofore guaranteed against federal intrusion by the first eight Amendments are henceforth guaranteed against state intrusion as well."

NOTES

1. In subsequent cases the Court has answered many of the questions suggested in *Duncan.*

    Recall in the right to counsel cases, § 4.2, the Court concluded that the judge must appoint counsel for an indigent only if the indigent in fact is imprisoned, no matter for how short a time. If the judge thought that a particular crime deserved imprisonment, the judge's failure to appoint counsel for an indigent would preclude a sentence of imprisonment. However, as to the jury issue, the touchstone is not the imprisonment that the judge actually imposed (if any). *Baldwin v. New York,* 399 U.S. 66, 90 S.Ct. 1886, 26 L.Ed.2d 437 (1970), made clear that if the statute authorizes imprisonment for more than six months, the accused has a constitutional right to jury. If the statute sets no maximum penalty—for example, if a judge sends someone to jail for criminal contempt—then a right to a jury trial exists only if the actual punishment is for more than six months. *Frank v. United States,* 395 U.S. 147, 89 S.Ct. 1503, 23 L.Ed.2d 162 (1969) (no jury trial for criminal contempt when sentence received is suspended, and the government agreed that the maximum penalty for violating probation was six months). If defendant is tried for several counts of criminal, and the sentences when added all together total more than six months, he also has a right to a jury trial. *Codispoti v. Pennsylvania,* 418 U.S. 506, 94 S.Ct. 2687, 41 L.Ed.2d 912 (1979).

    If the maximum sentence authorized is less than six months, a defendant may still have a right to a jury trial in some cases. Thus, the Supreme Court has suggested that one has a right of jury trial if the only punishment is a fine and the fine is of sufficient magnitude. *Muniz v. Hoffman,* 422 U.S. 454, 95 S.Ct. 2178, 45 L.Ed.2d 319 (1975) (fine of $10,000 on union of approximately 13,000 members does not warrant jury trial; the fine is less than $1 per member).

2. The Sixth Amendment, and the rule in *Duncan,* applies to criminal cases, not civil cases. In some instances the line between criminal and civil cases is not clear. In *McKeiver v. Pennsylvania,* 403 U.S. 528, 91 S.Ct. 1976, 29 L.Ed. 2d 647 (1971), the Court—with no majority opinion—concluded that the Fourteenth Amendment does not guarantee a jury trial in the adjudicative phase of a state court delinquency proceeding. The Court was concerned that imposing the jury requirement would not strengthen the fact-finding

function and would "provide an attrition of the juvenile court's assumed ability to function in a unique manner." Justice Douglas, joined by Justices Black and Marshall, dissented and argued that a constitutional right of a jury trial exists "for offenders charged in juvenile court and facing a possible incarceration until they reach their majority."

3. In *Williams v. Florida,* 399 U.S. 78, 90 S.Ct. 1893, 26 L.Ed.2d 446 (1970), the Court reconsidered one of the issues it raised in *Duncan.* The Court in *Williams* found no magic number in twelve and held that the Sixth Amendment allowed the use of six-person juries. Later the Court interpreted the Seventh Amendment—which had not been incorporated into the Fourteenth Amendment—to allow six-person juries in federal civil trials. *Colgrove v. Battin,* 413 U.S. 149, 93 S.Ct. 2448, 37 L.Ed.2d 522 (1973). On the other hand, a five-member jury in criminal cases does violate the Sixth Amendment. *Ballew v. Georgia,* 435 U.S. 223, 98 S.Ct. 1029, 55 L.Ed.2d 234 (1978). A line has to be drawn someplace, and the Court found "no significant state advantage in reducing the number of jurors from six to five." On the other side of the balance, empirical studies showed that "progressively smaller juries are less likely to foster effective group deliberation."

If defendant is entitled to twelve jurors, he may waive that right and be tried by only eleven, assuming of course that the waiver is "express and intelligent." *Patton v. United States,* 281 U.S. 276, 50 S.Ct. 253, 74 L.Ed. 854 (1930). In fact, defendant may waive the jury trial right entirely, but the government may constitutionally require that the trial judge and prosecutor consent to defendant's waiver of jury trial. If they refuse consent, "the result is that the defendant is subject to an impartial trial by jury—the very thing the Constitution guarantees him." *Singer v. United States,* 380 U.S. 24, 85 S.Ct. 783, 13 L.Ed.2d 630 (1965). The defendant, in short, does not have a federal right to a non-jury trial.

4. The Sixth Amendment does not require a jury of twelve, and it also does not require a unanimous verdict. *Apodaca v. Ohio,* 406 U.S. 404, 92 S.Ct. 1628, 32 L.Ed.2d 184 (1972) (defendant convicted of felonies by votes of eleven to one and ten to two). No majority opinion was given. Justice White's plurality cited *Williams v. Florida* and upheld Oregon's rule requiring that a verdict of guilty be reached only by ten of the twelve jurors. "Requiring unanimity would obviously produce hung juries in some situations where nonunanimous juries will convict or acquit. But in either case, the interest of the defendant in having the judgment of his peers interposed between

himself and the officers of the state who prosecute and judge him is equally well served." A majority of the Court did not say how substantial the majority for conviction must be. Justice Blackmun's concurrence said that only a seven-to-five vote to convict "would afford me great difficulty."

Subsequently, the Court invalidated a state law that allowed conviction by a nonunanimous jury of less than six. Louisiana allowed conviction by a vote of five in a six-person jury when the period of confinement was in excess of six months. The Court, with no dissents on this question, invalidated the law. *Burch v. Louisiana,* 441 U.S. 130, 99 S.Ct. 1623, 60 L.Ed. 2d 96 (1979). The Court said that "lines must be drawn somewhere." But "[w]e, of course, intimate no view as to the constitutionality of nonunanimous verdicts rendered by juries comprised of more than six members."

5. *Ludwig v. Massachusetts,* 427 U.S. 618, 96 S.Ct. 2781, 49 L.Ed.2d 732 (1976), reconsidered one of the issues raised in *Duncan,* and held that a state may constitutionally provide a nonjury trial in a case and then provide that the appeal from this nonjury trial consist of a completely new trial (a trial *de novo*) with a jury. At the retrial, the possibility of a more severe sentence altered the constitutional requirement. Massachusetts provided two basic levels of trial courts, with only the second level providing a jury. The Court distinguished *Callan v. Wilson* (cited in footnote 30 of *Duncan*) because *Callan* "unduly burdened" the defendant by requiring that the accused be "fully tried" in the first tier. Massachusetts, in contrast, allowed the defendant to skip the first tier if he admitted to "sufficient findings of fact." Stevens, Brennan, Stewart, & Marshall, JJ., dissented.

6. *Lewis v. United States*, 518 U.S. 322, 116 S.Ct. 2163, 135 L.Ed.2d 590 (1996) the defendant was prosecuted for obstructing the mail. Each count carried maximum authorized prison term of six months and thus was a "petty" offense. The Court held that the defendant was not constitutionally entitled to jury trial, even though he was charged with multiple counts in single proceeding so that aggregate maximum prison term exceeded six months.

4.6 CRUEL AND UNUSUAL PUNISHMENT

The Eighth Amendment prohibits "cruel and unusual punishments." Initially, it did not apply to the states. In *Louisiana ex rel. Francis v. Reswebar,* 329 U.S. 459, 67 S.Ct. 374, 91 L.Ed. 422 (1947), the Court, with no majority opinion, assumed, but did not decide, that the Fourteenth Amendment incorporated the cruel and unusual punishment clause. The Court ruled that Louisiana did *not* violate the Fourteenth Amendment when it sought to electrocute Willie Francis when the first attempt failed because of a defect in the apparatus. Justices Burton, Douglas, Murphy, and Rutledge dissented. At this first attempt, "Willie jumped. He strained against the straps. He groaned. [Then] Captain Foster, all in one motion, frantically threw the switch off and then on again. Those closest to Willie heard him strain out the words, 'Let me breath.' [The spectators] saw his lips puff out and swell like those of a pilot undergoing the stress of supersonic speeds."[4] After about two minutes the execution stopped, the hood was lifted from Willie Francis, and he got up. The dissent argued that the case should be remanded to determine whether Francis suffered from the electric current during this first execution attempt. The state claimed that "no current whatsoever reached Francis' body." Francis claimed otherwise.

Robinson v. California, 370 U.S. 660, 82 S.Ct. 1417, 8 L.Ed.2d 758 (1962), incorporated the cruel and unusual punishment clause into the Fourteenth Amendment and held that the clause was violated by a state statute that made the "status" of narcotic addiction a criminal offense. Narcotic addiction, said the Court, is an illness (a point "recognized" by counsel for the state), and that illness may be contracted innocently or involuntarily. The state could punish the sale or use of narcotics, but the state could not make it a criminal offense to have the status of an addict any more than it could make it a criminal offense to be "mentally ill, or a leper, or to be afflicted with a venereal disease. A State might determine that the general health and welfare require that the victims of these and other human afflictions be dealt with by compulsory treatment, involving quarantine, confinement, or sequestration. But in light of contemporary human knowledge, a law which made a criminal offense of such a disease would doubtless be universally thought to be an infliction of cruel and unusual punishment in violation of the Eighth and Fourteenth Amendments." Narcotic addiction is in "the same category."

The Court has not given *Robinson* an expanded meaning. Thus, five members of the Court, with no majority opinion, upheld the conviction of a person who was found guilty of being drunk in a "public place." Though he was a chronic alcoholic, he was not convicted of that status being drunk but of being "found in a state of intoxication in any public place." *Powell v. Texas,* 392 U.S. 514, 88 S.Ct. 2145, 20 L.Ed.2d 1254 (1968).

---

[4]   Prettyman, The Electric Chair Case, pp. 91–92, in The Third Branch of Government (C. Pritchett and A. Westin, eds., 1963).

In various cases the Supreme Court has said that the Eighth Amendment forbids various punishments that we would today call obviously cruel—although in olden times they were practiced with some frequency, possibly because they were so obviously cruel that the government thought it was effective in deterring crime. See, *e.g.*, *In re Kemmler*, 136 U.S. 436, 446–447, 10 S.Ct. 930, 933, 34 L.Ed. 519 (1890) ("torture or a lingering death," or "burning at the stake, crucifixion, breaking on the wheel, or the like") (dictum).

In *Weems v. United States*, 217 U.S. 349, 30 S.Ct. 544, 54 L.Ed. 793 (1910), the Court invalidated a Philippine punishment of "cadena temporal" imposed on one who falsified an official document. The punishment was at least twelve years and a day in chains, at hard and painful labor, loss of various basic civil rights, and lifetime surveillance. The Court found that the punishment was excessive, out of proportion to the crime. It "is a precept of justice that punishment for crime should be graduated and proportioned to the offense." *Weems* explained that the Eighth Amendment is not limited to eighteenth century barbarous methods of punishment. The "principle to be vital, must be capable of wider application than the mischief which gave it birth." The clause "is not fastened to the obsolete but may acquire meaning as public opinion becomes enlightened by a humane justice."

In an older case, the Supreme Court held that public shooting as "a mode of executing the death penalty for the crime of murder in the first degree" does not violate the Eighth Amendment. *Wilkerson v. Utah*, 99 U.S. 130, 25 L.Ed. 345 (1879). See also *In re Kemmler*, 136 U.S. 436, 10 S.Ct. 930, 34 L.Ed. 519 (1880) (death penalty by electrocution not violative of Eighth Amendment).

In *Trop v. Dulles*, 356 U.S. 86, 78 S.Ct. 590, 2 L.Ed.2d 630 (1958), Chief Justice Warren, in a plurality opinion, said that the Eighth Amendment was violated when a native-born American had to forfeit his citizenship because of his court-martial for wartime desertion. (The desertion was for less than one day; he willingly surrendered to an army officer when he was picked up walking back to the base.) Warren argued that any denaturalization as a punishment is barred by the Eighth Amendment. At the time of this decision, only the United States, the Philippines, and Turkey provided denaturalization as a punishment for desertion. Yet Warren added in dictum that capital punishment was not cruel and unusual because it has been "employed throughout our history" and is "still widely accepted."

GREGG V. GEORGIA
428 U.S. 153, 96 S.Ct. 2909, 49 L.Ed.2d 859 (1976)

[A jury found Troy Gregg guilty of armed robbery and murder. At the second stage of his trial, the sentencing stage, the trial judge instructed the same jury that it could not vote for the death penalty unless it found, beyond a reasonable doubt, one of various aggravating circumstances. The jury found two aggravating circumstances and imposed the death penalty for both the robbery and the murder. The Georgia Supreme Court affirmed both convictions and the death penalty for murder, but vacated the death penalty for robbery because "the death penalty had rarely been imposed in Georgia for that offense" and the jury had improperly considered the murder as aggravating the robberies while considering the armed robberies as aggravating the murders.]

Judgment of the Court, and opinion of JUSTICE STEWART, JUSTICE POWELL, and JUSTICE STEVENS, announced by Justice Stewart.

The issue in this case is whether the imposition of the sentence of death for the crime of murder under the law of Georgia violates the Eighth and Fourteenth Amendments. . . .

The Court on a number of occasions has both assumed and asserted the constitutionality of capital punishment. In several cases that assumption provided a necessary foundation for the decision, as the Court was asked to decide whether a particular method of carrying out a capital sentence would be allowed to stand under the Eighth Amendment. But until *Furman v. Georgia,* 408 U.S. 238, 92 S.Ct. 2726, 33 L.Ed.2d 346 (1972), the Court never confronted squarely the fundamental claim that the punishment of death always, regardless of the enormity of the offense or the procedure followed in imposing the sentence, is cruel and unusual punishment in violation of the Constitution. Although this issue was presented and addressed in *Furman,* it was not resolved by the Court. Four Justices would have held that capital punishment is not unconstitutional *per se;* two Justices would have reached the opposite conclusion; and three Justices, while agreeing that the statutes then before the Court were invalid as applied, left open the question whether such punishment may ever be imposed. We now hold that the punishment of death does not invariably violate the Constitution.

[T]he Eighth Amendment has not been regarded as a static concept. As Mr. Chief Justice Warren said, in an oft-quoted phrase, "[t]he Amendment must draw its meaning from the evolving standards of decency that mark the progress of a maturing society." *Trop v. Dulles.* Thus, an assessment of contemporary values concerning the infliction of a challenged sanction is relevant to the application of the Eighth Amendment. As we develop below more fully, this assessment does not call for a subjective judgment. It requires, rather, that we look to objective indicia that reflect the public attitude toward a given sanction.

But our cases also make clear that public perceptions of standards of decency with respect to criminal sanctions are not conclusive. A penalty also must accord with "the dignity of man," which is the "basic concept underlying the Eighth Amendment." *Trop v. Dulles* (plurality opinion). This means, at least, that the punishment not be "excessive." When a form of punishment in the abstract (in this case, whether capital punishment may ever be imposed as a sanction for murder) rather than in the particular (the propriety of death as a penalty to be applied to a specific defendant for a specific crime) is under consideration, the inquiry into "excessiveness" has two aspects. First, the punishment must not involve the unnecessary and wanton infliction of pain. See *Weems v. United States.* Second, the punishment must not be grossly out of proportion to the severity of the crime. *Trop v. Dulles* (plurality opinion) (dictum).

[W]hile we have an obligation to insure that constitutional bounds are not overreached, we may not act as judges as we might as legislators. [I]n assessing a punishment selected by a democratically elected legislature against the constitutional measure, we presume its validity. We may not require the legislature to select the least severe penalty possible so long as the penalty selected is not cruelly inhumane or disproportionate to the crime involved. And a heavy burden rests on those who would attack the judgment of the representatives of the people. . . . A decision that a given punishment is impermissible under the Eighth Amendment cannot be reversed short of a constitutional amendment. The ability of the people to express their preference through the normal democratic processes, as well as through ballot referenda, is shut off.

[H]istory and precedent [show] imposition of the death penalty for the crime of murder has a long history of acceptance both in the United States and in England. . . . It is apparent from the text of the Constitution itself that the existence of capital punishment was accepted by the Framers. At the time the Eighth Amendment was ratified, capital punishment was a common sanction in every State. Indeed, the First Congress of the United States enacted legislation providing death as the penalty for specified crimes. The Fifth Amendment, adopted at the same time as the Eighth, contemplated the continued existence of the capital sanction by imposing certain limits on the prosecution of capital cases. [T]he Fourteenth Amendment, adopted over three-quarters of a century later, similarly contemplates the existence of the capital sanction in providing that no State shall deprive any person of "life, liberty, or property" without due process of law. For nearly two centuries, this Court, repeatedly and often expressly, has recognized that capital punishment is not invalid *per se*. [See] *Wilkerson v. Utah*. . . .

Four years ago, the petitioners in *Furman* and its companion cases predicated their argument primarily upon the asserted proposition that standards of decency had evolved to the point where capital punishment no longer could be tolerated. [B]ut developments during the four years since *Furman* have undercut substantially the assumptions upon which their argument rested. Despite the continuing debate, dating back to the 19th century, over the morality and utility of capital punishment, it is now evident that a large proportion of American society continues to regard it as an appropriate and necessary criminal sanction. The most marked indication of society's endorsement of the death penalty for murder is the legislative response to *Furman*. The legislatures of at least 35 States have enacted new statutes that provide for the death penalty for at least some crimes that result in the death of another person. And the Congress of the United States, in 1974, enacted a statute providing the death penalty for aircraft piracy that results in death. . . .

The jury also is a significant and reliable objective index of contemporary values because it is so directly involved. . . . It may be true that evolving standards have influenced juries in recent decades to be more discriminating in imposing the sentence of death. But the relative infrequency of jury verdicts imposing the death sentence does not indicate rejection of capital punishment *per se*. Rather, the reluctance of juries in many cases to impose the sentence may well reflect the humane feeling that this most irrevocable of sanctions should be reserved for a small number of extreme cases. [T]he actions of juries in many States since *Furman* are fully compatible with the legislative judgments, reflected in the new statutes, as to the continued utility and necessity of capital punishment in appropriate cases. At the close of 1974 at least 254 persons had been sentenced to death since *Furman* and by the end of March 1976, more than 460 persons were subject to death sentences.

[T]he Eighth Amendment demands more than that a challenged punishment be acceptable to contemporary society. The Court also must ask whether it comports with the basic concept of human dignity at the core of the Amendment. [T]he sanction imposed cannot be so totally without penological justification that it results in the gratuitous infliction of suffering.

The death penalty is said to serve two principal social purposes: retribution and deterrence of capital crimes by prospective offenders.[28]

In part, capital punishment is an expression of society's moral outrage at particularly offensive conduct. This function may be unappealing to many, but it is essential in an ordered society that asks its citizens to rely on legal processes rather than self-help to vindicate their wrongs. . . .

Statistical attempts to evaluate the worth of the death penalty as a deterrent to crimes by potential offenders have occasioned a great deal of debate. The results simply have been inconclusive. [Although] some of the studies suggest that the death penalty may not function as a significantly greater deterrent than lesser penalties, there is no convincing empirical evidence either supporting or refuting this view. We may nevertheless assume safely that there are murderers, such as those who act in passion, for whom the threat of death has little or no deterrent effect. But for many others, the death penalty undoubtedly is a significant deterrent. . . .

In sum, we cannot say that the judgment of the Georgia Legislature that capital punishment may be necessary in some cases is clearly wrong. Considerations of federalism, as well as respect for the ability of a legislature to evaluate, in terms of its particular State, the moral consensus concerning the death penalty and its social utility as a sanction, require us to conclude, in the absence of more convincing evidence, that the infliction of death as a punishment for murder is not without justification and thus is not unconstitutionally severe.

Finally, we must consider whether the punishment of death is disproportionate in relation to the crime for which it is imposed. [W]e are concerned here only with the imposition of capital punishment for the crime of murder, and when a life has been taken deliberately by the offender, we cannot say that the punishment is invariably disproportionate to the crime. It is an extreme sanction, suitable to the most extreme of crimes.

We hold that the death penalty is not a form of punishment that may never be imposed, regardless of the circumstances of the offense, regardless of the character of the offender, and regardless of the procedure followed in reaching the decision to impose it.

We now consider whether Georgia may impose the death penalty on the petitioner in this case. . . . Because of the uniqueness of the death penalty, *Furman*

---

[28] Another purpose that has been discussed is the incapacitation of dangerous criminals and the consequent prevention of crimes that they may otherwise commit in the future.

held that it could not be imposed under sentencing procedures that created a substantial risk that it would be inflicted in an arbitrary and capricious manner. [T]he the death sentences examined by the Court in *Furman* were "cruel and unusual in the same way that being struck by lightning is cruel and unusual. For, of all the people convicted of [capital crimes], many just as reprehensible as these, the petitioners [in *Furman* were] among a capriciously selected random handful upon whom the sentence of death has in fact been imposed. [T]he Eighth and Fourteenth Amendments cannot tolerate the infliction of a sentence of death under legal systems that permit this unique penalty to be so wantonly and so freakishly imposed."

Furman mandates that where discretion is afforded a sentencing body on a matter so grave as the determination of whether a human life should be taken or spared, that discretion must be suitably directed and limited so as to minimize the risk of wholly arbitrary and capricious action. . . . Jury sentencing has been considered desirable in capital cases in order "to maintain a link between contemporary community values and the penal system—a link without which the determination of punishment could hardly reflect 'the evolving standards of decency that mark the progress of a maturing society.' " But it creates special problems. Much of the information that is relevant to the sentencing decision may have no relevance to the question of guilt, or may even be extremely prejudicial to a fair determination of that question. [T]herefore, [w]hen a human life is at stake and when the jury must have information prejudicial to the question of guilt but relevant to the question of penalty in order to impose a rational sentence, a bifurcated system is more likely to ensure elimination of the constitutional deficiencies identified in *Furman*. . . .

In summary, the concerns expressed in *Furman* that the penalty of death not be imposed in an arbitrary or capricious manner can be met by a carefully drafted statute that ensures that the sentencing authority is given adequate information and guidance. As a general proposition these concerns are best met by a system that provides for a bifurcated proceeding at which the sentencing authority is apprised of the information relevant to the imposition of sentence and provided with standards to guide its use of the information. . . .

We now turn to consideration of the constitutionality of Georgia's capital-sentencing procedures. In the wake of *Furman,* Georgia amended its capital punishment statute, but chose not to narrow the scope of its murder provisions. [I]n Georgia, "[a] person commits murder when he unlawfully and with malice aforethought, either express or implied, causes the death of another human being." All persons convicted of murder "shall be punished by death or by imprisonment for life."

Georgia did act, however, to narrow the class of murderers subject to capital punishment by specifying 10 statutory aggravating circumstances, one of which must be found by the jury to exist beyond a reasonable doubt before a death sentence can ever be imposed. In addition, the jury is authorized to consider any other appropriate aggravating or mitigating circumstances. The jury is not required to find any mitigating circumstance in order to make a recommendation of mercy that is binding on the trial court, but it must find a *statutory* aggravating circumstance before recommending a sentence of death.

. . . No longer can a Georgia jury do as *Furman's* jury did: reach a finding of the defendant's guilt and then, without guidance or direction, decide whether he should live or die. Instead, the jury's attention is directed to the specific circumstances of the crime: Was it committed in the course of another capital felony? Was it committed for money? Was it committed upon a peace officer or judicial officer? Was it committed in a particularly heinous way or in a manner that endangered the lives of many persons? In addition, the jury's attention is focused on the characteristics of the person who committed the crime: Does he have a record of prior convictions for capital offenses? Are there any special facts about this defendant that mitigate against imposing capital punishment (*e.g.*, his youth, the extent of his cooperation with the police, his emotional state at the time of the crime). As a result, while some jury discretion still exists, "the discretion to be exercised is controlled by clear and objective standards so as to produce non-discriminatory application." As an important additional safeguard against arbitrariness and caprice, the Georgia statutory scheme provides for automatic appeal of all death sentences to the State's Supreme Court. . . . On their face these procedures seem to satisfy the concerns of *Furman*. . . .

The petitioner contends, however, that the changes in the Georgia sentencing procedures are only cosmetic, that the arbitrariness and capriciousness condemned by *Furman* continue to exist in Georgia—both in traditional practices that still remain and in the new sentencing procedures adopted in response to *Furman*.

First, the petitioner focuses on the opportunities for discretionary action that are inherent in the processing of any murder case under Georgia law. He notes that the state prosecutor has unfettered authority to select those persons whom he wishes to prosecute for a capital offense and to plea bargain with them. Further, at the trial the jury may choose to convict a defendant of a lesser included offense rather than find him guilty of a crime punishable by death, even if the evidence would support a capital verdict. And finally, a defendant who is convicted and sentenced to die may have his sentence commuted by the Governor of the State and the Georgia Board of Pardons and Paroles.

The existence of these discretionary stages is not determinative of the issues before us. At each of these stages an actor in the criminal justice system makes a decision which may remove a defendant from consideration as a candidate for the death penalty. . . . Nothing in any of our cases suggests that the decision to afford an individual defendant mercy violates the Constitution. *Furman* held only that, in order to minimize the risk that the death penalty would be imposed on a capriciously selected group of offenders, the decision to impose it had to be guided by standards so that the sentencing authority would focus on the particularized circumstances of the crime and the defendant.

[W]e hold that the statutory system under which Gregg was sentenced to death does not violate the Constitution. Accordingly, the judgment of the Georgia Supreme Court is affirmed.

It is so ordered.

JUSTICE WHITE, with whom CHIEF JUSTICE BURGER and JUSTICE REHNQUIST join, concurring in the judgment.

Petitioner's argument that prosecutors behave in a standardless fashion in deciding which cases to try as capital felonies is unsupported by any facts. Petitioner simply asserts that since prosecutors have the power not to charge capital felonies they will exercise that power in a standardless fashion. This is untenable. Absent facts to the contrary it cannot be assumed that prosecutors will be motivated in their charging decision by factors other than the strength of their case and the likelihood that a jury would impose the death penalty if it convicts. . . .

Petitioner's argument that there is an unconstitutional amount of discretion in the system which separates those suspects who receive the death penalty from those who receive life imprisonment, a lesser penalty or are acquitted or never charged seems to be in final analysis an indictment of our entire system of justice. Petitioner has argued in effect that no matter how effective the death penalty may be as a punishment, government, created and run as it must be by humans, is inevitably incompetent to administer it. This cannot be accepted as a proposition of constitutional law. Imposition of the death penalty is surely an awesome responsibility for any system of justice and those who participate in it. Mistakes will be made and discriminations will occur which will be difficult to explain.

However, one of society's most basic tasks is that of protecting the lives of its citizens and one of the most basic ways in which it achieves the task is through criminal laws against murder. . . .

JUSTICE BRENNAN, dissenting:

. . . This Court inescapably has the duty, as the ultimate arbiter of the meaning of our Constitution, to say whether, when individuals condemned to death stand before our Bar, "moral concepts" require us to hold that the law has progressed to the point where we should declare that the punishment of death, like punishments on the rack, the screw, and the wheel, is no longer morally tolerable in our civilized society. . . . Death is not only an unusually severe punishment, unusual in its pain, in its finality, and in its enormity, but it serves no penal purpose more effectively than a less severe punishment; therefore the principle inherent in the Clause that prohibits pointless infliction of excessive punishment when less severe punishment can adequately achieve the same purposes invalidates the punishment.

The fatal constitutional infirmity in the punishment of death is that it treats "members of the human race as nonhumans, as objects to be toyed with and discarded. [It is] thus inconsistent with the fundamental premise of the Clause that even the vilest criminal remains a human being possessed of common human dignity." . . . I therefore would hold, on that ground alone, that death is today a cruel and unusual punishment prohibited by the Clause. "Justice of this kind is obviously no less shocking than the crime itself, and the new 'official' murder, far from offering redress for the offense committed against society, adds instead a second defilement to the first." . . .

JUSTICE MARSHALL, dissenting:

In *Furman v. Georgia*, I set forth at some length my views on the basic issue presented to the Court in these cases. The death penalty, I concluded, is a cruel and unusual punishment prohibited by the Eighth and Fourteenth Amendments. [T]he death penalty is constitutionally invalid for two reasons. First, the death penalty is excessive. And second, the American people, fully informed as to the purposes of the death penalty and its liabilities, would in my view reject it as morally unacceptable.

Since the decision in *Furman,* the legislatures of 35 States have enacted new statutes authorizing the imposition of the death sentence for certain crimes, and Congress has enacted a law providing the death penalty for air piracy resulting in death. I would be less than candid if I did not acknowledge that these developments have a significant bearing on a realistic assessment of the moral acceptability of the death penalty to the American people. But if the constitutionality of the death penalty turns, as I have urged, on the opinion of an *informed* citizenry, then even the enactment of new death statutes cannot be viewed as conclusive. [If Americans] were better informed they would consider it shocking, unjust, and unacceptable. . . .

The two purposes that sustain the death penalty as nonexcessive in the Court's view are general deterrence and retribution. [A] United Nations Committee [in 1968 concluded] "that the data which now exist show no correlation between the existence of capital punishment and lower rates of capital crime." [A] study by Isaac Ehrlich, reported a year after *Furman,* [is claimed] to support the contention that the death penalty does deter murder. . . . His tentative conclusion was that for the period from 1933 to 1967 each additional execution in the United States might have saved eight lives.

The methods and conclusions of the Ehrlich study have been severely criticized on a number of grounds. . . . The most compelling criticism of the Ehrlich study is that its conclusions are extremely sensitive to the choice of the time period included in the regression analysis. Analysis of Ehrlich's data reveals that all empirical support for the deterrent effect of capital punishment disappears when the five most recent years are removed from his time series. . . . The Ehrlich study, in short, is of little, if any, assistance in assessing the deterrent impact of the death penalty. . . .

The other principal purpose said to be served by the death penalty is retribution. [O]ur recognition that retribution plays a crucial role in determining who may be punished by no means requires approval of retribution as a general justification for punishment. It is the question whether retribution can provide a moral justification for punishment—in particular, capital punishment—that we must consider. "[T]here is no evidence whatever that utilization of imprisonment rather than death encourages private blood feuds and other disorders." It simply defies belief to suggest that the death penalty is necessary to prevent the American people from taking the law into their own hands. . . .

[The opinion of BLACKMUN, J., concurring in the judgment, is omitted.]

NOTES

1. In *Furman* Justice Marshall argued:

> It has often been noted that American citizens know almost
> nothing about capital punishment. Some of the conclusions
> [previously discussed] and the supporting evidence would be
> critical to an informed judgment on the morality of the death
> penalty: *e.g.,* that the death penalty is no more effective a deterrent
> than life imprisonment, that convicted murderers are rarely
> executed, but are usually sentenced to a term in prison; that
> convicted murderers usually are model prisoners, and that they
> almost always become law-abiding citizens upon their release from
> prison; that the costs of executing a capital offender exceed the
> costs of imprisoning him for life; that while in prison, a convict
> under sentence of death performs none of the useful functions that
> life prisoners perform; that no attempt is made in the sentencing
> process to ferret out likely recidivists for execution; and that the
> death penalty may actually stimulate criminal activity.

Does Justice Marshall have the approach of a philosopher-king?

2. *Woodson v. North Carolina,* 428 U.S. 280, 96 S.Ct. 2978, 49 L.Ed.2d 944 (1976),
    invalidated a state law that provided for a mandatory death penalty for first
    degree murder. There was no majority opinion. The Stewart plurality noted
    that when mandatory death penalty was common, juries often refused to
    convict. States responded by giving juries discretion. After *Furman* limited
    unbridled jury discretion, North Carolina reinstituted the mandatory death
    sentence. "The two crucial indicators of evolving standards of decency
    respecting the imposition of punishment in our society—jury determinations
    and legislative enactments—both point conclusively to the repudiation of
    automatic death sentences."

    Roberts v. Louisiana, 431 U.S. 633, 97 S.Ct. 1993, 52 L.Ed.2d 637 (1977),
    invalidated a state statute that imposed a mandatory death sentence for
    murder of a policeman or fireman. Mitigating circumstances can exist, "such
    as the youth of the offender, the absence of any prior conviction, the
    influence of drugs, alcohol or extreme emotional disturbance, and even the
    existence of circumstances which the offender reasonably believed provided
    a moral justification for his conduct. . . ."

Beck v. Alabama, 447 U.S. 625, 100 S.Ct. 2382, 65 L.Ed.2d 392 (1980) held that a statute that gives the jury only two alternatives—death penalty or acquittal—is invalid. The jury should be able to find the defendant guilty of a less serious homicide.

Lockett v. Ohio, 438 U.S. 586, 98 S.Ct. 2954, 57 L.Ed.2d 973 (1978), generally expanded the rule requiring discretion. The Court, with no majority opinion, concluded, "the Eighth and Fourteenth Amendments require that the sentencer, in all but the rarest kind of capital case, not be precluded from considering, *as a mitigating factor,* any aspect of a defendant's character or record and any of the circumstances of the offense that the defendant proffers as a basis for a sentence less than death." (footnotes omitted; emphasis in original).

3. In *Coker v. Georgia,* 433 U.S. 584, 97 S.Ct. 2861, 53 L.Ed.2d 982 (1977), the Court, with no majority opinion, concluded that to sentence someone to death for rape violated the Eighth Amendment. The penalty is unconstitutionally disproportionate, said the plurality, because "it does not compare with murder, which does involve the unjustified taking of human life." Chief Justice Burger, joined by Justice Rehnquist, dissented. The Eighth Amendment test "cannot have the primitive simplicity of 'life for life, eye for eye, tooth for tooth.'" The dissent was concerned that the "clear implication of today's holding appears to be that the death penalty may be properly imposed only as to crimes resulting in death of the victim. This casts serious doubt upon the constitutional validity of statutes imposing the death penalty for a variety of other conduct which, though dangerous, may not result in any immediate death, *e.g.,* treason, airplane hijacking, and kidnapping."

In *Edmunds v. Florida,* 458 U.S. 782, 102 S.Ct. 3368, 73 L.Ed.2d 1140 (1982), the Court, with no majority opinion, concluded that the death penalty may not be imposed on a participant in the crime (here, the driver in the getaway car) who did not pull the trigger, was not physically present at the murder, did not intend death, and did not anticipate that deadly force would be used.

4. In recent years, the Court has been very active in using the Eighth Amendment prohibition of cruel and unusual punishment to limit government power to execute and to sentence. Consider these areas:

Insanity. The Eight Amendment prohibits the government from imposing the death penalty upon a prisoner who is presently insane;

the government must provide a procedure designed to provide a fair hearing on the issue of a prisoner's insanity.[5]

Mental Status. *Atkins v. Virginia,*[6] (6 to 3) ruled that the Eighth Amendment prohibits the Government from imposing a death sentence on a person who is mentally retarded. *Atkins* abrogated the Court's earlier ruling in *Penry v. Lynaugh,*[7] which refused to prohibit executions of mentally retarded. While *Atkins* overruled that aspect of *Penry*, it did not alter the portion of *Penry* that required the Government to allow the defendant to present all information to a jury that might be considered mitigating evidence, including evidence of mental capacity and childhood abuse.

Age. Initially, the Court held that the Eighth Amendment does not prohibit the imposition of the death penalty on a person under 18 years old at the time that the individual committed the capital offense.[8] Then, *Roper v. Simmons,*[9] held that the Eight Amendment prohibits the execution of individuals under 18 at the time of their capital crimes. The facts were not favorable to the accused. As Justice Kennedy, speaking for the Court (5 to 4) explained:

> There is little doubt that Simmons was the instigator of the crime. Before its commission Simmons said he wanted to murder someone. In chilling, callous terms he talked about his plan, discussing it for the most part with two friends, Charles Benjamin and John Tessmer, then aged 15 and 16 respectively. Simmons proposed to commit burglary and murder by breaking and entering, tying up a victim, and throwing the victim off a bridge. Simmons assured his friends they could "get away with it" because they were minors.[10]

---

[5]   *Ford v. Wainwright*, 477 U.S. 399, 106 S.Ct. 2595, 91 L.Ed.2d 335 (1986) (majority opinion in part; plurality opinion in part).

[6]   *Atkins v. Virginia*, 536 U.S. 304, 122 S.Ct. 2242, 153 L.Ed.2d 335 (2002).

[7]   *Penry v. Lynaugh*, 492 U.S. 302, 109 S.Ct. 2934, 106 L.Ed.2d 256 (1989)

[8]   *Stanford v. Kentucky*, 492 U.S. 361, 109 S.Ct. 2969, 106 L.Ed.2d 306 (1989) (majority opinion in part and plurality opinion in part written by Justice Scalia)(4 dissenters).

[9]   *Roper v. Simmons*, 543 U.S. 551, 125 S.Ct. 1183, 161 L.Ed.2d 1 (2005).

[10]   *Roper v. Simmons*, 543 U.S. at 554, 125 S.Ct. at 1187.

The Eighth Amendment also prohibits sentencing a juvenile who committed a crime (other than homicide) life imprisonment without possibility of parole.[11]

5.   Professors Wayne LaFave, in his three-volume treatise, *Substantive Criminal Law*,[12] summarize some of the developments in the cruel and unusual punishment area:

> **Freedom from Cruel and Unusual Punishment.** [This] prohibition has three aspects: (1) it limits the methods which may be used to inflict punishment; (2) it limits the amount of punishment which may be prescribed for various offenses; and (3) it bars any and all penal sanctions in certain situations.
>
> As to the first of these, [s]terilization, found constitutional by some courts,[13] has been declared cruel and unusual by others,[14] which seems more in keeping with the Supreme Court's recent emphasis on the Eighth Amendment as protecting the "dignity of man."[15] Castration constitutes cruel and unusual punishment.[16] Flogging, condemned as cruel in dicta,[17] has been upheld,[18] although the fact that it is unique from all other authorized forms of punishment in that the aim is the infliction of severe pain strongly suggests the Supreme Court would declare it impermissible.[19] But solitary confinement, even when it must be served with no time out-of-doors, does not violate the Eighth Amendment.[20]

---

[11]   *Graham v. Florida*, 560 U.S. 48, 130 S. Ct. 2011, 176 L. Ed. 2d 825 (2010) (6 to 3).

[12]   Wayne R. LaFave, Substantive Criminal Law § 3.5(g)(West Thomson Reuters, 2nd ed. 2014 update), (footnotes renumbered or omitted).

[13]   *E.g., State v. Feilen*, 70 Wash. 65, 126 P. 75 (1912).

[14]   *E.g., Mickle v. Henrichs*, 262 F. 687 (D.Nev.1918).

[15]   *Trop v. Dulles*, 356 U.S. 86, 78 S.Ct. 590, 2 L.Ed.2d 630 (1958).

[16]   *State v. Brown*, 284 S.C. 407, 326 S.E.2d 410 (1985). This rule may not apply to As for whether this should be equally true of chemical castration, recently authorized as a punishment for sex offenders in a few states. . . .

[17]   *Weems v. United States*, 217 U.S. 349, 30 S.Ct. 544, 54 L.Ed. 793 (1910).

[18]   *State v. Cannon*, 55 Del. 587, 190 A.2d 514 (1963).

[19]   Cruel and unusual punishment arguments are sometimes directed at noncapital punishment which is not unique in this sense. See, *e.g.*, Note, 70 S.Cal.L.Rev. 1459 (1997) (claiming chain gangs are unconstitutional). Consider in this regard *Hope v. Pelzer*, 536 U.S. 730, 122 S.Ct. 2508, 153 L.Ed.2d 666 (2002) (handcuffing of prisoner to hitching post for disruptive behavior, after he already subdued, in sun for 7 hours without bathroom breaks and only 1–2 water breaks, cruel and unusual punishment, as it "amounts to gratuitous infliction of 'wanton and unnecessary' pain that our precedent clearly prohibits").

[20]   *Bass v. Perrin*, 170 F.3d 1312 (11th Cir.1999). *See also In re Long Term Admin. Segregation of Inmates Designated as Five Percenters*, 174 F.3d 464 (4th Cir.1999). For other challenges to the conditions of confinement,

[In general,] courts have shown considerable deference to the legislative judgment as to how severe a penalty should be authorized for specific classes of offenses. Illustrative of the usual response to a claim of excessive punishment is *Perkins v. North Carolina*,[21] where a federal court, although shocked at the sentence of from twenty to thirty years imposed for fellatio, upheld the sentence because it was within "the astounding statutory limit of 'not less than five nor more than sixty years.' "[22] While there are cases holding sentences invalid for being clearly out of proportion to the offense—for example, six years for picking flowers in a public park[23]—often these decisions have been based upon state constitutional provisions expressly prohibiting disproportionate sentences.

[The Supreme] Court on more than one occasion declined to strike down serious penalties other than death on lack-of-proportionality grounds.[24] But then came *Solem v. Helm*,[25] [where] the majority first concluded that the Eighth Amendment "principle that a criminal sentence must be proportionate to the crime for which the defendant has been convicted" was also applicable to felony prison sentences. Proportionality analysis, the Court next cautioned, "should be guided by objective criteria, including (i) the gravity of the offense and the harshness of the penalty; (ii) the sentences imposed on other criminals in the same jurisdiction; and (iii) the sentences imposed for commission of the same crime in other jurisdictions." In the instant case, Helm was convicted of uttering a "no account" check for $100, ordinarily punishable by a five year maximum term, but received a sentence of life imprisonment

---

see Glidden, Necessary Suffering: Weighing Government and Prisoner Interests in Determining What is Cruel and Unusual, 49 Am.Crim.L.Rev. 1815 (2012).

[21] *Perkins v. North Carolina*, 234 F.Supp. 333 (W.D.N.C.1964).

[22] . . . Compare *Humphrey v. Wilson*, 282 Ga. 520, 652 S.E.2d 501 (2007) (where 17-year-old boy who had oral sex with 15-year-old girl received 10-year sentence and mandatory sex offender registration, this deemed cruel and unusual punishment, considering that "most states either would not punish Wilson's conduct at all or would . . . punish it as a misdemeanor").

[23] *State ex rel. Garvey et al. v. Whitaker*, 48 La.Ann. 527, 19 So. 457 (1896).

[24] *Hutto v. Davis*, 454 U.S. 370, 102 S.Ct. 703, 70 L.Ed.2d 556 (1982) (granting of habeas corpus relief to prisoner sentenced to 40 years for possessing less than 9 ounces of marijuana an improper intrusion into the legislative line-drawing process); *Rummel v. Estelle*, 445 U.S. 263, 100 S.Ct. 1133, 63 L.Ed.2d 382 (1980) (mandatory life sentence after third felony of obtaining $120.27 by false pretenses, based on two earlier minor felonies, not cruel and unusual punishment).

[25] *Solem v. Helm*, 463 U.S. 277, 103 S.Ct. 3001, 77 L.Ed.2d 637 (1983).

without parole under the state's recidivist statute because of his prior convictions for six felonies, all of which were minor and nonviolent and none of which was a crime against a person. The Court concluded:

> Applying objective criteria, we find that Helm has received the penultimate sentence for relatively minor criminal conduct. He has been treated more harshly than other criminals in the State who have committed more serious crimes. He has been treated more harshly than he would have been in any other jurisdiction, with the possible exception of a single State. We conclude that his sentence is significantly disproportionate to his crime, and is therefore prohibited by the Eighth Amendment.

> *Solem* is unlikely to result in the invalidation of many legislatively-determined prison terms; as the Court cautioned, "outside the context of capital punishment, *successful* challenges to the proportionality of particular sentences [will be] exceedingly rare."[26]
> . . .

The third aspect of the constitutional ban on cruel and unusual punishment is that it bars the imposition of penal sanctions of any kind under certain circumstances. As such, the Eighth Amendment not only limits what legislatures may do by way of prescribing penalties for crime, but also what is permissible in terms of defining conduct as criminal. Thus, in *Robinson v. California*[27] [discussed above] the United States Supreme Court held unconstitutional a statute making it a crime for a person to "be addicted to the use of narcotics." . . .

---

[26] Quoting from *Rummel v. Estelle*, 445 U.S. 263, 100 S.Ct. 1133, 63 L.Ed.2d 382 (1980).

[27] *Robinson v. California*, 370 U.S. 660, 82 S.Ct. 1417, 8 L.Ed.2d 758 (1962).

CHAPTER 5

Equal Protection

Nearly a century ago, Justice Holmes labeled equal protection "the last resort of constitutional argument." *Buck v. Bell*, 274 U.S. 220, 208, 47 S.Ct. 584, 71 L.Ed. 1000 (1927). All laws classify to some extent. For example, a law that provides you cannot buy liquor until you are 21 years old distinguishes between those who are not yet 21 and those who are. People who are one day (or one hour) short of their 21st birthday cannot legally buy liquor, while those who are one day older can. One might argue that the law did not treat similar people (a different in age of mere hours) in a similar manner, but the Court would respond that it was "rational" for the legislature to draw the line where it did. The people were not similarly situated for the purposes to which the law applied.

In more modern times, the Court had been less deferential and has exercised a more active review *in certain areas*. The real question is how much deference the Court will give to the legislative judgment that makes classifications.

By the end of this chapter, you will learn that the Court has formally adopted three standards of review in equal protection cases. Since the Court Packing Plan of 1937, the Court has been extremely deferential in reviewing economic legislation challenged under the equal protection clause. If the classification is rational, the Court will uphold it. The Court calls this standard the "rational relationship" or "rational basis" test. Such laws have a strong presumption of constitutionality; the Court only invalidates the law if it has no rational relationship to any legitimate interest of government.

In other areas, the Court has practiced "strict scrutiny." In modern times and in earlier times (prior to *Plessy v. Ferguson*, § 5.2.1), laws that classify on the basis of race are "inherently suspect" and require the most exacting judicial examination. The Court requires that the state show that the law is narrowly tailored to promote a "compelling" or "overriding" governmental. The Court nearly always invalidates laws that draw distinctions based on race,[1] except in cases involving affirmative action.

In very recent times, the Court has developed yet another standard of review, sometimes called a middle-tier review to distinguish it from the two-tiered model (rational basis versus strict scrutiny). In modern cases involving classifications based on sex, classifications based on illegitimacy, and most classifications based on alienage, the Court applies middle tier review: Such classifications must be substantially related to an important government interest.

On which tier the law in question is placed goes a long way in deciding the result. An allegedly discriminatory law measured by the rational-basis test will almost certainly be upheld, while the law measured against strict scrutiny will almost certainly be invalidated. (The issue of affirmative action, or reverse discrimination, is the one area where a divided Court, applying strict scrutiny, has allowed distinctions on the basis of race.) Cases in the middle tier are harder to predict, but a careful reading of some of these cases should provide a sense of the evolution of Court thinking on equal protection.

5.1 TRADITIONAL EQUAL PROTECTION

RAILWAY EXPRESS AGENCY, INC. V. NEW YORK
336 U.S. 106, 69 S.Ct. 463, 93 L.Ed. 533 (1949)

JUSTICE DOUGLAS delivered the opinion of the Court.

Section 124 of the Traffic Regulations of the City of New York promulgated by the Police Commissioner provides:

> No person shall operate, or cause to be operated, in or upon any street an advertising vehicle; provided that nothing herein contained shall prevent the putting of business notices upon business delivery vehicles, so long as such vehicles are engaged in the usual business or regular work of the owner and not used merely or mainly for advertising.

---

[1] *E.g., Johnson v. California*, 543 U.S. 499, 125 S.Ct. 1141, 160 L.Ed.2d 949 (2005) applied strict scrutiny and invalidated a prison policy of placing new or transferred inmates with cellmates of the same race during their initial evaluation. The prison argued that this policy was necessary to prevent violence caused by racial gangs, but the Court noted that the Federal Government and almost all states manage prison systems without racial segregation. The prison should deal with security concerns by individualized consideration without using racial classifications unless it is warranted as a necessary and temporary response to a serious threat of race-related violence. Applying that test, *Hurd v. Garcia*, 454 F. Supp. 2d 1032 (S.D. Cal. 2006) upheld a temporary race-based lockdown of prisoners implemented because of a race riot between black and white inmates, which included a black inmate killing a white one. The prison lifted lockdown when the situation "gradually returned" to normal.

Appellant is engaged in a nation-wide express business. It operates about 1,900 trucks in New York City and sells the space on the exterior sides of these trucks for advertising. That advertising is for the most part unconnected with its own business. It was convicted in the magistrate's court and fined. . . .

The Court of Special Sessions concluded that advertising on vehicles using the streets of New York City constitutes a distraction to vehicle drivers and to pedestrians alike and therefore affects the safety of the public in the use of the streets. We do not sit to weigh evidence on the due process issue in order to determine whether the regulation is sound or appropriate; nor is it our function to pass judgment on its wisdom. . . .

The question of equal protection of the laws is pressed more strenuously on us. It is pointed out that the regulation draws the line between advertisements of products sold by the owner of the truck and general advertisements. It is argued that unequal treatment on the basis of such a distinction is not justified by the aim and purpose of the regulation. It is said, for example, that one of appellant's trucks carrying the advertisement of a commercial house would not cause any greater distraction of pedestrians and vehicle drivers than if the commercial house carried the same advertisement on its own truck. Yet the regulation allows the latter to do what the former is forbidden from doing. It is therefore contended that the classification which the regulation makes has no relation to the traffic problem since a violation turns not on what kind of advertisements are carried on trucks but on whose trucks they are carried.

That, however, is a superficial way of analyzing the problem, even if we assume that it is premised on the correct construction of the regulation. The local authorities may well have concluded that those who advertise their own wares on their trucks do not present the same traffic problem in view of the nature or extent of the advertising which they use. It would take a degree of omniscience which we lack to say that such is not the case. If that judgment is correct, the advertising displays that are exempt have less incidence on traffic than those of appellants.

We cannot say that that judgment is not an allowable one. Yet if it is, the classification has relation to the purpose for which it is made and does not contain the kind of discrimination against which the Equal Protection Clause affords protection. It is by such practical considerations based on experience rather than by theoretical inconsistencies that the question of equal protection is to be answered. And the fact that New York City sees fit to eliminate from traffic this kind of distraction but does not touch what may be even greater ones in a different category, such as the vivid displays on Times Square, is immaterial. It is no requirement of equal protection that all evils of the same genus be eradicated or none at all. . . .

Affirmed.

MR. JUSTICE RUTLEDGE acquiesces in the Court's opinion and judgment, *dubitante* on the question of equal protection of the laws.

JUSTICE JACKSON, concurring:

There are two clauses of the Fourteenth Amendment which this Court may invoke to invalidate ordinances by which municipal governments seek to solve their local problems. One says that no state shall "deprive any person of life, liberty, or property, without due process of law." The other declares that no state shall "deny to any person within its jurisdiction the equal protection of the laws."

My philosophy as to the relative readiness with which we should resort to these two clauses is almost diametrically opposed to the philosophy which prevails on this Court. While claims of denial of equal protection are frequently asserted, they are rarely sustained. But the Court frequently uses the due process clause to strike down measures taken by municipalities to deal with activities in their streets and public places which the local authorities consider as creating hazards, annoyances or discomforts to their inhabitants. . . .

The burden should rest heavily upon one who would persuade us to use the due process clause to strike down a substantive law or ordinance. Even its provident use against municipal regulations frequently disables all government—state, municipal and federal—from dealing with the conduct in question because the requirement of due process is also applicable to State and Federal Governments. Invalidation of a statute or an ordinance on due process grounds leaves ungoverned and ungovernable conduct which many people find objectionable.

Invocation of the equal protection clause, on the other hand, does not disable any governmental body from dealing with the subject at hand. It merely means that the prohibition or regulation must have a broader impact. I regard it as a salutary doctrine that cities, states and the Federal Government must exercise their powers so as not to discriminate between their inhabitants except upon some reasonable differentiation fairly related to the object of regulation. This equality is not merely abstract justice. The Framers of the Constitution knew, and we should not forget today, that there is no more effective practical guaranty against arbitrary and unreasonable government than to require that the principles of law which officials would impose upon a minority must be imposed generally. Conversely, nothing opens the door to arbitrary action so effectively as to allow those officials to pick and choose only a few to whom they will apply legislation and thus to escape the political retribution that might be visited upon them if larger numbers were affected. Courts can take no better measure to assure that laws will be just than to require that laws be equal in operation. . . .

[I]f the City of New York should assume that display of any advertising on vehicles tends and intends to distract the attention of persons using the highways and to increase the dangers of its traffic, I should think it fully within its constitutional powers to forbid it all. [Instead] the City seeks to reduce the hazard only by saying that while some may, others may not exhibit such appeals. The same display, for example, advertising cigarettes, which this appellant is forbidden to carry on its trucks, may be carried on the trucks of a cigarette dealer and might on the trucks of this appellant if it dealt in cigarettes. And almost an identical advertisement, certainly one of equal size, shape, color and appearance, may be carried by this appellant if it proclaims its own offer to transport cigarettes. But it may not be carried so long as the message is not its own but a cigarette dealer's offer to sell the same cigarettes. . . .

As a matter of principle and in view of my attitude toward the equal protection clause, I do not think differences of treatment under law should be approved on classification because of differences unrelated to the legislative purpose. The equal protection clause ceases to assure either equality or protection if it is avoided by any conceivable difference that can be pointed out between those bound and those left free. . . .

The question in my mind comes to this. Where individuals contribute to an evil or danger in the same way and to the same degree, may those who do so for hire be prohibited, while those who do so for their own commercial ends but not for hire be allowed to continue? I think the answer has to be that the hireling may be put in a class by himself and may be dealt with differently than those who act on their own. But this is not merely because such a discrimination will enable the lawmaker to diminish the evil. That might be done by many classifications, which I should think wholly unsustainable. It is rather because there is a real difference between doing in self-interest and doing for hire, so that it is one thing to tolerate action from those who act on their own and it is another thing to permit the same action to be promoted for a price.

NOTES

1. *Morey v. Doud,* 354 U.S. 457, 77 S.Ct. 1344, 1 L.Ed.2d 1485 (1957) invalidated a law giving arbitrary, economic advantage to one company. The Illinois Community Currency Exchange Act required that any firm selling or issuing money orders in the state must secure a license and submit to state regulation. However, the statute, by name, exempted from its coverage American Express Company money orders. The Court invalidated the law as a violation of equal protection. The purpose of the act was to afford the public continuing protection, but the "discrimination in favor of the American Express Company does not conform to this purpose." Although American Express "is a responsible institution operating on a worldwide basis," its exemption from regulation will continue (unless the statute is amended) "whether or not the American Express Company retains its present characteristics." Competitors will be subject to the act even if they are or become substantially identical to American Express. The Court reasoned that the statute created a closed class, and like those statutes giving an economic advantage to those who were engaged in a business as of a certain arbitrary date, it was a violation of equal protection. Black, Frankfurter, & Harlan, JJ., dissented.

2. Less than 20 years later, the Court overruled *Morey* in *City of New Orleans v. Dukes,* 427 U.S. 297, 96 S.Ct. 2513, 49 L.Ed.2d 511 (1976) (per curiam). A New Orleans ordinance excepted from the ordinance's prohibition against vendors selling foodstuffs from pushcarts in the Vieux Carre, French Quarter, those vendors who had continuously operated the same business there for eight or more years prior to January 1, 1972. The court of appeals invalidated the legislation and the Supreme Court reversed:

    > The record makes abundantly clear that the amended ordinance, including the "grandfather provision," is solely an economic regulation aimed at enhancing the vital role of the French Quarter's tourist-oriented charm in the economy of New Orleans. When local economic regulation is challenged solely as violating the Equal Protection Clause, this Court consistently defers to legislative determinations as to the desirability of particular statutory discriminations. Unless a classification trammels fundamental personal rights or is drawn upon inherently suspect distinctions such as race, religion, or alienage, our decisions presume the constitutionality of the statutory discriminations and require only

that the classification challenged be rationally related to a legitimate state interest. States are accorded wide latitude in the regulation of their local economies under their police powers, and rational distinctions may be made with substantially less than mathematical exactitude. Legislatures may implement their program step by step, in such economic areas, adopting regulations that only partially ameliorate a perceived evil and deferring complete elimination of the evil to future regulations. . . .

Nevertheless, relying on *Morey v. Doud,* as its "chief guide," the Court of Appeals held that even though the exemption of the two vendors was rationally related to legitimate city interests on the basis of facts extant when the ordinance was amended, the "grandfather clause" still could not stand because "the hypothesis that a present eight year veteran of the pushcart hot dog market in the Vieux Carre will continue to operate in a manner more consistent with the traditions of the Quarter than would any other operator is without foundation." Actually, the reliance on the statute's potential irrationality in *Morey v. Dowd,* as the dissenters in that case correctly pointed out, was a needlessly intrusive judicial infringement on the State's legislative powers, and we have concluded that the equal protection analysis employed in that opinion should no longer be followed. *Morey* was the only case in the last half century to invalidate a wholly economic regulation solely on equal protection grounds, and we are now satisfied that the decision was erroneous. *Morey* is, as appellee and the Court of Appeals properly recognized, essentially indistinguishable from this case, but the decision so far departs from proper equal protection analysis in cases of exclusively economic regulation that it should be and it is, overruled.

3. *Lindsley v. Natural Carbonic Gas Co.,* 220 U.S. 61, 31 S.Ct. 337, 55 L.Ed. 369 (1911) is a case still frequently cited with approval by the Court as setting the proper test to determine the constitutionality of laws challenged under traditional, economic equal protection:

1. The equal protection clause of the Fourteenth Amendment does not take from the State the power to classify in the adoption of police laws, but admits of the exercise of a wide scope of discretion in that regard, and avoids what is done only when it is

without any reasonable basis and therefore is purely arbitrary. **2.** A classification having some reasonable basis does not offend against that clause merely because it is not made with mathematical nicety or because in practice it results in some inequality. **3.** When the classification in such a law is called in question, if any state of facts reasonably can be conceived that would sustain it, the existence of that state of facts at the time the law was enacted must be assumed. **4.** One who assails the classification in such a law must carry the burden of showing that it does not rest upon any reasonable basis, but is essentially arbitrary.

5.2 RACE

5.2.1 The Beginnings

STRAUDER V. WEST VIRGINIA
100 U.S. 303, 25 L.Ed. 664 (1880)

JUSTICE STRONG delivered the opinion of the Court.

The plaintiff in error, a colored man was indicted for murder in the Circuit Court of Ohio County, in West Virginia, on the 20th of October, 1874, and upon trial was convicted and sentenced. [I]t is now, in substance, averred that at the trial in the State court [he] was denied rights to which he was entitled under the Constitution and laws of the United States [because under state law blacks are ineligible to serve on the grand or petit jury].

[The question] is not whether a colored man, when an indictment has been preferred against him, has a right to a grand or a petit jury composed in whole or in part of persons of his own race or color, but it is whether, in the composition or selection of jurors by whom he is to be indicted or tried, all persons of his race or color may be excluded by law, solely because of their race or color, so that by no possibility can any colored man sit upon the jury.

[The Fourteenth Amendment] is one of a series of constitutional provisions having a common purpose; namely, securing to a race recently emancipated, a race that through many generations had been held in slavery, all the civil rights that the superior race enjoy. . . . It was designed to assure to the colored race the enjoyment of all the civil rights that under the law are enjoyed by white persons, and to give to that race the protection of the general government, in that enjoyment, whenever it should be denied by the States. It not only gave citizenship and the privileges of citizenship to persons of color, but it denied to any State the power to withhold from them the equal protection of the laws. . . . What is this but declaring that the law in the States shall be the same for the black as for the white; that all persons, whether colored or white, shall stand equal before the laws of the States, and, in regard to the colored race, for whose protection the amendment was primarily designed, that no discrimination shall be made against them by law because of their color? The words of the amendment, it is true, are prohibitory, but they contain a necessary implication of a positive immunity, or right, most valuable to the colored race,—the right to exemption from unfriendly legislation against them distinctively as colored,—exemption from legal discriminations, implying inferiority in civil society, lessening the security of their enjoyment of the rights which others enjoy, and discriminations which are steps towards reducing them to the condition of a subject race.

That the West Virginia statute respecting juries—the statute that controlled the selection of the grand and petit jury in the case of the plaintiff in error—is such a discrimination ought not to be doubted. Nor would it be if the persons excluded by it were white men. . . . Nor if a law should be passed excluding all naturalized Celtic Irishmen, would there be any doubt of its inconsistency with the spirit of the amendment. The very fact that colored people are singled out and expressly denied by a statute all right to participate in the administration of the law, as jurors, because of their color, though they are citizens, and may be in other respects fully qualified, is practically a brand upon them, affixed by the law, an assertion of their inferiority, and a stimulant to that race prejudice which is an impediment to securing to individuals of the race that equal justice which the law aims to secure to all others. . . .

We do not say that within the limits from which it is not excluded by the amendment a State may not prescribe the qualifications of its jurors, and in so doing make discriminations. It may confine the selection to males, to freeholders, to citizens, to persons within certain ages, or to persons having educational qualifications. We do not believe the Fourteenth Amendment was ever intended to prohibit this. Looking at its history, it is clear it had no such purpose. Its aim was against discrimination because of race or color. . . . It is not easy to comprehend how it can be said that while every white man is entitled to a trial by a jury selected from persons of his own race or color, or, rather, selected without discrimination against his color, and a negro is not, the latter is equally protected by the law with the former. . . . The judgment of the Supreme Court of West Virginia will be reversed, and the case remitted with instructions to reverse the judgment of the Circuit Court of Ohio county; and it is So ordered.

[The dissenting opinion of FIELD, J., joined by CLIFFORD, J., is omitted.]

YICK WO V. HOPKINS

118 U.S. 356, 6 S.Ct. 1064, 30 L.Ed. 220 (1886)

[San Francisco ordinances, enacted in 1880, vested in the board of supervisors the discretion to grant or withhold their consent to the use of wooden buildings as laundries. There were no such restrictions on stone or brick buildings. Petitioner, a native of China and a subject of the Emperor, sought a writ of habeas corpus after he was imprisoned for violating the ordinances. He had been engaged in the laundry business on the same premises for 22 years, and the board of fire wardens and the health officer had inspected his facilities and found all arrangements to be proper. The city claimed the purpose of the ordinances was to protect the public against the danger of fire, though no such purpose appeared on the face of the statute. Of the 320 laundries in the city, Chinese persons owned and operated about 240; approximately 310 of the buildings were constructed of wood, the same material used for 90 percent of the houses in the city. The board had denied the application of all the Chinese (approximately 200) who had applied for licenses, all of whom had occupied and used the houses for laundries for more than 20 years. With one exception, the board had granted the applications of all the non-Chinese who had applied, about 80.]

JUSTICE MATTHEWS delivered the opinion of the Court.

[The ordinances] seem intended to confer, and actually do confer, not a discretion to be exercised upon a consideration of the circumstances of each case, but a naked and arbitrary power to give or withhold consent, not only as to places, but as to persons. So that, if an applicant for such consent, being in every way a competent and qualified person, and having complied with every reasonable condition demanded by any public interest, should, failing to obtain the requisite consent of the supervisors to the prosecution of his business, apply for redress by the judicial process . . . to require the supervisors to consider and act upon his case, it would be a sufficient answer for them to say that the law had conferred upon them authority to withhold their assent, without reason and without responsibility. The power given to them is not confided to their discretion in the legal sense of that term, but is granted to their mere will. It is purely arbitrary, and acknowledges neither guidance nor restraint. . . .

The rights of the petitioners, as affected by the proceedings of which they complain, are not less, because they are aliens and subjects of the Emperor of China. . . . The Fourteenth Amendment to the Constitution is not confined to the protection of citizens. [T]he very idea that one man may be compelled to hold his life, or the means of living, or any material right essential to the enjoyment of life, at the mere will of another, seems to be intolerable in any country where freedom prevails, as being the essence of slavery itself. There are many illustrations that might be given of this truth, which would make manifest that it was self-evident in the light of our system of jurisprudence. The case of the political franchise of voting is one. Though not regarded strictly as a natural right, but as a privilege merely conceded by society according to its will, under certain conditions, nevertheless it is regarded as a fundamental political right, because preservative of all rights.

[T]he cases present the ordinances in actual operation, and the facts shown establish an administration directed so exclusively against a particular class of persons as to warrant and require the conclusion, that, whatever may have been the intent of the ordinances as adopted, they are applied by the public authorities charged with their administration, and thus representing the State itself, with a mind so unequal and oppressive as to amount to a practical denial by the State of that equal protection of the laws which is secured to the petitioners, as to all other persons, by the broad and benign provisions of the Fourteenth Amendment to the Constitution of the United States. Though the law itself be fair on its face and impartial in appearance, yet, if it is applied and administered by public authority with an evil eye and an unequal hand, so as practically to make unjust and illegal discriminations between persons in similar circumstances, material to their rights, the denial of equal justice is still within the prohibition of the Constitution. . . .

The present cases, as shown by the facts disclosed in the record, are within this class. It appears that both petitioners have complied with every requisite, deemed by the law or by the public officers charged with its administration, necessary for the protection of neighboring property from fire, or as a precaution against injury to the public health. No reason whatever, except the will of the supervisors, is assigned why they should not be permitted to carry on, in the accustomed manner, their harmless and useful occupation, on which they depend for a livelihood. And while this consent of the supervisors is withheld from them and from two hundred others who have also petitioned, all of whom happen to be Chinese subjects, eighty others, not Chinese subjects, are permitted to carry on the same business under similar conditions. The fact of this discrimination is admitted. No reason for it is shown, and the conclusion cannot be resisted, that no reason for it exists except hostility to the race and nationality to which the petitioners belong, and which in the eye of the law is not justified. The discrimination is, therefore, illegal, and the public administration which enforces it is a denial of the equal protection of the laws and a violation of the Fourteenth Amendment of the Constitution. The imprisonment of the petitioners is, therefore, illegal, and they must be discharged. To this end, the judgment of the Supreme Court of California in the case of Yick Wo, and that of the Circuit Court of the United States for the District of California in the case of Wo Lee, are severally reversed, and the cases remanded, each to the proper court, with directions to discharge the petitioners from custody and imprisonment.

PLESSY V. FERGUSON
163 U.S. 537, 16 S.Ct. 1138, 41 L.Ed. 259 (1896)

MR. JUSTICE BROWN delivered the opinion of the Court.

This case turns upon the constitutionality of an act of the General Assembly of the State of Louisiana, passed in 1890, providing for separate [but equal] railway carriages for the white and colored races. . . .

The petition for the writ of prohibition averred that petitioner was seven eighths Caucasian and one eighth African blood; that the mixture of colored blood was not discernible in him, and that he was entitled to every right, privilege and immunity secured to citizens of the United States of the white race; and that, upon such theory, he took possession of a vacant seat in a coach where passengers of the white race were accommodated, and was ordered by the conductor to vacate said coach and take a seat in another assigned to persons of the colored race, and having refused to comply with such demand he was forcibly ejected with the aid of a police officer, and imprisoned in the parish jail to answer a charge of having violated the above act. . . .

The object of the [fourteenth] amendment was undoubtedly to enforce the absolute equality of the two races before the law, but in the nature of things it could not have been intended to abolish distinctions based upon color, or to enforce social, as distinguished from political equality, or a commingling of the two races upon terms unsatisfactory to either. Laws permitting, and even requiring, their separation in places where they are liable to be brought into contact do not necessarily imply the inferiority of either race to the other, and have been generally, if not universally, recognized as within the competency of the state legislatures in the exercise of their police power. The most common instance of this is connected with the establishment of separate schools for white and colored children, which has been held to be a valid exercise of the legislative power even by courts of States where the political rights of the colored race have been longest and most earnestly enforced. . . .

We consider the underlying fallacy of the plaintiff's argument to consist in the assumption that the enforced separation of the two races stamps the colored race with a badge of inferiority. If this be so, it is not by reason of anything found in the act, but solely because the colored race chooses to put that construction upon it. The argument necessarily assumes that if, as has been more than once the case, and is not unlikely to be so again, the colored race should become the dominant power in the state legislature, and should enact a law in precisely similar terms, it would thereby relegate the white race to an inferior position. We imagine that the white race, at least, would not acquiesce in this assumption. The argument also assumes that social prejudices may be overcome by legislation, and that equal rights cannot be secured to the negro except by an enforced commingling of the two races. We cannot accept this proposition. If the two races are to meet upon terms of social equality, it must be the result of natural affinities, a mutual appreciation of each other's merits and a voluntary consent of individuals. . . .

MR. JUSTICE HARLAN, dissenting.

[I]f this statute of Louisiana is consistent with the personal liberty of citizens, why may not the State require the separation in railroad coaches of native and naturalized citizens of the United States, or of Protestants and Roman Catholics? . . .

The white race deems itself to be the dominant race in this country. And so it is, in prestige, in achievements, in education, in wealth and in power. So, I doubt not, it will continue to be for all time, if it remains true to its great heritage and holds fast to the principles of constitutional liberty. But in view of the Constitution, in the eye of the law, there is in this country no superior, dominant, ruling class of citizens. There is no caste here. Our Constitution is color-blind, and neither knows nor tolerates classes among citizens. In respect of civil rights, all citizens are equal before the law. The humblest is the peer of the most powerful. The law regards man as man, and takes no account of his surroundings or of his color when his civil rights as guaranteed by the supreme law of the land are involved. It is, therefore, to be regretted that this high tribunal, the final expositor of the fundamental law of the land, has reached the conclusion that it is competent for a State to regulate the enjoyment by citizens of their civil rights solely upon the basis of race.

. . . Sixty millions of whites are in no danger from the presence here of eight millions of blacks. The destinies of the two races, in this country, are indissolubly linked together, and the interests of both require that the common government of all shall not permit the seeds of race hate to be planted under the sanction of law. What can more certainly arouse race hate, what more certainly create and perpetuate a feeling of distrust between these races, than state enactments, which, in fact, proceed on the ground that colored citizens are so inferior and degraded that they cannot be allowed to sit in public coaches occupied by white citizens? That, as all will admit, is the real meaning of such legislation as was enacted in Louisiana. . . .

MR. JUSTICE BREWER did not hear the argument or participate in the decision of this case.

NOTES

1. Before the Civil War, state law typically made it illegal to educate slaves, even if their owners wanted them educated. During Reconstruction, Congress created the Freemen's Bureau, which set up schools to educate the newly freed. These schools achieved "spectacular gains in literacy." Less than two months after the end of the war, they were educating 2,000 children in Richmond, Virginia. By the spring of 1866, at least 975 schools were educating more than 90,000 students in 15 Southern states. By late 1869, that number was more than 250,000. Freedmen's schools were open to whites, but few attended. "[M]ost parents preferred to consign their children to illiteracy rather than to see them educated alongside black children."[2]

2. After Lincoln's death, President Andrew Johnson issued executive orders that replaced Republican military officers "with compliant Democrats, many of whom averted their gaze when armed 'white leagues' drove teachers from their schools, assassinated local black leaders, and intimidated defenseless black and white Unionist voters."[3] The successes of Reconstruction faded into the era of Jim Crow.

SHELLEY V. KRAEMER
334 U.S. 1, 68 S.Ct. 836, 92 L.Ed. 1161 (1948)

MR. CHIEF JUSTICE VINSON delivered the opinion of the Court.

These cases present for our consideration questions relating to the validity of court enforcement of private agreements, generally described as restrictive covenants, which have as their purpose the exclusion of persons of designated

---

[2] Douglas R. Egerton, The Wars of Reconstruction: The Brief, Violent History of America's Most Progressive Era (Bloomsbury Publishing, 2014).

[3] Fergus M. Bordewich, A Moment of Possibility, Wall St. Journal, Jan 18–19, at C5.

race or color from the ownership or occupancy of real property. Basic constitutional issues of obvious importance have been raised. . . .

On August 11, 1945, pursuant to a contract of sale, petitioners Shelley, who are Negroes, for valuable consideration received from one Fitzgerald a warranty deed to the parcel in question. The trial court found that petitioners had no actual knowledge of the restrictive agreement at the time of the purchase.

On October 9, 1945, respondents, as owners of other property subject to the terms of the restrictive covenant, brought suit in the Circuit Court of the city of St. Louis praying that petitioners Shelley be restrained from taking possession of the property and that judgment be entered divesting title out of petitioners Shelley and revesting title in the immediate grantor or in such other person as the court should direct. The trial court denied the requested relief on the ground that the restrictive agreement, upon which respondents based their action, had never become final and complete because it was the intention of the parties to that agreement that it was not to become effective until signed by all property owners in the district, and signatures of all the owners had never been obtained. The Supreme Court of Missouri sitting *en banc* held the agreement effective and concluded that enforcement of its provisions violated no rights guaranteed to petitioners by the Federal Constitution. At the time the court rendered its decision, petitioners were occupying the property in question.

[R]estrictions on the right of occupancy of the sort sought to be created by the private agreements in these cases could not be squared with the requirements of the Fourteenth Amendment if imposed by state statute or local ordinance. We do not understand respondents to urge the contrary. In the case of *Buchanan v. Warley*, [245 U.S. 60, 38 S.Ct. 16, 62 L.Ed. 149 (1917)], a unanimous Court declared unconstitutional the provisions of a city ordinance which denied to colored persons the right to occupy houses in blocks in which the greater number of houses were occupied by white persons, and imposed similar restrictions on white persons with respect to blocks in which the greater number of houses were occupied by colored persons. During the course of the opinion in that case, this Court stated: "The Fourteenth Amendment and these statutes enacted in furtherance of its purpose operate to qualify and entitle a colored man to acquire property without state legislation discriminating against him solely because of color." . . .

But the present cases, unlike those just discussed, do not involve action by state legislatures or city councils. . . . Since the decision of this Court in the *Civil Rights Cases*, [109 U.S. 3, 3 S.Ct. 18, 27 L.Ed. 835 (1883)], the principle has become firmly embedded in our constitutional law that the action inhibited by the first section of the Fourteenth Amendment is only such action as may fairly be said to be that of the States. That Amendment erects no shield against merely private conduct, however discriminatory or wrongful. We conclude, therefore, that the restrictive agreements standing alone cannot be regarded as violative of any rights guaranteed to petitioners by the Fourteenth Amendment. So long as the purposes of those agreements are effectuated by voluntary adherence to their terms, it would appear clear that there has been no action by the State and the provisions of the Amendment have not been violated.

But here there was more. These are cases in which the purposes of the agreements were secured only by judicial enforcement by state courts of the restrictive terms of the agreements. . . . We have no doubt that there has been state action in these cases in the full and complete sense of the phrase. The undisputed facts disclose that petitioners were willing purchasers of properties upon which they desired to establish homes. The owners of the properties were willing sellers; and contracts of sale were accordingly consummated. It is clear that but for the active intervention of the state courts, supported by the full panoply of state power, petitioners would have been free to occupy the properties in question without restraint.

These are not cases, as has been suggested, in which the States have merely abstained from action, leaving private individuals free to impose such discriminations as they see fit. Rather, these are cases in which the States have made available to such individuals the full coercive power of government to deny to petitioners, on the grounds of race or color, the enjoyment of property rights in premises which petitioners are willing and financially able to acquire and which the grantors are willing to sell. The difference between judicial enforcement and nonenforcement of the restrictive covenants is the difference to petitioners between being denied rights of property available to other members of the community and being accorded full enjoyment of those rights on an equal footing.

The enforcement of the restrictive agreements by the state courts in these cases was directed pursuant to the common-law policy of the States as formulated by those courts in earlier decisions. [J]udicial action is not immunized from the operation of the Fourteenth Amendment simply because it is taken pursuant to the state's common-law policy. Nor is the Amendment ineffective simply because the particular pattern of discrimination, which the State has enforced, was defined initially by the terms of a private agreement. State action, as that phrase is understood for the purposes of the Fourteenth Amendment, refers to exertions of state power in all forms. And when the effect of that action is to deny rights subject to the protection of the Fourteenth Amendment, it is the obligation of this Court to enforce the constitutional commands.

We hold that in granting judicial enforcement of the restrictive agreements in these cases, the States have denied petitioners the equal protection of the laws and that, therefore, the action of the state courts cannot stand. We have noted that freedom from discrimination by the States in the enjoyment of property rights was among the basic objectives sought to be effectuated by the Framers of the Fourteenth Amendment. That such discrimination has occurred in these cases is clear. Because of the race or color of these petitioners they have been denied rights of ownership or occupancy enjoyed as a matter of course by other citizens of different race or color. . . .

Respondents urge, however, that since the state courts stand ready to enforce restrictive covenants excluding white persons from the ownership or occupancy of property covered by such agreements, enforcement of covenants excluding colored persons may not be deemed a denial of equal protection of the laws to the colored persons who are thereby affected.[28] This contention does not bear scrutiny. . . . The rights created by the first section of the Fourteenth Amendment are, by its terms, guaranteed to the individual. The rights established are personal rights. It is, therefore, no answer to these petitioners to say that the courts may also be induced to deny white persons rights of ownership and occupancy on grounds of race or color. Equal protection of the laws is not achieved through indiscriminate imposition of inequalities. . . .

Reversed.

Mr. Justice Reed, Mr. Justice Jackson, and Mr. Justice Rutledge took no part in the consideration or decision of these cases.

NOTES

1. No Justices dissented in *Shelley*. The three Justices who declined to participate did not explain why. (Generally, the Justices do not explain why.) They may have disqualified themselves because they owned property subject to restrictive covenants.

---

[28] It should be observed that the restrictions relating to residential occupancy contained in ordinances involved in the *Buchanan* [case], cited *supra*, and declared by this Court to be inconsistent with the requirements of the Fourteenth Amendment, applied equally to white persons and Negroes.

2.   In some states, when parties sought to enforce restrictive covenants, the state courts refused to do so on the grounds that the covenants violated state public policy. In Canada, the Ontario High Court ruled in 1945 that public policy forbids enforcement of a restrictive covenant against Jews. *In re Drummond Wren,* [1945] 4 D.L.R. 674. (In fact, the Canadian Court also cited the human rights provisions of the United Nations Charter.) Missouri, however, upheld the covenants.

On the same day that the Court decided *Shelley,* it invalidated racially restrictive covenants in the District of Columbia. The Fourteenth Amendment does not apply to the District (it is not a "state"), so the Court held that the racially restrictive covenant violated United States public policy and the Civil Rights Act of 1866. Section 1 of that act requires that all citizens have the same right "as is enjoyed by white citizens . . . to inherit, purchase, lease, sell, hold, and convey real and personal property." For federal courts to interfere with contracts of sale between willing black purchasers and willing sellers would violate that act. The Court did not find it necessary to reach the constitutional issue of whether federal judicial enforcement of racial covenants would violate the due process clause of the Fifth Amendment. *Hurd v. Hodge,* 334 U.S. 24, 68 S.Ct. 847, 92 L.Ed. 1187 (1948).

3.   As *Shelley* noted, the *Civil Rights Cases* (§ 6.1) held that in order for a Fourteenth Amendment violation to exist, there must be "state action." As Section 1 provides: "No State shall . . .; nor shall any State deprive. . . ." The *Civil Rights Cases* said: "[I]t is proper to state that civil rights, such as are guaranteed by the Constitution against State aggression, cannot be impaired by the wrongful acts of individuals unsupported by State authority in the shape of laws, customs, or judicial or executive proceedings." As *Shelley* noted, "[P]etitioners were willing purchasers of properties upon which they desired to establish homes. The owners of the properties were willing sellers. [B]ut for the active intervention of the state courts, supported by the full panoply of state power, petitioners would have been free to occupy the properties in question without restraint." The Court, in effect, said that the state court cannot use its injunctive powers to force a person to discriminate on racial grounds. No state action is involved when a white person refuses to sell to a black person.[4] *Shelley* does not hold that any judicial decree that disadvantages members of a racial minority violates the Fourteenth Amendment. A court can uphold trespass convictions based on a

---

[4]   Nowadays, state and federal statutes forbid racial discrimination in the sale or lease of real property.

homeowner's decision to refuse to open his home or other private property to a neighbor, even if the neighbor is a member of a racial minority. On the other hand, if of a homeowners' association rule prevents whites from inviting blacks into their homes, *Shelly* says no court can enforce that rule when a willing homeowner invites a guest in violation of that rule.

4. *Barrows v. Jackson*, 346 U.S. 249, 73 S.Ct. 1031, 97 L.Ed. 1586 (1953), held that courts cannot enforce racially restrictive covenants by injunction—as *Shelley* had held—or by damages. In this case, plaintiff sued defendant for damages when she sold her home to non-Caucasians, in violation of a restrictive covenant.

5. During the early 1960s, the Supreme Court heard a series of cases called the *Sit-In Cases*, which involved blacks convicted under state criminal trespass or disturbing the peace laws when they sat in the "white-only" section of various lunch counters and restaurants and refused to move after the restaurant ordered them to leave. Neither state nor federal laws at the time required the restaurants to serve blacks. The Supreme Court managed to reverse these convictions on narrow grounds without a Court majority ever adopting any broad state action theories.

In *Garner v. Louisiana,* 368 U.S. 157, 82 S.Ct. 248, 7 L.Ed.2d 207 (1961), for example, the court reversed the convictions (under a state disturbing the peace statute) of those who had engaged in a sit-in. Petitioners argued, *inter alia*, that "the participation of the police and the judiciary to enforce a state custom of segregation resulted in the use of 'state action.' . . ." The Court found it "unnecessary to reach the broader constitutional questions presented." It then reversed the convictions because the record was "totally devoid of evidentiary support" that petitioners caused any disturbance of the peace.

In *Peterson v. Greenville,* 373 U.S. 244, 83 S.Ct. 1119, 10 L.Ed.2d 323 (1963), the Court reversed the trespass conviction of blacks who engaged in a sit-in at a lunch counter. The store manager asked the blacks to leave because integrated service was "contrary to local customs" and also was a violation of a city ordinance. Given the law, the Court held that "these convictions cannot stand, even assuming, as respondent contends, that the manager would have acted as he did independently of the existence of the ordinance. [The state cannot save the convictions] by attempting to separate the mental urges of the discriminators."

Lombard v. Louisiana, 373 U.S. 267, 83 S.Ct. 1122, 10 L.Ed.2d 338 (1963), decided the same day, reversed the trespass convictions of three blacks and one white who sat in a privately owned restaurant that served only whites. The case involved no statutes or ordinances, but the police superintendent and the mayor had previously announced publicly that—in the words of the mayor—"no additional sit-in demonstrations . . . will be permitted." The Court held that because of the officials' pronouncements, "the city must be treated exactly as if it had an ordinance prohibiting such conduct. . . . The official command here was to direct continuance of segregated services in restaurants. . . ." Justice Douglas, concurring, would have decided on broader grounds. Relying on *Shelley v. Kraemer,* he argued that state action was present when the state judiciary "put criminal sanctions behind racial discrimination in public places."

Then Congress, under its commerce power, enacted the Civil Rights Act of 1964, 78 Stat. 241, which precluded such trespass prosecutions by creating substantive rights.[5] In *Hamm v. Rock Hill,* 379 U.S. 306, 85 S.Ct. 384, 13 L.Ed.2d 300 (1964), the Court applied that law to convictions rendered but not finalized before the law's passage. The Court followed the old common law rule of statutory construction that if, "subsequent to the judgment and before the decision of the appellate court, a law intervenes and positively changes the rule which governs, the law must be obeyed. [T]he court must decide according to existing laws, and if it be necessary to set aside a judgment, rightful when rendered, but which cannot be affirmed but in violation of law, the judgment must be set aside," quoting Chief Justice Marshall, in *United States v. The Peggy,* 5 U.S. (1 Cranch) 103, 110, 2 L.Ed. 49 (1801). The *Hamm* Court noted: "The great purpose of the civil rights legislation was to obliterate the effect of a distressing chapter in our history."

6. *Nixon v. Herndon,* 273 U.S. 536, 47 S.Ct. 446, 71 L.Ed. 759 (1927), invalidated, under the equal protection clause, a Texas law that expressly excluded blacks from voting in the state Democratic primary.

Texas responded to that decision by enacting in 1927 a statute providing that every political party in the state, through its executive committee, shall have the power, subject to some restrictions, to determine who would be qualified to vote or otherwise participate in the political party. The Democratic Party's state executive committee then adopted a resolution

---

[5] See *Heart of Atlanta Motel, Inc. v. United States,* § 6.3, *supra,* and *Katzenbach v. McClung,* § 6.3, *supra,* both decided the same day as *Hamm.*

excluding blacks from its primaries. The Court also invalidated this statute. "Whatever inherent power a State political party has to determine the content of its membership resides in the state convention." The statute changed that. "To this [executive] committee the statute here in controversy has attempted to confide authority to determine of its own motion the requisites of party membership and in so doing to speak for the party as a whole. . . . Whatever power of exclusion has been exercised by the members of the committee has come to them, therefore, not as delegates of the party, but as delegates of the State." Thus, the statute was unconstitutional under the Fourteenth Amendment owing to state action. *Nixon v. Condon*, 286 U.S. 73, 52 S.Ct. 484, 76 L.Ed. 984 (1932).

Texas once again responded. On May 24, 1932, the state Democratic Convention adopted a resolution allowing only whites to be party members. A state official thus refused to issue a ballot in the Democratic Party primary to petitioner because of his color. The Court held that since the state convention had declared the voter qualifications, the convention's actions were not state action. *Grovey v. Townsend*, 295 U.S. 45, 55 S.Ct. 622, 79 L.Ed. 1292 (1935).

The Court overruled *Grovey* less than a decade later in *Smith v. Allwright*, 321 U.S. 649, 64 S.Ct. 757, 88 L.Ed. 987 (1944), a case also arising in Texas. Between *Grovey* and *Smith*, the Court had decided *United States v. Classic*, 313 U.S. 299, 61 S.Ct. 1031, 85 L.Ed. 1368 (1941), holding that Art. I, § 4, cl. 1, authorized Congress to regulate primary as well as general elections to choose representatives in Congress, where the primary is by law made an integral part of the election machinery. *Allwright* said that *Classic* was also a "recognition of the place of the primary in the electoral scheme, [which] makes clear that state delegation to a party of the power to fix the qualifications of primary elections is delegation of a state function that may make the party's action the action of the state. . . . If the State requires a certain electoral procedure, prescribes a general election ballot made up of party nominees so chosen and limits the choice of the electorate in general elections for state offices, practically speaking, to those whose names appear on such a ballot, it endorses, adopts and enforces the discrimination against Negroes, practiced by a party entrusted by Texas law with the determination of the qualifications of participants in the primary. This is state action within the meaning of the Fifteenth Amendment."

Justice Roberts, the author of *Grovey*, dissented, protesting that "the instant decision, overruling that announced about nine years ago, tends to bring adjudications of this tribunal into the same class as a restricted railroad ticket, good for this day and train only."

7.   *Burton v. Wilmington Parking Authority*, 365 U.S. 715, 81 S.Ct. 856, 6 L.Ed. 2d 45 (1961), held that a private restaurant violated the equal protection clause when it refused to serve blacks. The restaurant had a lease in a building owned by the state through a state parking authority. The restaurant also benefited from the state-owned parking facilities in the building. And the building enjoyed a tax exemption. The state also profited from the rents paid by the restaurant. The Court found state action but offered no precise tests: "Only by sifting facts and weighing circumstances can the nonobvious involvement of the State in private conduct be attributed its true significance."

     In *Anderson v. Martin*, 375 U.S. 399, 84 S.Ct. 454, 11 L.Ed.2d 430 (1964), the Court invalidated a state law that required candidates to designate their race on the ballot. The law did not mandate private discrimination in voting, but requiring that candidates indicate their race on the ballot clearly facilitated it (and served no purpose except to facilitate private discrimination).

     In *Norwood v. Harrison*, 413 U.S. 455, 93 S.Ct. 2804, 37 L.Ed.2d 723 (1973), the Court prohibited Mississippi from supplying free textbooks to students attending racially discriminatory schools because the state action (providing free textbooks) was a form of financial aid to discrimination. "Textbooks are a basic educational tool and, like tuition grants, they are provided only in connection with schools; they are to be distinguished from generalized services government might provide to schools in common with others," like water, police, and fire protection. The state financial aid facilitated private discrimination.

8.   *Moose Lodge No. 107 v. Irvis*, 407 U.S. 163, 92 S.Ct. 1965, 32 L.Ed.2d 627 (1972), retreated from a broad state action view. It held that no state action was involved when a private club, the Moose Lodge, refused to serve blacks at its bar, even though Pennsylvania granted a liquor license to the Moose Lodge, giving it a semi-monopoly power. (Only establishments with liquor licenses can legally serve alcohol.) As Justice Douglas noted in his dissent, liquor licenses in Pennsylvania, unlike drivers' licenses, or marriage licenses, are not freely available; a state enforced scarcity operates, in this instance, to aid private discrimination. Moreover, "as Moose Lodge itself concedes,

without a liquor license a fraternal organization would be hard pressed to survive."

See also *Jackson v. Metropolitan Edison Co.,* 419 U.S. 345, 95 S.Ct. 449, 42 L.Ed.2d 477 (1974). Customer sued a privately owned and operated utility corporation, which held a certificate of public convenience issued by the Pennsylvania Utilities Commission. Plaintiff sought damages under the Civil Rights Act because the utility terminated her electric service allegedly before it have her procedural due process (notice, a hearing and an opportunity to pay any amounts found due.) The Court held that the actions of privately owned utility company are not state action, even though the utility enjoyed at least a partial monopoly.

5.2.2   The *Brown* Decisions and School Desegregation

BROWN V. BOARD OF EDUCATION [BROWN I]
347 U.S. 483, 74 S.Ct. 686, 98 L.Ed. 873 (1954)

CHIEF JUSTICE WARREN delivered the opinion of the Court.

These cases come to us from the States of Kansas, South Carolina, Virginia, and Delaware. They are premised on different facts and different local conditions, but a common legal question justifies their consideration together in this consolidated opinion.

In each of the cases, minors of the Negro race, through their legal representatives, seek the aid of the courts in obtaining admission to the public schools of their community on a nonsegregated basis. In each instance, they had been denied admission to schools attended by white children under laws requiring or permitting segregation according to race. This segregation was alleged to deprive the plaintiffs of the equal protection of the laws under the Fourteenth Amendment. In each of the cases other than the Delaware case, a three-judge federal district court denied relief to the plaintiffs on the so-called "separate but equal" doctrine announced by this Court in *Plessy v. Ferguson.* Under that doctrine, equality of treatment is accorded when the races are provided substantially equal facilities, even though these facilities be separate. In the Delaware case, the Supreme Court of Delaware adhered to that doctrine, but ordered that the plaintiffs be admitted to the white schools because of their superiority to the Negro schools.

The plaintiffs contend that segregated public schools are not "equal" and cannot be made "equal," and that hence they are deprived of the equal protection of the laws. Because of the obvious importance of the question presented, the Court took jurisdiction. Argument was heard in the 1952 Term, and reargument was heard this Term on certain questions propounded by the Court.

Reargument was largely devoted to the circumstances surrounding the adoption of the Fourteenth Amendment in 1868. It covered exhaustively consideration of the Amendment in Congress, ratification by the states, then existing practices in racial segregation, and the views of proponents and opponents of the Amendment. This discussion and our own investigation convince us that, although these sources cast some light, it is not enough to resolve the problem with which we are faced. At best, they are inconclusive. The most avid proponents of the post-War Amendments undoubtedly intended them to remove all legal distinctions among "all persons born or naturalized in the United States." Their opponents, just as certainly, were antagonistic to both the letter and the spirit of the Amendments and wished them to have the most limited effect. What others in Congress and the state legislatures had in mind cannot be determined with any degree of certainty.

An additional reason for the inconclusive nature of the Amendment's history, with respect to segregated schools, is the status of public education at that time. In the South, the movement toward free common schools, supported by general taxation, had not yet taken hold. Education of white children was largely in the hands of private groups. Education of Negroes was almost nonexistent, and practically all of the race were illiterate. In fact, any education of Negroes was forbidden by law in some states. Today, in contrast, many Negroes have achieved outstanding success in the arts and sciences as well as in the business and professional world. It is true that public school education at the time of the Amendment had advanced further in the North, but the effect of the Amendment on Northern States was generally ignored in the congressional debates. Even in the North, the conditions of public education did not approximate those existing today. The curriculum was usually rudimentary; ungraded schools were common in rural areas; the school term was but three months a year in many states; and compulsory school attendance was virtually unknown. As a consequence, it is not surprising that there should be so little in the history of the Fourteenth Amendment relating to its intended effect on public education.

In the first cases in this Court construing the Fourteenth Amendment, decided shortly after its adoption, the Court interpreted it as proscribing all state-imposed discriminations against the Negro race. The doctrine of "separate but equal" did not make its appearance in this Court until 1896 in the case of *Plessy v.*

Ferguson, involving not education but transportation. American courts have since labored with the doctrine for over half a century. In this Court, there have been six cases involving the "separate but equal" doctrine in the field of public education. In *Cumming v. County Board of Education*, 175 U.S. 528, 20 S.Ct. 197, 44 L.Ed. 262, and *Gong Lum v. Rice, 275* U.S. 78, 48 S.Ct. 91, 72 L.Ed. 172, the validity of the doctrine itself was not challenged. In more recent cases, all on the graduate school level, inequality was found in that specific benefits enjoyed by white students were denied to Negro students of the same educational qualifications. *Missouri ex rel. Gaines v. Canada*, 305 U.S. 337, 59 S.Ct. 232, 83 L.Ed. 208; *Sipuel v. Oklahoma*, 332 U.S. 631, 68 S.Ct. 299, 92 L.Ed. 247; *Sweatt v. Painter*, 339 U.S. 629, 70 S.Ct. 848, 94 L.Ed. 1114; *McLaurin v. Oklahoma State Regents*, 339 U.S. 637, 70 S.Ct. 851, 94 L.Ed. 1149. In none of these cases was it necessary to re-examine the doctrine to grant relief to the Negro plaintiff. And in *Sweatt v. Painter*, the Court expressly reserved decision on the question whether *Plessy v. Ferguson* should be held inapplicable to public education.

In the instant cases, that question is directly presented. Here, unlike *Sweatt v. Painter*, there are findings below that the Negro and white schools involved have been equalized, or are being equalized, with respect to buildings, curricula, qualifications and salaries of teachers, and other "tangible" factors. Our decision, therefore, cannot turn on merely a comparison of these tangible factors in the Negro and white schools involved in each of the cases. We must look instead to the effect of segregation itself on public education.

In approaching this problem, we cannot turn the clock back to 1868 when the Amendment was adopted, or even to 1896 when *Plessy v. Ferguson* was written. We must consider public education in the light of its full development and its present place in American life throughout the Nation. Only in this way can it be determined if segregation in public schools deprives these plaintiffs of the equal protection of the laws.

Today, education is perhaps the most important function of state and local governments. Compulsory school attendance laws and the great expenditures for education both demonstrate our recognition of the importance of education to our democratic society. It is required in the performance of our most basic public responsibilities, even service in the armed forces. It is the very foundation of good citizenship. Today it is a principal instrument in awakening the child to cultural values, in preparing him for later professional training, and in helping him to adjust normally to his environment. In these days, it is doubtful that any child may reasonably be expected to succeed in life if he is denied the opportunity of an education. Such an opportunity, where the state has undertaken to provide it, is a right which must be made available to all on equal terms.

We come then to the question presented: Does segregation of children in public schools solely on the basis of race, even though the physical facilities and other "tangible" factors may be equal, deprive the children of the minority group of equal educational opportunities? We believe that it does.

In *Sweatt v. Painter, supra*, in finding that a segregated law school for Negroes could not provide them equal educational opportunities, this Court relied in large part on "those qualities which are incapable of objective measurement but which make for greatness in a law school." In *McLaurin v. Oklahoma State Regents, supra*, the Court, in requiring that a Negro admitted to a white graduate school be treated like all other students, again resorted to intangible considerations: "his ability to study, to engage in discussions and exchange views with other students, and, in general, to learn his profession." Such considerations apply with added force to children in grade and high schools. To separate them from others of similar age and qualifications solely because of their race generates a feeling of inferiority as to their status in the community that may affect their hearts and minds in a way unlikely ever to be undone. The effect of this separation on their educational opportunities was well stated by a finding in the Kansas case by a court which nevertheless felt compelled to rule against the Negro plaintiffs:

> Segregation of white and colored children in public schools has a detrimental effect upon the colored children. The impact is greater when it has the sanction of the law; for the policy of separating the races is usually interpreted as denoting the inferiority of the negro group. A sense of inferiority affects the motivation of a child to learn. Segregation with the sanction of law, therefore, has a tendency to [retard] the educational and mental development of negro children and to deprive them of some of the benefits they would receive in a racial[ly] integrated school system.

Whatever may have been the extent of psychological knowledge at the time of *Plessy v. Ferguson*, this finding is amply supported by modern authority.[11] Any language in *Plessy v. Ferguson* contrary to this finding is rejected.

---

[11]   K. B. Clark, Effect of Prejudice and Discrimination on Personality Development (Midcentury White House Conference on Children and Youth, 1950); Witmer and Kotinsky, Personality in the Making (1952), c. VI; Deutscher and Chein, The Psychological Effects of Enforced Segregation: A Survey of Social Science Opinion, 26 J.Psychol. 259 (1948); Chein, What are the Psychological Effects of Segregation Under Conditions of Equal Facilities?, 3 Int.J.Opinion and Attitude Res. 229 (1949); Brameld, Educational Costs, in

We conclude that in the field of public education the doctrine of "separate but equal" has no place. Separate educational facilities are inherently unequal. Therefore, we hold that the plaintiffs and others similarly situated for whom the actions have been brought are, by reason of the segregation complained of, deprived of the equal protection of the laws guaranteed by the Fourteenth Amendment. This disposition makes unnecessary any discussion whether such segregation also violates the Due Process Clause of the Fourteenth Amendment.

Because these are class actions, because of the wide applicability of this decision, and because of the great variety of local conditions, the formulation of decrees in these cases presents problems of considerable complexity. On reargument, the consideration of appropriate relief was necessarily subordinated to the primary question—the constitutionality of segregation in public education. We have now announced that such segregation is a denial of the equal protection of the laws. In order that we may have the full assistance of the parties in formulating decrees, the cases will be restored to the docket, and the parties are requested to present further argument on Questions 4 and 5 previously propounded by the Court for the reargument this Term. The Attorneys General of the United States is again invited to participate. The Attorneys General of the states requiring or permitting segregation in public education will also be permitted to appear as *amici curiae* upon request to do so by September 15, 1954, and submission of briefs by October 1, 1954.

It is so ordered.

BOLLING V. SHARPE

347 U.S. 497, 74 S.Ct. 693, 98 L.Ed. 884 (1954)

CHIEF JUSTICE WARREN delivered the opinion of the Court.

This case challenges the validity of segregation in the public schools of the District of Columbia. The petitioners, minors of the Negro race, allege that such segregation deprives them of due process of law under the Fifth Amendment. . . .

We have this day held that the Equal Protection Clause of the Fourteenth Amendment prohibits the states from maintaining racially segregated public schools. The legal problem in the District of Columbia is somewhat different, however. The Fifth Amendment, which is applicable in the District of Columbia, does not contain an equal protection clause as does the Fourteenth Amendment which applies only to the states. But the concepts of equal protection and due

Discrimination and National Welfare (MacIver, ed., 1949), 44–48; Frazier, The Negro in the United States (1949), 674–681. And see generally Myrdal, An American Dilemma (1944).

process, both stemming from our American ideal of fairness, are not mutually exclusive. The "equal protection of the laws" is a more explicit safeguard of prohibited unfairness than "due process of law," and, therefore, we do not imply that the two are always interchangeable phrases. But, as this Court has recognized, discrimination may be so unjustifiable as to be violative of due process.

Classifications based solely upon race must be scrutinized with particular care, since they are contrary to our traditions and hence constitutionally suspect.[3] As long ago as 1896, this Court declared the principle "that the Constitution of the United States, in its present form, forbids, so far as civil and political rights are concerned, discrimination by the General Government, or by the States, against any citizen because of his race."[4] . . .

Although the Court has not assumed to define "liberty" with any great precision, that term is not confined to mere freedom from bodily restraint. Liberty under law extends to the full range of conduct which the individual is free to pursue, and it cannot be restricted except for a proper governmental objective. Segregation in public education is not reasonably related to any proper governmental objective, and thus it imposes on Negro children of the District of Columbia a burden that constitutes an arbitrary deprivation of their liberty in violation of the Due Process Clause.

In view of our decision that the Constitution prohibits the states from maintaining racially segregated public schools, it would be unthinkable that the same Constitution would impose a lesser duty on the Federal Government. We hold that racial segregation in the public schools of the District of Columbia is a denial of the due process of law guaranteed by the Fifth Amendment to the Constitution.

For the reasons set out in *Brown v. Board of Education,* this case will be restored to the docket for reargument on Questions 4 and 5 previously propounded by the Court.

It is so ordered.

---

[3]   *Korematsu v. United States,* 323 U.S. 214, 216, 65 S.Ct. 193, 194, 89 L.Ed. 194; *Hirabayashi v. United States,* 320 U.S. 81, 100, 63 S.Ct. 1375, 1385, 87 L.Ed. 1774.

[4]   *Gibson v. Mississippi,* 162 U.S. 565, 591, 16 S.Ct. 904, 910, 40 L.Ed. 1075. Cf. *Steele v. Louisville & Nashville R. Co.,* 323 U.S. 192, 198–199, 65 S.Ct. 226, 230, 89 L.Ed. 173.

NOTES

1. Following *Brown*, the Court applied the conclusions in that case to a host of other activities outside of the field of education. All were short *per curiam* opinions or orders, some without citation and others merely citing *Brown*. E.g., *Muir v. Louisville Park Theatrical Association*, 347 U.S. 971, 74 S.Ct. 783, 98 L.Ed. 1112 (1954) (*per curiam*) (amphitheater in city park); *Mayor and City Council of Baltimore v. Dawson*, 350 U.S. 877, 76 S.Ct. 133, 100 L.Ed. 774 (1955) (*per curiam*) (public beaches and bathhouses); *Holmes v. City of Atlanta*, 350 U.S. 879, 76 S.Ct. 141, 100 L.Ed. 776 (1955) (*per curiam*) (municipal golf courses); *Gayle v. Browder*, 352 U.S. 903, 77 S.Ct. 145, 1 L.Ed.2d 114 (1956) (*per curiam*) (municipal buses); *New Orleans Park Development Association v. Detiege*, 358 U.S. 54, 79 S.Ct. 99, 3 L.Ed.2d 46 (1958) (*per curiam*) (public parks and golf courses); *State Athletic Commission v. Dorsey*, 359 U.S. 533, 79 S.Ct. 1137, 3 L.Ed.2d 1028 (1959) (*per curiam*) (athletic contests); *Turner v. City of Memphis*, 369 U.S. 350, 82 S.Ct. 805, 7 L.Ed.2d 762 (1962) (*per curiam*) (municipal airport restaurants); *Johnson v. Virginia*, 373 U.S. 61, 83 S.Ct. 1053, 10 L.Ed.2d 195 (1963) (*per curiam*) (courtroom seating); and *Schiro v. Bynum*, 375 U.S. 395, 84 S.Ct. 452, 11 L.Ed.2d 412 (1964) (*per curiam*) (municipal auditoriums).

2. In *Korematsu* and *Hirabayashi*, cited in *Bolling* in footnote 3, the Court, relying on the war powers, *upheld* racial classifications involving curfews and relocations imposed on Japanese-Americans, given the special facts of those cases. In *Korematsu*, Roberts, Murphy, and Jackson, JJ., each filed vigorous dissents. Justice Black, for the Court, in upholding the law, did say that racial classifications are "immediately suspect," and—although not invalid per se— must be subjected to "the most rigid scrutiny." One would never suspect from the way the Court has typically cited *Korematsu* and *Hirabayashi* in *Brown* and subsequent cases that the U.S. citizens of Japanese ancestry lost.

BROWN V. BOARD OF EDUCATION [BROWN II]
349 U.S. 294, 75 S.Ct. 753, 99 L.Ed. 1083 (1955)

CHIEF JUSTICE WARREN delivered the opinion of the Court.

These cases were decided on May 17, 1954. The opinions of that date, declaring the fundamental principle that racial discrimination in public education is unconstitutional, are incorporated herein by reference. All provisions of federal, state, or local law requiring or permitting such discrimination must yield to this principle. There remains for consideration the manner in which relief is to be accorded.

Because these cases arose under different local conditions and their disposition will involve a variety of local problems, we requested further argument on the question of relief.[2] In view of the nationwide importance of the decision, we invited the Attorney General of the United States and the Attorneys General of all states requiring or permitting racial discrimination in public education to present their views on that question. The parties, the United States, and the States of Florida, North Carolina, Arkansas, Oklahoma, Maryland, and Texas filed briefs and participated in the oral argument.

These presentations were informative and helpful to the Court in its consideration of the complexities arising from the transition to a system of public education freed of racial discrimination. The presentations also demonstrated that substantial steps to eliminate racial discrimination in public schools have already been taken, not only in some of the communities in which these cases arose, but in some of the states appearing as *amici curiae*, and in other states as well. Substantial progress has been made in the District of Columbia and in the communities in Kansas and Delaware involved in this litigation. The defendants in the cases coming to us from South Carolina and Virginia are awaiting the decision of this Court concerning relief.

Full implementation of these constitutional principles may require solution of varied local school problems. School authorities have the primary responsibility for elucidating, assessing, and solving these problems; courts will have to consider whether the action of school authorities constitutes good faith implementation of the governing constitutional principles. Because of their proximity to local conditions and the possible need for further hearings, the courts which originally

---

2   Further argument was requested on the following questions previously propounded by the Court:

4   Assuming it is decided that segregation in public schools violates the Fourteenth Amendment

(*a*) would a decree necessarily follow providing that, within the limits set by normal geographic school districting, Negro children should forthwith be admitted to schools of their choice, or

(*b*) may this Court, in the exercise of its equity powers, permit an effective gradual adjustment to be brought about from existing segregated systems to a system not based on color distinctions?

5   On the assumption on which questions 4(*a*) and (*b*) are based, and assuming further that this Court will exercise its equity powers to the end described in question 4(*b*),

(*a*) should this Court formulate detailed decrees in these cases;

(*b*) if so, what specific issues should the decrees reach;

(*c*) should this Court appoint a special master to hear evidence with a view to recommending specific terms for such decrees;

(*d*) should this Court remand to the courts of first instance with directions to frame decrees in these cases, and if so what general directions should the decrees of this Court include and what procedures should the courts of first instance follow in arriving at the specific terms of more detailed decrees?

heard these cases can best perform this judicial appraisal. Accordingly, we believe it appropriate to remand the cases to those courts.

In fashioning and effectuating the decrees, the courts will be guided by equitable principles. Traditionally, equity has been characterized by a practical flexibility in shaping its remedies and by a facility for adjusting and reconciling public and private needs. These cases call for the exercise of these traditional attributes of equity power. At stake is the personal interest of the plaintiffs in admission to public schools as soon as practicable on a nondiscriminatory basis. To effectuate this interest may call for elimination of a variety of obstacles in making the transition to school systems operated in accordance with the constitutional principles set forth in our May 17, 1954, decision. Courts of equity may properly take into account the public interest in the elimination of such obstacles in a systematic and effective manner. But it should go without saying that the vitality of these constitutional principles cannot be allowed to yield simply because of disagreement with them.

While giving weight to these public and private considerations, the courts will require that the defendants make a prompt and reasonable start toward full compliance with our May 17, 1954, ruling. Once such a start has been made, the courts may find that additional time is necessary to carry out the ruling in an effective manner. The burden rests upon the defendants to establish that such time is necessary in the public interest and is consistent with good faith compliance at the earliest practicable date. To that end, the courts may consider problems related to administration, arising from the physical condition of the school plant, the school transportation system, personnel, revision of school districts and attendance areas into compact units to achieve a system of determining admission to the public schools on a nonracial basis, and revision of local laws and regulations which may be necessary in solving the foregoing problems. They will also consider the adequacy of any plans the defendants may propose to meet these problems and to effectuate a transition to a racially nondiscriminatory school system. During this period of transition, the courts will retain jurisdiction of these cases.

The judgments below, except that in the Delaware case, are accordingly reversed and the cases are remanded to the District Courts to take such proceedings and enter such orders and decrees consistent with this opinion as are necessary and proper to admit to public schools on a racially nondiscriminatory basis with all deliberate speed the parties to these cases. The judgment in the Delaware case—ordering the immediate admission of the plaintiffs to schools previously attended only by white children—is affirmed on the basis of the principles stated in our May 17, 1954, opinion, but the case is remanded to the Supreme Court of Delaware for such further proceedings as that Court may deem necessary in light of this opinion.

It is so ordered.

NOTES

1. *Brown II* was not the first case that invoked the "all deliberate speed" language.[6] Yet it was the first case to invoke it in a civil liberties context. How could the Court hold that a state is depriving blacks of equal protection of the law and still allow the state to continue the deprivation for a time? When the Court, for example, invalidated state laws forbidding the sale of birth control pills (see § 2.4.2), such laws were declared unenforceable at once. The state did not have the option of eliminating those laws with all deliberate speed. Should the Court in *Brown II* simply have declared unenforceable all state or local laws requiring segregation in education?[7]

2. In *Cooper v. Aaron*, 358 U.S. 1, 78 S.Ct. 1401, 3 L.Ed.2d 5 (1958), Arkansas state authorities actively obstructed a school board's court-approved desegregation plan. Among other things, the governor called on the National Guard to prevent nine black children from entering the previously all-white

---

[6] See *Virginia v. West Virginia,* 222 U.S. 17, 19–20, 32 S.Ct. 4, 5–6, 56 L.Ed. 71 (1911) (Justice Holmes): "A question like the present should be disposed of without undue delay. But a State cannot be expected to move with the celerity of a private business man; it is enough if it proceeds, in the language of the English Chancery, with all deliberate speed." See also *Radio Station WOW v. Johnson,* 326 U.S. 120, 132, 65 S.Ct. 1475, 1482, 89 L.Ed. 2092 (1945) (Justice Frankfurter): "We think that State power is amply respected if it is qualified merely to the extent of requiring it to withhold execution of that portion of its decree requiring retransfer of the physical properties until steps are ordered to be taken, with all deliberate speed, to enable the [Federal Communications] Commission to deal with new applications in connection with the station." Cf. The Hound of Heaven, 1 The Works of Francis Thompson 107 (1913): "But with unhurrying chase,/ and unperturbed pace,/ Deliberate speed, majestic instancy. . . ."

[7] See Bernard Schwartz, Super Chief: Earl Warren and His Supreme Court—A Judicial Biography 124 (Unabridged ed. 1983): "In his later years, Warren concluded that he had been sold a bill of goods when Frankfurter induced him to use the phrase. It would have been better, he came to believe, to have ordered desegregation forthwith. By then, however, Black's prediction of the 'glacial' pace of desegregation had proved, if anything, overoptimistic. The Justices had, to be sure, not expected enthusiastic compliance by the South. But the extent of opposition was something that had not been foreseen. Looking back, Warren, at least, felt that much of the defiance could have been avoided if the South had not been led to believe that 'deliberate speed' would countenance indefinite delay. When a comparable problem arose in 1964 in connection with enforcement of the 'one man-one vote' principle in legislative apportionments, the Chief did not hesitate to urge immediate enforcement, regardless of the problems in individual states in adapting to the new rule." When Warren first arrived at the Supreme Court, it had separate restrooms for blacks. One of the first things he did was to end that practice.

Little Rock high school. President Eisenhower dispatched federal troops to effect the admission of the blacks and to control the large crowds. The school board later asked for a two-and-one-half-year postponement of the desegregation plan "because of extreme public hostility," engendered largely by the governor and other state officials. The district court granted the delay, but the court of appeals reversed, and the Supreme Court affirmed the appellate decision. "The constitutional rights of respondents are not to be sacrificed or yielded to the violence of the Governor and Legislature," and "law and order are not here preserved by depriving the Negro children of their constitutional rights." The district court, when it considers all the factors to determine "deliberate speed," should exclude "hostility to racial desegregation.

The National Guard escorted the nine black children into a hate-filled Arkansas high school. The first was Elizabeth Eckford. The vice principal for girls at Central High School wrote in her diary, "Saw the awful pictures—the dignity of the rejected Negro girl, the obscenity of the faces of her tormentors." Other diary entries: "October 28: Elizabeth shoved in hall. November 20: Elizabeth jostled in gym. November 21: Elizabeth hit with paper clip. December 10: Elizabeth kicked. December 18: Elizabeth punched. January 10: Elizabeth shoved on the stairs. January 14: Elizabeth knocked flat. January 22: Elizabeth spat upon. January 29: Elizabeth attacked with spitballs. January 31: Elizabeth asks grandfather to take her home after girls serenade her with humiliating songs in gym class. February 4: Elizabeth has soda bottle thrown at her. February 14: Elizabeth attacked with rock-filled snowballs. March 7: Elizabeth hit by egg. March 12: Elizabeth hit by tomato. 'She said that except for some broken glass thrown at her during lunch, she really had had a wonderful day.' " Another was Minnijean Brown, whom the school later expelled for calling one of her tormentors, "white trash." Brown described how the students "spill ink on your clothes, they call you 'nigger,' they just keep bothering you every five minutes."[8]

3. *Goss v. Board of Education*, 373 U.S. 683, 83 S.Ct. 1405, 10 L.Ed.2d 632 (1963), invalidated a portion of a desegregation plan that allowed a student to transfer from a school in which he was a member of a racial minority to a school where he was in the racial majority. Over nine years had passed since *Brown I*, and thus "the context in which we must interpret and apply this language ['all deliberate speed'] has been significantly altered."

---

[8]   David Margolick, Elizabeth and Hazel: Two Women of Little Rock 65, 132–34 (Yale U. Press 2011).

Griffin v. School Board of Prince Edward County, 377 U.S. 218, 84 S.Ct. 1226, 12 L.Ed.2d 256 (1964), had been one of the cases that *Brown II* had remanded for further relief. Virginia responded in various ways, such as cutting off state funds to public schools where whites and blacks attended together, closing such schools, paying tuition grants to children in nonsectarian private schools, and extending state retirement benefits to teachers in newly created private schools. After the state court invalidated the laws cutting off state funds and closing mixed schools, the state adopted other tactics, including a new tuition grant program and repeal of the compulsory attendance laws. The supervisors of Prince Edward County then responded to a court desegregation order by refusing to levy any school taxes for the 1959–1960 school year because, they said, they were confronted with the court decree. The public schools in that county were closed and remained closed. Meanwhile, a private school for white children opened in 1960, supported primarily by state and county tuition grants. The county also provided property tax credits for contributions to any "nonprofit, nonsectarian private school." Blacks were without formal schooling from 1959 to 1963.

The Supreme Court affirmed the district court's order enjoining the county from paying tuition grants or giving tax credits so long as public schools remained closed. The Court added that the district court "may, if necessary to prevent further racial discrimination, require the Supervisors to exercise the power that is theirs to levy taxes to raise funds adequate to reopen, operate, and maintain without racial discrimination a public school system in Prince Edward County like that operated in other counties in Virginia."

The Court added: "An order of this kind is within the court's power if required to assure these petitioners that their constitutional rights will no longer be denied them. The time for mere 'deliberate speed' has run out, and that phrase can no longer justify denying these Prince Edward County school children their constitutional rights to an education equal to that afforded by the public schools in other parts of Virginia."

Some states responded to *Brown II* by instituting desegregation at a pace of one grade a year. After *Griffin* the Court invalidated such plans as too slow. *Rogers v. Paul*, 382 U.S. 198, 86 S.Ct. 358, 15 L.Ed.2d 265 (1965). Other states responded with a "freedom-of-choice" plan, allowing a pupil to choose his or her own public school. *Green v. New Kent County School Board*, 391 U.S. 430, 88 S.Ct. 1689, 20 L.Ed.2d 716 (1968), invalidated such a plan. The county for many years had a history of a dual school system extending to every facet of school operations, "faculty, staff, transportation, extracurricular activities and faculties." Given the county's long history of segregation it was insufficient for the board merely to open its white school to blacks and its black school to whites. Under *Brown II,* school boards "such as the respondent then operating state-controlled dual systems were ... clearly charged with the affirmative duty to take whatever steps might be necessary to convert to a unitary system in which racial discrimination would be eliminated root and branch."

The Court did not invalidate all freedom-of-choice plans; however, given the history of the case before it, such a plan was unacceptable. "The burden on a school board today is to come forward with a plan that promises realistically to work, and promises realistically to work *now*." (emphasis in original). The plan must promise "meaningful and immediate progress towards disestablishing state-imposed segregation." The history of the freedom-of-choice plan in this county offered no such promise of "immediate progress." The black school enrolled 85% of all the black children but not one white. Other plans, such as zoning, must be used if they are a "speedier" means of converting to a unitary school system. The board must fashion steps "to convert promptly to a system without a 'white' school and a 'Negro' school, but just schools."

In *Carter v. Western Feliciana Parish School Board,* 396 U.S. 290, 90 S.Ct. 608, 24 L.Ed.2d 477 (1970) (*per curiam*), the Court reversed a Fifth Circuit opinion that had allowed a one-semester delay in the implementation of a desegregation order because the order had been issued in the middle of the school year. Two members of the Court thought that the time between a finding of noncompliance and the effect of the remedy, including any judicial review, should not exceed eight weeks. Four others thought that even that delay was too long.

4. In *Swann v. Charlotte-Mecklenburg Board of Education,* 402 U.S. 1, 91 S.Ct. 1267, 28 L.Ed.2d 554 (1971), the Supreme Court, per Chief Justice Burger, carefully examined the broad range of judicial alternatives to eliminate the last vestiges of a school system long segregated by law. Given a history of such segregation, if it is possible to identify a white or a black school "simply by reference to the racial composition of teachers and staff, the quality of school buildings and equipment, or the organization of sports activities, a *prima facie* case of violation of substantive constitutional rights under the Equal

Protection Clause is shown." The first remedial responsibility is to eliminate any invidious racial distinctions. With respect to transportation, supporting personnel, extracurricular activities, maintenance of buildings, and the distribution of equipment, the corrective action is straightforward. "Something more must be said, however, as to faculty assignment and new school construction."

As to the assignment of teachers, the Court rejected the argument that district courts should not use their equity power to order teacher assignments to achieve faculty desegregation. In order to achieve a plan that "promises realistically to work *now*," the district court need not be color-blind in assigning teachers, given the past history of legal segregation.

The Court recognized that some school boards made decisions regarding the construction of new schools and the closing of old ones, as a "potent weapon" to create or maintain segregated schools, *e.g.*, by closing schools as they become racially mixed and by building new schools in white suburban areas farthest from black population centers. Such choices are evidence of the existence of legally imposed school segregation, and the district court has the responsibility to assure that future school construction and abandonment do not perpetuate or reestablish a dual school system. Then the Court turned to the assignment of students:

> 1.   *Racial balance.* The district court, said *Swann*, may not require as a substantive constitutional right any particular degree of racial balance. Every school need not always reflect the racial composition of the school system as a whole. Yet, the district court did not err when it sought a 71–29 ratio of white to black in each school, reflecting the fact that the pupils of the school system of 107 schools were approximately 71% white and 29% black. Under the circumstances of this case, the "limited use made of mathematical ratios" was within the court's equitable discretion. "Awareness of the racial composition of the whole school system is likely to be a useful starting point in shaping a remedy to correct past constitutional violations."

> 2.   *One-race schools.* That there are schools primarily or totally of one race in a school system is not evidence of segregation imposed by law, but if the district has a history of such segregation, a presumption against such schools is justified. The school system converting to a unitary system has "the burden of showing that

such school assignments are genuinely nondiscriminatory" and not the product of present or past discrimination. Also, an "optional majority-to-minority transfer provision has long been recognized as a useful part of every desegregation plan."

3. *Remedial altering of attendance zones.* "[O]ne of the principal tools employed by school planners and by courts to break up the dual school system has been a frank—and sometimes—drastic gerrymandering of school districts and attendance zones. An additional step was pairing, 'clustering,' or 'grouping' to accomplish the transfer of Negro students out of formerly segregated Negro schools and transfer of white students to formerly all-Negro schools. More often than not, these zones are neither compact nor contiguous; indeed they may be on opposite ends of the city. As an interim corrective measure, this cannot be said to be beyond the broad remedial powers of a court." In this area the Supreme Court will rely "on the informed judgment of the district courts in the first instance and on courts of appeals."

4. *Transportation of students.* "Bus transportation has been an integral part of the public education system for years, [and the] importance of bus transportation as a normal and accepted tool of educational policy is readily discernible in this and the companion case. . . . In these circumstances, we find no basis for holding that the local school authorities may not be required to employ bus transportation as one tool of desegregation. Desegregation plans cannot be limited to the walk-in school. An objection to transportation of students may have validity when the time or distance of travel is so great as to either risk the health of the children or significantly impinge on the educational process."

5. The following year the Court further broadened lower court powers in two cases decided the same day, *Wright v. Council of the City of Emporia*, 407 U.S. 451, 92 S.Ct. 2196, 33 L.Ed.2d 51 (1972), and *United States v. Scotland Neck City Board of Education*, 407 U.S. 484, 92 S.Ct. 2214, 33 L.Ed.2d 75 (1972). The first case was a five-to-four opinion; the four dissenters in the first case concurred in the result in the second. In both cases the Court upheld lower court orders enjoining, under the facts of those cases, state or local officials from carving out a new school district from an existing one when the district had not yet completed the process of dismantling a system of legally enforced

school segregation, and the creation of the new districts would have the effect of hindering the process of desegregation.

In *Emporia,* the lower court found that "if Emporia were allowed to establish an independent system, Negroes remaining in the county schools would be deprived of what *Brown II* promised them: a school system in which all vestiges of enforced racial segregation have been eliminated." The Supreme Court said, "Only when it became clear—15 years after our decision in *Brown I*—that segregation in the county system was finally to be abolished, did Emporia attempt to take its children out of the county system. Under these circumstances, the power of the District Court to enjoin Emporia's withdrawal from that system need not rest upon an independent constitutional violation."

In *Scotland Neck,* the Court noted that the respondents' primary argument in support of carving out a new school district from an old one "was that separation of the Scotland Neck schools from those of Halifax County was necessary to avoid 'white flight' by Scotland Neck residents into private schools that would follow complete dismantling of the dual school system. . . . But while this development may be cause for deep concern to the respondents, it cannot . . . be accepted as a reason for achieving anything less than complete uprooting of the dual public school system."†

5.2.3　Motive, Purpose, and Effect

WASHINGTON V. DAVIS
426 U.S. 229, 96 S.Ct. 2040, 48 L.Ed.2d 597 (1976)

JUSTICE WHITE delivered the opinion of the Court.

This case involves the validity of a qualifying test administered to applicants for positions as police officers in the District of Columbia Metropolitan Police Department. The test was sustained by the District Court but invalidated by the Court of Appeals. We are in agreement with the District Court and hence reverse the judgment of the Court of Appeals.

---

†　Compare. *Palmore v. Sidoti,* 466 U.S. 429, 104 S.Ct. 1879, 80 L.Ed.2d 412 (1984), holding that if a state court divests a natural mother of custody of her infant because of remarriage to a person of a different race, there is a violation of equal protection. The state court had referred to the child's peer pressures and social stigmatization: "The Constitution cannot control such prejudices but neither can it tolerate them. . . . 'Public officials sworn to uphold the Constitution may not avoid a constitutional duty by bowing to the hypothetical effects of private racial prejudice that they assume to be both widely and deeply held.' "

[The test, known as "Test 21," is used generally throughout the federal service and was developed by the Civil Service Commission to test "verbal ability, vocabulary, reading and comprehension." The court of appeals declared] that lack of discriminatory intent in designing and administering Test 21 was irrelevant; the critical fact was rather that a far greater proportion of blacks—four times as many—failed the test than did whites. This disproportionate impact, standing alone and without regard to whether it indicated a discriminatory purpose, was held sufficient to establish a constitutional violation, absent proof by petitioners that the test was an adequate measure of job performance in addition to being an indicator of probable success in the training program, a burden which the court ruled petitioners had failed to discharge. That the Department had made substantial efforts to recruit blacks was held beside the point. . . .

The central purpose of the Equal Protection Clause of the Fourteenth Amendment is the prevention of official conduct discriminating on the basis of race. It is also true that the Due Process Clause of the Fifth Amendment contains an equal protection component prohibiting the United States from invidiously discriminating between individuals or groups. *Bolling v. Sharpe*. But our cases have not embraced the proposition that a law or other official act, without regard to whether it reflects a racially discriminatory purpose, is unconstitutional *solely* because it has a racially disproportionate impact.

The school desegregation cases have also adhered to the basic equal protection principle that the invidious quality of a law claimed to be racially discriminatory must ultimately be traced to a racially discriminatory purpose. That there are both predominantly black and predominantly white schools in a community is not alone violative of the Equal Protection Clause. The essential element of *de jure* segregation is "a current condition of segregation resulting from intentional state action." *Keyes v. School Dist. No. 1*. "The differentiating factor between *de jure* segregation and so-called *de facto* segregation . . . is *purpose* or *intent* to segregate." . . . This is not to say that the necessary discriminatory racial purpose must be express or appear on the face of the statute, or that a law's disproportionate impact is irrelevant in cases involving Constitution-based claims of racial discrimination. A statute, otherwise neutral on its face, must not be applied so as invidiously to discriminate on the basis of race. *Yick Wo v. Hopkins*. . . .

Necessarily, an invidious discriminatory purpose may often be inferred from the totality of the relevant facts, including the fact, if it is true, that the law bears more heavily on one race than another. It is also not infrequently true that the discriminatory impact—in the jury cases for example, the total or seriously disproportionate exclusion of Negroes from jury venires—may for all practical purposes demonstrate unconstitutionality because in various circumstances the discrimination is very difficult to explain on nonracial grounds. Nevertheless, we have not held that a law, neutral on its face and serving ends otherwise within the power of government to pursue, is invalid under the Equal Protection Clause simply because it may affect a greater proportion of one race than of another. Disproportionate impact is not irrelevant, but it is not the sole touchstone of an invidious racial discrimination forbidden by the Constitution. Standing alone, it does not trigger the rule, that racial classifications are to be subjected to the strictest scrutiny and are justifiable only by the weightiest of considerations. . . .

As an initial matter, we have difficulty understanding how a law establishing a racially neutral qualification for employment is nevertheless racially discriminatory and denies "any person . . . equal protection of the laws" simply because a greater proportion of Negroes fail to qualify than members of other racial or ethnic groups. . . . Test 21, which is administered generally to prospective Government employees, concededly seeks to ascertain whether those who take it have acquired a particular level of verbal skill; and it is untenable that the Constitution prevents the Government from seeking modestly to upgrade the communicative abilities of its employees rather than to be satisfied with some lower level of competence, particularly where the job requires special ability to communicate orally and in writing. Respondents, as Negroes, could no more successfully claim that the test denied them equal protection than could white applicants who also failed. The conclusion would not be different in the face of proof that more Negroes than whites had been disqualified by Test 21. That other Negroes also failed to score well would, alone, not demonstrate that respondents individually were being denied equal protection of the laws by the application of an otherwise valid qualifying test being administered to prospective police recruits.

Nor on the facts of the case before us would the disproportionate impact of Test 21 warrant the conclusion that it is a purposeful device to discriminate against Negroes and hence an infringement of the constitutional rights of respondents as well as other black applicants. As we have said, the test is neutral on its face and rationally may be said to serve a purpose the Government is constitutionally empowered to pursue. Even agreeing with the District Court that the differential racial effect of Test 21 called for further inquiry, we think the District Court correctly held that the affirmative efforts of the Metropolitan Police Department to recruit black officers, the changing racial composition of the recruit classes and of the force in general, and the relationship of the test to the training program negated any inference that the Department discriminated on the basis of race or that "a police officer qualifies on the color of his skin rather than ability."

Under Title VII, Congress provided that when hiring and promotion practices disqualifying substantially disproportionate numbers of blacks are challenged, discriminatory purpose need not be proved, and that it is an insufficient response to demonstrate some rational basis for the challenged practices. It is necessary, in addition, that they be "validated" in terms of job performance in any one of several ways, perhaps by ascertaining the minimum skill, ability, or potential necessary for the position at issue and determining whether the qualifying tests are appropriate for the selection of qualified applicants for the job in question. However this process proceeds, it involves a more probing judicial review of, and less deference to, the seemingly reasonable acts of administrators and executives than is appropriate under the Constitution where special racial impact, without discriminatory purpose, is claimed. We are not disposed to adopt this more rigorous [statutory] standard for the purposes of applying the Fifth and the Fourteenth Amendments in cases such as this.

A rule that a statute designed to serve neutral ends is nevertheless invalid, absent compelling justification, if in practice it benefits or burdens one race more than another would be far reaching and would raise serious questions about, and perhaps invalidate, a whole range of tax, welfare, public service, regulatory, and licensing statutes that may be more burdensome to the poor and to the average black than to the more affluent white. Given that rule, such consequences would perhaps be likely to follow. However, in our view, extension of the rule beyond those areas where it is already applicable by reason of statute, such as in the field of public employment, should await legislative prescription.

JUSTICE STEVENS, concurring:

Frequently the most probative evidence of intent will be objective evidence of what actually happened rather than evidence describing the subjective state of mind of the actor. For normally the actor is presumed to have intended the natural consequences of his deeds. This is particularly true in the case of governmental action which is frequently the product of compromise, of collective decisionmaking, and of mixed motivation. It is unrealistic, on the one hand, to require the victim of alleged discrimination to uncover the actual subjective intent of the decisionmaker or, conversely, to invalidate otherwise legitimate action simply because an improper motive affected the deliberation of a participant in the decisional process. A law conscripting clerics should not be invalidated because an atheist voted for it. . . . On the other hand, when the disproportion is as dramatic as in *Yick Wo v. Hopkins*, it really does not matter whether the standard is phrased in terms of purpose or effect.

. . . I do not rely at all on the evidence of good-faith efforts to recruit black police officers. In my judgment, neither those efforts nor the subjective good faith of the District administration, would save Test 21 if it were otherwise invalid. There are two reasons why I am convinced that the challenge to Test 21 is insufficient. First, the test serves the neutral and legitimate purpose of requiring all applicants to meet a uniform minimum standard of literacy. Reading ability is manifestly relevant to the police function, there is no evidence that the required passing grade was set at an arbitrarily high level, and there is sufficient disparity among high schools and high school graduates to justify the use of a separate uniform test. Second, the same test is used throughout the federal service. The applicants for employment in the District of Columbia Police Department represent such a small fraction of the total number of persons who have taken the test that their experience is of minimal probative value in assessing the neutrality of the test itself. That evidence, without more, is not sufficient to overcome the presumption that a test which is this widely used by the Federal Government is in fact neutral in its effect as well as its "purpose" as that term is used in constitutional adjudication. . . .

[The dissenting opinion of BRENNAN, J., joined by MARSHALL, J., is omitted. They dissented on a statutory issue. STEWART, J., joined the opinion of the Court only as to the constitutional issue.]

NOTES

1. *Rogers v. Lodge,* 458 U.S. 613, 102 S.Ct. 3272, 73 L.Ed.2d 1012 (1982), upheld a trial court ruling that the at-large system of voting in a Georgia county violated the Fourteenth Amendment rights of blacks because it was "maintained for invidious purposes" even though it was racially neutral when adopted. Therefore, the trial court divided the county into five districts for purposes of electing County Commissioners. The majority reviewed the trial court's findings and ruled that they supported the ultimate finding of intentional discrimination.

   Stevens wrote a separate dissenting opinion, warning that "in the long run constitutional adjudication that is premised on a case-by-case appraisal of the subjective intent of local decisionmakers cannot possibly satisfy the requirement of impartial administration of the law that is embodied in the

Equal Protection Clause of the Fourteenth Amendment." Justices Powell and Rehnquist dissented because they believed that the evidence of intentional discrimination marshaled in the case was insufficient.

2. In *Village of Arlington Heights v. Metropolitan Housing Development Corp.*, 429 U.S. 252, 97 S.Ct. 555, 50 L.Ed.2d 450 (1977), a nonprofit real estate developer contracted to purchase a tract of land to build racially integrated low and moderate income housing. It sued, alleging that local authorities' refusal to change the tract from a single-family to a multi-family classification was racially discriminatory. The Court held that the plaintiffs failed to prove that racially discriminatory intent or purpose was a motivating factor in the rezoning decision. In the course of this decision, the Court dropped a significant footnote that explained the plaintiff's burden of proof:

> Proof that the decision by the Village was motivated in part by a racially discriminatory purpose would not necessarily have required invalidation of the challenged decision. Such proof would, however, have shifted to the Village the burden of establishing that the same decision would have resulted even had the impermissible purpose not been considered. If this were established, the complaining party in a case of this kind no longer fairly could attribute the injury complained of to improper consideration of a discriminatory purpose. In such circumstances, there would be no justification for judicial interference with the challenged decision. But in this case respondents failed to make the required threshold showing.

HUNTER V. UNDERWOOD
471 U.S. 222, 105 S.Ct. 1916, 85 L.Ed.2d 222 (1985)

JUSTICE REHNQUIST delivered the opinion of the Court.

We are required in this case to decide the constitutionality of Art. VIII, § 182, of the Alabama Constitution of 1901, which provides for the disenfranchisement of persons convicted of, among other offenses, "any crime . . . involving moral turpitude." . . . Edwards and Underwood sued . . . for a declaration invalidating § 182 as applied to persons convicted of crimes not punishable by imprisonment in the state penitentiary (misdemeanors) and an injunction against its future application to such persons. . . .

The predecessor to § 182 was Art. VIII, § 3, of the Alabama Constitution of 1875, which denied persons "convicted of treason, embezzlement of public funds, malfeasance in office, larceny, bribery, or other crime punishable by imprisonment in the penitentiary" the right to register, vote or hold public office. These offenses were largely, if not entirely, felonies. The drafters of § 182, which was adopted by the 1901 convention, expanded the list of enumerated crimes substantially [and] retained the general felony provision—"any crime punishable by imprisonment in the penitentiary"—but also added a new catch-all provision covering "any . . . crime involving moral turpitude." This latter phrase is not defined, but it was subsequently interpreted by the Alabama Supreme Court to mean an act that is "immoral in itself, regardless of the fact whether it is punishable by law. The doing of the act itself, and not its prohibition by statute fixes, the moral turpitude." *Pippin v. State*, 197 Ala. 613, 616, 73 So. 340, 342 (1916) (quoting *Fort v. Brinkley*, 87 Ark. 400, 112 S.W. 1084 (1908)). . . . Various minor nonfelony offenses such as presenting a worthless check and petty larceny fall within the sweep of § 182, while more serious nonfelony offenses such as second-degree manslaughter, assault on a police officer, mailing pornography, and aiding the escape of a misdemeanant do not because they are neither enumerated in § 182 nor considered crimes involving moral turpitude. It is alleged, and the Court of Appeals found, that the crimes selected for inclusion in § 182 were believed by the delegates to be more frequently committed by blacks.

Section 182 on its face is racially neutral, applying equally to anyone convicted of one of the enumerated crimes or a crime falling within one of the catch-all provisions. Appellee Edwards nonetheless claims that the provision has had a racially discriminatory impact. [T]he Court of Appeals implicitly found the evidence of discriminatory impact indisputable:

> The registrars' expert estimated that by January 1903 section 182 had disfranchised approximately ten times as many blacks as whites. This disparate effect persists today. In Jefferson and Montgomery Counties blacks are by even the most modest estimates at least 1.7 times as likely as whites to suffer disfranchisement under section 182 for the commission of nonprison offenses.

. . . Presented with a neutral state law that produces disproportionate effects along racial lines, the Court [must] determine whether the law violates the Equal Protection Clause of the Fourteenth Amendment: "[O]fficial action will not be held unconstitutional solely because it results in a racially disproportionate impact. . . . Proof of racially discriminatory intent or purpose is required to show a violation of the Equal Protection Clause." See *Washington v. Davis*. Once racial discrimination is shown to have been a "substantial" or "motivating" factor behind enactment of the law, the burden shifts to the law's defenders to demonstrate that the law would have been enacted without this factor.

Proving the motivation behind official action is often a problematic undertaking. See *Rogers v. Lodge*. When we move from an examination of a board of county commissioners such as was involved in *Rogers* to a body the size of the Alabama Constitutional Convention of 1901, the difficulties in determining the actual motivations of the various legislators that produced a given decision increase. With respect to Congress, the Court said in *United States v. O'Brien*, 391 U.S. 367, 88 S.Ct. 1673, 20 L.Ed.2d 672 (1968)[§ 7.9.1]:

> Inquiries into congressional motives or purposes are a hazardous matter. When the issue is simply the interpretation of legislation, the Court will look to statements by legislators for guidance as to the purpose of the legislature, because the benefit to sound decision-making in this circumstance is thought sufficient to risk the possibility of misreading Congress' purpose. It is entirely a different matter when we are asked to void a statute that is, under well-settled criteria, constitutional on its face, on the basis of what fewer than a handful of Congressmen said about it. What motivates one legislator to make a speech about a statute is not necessarily what motivates scores of others to enact it, and the stakes are sufficiently high for us to eschew guesswork.

But the sort of difficulties of which the Court spoke in *O'Brien* do not obtain in this case. Although understandably no "eye witnesses" to the 1901 proceedings testified, testimony and opinions of historians were offered and received without objection. These showed that the Alabama Constitutional Convention of 1901 was part of a movement that swept the post-Reconstruction South to disenfranchise blacks. The delegates to the all-white convention were not secretive about their purpose. John B. Knox, president of the convention, stated in his opening address:

> And what is it that we want to do? Why it is within the limits imposed by the Federal Constitution, to establish white supremacy in this State."
> 1 Official Proceedings of the Constitutional Convention of the State of Alabama, May 21st, 1901, to September 3rd, 1901, p. 8 (1940).

. . . The evidence of legislative intent available to the courts below consisted of the proceedings of the convention, several historical studies, and the testimony of two expert historians. Having reviewed this evidence, we are persuaded that the Court of Appeals was correct in its assessment. That court's opinion presents a thorough analysis of the evidence and demonstrates conclusively that § 182 was enacted with the intent of disenfranchising blacks. We see little purpose in repeating that factual analysis here. At oral argument in this Court appellants' counsel essentially conceded this point, stating: "I would be very blind and naive [to] try to come up and stand before this Court and say that race was not a factor in the enactment of Section 182; that race did not play a part in the decisions of those people who were at the constitutional convention of 1901 and I won't do that."

In their brief to this Court, appellants maintain on the basis of their expert's testimony that the real purpose behind § 182 was to disenfranchise poor whites as well as blacks. The Southern Democrats, in their view, sought in this way to stem the resurgence of Populism which threatened their power. . . . Even were we to accept this explanation as correct, it hardly saves § 182 from invalidity. The explanation concedes both that discrimination against blacks, as well as against poor whites, was a motivating factor for the provision and that § 182 certainly would not have been adopted by the convention or ratified by the electorate in the absence of the racially discriminatory motivation. [A]n additional purpose to discriminate against poor whites would not render nugatory the purpose to discriminate against all blacks, and it is beyond peradventure that the latter was a "but-for" motivation for the enactment of § 182.

Appellants contend that the State has a legitimate interest in denying the franchise to those convicted of crimes involving moral turpitude, and that § 182 should be sustained on that ground. The Court of Appeals convincingly demonstrated that such a purpose simply was not a motivating factor of the 1901 convention. . . .

At oral argument in this Court, the State suggested that, regardless of the original purpose of § 182, events occurring in the succeeding 80 years had legitimated the provision. . . . Without deciding whether § 182 would be valid if enacted today without any impermissible motivation, we simply observe that its original enactment was motivated by a desire to discriminate against blacks on account of race and the section continues to this day to have that effect. As such, it violates equal protection. . . .

Finally, appellants contend that the State is authorized by the Tenth Amendment and § 2 of the Fourteenth Amendment to deny the franchise to persons who commit misdemeanors involving moral turpitude. For the reasons we have stated, the enactment of § 182 violated the Fourteenth Amendment, and the Tenth Amendment cannot save legislation prohibited by the subsequently enacted Fourteenth Amendment. The single remaining question is whether § 182 is excepted from the operation of the Equal Protection Clause of § 1 of the Fourteenth Amendment by the "other crime" provision of § 2 of that Amendment. Without again considering the implicit authorization of § 2 to deny the vote to citizens "for participation in rebellion, or other crime," we are confident that § 2 was not designed to permit the purposeful racial discrimination attending the enactment and operation of § 182 which otherwise violates § 1 of the Fourteenth Amendment. . . .

The judgment of the Court of Appeals is

Affirmed.

JUSTICE POWELL took no part in the consideration or decision of this case.

5.2.4   Affirmative Action/Reverse Discrimination

Does the Constitution allow affirmative action, or reverse discrimination—that is, the use of racial classification—in order to help a racial minority? Or, is the Constitution color-blind? If the state enacts a law that uses a racial classification to help one racial group to enjoy a limited resource (*e.g.*, admission to college), does that not mean that it is using race to hurt another racial group? The best way to approach this problem may be to distinguish several types of cases.

First, there are the school desegregation cases—kindergarten through 12th grade—where courts often use race in fashioning a remedy. However, in those cases, the court first judicially determines that the school board has violated the equal protection clause. Then, the Court looks at race to make sure that the burdens of discrimination are faced equally (*e.g.*, not only blacks should be forced to ride the school bus). The court must look at race to see if the school desegregation plan has in fact eliminated segregation root and branch. Because the obligation of the courts is to desegregate now (the time for "all deliberate speed" has passed), courts may look at the race of the teachers and students to make sure the school is desegregating. Finally, these plans deprive no one of going to a school. Not every schoolchild may go to the closest neighborhood public school, but everyone does go to a public school.

Employment discrimination cases are also different in kind from the typical reverse discrimination case. In the employment discrimination case, a court first finds that a state's past discrimination (in hiring police, teachers, firefighters, etc.) has prejudiced a racial minority (*e.g.*, blacks) in the hiring process. When the court orders that the employer give retroactive seniority to put the blacks where they would have been if no discrimination had occurred, the white employees are hurt, even though these employees did not cause the racial discrimination. However, a white who lose his place in the seniority line has benefitted from the past discrimination. The intent of the court order is to assure that the whites gain no advantage by the past wrong; whites lose only to the extent that the court order places them where they would have been in the seniority line *if* no racial discrimination had occurred.

When the Court deals with affirmative action, or reverse discrimination, it deals with a different fact setting. An administrative or legislative body decides to (1) set aside a certain number of places in a state school of higher education, or (2) set aside a certain number of contracts in a government procurement program, or (3) reserve a certain number of places in a government housing development for members of one or more racial groups. The racial groups include blacks and often other racial minorities, such as Hispanic, American Indian, Aleuts, etc. The majority racial group includes all those not in the racial minority group, such as whites, Asians and any other group that the state does not as part of the favored racial minority. For simplicity, we often refer only to blacks and whites, but we should understand that there are other racial or ethnic groups. There is no court-approved list of minorities; instead, the agency implementing the affirmative action program creates the list of the favored minorities. In all cases, there is no judicial finding of past racial discrimination. In addition, in all cases, the administrators or legislators are passing out a scarce resource (a limited number of university admissions, a limited number of jobs as firefighter) on the basis of race. The affirmative action plan burdens other racial groups (*e.g.*, whites, Asians) because of their race, even though they did not cause or take advantage of the past wrongs.

Sometimes the percentage reserved for the racial minority is called a "goal," and sometimes, a "quota." Typically, the Court uses "quota" to mean that that the government entity (the state university, the fire department, etc.) has reserved a set number of spaces (let us say, 10%) for racial minorities. The racial majority (whites) can compete for other spaces but only the racial minority can compete for the 10%. In the case of a "goal," the theory is that all races can compete for all places, but the employer has a goal of, *e.g.*, 10%, for racial minorities. In the case of a goal, the theory is that the school takes into account a host of factors (including race) in granting admission; a member of the non-favored race may be such a good violin player that it enough to override the interest in racial diversity.

The Supreme Court has had difficulty with this issue although a majority does now conclude that some affirmative action programs are constitutional and subject to strict scrutiny. First, there is the case of higher education. Universities already pick their students. Unless a school has "open admissions" (accept all who apply), not everyone can attend any particular university. As we shall see, a majority of the Court now allows universities to take into account race as part of a program to secure a diverse group of students, although the Court majority has now said that these plans cannot continue forever, but should end about 2028. (*Grutter v. Bollinger* (2003), which we read in this section, the majority said that affirmative action must meet the strict requirements of that case and should end in 25 years.) A majority of the Court has also limited affirmative action of higher education.

In the case of affirmative action in employment, the Court, after several false starts, has now made it very difficult if not virtually impossible for an affirmative action case to survive Supreme Court review.

To be distinguished from this type of affirmative action is the situation in which the set-aside for racial minorities is not only a floor but also a ceiling. *Otero v. New York Housing Authority,* 484 F.2d 1122 (2d Cir. 1973), concerned such a situation. A low-cost public housing project set a "benign quota" for blacks to prevent reaching what managers called the "tipping point." The Housing Project contended that once a certain percentage of blacks populate a housing project, the blacks tip the racial balance and the departure of whites (the "white flight") is accelerated. The Housing Authority therefore placed a quota on blacks to keep the housing project integrated. The Second Circuit held that the Housing Authority "may limit the number of apartments to be made available to persons of white or non-white races, including minority groups, where it can show that such action is essential to promote a racially balanced community and to avoid concentrated racial pockets that will result in a segregated community." The parties did not seek review before the Supreme Court. The Court, not since *Brown v. Board of Education* ever approved an *Otero*-type situation, where the government uses race to burden racial minorities. *Otero* justified a government program that denied a black family housing because family is black! And, it did that so that the white racists (who liked subsidized housing but would reject it if the housing project has "too many" blacks) would not leave. This case illustrates the risk whenever the government can pass out benefits or burdens on the basis of color.

The first case we read is *Bakke*. Although it is decades old, it still lays out the arguments for and against affirmative action in the context of higher education. Thus, it remains relevant.

5.2.4.1 Higher Education

REGENTS OF THE UNIVERSITY OF CALIFORNIA V. BAKKE
438 U.S. 265, 98 S.Ct. 2733, 57 L.Ed.2d 750 (1978)

[The University of California at Davis opened up a medical school in 1968. It never discriminated on the basis of race and initially had no special admissions program for minorities. The first class contained three Asians but no blacks, Mexican-Americans, or American Indians. Then the school created a special admissions program and special committee to administer it. The 1974 application form asked candidates whether they wished to be considered as "Blacks," "Chicanos," "Asians," or "American Indians." If the candidate said yes, the application was sent to the special committee. When the overall class size was fifty, the "prescribed number" of special admissions candidates was eight. When the class size doubled to one hundred, the special admissions program doubled to sixteen. No white ever received admission through the special admissions process.

[Allan Bakke, a white male, applied to the Davis Medical School in both 1973 and 1974. In 1973 Bakke's application came late in the year, causing his rejection. After his rejection, Bakke wrote the associate dean and protested the special admissions program. In 1974 his faculty interviewer by coincidence was the associate dean, who gave Bakke the lowest of his six ratings. Again he was rejected and he filed suit. The California Supreme Court, relying only on the equal protection clause, ordered Bakke admitted.

[When the U.S. Supreme court heard the case, Chief Justice Burger and Justices Stewart, Rehnquist, and Stevens believed that the Davis program violated Title VI of the Civil Rights Act of 1964. These Justices therefore did not need to reach the constitutional issue. The other Justices believed that Title VI meant to prohibit only that racial discrimination which is forbidden by the equal protection clause. Thus, they reached the constitutional issues in separate opinions that drew no majority. Although Justice Powell expressed his belief that some affirmative action programs are constitutional, he concluded that Davis' particular affirmative action program was unconstitutional. Justice Powell's vote joined with the votes of Justices Burger, Stewart, Rehnquist, and Stevens to admit Bakke to the Medical School.]

MR. JUSTICE POWELL announced the judgment of the Court.

[T]he parties fight a sharp preliminary action over the proper characterization of the special admissions program. Petitioner prefers to view it as establishing a "goal" of minority representation in the Medical School. Respondent, echoing the courts below, labels it a racial quota. This semantic distinction is beside the point: The special admissions program is undeniably a classification based on race and ethnic background. To the extent that there existed a pool of at least minimally qualified minority applicants to fill the 16 special admissions seats, white applicants could compete only for 84 seats in the entering class, rather than the 100 open to minority applicants. Whether this limitation is described as a quota or a goal, it is a line drawn on the basis of race and ethnic status.

. . . The guarantee of equal protection cannot mean one thing when applied to one individual and something else when applied to a person of another color. If both are not accorded the same protection, then it is not equal. Nevertheless, petitioner argues that the court below erred in applying strict scrutiny to the special admissions program because white males, such as respondent, are not a "discrete and insular minority" requiring extraordinary protection from the majoritarian political process. This rationale, however, has never been invoked in our decisions as a prerequisite to subjecting racial or ethnic distinctions to strict scrutiny. . . . These characteristics may be relevant in deciding whether or not to add new types of classifications to the list of "suspect" categories or whether a particular classification survives close examination. Racial and ethnic classifications, however, are subject to stringent examination without regard to these additional characteristics. . . . Racial and ethnic distinctions of any sort are inherently suspect and thus call for the most exacting judicial examination. . . .

Petitioner urges us to adopt for the first time a more restrictive view of the Equal Protection Clause and hold that discrimination against members of the white "majority" cannot be suspect if its purpose can be characterized as "benign."[34] . . . It is far too late to argue that the guarantee of equal protection to

---

[34] In the view of Mr. Justice Brennan [et al.], the pliable notion of "stigma" is the crucial element in analyzing racial classifications. The Equal Protection Clause is not framed in terms of "stigma." Certainly the word has not clearly defined constitutional meaning. It reflects a subjective judgment that is standard-less. *All* state-imposed classifications that rearrange burdens and benefits on the basis of race are likely to be viewed with deep resentment by the individuals burdened. The denial to innocent persons of equal rights and opportunities may outrage those so deprived and therefore may be perceived as invidious. These individuals are likely to find little comfort in the notion that the deprivation they are asked to endure is merely the price of membership in the dominant majority and that its imposition is inspired by the supposedly benign purpose of aiding others. One should not lightly dismiss the inherent unfairness of, and the perception of mistreatment that accompanies, a system of allocating benefits and privileges on the basis of skin color and ethnic origin. Moreover, Mr. Justice Brennan [et al.] offer no principle for deciding whether preferential classifications reflect

all persons permits the recognition of special wards entitled to a degree of protection greater than that accorded others. . . .[35]

Once the artificial line of a "two-class theory" of the Fourteenth Amendment is put aside, the difficulties entailed in varying the level of judicial review according to a perceived "preferred" status of a particular racial or ethnic minority are intractable. The concepts of "majority" and "minority" necessarily reflect temporary arrangements and political judgments. [T]he white "majority" itself is composed of various minority groups, most of which can lay claim to a history of prior discrimination at the hands of the State and private individuals. Not all of these groups can receive preferential treatment and corresponding judicial tolerance of distinctions drawn in terms of race and nationality, for then the only "majority" left would be a new minority of white Anglo-Saxon Protestants. There is no principled basis for deciding which groups would merit "heightened judicial solicitude" and which would not. Courts would be asked to evaluate the extent of the prejudice and consequent harm suffered by various minority groups. Those whose societal injury is thought to exceed some arbitrary level of tolerability then would be entitled to preferential classifications at the expense of individuals belonging to other groups. Those classifications would be free from exacting judicial scrutiny. As these preferences began to have their desired effect, and the consequences of past discrimination were undone, new judicial rankings would be necessary. The kind of variable sociological and political analysis necessary to produce such rankings simply does not lie within the judicial competence—even if they otherwise were politically feasible and socially desirable.

Moreover, there are serious problems of justice connected with the idea of preference itself. First, it may not always be clear that a so-called preference is in fact benign. . . . Second, preferential programs may only reinforce common stereotypes holding that certain groups are unable to achieve success without special protection based on a factor having no relationship to individual worth.

---

a benign remedial purpose or a malevolent stigmatic classification, since they are willing in this case to accept more *post hoc* declarations by an isolated state entity—a medical school faculty—unadorned by particularized findings of past discrimination, to establish such a remedial purpose.

[35] Professor Bickel noted the self-contradiction of that view:

"The lesson of the great decisions of the Supreme Court and the lesson of contemporary history have been the same for at least a generation: discrimination on the basis of race is illegal, immoral, unconstitutional, inherently wrong, and destructive of democratic society. Now this is to be unlearned and we are told that this is not a matter of fundamental principle but only a matter of whose ox is gored. Those for whom racial equality was demanded are to be more equal than others. Having found support in the Constitution for equality, they now claim support for inequality under the same Constitution." A. Bickel, The Morality of Consent 133 (1975).

Third, there is a measure of inequity in forcing innocent persons in respondent's position to bear the burdens of redressing grievances not of their making.

By hitching the meaning of the Equal Protection Clause to these transitory considerations, we would be holding, as a constitutional principle, that judicial scrutiny of classifications touching on racial and ethnic background may vary with the ebb and flow of political forces. . . .

[I]n "order to justify the use of a suspect classification, a State must show that its purpose or interest is both constitutionally permissible and substantial, and that its use of the classification is 'necessary . . . to the accomplishment' of its purpose or the safeguarding of its interest." The special admissions program purports to serve the purposes of: (i) "reducing the historic deficit of traditionally disfavored minorities in medical schools and in the medical profession;" (ii) countering the effects of societal discrimination; (iii) increasing the number of physicians who will practice in communities currently underserved; and (iv) obtaining the educational benefits that flow from an ethnically diverse student body. It is necessary to decide which, if any, of these purposes is substantial enough to support the use of a suspect classification.

If petitioner's purpose is to assure within its student body some specified percentage of a particular group merely because of its race or ethnic origin, such a preferential purpose must be rejected not as insubstantial but as facially invalid. Preferring members of any one group for no reason other than race or ethnic origin is discrimination for its own sake. This the Constitution forbids.

. . . We have never approved a classification that aids persons perceived as members of relatively victimized groups at the expense of other innocent individuals in the absence of judicial, legislative, or administrative findings of constitutional or statutory violations. . . . Petitioner does not purport to have made, and is in no position to make, such findings. Its broad mission is education, not the formulation of any legislative policy or the adjudication of particular claims of illegality. . . .[45] Petitioner simply has not carried its burden of demonstrating that it must prefer members of particular ethnic groups over all other individuals in order to promote better health-care delivery to deprived citizens. Indeed, petitioner has not shown that its preferential classification is likely to have any significant effect on the problem.

---

[45] For example, the University is unable to explain its selection of only the four favored groups—Negroes, Mexican-Americans, American Indians, and Asians—for preferential treatment. The inclusion of the last group is especially curious in light of the substantial numbers of Asians admitted through the regular admissions process.

The fourth goal asserted by petitioner is the attainment of a diverse student body. This clearly is a constitutionally permissible goal for an institution of higher education. Academic freedom [is] a special concern of the First Amendment. The freedom of a university to make its own judgments as to education includes the selection of its student body. [I]n arguing that its universities must be accorded the right to select those students who will contribute the most to the "robust exchange of ideas," petitioner invokes a countervailing constitutional interest, that of the First Amendment. In this light, petitioner must be viewed as seeking to achieve a goal that is of paramount importance in the fulfillment of its mission.

. . . Ethnic diversity, however, is only one element in a range of factors a university properly may consider in attaining the goal of a heterogeneous student body. [T]he interest of diversity is compelling in the context of a university's admissions program, the question remains whether the program's racial classification is necessary to promote this interest.

[D]iversity that furthers a compelling state interest encompasses a far broader array of qualifications and characteristics of which racial or ethnic origin is but a single though important element. Petitioner's special admissions program, focused *solely* on ethnic diversity, would hinder rather than further attainment of genuine diversity. Nor would the state interest in genuine diversity be served by expanding petitioner's two-track system into a multitrack program with a prescribed number of seats set aside for each identifiable category of applicants. Indeed, it is inconceivable that a university would thus pursue the logic of petitioner's two-track program to the illogical end of insulating each category of applicants with certain desired qualifications from competition with all other applicants. The experience of other university admissions programs, which take race into account in achieving the educational diversity valued by the First Amendment, demonstrates that the assignment of a fixed number of places to a minority group is not a necessary means toward that end. An illuminating example is found in the Harvard College program:

> In recent years Harvard College has expanded the concept of diversity to include students from disadvantaged economic, racial and ethnic groups. . . . In practice, this new definition of diversity has meant that race has been a factor in some admission decisions. [T]he race of an applicant may tip the balance in his favor just as geographic origin or a life spent on a farm may tip the balance in other candidates' cases. A farm boy from Idaho can bring something to Harvard College that a Bostonian cannot offer. Similarly, a black student can usually bring

something that a white person cannot offer. [The] awareness [of the necessity of including more than a token number of black students] does not mean that the Committee sets a minimum number of blacks or of people from west of the Mississippi who are to be admitted.

In such an admissions program, race or ethnic background may be deemed a "plus" in a particular applicant's file, yet it does not insulate the individual from comparison with all other candidates for the available seats. The file of a particular black applicant may be examined for his potential contribution to diversity without the factor of race being decisive when compared, for example, with that of an applicant identified as an Italian-American if the latter is thought to exhibit qualities more likely to promote beneficial educational pluralism. Such qualities could include exceptional personal talents, unique work or service experience, leadership potential, maturity, demonstrated compassion, a history of overcoming disadvantage, ability to communicate with the poor, or other qualifications deemed important. . . .

This kind of program treats each applicant as an individual in the admissions process. The applicant who loses out on the last available seat to another candidate receiving a "plus" on the basis of ethnic background will not have been foreclosed from all consideration for that seat simply because he was not the right color or had the wrong surname. It would mean only that his combined qualifications, which may have included similar nonobjective factors, did not outweigh those of the other applicant. His qualifications would have been weighed fairly and competitively, and he would have no basis to complain of unequal treatment under the Fourteenth Amendment.

It has been suggested that an admissions program which considers race only as one factor is simply a subtle and more sophisticated—but no less effective—means of according racial preference than the Davis program. A facial intent to discriminate, however, is evident in petitioner's preference program and not denied in this case. No such facial infirmity exists in an admissions program where race or ethnic background is simply one element—to be weighed fairly against other elements—in the selection process. [A] court would not assume that a university, professing to employ a facially nondiscriminatory admissions policy, would operate it as a cover for the functional equivalent of a quota system. In short, good faith would be presumed in the absence of a showing to the contrary in the manner permitted by our cases. See, *e.g., Washington v. Davis.*

In summary, it is evident that the Davis special admissions program involves the use of an explicit racial classification never before countenanced by this Court.

It tells applicants who are not Negro, Asian, or Chicano that they are totally excluded from a specific percentage of the seats in an entering class. No matter how strong their qualifications, quantitative and extracurricular, including their own potential for contribution to educational diversity, they are never afforded the chance to compete with applicants from the preferred groups for the special admissions seats. At the same time, the preferred applicants have the opportunity to compete for every seat in the class.

The fatal flaw in petitioner's preferential program is its disregard of individual rights as guaranteed by the Fourteenth Amendment. *Shelley v. Kramer.* Such rights are not absolute. But when a State's distribution of benefits or imposition of burdens hinges on ancestry or the color of a person's skin or ancestry, that individual is entitled to a demonstration that the challenged classification is necessary to promote a substantial state interest. Petitioner has failed to carry this burden. For this reason, that portion of the California court's judgment holding petitioner's special admissions program invalid under the Fourteenth Amendment must be affirmed.

In enjoining petitioner from ever considering the race of any applicant, however, the courts below failed to recognize that the State has a substantial interest that legitimately may be served by a properly devised admissions program involving the competitive consideration of race and ethnic origin. For this reason, so much of the California court's judgment as enjoins petitioner from any consideration of the race of any applicant must be reversed. . . .

Opinion of Justice Brennan, Justice White, Justice Marshall, and Justice Blackmun, concurring in the judgment in part and dissenting in part:

[The multiple opinions in this case should not] mask the central meaning of today's opinions: Government may take race into account when it acts not to demean or insult any racial group, but to remedy disadvantages cast on minorities by past racial prejudice, at least when appropriate findings have been made by judicial, legislative, or administrative bodies with competence to act in this area. . . .

[W]e cannot . . . let color blindness become myopia which masks the reality that many "created equal" have been treated within our lifetimes as inferior both by the law and by their fellow citizens. . . . The assertion of human equality is closely associated with the proposition that differences in color or creed, birth or status, are neither significant nor relevant to the way in which persons should be treated. Nonetheless, the position that such factors must be "constitutionally an irrelevance," summed up by the shorthand phrase "[o]ur Constitution is color-blind," *Plessy v. Ferguson*, (Justice Harlan, dissenting), has never been adopted by this Court as the proper meaning of the Equal Protection Clause. Indeed, we have expressly rejected this proposition on a number of occasions.

Our cases have always implied that an "overriding statutory purpose," could be found that would justify racial classifications. See, *e.g.*, *Korematsu v. United States; Hirabayashi v. United States*. [Therefore,] racial classifications are not *per se* invalid under the Fourteenth Amendment. Accordingly, we turn to the problem of articulating what our role should be in reviewing state action that expressly classifies by race.

[W]hites as a class [do not] have any of the "traditional indicia of suspectness: the class is not saddled with such disabilities, or subjected to such a history of purposeful unequal treatment, or relegated to such a position of political powerlessness as to command extraordinary protection from the majoritarian political process." [No one has] suggested that the University's purposes contravene the cardinal principle that racial classifications that stigmatize— because they are drawn on the presumption that one race is inferior to another or because they put the weight of government behind racial hatred and separatism— are invalid without more.[33]

[B]ecause of the significant risk that racial classifications established for ostensibly benign purposes can be misused, causing effects not unlike those created by invidious classifications, it is inappropriate to inquire only whether there is any conceivable basis that might sustain such a classification. Instead, to justify such a classification an important and articulated purpose for its use must be shown. In addition, any statute must be stricken that stigmatizes any group or that singles out those least well represented in the political process to bear the brunt of a benign program. Thus, our review under the Fourteenth Amendment should be strict—not " 'strict' in theory and fatal in fact," because it is stigma that causes fatality—but strict and searching nonetheless.

Davis' articulated purpose of remedying the effects of past societal discrimination is, under our cases, sufficiently important to justify the use of race-conscious admissions programs where there is a sound basis for concluding that minority underrepresentation is substantial and chronic, and that the handicap of past discrimination is impeding access of minorities to the Medical School.

---

[33] Indeed, even in *Plessy v. Ferguson*, the Court recognized that a classification by race that presumed one race to be inferior to another would have to be condemned.

[A] requirement of a judicial determination of a constitutional or statutory violation as a predicate for race-conscious remedial actions would be self-defeating. Such a requirement would severely undermine efforts to achieve voluntary compliance with the requirements of law. . . .

. . . Until at least 1973, the practice of medicine in this country was, in fact, if not in law, largely the prerogative of whites. In 1950, for example, while Negroes constituted 10% of the total population, Negro physicians constituted only 2.2% of the total number of physicians. . . . By 1970, the . . . number of Negroes employed in medicine remained frozen at 2.2% while the Negro population had increased to 11.1% . . . .

The second prong of our test—whether the Davis program stigmatizes any discrete group or individual and whether race is reasonably used in light of the program's objectives—is clearly satisfied by the Davis program. It is not even claimed that Davis' program in any way operates to stigmatize or single out any discrete and insular, or even any identifiable, nonminority group. . . . True, whites are excluded from participation in the special admissions program, but this fact only operates to reduce the number of whites to be admitted in the regular admissions program in order to permit admission of a reasonable percentage—less than their proportion of the California population—of otherwise underrepresented qualified minority applicants.

Nor was Bakke in any sense stamped as inferior by the Medical School's rejection of him. Indeed, it is conceded by all that he satisfied those criteria regarded by the school as generally relevant to academic performance better than most of the minority members who were admitted. . . .

In addition, there is simply no evidence that the Davis program discriminates intentionally or unintentionally against any minority group which it purports to benefit. The program does not establish a quota in the invidious sense of a ceiling on the number of minority applicants to be admitted. Nor can the program reasonably be regarded as stigmatizing the program's beneficiaries or their race as inferior. . . . Once admitted, these students must satisfy the same degree requirements as regularly admitted students.

[With] respect to any factor (such as poverty or family educational background) that may be used as a substitute for race as an indicator of past discrimination, whites greatly outnumber racial minorities simply because whites make up a far larger percentage of the total population and therefore far outnumber minorities in absolute terms at every socioeconomic level. For example, of a class of recent medical school applicants from families with less than

$10,000 income, at least 71% were white. Of all 1970 families headed by a person *not* a high school graduate which included related children under 18, 80% were white and 20% were racial minorities. Moreover, while race is positively correlated with differences in GPA and MCAT scores, economic disadvantage is not. [T]he University's purpose to integrate its classes by compensating for past discrimination could not be achieved by a general preference for the economically disadvantaged or the children of parents of limited education unless such groups were to make up the entire class.

Finally, Davis' special admissions program cannot be said to violate the Constitution simply because it has set aside a predetermined number of places for qualified minority applicants rather than using minority status as a positive factor to be considered in evaluating the applications of disadvantaged minority applicants. For purposes of constitutional adjudication, there is no difference between the two approaches. In any admissions program which accords special consideration to disadvantaged racial minorities, a determination of the degree of preference to be given is unavoidable, and any given preference that results in the exclusion of a white candidate is no more or less constitutionally acceptable than a program such as that at Davis. . . . That the Harvard approach does not also make public the extent of the preference and the precise workings of the system while the Davis program employs a specific, openly stated number, does not condemn the latter plan for purposes of Fourteenth Amendment adjudication. . . .

JUSTICE MARSHALL.

Three hundred and fifty years ago, the Negro was dragged to this country in chains to be sold into slavery. Uprooted from his homeland and thrust into bondage for forced labor, the slave was deprived of all legal rights. It was unlawful to teach him to read; he could be sold away from his family and friends at the whim of his master; and killing or maiming him was not a crime. The system of slavery brutalized and dehumanized both master and slave. . . . The position of the Negro today in America is the tragic but inevitable consequence of centuries of unequal treatment. . . . Although Negroes represent 11.5% of the population, they are only 1.2% of the lawyers and judges, 2% of the physicians, 2.3% of the dentists, 1.1% of the engineers and 2.6% of the college and university professors. . . . These differences in the experience of the Negro make it difficult for me to accept that Negroes cannot be afforded greater protection under the Fourteenth Amendment where it is necessary to remedy the effects of past discrimination. . . .

JUSTICE BLACKMUN.

. . . In order to get beyond racism, we must first take account of race. There is no other way. And in order to treat some persons equally, we must treat them differently. We cannot—we dare not—let the Equal Protection Clause perpetrate racial supremacy.

JUSTICE STEVENS, with whom CHIEF JUSTICE BURGER, JUSTICE STEWART, and JUSTICE REHNQUIST join, concurring in the judgment in part and dissenting in part.

It is always important at the outset to focus precisely on the controversy before the Court.[1] . . . Section 601 of the Civil Rights Act of 1964, 78 Stat. 252, 42 U.S.C.A. § 2000d, provides:

> No person in the United States shall, on the ground of race, color, or national origin, be excluded from participation in, be denied the benefits of, or be subjected to discrimination under any program or activity receiving Federal financial assistance.

The University, through its special admissions policy, excluded Bakke from participation in its program of medical education because of his race. The University also acknowledges that it was, and still is, receiving federal financial assistance. The plain language of the statute therefore requires affirmance of the judgment below. . . . In the words of the House Report, Title VI stands for "the general principle that *no person* . . . be excluded from participation . . . on the ground of race, color, or national origin under any program or activity receiving Federal financial assistance." H.R, Rep. No. 914, pt. 1, 88th Cong., 1st Sess., 25 (1963) (emphasis added). This same broad view of Title VI and § 601 was echoed throughout the congressional debate and was stressed by every one of the major spokesmen for the Act. . . .

[The separate opinion of WHITE, J., is omitted.]

NOTES

1. *United Steel Workers v. Weber,* 443 U.S. 193, 99 S.Ct. 2721, 61 L.Ed.2d 480 (1979), interpreted Title VII of the Civil Rights Act of 1964 to allow private employers and unions to take race-conscious steps to eliminate racial imbalances in traditionally segregated job categories. The union and employer

---

[1]   Four Members of the Court have undertaken to announce the legal and constitutional effect of this Court's judgment. See opinion of Justices Brennan, White, Marshall, and Blackmun. It is hardly necessary to state that only a majority can speak for the Court or determine what is the "central meaning" of any judgment of the Court.

bargained for an affirmative action plan that reserved for blacks 50% of the openings in an in-plant craft-training program until the percentage of black craft workers in the plant would equal the percentage of blacks in the local labor force.

The Court (5 to 2) emphasized the narrowness of its holding by noting that the affirmative action plan did not involve state action. Nor was the Court "concerned with what Title VII requires or with what a court might order to remedy a past proven violation of the Act." The Court interpreted Title VII—which makes it unlawful to discriminate because of race in hiring, and which protects whites as well as blacks—to mean that the law does not prohibit bona fide affirmative action plans that private parties voluntarily adopt to eliminate traditional patterns of racial discrimination.

2. The Harvard Plan, to which Justice Powell endorses in *Bakke*, originated in 1922. President A. Lawrence Lowell of Harvard called for a quota system to limit the number of Jews attending Harvard. (By that time, the proportion had reached 22%.) The Harvard Overseers and faculty formally rejected the proposal, so Lowell "imposed a limit of 1,000 students in each incoming class and then urged his admissions officials to seek a broad geographical distribution—that is, to accept more students from Southern and Western states where comparatively few Jews lived. By the time Lowell retired in 1933, the proportion of Jews had shrunk to 10%."[9]

3. In 1992, the Department of Education's Office of Civil Rights found that Boalt Hall, the University of California's law school at Berkeley, had been violating *Bakke* ever since 1978. The challenged procedures called for a "goal" of 8%–10% African-Americans, 8%–10% Hispanic-Americans; 5%–7% Asian-Americans; and 1% Native-Americans. Pursuant to these procedures, which excluded a large number of highly qualified Asian-Americans, Boalt Hall "segregated the applicant pools: minority students competed only with applicants from their own racial background. The school covered shortfalls of minority students by pulling applicants off equally segregated waiting lists." Until 1989, it explicitly informed applicants about

---

[9] Time Magazine, Sept. 18, 1986, at 65. In 1988, Harvard denied that it used quotas to limit Asian-Americans. It conceded that Asian-Americans (both applicants and admitted students) typically scored about 40 points higher than any other group on the combined SAT verbal and mathematics test, and that, over the last decade, there has been a 3.7% difference between the admission rate at Harvard and Radcliffe for Asian-Americans and whites. However, Harvard said, the different admission rates are not the result of a quota: although "Asian-Americans are slightly stronger than whites on academic criteria, they are slightly less strong on extracurricular criteria." In addition, fewer Asian-Americans were children of alums. Harvard Statement on Asian-American Admissions (Jan. 1988).

their status on these lists by stating, *e.g.*, "You are presently in the bottom half of the Asian waiting list."[10] Boalt Hall, while not admitting guilt, agreed to change its procedures.

GRATZ V. BOLLINGER
539 U.S. 244, 123 S.Ct. 2411, 156 L.Ed.2d 257 (2003)

CHIEF JUSTICE REHNQUIST delivered the opinion of the Court.

We granted certiorari in this case to decide whether "the University of Michigan's use of racial preferences in undergraduate admissions violate[s] the Equal Protection Clause of the Fourteenth Amendment, Title VI of the Civil Rights Act of 1964, or 42 U.S.C. § 1981." Because we find that the manner in which the University considers the race of applicants in its undergraduate admissions guidelines violates these constitutional and statutory provisions, we reverse that portion of the District Court's decision upholding the guidelines.

Petitioners Jennifer Gratz and Patrick Hamacher both applied for admission to the University of Michigan's (University) College of Literature, Science, and the Arts (LSA) as residents of the State of Michigan. [LSA denied them admission. The class action included] "those individuals who applied for and were not granted admission to the College of Literature, Science and the Arts of the University of Michigan for all academic years from 1995 forward and who are members of those racial or ethnic groups, including Caucasian, that defendants treated less favorably on the basis of race in considering their application for admission." [T]he University has considered African-Americans, Hispanics, and Native Americans to be "underrepresented minorities," and it is undisputed that the University admits "virtually every qualified . . . applicant" from these groups. . . .

Beginning with the 1998 academic year, . . . an applicant could score a maximum of 150 points. This index was divided linearly into ranges generally calling for admissions dispositions as follows: 100–150 (admit); 95–99 (admit or postpone); 90–94 (postpone or admit); 75–89 (delay or postpone); 74 and below (delay or reject).

Each application received points based on high school grade point average, standardized test scores, academic quality of an applicant's high school, strength or weakness of high school curriculum, in-state residency, alumni relationship, personal essay, and personal achievement or leadership. Of particular significance

---

[10]   Greve, The Newest Move in Law Schools' Quota Game, Wall St. Journal., Oct. 5, 1992, at A12, col. 3–6.

here, under a "miscellaneous" category, an applicant was entitled to 20 points based upon his or her membership in an underrepresented racial or ethnic minority group. . . .

It is by now well established that "all racial classifications reviewable under the Equal Protection Clause must be strictly scrutinized." To withstand our strict scrutiny analysis, respondents must demonstrate that the University's use of race in its current admission program employs "narrowly tailored measures that further compelling governmental interests." [T]he University's policy, which automatically distributes 20 points, or one-fifth of the points needed to guarantee admission, to every single "underrepresented minority" applicant solely because of race, is not narrowly tailored to achieve the interest in educational diversity that respondents claim justifies their program. . . . Even if student C's "extraordinary artistic talent" rivaled that of Monet or Picasso, the applicant would receive, at most, five points under the LSA's system. At the same time, every single underrepresented minority applicant, including students A and B, would automatically receive 20 points for submitting an application. . . .

Respondents contend that "[t]he volume of applications and the presentation of applicant information make it impractical for [LSA] to use the . . . admissions system" upheld by the Court today in *Grutter*. But the fact that the implementation of a program capable of providing individualized consideration might present administrative challenges does not render constitutional an otherwise problematic system. [Prior cases reject] " 'administrative convenience' " as a determinant of constitutionality in the face of a suspect classification. . . .

[B]ecause the University's use of race in its current freshman admissions policy is not narrowly tailored to achieve respondents' asserted compelling interest in diversity, the admissions policy violates the Equal Protection Clause of the Fourteenth Amendment.[22] We further find that the admissions policy also violates Title VI and 42 U.S.C. § 1981.[23] . . .

---

[22] Justice Ginsburg in her dissent observes that "[o]ne can reasonably anticipate . . . that colleges and universities will seek to maintain their minority enrollment . . . whether or not they can do so in full candor through adoption of affirmative action plans of the kind here at issue." She goes on to say that "[i]f honesty is the best policy, surely Michigan's accurately described, fully disclosed College affirmative action program is preferable to achieving similar numbers through winks, nods, and disguises." These observations are remarkable for two reasons. First, they suggest that universities—to whose academic judgment we are told in *Grutter v. Bollinger, post*, we should defer—will pursue their affirmative-action programs whether or not they violate the United States Constitution. Second, they recommend that these violations should be dealt with, not by requiring the universities to obey the Constitution, but by changing the Constitution so that it conforms to the conduct of the universities.

[23] [D]iscrimination that violates the Equal Protection Clause of the Fourteenth Amendment committed by an institution that accepts federal funds also constitutes a violation of Title VI. [§ 1981] was "meant, by its

JUSTICE THOMAS, concurring.

I join the Court's opinion because I believe it correctly applies our precedents, including today's decision in *Grutter v. Bollinger, post.* . . . Under today's decisions, a university may not racially discriminate between the groups constituting the critical mass. *Grutter, post* (opinion of the Court) (stating that such "racial balancing . . . is patently unconstitutional"). . . .

JUSTICE GINSBURG, with whom JUSTICE SOUTER joins, dissenting.

. . . There is no suggestion that the . . . College's program unduly constricts admissions opportunities for students who do not receive special consideration based on race.[10] . . . Without recourse to [candid affirmative action] plans, institutions of higher education may resort to camouflage. For example, schools may encourage applicants to write of their cultural traditions in the essays they submit, or to indicate whether English is their second language. [A] fully disclosed College affirmative action program is preferable to achieving similar numbers through winks, nods, and disguises. . . .

[The opinion of O'CONNOR, J., concurring, and the opinion of BREYER, J., concurring in the judgment, are omitted. The dissenting opinion of STEVENS, J., joined by SOUTER, J., and the dissenting opinion of SOUTER, J., joined in part by GINSBURG J., is omitted.]

GRUTTER V. BOLLINGER

539 U.S. 306, 123 S.Ct. 2325, 156 L.Ed.2d 304 (2003)

JUSTICE O'CONNOR delivered the opinion of the Court.

This case requires us to decide whether the use of race as a factor in student admissions by the University of Michigan Law School (Law School) is unlawful.

The Law School ranks among the Nation's top law schools. It receives more than 3,500 applications each year for a class of around 350 students. . . . In reviewing an applicant's file, admissions officials must consider the applicant's undergraduate grade point average (GPA) and Law School Admissions Test (LSAT) score because they are important (if imperfect) predictors of academic

---

broad terms, to proscribe discrimination in the making or enforcement of contracts against, or in favor of, any race."

   [10]   The United States points to the "percentage plans" used in California, Florida, and Texas as one example of a "race-neutral alternativ[e]" that would permit the College to enroll meaningful numbers of minority students. (percentage plans guarantee admission to state universities for a fixed percentage of the top students from high schools in the State). Calling such 10 or 20% plans "race-neutral" seems to me disingenuous, for they "unquestionably were adopted with the specific purpose of increasing representation of African-Americans and Hispanics in the public higher education system." . . .

success in law school. [E]ven the highest possible score does not guarantee admission to the Law School. Nor does a low score automatically disqualify an applicant. [The admissions policy reaffirms] the Law School's longstanding commitment to "one particular type of diversity," that is, "racial and ethnic diversity with special reference to the inclusion of students from groups which have been historically discriminated against, like African-Americans, Hispanics and Native Americans, who without this commitment might not be represented in our student body in meaningful numbers." By enrolling a " 'critical mass' of [underrepresented] minority students," the Law School seeks to "ensur[e] their ability to make unique contributions to the character of the Law School." . . .

Petitioner Barbara Grutter is a white Michigan resident who applied to the Law School in 1996 with a 3.8 grade point average and 161 LSAT score. The Law School . . . rejected her application. [She sued, and] alleged that her application was rejected because the Law School uses race as a "predominant" factor, giving applicants who belong to certain minority groups "a significantly greater chance of admission than students with similar credentials from disfavored racial groups." . . .

. . . During the 15-day bench trial, the parties introduced extensive evidence concerning the Law School's use of race in the admissions process. Dennis Shields, Director of Admissions when petitioner applied to the Law School, testified that he did not direct his staff to admit a particular percentage or number of minority students, but rather to consider an applicant's race along with all other factors. [A]t the height of the admissions season, he would frequently consult the so-called "daily reports" that kept track of the racial and ethnic composition of the class (along with other information such as residency status and gender). This was done, Shields testified, to ensure that a critical mass of underrepresented minority students would be reached so as to realize the educational benefits of a diverse student body. [Professor Richard Lempert who chaired the faculty committee that drafted the affirmative action admissions policy] emphasized that the Law School seeks students with diverse interests and backgrounds to enhance classroom discussion and the educational experience both inside and outside the classroom. [He] acknowledged that other groups, such as Asians and Jews, have experienced discrimination, but explained they were not mentioned in the policy because individuals who are members of those groups were already being admitted to the Law School in significant numbers.

[Another law professor testified] that when a critical mass of underrepresented minority students is present, racial stereotypes lose their force because nonminority students learn there is no " 'minority viewpoint' " but rather a variety of viewpoints among minority students. [T]he Law School's expert, [testified that under] a race-blind admissions system ... underrepresented minority students would have comprised 4 percent of the entering class in 2000 instead of the actual figure of 14.5 percent. . . .

We last addressed the use of race in public higher education over 25 years ago. . . . Since this Court's splintered decision in *Bakke*, Justice Powell's opinion announcing the judgment of the Court has served as the touchstone for constitutional analysis of race-conscious admissions policies. [F]or the reasons set out below, today we endorse Justice Powell's view that student body diversity is a compelling state interest that can justify the use of race in university admissions.

The Equal Protection Clause provides that no State shall "deny to any person within its jurisdiction the equal protection of the laws." Because the Fourteenth Amendment "protect[s] *persons*, not *groups*," all "governmental action based on race—a *group* classification long recognized as in most circumstances irrelevant and therefore prohibited—should be subjected to detailed judicial inquiry to ensure that the *personal* right to equal protection of the laws has not been infringed." [Hence,] government may treat people differently because of their race only for the most compelling reasons. . . . We apply strict scrutiny to all racial classifications to " 'smoke out' illegitimate uses of race by assuring that [government] is pursuing a goal important enough to warrant use of a highly suspect tool." . . .

[R]espondents assert only one justification for their use of race in the admissions process: obtaining "the educational benefits that flow from a diverse student body." In other words, the Law School asks us to recognize, in the context of higher education, a compelling state interest in student body diversity. [W]e hold that the Law School has a compelling interest in attaining a diverse student body.

The Law School's educational judgment that such diversity is essential to its educational mission is one to which we defer. [A]ttaining a diverse student body is at the heart of the Law School's proper institutional mission, and that "good faith" on the part of a university is "presumed" absent "a showing to the contrary."

As part of its goal of "assembling a class that is both exceptionally academically qualified and broadly diverse," the Law School seeks to "enroll a 'critical mass' of minority students." The Law School's interest is not simply "to assure within its student body some specified percentage of a particular group merely because of its race or ethnic origin." *Bakke.* That would amount to outright racial balancing, which is patently unconstitutional. *Ibid.* Rather, the Law School's concept of critical mass is defined by reference to the educational benefits that diversity is designed to produce.

[T]he Law School's admissions policy promotes "cross-racial understanding," helps to break down racial stereotypes, and "enables [students] to better understand persons of different races." These benefits are "important and laudable," because "classroom discussion is livelier, more spirited, and simply more enlightening and interesting" when the students have "the greatest possible variety of backgrounds." . . .

[M]ajor American businesses have made clear that the skills needed in today's increasingly global marketplace can only be developed through exposure to widely diverse people, cultures, ideas, and viewpoints. Brief for 3M et al. as *Amici Curiae.* [H]igh-ranking retired officers and civilian leaders of the United States military assert that, "[b]ased on [their] decades of experience," a "highly qualified, racially diverse officer corps . . . is essential to the military's ability to fulfill its principle mission to provide national security." Brief for Julius W. Becton, Jr. et al. as *Amici Curiae* 27. The primary sources for the Nation's officer corps are the service academies and the Reserve Officers Training Corps (ROTC), the latter comprising students already admitted to participating colleges and universities. At present, "the military cannot achieve an officer corps that is *both* highly qualified *and* racially diverse unless the service academies and the ROTC used limited race-conscious recruiting and admissions policies." *Ibid.* (emphasis in original). . . .

The Law School does not premise its need for critical mass on "any belief that minority students always (or even consistently) express some characteristic minority viewpoint on any issue." To the contrary, diminishing the force of such stereotypes is both a crucial part of the Law School's mission, and one that it cannot accomplish with only token numbers of minority students. Just as growing up in a particular region or having particular professional experiences is likely to affect an individual's views, so too is one's own, unique experience of being a racial minority in a society, like our own, in which race unfortunately still matters. The Law School has determined, based on its experience and expertise, that a "critical mass" of underrepresented minorities is necessary to further its compelling interest in securing the educational benefits of a diverse student body. . . .

To be narrowly tailored, a race-conscious admissions program cannot use a quota system—it cannot "insulat[e] each category of applicants with certain desired qualifications from competition with all other applicants." *Bakke* (opinion of Powell, J.). . . . We are satisfied that the Law School's admissions program, like the Harvard plan described by Justice Powell, does not operate as a quota. Properly understood, a "quota" is a program in which a certain fixed number or proportion of opportunities are "reserved exclusively for certain minority groups." . . .

Here, the Law School engages in a highly individualized, holistic review of each applicant's file, giving serious consideration to all the ways an applicant might contribute to a diverse educational environment. The Law School affords this individualized consideration to applicants of all races. There is no policy, either *de jure* or *de facto*, of automatic acceptance or rejection based on any single "soft" variable. Unlike the program at issue in *Gratz v. Bollinger, ante,* the Law School awards no mechanical, predetermined diversity "bonuses" based on race or ethnicity. . . .

The District Court took the Law School to task for failing to consider race-neutral alternatives such as "using a lottery system" or "decreasing the emphasis for all applicants on undergraduate GPA and LSAT scores." But these alternatives would require a dramatic sacrifice of diversity, the academic quality of all admitted students, or both. . . .

We acknowledge that "there are serious problems of justice connected with the idea of preference itself." *Bakke* (opinion of Powell, J.). Narrow tailoring, therefore, requires that a race-conscious admissions program not unduly harm members of any racial group. [I]n the context of its individualized inquiry into the possible diversity contributions of all applicants, the Law School's race-conscious admissions program does not unduly harm nonminority applicants.

We are mindful, however, that "[a] core purpose of the Fourteenth Amendment was to do away with all governmentally imposed discrimination based on race." Accordingly, race-conscious admissions policies must be limited in time. [R]acial classifications, however compelling their goals, are potentially so dangerous that they may be employed no more broadly than the interest demands. Enshrining a permanent justification for racial preferences would offend this fundamental equal protection principle. We see no reason to exempt race-conscious admissions programs from the requirement that all governmental use of race must have a logical end point. The Law School, too, concedes that all "race-conscious programs must have reasonable durational limits."

In the context of higher education, the durational requirement can be met by sunset provisions in race-conscious admissions policies and periodic reviews to determine whether racial preferences are still necessary to achieve student body diversity. . . . It has been 25 years since Justice Powell first approved the use of race to further an interest in student body diversity in the context of public higher education. Since that time, the number of minority applicants with high grades and test scores has indeed increased. We expect that 25 years from now, the use of racial preferences will no longer be necessary to further the interest approved today.

In summary, the Equal Protection Clause does not prohibit the Law School's narrowly tailored use of race in admissions decisions to further a compelling interest in obtaining the educational benefits that flow from a diverse student body. Consequently, petitioner's statutory claims based on Title VI and 42 U.S.C. § 1981 also fail. The judgment of the Court of Appeals for the Sixth Circuit, accordingly, is affirmed.

It is so ordered.

JUSTICE GINSBURG, with whom JUSTICE BREYER joins, concurring.

The Court's observation that race-conscious programs "must have a logical end point," accords with the international understanding. [See] The International Convention on the Elimination of All Forms of Racial Discrimination, ratified by the United States in 1994. . . . From today's vantage point, one may hope, but not firmly forecast, that over the next generation's span, progress toward nondiscrimination and genuinely equal opportunity will make it safe to sunset affirmative action.

JUSTICE SCALIA, with whom JUSTICE THOMAS joins, concurring in part and dissenting in part. . . .

Unlike a clear constitutional holding that racial preferences in state educational institutions are impermissible, or even a clear anticonstitutional holding that racial preferences in state educational institutions are OK, today's *Grutter-Gratz* split double header seems perversely designed to prolong the controversy and the litigation. Some future lawsuits will presumably focus on whether the discriminatory scheme in question contains enough evaluation of the applicant "as an individual," and sufficiently avoids "separate admissions tracks" to fall under *Grutter* rather than *Gratz*. [O]ther suits may challenge the bona fides of the institution's expressed commitment to the educational benefits of diversity that immunize the discriminatory scheme in *Grutter*. (Tempting targets, one would suppose, will be those universities that talk the talk of multiculturalism and racial diversity in the courts but walk the walk of tribalism and racial segregation on their campuses—through minority-only student organizations, separate minority housing opportunities, separate minority student centers, even separate minority-only graduation ceremonies.) And still other suits may claim that the institution's racial preferences have gone below or above the mystical *Grutter*-approved "critical mass." Finally, litigation can be expected on behalf of minority groups intentionally short changed in the institution's composition of its generic minority "critical mass." . . . The Constitution proscribes government discrimination on the basis of race, and state-provided education is no exception.

JUSTICE THOMAS, with whom JUSTICE SCALIA joins as to Parts I-VII, concurring in part and dissenting in part.

Frederick Douglass, speaking to a group of abolitionists almost 140 years ago, delivered a message lost on today's majority:

> ". . . The American people have always been anxious to know what they shall do with us. . . . I have had but one answer from the beginning. Do nothing with us! Your doing with us has already played the mischief with us. Do nothing with us! If the apples will not remain on the tree of their own strength, if they are worm-eaten at the core, if they are early ripe and disposed to fall, let them fall! [I]f the negro cannot stand on his own legs, let him fall also. All I ask is, give him a chance to stand on his own legs! Let him alone! . . . [Y]our interference is doing him positive injury."
> What the Black Man Wants: An Address Delivered in Boston, Massachusetts, on 26 January 1865.

Like Douglass, I believe blacks can achieve in every avenue of American life without the meddling of university administrators. . . .

. . . I agree with the Court insofar as its decision, which approves of only one racial classification, confirms that further use of race in admissions remains unlawful. Second, I agree with the Court's holding that racial discrimination in higher education admissions will be illegal in 25 years. . . . I respectfully dissent from the remainder of the Court's opinion and the judgment, however, because I believe that the Law School's current use of race violates the Equal Protection Clause and that the Constitution means the same thing today as it will in 300 months.

I.   The majority agrees that the Law School's racial discrimination should be subjected to strict scrutiny. . . .

VII. [I] find two points on which I agree. First, [u]nder today's decision, it is still the case that racial discrimination that does not help a university to enroll an unspecified number, or "critical mass," of underrepresented minority students is unconstitutional. Thus, the Law School may not discriminate in admissions between similarly situated blacks and Hispanics, or between whites and Asians. This is so because preferring black to Hispanic applicants, for instance, does nothing to further the interest recognized by the majority today. Indeed, the majority describes such racial balancing as "patently unconstitutional." . . .

The Court also holds that racial discrimination in admissions should be given another 25 years before it is deemed no longer narrowly tailored to the Law School's fabricated compelling state interest. . . . The majority does not and cannot rest its time limitation on any evidence that the gap in credentials between black and white students is shrinking or will be gone in that timeframe. In recent years there has been virtually no change, for example, in the proportion of law school applicants with LSAT scores of 165 and higher who are black. In 1993 blacks constituted 1.1% of law school applicants in that score range, though they represented 11.1% of all applicants. In 2000 the comparable numbers were 1.0% and 11.3%. No one can seriously contend, and the Court does not, that the racial gap in academic credentials will disappear in 25 years. Nor is the Court's holding that racial discrimination will be unconstitutional in 25 years made contingent on the gap closing in that time. . . . I therefore can understand the imposition of a 25-year time limit only as a holding that the deference the Court pays to the Law School's educational judgments and refusal to change its admissions policies will itself expire. . . .

CHIEF JUSTICE REHNQUIST, with whom JUSTICE SCALIA, JUSTICE KENNEDY, and JUSTICE THOMAS join, dissenting. . . .

From 1995 through 2000, the Law School admitted between 1,130 and 1,310 students. Of those, between 13 and 19 were Native American, between 91 and 108 were African-Americans, and between 47 and 56 were Hispanic. If the Law School is admitting between 91 and 108 African-Americans in order to achieve "critical mass," thereby preventing African-American students from feeling "isolated or like spokespersons for their race," one would think that a number of the same order of magnitude would be necessary to accomplish the same purpose for Hispanics and Native Americans. Similarly, even if all of the Native American applicants admitted in a given year matriculate, which the record demonstrates is not at all the case,* how can this possibly constitute a "critical mass" of Native Americans in a class of over 350 students? . . .

---

* Indeed, during this 5-year time period, enrollment of Native American students dropped to as low as *three* such students. Any assertion that such a small group constituted a "critical mass" of Native Americans is simply absurd.

[I]n 2000, 12 Hispanics who scored between a 159–160 on the LSAT and earned a GPA of 3.00 or higher applied for admission and only 2 were admitted. Meanwhile, 12 African-Americans in the same range of qualifications applied for admission and all 12 were admitted. . . . Respondents have *never* offered any race-specific arguments explaining why significantly more individuals from one underrepresented minority group are needed in order to achieve "critical mass" or further student body diversity. [T]he Law School's disparate admissions practices with respect to these minority groups demonstrate that its alleged goal of "critical mass" is simply a sham. . . .

JUSTICE KENNEDY, dissenting.

. . . Dean Allan Stillwagon, who directed the Law School's Office of Admissions from 1979 to 1990, . . . testified that faculty members were "breathtakingly cynical" in deciding who would qualify as a member of underrepresented minorities. An example he offered was faculty debate as to whether Cubans should be counted as Hispanics: One professor objected on the grounds that Cubans were Republicans. . . .

NOTES

1. The plaintiff in *Grutter*, was a 49-year-old wife, mother, and proprietor of a small business: "She is one of nine children, the daughter of an itinerant, financially struggling Protestant minister. She worked in an inner-city clinic for two years to save money for community college. She didn't have a college counselor in high school, hadn't heard of such things as SAT prep classes— or even the SAT college-admissions test. Even though she is white, Barbara Grutter thinks she should have been 'a prime candidate' for an affirmative-action plan designed to promote campus diversity."[11] Would an affirmative action for underprivileged whites like Barbara Grutter be constitutional?

2. Many college admissions officials say, "they don't verify applicants' claims of minority status. 'Schools don't ask—and don't really want to know—just how 'ethnic' a self-reported minority applicant really is,' says Anna Ivey, former dean of admissions at Chicago law school. 'A formal policy—one-half? one-fourth? one drop?—would smack too much of different regimes and times and places that we don't want to live in.' "[12]

---

[11] June Kronholz, Does a White Mom Add Diversity?, Wall Street Journal, June 25, 2003, at B3.

[12] Daniel Golden and Charles Forelle, How Far Does Diversity Go?—Justices' Ruling May Spur Others to Seek Preferences; Recruiting Southeast Asians, Wall Street Journal, June 25, 2003, at B1.

3. Justice Ginsburg, dissenting in *Gratz*, at footnote 10, argued that one of the
    "perverse incentives" of the "percentage plans" used in several states such as
    California, is that they "encourage parents to keep their children in low-
    performing segregated schools." If such plans encourage white parents to
    send their children to predominately minority schools to take advantage of
    the percentage plans, would that not reduce *de facto* segregation? That result
    is not perverse, is it?

4. In *Grutter*, O'Connor said, by enrolling "a 'critical mass' of
    [underrepresented] minority students," the Law School seeks to "ensur[e]
    their ability to make unique contributions to the character of the Law
    School." Later, she emphasized that the Director of Admissions testified that
    the school needed "a critical mass of underrepresented minority students" to
    "enhance classroom discussion." Yet, O'Connor also relied on a law
    professor who testified that when there is "a critical mass of
    underrepresented minority students," then "nonminority students learn there
    is no 'minority viewpoint.'" Are those two arguments consistent? Is she
    saying the school needs more minority students to show the nonminority
    students that there is no minority viewpoint? If so, why is it that the school
    needs so few Native Americans to make that point. Recall Rehnquist said,
    out of between 1,130 and 1,310 students, only 13 and 19 were Native
    American.

5. *Parents Involved in Community Schools v. Seattle School District No. 1*, 551 U.S. 701,
    127 S.Ct. 2738, 168 L.Ed.2d 508 (2007) involved affirmative action in K
    through 12th grade, not higher education. Parents sued, arguing that it
    violates equal protection for schools to use the race of the students to allocate
    slots in grade schools and high schools. Roberts, C.J., for the Court (5 to 4)
    held that the schools acted unconstitutionally. Unlike *Grutter*, the schools do
    not consider race "as part of a broader effort to achieve 'exposure to widely
    diverse people, cultures, ideas, and viewpoints,' race, for some students, is
    determinative standing alone." The *Grutter* Court held that racial
    classifications as "an effort to achieve racial balance," is "patently
    unconstitutional." Roberts repeatedly emphasized that the diversity interest
    in higher education does not apply to allow racial balancing in K-12th grade.
    The interest "we have recognized as compelling for purposes of strict
    scrutiny is the interest in diversity in higher education upheld in *Grutter*. The
    specific interest found compelling in *Grutter* was student body diversity 'in
    the context of higher education.'" *Grutter* "relied upon considerations unique
    to institutions of higher education," and because of "the expansive freedoms

of speech and thought associated with the university environment," they "occupy a special niche in our constitutional tradition." *Grutter* "repeatedly noted that it was addressing the use of race 'in the context of higher education.' " "*Grutter* expressly articulated key limitations on its holding— defining a specific type of broad-based diversity and noting the unique context of higher education—but these limitations were largely disregarded by the lower courts in extending *Grutter* to uphold race-based assignments in elementary and secondary schools. The present cases are not governed by *Grutter*." The *Grutter* factors are not "present in elementary and secondary schools. Those schools do not select their own students, and education in the elementary and secondary environment generally does not involve the free interchange of ideas thought to be an integral part of higher education. Extending *Grutter* to this context would require us to cut that holding loose from its theoretical moorings."

Justice Kennedy concurred in part and in the judgment:

School boards may pursue the goal of bringing together students of diverse backgrounds and races through other means, including strategic site selection of new schools; drawing attendance zones with general recognition of the demographics of neighborhoods; allocating resources for special programs; recruiting students and faculty in a targeted fashion; and tracking enrollments, performance, and other statistics by race. These mechanisms are race conscious but do not lead to different treatment based on a classification that tells each student he or she is to be defined by race, so it is unlikely any of them would demand strict scrutiny to be found permissible.

Breyer, J., joined by Stevens, Souter, & Ginsburg, JJ., dissented. This case "is not one in which race-conscious limits stigmatize or exclude; the limits at issue do not pit the races against each other or otherwise significantly exacerbate racial tensions."

5.2.4.2 *Employment*

In *Fullilove v. Klutznick*, 448 U.S. 448, 100 S.Ct. 2758, 65 L.Ed.2d 902 (1980), a fragmented Court, with no majority opinion, rejected a facial challenge to the federal minority business enterprise (MBE) "set-aside" program of the Public Works Employment Act of 1977. The law required that (unless there was an administrative waiver) at least 10% of federal funds granted for local public works projects would be set aside for state or local grantees to purchase business or supplies by MBEs. The law defined MBEs as at least 50% owned by "minority" group members, which the law defined as "citizens of the United States who are Negroes, Spanish-speaking, Orientals, Indians, Eskimos, and Aleuts." A splintered Court upheld the law.[13]

Stewart, J., joined by Rehnquist, J., dissented, "Our Constitution is color-blind," and even "good faith racial discrimination" is bad. Stevens argued that the statute was not "narrowly tailored" because it raised many questions—"why were these six racial classifications and no others, included;" "what percentage of Oriental blood" is required. Stevens, J. also dissented. In a footnote, he said, "the National Government is to make a serious effort to define racial classes by criteria that can be administered objectively, it must study precedents such as the First Regulation to the Reich Citizenship Law of November 14, 1935, translated in 4 Nazi Conspiracy and Aggression, Document No. 1417–PS, pp. 8–9 (1946)[defining 'Jew']."

Then came *Wygant v. Jackson Board of Education*, 476 U.S. 267, 106 S.Ct. 1842, 90 L.Ed.2d 260 (1986). This time, another divided Court, with no majority opinion, invalidated a race-based provision in a collective bargaining agreement giving preferential treatment to certain minorities. It required that the school board, in laying off teachers, must lay off the least senior first, *except* that at no time would there be a greater percentage of minority personnel laid off than the current percentage of minority personnel employed at the time of the layoff. Powell, J., announced the judgment of the Court:

> [T]he role model theory employed by the District Court has no logical stopping point. [T]he idea that black students are better off with black teachers could lead to the very system the Court rejected in *Brown v. Board of Education*.

Richmond v. J.A. Croson Co., 488 U.S. 469, 109 S.Ct. 706, 102 L.Ed.2d 854 (1989), Court invalidated an MBE set-aside program that the City Council of Richmond, Virginia adopted. Richmond patterned this law after the federal law. It required prime contractors (other than minority-owned prime contractors) awarded city construction contracts, to subcontract at least 30% of the dollar amount of such contracts to one or more MBEs, defined as a business at least 51% owned by "[c]itizens of the United States, who are Blacks, Spanish-speaking,

---

[13] Burger, C.J., joined by White & Powell, JJ., wrote the plurality. Marshall, J., joined by Brennan & Blackmun, JJ., concurred in the judgment.

Orientals, Indians, Eskimos, or Aleuts." O'Connor, J., (in a portion of her opinion that attracted a majority of the Court) said:

> [In *Fullilove*] Congress was exercising its power under § 5 of the Fourteenth Amendment in making a finding that past discrimination would cause federal funds to be distributed in a manner which reinforced prior patterns of discrimination. . . . If all a state or local government need do is find a congressional report on the subject to enact a set-aside program, the constraints of the Equal Protection Clause will, in effect, have been rendered a nullity. [Moreover, there] is *absolutely no evidence* of past discrimination against Spanish-speaking, Oriental, Indian, Eskimo, or Aleut persons in any aspect of the Richmond construction industry. [Perhaps] Richmond has never had an Aleut or Eskimo citizen.

Kennedy, J., concurring in part and in the judgment, rejected this reasoning. "The process by which a law that is an equal protection violation when enacted by a State becomes transformed to an equal protection guarantee when enacted by Congress poses a difficult proposition for me. . . ."

In *Metro Broadcasting, Inc. v. Federal Communications Commission*, 497 U.S. 547, 110 S.Ct. 2997, 111 L.Ed.2d 445 (1990), Brennan, J., wrote the opinion for the Court (5 to 4). He held that a federal affirmative action program and minority preference policies of the Federal Communications Commission did not violate the equal protection component of the Fifth Amendment because Congress wanted to promote minority participation in the broadcast industry. O'Connor, J. joined by Rehnquist, C.J., Scalia & Kennedy, J.J., dissented.

> The Court's emphasis on "benign racial classifications" suggests confidence in its ability to distinguish good from harmful governmental uses of racial criteria. History should teach greater humility.

Five years later, *Adarand* overruled *Metro Broadcasting*.

ADARAND CONSTRUCTORS, INC. V. PENA

515 U.S. 200, 115 S.Ct. 2097, 132 L.Ed.2d 158 (1995)

JUSTICE O'CONNOR announced the judgment of the Court and delivered an opinion with respect to Parts I, II, III-A, III-B, III-D, and IV, which is for the Court except insofar as it might be inconsistent with the views expressed in JUSTICE SCALIA's concurrence, and an opinion with respect to Part III-C in which

JUSTICE KENNEDY joins. [Part III-C, which is not an opinion of the Court, is omitted.]

Petitioner Adarand Constructors, Inc., claims that the Federal Government's practice of giving general contractors on government projects a financial incentive to hire subcontractors controlled by "socially and economically disadvantaged individuals," and in particular, the Government's use of race-based presumptions in identifying such individuals, violates the equal protection component of the Fifth Amendment's Due Process Clause. The Court of Appeals rejected Adarand's claim [but we] vacate the Court of Appeals' judgment and remand the case for further proceedings.

I.

In 1989, the Central Federal Lands Highway Division (CFLHD), which is part of the United States Department of Transportation (DOT), awarded the prime contract for a highway construction project in Colorado to Mountain Gravel & Construction Company. Mountain Gravel then solicited bids from subcontractors for the guardrail portion of the contract. Adarand, a Colorado-based highway construction company specializing in guardrail work, submitted the low bid. Gonzales Construction Company also submitted a bid.

The prime contract's terms provide that Mountain Gravel would receive additional compensation if it hired subcontractors certified as small businesses controlled by "socially and economically disadvantaged individuals." Gonzales is certified as such a business; Adarand is not. Mountain Gravel awarded the subcontract to Gonzales, despite Adarand's low bid, and Mountain Gravel's Chief Estimator has submitted an affidavit stating that Mountain Gravel would have accepted Adarand's bid, had it not been for the additional payment it received by hiring Gonzales instead. Federal law requires that a subcontracting clause similar to the one used here must appear in most federal agency contracts, and it also requires the clause to state that "[t]he contractor shall presume that socially and economically disadvantaged individuals include Black Americans, Hispanic Americans, Native Americans, Asian Pacific Americans, and other minorities, or any other individual found to be disadvantaged by the [Small Business] Administration pursuant to section 8(a) of the Small Business Act." Adarand claims that the presumption set forth in that statute discriminates on the basis of race in violation of the Federal Government's Fifth Amendment obligation not to deny anyone equal protection of the laws.

[The lower court understood] *Fullilove v. Klutznick* (1980), to have adopted "a lenient standard, resembling intermediate scrutiny, in assessing" the constitutionality of federal race-based action. Applying that "lenient standard," as further developed in *Metro Broadcasting, Inc. v. FCC* (1990), the Court of Appeals upheld the use of subcontractor compensation clauses. We granted certiorari.

III.

Adarand's claim arises under the Fifth Amendment to the Constitution. . . .

A. [*Bolling v. Sharpe* (1954)] concerned school desegregation, but its reasoning was not so limited. [It] reiterated " 'that the Constitution of the United States, in its present form, forbids, so far as civil and political rights are concerned, discrimination *by the General Government, or by the States,* against any citizen because of his race.' " [T]he resulting imposition on the Federal Government of an obligation equivalent to that of the States, followed as a matter of course. . . .

B. . . . *Richmond v. J.A. Croson Co.* (1989) concerned a city's determination that 30% of its contracting work should go to minority-owned businesses. [In] *Croson,* the Court finally agreed that the Fourteenth Amendment requires strict scrutiny of all race-based action by state and local governments. [T]he Court's cases through *Croson* had established three general propositions with respect to governmental racial classifications. First, skepticism: " '[a]ny preference based on racial or ethnic criteria must necessarily receive a most searching examination,' " *Wygant* (plurality opinion of Powell, J.). Second, consistency: "the standard of review under the Equal Protection Clause is not dependent on the race of those burdened or benefitted by a particular classification," *Croson* (plurality opinion). And third, congruence: "[e]qual protection analysis in the Fifth Amendment area is the same as that under the Fourteenth Amendment," *Bolling v. Sharpe*. Taken together, these three propositions lead to the conclusion that any person, of whatever race, has the right to demand that any governmental actor subject to the Constitution justify any racial classification subjecting that person to unequal treatment under the strictest judicial scrutiny. . . .

A year [after *Croson*], the Court took a surprising turn. *Metro Broadcasting, Inc. v. FCC* (1990), involved a Fifth Amendment challenge to two race-based policies of the Federal Communications Commission. In *Metro Broadcasting,* the Court repudiated the long-held notion that "it would be unthinkable that the same Constitution would impose a lesser duty on the Federal Government" than it does on a State to afford equal protection of the laws, *Bolling*. . . .

By adopting intermediate scrutiny as the standard of review for congressionally mandated "benign" racial classifications, *Metro Broadcasting* departed from prior cases in two significant respects. First, it turned its back on

Croson's explanation of why strict scrutiny of all governmental racial classifications is essential because "it may not always be clear that a so-called preference is in fact benign," *Bakke* (opinion of Powell, J.). "[M]ore than good motives should be required when government seeks to allocate its resources by way of an explicit racial classification system." Days, *Fullilove*, 96 Yale L.J. 453, 485 (1987).

Second, *Metro Broadcasting* squarely rejected one of the three propositions established by the Court's earlier equal protection cases, namely, congruence between the standards applicable to federal and state racial classifications, and in so doing also undermined the other two—skepticism of all racial classifications, and consistency of treatment irrespective of the race of the burdened or benefitted group. . . .

The three propositions undermined by *Metro Broadcasting* all derive from the basic principle that the Fifth and Fourteenth Amendments to the Constitution protect *persons,* not *groups*. It follows from that principle that all governmental action based on race—a *group* classification long recognized as "in most circumstances irrelevant and therefore prohibited"—should be subjected to detailed judicial inquiry to ensure that the *personal* right to equal protection of the laws has not been infringed. . . . Accordingly, we hold today that all racial classifications, imposed by whatever federal, state, or local governmental actor, must be analyzed by a reviewing court under strict scrutiny. [S]uch classifications are constitutional only if they are narrowly tailored measures that further compelling governmental interests. To the extent that *Metro Broadcasting* is inconsistent with that holding, it is overruled. . . .

. . . Justice Stevens himself has already explained in his dissent in *Fullilove* why "good intentions" alone are not enough to sustain a supposedly "benign" racial classification: "[E]ven though it is not the actual predicate for this legislation, a statute of this kind inevitably is perceived by many as resting on an assumption that those who are granted this special preference are less qualified in some respect that is identified purely by their race. Because that perception—*especially when fostered by the Congress of the United States*—can only exacerbate rather than reduce racial prejudice, it will delay the time when race will become a truly irrelevant, or at least insignificant, factor. *Unless Congress clearly articulates the need and basis* for a racial classification, *and also tailors the classification to its justification*, the Court should not uphold this kind of statute." *Fullilove, supra* (dissenting opinion) (emphasis added; footnote omitted). . . .

D. [F]ederal racial classifications, like those of a State, must serve a compelling governmental interest, and must be narrowly tailored to further that interest. [T]o the extent (if any) that *Fullilove* held federal racial classifications to be subject to a less rigorous standard, it is no longer controlling. . . . Finally, we wish to dispel the notion that strict scrutiny is "strict in theory, but fatal in fact." [In] 1987, for example, every Justice of this Court agreed that the Alabama Department of Public Safety's "pervasive, systematic, and obstinate discriminatory conduct" justified a narrowly tailored race-based remedy. See *United States v. Paradise*, 480 U.S. 149, 107 S.Ct. 1053, 94 L.Ed.2d 203 (1987) [noted below]. When race-based action is necessary to further a compelling interest, such action is within constitutional constraints if it satisfies the "narrow tailoring" test this Court has set out in previous cases.

IV.

[We] remand the case to the lower courts for further consideration in light of the principles we have announced. . . .

It is so ordered.

JUSTICE SCALIA, concurring in part and concurring in the judgment.

I join the opinion of the Court, except Part III-C [omitted], and except insofar as it may be inconsistent with the following: In my view, government can never have a "compelling interest" in discriminating on the basis of race in order to "make up" for past racial discrimination in the opposite direction. Individuals who have been wronged by unlawful racial discrimination should be made whole; but under our Constitution there can be no such thing as either a creditor or a debtor race. That concept is alien to the Constitution's focus upon the individual, see Amdt. 14, § 1 ("[N]or shall any State . . . deny *to any person*" the equal protection of the laws) (emphasis added), and its rejection of dispositions based on race, see Amdt. 15, § 1 (prohibiting abridgment of the right to vote "on account of race") or based on blood, see Art. III, § 3 ("[N]o Attainder of Treason shall work Corruption of Blood"); Art. I, § 9 ("No Title of Nobility shall be granted by the United States"). In the eyes of government, we are just one race here. It is American.

It is unlikely, if not impossible, that the challenged program would survive under this understanding of strict scrutiny, but I am content to leave that to be decided on remand.

JUSTICE STEVENS, with whom JUSTICE GINSBURG joins, dissenting. . . .

The Court's explanation for treating dissimilar race-based decisions as though they were equally objectionable is a supposed inability to differentiate between "invidious" and "benign" discrimination. But the term "affirmative action" is common and well understood. . . .

[The opinion of THOMAS, J., concurring in part and in the judgment, and the dissenting opinion of SOUTER, J., joined by GINSBURG & BREYER, JJ., is omitted.]

NOTES

1. The article on *Fullilove*, which the Court cited in section III(B), was written by Drew Days (Professor at Yale when he wrote the article), who was the U.S. Solicitor General who argued this case.

2. In *United States v. Paradise*, 480 U.S. 149, 107 S.Ct. 1053, 94 L.Ed.2d 203 (1987) (5 to 4), which the Court cites as an example of permissible affirmative action, the trial court found, in 1972, that the Alabama Department of Public Safety systematically excluded blacks from employment as state troopers in violation of the Fourteenth Amendment. By 1979, five years after the trial court ordered the Department to refrain from employment discrimination, including promotions, there still were no blacks in the upper ranks of the department. It was not until 1983 that the department agreed to promote four blacks to corporal (among 15 new corporals). The trial court then ordered that, "for a period of time," at least 50% of those promoted to corporal must be black, if qualified black candidates were available. The trial court also imposed a 50% promotional requirement in the other upper ranks, but only if (1) there were qualified black candidates available, *and if* (2) a particular rank were less than 25% black, *and if* (3) the Department had not developed and implemented a promotion plan that did not have adverse impact for the relevant rank. Pursuant to this order, the Department promoted eight blacks and eight whites, and submitted its proposed corporal and sergeant promotional procedures for corporal and sergeant. The trial court then suspended the 50% requirement.

    The Supreme Court, with no majority, affirmed the one-for-one promotional requirement. O'Connor, J., dissenting, joined by Scalia, J. and Rehnquist, C.J., arguing that the trial court's action was not narrowly tailored. (White, J., also dissented on similar grounds.) The dissent argued that the "one-for-one promotion quota used in this case far exceeded the percentage of blacks in the trooper force, and there is no evidence in the record that such an extreme quota was necessary to eradicate the effects of the Department's delay." The plurality argued that the one-for-one promotion, when compared to the 25% minority labor pool, was not arbitrary, because the 50% figure was not the goal but merely determined the speed at which the 25% goal would be achieved.

3.   After the decision in *Richmond v. J.A. Croson Co.,* discussed in *Adarand Constructors,* about 50 of the approximately 200 affirmative action plans of state and local governments were voluntarily dropped. Lower court decisions eliminated approximately another dozen plans. In Richmond, the percentage of the city's construction contracts dropped from more than 30% to the low single digits.'

5.3 ALIENAGE

AMBACH V. NORWICK
441 U.S. 68, 99 S.Ct. 1589, 60 L.Ed.2d 49 (1979)

JUSTICE POWELL delivered the opinion of the Court.

This case presents the question whether a State, consistently with the Equal Protection Clause of the Fourteenth Amendment, may refuse to employ as elementary and secondary school teachers aliens who are eligible for United States citizenship but who refuse to seek naturalization. . . .

The decisions of this Court regarding the permissibility of statutory classifications involving aliens have not formed an unwavering line over the years. State regulation of the employment of aliens long has been subject to constitutional constraints. In *Yick Wo v. Hopkins,* the Court struck down an ordinance which was applied to prevent aliens from running laundries, and in *Truax v. Raich,* 239 U.S. 33, 36 S.Ct. 7, 60 L.Ed. 131 (1915), a law requiring at least 80% of the employees of certain businesses to be citizens was held to be an unconstitutional infringement of an alien's "right to work for a living in the common occupations of the community. . . ." At the same time, however, the Court also has recognized a greater degree of latitude for the States when aliens were sought to be excluded from public employment. At the time *Truax* was decided, the governing doctrine permitted States to exclude aliens from various activities when the restriction pertained to "the regulation or distribution of the public domain, or of the common property or resources of the people of the State. . . ." Hence, as part of a larger authority to forbid aliens from owning land, *Terrace v. Thompson,* 263 U.S. 197, 44 S.Ct. 15, 68 L.Ed. 255 (1923); harvesting wildlife *McCready v. Virginia,* 4 Otto 391, 94 U.S. 391, 24 L.Ed. 248 (1877); or maintaining an inherently dangerous enterprise, *Ohio ex rel. Clarke v. Deckebach,* 274

U.S. 392, 47 S.Ct. 630, 71 L.Ed. 1115 (1927), States permissibly could exclude aliens from working on public construction projects, *Crane v. New York,* 239 U.S. 195, 36 S.Ct. 85, 60 L.Ed. 218 (1915), and, it appears, from engaging in any form of public employment at all, see *Truax, supra.*

Over time, the Court's decisions gradually have restricted the activities from which States are free to exclude aliens. The first sign that the Court would question the constitutionality of discrimination against aliens even in areas affected with a "public interest" appeared in *Oyama v. California,* 332 U.S. 633, 68 S.Ct. 269, 92 L.Ed. 249 (1948). The Court there held that statutory presumptions designed to discourage evasion of California's ban on alien landholding discriminated against the citizen children of aliens. The same Term, the Court held that the "ownership" a State exercises over fish found in its territorial waters "is inadequate to justify California in excluding any or all aliens who are lawful residents of the State from making a living by fishing in the ocean off its shores while permitting all others to do so." *Takahashi v. Fish & Game Comm'n,* 334 U.S. 410, 421, 68 S.Ct. 1138, 1144, 92 L.Ed. 1478 (1948). This process of withdrawal from the former doctrine culminated in *Graham v. Richardson,* [403 U.S. 365, 91 S.Ct. 1848, 29 L.Ed.2d 534 (1971)], which for the first time treated classifications based on alienage as "inherently suspect and subject to close judicial scrutiny." Applying *Graham,* this Court has held invalid statutes that prevented aliens from entering a State's classified civil service, *Sugarman v. Dougall,* 413 U.S. 634, 93 S.Ct. 2842, 37 L.Ed.2d 853 (1973), practicing law, *In re Griffiths,* 413 U.S. 717, 93 S.Ct. 2851, 37 L.Ed.2d 910 (1973), working as an engineer, *Examining Board v. Flores de Otero,* 426 U.S. 572, 96 S.Ct. 2264, 49 L.Ed.2d 65 (1976), and receiving state educational benefits, *Nyquist v. Mauclet,* 432 U.S. 1, 97 S.Ct. 2120, 53 L.Ed.2d 63 (1977).

Although our more recent decisions have departed substantially from the public-interest doctrine of Truax's day, they have not abandoned the general principle that some state functions are so bound up with the operation of the State as a governmental entity as to permit the exclusion from those functions of all persons who have not become part of the process of self-government. In *Sugarman,* we recognized that a State could, "in an appropriately defined class of positions, require citizenship as a qualification for office." We went on to observe:

> Such power inheres in the State by virtue of its obligation, already noted above, to preserve the basic conception of a political community. . . . And this power and responsibility of the State applies, not only to the qualifications of voters, but also to persons holding state elective or important nonelective executive, legislative, and judicial

positions, for officers who participate directly in the formulation, execution, or review of broad public policy perform functions that go to the heart of representative government.

The exclusion of aliens from such governmental positions would not invite as demanding scrutiny from this Court.

Applying the rational-basis standard, we held last Term that New York could exclude aliens from the ranks of its police force. *Foley v. Connelie,* 435 U.S. 291, 98 S.Ct. 1067, 55 L.Ed.2d 287 (1978). Because the police function fulfilled "a most fundamental obligation of government to its constituency" and by necessity cloaked policemen with substantial discretionary powers, we viewed the police force as being one of those appropriately defined classes of positions for which a citizenship requirement could be imposed. Accordingly, the State was required to justify its classification only "by a showing of some rational relationship between the interest sought to be protected and the limiting classification."

The rule for governmental functions, which is an exception to the general standard applicable to classifications based on alienage, rests on important principles inherent in the Constitution. The distinction between citizens and aliens, though ordinarily irrelevant to private activity, is fundamental to the definition and government of a State. [A]n oath of allegiance or similar ceremony cannot substitute for the unequivocal legal bond citizenship represents. It is because of this special significance of citizenship that governmental entities, when exercising the functions of government have wider latitude in limiting the participation of noncitizens.

In determining whether, for purposes of equal protection analysis, teaching in public schools constitutes a governmental function, we look to the role of public education and to the degree of responsibility and discretion teachers possess in fulfilling that role. See *Foley v. Connelie, supra.* Each of these considerations supports the conclusion that public school teachers may be regarded as performing a task "that go[es] to the heart of representative government." *Sugarman v. Dougall, supra.*[6]

Public education, like the police function, "fulfills a most fundamental obligation of government to its constituency." The importance of public schools

---

[6]   . . . New York's citizenship requirement is limited to a governmental function because it applies only to teachers employed by and acting as agents of the State. The Connecticut statute held unconstitutional in *In re Griffiths,* 413 U.S. 717, 93 S.Ct. 2851, 37 L.Ed.2d 910 (1973), by contrast, applied to all attorneys, most of whom do not work for the government. The exclusion of aliens from access to the bar implicated the right to pursue a chosen occupation, not access to public employment. . . .

in the preparation of individuals for participation as citizens, and in the preservation of the values on which our society rests, long has been recognized by our decisions.... Other authorities have perceived public schools as an "assimilative force" by which diverse and conflicting elements in our society are brought together on a broad but common ground.... This influence [of the teacher] is crucial to the continued good health of a democracy.

Furthermore, it is clear that all public school teachers, and not just those responsible for teaching the courses most directly related to government, history, and civic duties, should help fulfill the broader function of the public school system. Teachers, regardless of their specialty, may be called upon to teach other subjects, including those expressly dedicated to political and social subjects. More importantly, a State properly may regard all teachers as having an obligation to promote civic virtues and understanding in their classes, regardless of the subject taught. Certainly a State also may take account of a teacher's function as an example for students, which exists independently of particular classroom subjects. In light of the foregoing considerations, we think it clear that public school teachers come well within the "governmental function" principle recognized in *Sugarman* and *Foley*. Accordingly, the Constitution requires only that a citizenship requirement applicable to teaching in the public schools bear a rational relationship to a legitimate state interest.

As the legitimacy of the State's interest in furthering the educational goals outlined above is undoubted, it remains only to consider whether § 3001(3) bears a rational relationship to this interest. The restriction is carefully framed to serve its purpose, as it bars from teaching only those aliens who have demonstrated their unwillingness to obtain United States citizenship. Appellees, and aliens similarly situated, in effect have chosen to classify themselves.

JUSTICE BLACKMUN, with whom JUSTICE BRENNAN, JUSTICE MARSHALL, and JUSTICE STEVENS join, dissenting:

Once again the Court is asked to rule upon the constitutionality of one of New York's many statutes that impose a requirement of citizenship upon a person before that person may earn his living in a specified occupation.[1] These New York statutes, for the most part, have their origin in the frantic and overreactive days of the First World War when attitudes of parochialism and fear of the foreigner were the order of the day.... We are concerned here with elementary and secondary education in the public schools of New York State. We are not concerned with

---

[1] ... Among [such statutes still in effect] are those relating to the occupations of inspector, certified shorthand reporter, funeral director, masseur, physical therapist, and animal technician.

teaching at the college or graduate levels. It seems constitutionally absurd, to say the least, that in these lower levels of public education a Frenchman may not teach French or, indeed, an Englishwoman may not teach the grammar of the English language. [I]t is logically impossible to differentiate between this case concerning teachers and *In re Griffiths* concerning attorneys. If a resident alien *may not* constitutionally be barred from taking a state bar examination and thereby becoming qualified to practice law in the courts of a State, how is one to comprehend why a resident alien *may* constitutionally be barred from teaching in the elementary and secondary levels of a State's public schools? . . .

PLYLER V. DOE

457 U.S. 202, 102 S.Ct. 2382, 72 L.Ed.2d 786 (1982)

JUSTICE BRENNAN delivered the opinion of the Court.

The question presented by these cases is whether, consistent with the Equal Protection Clause of the Fourteenth Amendment, Texas may deny to undocumented school-age children the free public education that it provides to children who are citizens of the United States or legally admitted aliens. . . .

In May 1975, the Texas legislature revised its education laws to withhold from local school districts any state funds for the education of children who were not "legally admitted" into the United States. The 1975 revision also authorized local school districts to deny enrollment in their public schools to children not "legally admitted" to the country. These cases involve constitutional challenges to those provisions. . . .

. . . That a person's initial entry into a State, or into the United States, was unlawful, and that he may for that reason be expelled, cannot negate the simple fact of his presence within the State's territorial perimeter. Given such presence, he is subject to the full range of obligations imposed by the State's civil and criminal laws. And until he leaves the jurisdiction—either voluntarily, or involuntarily in accordance with the Constitution and laws of the United States—he is entitled to the equal protection of the laws that a State may choose to establish. . . .

Sheer incapability or lax enforcement of the laws barring entry into this country, coupled with the failure to establish an effective bar to the employment of undocumented aliens, has resulted in the creation of a substantial "shadow population" of illegal migrants—numbering in the millions—within our borders. This situation raises the specter of a permanent caste of undocumented resident aliens, encouraged by some to remain here as a source of cheap labor, but nevertheless denied the benefits that our society makes available to citizens and lawful residents. The existence of such an underclass presents most difficult problems for a Nation that prides itself on adherence to principles of equality under law.[19]

The children who are plaintiffs in these cases are special members of this underclass. Persuasive arguments support the view that a State may withhold its beneficence from those whose very presence within the United States is the product of their own unlawful conduct. These arguments do not apply with the same force to classifications imposing disabilities on the minor *children* of such illegal entrants. At the least, those who elect to enter our territory by stealth and in violation of our law should be prepared to bear the consequences, including, but not limited to, deportation. But the children of those illegal entrants are not comparably situated. [T]he children who are plaintiffs in these cases "can affect neither their parents' conduct nor their own status." Even if the State found it expedient to control the conduct of adults by acting against their children, legislation directing the onus of a parent's misconduct against his children does not comport with fundamental conceptions of justice. "[N]o child is responsible for his birth and penalizing the . . . child is an ineffectual—as well as unjust—way of deterring the parent."

Of course, undocumented status is not irrelevant to any proper legislative goal. Nor is undocumented status an absolutely immutable characteristic since it is the product of conscious, indeed unlawful, action. But § 21.031 is directed against children, and imposes its discriminatory burden on the basis of a legal characteristic over which children can have little control. It is thus difficult to conceive of a rational justification for penalizing these children for their presence within the United States. Yet that appears to be precisely the effect of § 21.031.

Public education is not a "right" granted to individuals by the Constitution. But neither is it merely some governmental "benefit" indistinguishable from other forms of social welfare legislation. Both the importance of education in maintaining our basic institutions, and the lasting impact of its deprivation on the

---

[19]   We reject the claim that "illegal aliens" are a "suspect class." [E]ntry into this class, by virtue of entry into this country, is the product of voluntary action. Indeed, entry into the class is itself a crime. In addition, it could hardly be suggested that undocumented status is a "constitutional irrelevancy." With respect to the actions of the federal government, alienage classifications may be intimately related to the conduct of foreign policy, to the federal prerogative to control access to the United States, and to the plenary federal power to determine who has sufficiently manifested his allegiance to become a citizen of the Nation. No State may independently exercise a like power. But if the Federal Government has by uniform rule prescribed what it believes to be appropriate standards for the treatment of an alien subclass, the States may, of course, follow the federal direction.

life of the child, mark the distinction. . . . We cannot ignore the significant social costs borne by our Nation when select groups are denied the means to absorb the values and skills upon which our social order rests. . . .

These well-settled principles allow us to determine the proper level of deference to be afforded § 21.031. Undocumented aliens cannot be treated as a suspect class because their presence in this country in violation of federal law is not a "constitutional irrelevancy." Nor is education a fundamental right; a State need not justify by compelling necessity every variation in the manner in which education is provided to its population. See *San Antonio School Dist. v. Rodriguez*, 411 U.S. 1, 28–39, 93 S.Ct. 1278, 36 L.Ed.2d 16 (1973). But more is involved in this case than the abstract question whether § 21.031 discriminates against a suspect class, or whether education is a fundamental right. Section 21.031 imposes a lifetime hardship on a discrete class of children not accountable for their disabling status. The stigma of illiteracy will mark them for the rest of their lives. By denying these children a basic education, we deny them the ability to live within the structure of our civic institutions, and foreclose any realistic possibility that they will contribute in even the smallest way to the progress of our Nation. In determining the rationality of § 21.031, we may appropriately take into account its costs to the Nation and to the innocent children who are its victims. In light of these countervailing costs, the discrimination contained in § 21.031 can hardly be considered rational unless it furthers some substantial goal of the State. . . .

[W]e are unable to find in the congressional immigration scheme any statement of policy that might weigh significantly in arriving at an equal protection balance concerning the State's authority to deprive these children of an education. . . . The State does not claim that the conservation of state educational resources was ever a congressional concern in restricting immigration. . . . In light of the discretionary federal power to grant relief from deportation, a State cannot realistically determine that any particular undocumented child will in fact be deported until after deportation proceedings have been completed. It would of course be most difficult for the State to justify a denial of education to a child enjoying an inchoate federal permission to remain.

We are reluctant to impute to Congress the intention to withhold from these children, for so long as they are present in this country through no fault of their own, access to a basic education. In other contexts, undocumented status, coupled with some articulable federal policy, might enhance State authority with respect to the treatment of undocumented aliens. But in the area of special constitutional sensitivity presented by this case, and in the absence of any contrary indication fairly discernible in the present legislative record, we perceive no national policy that supports the State in denying these children an elementary education. . . .

Appellants argue that the classification at issue furthers an interest in the "preservation of the state's limited resources for the education of its lawful residents." [But] a concern for the preservation of resources standing alone can hardly justify the classification used in allocating those resources. Apart from the asserted state prerogative to act against undocumented children solely on the basis of their undocumented status—an asserted prerogative that carries only minimal force in the circumstances of this case—we discern three colorable state interests that might support § 21.031.

First, appellants appear to suggest that the State may seek to protect the State from an influx of illegal immigrants. . . . There is no evidence in the record suggesting that illegal entrants impose any significant burden on the State's economy. To the contrary, the available evidence suggests that illegal aliens underutilize public services, while contributing their labor to the local economy and tax money to the State fisc. The dominant incentive for illegal entry into the State of Texas is the availability of employment; few if any illegal immigrants come to this country, or presumably to the State of Texas, in order to avail themselves of a free education. . . .

Second . . . appellants suggest that undocumented children are appropriately singled out for exclusion because of the special burdens they impose on the State's ability to provide high quality public education. But the record in no way supports the claim that exclusion of undocumented children is likely to improve the overall quality of education in the State. [E]ven if improvement in the quality of education were a likely result of barring some *number* of children from the schools of the State, the State must support its selection of *this* group as the appropriate target for exclusion. In terms of educational cost and need, however, undocumented children are "basically indistinguishable" from legally resident alien children.

Finally, appellants suggest that undocumented children are appropriately singled out because their unlawful presence within the United States renders them less likely than other children to remain within the boundaries of the State, and to put their education to productive social or political use within the State. Even assuming that such an interest is legitimate, it is an interest that is most difficult to quantify. The State has no assurance that any child, citizen or not, will employ the education provided by the State within the confines of the State's borders. . . .

If the State is to deny a discrete group of innocent children the free public education that it offers to other children residing within its borders, that denial must be justified by a showing that it furthers some substantial state interest. No such showing was made here. Accordingly, the judgment of the Court of Appeals in each of these cases is

Affirmed.

JUSTICE POWELL, concurring:

[T]he exclusion of appellee's class[5] of children from state-provided education is a type of punitive discrimination based on status that is impermissible under the Equal Protection Clause. [I]t hardly can be argued rationally that anyone benefits from the creation within our borders of a subclass of illiterate persons many of whom will remain in the State, adding to the problems and costs of both State and National Governments attendant upon unemployment, welfare and crime.

CHIEF JUSTICE BURGER, with whom JUSTICE WHITE, JUSTICE REHNQUIST, and JUSTICE O'CONNOR join, dissenting:

Were it our business to set the Nation's social policy, I would agree without hesitation that it is senseless for an enlightened society to deprive any children—including illegal aliens—of an elementary education. I fully agree that it would be folly—and wrong—to tolerate creation of a segment of society made up of illiterate persons, many having a limited or no command of our language. However, the Constitution does not constitute us as "Platonic Guardians" nor does it vest in this Court the authority to strike down laws because they do not meet our standards of desirable social policy, "wisdom," or "common sense." [I]t is not the function of the judiciary to provide "effective leadership" simply because the political branches of government fail to do so. . . .

The dispositive issue in these cases, simply put, is whether, for purposes of allocating its finite resources, a State has a legitimate reason to differentiate between persons who are lawfully within the State and those who are unlawfully there. The distinction the State of Texas has drawn—based not only upon its own legitimate interests but on classifications established by the federal government in its immigration laws and policies—is not unconstitutional. . . . Yet by patching together bits and pieces of what might be termed quasi-suspect-class and quasifundamental-rights analysis, the Court spins out a theory custom-tailored to the facts of these cases. In the end, we are told little more than that the level of scrutiny employed to strike down the Texas law applies only when illegal alien

---

[5]   . . . A different case would be presented in the unlikely event that a minor, old enough to be responsible for illegal entry and yet still of school age, entered this country illegally on his own volition.

children are deprived of a public education.[3] If ever a court was guilty of an unabashedly result-oriented approach, this case is a prime example.

The Court first suggests that these illegal alien children, although not a suspect class, are entitled to special solicitude under the Equal Protection Clause because they lack "control" over or "responsibility" for their unlawful entry into this country. Similarly, the Court appears to take the position that § 21.031 is presumptively "irrational" because it has the effect of imposing "penalties" on "innocent" children.[4] However, the Equal Protection Clause does not preclude legislators from classifying among persons on the basis of factors and characteristics over which individuals may be said to lack "control." Indeed, in some circumstances persons generally, and children in particular, may have little control over or responsibility for such things as their ill-health, need for public assistance, or place of residence. Yet a state legislature is not barred from considering, for example, relevant differences between the mentally-healthy and the mentally-ill, or between the residents of different counties, simply because these may be factors unrelated to individual choice or to any "wrongdoing." The Equal Protection Clause protects against arbitrary and irrational classifications, and against invidious discrimination stemming from prejudice and hostility; it is not an all-encompassing "equalizer" designed to eradicate every distinction for which persons are not "responsible." . . .

The second strand of the Court's analysis rests on the premise that, although public education is not a constitutionally-guaranteed right, "neither is it merely some governmental 'benefit' indistinguishable from other forms of social welfare legislation." Whatever meaning or relevance this opaque observation might have in some other context, it simply has no bearing on the issues at hand. . . . Is the Court suggesting that education is more "fundamental" than food, shelter, or medical care?

Once it is conceded—as the Court does—that illegal aliens are not a suspect class, and that education is not a fundamental right, our inquiry should focus on and be limited to whether the legislative classification at issue bears a rational relationship to a legitimate state purpose. [I]t simply is not "irrational" for a State

---

[3]   The Court implies, for example, that the Fourteenth Amendment would not require a State to provide welfare benefits to illegal aliens.

[4]   Both the opinion of the Court and Justice Powell's concurrence imply that appellees are being "penalized" because their *parents* are illegal entrants. However, Texas has classified appellees on the basis of *their own* illegal status, not that of their parents. Children born in this country to illegal alien parents, including some of appellees' siblings, are not excluded from the Texas schools. Nor does Texas discriminate against appellees because of their Mexican origin or citizenship. Texas provides a free public education to countless thousands of Mexican immigrants who are lawfully in this country.

to conclude that it does not have the same responsibility to provide benefits for persons whose very presence in the State and this country is illegal as it does to provide for persons lawfully present. By definition, illegal aliens have no right whatever to be here, and the State may reasonably, and constitutionally, elect not to provide them with governmental services at the expense of those who are lawfully in the State. . . .

It is significant that the federal government has seen fit to exclude illegal aliens from numerous social welfare programs, such as the food stamp program, 7 U.S.C.A. § 2015(f) and 7 CFR § 273.4 (1981), the old age assistance, aid to families with dependent children, aid to the blind, aid to the permanently and totally disabled, and supplemental security income programs, 45 CFR § 233.50 (1981), the Medicare hospital insurance benefits program, 42 U.S.C.A. § 1395i–2 and 42 CFR § 405.205(b) (1981), and the Medicaid hospital insurance benefits for the aged and disabled program, 42 U.S.C.A. § 1395o and 42 CFR § 405.103(a)(4) (1981). Although these exclusions do not conclusively demonstrate the constitutionality of the State's use of the same classification for comparable purposes, at the very least they tend to support the rationality of excluding illegal alien residents of a State from such programs so as to preserve the State's finite revenues for the benefit of lawful residents. . . .

The concurring opinions of MARSHALL & BLACKMUN, JJ., are omitted.

NOTES

1. *Graham v. Richardson,* 403 U.S. 365, 91 S.Ct. 1848, 29 L.Ed.2d 534 (1971), held that state statutes that deny welfare benefits to resident aliens, or to aliens not meeting a requirement of durational residence within the United States, violate the equal protection clause of the Fourteenth Amendment and encroach upon the exclusive federal power over the entrance and residence of aliens.

   Graham dealt with *state* power over aliens. Federal power is much greater. In *Mathews v. Diaz,* 426 U.S. 67, 96 S.Ct. 1883, 48 L.Ed.2d 478 (1976), a unanimous Court held that Congress could constitutionally condition an alien's eligibility for participation in a federal medical insurance program on continuous residence in the United States for a five-year period and admission for permanent residence. The Court readily agreed that the Fifth Amendment, like the Fourteenth, protects aliens. "Even one whose presence in the country is unlawful, involuntary, or transitory is entitled to that constitutional protection." But that fact does not lead to the conclusion that "all aliens are entitled to enjoy all the advantages of citizenship" because of Congress' broad power over immigration and naturalization:

> For reasons long recognized as valid, the responsibility for regulating the relationship between the United States and our alien visitors has been committed to the political branches of the Federal Government. . . . Any rule of constitutional law that would inhibit the flexibility of the political branches of government to respond to changing world conditions should be adopted only with the greatest caution. The reasons that preclude judicial review of political questions also dictate a narrow standard of review of decisions made by the Congress or the President in the area of immigration and naturalization. . . . In short, it is unquestionably reasonable for Congress to make an alien's eligibility depend on both the character and the duration of his residence. Since neither requirement is wholly irrational, this case essentially involves nothing more than a claim that it would have been more reasonable for Congress to select somewhat different requirements of the same kind.

2. In *Hampton v. Mow Sun Wong*, 426 U.S. 88, 96 S.Ct. 1895, 48 L.Ed.2d 495 (1976), decided the same day as *Diaz*, Justice Stevens again wrote the opinion of the Court. Unlike the unanimous *Diaz* opinion, *Mow Sun Wong* drew four dissents. Five lawful, permanently residing aliens challenged the constitutionality of U.S. Civil Service regulations barring resident aliens from employment in the federal competitive civil service. Earlier, *Sugarman v. Dougall*, 413 U.S. 634, 93 S.Ct. 2842, 37 L.Ed.2d 853 (1973), invalidated a *state* law excluding aliens from permanent positions in all of the state's competitive civil service. The law swept indiscriminately and was not carefully tailored to serve substantial state interests. The Court in *Mow Sun Wong* reasoned, "the paramount federal power over immigration and naturalization forecloses a simple extension of the holding in *Sugarman*," because "overriding national interests may provide a justification for a citizenship requirement in the federal service even though an identical requirement may not be enforced by a State."

The U.S. Civil Service broad employment prohibition, the Court acknowledged, could serve various interests: giving the President a bargaining chip in seeking reciprocal concessions in his negotiations with foreign powers; giving aliens an incentive to qualify for naturalization; and avoiding the administrative effort of classifying sensitive positions that only citizens should hold. However, the Civil Service Commission has no responsibility for foreign affairs, treaty negotiation, or naturalization policies. Because Congress had not delegated to the Civil Service Commission the authority to make such policy judgments regarding aliens, and the President and Congress did not mandated such restrictions themselves, the Court invalidated the U.S. Civil Service rule. Three months after this decision, President Ford issued an executive order barring, with certain exceptions, noncitizens from employment in the federal civil service. Executive Order 11935, 41 Fed. Reg. 37301 (Sept. 2, 1976), 5 C.F.R., Part 7, § 7.4. On remand the district court upheld the constitutionality of the executive order. *Mow Sun Wong v. Hampton*, 435 F.Supp. 37, 42–46 (N.D.Cal.1977); see also *Vergara v. Hampton*, 581 F.2d 1281, 1286–87 (7th Cir. 1978), cert, denied 441 U.S. 905, 99 S.Ct. 1993, 60 L.Ed.2d 373 (1979); *Jalil v. Campbell*, 590 F.2d 1120, 1123 n. 3 (D.C.C.ir.1978).

3.   When we consider this entire series of cases, we can formulate a rule that generally explains what the present law is. FIRST, when state or local laws classify persons on the basis of United States citizenship for the purpose of distributing economic benefits, or limiting the opportunity to engage in private sector economic activity, the Court will subject the law to strict judicial scrutiny. These classifications based on alienage are "suspect" and upheld only if necessary to promote a compelling or overriding interest. It will be very difficult for the state to meet this test because in almost all instances the lawfully resident noncitizen is subject to federal and state taxation just as is the resident citizen. The lawfully resident alien is not reasonably distinguishable from the citizen in terms of legitimate, nondiscriminatory economic goals of the state.

SECOND, if the state uses alienage classification to allocate power or positions in the political process, the Court will uphold the law under the traditional rational basis test. *Ambach v. Norwick* said it will apply the traditional rational basis test to "state elective or important nonelective executive, legislative, and judicial positions, for officers who participate directly in the formulation, execution, or review of broad public policy perform functions that go to the heart of representative government." Without selling public school teachers short, one wonders why the Court concludes, "public school teachers may be regarded as performing a task 'that go[es] to the heart of representative government.' " (In *Ambach*, footnote 6, the Court says it is only talking about *public* school teachers, not teachers in private schools.) However, states may not use a United States citizenship classification to exclude lawfully resident aliens from employment in government positions that are purely functionary and are not related to the interest in self-governance.

THIRD, the Court will subject alienage classifications created by federal law to the rational basis standard of review because the federal government has interests and powers over aliens that the states do not share.

5.4 ILLEGITIMACY

Historically, laws have burdened illegitimate children, who suffer because their parents were not married. Under the common law of England, a child born out of wedlock was *nullius filius*, the "son of nobody." These children could not be the heir to anyone, and their parents owe them no obligation of support. One legal analysis concluded, in 1923, "Except in Connecticut, a bastard cannot, in the absence of legislative provision, inherit from his ancestors or collateral relatives."[14] Over the years, some states removed some of the restrictions but others did not. For example, the 1969 Louisiana Civil Code, article 920, stated, "Bastard, adulterous or incestuous children shall not enjoy the right of inheriting the estate of their natural father or mother . . ."

In a series of cases beginning in the 1970's, the Court began to examine carefully, and invalidate, laws that discriminated against illegitimates. For example, *Weber v. Aetna Casualty & Surety Co.,* 406 U.S. 164, 92 S.Ct. 1400, 31 L.Ed.2d 768 (1972) invalidated a Louisiana law that denied to dependent, unacknowledged, illegitimate children a right to recover benefits under Louisiana's workmen's compensation law for the death of their biological father on an equal footing with the father's dependent legitimate children. Under the state law, the biological father could not have acknowledged his illegitimate children living in his household even if he had desired to do so: the state prohibited acknowledgment of children if the parents were incapable of contracting marriage at the time of conception. This biological father could not marry the mother because he remained married to his first wife.

The state law did not serve any interest the state has in reducing false claims because of the difficulty of proof of parentage: "By limiting recovery to dependents of the deceased, Louisiana substantially lessens the possible problems of locating illegitimate children and of determining uncertain claims of

---

[14]   24 American Law Reports 570.

parenthood." The law also did not serve the state's interest in encouraging legitimate family relationships: "no child is responsible for his birth and penalizing the illegitimate child is an ineffective—as well as an unjust—way of deterring the parent." Justice Rehnquist was the sole dissent.

In *Trimble v. Gordon*, 430 U.S. 762, 97 S.Ct. 1459, 52 L.Ed.2d 31 (1977), an Illinois statute allowed a child born out of wedlock to inherit from his "intestate father" (a father who had no will) only if the father had "acknowledged" the child and the parents' marriage legitimated the child. The appellant in *Trimble* was a child born out of wedlock whose father neither had acknowledged her nor married her mother. However, a judicial decree found him to be her father and ordered him to contribute to her support. When the father died intestate, the child was excluded as an heir because the statutory requirements for inheritance had not been met. The Court held that the Illinois statute discriminated against illegitimate children in violation of the Equal Protection Clause. The difficulties in proving paternity in some situations did not justify total statutory disinheritance of children born out of wedlock.

Pickett v. Brown, 462 U.S. 1, 103 S.Ct. 2199, 76 L.Ed.2d 372 (1983) unanimously invalidated a Tennessee law requiring that certain paternity and support actions be filed within two years after the child's birth. The state's interest in preventing stale claims is becoming "more attenuated as scientific advances in blood testing have alleviated the problem of proof surrounding paternity actions." In these series of cases, the Justices often disagreed on what test courts should use to determine if a state law violates equal protection. Finally, the Court agreed on a test (and it did so *unanimously*), in *Clark v. Jetter*.

CLARK V. JETER

486 U.S. 456, 108 S.Ct. 1910, 100 L.Ed.2d 465 (1988)

[A Pennsylvania law ordinarily required an illegitimate child to establish paternity within six years of the illegitimate child's birth, while a legitimate child could seek support from his or her parents at any time. The Court held that the six-year statute of limitations was not substantially related to Pennsylvania's legitimate interest in avoiding stale or fraudulent claims. First, in some other cases it places no limit on when the paternity issue may be litigated (*e.g.*, at any time, under the intestacy statute, if there is "clear and convincing evidence that the man was the father of the child"). Second, while the state has interest in the proof of paternity, "increasingly sophisticated tests for genetic markers permit the exclusion of over 99% of those who might be accused of paternity, regardless of the age of the child." Then, the Court explained the proper "intermediate scrutiny" test to use under the Equal Protection Clause when courts examine state legislation discriminating against illegitimates.]

O'CONNOR, J., delivered the opinion for a unanimous Court. . . .

In considering whether state legislation violates the Equal Protection Clause of the Fourteenth Amendment, U.S. Const., Amdt. 14, § 1, we apply different levels of scrutiny to different types of classifications. At a minimum, a statutory classification must be rationally related to a legitimate governmental purpose. Classifications based on race or national origin, and classifications affecting fundamental rights, are given the most exacting scrutiny. Between these extremes of rational basis review and strict scrutiny lies a level of intermediate scrutiny, which generally has been applied to discriminatory classifications based on sex or illegitimacy.

To withstand intermediate scrutiny, a statutory classification must be substantially related to an important governmental objective. Consequently we have invalidated classifications that burden illegitimate children for the sake of punishing the illicit relations of their parents, because "visiting this condemnation on the head of an infant is illogical and unjust. [T]his Court acknowledged that it might be appropriate to treat illegitimate children differently in the support context because of "lurking problems with respect to proof of paternity."

[However,] increasingly sophisticated tests for genetic markers permit the exclusion of over 99% of those who might be accused of paternity, regardless of the age of the child. H.R.Rep. No. 98–527, p. 38 (1983). This scientific evidence is available throughout the child's minority, and it is an additional reason to doubt that Pennsylvania had a substantial reason for limiting the time within which paternity and support actions could be brought.

We conclude that the Pennsylvania statute does not withstand heightened scrutiny under the Equal Protection Clause. We therefore find it unnecessary to reach Clark's due process claim. The judgment of the Superior Court is reversed, and the case is remanded for further proceedings not inconsistent with this opinion.

5.5 SEX

In *Bradwell v. Illinois*, 83 U.S. (16 Wall.) 130, 21 L.Ed. 442 (1873), the Supreme Court, with a sole dissent (Chief Justice Chase), upheld the constitutional power of Illinois to refuse to license a woman to practice law simply because she was a woman. Justice Bradley, in a separate opinion concurring in the judgment, felt the need to say that the "natural and proper timidity and delicacy which belongs to the female sex evidently unfits it for many of the occupants of civil life." He added, the "paramount destiny and mission of womanhood are to fulfill the noble and benign offices of wife and mother. This is the law of the creator." Recall in *Strauder v. West Virginia*, section 5.2, *supra*, the Court invalidated, as a denial of equal protection, a state law that precluded blacks from serving on the jury. However, said the Court, the state "may confine the selection to *males*, to freeholders. . . ." (Emphasis added.)

While this litigation was going on, Alta M. Hulett also sought admission to the bar. Supported by Ms. Bradwell, the legal newspaper that she had founded in 1868, and others, she persuaded the Illinois legislature to enact a law providing that no person could be precluded from any occupation except the military on the grounds of sex. In March 1872 (a year before the Court's decision in *Bradwell*), the 18-years old, Ms. Hulett, became the first woman lawyer in Illinois. The Illinois legislature, the popular branch of government, reversed the effect of the state court decision.

There is more to the story. The Illinois Supreme Court, on its own motion, granted Myra Bradwell her license to practice law in 1890. Two years later she was admitted to practice before the United States Supreme Court. She died in 1894, "survived by a son and a daughter, Bessie Bradwell Helmer. Both of her children were lawyers."[15]

In *Goesaert v. Cleary*, 335 U.S. 464, 69 S.Ct. 198, 93 L.Ed. 163 (1948), the Court upheld a Michigan statute that would not license a female as a bartender unless she was the wife or daughter of the male owner of the bar. Justice Frankfurter, for the Court, began with the assumption that the state could bar all women. In dissent, Justice Rutledge, joined by Justices Douglas and Murphy, argued that the statute was irrational:

> The statute arbitrarily discriminates between male and female owners of liquor establishments. A male owner, although he himself is always absent from his bar, may employ his wife and daughter as barmaids. A female owner may neither work as a barmaid herself nor employ her daughter in that position, even if a man is always present in the establishment to keep order. This inevitable result of the classification belies the assumption that the statute was motivated by a legislative

[15] Karen Berger Morello, The Invisible Bar: The Woman Lawyer In America 1638–1986 (Random House, 1986), at p. 21.

solicitude for the moral and physical well-being of women who, but for the law, would be employed as barmaids. Since there could be no other conceivable justification for such discrimination against women owners of liquor establishments, the statute should be held invalid as a denial of equal protection.

Frankfurter responded by arguing that the Court was dealing in an "historic calling. We meet the alewife, sprightly and ribald, in Shakespeare, but centuries before him she played a role in the social life of England." As to the issue of equal protection, "to state the question is in effect to answer it."

Section 1 of the Fourteenth Amendment guarantees equal protection to "any person." Early on, the Supreme Court applied that clause to protect aliens, such as Yick Wo, "a native of China and a subject of the Emperor." See *Yick Wo v. Hopkins*, section 5.2, *supra*. Does "person" mean only "male"? The Framers of the Fourteenth Amendment specifically used "male" in § 2 of the Fourteenth Amendment, but not in § 1. Perhaps inevitably, the Court would have to apply the equal protection clause to discrimination based on sex.

In *Reed v. Reed*, 404 U.S. 71, 92 S.Ct. 251, 30 L.Ed.2d 225 (1971), a unanimous Court invalidated an Idaho statute that provided that, as between persons equally qualified to administer the estate of one who dies without leaving a will, the probate court must prefer males to females. Chief Justice Burger ruled that the statute was arbitrary, in violation of equal protection, and that the state's purpose (to avoid the need to hold hearings to determine who is better qualified) did not save the statute from being arbitrary. Because the alleged administrative efficiency of the statute (it avoided the need to hold hearings) was not sufficient to prevent the statute from being held irrational, many commentators thought that the court was using a new definition of "rational." After all, it is not irrational for the state to provide that, as between two equally qualified people, the court (for administrative efficiency) should choose by flipping a coin. The Court did not cite *Goesaert*.

In *Frontiero v. Richardson*, 411 U.S. 677, 93 S.Ct. 1764, 36 L.Ed.2d 583 (1973), the Court invalidated a federal statute (under the due process clause of the Fifth Amendment) because it did not put women on an equal footing with men in the armed forces with respect to certain fringe benefits. The law allowed a serviceman to claim his wife as a "dependent" for the purposes of obtaining increased living quarters without regard to whether she was in fact dependent on him for any part of her support. In contrast, a servicewoman could not claim her husband as a dependent unless he was in fact dependent for over one-half of his support. The

Court could produce no majority because the Justices could not agree on the proper test for the law. Brennan, J., joined by Douglas, White, & Marshall, JJ., argued for strict scrutiny because "sex, like race and national origin, is an immutable characteristic determined solely by the accident of birth," and unlike intelligence or physical disability, sex "frequently bears no relation to ability to perform or contribute to society." Brennan complained that the nation's long history of sex discrimination rationalized by an attitude of "romantic paternalism . . . put women, not on a pedestal, but in a cage." As to the justification of administrative efficiency (women, the government argued, are more likely to be dependent on men), Brennan said: "[W]hen we enter the realm of 'strict judicial scrutiny,' there can be no doubt that 'administrative convenience' is not a shibboleth."

Brennan could not muster a majority for strict scrutiny, because all of the other Justices (except for Rehnquist, who dissented), while agreeing that the statute was unconstitutional, objected to the strict scrutiny standard. Finally, in the following case the Court agreed on a standard of review for sex discrimination cases. It is the same test the Court now uses in illegitimacy cases, the middle tier analysis: the classification must "be substantially related to important governmental objectives."

CRAIG V. BOREN

429 U.S. 190, 97 S.Ct. 451, 50 L.Ed.2d 397 (1976)

JUSTICE BRENNAN delivered the opinion of the Court.

The interaction of two sections of an Oklahoma statute prohibits the sale of "nonintoxicating" 3.2% beer to males under the age of 21 and to females under the age of 18. The question to be decided is whether such a gender-based differential constitutes a denial to males 18–20 years of age of the equal protection of the laws in violation of the Fourteenth Amendment. . . . To withstand constitutional challenge, previous cases establish that classifications by gender must serve important governmental objectives and must be substantially related to achievement of those objectives. [As in] *Reed v. Reed* [the state may not employ] gender as an inaccurate proxy for other, more germane bases of classification. Hence, "archaic and overbroad" generalizations, concerning the financial position of servicewomen, *Frontiero v. Richardson,* and working women, could not justify use of a gender line in determining eligibility for certain governmental entitlements. Similarly, increasingly outdated misconceptions concerning the role of females in the home rather than in the "marketplace and world of ideas" were rejected as loose-fitting characterizations incapable of supporting state statutory schemes that were premised upon their accuracy. In light of the weak congruence between gender and the characteristic or trait that gender purported to represent, it was necessary that the legislatures choose either to realign their substantive laws in a gender-neutral fashion, or to adopt procedures for identifying those instances where the sex-centered generalization actually comported with fact.

. . . We turn then to the question whether, under *Reed*, the difference between males and females with respect to the purchase of 3.2% beer warrants the differential in age drawn by the Oklahoma statute. We conclude that it does not. . . . We accept for purposes of discussion the District Court's identification of the objective underlying §§ 241 and 245 as the enhancement of traffic safety. Clearly, the protection of public health and safety represents an important function of state and local governments. However, appellees' statistics in our view cannot support the conclusion that the gender-based distinction closely serves to achieve that objective and therefore the distinction cannot under *Reed* withstand equal protection challenge.

The appellees introduced a variety of statistical surveys. First, an analysis of arrest statistics for 1973 demonstrated that 18-20-year-old male arrests for "driving under the influence" and "drunkenness" substantially exceeded female arrests for that same age.[8] Similarly, youths aged 17–21 were found to be overrepresented among those killed or injured in traffic accidents, with males again numerically exceeding females in this regard. . . .

Even were this statistical evidence accepted as accurate, it nevertheless offers only a weak answer to the equal protection question presented here. The most focused and relevant of the statistical surveys, arrests of 18-20-year-olds for alcohol-related driving offenses, exemplifies the ultimate unpersuasiveness of this evidentiary record. Viewed in terms of the correlation between sex and the actual activity that Oklahoma seeks to regulate—driving while under the influence of alcohol—the statistics broadly establish that .18% of females and 2% of males in that age group were arrested for that offense. While such a disparity is not trivial in a statistical sense, it hardly can form the basis for employment of a gender line as a classifying device. Certainly if maleness is to serve as a proxy for drinking and driving, a correlation of 2% must be considered an unduly tenuous "fit." Indeed, prior cases have consistently rejected the use of sex as a decisionmaking factor

---

8   . . . Even if we assume that a legislature may rely on such arrest data in some situations, these figures do not offer support for a differential age line, for the disproportionate arrests of males persisted at older ages; indeed, in the case of arrests for drunkenness, the figures for all ages indicated "even more male involvement in such arrests at later ages."

even though the statutes in question certainly rested on far more predictive empirical relationships than this. . . .

There is no reason to belabor this line of analysis. It is unrealistic to expect either members of the judiciary or state officials to be well versed in the rigors of experimental or statistical technique. But this merely illustrates that providing broad sociological propositions by statistics is a dubious business, and one that inevitably is in tension with the normative philosophy that underlies the Equal Protection Clause. Suffice to say that the showing offered by the appellees does not satisfy us that sex represents a legitimate, accurate proxy for the regulation of drinking and driving. In fact, when it is further recognized that Oklahoma's statute prohibits only the selling of 3.2% beer to young males and not their drinking the beverage once acquired (even after purchase by their 18-20-year-old female companions), the relationship between gender and traffic safety becomes far too tenuous to satisfy *Reed's* requirement that the gender-based difference be substantially related to achievement of the statutory objective.

We hold, therefore, that under *Reed*, Oklahoma's 3.2% beer statute invidiously discriminates against males 18-20 years of age.

Appellees argue, however, that §§ 241 and 245 enforce state policies concerning the sale and distribution of alcohol and by force of the Twenty-first Amendment should therefore be held to withstand the equal protection challenge. . . . Once passing beyond consideration of the Commerce Clause, the relevance of the Twenty-first Amendment to other constitutional provisions becomes increasingly doubtful. [S]ocial science studies that have uncovered quantifiable differences in drinking tendencies dividing along both racial and ethnic lines strongly suggest the need for application of the Equal Protection Clause in preventing discriminatory treatment that almost certainly would be perceived as invidious.[22] In sum, the principles embodied in the Equal Protection Clause are not to be rendered inapplicable by statistically measured but loose-fitting generalities concerning the drinking tendencies of aggregate groups. We thus hold that the operation of the Twenty-first Amendment does not alter the application of equal protection standards that otherwise govern this case.

---

[22] Thus, if statistics were to govern the permissibility of state alcohol regulation without regard to the Equal Protection Clause as a limiting principle, it might follow that States could freely favor Jews and Italian Catholics at the expense of all other Americans, since available studies regularly demonstrate that the former two groups exhibit the lowest rates of problem drinking. . . .

We conclude that the gender-based differential contained in Okla.Stat., Tit. 37, § 245 (1976 Supp.) constitutes a denial of the equal protection of the laws to males aged 18–20 and reverse the judgment of the District Court.[26]

It is so ordered.

JUSTICE STEVENS, concurring.

[This classification] is objectionable because it is based on an accident of birth, because it is a mere remnant of the now almost universally rejected tradition of discriminating against males in this age bracket, and because, to the extent it reflects any physical difference between males and females, it is actually perverse.[4] The question then is whether the traffic safety justification put forward by the State is sufficient to make an otherwise offensive classification acceptable. The classification is not totally irrational. [E]ven assuming some such slight benefit, it does not seem to me that an insult to all of the young men of the State can be justified by visiting the sins of the 2% on the 98%.

JUSTICE REHNQUIST, dissenting:

The Court's disposition of this case is objectionable on two grounds. First is its conclusion that *men* challenging a gender-based statute which treats them less favorably than women may invoke a more stringent standard of judicial review than pertains to most other types of classifications. Second is the Court's enunciation of this standard, without citation to any source, as being that "classifications by gender must serve *important* governmental objectives and must be *substantially* related to achievement of those objectives." Ante (emphasis added). The only redeeming feature of the Court's opinion, to my mind, is that it apparently signals a retreat by those who joined the plurality opinion in *Frontiero v. Richardson*, from their view that sex is a "suspect" classification for purposes of equal protection analysis. I think the Oklahoma statute challenged here need pass only the "rational basis" equal protection analysis and I believe that it is constitutional under that analysis. . . .

The Court's conclusion that a law which treats males less favorably than females "must serve important governmental objectives and must be substantially related to achievement of those objectives" apparently comes out of thin air. The Equal Protection Clause contains no such language, and none of our previous cases adopt that standard. I would think we have had enough difficulty with the

---

[26] [T]he Oklahoma Legislature is free to redefine any cutoff age for the purchase and sale of 3.2% beer that it may choose, provided that the redefinition operates in a gender-neutral fashion.

[4] Because males are generally heavier than females, they have a greater capacity to consume alcohol without impairing their driving ability than do females.

two standards of review which our cases have recognized—the norm of "rational basis," and the "compelling state interest" required where a "suspect classification" is involved—so as to counsel weightily against the insertion of still another "standard" between those two.

[The opinion of POWELL, J., concurring, BLACKMUN, J., concurring in part, of STEWART, J., concurring in the judgment, and of BURGER, C.J., dissenting, are omitted.]

NOTES

1. The issue in *Geduldig v. Aiello*, 417 U.S. 484, 94 S.Ct. 2485, 41 L.Ed.2d 256 (1974), was whether California's disability insurance program invidiously discriminated against women by not paying insurance benefits for disability that accompanies normal pregnancy and childbirth. The State intended the program to be self-supporting by the covered employees, and it chose a contribution rate "to maintain the solvency of the program" and "to permit low-income employees to participate with minimal personal sacrifice." If the state were to pay disability benefits for normal pregnancy and delivery, the increased costs to the program would be substantial.

   The Court held that the state insurance program did not violate equal protection. "There is no risk from which men are protected and women are not. Likewise, there is no risk from which women are protected and men are not." This case thus is "a far cry from cases like *Reed v. Reed* and *Frontiero v. Richardson,* involving discrimination based upon gender as such. The California insurance program does not exclude anyone from benefit eligibility because of gender but merely removes one physical condition—pregnancy— from the list of compensable disabilities." The Court said that pregnancy is not a sex-based classification! "While it is true that only women can become pregnant, it does not follow that every legislative classification concerning pregnancy is a sex-based classification." Unless the discrimination based on pregnancy is a mere "pretext designed to effect an invidious discrimination against the members of one sex or the other," lawmakers are constitutionally free to make such distinctions "on any reasonable basis." The California program "divides potential recipients into two groups—pregnant women and nonpregnant persons. While the first group is exclusively female, the second includes members of both sexes. The fiscal and actuarial benefits of the program thus accrue to members of both sexes." Justices Brennan, Douglas, and Marshall dissented.

Two years later the Court ruled that such pregnancy distinctions in disability benefit plans do not constitute gender discrimination under Title VII of the Civil Rights Act of 1964. *General Electric Co. v. Gilbert*, 429 U.S. 125, 97 S.Ct. 401, 50 L.Ed.2d 343 (1976). Congress reversed that result by amending the statute in 1978. Pub.L. 95–555, amending 42 U.S.C.A. § 2000e.

2. Congress submitted the Equal Rights Amendment to the states for ratification on March 22, 1972. Not enough states voted to ratify the E.R.A., which provided:

> Section 1. Equality of rights under the law shall not be denied or abridged by the United States or by any State on account of sex.

> Section 2. The Congress shall have the power to enforce, by appropriate legislation, the provisions of this article.

> Section 3. This amendment shall take effect two years after the date of ratification.

3. In *Michael M. v. Superior Court*, 450 U.S. 464, 101 S.Ct. 1200, 67 L.Ed.2d 437 (1981), the Court, without a majority opinion, ruled that California's "statutory rape" law did not violate equal protection even though the statute made men alone criminally liable for illegal intercourse, which the law defined as intercourse "with a female not the wife of the perpetrator, where the female is under the age of 18 years." Michael M. was 17½ and had intercourse with a female also under 18.

Rehnquist, J., for the plurality, noted that the purpose of the statute, as offered by the state and as accepted by the California Supreme Court, was legitimate: to prevent illegitimate teenage pregnancies. "Moreover, the risk of pregnancy itself constitutes a substantial deterrence to young females. No similar natural sanctions deter males. A criminal sanction imposed solely on males thus serves to roughly 'equalize' the deterrents on the sexes. [A] gender-neutral statute would frustrate its interest in effective enforcement [because] a female is surely less likely to report violations of the statute if she herself would be subject to criminal prosecution."

Stewart, J., concurring, emphasized "the substantial physical risks for prepubescent females that are not shared by their male counterparts." Empirical evidence also showed that sexual abuse of young females is a more serious problem than sexual abuse of young males.

Brennan, J., joined by White and Marshall, JJ., dissented, argued that the California statute is not substantially related to the achievement of the asserted goal of preventing teenage pregnancies. For example, other jurisdictions have a gender—neutral statutory rape law. Even if it is more difficult to enforce a gender-neutral law, "the State has still not shown that those enforcement problems would make such a statute less effective than a gender-based statute in deterring minor females from engaging in sexual intercourse." This dissent also criticized the California Supreme Court for engaging in "a remarkable display of sexual stereotyping" when it stated: "The Legislature is well within its power in imposing criminal sanctions against males, alone, because they are the *only* persons who may physiologically cause the result which the law properly seeks to avoid." (Emphasis in original).

4. In *Personnel Administrator v. Feeney*, 442 U.S. 256, 99 S.Ct. 2282, 60 L.Ed.2d 870 (1979), Justice Stewart for the Court upheld a Massachusetts law that gave all veterans who qualify for state civil service positions an absolute lifetime preference over qualified nonveterans. The statute was sex-neutral on its face, but the preference operated overwhelmingly to the advantage of males, because less than 2% of women in Massachusetts are veterans. The majority applied the test of *Washington v. Davis,* § 5.2, and ruled that no evidence proved that a state created this preference because it had gender-based discriminatory purpose. The state's "legitimate and worthy purpose" was to help veterans. While "few women benefit from the preference, the nonveteran class is not substantially all female." The statute adversely affected too many men (those not veterans) "to permit the inference" that it was "but a pretext for preferring men over women." Only Justices Marshall and Brennan, dissented because the statute's disproportionate impact flows "inexorably" from "the long history of policies severely limiting women's participation in the military."

5. *Mississippi University for Women v. Hogan,* 458 U.S. 718, 102 S.Ct. 3331, 73 L.Ed.2d 1090 (1982) (5 to 4), invalidated a state statute excluding males from a state nursing school. The state justified the male exclusion as a form of affirmative action for women, but Justice O'Connor for the Court responded that the state could not prove that women lacked opportunities in nursing. In fact, over 98 percent of nursing degrees earned nationwide are already earned by women, and the state university's policy, rather "than compensat[ing] for discriminatory barriers faced by women," served "to perpetuate the stereotyped view of nursing as an exclusively woman's job."

6. *United States v. Virginia,* 518 U.S. 515, 116 S.Ct. 2264, 135 L.Ed.2d 735 (1996). The Virginia Military Institute (VMI) was a single-sex male college that the Commonwealth of Virginia operated. The United States sued VMI, claiming that its male-only policy violated equal protection. In response, Virginia proposed to establish what it called a parallel program for women (called the Virginia Women's Institute for Leadership, or VWIL) to be located at a private liberal arts college for women. The Fourth Circuit affirmed, after finding that the VMI and VWIL students would receive "substantially comparable" benefits, although even the VWIL degree lacked the prestige and historical benefit of the VMI degree.

    Ginsburg, J., for the Court, reversed and held that equal protection precluded Virginia from reserving exclusively to men the "unique educational opportunities VMI affords." Virginia argued that offering an option for single-sex education fostered diversity in education, but Virginia did not demonstrate that VMI created or maintained its all-male policy in order to diversify educational opportunities within the state. Virginia also argued that its all-male policy was necessary to VMI's mission of producing "citizen-soldiers" by using an "adversative method" of training (involving physical and mental discipline and loss of privacy). The Court agreed that the admission of women into VMI would require accommodations, primarily in terms of arranging housing assignments (to give "each sex privacy from the other sex in living arrangements") and changing physical training programs for female cadets (because of "physiological differences between male and female individuals"). However, VMI's goal of creating citizen-soldiers and its implementing methodology is not "inherently unsuitable" to women. VMI could not exclude all women from a program from which some were qualified. VWIL's creation did not cure the constitutional violation because it was unequal in both tangible and intangible factors (*e.g.*, curricular choices, faculty stature, funding, prestige, alumni support, and influence) and did not afford females the pressures, hazards, and psychological bonding characteristic of VMI's adversative training. The Court assumed that "most women would not choose VMI's adversative method," but "the question is whether the State can constitutionally deny to women who have the will and capacity, the training and attendant opportunities that VMI uniquely affords." In a footnote, the Court quoted footnote 1 of *Mississippi University for Women,* which said, "we are not faced with the question of whether States can provide 'separate but equal' undergraduate institutions for males and females."

Scalia, J., filed the only dissent. He criticized the Court for writing into the Constitution "the smug assurances" of the present age, and noted that the Court provided no example of a program "that *would* pass muster under its reasoning today: not even, for example, a football or wrestling program. On the Court's theory, any woman ready, willing, and physically able to participate in such a program would, *as a constitutional matter*, be entitled to do so." [Emphasis added.]

5.6 WEALTH, AGE, MENTAL RETARDATION, AND THE MENTALLY ILL

DANDRIDGE V. WILLIAMS
397 U.S. 471, 90 S.Ct. 1153, 25 L.Ed.2d 491 (1970)

JUSTICE STEWART delivered the opinion of the Court.

This case involves the validity of a method used by Maryland, in the administration of an aspect of its public welfare program, to reconcile the demands of its needy citizens with the finite resources available to meet those demands. Like every other State in the Union, Maryland participates in the Federal Aid to Families With Dependent Children (AFDC) program, which originated with the Social Security Act of 1935. . . .

The operation of the Maryland welfare system is not complex. . . . It computes the standard of need for each eligible family based on the number of children in the family and the circumstances under which the family lives. In general, the standard of need increases with each additional person in the household, but the increments become proportionately smaller. The regulation here in issue imposes upon the grant that any single family may receive an upper limit of $250 per month in certain counties and Baltimore City, and of $240 per month elsewhere in the State. The appellees all have large families, so that their standards of need as computed by the State substantially exceed the maximum grants that they actually receive under the regulation. The appellees urged in the District Court that the maximum grant limitation operates to discriminate against them merely because of the size of their families, in violation of the Equal Protection Clause of the Fourteenth Amendment. . . .

[This] regulation can be clearly justified, Maryland argues, in terms of legitimate state interests in encouraging gainful employment, in maintaining an equitable balance in economic status as between welfare families and those supported by a wage-earner, in providing incentives for family planning, and in allocating available public funds in such a way as fully to meet the needs of the largest possible number of families. The District Court, while apparently recognizing the validity of at least some of these state concerns, nonetheless held that the regulation "is invalid on its face for overreaching," that it violates the Equal Protection Clause "[b]ecause it cuts too broad a swath on an indiscriminate basis as applied to the entire group of AFDC eligibles to which it purports to apply. . . ."

If this were a case involving government action claimed to violate the First Amendment guarantee of free speech, a finding of "overreaching" would be significant and might be crucial. For when otherwise valid governmental regulation sweeps so broadly as to impinge upon activity protected by the First Amendment, its very overbreadth may make it unconstitutional. But the concept of "overreaching" has no place in this case. For here we deal with state regulation in the social and economic field, not affecting freedoms guaranteed by the Bill of Rights, and claimed to violate the Fourteenth Amendment only because the regulation results in some disparity in grants of welfare payments to the largest AFDC families. For this Court to approve the invalidation of state economic or social regulation as "overreaching" would be far too reminiscent of an era when the Court thought the Fourteenth Amendment gave it power to strike down state laws "because they may be unwise, improvident, or out of harmony with a particular school of thought." *Williamson v. Lee Optical Co.,* 348 U.S. 483, 488, 75 S.Ct. 461, 464, 99 L.Ed. 563. That era long ago passed into history. *Ferguson v. Skrupa.*

In the area of economics and social welfare, a State does not violate the Equal Protection Clause merely because the classifications made by its laws are imperfect. If the classification has some "reasonable basis," it does not offend the Constitution simply because the classification "is not made with mathematical nicety or because in practice it results in some inequality." *Lindsley v. Natural Carbonic Gas Co.* "The problems of government are practical ones and may justify, if they do not require, rough accommodations—illogical, it may be, and unscientific." "A statutory discrimination will not be set aside if any state of facts reasonably may be conceived to justify it."

To be sure, the cases cited, and many others enunciating this fundamental standard under the Equal Protection Clause, have in the main involved state regulation of business or industry. The administration of public welfare assistance, by contrast, involves the most basic economic needs of impoverished human beings. We recognize the dramatically real factual difference between the cited cases and this one, but we can find no basis for applying a different constitutional standard. It is a standard that has consistently been applied to state legislation restricting the availability of employment opportunities. And it is a standard that is true to the principle that the Fourteenth Amendment gives the federal courts no power to impose upon the States their views of what constitutes wise economic or social policy.

Under this long-established meaning of the Equal Protection Clause, it is clear that the Maryland maximum grant regulation is constitutionally valid. We need not explore all the reasons that the State advances in justification of the regulation. It is enough that a solid foundation for the regulation can be found in the State's legitimate interest in encouraging employment and in avoiding discrimination between welfare families and the families of the working poor. By combining a limit on the recipient's grant with permission to retain money earned, without reduction in the amount of the grant, Maryland provides an incentive to seek gainful employment. And by keying the maximum family AFDC grants to the minimum wage a steadily employed head of a household receives, the State maintains some semblance of an equitable balance between families on welfare and those supported by an employed breadwinner.

It is true that in some AFDC families there may be no person who is employable. It is also true that with respect to AFDC families whose determined standard of need is below the regulatory maximum, and who therefore receive grants equal to the determined standard, the employment incentive is absent. But the Equal Protection Clause does not require that a State must choose between attacking every aspect of a problem or not attacking the problem at all. *Lindsley v. Natural Carbonic Gas Co.* It is enough that the State's action be rationally based and free from invidious discrimination. The regulation before us meets that test.

We do not decide today that the Maryland regulation is wise, that it best fulfills the relevant social and economic objectives that Maryland might ideally espouse, or that a more just and humane system could not be devised. Conflicting claims of morality and intelligence are raised by opponents and proponents of almost every measure, certainly including the one before us. But the intractable economic, social, and even philosophical problems presented by public welfare assistance programs are not the business of this Court. The Constitution may impose certain procedural safeguards upon systems of welfare administration. But the Constitution does not empower this Court to second-guess state officials charged with the difficult responsibility of allocating limited public welfare funds among the myriad of potential recipients.

The judgment is reversed.

[The concurring opinions of BLACK, J., joined by BURGER, C.J., and HARLAN, J., and the dissenting opinion of MARSHALL, J., joined by BRENNAN, J., are omitted.]

NOTES

1. *San Antonio Independent School District v. Rodriguez,* 411 U.S. 1, 93 S.Ct. 1278, 36 L.Ed.2d 16 (1973), rejected (5 to 4) a lawsuit attacking the constitutionality of the Texas system of financing public education. The system, a typical one, relied on assessed property value. The average assessed property value per pupil of the poorest district was $5,960, and the median family income was $4,686 (compared to figures of $49,000 and $8,000, respectively, in the most affluent school district). The poorest district had a tax rate of $1.05 per $100 of assessed property, contributing $26 per child. The tax rate for the richest district was 85 cents per $100, which yielded $333 per pupil. By adding state and federal funds to these figures, the poorest district (which was 90% Mexican-American and over 6% black) spent $356 per pupil, and the richest district (which was 18% Mexican-American and less than 1% black) spent $594 per pupil. The majority concluded, "to the extent that the Texas system of school financing results in unequal expenditures between children who happen to reside in different districts, we cannot say that such disparities are the product of a system that is so irrational as to be invidiously discriminatory."

2. *Papasan v. Allain,* 478 U.S. 265, 106 S.Ct. 2932, 92 L.Ed.2d 209 (1986), held that plaintiffs have stated a cause of action by alleging that unequal distribution of funds for education were not rationally related to a legitimate state interest. The Court said that *Rodriguez* did not uphold all funding decisions. It "held merely that the variations that resulted from allowing local control over local property tax funding of the public schools were constitutionally permissible in that case." *Papasan* said that plaintiffs would have to prove that the differential treatment was not rationally related to a legitimate state interest. Powell, J., joined by Burger. C.J., and Rehnquist, J., objected and concluded that *Rodriguez* should foreclose attacks on the system of financing public schools.

3. Compare, *Connecticut Department of Public Safety v. Doe,* 538 U.S. 1, 123 S.Ct. 1160, 155 L.Ed.2d 98 (2003). Connecticut's "Megan's Law" requires persons

convicted of sexual offenses to register with the Department of Public Safety when released into the community. The Department then posts a sex offender registry on the Internet containing the registrants' names, addresses, photographs, and descriptions. The Second Circuit permanently enjoined Megan's Law after concluding that the required disclosure deprived sex offenders of a liberty interest and violated the due process clause because the statute did not allow hearings prior to posting to determine whether offenders are "currently dangerous." Rehnquist, C.J., for a unanimous Court, reversed. Plaintiffs who assert a due process right to a hearing must show that facts they seek to establish in that hearing are relevant under the statutory scheme.

Souter, J., concurring, joined by Ginsberg, J., added:

> "I write separately only to note that a substantive due process claim may not be the only one still open to a test by those in the respondents' situation. . . . The line drawn by the legislature between offenders who are sensibly considered eligible to seek discretionary relief from the courts and those who are not is, like all legislative choices affecting individual rights, open to challenge under the Equal Protection Clause. See, *e.g.*, 3 R. Rotunda & J. Nowak, Treatise on Constitutional Law § 17.6 (3d ed.1999)."

4.   **AGE DISCRIMINATION.** State law forced Robert Murgia, an officer in the uniformed Massachusetts State Police, to retire at age 50. Because police work can be arduous, the state required uniformed officers to pass a comprehensive physical examination biennially until age 40. After that, the officers had to pass a more rigorous examination annually. Murgia passed such an examination four months before he was forced to retire. Since there was no dispute that he had excellent physical and mental health and was capable of performing his duties, he challenged the mandatory retirement law as denying him equal protection. The Supreme Court rejected the challenge, over the dissent of Justice Marshall. *Massachusetts Board of Retirement v. Murgia,* 427 U.S. 307, 96 S.Ct. 2562, 49 L.Ed.2d 520 (1976) (*per curiam*).

Citing *Dandridge v. Williams* and *San Antonio Independent School District v. Rodriguez,* the Court stated that the right of governmental employment is not *per se* fundamental. The Court went on to explain:

> Nor does the class of uniformed state police officers over 50 constitute a suspect class for purposes of equal protection analysis. *Rodriguez, supra,* observed that a suspect class is one saddled with

such disabilities, or subject to such a history of purposeful unequal treatment, or relegated to such a position of political powerlessness as to command extraordinary protection from the majoritarian political process. While the treatment of the aged in this Nation has not been wholly free of discrimination, such persons, unlike, say, those who have been discriminated against on the basis of race or national origin, have not experienced a history of purposeful unequal treatment or been subjected to unique disabilities on the basis of stereotyped characteristics not truly indicative of their abilities. The class subject to the compulsory retirement feature of the Massachusetts statute consists of uniformed state police officers over the age of 50. It cannot be said to discriminate only against the elderly. Rather, it draws the line at a certain age in middle life. But even old age does not define a discrete and insular group, *United States v. Carotene Products Co.,* [Chapter 6, *supra*], in need of "extraordinary protection from the majoritarian political process." Instead, it marks a stage that each of us will reach if we live out our normal span. Even if the statute could be said to impose a penalty upon a class defined as the aged, it would not impose a distinction sufficiently akin to those classifications that we have found suspect to call for strict judicial scrutiny.

The Court then upheld this state classification under the rational-basis standard. The purpose of the state retirement law is to assure physical preparedness of its uniformed police; physical ability declines with age; and 50 years marks a cutoff that is not irrational. "That the State chooses not to determine fitness more precisely through individualized testing after age 50 is not to say that the objective of assuring physical fitness is not rationally furthered by a maximum-age limitation. It is only to say that with regard to the interest of all concerned, the State perhaps has not chosen the best means to accomplish this purpose."

5. **THE MENTALLY RETARDED.** *City of Cleburne v. Cleburne Living Center,* 473 U.S. 432, 105 S.Ct. 3249, 87 L.Ed.2d 313 (1985) rejected (6 to 3) any intermediate standard of review for the mentally retarded. However, it then held that the denial by Cleburne, Texas, of a special use permit under its zoning laws to a group home for the mentally retarded was unconstitutional under Equal Protection because it was "irrational." The city would have permitted the group home if it were not for the mentally retarded. The city

did not require a special use permit for fraternity houses, boarding houses, nursing homes for convalescents, etc.

Legislation "singling out the retarded for special treatment reflects the real and undeniable differences between the retarded and others." However, differences regarding the mentally retarded as a group "are largely irrelevant" unless the home threatens "legitimate interests of the city in a way that other permitted uses such as boarding houses and hospitals do not." The Court invalidated the ordinance as applied because there was no rational basis to believe that this home for the mentally retarded posed "any special threat to the city's legitimate interest." The home was also across the street from a high school, and the city was concerned that the high school students might harass the residents of the home but "the school itself is attended by about 30 mentally retarded students, and denying a permit based on such vague, undifferentiated fears is" improper. The city claimed concern because the home would be on a 500-year flood plain, but only the home had to obtain a special use permit, and other uses—such as boarding houses—did not.

Heller v. Doe, 509 U.S. 312, 113 S.Ct. 2637, 125 L.Ed.2d 257 (1993). Kentucky's involuntary commitment procedure allows mentally *retarded* individuals to be institutionalized if there is "clear and convincing" evidence of their retardation. However, the state may commit mentally *ill* individuals only by proof "beyond a reasonable doubt." The Court held that this distinction is rational and thus does not violate the Equal Protection Clause. The two conditions are different: it is easier to diagnose mental retardation; it is easier to determine, in the case of mental retardation, whether the subject is dangerous to self or others; and the prevailing ways of treating mental retardation are less invasive from those treating mental illness. It is also rational (and therefore constitutional) for the state to allow close relatives to participate in involuntary commitment proceedings of the mentally retarded but not the mentally ill because mental retardation appears in one's development period where relatives or guardians are likely to have intimate knowledge of the subject's abilities, while mental illness may manifest itself after minority.

5.7 VOTING

5.7.1   One Person, One Vote

REYNOLDS V. SIMS

377 U.S. 533, 84 S.Ct. 1362, 12 L.Ed.2d 506 (1964)

[Alabama plaintiffs, suing various state and political party officials charged with performance of certain duties in connection with state elections, claimed, *inter alia,* that the malapportioned state legislature violated the equal protection clause. Since the last reapportionment of the state legislature was based on the 1900 census, and the population growth had been uneven, plaintiffs claimed serious discrimination in the allocation of legislative representation. After the Supreme Court found such a claim justiciable (see *Baker v. Carr,* § 1.8.21.2, *supra*), the district court held that the inequality of existing representation violated equal protection and that the proposed state legislative reapportionment was inadequate. It ordered into effect a temporary reapportionment plan for the 1962 election, and retained jurisdiction.]

CHIEF JUSTICE WARREN delivered the opinion of the Court.

In *Gray v. Sanders,* 372 U.S. 368, 83 S.Ct. 801, 9 L.Ed.2d 821 [1963], we held that the Georgia county unit system, applicable in statewide primary elections, was unconstitutional since it resulted in a dilution of the weight of the votes of certain Georgia voters merely because of where they resided. After indicating that the Fifteenth and Nineteenth Amendments prohibit a State from overweighting or diluting votes on the basis of race or sex, we stated:

> How then can one person be given twice or ten times the voting power of another person in a statewide election merely because he lives in a rural area or because he lives in the smallest rural county? Once the geographical unit for which a representative is to be chosen is designated, all who participate in the election are to have an equal vote— whatever their race, whatever their sex, whatever their occupation, whatever their income, and wherever their home may be in that geographical unit. This is required by the Equal Protection Clause of the Fourteenth Amendment. The concept of 'we the people' under the Constitution visualizes no preferred class of voters but equality among those who meet the basic qualifications. The idea that every voter is equal to every other voter in his State, when he casts his ballot in favor of one of several competing candidates, underlies many of our decisions.

Continuing, we stated that "there is no indication in the Constitution that homesite or occupation affords a permissible basis for distinguishing between qualified voters within the State." And, finally, we concluded: "The conception of political equality from the Declaration of Independence, to Lincoln's Gettysburg Address, to the Fifteenth, Seventeenth, and Nineteenth Amendments can mean only one thing—one person, one vote." . . .

In *Wesberry v. Sanders,* 376 U.S. 1, 84 S.Ct. 526, 11 L.Ed.2d 481, decided earlier this Term, we held that attacks on the constitutionality of congressional districting plans enacted by state legislatures do not present non justiciable questions and should not be dismissed generally for "want of equity." We determined that the constitutional test for the validity of congressional districting schemes was one of substantial equality of population among the various districts established by a state legislature for the election of members of the Federal House of Representatives.

In that case we decided that an apportionment of congressional seats which "contracts the value of some votes and expands that of others" is unconstitutional, since "the Federal Constitution intends that when qualified voters elect members of Congress each vote be given as much weight as any other vote. . . ." We concluded that the constitutional prescription for election of members of the House of Representatives "by the People," construed in its historical context, "means that as nearly as is practicable one man's vote in a congressional election is to be worth as much as another's." [U.S. Const., Art. I, § 2, cl. 1].

Gray and *Wesberry* are of course not dispositive of or directly controlling on our decision in these cases involving state legislative apportionment controversies. Admittedly, those decisions, in which we held that, in statewide and in congressional elections, one person's vote must be counted equally with those of all other voters in a State, were based on different constitutional considerations and were addressed to rather distinct problems. But neither are they wholly inapposite. *Gray,* though not determinative here since involving the weighting of votes in statewide elections, established the basic principle of equality among voters within a State, and held that voters cannot be classified, constitutionally, on the basis of where they live, at least with respect to voting in statewide elections. And our decision in *Wesberry* was of course grounded on that language of the Constitution which prescribes that members of the Federal House of Representatives are to be chosen "by the People," while attacks on state legislative apportionment schemes, such as that involved in the instant cases, are principally based on the Equal Protection Clause of the Fourteenth Amendment. . . .

A predominant consideration in determining whether a State's legislative apportionment scheme constitutes an invidious discrimination violative of rights asserted under the Equal Protection Clause is that the rights allegedly impaired are individual and personal in nature. . . . Undoubtedly, the right of suffrage is a fundamental matter in a free and democratic society. Especially since the right to exercise the franchise in a free and unimpaired manner is preservative of other basic civil and political rights, any alleged infringement of the right of citizens to vote must be carefully and meticulously scrutinized. Almost a century ago, in *Yick Wo v. Hopkins,* [section 4.2, *supra*], the Court referred to "the political franchise of voting" as "a fundamental political right, because preservative of all rights."

Legislators represent people, not trees or acres. Legislators are elected by voters, not farms or cities or economic interests. As long as ours is a representative form of government, and our legislatures are those instruments of government elected directly by and directly representative of the people, the right to elect legislators in a free and unimpaired fashion is a bedrock of our political system. It could hardly be gainsaid that a constitutional claim had been asserted by an allegation that certain otherwise qualified voters had been entirely prohibited from voting for members of their state legislature. And, if a State should provide that the votes of citizens in one part of the State should be given two times, or five times, or ten times the weight of votes of citizens in another part of the State, it could hardly be contended that the right to vote of those residing in the disfavored areas had not been effectively diluted. . . . Of course, the effect of state legislative districting schemes which give the same number of representatives to unequal numbers of constituents is identical. Overweighting and overvaluation of the votes of those living here has the certain effect of dilution and undervaluation of the votes of those living there. . . .

Logically, in a society ostensibly grounded on representative government, it would seem reasonable that a majority of the people of a State could elect a majority of that State's legislators [T]he concept of equal protection has been traditionally viewed as requiring the uniform treatment of persons standing in the same relation to the government action questioned or challenged. With respect to the allocation of legislative representation, all voters, as citizens of a State, stand in the same relation regardless of where they live. Any suggested criteria for the differentiation of citizens are insufficient to justify any discrimination, as to the weight of their votes, unless relevant to the permissible purposes of legislative apportionment. Since the achieving of fair and effective representation for all citizens is concededly the basic aim of legislative apportionment, we conclude that the Equal Protection Clause guarantees the opportunity for equal participation by all voters in the election of state legislators. Diluting the weight of votes because of place of residence impairs basic constitutional rights under the Fourteenth Amendment just as much as invidious discriminations based upon factors such as race. . . . Our constitutional system amply provides for the protection of minorities by means other than giving them majority control of state legislatures. And the democratic ideals of equality and majority rule, which have served this Nation so well in the past, are hardly of any less significance for the present and the future.

We are told that the matter of apportioning representation in a state legislature is a complex and many-faceted one. We are advised that States can rationally consider factors other than population in apportioning legislative representation. We are admonished not to restrict the power of the States to impose differing views as to political philosophy on their citizens. We are cautioned about the dangers of entering into political thickets and mathematical quagmires. Our answer is this: a denial of constitutionally protected rights demands judicial protection; our oath and our office require no less of us. . . . Population is, of necessity, the starting point for consideration and the controlling criterion for judgment in legislative apportionment controversies. . . .

We hold that, as a basic constitutional standard, the Equal Protection Clause requires that the seats in both houses of a bicameral state legislature must be apportioned on a population basis. Simply stated, an individual's right to vote for state legislators is unconstitutionally impaired when its weight is in a substantial fashion diluted when compared with votes of citizens living in other parts of the State. . . . Much has been written since our decision in *Baker v. Carr* about the applicability of the so-called federal analogy to state legislative apportionment arrangements. [W]e find the federal analogy inapposite and irrelevant to state legislative districting schemes. Attempted reliance on the federal analogy appears often to be little more than an after-the-fact rationalization offered in defense of maladjusted state apportionment arrangements. The original constitutions of 36 of our States provided that representation in both houses of the state legislatures would be based completely, or predominantly, on population. And the Founding Fathers clearly had no intention of establishing a pattern or model for the apportionment of seats in state legislatures when the system of representation in the Federal Congress was adopted. Demonstrative of this is the fact that the Northwest Ordinance, adopted in the same year, 1787, as the Federal Constitution, provided for the apportionment of seats in territorial legislatures solely on the basis of population.

The system of representation in the two Houses of the Federal Congress is one ingrained in our Constitution, as part of the law of the land. It is one conceived out of compromise and [arises] from unique historical circumstances. . . . Since we find the so-called federal analogy inapposite to a consideration of the constitutional validity of state legislative apportionment schemes, we necessarily hold that the Equal Protection Clause requires both houses of a state legislature to be apportioned on a population basis. The right of a citizen to equal representation and to have his vote weighted equally with those of all other citizens in the election of members of one house of a bicameral state legislature would amount to little if States could effectively submerge the equal-population principle in the apportionment of seats in the other house. . . .

We do not believe that the concept of bicameralism is rendered anachronistic and meaning less when the predominant basis of representation in the two state legislative bodies is required to be the same—population. . . . One body could be composed of single-member districts while the other could have at least some multimember districts. The length of terms of the legislators in the separate bodies could differ. The numerical size of the two bodies could be made to differ, even significantly, and the geographical size of districts from which legislators are elected could also be made to differ. And apportionment in one house could be arranged so as to balance off minor inequities in the representation of certain areas in the other house. In summary, these and other factors could be, and are presently in many States, utilized to engender differing complexions and collective attitudes in the two bodies of a state legislature, although both are apportioned substantially on a population basis.

By holding that as a federal constitutional requisite both houses of a state legislature must be apportioned on a population basis, we mean that the Equal Protection Clause requires that a State make an honest and good faith effort to construct districts, in both houses of its legislature, as nearly of equal population as is practicable. We realize that it is a practical impossibility to arrange legislative districts so that each one has an identical number of residents, or citizens, or voters. Mathematical exactness or precision is hardly a workable constitutional requirement. . . . Since, almost invariably, there is a significantly larger number of seats in state legislative bodies to be distributed within a State than congressional seats, it may be feasible to use political subdivision lines to a greater extent in establishing state legislative districts than in congressional districting while still affording adequate representation to all parts of the State. To do so would be constitutionally valid, so long as the resulting apportionment was one based substantially on population and the equal-population principle was not diluted in any significant way. Somewhat more flexibility may therefore be constitutionally permissible with respect to state legislative apportionment than in congressional districting. . . . A State may legitimately desire to maintain the integrity of various political subdivisions, insofar as possible, and provide for compact districts of contiguous territory in designing a legislative apportionment scheme. Valid considerations may underlie such aims. . . .

History indicates, however, that many States have deviated, to a greater or lesser degree, from the equal-population principle in the apportionment of seats in at least one house of their legislatures. So long as the divergences from a strict population standard are based on legitimate considerations incident to the effectuation of a rational state policy, some deviations from the equal-population principle are constitutionally permissible with respect to the apportionment of seats in either or both of the two houses of a bicameral state legislature. But neither history alone, nor economic or other sorts of group interests, are permissible factors in attempting to justify disparities from population-based representation. Citizens, not history or economic interests, cast votes. Considerations of area alone provide an insufficient justification for deviations from the equal-population principle. Again, people, not land or trees or pastures, vote. Modern developments and improvements in transportation and communications make rather hollow, in the mid-1960s, most claims that deviations from population-based representation can validly be based solely on geographical considerations. Arguments for allowing such deviations in order to insure effective representation for sparsely settled areas and to prevent legislative districts from becoming so large that the availability of access of citizens to their representatives is impaired are today, for the most part, unconvincing.

A consideration that appears to be of more substance in justifying some deviations from population-based representation in state legislatures is that of insuring some voice to political subdivisions, as political subdivisions. . . . But if, even as a result of a clearly rational state policy of according some legislative representation to political subdivisions, population is submerged as the controlling consideration in the apportionment of seats in the particular legislative body, then the right of all of the State's citizens to case an effective and adequately weighted vote would be unconstitutionally impaired. . . .

That the Equal Protection Clause requires that both houses of a state legislature be apportioned on a population basis does not mean that States cannot adopt some reasonable plan for periodic revision of their apportionment schemes. Decennial reapportionment appears to be a rational approach to readjustment of legislative representation in order to take into account population shifts and growth. . . . And we do not mean to intimate that more frequent reapportionment would not be constitutionally permissible or practicably desirable. But if reapportionment were accomplished with less frequency, it would assuredly be constitutionally suspect. . . .

We do not consider here the difficult question of the proper remedial devices which federal courts should utilize in state legislative apportionment cases. Remedial techniques in this new and developing area of the law will probably often differ with the **circumstances** of the challenged apportionment and a variety of local conditions. It is enough to say now that, once a State's legislative apportionment scheme has been found to be unconstitutional, it would be the unusual case in which a court would be justified in not taking appropriate action to insure that no further elections are conducted under the invalid plan. However, under certain circumstances, such as where an impending election is imminent and a State's election machinery is already in progress, equitable considerations might justify a court in withholding the granting of immediately effective relief in a legislative apportionment case, even though the existing apportionment scheme was found invalid. In awarding or withholding immediate relief, a court is entitled to and should consider the proximity of a forthcoming election and the mechanics and complexities of state election laws, and should act and rely upon general equitable principles. With respect to the timing of relief, a court can reasonably endeavor to avoid a disruption of the election process which might result from requiring precipitate changes that could make unreasonable or embarrassing demands on a State in adjusting to the requirements of the court's decree. As stated by Mr. Justice Douglas, concurring in *Baker v. Carr,* "any relief accorded can be fashioned in the light of well-known principles of equity."

. . . Since the District Court evinced its realization that its ordered reapportionment could not be sustained as the basis for conducting the 1966 election of Alabama legislators, and avowedly intends to take some further action should the reapportioned Alabama Legislature fail to enact a constitutionally valid, permanent apportionment scheme in the interim, we affirm the judgment below and remand the cases for further proceedings consistent with the views stated in this opinion.

It is so ordered.

JUSTICE HARLAN, dissenting.

[T]he Court's argument boils down to the assertion that appellees' right to vote has been invidiously "debased" or "diluted" by systems of apportionment which entitle them to vote for fewer legislators than other voters, an assertion which is tied to the Equal Protection Clause only by the constitutionally frail tautology that "equal" means "equal." . . .

[T]he Court declares it unconstitutional for a State to give effective consideration to any of the following in establishing legislative districts:

(1) history;

(2) "economic or other sorts of group interests";

(3) area;

(4) geographical considerations;

(5) a desire "to insure effective representation for sparsely settled areas";

(6) "availability of access of citizens to their representatives";

(7) theories of bicameralism (except those approved by the Court);

(8) occupation;

(9) "an attempt to balance urban and rural power;"

(10) the preference of a majority of voters in the State.

So far as presently appears, the *only* factor which a State may consider, apart from numbers, is political subdivisions. But even "a clearly rational state policy" recognizing this factor is unconstitutional if "population is submerged as the controlling consideration. . . ."

[T]hese decisions give support to a current mistaken view of the Constitution and the constitutional function of this Court. This view, in a nutshell, is that every major social ill in this country can find its cure in some constitutional "principle," and that this Court should "take the lead" in promoting reform when other branches of government fail to act. The Constitution is not a panacea for every blot upon the public welfare, nor should this Court, ordained as a judicial body, be thought of as a general haven for reform movements. The Constitution is an instrument of government, fundamental to which is the premise that in a diffusion of governmental authority lies the greatest promise that this Nation will realize liberty for all its citizens. This Court, limited in function in accordance with that premise, does not serve its high purpose when it exceeds its authority, even to satisfy justified impatience with the slow workings of the political process. For when, in the name of constitutional interpretation, the Court *adds* something to the Constitution that was deliberately excluded from it, the Court in reality substitutes its view of what should be so for the amending process.

[The opinion of CLARK, J., concurring in the affirmance, and the separate opinion of STEWART, J., are omitted.]

NOTES

1. On the same day that it decided the *Reynolds* case involving Alabama, the Court decided *Lucas v. Forty-Fourth General Assembly of Colorado*, 377 U.S. 713, 84 S.Ct. 1459, 12 L.Ed.2d 632 (1964). Colorado voters adopted by a wide margin a state constitutional amendment (No. 7) providing for the apportionment of the state house on the basis of population and the state senate on the basis of population *and* a variety of other factors. At the same time the voters rejected, also by a wide margin, an amendment (No. 8) apportioning both houses on a population basis. A majority of the voters in every county of the State voted in favor of No. 7 and against No. 8. However,

    > An individual's constitutionally protected right to cast an equally weighted vote cannot be denied even by a vote of a majority of a State's electorate, if the apportionment scheme adopted by the voters fails to measure up to the requirements of the Equal Protection Clause. Manifestly, the fact that an apportionment plan is adopted in a popular referendum is insufficient to sustain its constitutionality or to induce a court of equity to refuse to act. . . . A citizen's constitutional rights can hardly be infringed because a majority of the people choose that it be. We hold that the fact that a challenged legislative apportionment plan was approved by the electorate is without federal constitutional significance, if the scheme adopted fails to satisfy the basic requirements of the Equal Protection Clause, as delineated in our opinion in *Reynolds v. Sims*.

2. After several false starts the Court finally settled on a test to determine when *Reynolds* applies to local governmental units. *Reynolds* applies if the officials are selected by popular vote. As stated in *Hadley v. Junior College District*, 397 U.S. 50, 90 S.Ct. 791, 25 L.Ed.2d 45 (1970) (*Reynolds* applicable to trustees of junior college district selected by popular vote):

    > [A]s a general rule, whenever a state or local government decides to select persons by popular election to perform governmental functions, the Equal Protection Clause of the Fourteenth

Amendment requires that each qualified voter must be given an equal opportunity to participate in that election, and when members of an elected body are chosen from separate districts, each district must be established on a basis that will insure, so far as is practicable, that equal numbers of voters can vote for proportionally equal numbers of officials. It is of course possible that there might be some case in which a State elects certain functionaries whose duties are so far removed from normal governmental activities and so disproportionately affect different groups that a popular election in compliance with *Reynolds* might not be required.

Contrast *Fortson v. Morris*, 385 U.S. 231, 87 S.Ct. 446, 17 L.Ed.2d 330 (1966) (*Reynolds* not applicable when state constitution requires the General Assembly to select the Governor in a situation where, after two primaries and one general election, no candidate had received a majority of the popular votes cast).

3.   Recall that *Reynolds* said, "[s]omewhat more flexibility" may be permissible with respect to state legislative apportionment than in congressional districting. Also, the Court based *Reynolds* on the equal protection guarantee while it based *Wesberry* on Art. 1, § 2, cl. 1, providing that U.S. Representatives shall be chosen "by the People." Thus, the Court in subsequent cases has been more tolerant of slight malapportionment in elections for state office than it has been for elections to Congress.

Karsher v. Daggett, 462 U.S. 725, 103 S.Ct. 2653, 77 L.Ed.2d 133 (1983) (5 to 4) held that Art. I, § 2, permits only those limited population variances that are unavoidable despite a good faith effort to achieve absolute equality, or for which special justification is shown. The maximum population difference between the smallest and the largest district in New Jersey was 3,674 people or only .6984 percent of the average district. However, the New Jersey legislature had rejected another plan with a maximum population difference of 2,375 or .4514 percent. Even though the maximum deviation in New Jersey was less than the predictable undercount in available census data, the legislature should use the best actual census data available. There is no *de minimis* level that does not need special justification. "[A]bsolute population equality" is the "paramount objective of apportionment" in the case of congressional districts. Because New Jersey did not prove that the minor (but real) statistical disparity was unavoidable and did not prove that the deviations were necessary to achieve a legitimate state objective (*e.g.*, "making districts compact, respecting municipal boundaries, preserving the cores of prior districts, and avoiding contests between incumbent Representatives"), then the plan failed.

Stevens, J., who joined the majority opinion, wrote a concurring opinion in which he also objected to the "bizarre" shapes of the districts and expressed an interest in requiring compactness as well as population equality as a constitutional standard.

Compare *Mahan v. Howell*, 410 U.S. 315, 93 S.Ct. 979, 35 L.Ed.2d 320 (1973), modified 411 U.S. 922, 93 S.Ct. 1475, 36 L.Ed.2d 316 (1973), involving apportionment of the Virginia Senate and House of Delegates. The Court found that the desire of the General Assembly to maintain the integrity of traditional county and city boundaries justified a total percentage deviation of 16.4 percent. In *Connor v. Finch*, 431 U.S. 407, 97 S.Ct. 1828, 52 L.Ed.2d 465 (1977), the Court did not accept a reapportionment plan of 16.5% in the Mississippi Senate and 19.3% in the House. Unlike *Mahan*, in which the legislature's plan produced the minimum deviations while keeping intact political boundaries, another plan would have cut across fewer county boundaries and have had a smaller percentage deviation.

Smaller deviations do not even require special justification. *White v. Regester*, 412 U.S. 755, 93 S.Ct. 2332, 37 L.Ed.2d 314 (1973) (9.9 percent deviation allowed in election for Texas House of Representatives).

4. **VOTER I.D.** *Crawford v. Marion County Election Board*, 553 U.S. 181, 128 S.Ct. 1610, 170 L.Ed.2d 574 (2008). The issue before the Court was the constitutionality of an Indiana statute requiring citizens who vote in person on election day, or who cast a ballot in person at the office of the circuit court clerk prior to election day, to present a free photo identification (voter ID) issued by the government. Plaintiffs, including the Democratic Party, sued, claiming that this requirement violated the Voting Rights Act and the Fourteenth Amendment. A majority of the Court (6 to 3) rejected those claims, but without a majority opinion.

The voter ID statute does not apply to absentee ballots or to persons living and voting in a state licensed facility, such as a nursing home. A person who is indigent or has a religious objection to being photographed may cast a provisional ballot that is counted if the person executes an appropriate affidavit within 10 days of the election. One who has a photo ID but cannot present it for identification may also cast a provisional ballot if she brings her photo ID within 10 days. There is no photo ID requirement in order to register to vote, and the state offers free photo ID of qualified voters who establish their residence and identity.

The district court found that the plaintiffs had "not introduced evidence of a single individual Indiana resident who will be unable to vote as a result of" voter ID. She rejected this facial challenge to the law. Stevens, J., for the plurality, relied on *Harper v. Virginia Board of Elections*, affirmed. Stevens concluded that even rational restrictions on the right to vote are invidious if they are unrelated to voter qualifications. He relied on *Harper v. Virginia State Board of Elections*, 383 U.S. 663, 86 S.Ct. 1079, 16 L.Ed.2d 169 (1966), which held that the Fourteenth Amendment made unconstitutional the poll tax in all elections, state as well as federal. (A poll tax is a tax the voter must pay in order to vote. Stevens said, " 'evenhanded restrictions that protect the integrity and reliability of the electoral process itself' are not invidious and satisfy the standard set forth in *Harper*."

Indiana meets this test. First, there is the interest in deterring and detecting voter fraud. The evidence showed that 19 of 92 Indiana counties had registration totals exceeding 100% of the 2004 voting-age population. The record did not show that in-person voting fraud occurred in Indiana, but such fraud has occurred in other parts of the country. The Court relied on the Commission on Federal Election Reform chaired by former President Jimmy Carter and former Secretary of State James A. Baker III, which concluded, "The electoral system cannot inspire public confidence if no safeguards exist to deter or detect fraud or to confirm the identity of voters. Photo identification cards currently are needed to board a plane, enter federal buildings, and cash a check. Voting is equally important."

The burden the state imposes would be significant if the state required voters to pay a tax or fee to obtain a voter ID, but Indiana's voter ID is free. There may be a "somewhat heavier burden" on a few people (such as indigents who find it difficult to obtain state-issued identification), but that is not enough to validate the statute on its face.

Scalia, J., joined by Thomas & Alito, JJ., concurred in the judgment. "The Indiana photo-identification law is a generally applicable, nondiscriminatory voting regulation, and our precedents refute the view that individual impacts are relevant to determining the severity of the burden it imposes." Breyer, J., dissented, arguing that this burden is "out of proportion" to the benefits of the law. Souter, J., joined by Ginsburg, J., also dissented.

In the 2008 election, the voter turnout for Indiana and Georgia (the two states with the strictest voter ID) was higher than previously, and higher than the turnout in the states that had not instituted voter ID. A former commissioner on the Federal Election Commission studied the figures and said, "With every election that has occurred since states have begun to implement voter ID, the evidence is overwhelming that it does not depress the turnout of voters. Indeed, it may actually increase the public's confidence that their votes will count."[16]

5.7.2   Counting the Votes—The Presidential Election of 2000

BUSH V. GORE
531 U.S. 98, 121 S.Ct. 525, 148 L.Ed.2d 388 (2000)

[The results of the 2000 Presidential Election depended on Florida's electoral votes, which set off a flurry of litigation. Vice President Albert Gore, the Democratic candidate for President, sued in state court contesting Florida's certification of its results in the presidential election. The Florida trial court denied all relief, and Gore appealed to the Florida Supreme Court, which issued its decision on December 8, 2000.]

PER CURIAM.

I.   . . . The proceedings leading to the present controversy are discussed in some detail in our opinion in *Bush v. Palm Beach County Canvassing Bd.*, 531 U.S. 70, 121 S.Ct. 471, 148 L.Ed.2d 366 (Dec. 4, 2000) (per curiam) (*Bush I*). On November 8, 2000, the day following the Presidential election, the Florida Division of Elections reported that petitioner, Governor Bush, had received 2,909,135 votes, and respondent, Vice President Gore, had received 2,907,351 votes, a margin of 1,784 for Governor Bush. Because Governor Bush's margin of victory was less than "one-half of a percent . . . of the votes cast," an automatic machine recount was conducted under § 102.141(4) of the [Florida] election code, the results of which showed Governor Bush still winning the race but by a diminished margin. Vice President Gore then sought manual recounts in Volusia, Palm Beach, Broward, and Miami-Dade Counties, pursuant to Florida's election protest

---

[16]   Hans von Spakovsky, *Voter ID Was a Success in November*, Wall St. Journal, Jan. 20, 2009, at A 23.

provisions. A dispute arose concerning the deadline for local county canvassing boards to submit their returns to the Secretary of State (Secretary). The Secretary declined to waive the November 14 deadline imposed by statute. The Florida Supreme Court, however, set the deadline at November 26. We granted certiorari and vacated the Florida Supreme Court's decision [on Dec. 4], finding considerable uncertainty as to the grounds on which it was based. *Bush I.* On December 11, the Florida Supreme Court issued a decision on remand reinstating that date.

On November 26, the Florida Elections Canvassing Commission certified the results of the election and declared Governor Bush the winner of Florida's 25 electoral votes. On November 27, Vice President Gore, pursuant to Florida's contest provisions, filed a complaint in Leon County Circuit Court contesting the certification. He sought relief pursuant to § 102.168(3)(c), which provides that "[r]eceipt of a number of illegal votes or rejection of a number of legal votes sufficient to change or place in doubt the result of the election" shall be grounds for a contest.

[The Florida Supreme Court] held that Vice President Gore had satisfied his burden of proof under § 102.168(3)(c) with respect to his challenge to Miami-Dade County's failure to tabulate, by manual count, 9,000 ballots on which the machines had failed to detect a vote for President ("undervotes"). . . . A "legal vote," as determined by the [Florida] Supreme Court, is "one in which there is a 'clear indication of the intent of the voter.'" The court therefore ordered a hand recount of the 9,000 ballots in Miami-Dade County. [The Florida] Supreme Court further held that the Circuit Court could order "the Supervisor of Elections and the Canvassing Boards, as well as the necessary public officials, in all counties that have not conducted a manual recount or tabulation of the undervotes . . . to do so forthwith, said tabulation to take place in the individual counties where the ballots are located." . . .

The petition presents the following questions: whether the Florida Supreme Court established new standards for resolving Presidential election contests, thereby violating Art. II, § 1, cl. 2, of the United States Constitution and failing to comply with 3 U.S.C. § 5, and whether the use of standardless manual recounts violates the Equal Protection and Due Process Clauses. With respect to the equal protection question, we find a violation of the Equal Protection Clause.

II. . . . Nationwide statistics reveal that an estimated 2% of ballots cast do not register a vote for President for whatever reason, including deliberately choosing no candidate at all or some voter error, such as voting for two candidates or insufficiently marking a ballot. In certifying election results, the votes eligible for inclusion in the certification are the votes meeting the properly established legal requirements. This case has shown that punch card balloting machines can produce an unfortunate number of ballots which are not punched in a clean, complete way by the voter. After the current counting, it is likely legislative bodies nationwide will examine ways to improve the mechanisms and machinery for voting.

The individual citizen has no federal constitutional right to vote for electors for the President of the United States unless and until the state legislature chooses a statewide election as the means to implement its power to appoint members of the Electoral College. U.S. Const., Art. II, § 1. This is the source for the statement in *McPherson v. Blacker*, 146 U.S. 1, 35, 13 S.Ct. 3, 36 L.Ed. 869 (1892), that the State legislature's power to select the manner for appointing electors is plenary; it may, if it so chooses, select the electors itself, which indeed was the manner used by State legislatures in several States for many years after the Framing of our Constitution. History has now favored the voter, and in each of the several States the citizens themselves vote for Presidential electors. When the state legislature vests the right to vote for President in its people, the right to vote as the legislature has prescribed is fundamental; and one source of its fundamental nature lies in the equal weight accorded to each vote and the equal dignity owed to each voter. . . .

. . . Having once granted the right to vote on equal terms, the State may not, by later arbitrary and disparate treatment, value one person's vote over that of another. See, *e.g., Harper v. Virginia Bd. of Elections* (1966). [The] "right of suffrage can be denied by a debasement or dilution of the weight of a citizen's vote just as effectively as by wholly prohibiting the free exercise of the franchise." *Reynolds v. Sims* (1964). [Therefore, the question] is whether the recount procedures the Florida Supreme Court has adopted are consistent with its obligation to avoid arbitrary and disparate treatment of the members of its electorate.

Much of the controversy seems to revolve around ballot cards designed to be perforated by a stylus but which, either through error or deliberate omission, have not been perforated with sufficient precision for a machine to count them. In some cases a piece of the card—a chad—is hanging, say by two corners. In other cases there is no separation at all, just an indentation.

The Florida Supreme Court has ordered that the intent of the voter be discerned from such ballots. . . . The recount mechanisms implemented in response to the decisions of the Florida Supreme Court do not satisfy the minimum requirement for non-arbitrary treatment of voters necessary to secure the fundamental right. Florida's basic command for the count of legally cast votes is to consider the "intent of the voter." *Gore v. Harris*, 772 So.2d, at 1254. This is unobjectionable as an abstract proposition and a starting principle. The problem inheres in the absence of specific standards to ensure its equal application. The formulation of uniform rules to determine intent based on these recurring circumstances is practicable and, we conclude, necessary.

[T]he question is not whether to believe a witness but how to interpret the marks or holes or scratches on an inanimate object, a piece of cardboard or paper which, it is said, might not have registered as a vote during the machine count. The factfinder confronts a thing, not a person. The search for intent can be confined by specific rules designed to ensure uniform treatment.

The want of those rules here has led to unequal evaluation of ballots in various respects. See *Gore v. Harris*, 772 So.2d at 1267 (Wells, J., dissenting) ("Should a county canvassing board count or not count a 'dimpled chad' where the voter is able to successfully dislodge the chad in every other contest on that ballot? Here, the county canvassing boards disagree"). [T]he standards for accepting or rejecting contested ballots might vary not only from county to county but indeed within a single county from one recount team to another.

The record provides some examples. A monitor in Miami-Dade County testified at trial that he observed that three members of the county canvassing board applied different standards in defining a legal vote. [A]t least one county changed its evaluative standards during the counting process. Palm Beach County, for example, began the process with a 1990 guideline which precluded counting completely attached chads, switched to a rule that considered a vote to be legal if any light could be seen through a chad, changed back to the 1990 rule, and then abandoned any pretense of a *per se* rule, only to have a court order that the county consider dimpled chads legal. This is not a process with sufficient guarantees of equal treatment.

An early case in our one person, one vote jurisprudence arose when a State accorded arbitrary and disparate treatment to voters in its different counties. *Gray v. Sanders*, 372 U.S. 368, 83 S.Ct. 801, 9 L.Ed.2d 821 (1963). The Court found a constitutional violation. We relied on these principles in the context of the Presidential selection process in *Moore v. Ogilvie*, 394 U.S. 814, 89 S.Ct. 1493, 23 L.Ed.2d 1 (1969), where we invalidated a county-based procedure that diluted the influence of citizens in larger counties in the nominating process. There we observed that "[t]he idea that one group can be granted greater voting strength than another is hostile to the one man, one vote basis of our representative government."

The State Supreme Court ratified this uneven treatment. It mandated that the recount totals from two counties, Miami-Dade and Palm Beach, be included in the certified total. The court also appeared to hold *sub silentio* that the recount totals from Broward County, which were not completed until after the original November 14 certification by the Secretary of State, were to be considered part of the new certified vote totals even though the county certification was not contested by Vice President Gore. Yet each of the counties used varying standards to determine what was a legal vote. Broward County used a more forgiving standard than Palm Beach County, and uncovered almost three times as many new votes, a result markedly disproportionate to the difference in population between the counties.

In addition, the recounts in these three counties were not limited to so-called undervotes but extended to all of the ballots. The distinction has real consequences. A manual recount of all ballots identifies not only those ballots which show no vote but also those which contain more than one, the so-called overvotes. Neither category will be counted by the machine. This is not a trivial concern. At oral argument, respondents estimated there are as many as 110,000 overvotes statewide. As a result, the citizen whose ballot was not read by a machine because he failed to vote for a candidate in a way readable by a machine may still have his vote counted in a manual recount; on the other hand, the citizen who marks two candidates in a way discernable by the machine will not have the same opportunity to have his vote count, even if a manual examination of the ballot would reveal the requisite indicia of intent. . . . The State Supreme Court's inclusion of vote counts based on these variant standards exemplifies concerns with the remedial processes that were under way.

That brings the analysis to yet a further equal protection problem. The votes certified by the court included a partial total from one county, Miami-Dade. The Florida Supreme Court's decision thus gives no assurance that the recounts included in a final certification must be complete. Indeed, it is respondent's submission that it would be consistent with the rules of the recount procedures to include whatever partial counts are done by the time of final certification. . . . A desire for speed is not a general excuse for ignoring equal protection guarantees.

In addition to these difficulties the actual process by which the votes were to be counted under the Florida Supreme Court's decision raises further concerns. [C]ounty canvassing boards were forced to pull together ad hoc teams comprised of judges from various Circuits who had no previous training in handling and interpreting ballots. Furthermore, while others were permitted to observe, they were prohibited from objecting during the recount.

The recount process, in its features here described, is inconsistent with the minimum procedures necessary to protect the fundamental right of each voter in the special instance of a statewide recount under the authority of a single state judicial officer. Our consideration is limited to the present circumstances, for the problem of equal protection in election processes generally presents many complexities.

[A] state court with the power to assure uniformity has ordered a statewide recount with minimal procedural safeguards. When a court orders a statewide remedy, there must be at least some assurance that the rudimentary requirements of equal treatment and fundamental fairness are satisfied.

Given the Court's assessment that the recount process underway was probably being conducted in an unconstitutional manner, the Court stayed the order directing the recount so it could hear this case and render an expedited decision. The contest provision, as it was mandated by the State Supreme Court, is not well calculated to sustain the confidence that all citizens must have in the outcome of elections. . . .

[T]he recount cannot be conducted in compliance with the requirements of equal protection and due process without substantial additional work. It would require not only the adoption (after opportunity for argument) of adequate statewide standards for determining what is a legal vote, and practicable procedures to implement them, but also orderly judicial review of any disputed matters that might arise. In addition, the Secretary of State has advised that the recount of only a portion of the ballots requires that the vote tabulation equipment be used to screen out undervotes, a function for which the machines were not designed. If a recount of overvotes were also required, perhaps even a second screening would be necessary. Use of the equipment for this purpose, and any new software developed for it, would have to be evaluated for accuracy by the Secretary of State, as required by Fla. Stat. § 101.015 (2000).

The Supreme Court of Florida has said that the legislature intended the State's electors to "participat[e] fully in the federal electoral process," as provided in 3 U.S.C. § 5. 772 So.2d, at 1253; see also *Palm Beach Canvassing Bd. v. Harris*, 772 So.2d 1220, 1237 (Fla.2000). That statute, in turn, requires that any controversy or contest that is designed to lead to a conclusive selection of electors be completed by December 12. That date is upon us, and there is no recount procedure in place under the State Supreme Court's order that comports with minimal constitutional standards. Because it is evident that any recount seeking to meet the December 12 date will be unconstitutional for the reasons we have discussed, we reverse the judgment of the Supreme Court of Florida ordering a recount to proceed.

Seven Justices of the Court agree that there are constitutional problems with the recount ordered by the Florida Supreme Court that demand a remedy. See *post* (Souter, J., dissenting); *post* (Breyer, J., dissenting). The only disagreement is as to the remedy. Because the Florida Supreme Court has said that the Florida Legislature intended to obtain the safe-harbor benefits of 3 U.S.C. § 5, Justice Breyer's proposed remedy—remanding to the Florida Supreme Court for its ordering of a constitutionally proper contest until December 18—contemplates action in violation of the Florida election code, and hence could not be part of an "appropriate" order authorized by Fla. Stat. § 102.168(8) (2000). . . .

The judgment of the Supreme Court of Florida is reversed, and the case is remanded for further proceedings not inconsistent with this opinion. Pursuant to this Court's Rule 45.2, the Clerk is directed to issue the mandate in this case forthwith.

It is so ordered.

CHIEF JUSTICE REHNQUIST, with whom JUSTICE SCALIA and JUSTICE THOMAS join, concurring.

We join the *per curiam* opinion. We write separately because we believe there are additional grounds that require us to reverse the Florida Supreme Court's decision.

I. [T]here are a few exceptional cases in which the Constitution imposes a duty or confers a power on a particular branch of a State's government. This is one of them. Article II, § 1, cl. 2, provides that "[e]ach State shall appoint, in such Manner as the *Legislature* thereof may direct," electors for President and Vice President. (Emphasis added.) Thus, the text of the election law itself, and not just its interpretation by the courts of the States, takes on independent significance. . . .

In order to determine whether a state court has infringed upon the legislature's authority, we necessarily must examine the law of the State as it existed prior to the action of the court. Though we generally defer to state courts on the interpretation of state law there are of course areas in which the Constitution requires this Court to undertake an independent, if still deferential, analysis of state law. For example, in *NAACP v. Alabama ex rel. Patterson*, 357 U.S.

449, 78 S.Ct. 1163, 2 L.Ed.2d 1488 (1958), it was argued that we were without jurisdiction because the petitioner had not pursued the correct appellate remedy in Alabama's state courts. . . . We found this state-law ground inadequate to defeat our jurisdiction because we were "unable to reconcile the procedural holding of the Alabama Supreme Court" with prior Alabama precedent. The purported state-law ground was so novel, in our independent estimation, that "petitioner could not fairly be deemed to have been apprised of its existence." . . .[1] This inquiry does not imply a disrespect for state *courts* but rather a respect for the constitutionally prescribed role of state *legislatures*. . . .

II. [T]he [Florida] court's interpretation of "legal vote," and hence its decision to order a contest-period recount, plainly departed from the legislative scheme. Florida statutory law cannot reasonably be thought to *require* the counting of improperly marked ballots. Each Florida precinct before election day provides instructions on how properly to cast a vote, § 101.46; . . . voters are instructed to punch out the ballot cleanly:

> AFTER VOTING, CHECK YOUR BALLOT CARD TO BE SURE YOUR VOTING SELECTIONS ARE CLEARLY AND CLEANLY PUNCHED AND THERE ARE NO CHIPS LEFT HANGING ON THE BACK OF THE CARD.

No reasonable person would call it "an error in the vote tabulation," Fla. Stat. § 102.166(5), or a "rejection of legal votes," Fla. Stat. § 102.168(3)(c), when electronic or electromechanical equipment performs precisely in the manner designed, and fails to count those ballots that are not marked in the manner that these voting instructions explicitly and prominently specify. The scheme that the Florida Supreme Court's opinion attributes to the legislature is one in which machines are *required* to be "capable of correctly counting votes," § 101.5606(4), but which nonetheless regularly produces elections in which legal votes are predictably *not* tabulated, so that in close elections manual recounts are regularly required. This is of course absurd. The Secretary of State, who is authorized by law to issue binding interpretations of the election code, rejected this peculiar reading of the statutes. See DE 00–13 (opinion of the Division of Elections). The Florida Supreme Court, although it must defer to the Secretary's interpretations, see *Krivanek v. Take Back Tampa Political Committee*, 625 So.2d 840, 844 (Fla.1993),

---

[1]   [The Fifth Amendment's Taking Clause would] afford no protection against state power if our inquiry could be concluded by a state supreme court holding that state property law accorded the plaintiff no rights. [W]e similarly made an independent evaluation of state law in order to protect federal treaty guarantees. . . . *Fairfax's Devisee v. Hunter's Lessee* (1813). . . .

rejected her reasonable interpretation and embraced the peculiar one. See *Palm Beach County Canvassing Board v. Harris*, 772 So.2d 1273 (Dec. 11, 2000) (*Harris III*).

[T]he State's Attorney General (who was supporting the Gore challenge) confirmed in oral argument here that never before the present election had a manual recount been conducted on the basis of the contention that "undervotes" should have been examined to determine voter intent. cf. *Broward County Canvassing Board v. Hogan*, 607 So.2d 508, 509 (Fla.Ct.App.1992) (denial of recount for failure to count ballots with "hanging paper chads"). . . .

III. The scope and nature of the remedy ordered by the Florida Supreme Court jeopardizes the "legislative wish" to take advantage of the safe harbor provided by 3 U.S.C. § 5. December 12, 2000, is the last date for a final determination of the Florida electors that will satisfy § 5. Yet in the late afternoon of December 8th—four days before this deadline—the Supreme Court of Florida ordered recounts of tens of thousands of so-called "undervotes" spread through 64 of the State's 67 counties . . .

JUSTICE STEVENS, with whom JUSTICE GINSBURG and JUSTICE BREYER join, dissenting. . . .

Admittedly, the use of differing sub-standards for determining voter intent in different counties employing similar voting systems may raise serious concerns. [A]s a general matter, "[t]he interpretation of constitutional principles must not be too literal. We must remember that the machinery of government would not work if it were not allowed a little play in its joints." . . . Even assuming that aspects of the remedial scheme might ultimately be found to violate the Equal Protection Clause, I could not subscribe to the majority's disposition of the case. . . . Although we may never know with complete certainty the identity of the winner of this year's Presidential election, the identity of the loser is perfectly clear. It is the Nation's confidence in the judge as an impartial guardian of the rule of law. I respectfully dissent.

JUSTICE SOUTER, with whom JUSTICE BREYER joins and with whom JUSTICE STEVENS and JUSTICE GINSBURG join with regard to all but Part C, dissenting. . . .

C. [E]vidence in the record here suggests that a different order of disparity obtains under rules for determining a voter's intent that have been applied (and could continue to be applied) to identical types of ballots used in identical brands of machines and exhibiting identical physical characteristics (such as "hanging" or "dimpled" chads). I can conceive of no legitimate state interest served by these differing treatments of the expressions of voters' fundamental rights. The differences appear wholly arbitrary.

. . . To recount these manually would be a tall order, but [t]here is no justification for denying the State the opportunity to try to count all disputed ballots now. I respectfully dissent.

JUSTICE BREYER, with whom JUSTICE STEVENS and JUSTICE GINSBURG join except as to Part I-A-1, and with whom JUSTICE SOUTER joins as to Part I, dissenting. . . .

1.   The majority raises three Equal Protection problems with . . . the absence of a uniform, specific standard to guide the recounts. [This] concern does implicate principles of fundamental fairness. [I]n these very special circumstances, basic principles of fairness may well have counseled the adoption of a uniform standard to address the problem. In light of the majority's disposition, I need not decide whether, or the extent to which, as a remedial matter, the Constitution would place limits upon the content of the uniform standard.

2.   . . . Whether there is time to conduct a recount prior to December 18, when the electors are scheduled to meet, is a matter for the state courts to determine. . . .

[The dissenting opinion of GINSBURG, J., joined by STEVENS, J. and in part by SOUTER & BREYER, JJ., is omitted.]

NOTES

1.   After this case, several newspapers hired auditors who examined the ballots and reported their findings in April 2001. The *Miami Herald*, a major sponsor of this recount, concluded that a "comprehensive review of 64,248 ballots in all 67 Florida counties by *The Herald*" in partnership with *USA Today*, "found that Bush's slender margin of 537 votes would have tripled to 1,665 votes under the generous counting standards advocated by Democrat Al Gore."[17] The *Herald*'s team began counting the undervotes on December 18, 2000, and was not able to conclude until March 13, 2001.[18] The *Herald*'s reviewers "also discovered that canvassing boards in Palm Beach and Broward counties

---

[17]   Martin Merzer, Review Shows Ballots Say Bush, Miami Herald, April 4, 2001, p. A1.

[18]   CNN, Recount of Florida Undervotes Confirms Bush Victory, April 4, 2001, http://www.cnn.com/2001/ALLPOLITICS/04/03/florida.recount/

threw out hundreds of ballots that had marks that were no different from ballots deemed to be valid."[19]

2. At the end of the Per Curiam opinion, the Court cited the Florida Supreme Court as indicating that Florida wanted to take advantage of the "safe harbor" provisions of the federal statute, 3 U.S.C.A. § 5, which requires electors to be selected by December 12, six days before the electors vote for President. The Court cited two Florida opinions. In the first citation, *Gore v. Harris*, 772 So.2d 1243, 1253 n. 11 (Fla.2000), the Florida Court said: "Of course, because the selection and participation of Florida's electors in the presidential election process is subject to a stringent calendar controlled by federal law, the Florida election law scheme must yield in the event of a conflict." In the second citation, *Palm Beach County Canvassing Board v. Harris*, 772 So.2d 1220, 1237 (Fla.2000), the Florida Court said: "Ignoring the county's returns is a drastic measure and is appropriate only if the returns are submitted to the Department so late that their inclusion will compromise the integrity of the electoral process in either of two ways: (1) by precluding a candidate, elector, or taxpayer from contesting the certification of an election pursuant to section 102.168; or (2) by precluding Florida voters from participating fully in the federal electoral process." (Footnote omitted, citing 3 U.S.C.A. §§ 1– 10).

---

[19] Id.

Congressional Enforcement of Civil Rights

6.1 THE FOURTEENTH AMENDMENT

THE CIVIL RIGHTS CASES (UNITED STATES V. STANLEY; UNITED STATES V. RYAN; UNITED STATES V. NICHOLS; UNITED STATES V. SINGLETON; ROBINSON V. MEMPHIS & CHARLESTON R. CO.)

109 U.S. 3, 3 S.Ct. 18, 27 L.Ed. 835 (1883)

[These cases involve application of the first two sections of the Civil Rights Act, passed March 1st, 1875, entitled "An Act to protect all citizens in their civil and legal rights." In two cases, the Government indicted Stanley and Nichols, for denying to "persons of color the accommodations and privileges of an inn or hotel." Another case involved an information against Ryan "for refusing a colored person a seat in the dress circle of Maguire's theatre in San Francisco." The Government also indicted Singleton "for denying to another person, whose color was not stated, the full enjoyment of" the New York Grand Opera House, "said denial not being made for any reasons by law applicable to citizens of every race and color, and regardless of any previous condition of servitude." Another case involved an action by "Robinson and wife against the Memphis & Charleston R.R. Company," to recover a $500 penalty given by the second section of the act. The "gravamen was the refusal by the conductor of the railroad company to allow the wife to ride in the ladies' car, for the reason, as stated in one of the counts, that she was a person of African descent."]

JUSTICE BRADLEY delivered the opinion of the Court.

It is obvious that the primary and important question in all the cases is the constitutionality of the law: for if the law is unconstitutional none of the prosecutions can stand.

The sections of the law referred to provide as follows:

Sec. 1.   That all persons within the jurisdiction of the United States shall be entitled to the full and equal enjoyment of the accommodations, advantages, facilities, and privileges of inns, public conveyances on land or water, theatres, and other places of public amusement; subject only to the conditions and limitations established by law, and applicable alike to citizens of every race and color, regardless of any previous condition of servitude.

Sec. 2.   That any person who shall violate the foregoing section . . . shall for every such offence forfeit and pay the sum of five hundred dollars to the person aggrieved thereby, to be recovered in an action of debt, with full costs; and shall also, for every such offence, be deemed guilty of a misdemeanor, and, upon conviction thereof, shall be fined not less than five hundred nor more than one thousand dollars, or shall be imprisoned not less than thirty days nor more than one year. . . .

Has Congress constitutional power to make such a law? Of course, no one will contend that the power to pass it was contained in the Constitution before the adoption of the last three amendments. The power is sought, first, in the Fourteenth Amendment, and the views and arguments of distinguished Senators, advanced whilst the law was under consideration, claiming authority to pass it by virtue of that amendment, are the principal arguments adduced in favor of the power.

[Under the Fourteenth Amendment, it] is State action of a particular character that is prohibited. Individual invasion of individual rights is not the subject-matter of the amendment. It has a deeper and broader scope. It nullifies and makes void all State legislation, and State action of every kind, which impairs the privileges and immunities of citizens of the United States, or which injures them in life, liberty or property without due process of law, or which denies to any of them the equal protection of the laws. It not only does this, but, in order that the national will, thus declared, may not be a mere *burtum fulmen,* the last section of the amendment invests Congress with power to enforce it by appropriate legislation. To enforce what? To enforce the prohibition. To adopt appropriate legislation for correcting the effects of such prohibited State laws and

State acts, and thus to render them effectually null, void, and innocuous. This is the legislative power conferred upon Congress, and this is the whole of it. . . .

[U]ntil some State law has been passed, or some State action through its officers or agents has been taken, adverse to the rights of citizens sought to be protected by the Fourteenth Amendment, no legislation of the United States under said amendment, nor any proceeding under such legislation, can be called into activity: for the prohibitions of the amendment are against State laws and acts done under State authority. . . .

If this legislation is appropriate for enforcing the prohibitions of the amendment, it is difficult to see where it is to stop. Why may not Congress with equal show of authority enact a code of laws for the enforcement and vindication of all rights of life, liberty, and property? If it is supposable that the States may deprive persons of life, liberty, and property without due process of law (and the amendment itself does suppose this), why should not Congress proceed at once to prescribe due process of law for the protection of every one of these fundamental rights, in every possible case, as well as to prescribe equal privileges in inns, public conveyances, and theatres? The truth is, that the implication of a power to legislate in this manner is based upon the assumption that if the States are forbidden to legislate or act in a particular way on a particular subject, and power is conferred upon Congress to enforce the prohibition, this gives Congress power to legislate generally upon that subject, and not merely power to provide modes of redress against such State legislation or action. The assumption is certainly unsound. It is repugnant to the Tenth Amendment of the Constitution, which declares that powers not delegated to the United States by the Constitution, nor prohibited by it to the States, are reserved to the States respectively or to the people. . . .

In this connection it is proper to state that civil rights, such as are guaranteed by the Constitution against State aggression, cannot be impaired by the wrongful acts of individuals, unsupported by State authority in the shape of laws, customs, or judicial or executive proceedings. . . .

Of course, these remarks do not apply to those cases in which Congress is clothed with direct and plenary powers of legislation over the whole subject, accompanied with an express or implied denial of such power to the States, as in the regulation of commerce with foreign nations, among the several States, and with the Indian tribes, the coining of money. [I]t is clear that the law in question cannot be sustained by any grant of legislative power made to Congress by the Fourteenth Amendment. . . . Whether the law would be a valid one as applied to the Territories and the District is not a question for consideration in the cases before us: they all being cases arising within the limits of States. And whether Congress, in the exercise of its power to regulate commerce amongst the several States, might or might not pass a law regulating rights in public conveyances passing from one State to another, is also a question which is not now before us, as the sections in question are not conceived in any such view.

But the power of Congress to adopt direct and primary, as distinguished from corrective legislation, on the subject in hand, is sought, in the second place, from the Thirteenth Amendment. . . . By its own unaided force and effect it abolished slavery, and established universal freedom. Still, legislation may be necessary and proper to meet all the various cases and circumstances to be affected by it, and to prescribe proper modes of redress for its violation in letter or spirit. And such legislation may be primary and direct in its character; for the amendment is not a mere prohibition of State laws establishing or upholding slavery, but an absolute declaration that slavery or involuntary servitude shall not exist in any part of the United States.

It is true, that slavery cannot exist without law, any more than property in lands and goods can exist without law: and, therefore, the Thirteenth Amendment may be regarded as nullifying all State laws which establish or uphold slavery. But it has a reflex character also, establishing and decreeing universal civil and political freedom throughout the United States; and it is assumed, that the power vested in Congress to enforce the article by appropriate legislation, clothes Congress with power to pass all laws necessary and proper for abolishing all badges and incidents of slavery in the United States: and upon this assumption it is claimed, that this is sufficient authority for declaring by law that all persons shall have equal accommodations and privileges in all inns, public conveyances, and places of amusement; the argument being, that the denial of such equal accommodations and privileges is, in itself, a subjection to a species of servitude within the meaning of the amendment. Conceding the major proposition to be true, that Congress has a right to enact all necessary and proper laws for the obliteration and prevention of slavery with all its badges and incidents, is the minor proposition also true, that the denial to any person of admission to the accommodations and privileges of an inn, a public conveyance, or a theatre, does subject that person to any form of servitude, or tend to fasten upon him any badge of slavery? If it does not, then power to pass the law is not found in the Thirteenth Amendment. . . .

The long existence of African slavery in this country gave us very distinct notions of what it was, and what were its necessary incidents. . . . Congress, as we have seen, by the Civil Rights Bill of 1866, passed in view of the Thirteenth Amendment, before the Fourteenth was adopted, undertook to wipe out these burdens and disabilities, the necessary incidents of slavery, constituting its substance and visible form; and to secure to all citizens of every race and color, and without regard to previous servitude, those fundamental rights which are the essence of civil freedom, namely, the same right to make and enforce contracts, to sue, be parties, give evidence, and to inherit, purchase, lease, sell and convey property, as is enjoyed by white citizens. Whether this legislation was fully authorized by the Thirteenth Amendment alone, without the support which it afterward received from the Fourteenth Amendment, after the adoption of which it was reenacted with some additions, it is not necessary to inquire. It is referred to for the purpose of showing that at that time (in 1866) Congress did not assume, under the authority given by the Thirteenth Amendment, to adjust what may be called the social rights of men and races in the community; but only to declare and vindicate those fundamental rights which appertain to the essence of citizenship, and the enjoyment or deprivation of which constitutes the essential distinction between freedom and slavery. . . .

The only question under the present head, therefore, is, whether the refusal to any persons of the accommodations of an inn, or a public conveyance, or a place of public amusement, by an individual, and without any sanction or support from any State law or regulation, does inflict upon such persons any manner of servitude, or form of slavery, as those terms are understood in this country? [S]uch an act of refusal has nothing to do with slavery or involuntary servitude, and that if it is violative of any right of the party, his redress is to be sought under the laws of the State; or if those laws are adverse to his rights and do not protect him, his remedy will be found in the corrective legislation which Congress has adopted, or may adopt, for counteracting the effect of State laws, or State action, prohibited by the Fourteenth Amendment. It would be running the slavery argument into the ground to make it apply to every act of discrimination which a person may see fit to make as to the guests he will entertain, or as to the people he will take into his coach or cab or car, or admit to his concert or theatre, or deal with in other matters of intercourse or business. Innkeepers and public carriers, by the laws of all the States, so far as we are aware, are bound, to the extent of their facilities, to furnish proper accommodation to all unobjectionable persons who in good faith apply for them. If the laws themselves make any unjust discrimination, amenable to the prohibitions of the Fourteenth Amendment, Congress has full power to afford a remedy under that amendment and in accordance with it.

When a man has emerged from slavery, and by the aid of beneficent legislation has shaken off the inseparable concomitants of that state, there must be some stage in the progress of his elevation when he takes the rank of a mere citizen, and ceases to be the special favorite of the laws, and when his rights as a citizen, or a man, are to be protected in the ordinary modes by which other men's rights are protected. There were thousands of free colored people in this country before the abolition of slavery, enjoying all the essential rights of life, liberty and property the same as white citizens; yet no one, at that time, thought that it was any invasion of his personal status as a freeman because he was not admitted to all the privileges enjoyed by white citizens, or because he was subjected to discriminations in the enjoyment of accommodations in inns, public conveyances and places of amusement. Mere discriminations on account of race or color were not regarded as badges of slavery.

[Thus,] the first and second sections of the act of Congress of March 1st, 1875, entitled "An Act to protect all citizens in their civil and legal rights," are unconstitutional and void, and that judgment should be rendered upon the several indictments in those cases accordingly.

And it is so ordered.

JUSTICE HARLAN, dissenting.

The opinion in these cases proceeds, it seems to me, upon grounds entirely two narrow and artificial. I cannot resist the conclusion that the substance and spirit of the recent amendments of the Constitution have been sacrificed by a subtle and ingenious verbal criticism.

[T]here are burdens and disabilities which constitute badges of slavery and servitude, and . . . such discrimination practised by corporations and individuals in the exercise of their public or quasi-public functions is a badge of servitude the imposition of which Congress may prevent under its power, by appropriate legislation, to enforce the Thirteenth Amendment; and, consequently, without reference to its enlarged power under the Fourteenth Amendment, the act of March 1, 1875, is not, in my judgment, repugnant to the Constitution.

It remains now to consider these cases with reference to the power Congress has possessed since the adoption of the Fourteenth Amendment. . . . The assumption that this amendment consists wholly of prohibitions upon State laws and State proceedings in hostility to its provisions, is unauthorized by its language. . . . because the power of Congress is not restricted to the enforcement of prohibitions upon State laws or State action. It is, in terms distinct and positive, to enforce "the *provisions of this article*" of amendment; not simply those of a prohibitive character, but the provisions—*all* of the provisions—affirmative and prohibitive, of the amendment. . . .

[W]hat was secured to colored citizens of the United States—as between them and their respective States—by the national grant to them of State citizenship? With what rights, privileges, or immunities did this grant invest them? There is one, if there be no other—exemption from race discrimination in respect of any civil right belonging to citizens of the white race in the same State. That, surely, is their constitutional privilege when within the jurisdiction of other States. And such must be their constitutional right, in their own State, unless the recent amendments be splendid baubles, thrown out to delude those who deserved fair and generous treatment at the hands of the nation. Citizenship in this country necessarily imports at least equality of civil rights among citizens of every race in the same State. . . .

The court, in its opinion, reserves the question whether Congress, in the exercise of its power to regulate commerce amongst the several States, might or might not pass a law regulating rights in public conveyances passing from one State to another. . . . Might not the act of 1875 be maintained in that case, as applicable at least to commerce between the States, notwithstanding it does not, upon its face, profess to have been passed in pursuance of the power of Congress to regulate commerce? Has it ever been held that the judiciary should overturn a statute, because the legislative department did not accurately recite therein the particular provision of the Constitution authorizing its enactment? We have often enforced municipal bonds in aid of railroad subscriptions, where they failed to recite the statute authorizing their issue, but recited one which did not sustain their validity. The inquiry in such cases has been, was there, in any statute, authority for the execution of the bonds? . . .

NOTES

1. In *Bell v. Maryland,* 378 U.S. 226, 84 S.Ct. 1814, 12 L.Ed.2d 822 (1964), twelve black students entered a restaurant and sought service. When an employee asked them to leave solely because of their race, they refused, and were convicted of criminal trespass. After the state courts affirmed the conviction, Baltimore and Maryland enacted public accommodations laws making it unlawful for restaurants to deny service because of race. The Court, per Justice Brennan, then remanded the case so that the state court could consider whether to nullify the convictions in view of the change in state law,

which would apply to any case pending at the time of the supervening legislation. Of the various opinions written, Justice Goldberg's concurrence, joined by Chief Justice Warren, and in part by Justice Douglas, considered the historical background of the *Civil Rights Cases*. In those rulings, Justice Bradley stated: "Innkeepers and public carriers, by the laws of all the States, so far as we are aware, are bound, to the extent of their facilities, to furnish proper accommodation to all unobjectionable persons who in good faith apply for them." According to Justice Goldberg:

> This assumption, whatever its validity at the time of the 1883 decision, has proved to be unfounded. Although reconstruction ended in 1877, six years before the *Civil Rights Cases,* there was little immediate action in the South to establish segregation, in law or in fact, in places of public accommodation.[26] This benevolent, or perhaps passive, attitude endures about a decade and then in the late 1880s States began to enact laws mandating unequal treatment in public places. Finally, three-quarters of a century later, after this Court declared such legislative action invalid, some States began to utilize and make available their common law to sanction similar discriminatory treatment.
>
> A State applying its statutory or common law to deny rather than protect the right of access to public accommodations has clearly made the assumption of the opinion in the *Civil Rights Cases* inapplicable and has, as the author of that opinion would himself have recognized, denied the constitutionally intended equal protection. Indeed, in light of the assumption so explicitly stated in the *Civil Rights Cases,* it is significant that Mr. Justice Bradley, who spoke for the Court had earlier in correspondence with Circuit Judge Woods expressed the view that the Fourteenth Amendment "not only prohibits the making or enforcing of laws which shall abridge the privileges of the citizen; but prohibits the states from denying to all persons within its jurisdiction the equal protection of the laws." In taking this position, which is consistent with his opinion and the assumption in the *Civil Rights Cases,* he concluded

---

[26] Woodward, The Strange Career of Jim Crow (1955), 15–26, points out that segregation in its modern and pervasive form is a relatively recent phenomenon. Although the speed of the movement varied, it was not until 1904, for example, that Maryland, the respondent in this case, extended Jim Crow legislation to railroad coaches and other common carriers. In the 1870s Negroes in Baltimore, Maryland, successfully challenged attempts to segregate transit facilities.

that: "Denying includes inaction as well as action. And denying the equal protection of the laws includes the omission to protect, as well as the omission to pass laws for protection." These views are fully consonant with this Court's recognition that state conduct which might be described as "inaction" can nevertheless constitute responsible "state action" within the meaning of the Fourteenth Amendment.

2.   In *Katzenbach v. Morgan*, the Court upheld federal power under § 5 to override a *state* law.

KATZENBACH V. MORGAN
384 U.S. 641, 86 S.Ct. 1717, 16 L.Ed.2d 828 (1966)

MR. JUSTICE BRENNAN delivered the opinion of the Court.

These cases concern the constitutionality of § 4(e) of the Voting Rights Act of 1965. That law, in the respects pertinent in these cases, provides that no person who has successfully completed the sixth primary grade in a public school in, or a private school accredited by, the Commonwealth of Puerto Rico in which the language of instruction was other than English shall be denied the right to vote in any election because of his inability to read or write English. Appellees, registered voters in New York City, brought this suit to challenge the constitutionality of § 4(e) insofar as it *pro tanto* prohibits the enforcement of the election laws of New York requiring an ability to read and write English as a condition of voting. Under these laws many of the several hundred thousand New York City residents who have migrated there from the Commonwealth of Puerto Rico had previously been denied the right to vote, and appellees attack § 4(e) insofar as it would enable many of these citizens to vote. . . . We hold that, in the application challenged in these cases, § 4(e) is a proper exercise of the powers granted to Congress by § 5 of the Fourteenth Amendment and that by force of the Supremacy Clause, Article VI, the New York English literacy requirement cannot be enforced to the extent that it is inconsistent with § 4(e). . . .

The Attorney General of the State of New York argues that an exercise of congressional power under § 5 of the Fourteenth Amendment that prohibits the enforcement of a state law can only be sustained if the judicial branch determines that the state law is prohibited by the provisions of the Amendment that Congress sought to enforce. . . . We disagree. Neither the language nor history of § 5 supports such a construction. As was said with regard to § 5 in *Ex parte Com. of Virginia,* 100 U.S. 339, 345, 25 L.Ed. 676, "It is the power of Congress which has been enlarged. Congress is authorized to *enforce* the prohibitions by appropriate legislation. Some legislation is contemplated to make the amendments fully effective." A construction of § 5 that would require a judicial determination that the enforcement of the state law precluded by Congress violated the Amendment, as a condition of sustaining the congressional enactment, would depreciate both congressional resourcefulness and congressional responsibility for implementing the Amendment. It would confine the legislative power in this context to the insignificant role of abrogating only those state laws that the judicial branch was prepared to adjudge unconstitutional, or of merely informing the judgment of the judiciary by particularizing the "majestic generalities" of § 1 of the Amendment.

Thus our task in this case is not to determine whether the New York English literacy requirement as applied to deny the right to vote to a person who successfully completed the sixth *grade* in a Puerto Rican school violates the Equal Protection Clause. Accordingly, our decision in *Lassiter v. Northampton County Bd. of Election,* 360 U.S. 45, 79 S.Ct. 985, 3 L.Ed.2d 1072, sustaining the North Carolina English literacy requirement as not in all circumstances prohibited by the first sections of the Fourteenth and Fifteenth Amendments, is inapposite. *Lassiter* did not present the question before us here: Without regard to whether the judiciary would find that the Equal Protection Clause itself nullifies New York's English literacy requirement as so applied, could Congress prohibit the enforcement of the state law by legislating under § 5 of the Fourteenth Amendment? In answering this question, our task is limited to determining whether such legislation is, as required by § 5, appropriate legislation to enforce the Equal Protection Clause.

By including § 5 the draftsmen sought to grant to Congress, by a specific provision applicable to the Fourteenth Amendment, the same broad powers expressed in the Necessary and Proper Clause, Art. I, § 8, cl. 18. The classic formulation of the reach of those powers was established by Chief Justice Marshall in *McCulloch v. Maryland. Ex parte Com. of Virginia,* decided 12 years after the adoption of the Fourteenth Amendment, held that congressional power under § 5 had this same broad scope. [T]he *McCulloch v. Maryland* standard is the measure of what constitutes "appropriate legislation" under § 5 of the Fourteenth Amendment. Correctly viewed, § 5 is a positive grant of legislative power authorizing Congress to exercise its discretion in determining whether and what legislation is needed to secure the guarantees of the Fourteenth Amendment. . . .[10]

---

[10] Contrary to the suggestion of the dissent, § 5 does not grant Congress power to exercise discretion in the other direction and to enact "statutes so as in effect to dilute equal protection and due process decisions of this Court." We emphasize that Congress' power under § 5 is limited to adopting measures to enforce the guarantees of the Amendment; § 5 grants Congress no power to restrict, abrogate, or dilute these guarantees.

There can be no doubt that § 4(e) may be regarded as an enactment to enforce the Equal Protection Clause. Congress explicitly declared that it enacted § 4(e) "to secure the rights under the fourteenth amendment of persons educated in American-flag schools in which the predominant classroom language was other than English." . . . More specifically, § 4(e) may be viewed as a measure to secure for the Puerto Rican community residing in New York nondiscriminatory treatment by government—both in the imposition of voting qualifications and the provision or administration of governmental services, such as public schools, public housing and law enforcement.

Section 4(e) may be readily seen as "plainly adapted" to furthering these aims of the Equal Protection Clause. The practical effect of § 4(e) is to prohibit New York from denying the right to vote to large segments of its Puerto Rican community. Congress has thus prohibited the State from denying to that community the right that is "preservative of all rights." This enhanced political power will be helpful in gaining nondiscriminatory treatment in public services for the entire Puerto Rican community.[11] . . . It was for Congress, as the branch that made this judgment, to assess and weigh the various conflicting considerations—the risk or pervasiveness of the discrimination in governmental services, the effectiveness of eliminating the state restriction on the right to vote as a means of dealing with the evil, the adequacy or availability of alternative remedies, and the nature and significance of the state interests that would be affected by the nullification of the English literacy requirement as applied to residents who have successfully completed the sixth grade in a Puerto Rican school. It is not for us to review the congressional resolution of these factors. It is enough that we be able to perceive a basis upon which the Congress might resolve the conflict as it did. There plainly was such a basis to support § 4(e) in the application in question in this case. Any contrary conclusion would require us to be blind to the realities familiar to the legislators.

Thus, for example, an enactment authorizing the States to establish racially segregated systems of education would not be—as required by § 5—a measure "to enforce" the Equal Protection Clause since that clause of its own force prohibits such state laws.

[11]   Cf. *James Everard's Breweries v. Day,* [265 U.S. 545, 44 S.Ct. 628, 68 L.Ed. 1174], which held that, under the Enforcement Clause of the Eighteenth Amendment, Congress could prohibit the prescription of intoxicating malt liquor for medicinal purposes even though the Amendment itself only prohibited the manufacture and sale of intoxicating liquors for beverage purposes. Cf. also the settled principle applied in the *Shreveport Case (Houston, E. & W. T.R. Co. v. United States)* and expressed in *United States v. Darby* that the power of Congress to regulate interstate commerce "extends to those activities intrastate which so affect interstate commerce or the exercise of the power of Congress over it as to make regulation of them appropriate means to the attainment of a legitimate end. . . ."

The result is no different if we confine our inquiry to the question whether § 4(e) was merely legislation aimed at the elimination of an invidious discrimination in establishing voter qualifications. We are told that New York's English literacy requirement originated in the desire to provide an incentive for non-English speaking immigrants to learn the English language and in order to assure the intelligent exercise of the franchise. Yet Congress might well have questioned, in light of the many exemptions provided,[13] and some evidence suggesting that prejudice played a prominent role in the enactment of the requirement, whether these were actually the interests being served. Congress might have also questioned whether denial of a right deemed so precious and fundamental in our society was a necessary or appropriate means of encouraging persons to learn English, or of furthering the goal of an intelligent exercise of the franchise. Finally, Congress might well have concluded that as a means of furthering the intelligent exercise of the franchise, an ability to read or understand Spanish is as effective as ability to read English for those to whom Spanish-language newspapers and Spanish-language radio and television programs are available to inform them of election issues and governmental affairs. Since Congress undertook to legislate so as to preclude the enforcement of the state law, and did so in the context of a general appraisal of literacy requirements for voting, to which it brought a specially informed legislative competence, it was Congress' prerogative to weigh these competing considerations. Here again, it is enough that we perceive a basis upon which Congress might predicate a judgment that the application of New York's English literacy requirement to deny the right to vote to a person with a sixth grade education in Puerto Rican schools in which the language of instruction was other than English constituted an invidious discrimination in violation of the Equal Protection Clause.

There remains the question whether the congressional remedies adopted in § 4(e) constitute means which are not prohibited by, but are consistent "with the letter and spirit of the constitution." The only respect in which appellees contend that § 4(e) fails in this regard is that the section itself works an invidious discrimination in violation of the Fifth Amendment by prohibiting the enforcement of the English literacy requirement only for those educated in American-flag schools (schools located within United States jurisdiction) in which the language of instruction was other than English, and not for those educated in schools beyond the territorial limits of the United States in which the language of instruction was also other than English. This is not a complaint that Congress, in

---

[13] The principal exemption complained of is that for persons who had been eligible to vote before January 1, 1922.

enacting § 4(e), has unconstitutionally denied or diluted anyone's right to vote but rather that Congress violated the Constitution by not extending the relief effected in § 4(e) to those educated in non-American-flag schools.

[W]e are guided by the familiar principles that a "statute is not invalid under the Constitution because it might have gone farther than it did," that a legislature need not "strike at all evils at the same time," and that "reform may take one step at a time, addressing itself to the phase of the problem which seems most acute to the legislative mind."

Guided by these principles, we are satisfied that appellees' challenge to this limitation in § 4(e) is without merit. In the context of the case before us, the congressional choice to limit the relief effected in § 4(e) may, for example, reflect Congress' greater familiarity with the quality of instruction in American-flag schools. [T]he limitation on relief effected in § 4(e) does not constitute a forbidden discrimination since these factors might well have been the basis for the decision of Congress to go "no farther than it did."

We therefore conclude that § 4(e), in the application challenged in this case, is appropriate legislation to enforce the Equal Protection Clause and that the judgment of the District Court must be and hereby is

Reversed.

MR. JUSTICE DOUGLAS joins the Court's opinion except for the discussion of the question whether the congressional remedies adopted in § 4(e) constitute means which are not prohibited by, but are consistent with "the letter and spirit of the constitution." On that question, he reserves judgment until such time as it is presented by a member of the class against which that particular discrimination is directed.

MR. JUSTICE HARLAN, whom MR. JUSTICE STEWART joins, dissenting. . . .

When recognized state violations of federal constitutional standards have occurred, Congress is of course empowered by § 5 to take appropriate remedial measures to redress *and* prevent the wrongs. But it is a judicial question whether the condition with which Congress has thus sought to deal is in truth an infringement of the Constitution, something that is the necessary prerequisite to bringing the § 5 power into play at all. Thus, in *Ex parte Virginia, supra,* involving a federal statute making it a federal crime to disqualify anyone from jury service because of race, the Court first held as a matter of constitutional law that "the Fourteenth Amendment secures, among other civil rights, to colored men, when charged with criminal offences against a State, an impartial jury trial, by jurors indifferently selected or chosen without discrimination against such jurors because of their color." Only then did the Court hold that to enforce this prohibition upon state discrimination, Congress could enact a criminal statute of the type under consideration. . . .

Section 4(e), however, presents a significantly different type of congressional enactment. The question here is not whether the statute is appropriate remedial legislation to cure an established violation of a constitutional command, but whether there has in fact been an infringement of that constitutional command, that is, whether a particular state practice or, as here, a statute is so arbitrary or irrational as to offend the command of the Equal Protection Clause of the Fourteenth Amendment. That question is one for the judicial branch ultimately to determine. Were the rule otherwise, Congress would be able to qualify this Court's constitutional decisions under the Fourteenth and Fifteenth Amendments, let alone those under other provisions of the Constitution, by resorting to congressional power under the Necessary and Proper Clause. In view of this Court's holding in *Lassiter, supra,* that an English literacy test is a permissible exercise of state supervision over its franchise, I do not think it is open to Congress to limit the effect of that decision as it has undertaken to do by § 4(e). In effect the Court reads § 5 of the Fourteenth Amendment as giving Congress the power to define the *substantive* scope of the Amendment. If that indeed be the true reach of § 5, then I do not see why Congress should not be able as well to exercise its § 5 "discretion" by enacting statutes so as in effect to dilute equal protection and due process decisions of this Court. In all such cases there is room for reasonable men to differ as to whether or not a denial of equal protection or due process has occurred, and the final decision is one of judgment. Until today this judgment has always been one for the judiciary to resolve.

I do not mean to suggest in what has been said that a legislative judgment of the type incorporated in § 4(e) is without any force whatsoever. Decisions on questions of equal protection and due process are based not on abstract logic, but on empirical foundations. To the extent "legislative facts" are relevant to a judicial determination, Congress is well equipped to investigate them, and such determinations are of course entitled to due respect. . . . But no such factual data provide a legislative record supporting § 4(e)[9] by way of showing that Spanish-speaking citizens are fully as capable of making informed decisions in a New York election as are English-speaking citizens. . . . There is simply no legislative record

---

[9]   There were no committee hearings or reports referring to this section, which was introduced from the floor during debate on the full Voting Rights Act.

supporting such hypothesized discrimination of the sort we have hitherto insisted upon when congressional power is brought to bear on constitutionally reserved state concerns. . . .

NOTES

1. *Oregon v. Mitchell*, 400 U.S. 112, 91 S.Ct. 260, 27 L.Ed.2d 272 (1970), responded to a lawsuit brought by Oregon and other states resisting compliance with the Voting Rights Amendments of 1970. This law lowered the minimum voting age in state and federal elections from twenty-one to eighteen, barred the use of literacy tests under certain circumstances, and forbade state imposition of residency requirements for presidential and vice-presidential elections.

   The Justices all agreed that Congress has the power, under the enforcement clause of the Fifteenth Amendments, to prohibit the use of literacy tests or other devices used to discriminate against voters on account of their race in both state and federal elections. All the Justices except Harlan also agreed that Congress could set residency requirements and provide for absentee balloting in the election for presidential and vice-presidential electors. But the Justices split several different ways and wrote five separate opinions on the question whether Congress could extend the franchise to eighteen-year-olds in state and federal elections. Only a minority (4) members of the Court—Douglas, Brennan, White, and Marshall—maintained that Congress had the power under § 5 of the Fourteenth Amendment to mandate that eighteen-to-twenty-one-year-olds vote in state and federal elections.

   Stewart, J., joined by Burger, C.J., and Blackmun, J., said that Congress could not usurp the role of the courts by determining the boundaries of the equal protection clause. Rather than reading *Morgan* as granting Congress power to define the reach of the equal protection clause, Stewart said that *Morgan* only accepted (as undoubtedly correct) the congressional conclusion that a state statute denying a racial group the right to vote amounts to invidious discrimination under equal protection. Harlan agreed that Congress cannot define the reach of equal protection because constitutional interpretation by the Congress conflicts with the procedures for amending the Constitution. Black upheld the power of Congress to set the voting age in national elections (congressional, senatorial, vice-presidential, and presidential elections) but not in state and local elections. (Black relied not on § 5 but on Article I, § 4, augmented by the necessary and proper clause.) Based on differing reasons, none of which attracted a majority, the Court ruled that the 18-year-old vote provisions were constitutional only insofar as they pertained to federal elections and unconstitutional insofar as they pertained to state and local elections.

2. In 1971 the Twenty-sixth Amendment became part of the Constitution; it prohibits *citizens* eighteen years old and older from being denied the right to vote because of age.

3. *Mississippi University for Women v. Hogan,* 458 U.S. 718, 102 S.Ct. 3331, 73 L.Ed.2d 1090 (1982), invalidated, under the equal protection clause, a state statute that excluded males from enrolling in a state-supported professional nursing school. The state justified its exclusion of men in part on the basis of Title IX of the Educational Amendments of 1972. This title prohibits gender discrimination in schools receiving federal aid, but exempts the admissions policies of undergraduate schools that "traditionally" were open only to one gender. The Court held, first, this section of Title IX did not exempt any university from constitutional requirements but only from the requirements of Title IX. Second, even "if Congress envisioned a constitutional exemption, the State's argument would fail" because Congress can only enforce the guarantees of the Fourteenth Amendment. Congress has no power "to restrict, abrogate, or dilute these guarantees."

4. In *United States v. Guest,* 383 U.S. 745, 86 S.Ct. 1170, 16 L.Ed.2d 239 (1966), a majority of the Justices, *in dictum,* expressed the view, that § 5 of the Fourteenth Amendment authorizes Congress to enact laws punishing conspiracies to interfere with the exercise of Fourteenth Amendment rights, whether or not anyone was acting under color of law. However, the Supreme Court never adopted that principle as a holding and later specifically rejected it, in *City of Boerne v. Flores* (1997).

CITY OF BOERNE V. FLORES

521 U.S. 507, 117 S.Ct. 2157, 138 L.Ed.2d 624 (1997)

JUSTICE KENNEDY delivered the opinion of the Court.

[Local zoning authorities denied the Catholic Archbishop a building permit to enlarge a church because of an ordinance governing historic preservation. The Archbishop sued, challenging the ordinance under the Religious Freedom Restoration Act of 1993 (RFRA).] The case calls into question the authority of Congress to enact RFRA. We conclude the statute exceeds Congress' power . . .

Congress enacted RFRA in direct response to the Court's decision in *Employment Div., Dept. of Human Resources of Ore. v. Smith*, 494 U.S. 872, 110 S.Ct. 1595, 108 L.Ed.2d 876 (1990). There we considered a Free Exercise Clause claim brought by members of the Native American Church who were denied unemployment benefits when they lost their jobs because they had used peyote. Their practice was to ingest peyote for sacramental purposes in violation of the state's controlled substance law, which banned all use of peyote. Plaintiffs challenged this Oregon statute of general applicability, which made use of the drug criminal. . . . *Smith* held that neutral, generally applicable laws may be applied to religious practices even when not supported by a compelling governmental interest.

[RFRA's] stated purposes are:

"(1) to restore the compelling interest test as set forth in *Sherbert v. Verner* (1963) and *Wisconsin v. Yoder* (1972) and to guarantee its application in all cases where free exercise of religion is substantially burdened; and

"(2) to provide a claim or defense to persons whose religious exercise is substantially burdened by government."

RFRA prohibits "[g]overnment" from "substantially burden[ing]" a person's exercise of religion even if the burden results from a rule of general applicability unless the government can demonstrate the burden "(1) is in furtherance of a compelling governmental interest; and (2) is the least restrictive means of furthering that compelling governmental interest." The Act's mandate applies to any "branch, department, agency, instrumentality, and official (or other person acting under color of law) of the United States," as well as to any "State, or . . . subdivision of a State." . . .

. . . Congress relied on its Fourteenth Amendment enforcement power in enacting the most far reaching and substantial of RFRA's provisions, those which impose its requirements on the States. [R]espondent contends, with support from the United States as *amicus*, that RFRA is permissible enforcement legislation. Congress, it is said, is only protecting by legislation one of the liberties guaranteed by the Fourteenth Amendment's Due Process Clause, the free exercise of religion, beyond what is necessary under *Smith*. . . .

All must acknowledge that § 5 is "a positive grant of legislative power" to Congress, *Katzenbach v. Morgan* (1966). . . . Legislation which deters or remedies constitutional violations can fall within the sweep of Congress' enforcement power even if in the process it prohibits conduct which is not itself unconstitutional and intrudes into "legislative spheres of autonomy previously reserved to the States."

"[A]s broad as the congressional enforcement power is, it is not unlimited." In assessing the breadth of § 5's enforcement power, we begin with its text. Congress has been given the power "to enforce" the "provisions of this article." . . . Congress can enact legislation under § 5 enforcing the constitutional right to the free exercise of religion. The "provisions of this article," to which § 5 refers, include the Due Process Clause of the Fourteenth Amendment [which incorporates the Free Exercise Clause].

Congress' power under § 5, however, extends only to "enforc[ing]" the provisions of the Fourteenth Amendment. The Court has described this power as "remedial." The design of the Amendment and the text of § 5 are inconsistent with the suggestion that Congress has the power to decree the substance of the Fourteenth Amendment's restrictions on the States. Legislation which alters the meaning of the Free Exercise Clause cannot be said to be enforcing the Clause. Congress does not enforce a constitutional right by changing what the right is. It has been given the power "to enforce," not the power to determine what constitutes a constitutional violation. Were it not so, what Congress would be enforcing would no longer be, in any meaningful sense, the "provisions of [the Fourteenth Amendment]."

While the line between measures that remedy or prevent unconstitutional actions and measures that make a substantive change in the governing law is not easy to discern, and Congress must have wide latitude in determining where it lies, the distinction exists and must be observed. There must be a congruence and proportionality between the injury to be prevented or remedied and the means adopted to that end. Lacking such a connection, legislation may become substantive in operation and effect. History and our case law support drawing the distinction, one apparent from the text of the Amendment.

The Fourteenth Amendment's history confirms the remedial, rather than substantive, nature of the Enforcement Clause. The Joint Committee on Reconstruction of the 39th Congress began drafting what would become the Fourteenth Amendment in January 1866. . . . Members of Congress from across the political spectrum criticized the Amendment, and the criticisms had a common theme: The proposed Amendment gave Congress too much legislative power at the expense of the existing constitutional structure. . . . Under the revised Amendment, Congress' power was no longer plenary but remedial. Congress was granted the power to make the substantive constitutional prohibitions against the States effective. [This] revised Amendment proposal did not raise the concerns expressed earlier regarding broad congressional power to prescribe uniform national laws with respect to life, liberty, and property. [T]he new measure passed both Houses and was ratified in July 1868 as the Fourteenth Amendment. [It] confers substantive rights against the States which, like the provisions of the Bill of Rights, are self-executing. The power to interpret the Constitution in a case or controversy remains in the Judiciary.

The remedial and preventive nature of Congress' enforcement power, and the limitation inherent in the power, were confirmed in our earliest cases on the Fourteenth Amendment. In the *Civil Rights Cases* (1883), the Court invalidated sections of the Civil Rights Act of 1875 which prescribed criminal penalties for denying to any person "the full enjoyment of" public accommodations and conveyances, on the grounds that it exceeded Congress' power by seeking to regulate private conduct. The Enforcement Clause, the Court said, did not authorize Congress to pass "general legislation upon the rights of the citizen, but corrective legislation; that is, such as may be necessary and proper for counteracting such laws as the States may adopt or enforce, and which, by the amendment, they are prohibited from making or enforcing. . . ." . . .

Any suggestion that Congress has a substantive, non-remedial power under the Fourteenth Amendment is not supported by our case law. . . . There is language in our opinion in *Katzenbach v. Morgan* (1966) which could be interpreted as acknowledging a power in Congress to enact legislation that expands the rights contained in § 1 of the Fourteenth Amendment. This is not a necessary interpretation, however, or even the best one. . . . The Court provided two related rationales for its conclusion that § 4(e) could "be viewed as a measure to secure for the Puerto Rican community residing in New York nondiscriminatory treatment by government." Under the first rationale, Congress could prohibit New York from denying the right to vote to large segments of its Puerto Rican community, in order to give Puerto Ricans "enhanced political power" that would be "helpful in gaining nondiscriminatory treatment in public services for the entire Puerto Rican community." Section 4(e) thus could be justified as a remedial measure to deal with "discrimination in governmental services." The second rationale, an alternative holding, did not address discrimination in the provision of public services but "discrimination in establishing voter qualifications." The Court perceived a factual basis on which Congress could have concluded that New York's literacy requirement "constituted an invidious discrimination in violation of the Equal Protection Clause." Both rationales for upholding § 4(e) rested on unconstitutional discrimination by New York and Congress' reasonable attempt to combat it. [I]nterpreting *Morgan* to give Congress the power to interpret the Constitution "would require an enormous extension of that decision's rationale."

If Congress could define its own powers by altering the Fourteenth Amendment's meaning, no longer would the Constitution be "superior paramount law, unchangeable by ordinary means." It would be "on a level with ordinary legislative acts, and, like other acts, . . . alterable when the legislature shall please to alter it." *Marbury v. Madison*. Under this approach, it is difficult to conceive of a principle that would limit congressional power. . . .

We now turn to consider whether RFRA can be considered enforcement legislation under § 5 of the Fourteenth Amendment.

Respondent contends that RFRA is a proper exercise of Congress' remedial or preventive power. The Act, it is said, is a reasonable means of protecting the free exercise of religion as defined by *Smith*. It prevents and remedies laws which are enacted with the unconstitutional object of targeting religious beliefs and practices. To avoid the difficulty of proving such violations, it is said, Congress can simply invalidate any law which imposes a substantial burden on a religious practice unless it is justified by a compelling interest and is the least restrictive means of accomplishing that interest. If Congress can prohibit laws with discriminatory effects in order to prevent racial discrimination in violation of the Equal Protection Clause, then it can do the same, respondent argues, to promote religious liberty.

While preventive rules are sometimes appropriate remedial measures, there must be a congruence between the means used and the ends to be achieved. The appropriateness of remedial measures must be considered in light of the evil presented. Strong measures appropriate to address one harm may be an unwarranted response to another, lesser one.

. . . RFRA's legislative record lacks examples of modern instances of generally applicable laws passed because of religious bigotry. The history of persecution in this country detailed in the hearings mentions no episodes occurring in the past 40 years. See, *e.g.,* Religious Freedom Restoration Act of 1991, Hearings on H. R. 2797 before the Subcommittee on Civil and Constitutional Rights of the House Committee on the Judiciary, 102d Cong., 2d Sess., 331–334 (1993). Rather, the emphasis of the hearings was on laws of general applicability which place incidental burdens on religion. Much of the discussion centered upon anecdotal evidence of autopsies performed on Jewish individuals and Hmong immigrants in violation of their religious beliefs, and on zoning regulations and historic preservation laws (like the one at issue here), which as an incident of their normal operation, have adverse effects on churches and synagogues. It is difficult to maintain that they are examples of legislation enacted or enforced due to animus or hostility to the burdened religious practices or that they indicate some widespread pattern of religious discrimination in this country. Congress' concern was with the incidental burdens imposed, not the object or purpose of the legislation. This lack of support in the legislative record, however, is not RFRA's most serious shortcoming. Judicial deference, in most cases, is based not on the state of the legislative record Congress compiles but "on due regard for the decision of the body constitutionally appointed to decide." As a general matter, it is for Congress to determine the method by which it will reach a decision.

Regardless of the state of the legislative record, RFRA cannot be considered remedial, preventive legislation, if those terms are to have any meaning. RFRA is so out of proportion to a supposed remedial or preventive object that it cannot be understood as responsive to, or designed to prevent, unconstitutional behavior. It appears, instead, to attempt a substantive change in constitutional protections. Preventive measures prohibiting certain types of laws may be appropriate when there is reason to believe that many of the laws affected by the congressional enactment have a significant likelihood of being unconstitutional. . . .

RFRA is not so confined. Sweeping coverage ensures its intrusion at every level of government, displacing laws and prohibiting official actions of almost every description and regardless of subject matter. RFRA's restrictions apply to every agency and official of the Federal, State, and local Governments. RFRA applies to all federal and state law, statutory or otherwise, whether adopted before or after its enactment. RFRA has no termination date or termination mechanism. Any law is subject to challenge at any time by any individual who alleges a substantial burden on his or her free exercise of religion. . . .

The stringent test RFRA demands of state laws reflects a lack of proportionality or congruence between the means adopted and the legitimate end to be achieved. [RFRA's substantial burden test] is not even a discriminatory effects or disparate impact test. It is a reality of the modern regulatory state that numerous state laws, such as the zoning regulations at issue here, impose a substantial burden on a large class of individuals. When the exercise of religion has been burdened in an incidental way by a law of general application, it does not follow that the persons affected have been burdened any more than other citizens, let alone burdened because of their religious beliefs. In addition, the Act imposes in every case a least restrictive means requirement—a requirement that was not used in the pre-*Smith* jurisprudence RFRA purported to codify—which also indicates that the legislation is broader than is appropriate if the goal is to prevent and remedy constitutional violations.

[C]ourts retain the power, as they have since *Marbury v. Madison*, to determine if Congress has exceeded its authority under the Constitution. Broad as the power of Congress is under the Enforcement Clause of the Fourteenth Amendment, RFRA contradicts vital principles necessary to maintain separation of powers and the federal balance. The judgment of the Court of Appeals sustaining the Act's constitutionality is reversed.

It is so ordered.

[The concurring opinion of STEVENS, J.; the opinion concurring in part by SCALIA, J., joined in part by STEVENS, J.; the dissenting opinions of SOUTER & BREYER, JJ., are omitted. O'CONNOR, J., filed a dissenting opinion that BREYER, J., joined in part. In the part that BREYER did not join, O'CONNOR said, "Indeed, if I agreed with the Court's standard in *Smith*, I would join the opinion. As the Court's careful and thorough historical analysis shows, Congress lacks the 'power to decree the *substance* of the Fourteenth Amendment's restrictions on the States.' " (emphasis by O'Connor).]

NOTES

1. RFRA, by its terms, "applies to all Federal and State law, and the implementation of that law." This decision does not invalidate RFRA as to federal laws but only as to state laws.

2. The Age Discrimination in Employment Act (ADEA) stated that it was subjecting the states to the ADEA and taking away their Eleventh Amendment immunity. *Kimel v. Florida Board of Regents*, 528 U.S. 62, 120 S.Ct. 631, 145 L.Ed.2d 522 (2000), held that Congress could not constitutionally use § 5 in this manner because the abrogation exceeded federal power. Age is not a suspect class under the equal protection clause and therefore an age classification is constitutional if it is rational. Congress cannot annul the states' Eleventh Amendment immunity merely by stating that it is enforcing the Fourteenth Amendment; the law must actually enforce (not redefine) section 1.

3. *United States v. Morrison*, 529 U.S. 598, 120 S.Ct. 1740, 146 L.Ed.2d 658 (2000), held that § 5 could not justify the Violence Against Women Act, 42 U.S.C.A. § 13981, which provided a tort remedy for victims (whether men or women)

of "gender-motivated violence." The Fourteenth Amendment, "by its very terms, prohibits only state action." But § 13981 "is directed not at any State or state actor, but at individuals who have committed criminal acts motivated by gender bias." The Court added:

> Section 13981 is also different from these previously upheld remedies in that it applies uniformly throughout the Nation. Congress' findings indicate that the problem of discrimination against the victims of gender-motivated crimes does not exist in all States, or even most States. By contrast, the § 5 remedy upheld in *Katzenbach* v. *Morgan*, was directed only to the State where the evil found by Congress existed. . . .

4. In *Tennessee v. Lane*, 541 U.S. 509, 124 S.Ct. 1978, 158 L.Ed.2d 820 (2004), paraplegics sued for damages and equitable relief, alleging that Tennessee and a number of its counties had denied them physical access to that State's courts in violation of Title II of the Americans with Disabilities Act. The Court held (5 to 4) that, "Title II, as it applies to the class of cases implicating the fundamental right of access to the courts, constitutes a valid exercise of Congress' § 5 authority to enforce the guarantees of the Fourteenth Amendment."

5. *United States v. Georgia*, 546 U.S. 151, 126 S.Ct. 877, 163 L.Ed.2d 650 (2006). Scalia, J., for a unanimous Court, held that Title II of the Americans with Disabilities Act validly abrogates state sovereign immunity insofar as it authorizes a disabled prisoner to sue for money damages for the state's alleged cruel and unusual punishment. Congress may validly abrogate state sovereign immunity for Eight Amendment claims in state prisons because such conduct actually violates § 1 of the Fourteenth Amendment: "no one doubts that § 5 grants Congress the power to 'enforce . . . the provisions' of the Amendment by creating private remedies against the States for *actual* violations of those provisions." (emphasis by the Court).

6.2 THE FIFTEENTH AMENDMENT

SOUTH CAROLINA V. KATZENBACH

383 U.S. 301, 86 S.Ct. 803, 15 L.Ed.2d 769 (1966)

CHIEF JUSTICE WARREN delivered the opinion of the Court.

By leave of the Court, South Carolina has filed a bill of complaint, seeking a declaration that selected provisions of the Voting Rights Act of 1965 violate the

Federal Constitution, and asking for an injunction against enforcement of these provisions by the Attorney General. Original jurisdiction is founded on the presence of a controversy between a State and a citizen of another State under Art. III, § 2, of the Constitution. . . .

The constitutional propriety of the Voting Rights Act of 1965 must be judged with reference to the historical experience which it reflects. . . . The Voting Rights Act of 1965 reflects Congress' firm intention to rid the country of racial discrimination in voting. The heart of the Act is a complex scheme of stringent remedies aimed at areas where voting discrimination has been most flagrant. Section 4(a)–(d) lays down a formula defining the States and political subdivisions to which these new remedies apply. The first of the remedies, contained in § 4(a), is the suspension of literacy tests and similar voting qualifications for a period of five years from the last occurrence of substantial voting discrimination. Section 5 prescribes a second remedy, the suspension of all new voting regulations pending review by federal authorities to determine whether their use would perpetuate voting discrimination. The third remedy, covered in §§ 6(b), 7, 9, and 13(a), is the assignment of federal examiners on certification by the Attorney General to list qualified applicants who are thereafter entitled to vote in all elections. . . .

These provisions of the Voting Rights Act of 1965 are challenged on the fundamental ground that they exceed the powers of Congress and encroach on an area reserved to the States by the Constitution. South Carolina and certain of the *amici curiae* also attack specific sections of the Act for more particular reasons. . . . Some of these contentions may be dismissed at the outset. The word "person" in the context of the Due Process Clause of the Fifth Amendment cannot, by any reasonable mode of interpretation, be expanded to encompass the States of the Union, and to our knowledge this has never been done by any court. Likewise, courts have consistently regarded the Bill of Attainder Clause of Article I and the principle of the separation of powers only as protections for individual persons and private groups, those who are peculiarly vulnerable to nonjudicial determinations of guilt. Nor does a State have standing as the parent of its citizens to invoke these constitutional provisions against the Federal Government, the ultimate *parens patriae* of every American citizen. The objections to the Act which are raised under these provisions may therefore be considered only as additional aspects of the basic question presented by the case: Has Congress exercised its powers under the Fifteenth Amendment in an appropriate manner with relation to the States?

The ground rules for resolving this question are clear. [A]gainst the reserved powers of the States, Congress may use any rational means to effectuate the constitutional prohibition of racial discrimination in voting. . . . The basic test to be applied in a case involving § 2 of the Fifteenth Amendment is the same as in all cases concerning the express powers to Congress with relation to the reserved powers of the States. Chief Justice Marshall laid down the classic formulation [in] *McCulloch v. Maryland*. The Court has subsequently echoed his language in describing each of the Civil War Amendments. . . .

Congress exercised its authority under the Fifteenth Amendment in an inventive manner when it enacted the Voting Rights Act of 1965. First: The measure prescribes remedies for voting discrimination which go into effect without any need for prior adjudication. This was clearly a legitimate response to the problem, for which there is ample precedent under other constitutional provisions. See *Katzenbach v. McClung*. Congress had found that case-by-case litigation was inadequate to combat widespread and persistent discrimination in voting, because of the inordinate amount of time and energy required to overcome the obstructionist tactics invariably encountered in these lawsuits. . . .

Second: The Act intentionally confines these remedies to a small number of States and political subdivisions which in most instances were familiar to Congress by name. This, too, was a permissible method of dealing with the problem. . . . The doctrine of the equality of States, invoked by South Carolina, does not bar this approach, for that doctrine applies only to the terms upon which States are admitted to the Union, and not to the remedies for local evils which have subsequently appeared. See *Coyle v. Smith,* and cases cited therein.

COVERAGE FORMULA

We now consider the related question of whether the specific States and political subdivisions within § 4(b) of the Act were an appropriate target for the new remedies. South Carolina contends that the coverage formula is awkwardly designed in a number of respects and that it disregards various local conditions which have nothing to do with racial discrimination. These arguments, however, are largely beside the point. [The areas] for which there was evidence of actual voting discrimination, share two characteristics incorporated by Congress into the coverage formula: the use of tests and devices for voter registration, and a voting rate in the 1964 presidential election at least 12 points below the national average. Tests and devices are relevant to voting discrimination because of their long history as a tool for perpetrating the evil; a low voting rate is pertinent for the obvious reason that widespread disenfranchisement must inevitably affect the number of actual voters. Accordingly, the coverage formula is rational in both practice and theory. It was therefore permissible to impose the new remedies on the few remaining States and political subdivisions covered by the formula, at least in the absence of proof that they have been free of substantial voting discrimination in recent years. Congress is clearly not bound by the rules relating to statutory presumptions in criminal cases when it prescribes civil remedies against other organs of government under § 2 of the Fifteenth Amendment.

It is irrelevant that the coverage formula excludes certain localities which do not employ voting tests and devices but for which there is evidence of voting discrimination by other means. . . . Legislation need not deal with all phases of a problem in the same way, so long as the distinctions drawn have some basis in practical experience. There are no States or political subdivisions exempted from coverage under § 4(b) in which the record reveals recent racial discrimination involving tests and devices. This fact confirms the rationality of the formula.

Acknowledging the possibility of over-breadth, the Act provides for termination of special statutory coverage at the behest of States and political subdivisions in which the danger of substantial voting discrimination has not materialized during the preceding five years. Despite South Carolina's argument to the contrary, Congress might appropriately limit litigation under this provision to a single court in the District of Columbia, pursuant to its constitutional power under Art. III, § 1, to "ordain and establish" inferior federal tribunals. . . .

The Act bars direct judicial review of the findings by the Attorney General and the Director of the Census which trigger application of the coverage formula. . . . In this instance, the findings not subject to review consist of objective statistical determinations by the Census Bureau and a routine analysis of state statutes by the Justice Department. These functions are unlikely to arouse any plausible dispute, as South Carolina apparently concedes. In the event that the formula is improperly applied, the area affected can always go into court and obtain termination of coverage under § 4(b), provided of course that it has not been guilty of voting discrimination in recent years. This procedure serves as a partial substitute for direct judicial review.

SUSPENSION OF TESTS

We now arrive at consideration of the specific remedies prescribed by the Act for areas included within the coverage formula. South Carolina assails the temporary suspension of existing voting qualifications, reciting the rule laid down by *Lassiter v. Northampton County Bd. of Elections*, 360 U.S. 45, 79 S.Ct. 985, 3 L.Ed.2d 1072, that literacy tests and related devices are not in themselves contrary to the

Fifteenth Amendment. [H]owever, the Court went on to say, "Of course a literacy test, fair on its face, may be employed to perpetuate that discrimination which the Fifteenth Amendment was designed to uproot." . . .

The Act suspends literacy tests and similar devices for a period of five years from the last occurrence of substantial voting discrimination. . . . States and political subdivisions which had been allowing white illiterates to vote for years could not sincerely complain about "dilution" of their electorates through the registration of Negro illiterates. Congress knew that continuance of the tests and devices in use at the present time, no matter how fairly administered in the future, would freeze the effect of past discrimination in favor of unqualified white registrants. Congress permissibly rejected the alternative of requiring a complete re-registration of all voters, believing that this would be too harsh on many whites who had enjoyed the franchise for their entire adult lives.

REVIEW OF NEW RULES

The Act suspends new voting regulations pending scrutiny by federal authorities to determine whether their use would violate the Fifteenth Amendment. This may have been an uncommon exercise of congressional power, as South Carolina contends, but the Court has recognized that exceptional conditions can justify legislative measures not otherwise appropriate. . . . Nor has Congress authorized the District Court to issue advisory opinions, in violation of the principles of Article III invoked by Georgia as *amicus curiae*. The Act automatically suspends the operation of voting regulations enacted after November 1, 1964, and furnishes mechanisms for enforcing the suspension. A State or political subdivision wishing to make use of a recent amendment to its voting laws therefore has a concrete and immediate "controversy" with the Federal Government. An appropriate remedy is a judicial determination that continued suspension of the new rule is unnecessary to vindicate rights guaranteed by the Fifteenth Amendment.

FEDERAL EXAMINERS

The Act authorizes the appointment of federal examiners to list qualified applicants who are thereafter entitled to vote, subject to an expeditious challenge procedure. This was clearly an appropriate response to the problem, closely related to remedies authorized in prior cases. In many of the political subdivisions covered by § 4(b) of the Act, voting officials have persistently employed a variety of procedural tactics to deny Negroes the franchise, often in direct defiance or evasion of federal court decrees. Congress realized that merely to suspend voting rules which have been misused or are subject to misuse might leave this localized evil undisturbed. . . .

[We] hold that the portions of the Voting Rights Act properly before us are a valid means for carrying out the commands of the Fifteenth Amendment. Hopefully, millions of non-white Americans will now be able to participate for the first time on an equal basis in the government under which they live. . . . The bill of complaint is

Dismissed.

MR. JUSTICE BLACK, concurring and dissenting.

I agree with substantially all of the Court's opinion sustaining the power of Congress under § 2 of the Fifteenth Amendment to suspend state literacy tests and similar voting qualifications and to authorize the Attorney General to secure the appointment of federal examiners to register qualified voters in various sections of the country. . . . I dissent from its holding that every part of § 5 of the Act is constitutional.

[T]he States [should] have power to pass laws and amend their constitutions without first sending their officials hundreds of miles away to beg federal authorities to approve them. Moreover, it seems to me that § 5 which gives federal officials power to veto state laws they do not like is in direct conflict with the clear command of our Constitution that "The United States shall guarantee to every State in this Union a Republican Form of Government." [T]he inevitable effect of any such law . . . is to create the impression that the State or States treated in this way are little more than conquered provinces . . .

SHELBY COUNTY V. HOLDER
570 U.S. ___, 133 S.Ct. 2612, 186 L.Ed.2d 651 (2013)

CHIEF JUSTICE ROBERTS delivered the opinion of the Court.

The Voting Rights Act of 1965 employed extraordinary measures to address an extraordinary problem. Section 5 of the Act required States to obtain federal permission before enacting any law related to voting—a drastic departure from basic principles of federalism. And § 4 of the Act applied that requirement only to some States—an equally dramatic departure from the principle that all States enjoy equal sovereignty. This was strong medicine, but Congress determined it was needed to address entrenched racial discrimination in voting, "an insidious and pervasive evil which had been perpetuated in certain parts of our country through unremitting and ingenious defiance of the Constitution." *South Carolina*

v. *Katzenbach* (1966). As we explained in upholding the law, "exceptional conditions can justify legislative measures not otherwise appropriate." Reflecting the unprecedented nature of these measures, they were scheduled to expire after five years. See Voting Rights Act of 1965, § 4(a).

Nearly 50 years later, they are still in effect; indeed, they have been made more stringent, and are now scheduled to last until 2031. There is no denying, however, that the conditions that originally justified these measures no longer characterize voting in the covered jurisdictions. By 2009, "the racial gap in voter registration and turnout [was] lower in the States originally covered by § 5 than it [was] nationwide." *Northwest Austin Municipal Util. Dist. No. One* v. *Holder*, 557 U.S. 193, 129 S.Ct. 2504, 174 L.Ed.2d 140 (2009). Since that time, Census Bureau data indicate that African-American voter turnout has come to exceed white voter turnout in five of the six States originally covered by § 5, with a gap in the sixth State of less than one half of one percent.

At the same time, voting discrimination still exists; no one doubts that. The question is whether the Act's extraordinary measures, including its disparate treatment of the States, continue to satisfy constitutional requirements. As we put it a short time ago, "the Act imposes current burdens and must be justified by current needs." *Northwest Austin.* . . .

Inspired to action by the civil rights movement, Congress responded in 1965 with the Voting Rights Act. Section 2 was enacted to forbid, in all 50 States, any "standard, practice, or procedure . . . imposed or applied . . . to deny or abridge the right of any citizen of the United States to vote on account of race or color." The current version forbids any "standard, practice, or procedure" that "results in a denial or abridgement of the right of any citizen of the United States to vote on account of race or color." Both the Federal Government and individuals have sued to enforce § 2, and injunctive relief is available in appropriate cases to block voting laws from going into effect. Section 2 is permanent, applies nationwide, and is not at issue in this case.

Other sections targeted only some parts of the country. At the time of the Act's passage, these "covered" jurisdictions were those States or political subdivisions that had maintained a test or device as a prerequisite to voting as of November 1, 1964, and had less than 50 percent voter registration or turnout in the 1964 Presidential election. § 4(b). Such tests or devices included literacy and knowledge tests, good moral character requirements, the need for vouchers from registered voters, and the like. § 4(c). A covered jurisdiction could "bail out" of coverage if it had not used a test or device in the preceding five years "for the purpose or with the effect of denying or abridging the right to vote on account of race or color." § 4(a). In 1965, the covered States included Alabama, Georgia, Louisiana, Mississippi, South Carolina, and Virginia. The additional covered subdivisions included 39 counties in North Carolina and one in Arizona.

In those jurisdictions, § 4 of the Act banned all such tests or devices. § 4(a). Section 5 provided that no change in voting procedures could take effect until it was approved by federal authorities in Washington, D.C.—either the Attorney General or a court of three judges. A jurisdiction could obtain such "preclearance" only by proving that the change had neither "the purpose [nor] the effect of denying or abridging the right to vote on account of race or color."

Sections 4 and 5 were intended to be temporary; they were set to expire after five years. See § 4(a). In *South Carolina* v. *Katzenbach*, we upheld the 1965 Act against constitutional challenge, explaining that it was justified to address "voting discrimination where it persists on a pervasive scale." In 1970, Congress reauthorized the Act for another five years, and extended the coverage formula in § 4(b) to jurisdictions that had a voting test and less than 50 percent voter registration or turnout as of 1968. That swept in several counties in California, New Hampshire, and New York. Congress also extended the ban in § 4(a) on tests and devices nationwide.

In 1975, Congress reauthorized the Act for seven more years, and extended its coverage to jurisdictions that had a voting test and less than 50 percent voter registration or turnout as of 1972. Congress also amended the definition of "test or device" to include the practice of providing English-only voting materials in places where over five percent of voting-age citizens spoke a single language other than English. As a result of these amendments, the States of Alaska, Arizona, and Texas, as well as several counties in California, Florida, Michigan, New York, North Carolina, and South Dakota, became covered jurisdictions. Congress correspondingly amended sections 2 and 5 to forbid voting discrimination on the basis of membership in a language minority group, in addition to discrimination on the basis of race or color. Finally, Congress made the nationwide ban on tests and devices permanent.

In 1982, Congress reauthorized the Act for 25 years, but did not alter its coverage formula.... We upheld each of these reauthorizations against constitutional challenge. See *Georgia v. United States*, 411 U.S. 526 (1973); *City of Rome v. United States*, 446 U.S. 156 (1980); *Lopez v. Monterey County*, 525 U.S. 266 (1999).

In 2006, Congress again reauthorized the Voting Rights Act for 25 years, again without change to its coverage formula. Congress also amended § 5 to prohibit more conduct than before. Section 5 now forbids voting changes with "any discriminatory purpose" as well as voting changes that diminish the ability of citizens, on account of race, color, or language minority status, "to elect their preferred candidates of choice." . . .

Shelby County is located in Alabama, a covered jurisdiction. [It sought] a declaratory judgment that sections 4(b) and 5 of the Voting Rights Act are facially unconstitutional, as well as a permanent injunction against their enforcement. The District Court [and the D.C. Circuit upheld §§ 4 and 5]. Judge Williams dissented. He found "no positive correlation between inclusion in § 4(b)'s coverage formula and low black registration or turnout." Rather, to the extent there was any correlation, it actually went the other way: "condemnation under § 4(b) is a marker of *higher* black registration and turnout." (emphasis added). Judge Williams also found that "[c]overed jurisdictions have *far more* black officeholders as a proportion of the black population than do uncovered ones." As to the evidence of successful § 2 suits, "[t]he five worst uncovered jurisdictions . . . have worse records than eight of the covered jurisdictions." He also noted that two covered jurisdictions—Arizona and Alaska—had not had any successful reported § 2 suit brought against them during the entire 24 years covered by the data. Judge Williams would have held the coverage formula of § 4(b) "irrational" and unconstitutional. . . .

Not only do States retain sovereignty under the Constitution, there is also a "fundamental principle of *equal* sovereignty" among the States. . . . The Voting Rights Act sharply departs from these basic principles. It suspends "*all* changes to state election law—however innocuous—until they have been precleared by federal authorities in Washington, D. C." States must beseech the Federal Government for permission to implement laws that they would otherwise have the right to enact and execute on their own, subject of course to any injunction in a § 2 action. . . . If a State seeks preclearance from a three-judge court, the process can take years.

And despite the tradition of equal sovereignty, the Act applies to only nine States (and several additional counties). While one State waits months or years and expends funds to implement a validly enacted law, its neighbor can typically put the same law into effect immediately, through the normal legislative process. [T]he preclearance proceeding "not only switches the burden of proof to the supplicant jurisdiction, but also applies substantive standards quite different from those governing the rest of the nation."

. . . Shortly before enactment of the Voting Rights Act, only 19.4 percent of African-Americans of voting age were registered to vote in Alabama, only 31.8 percent in Louisiana, and only 6.4 percent in Mississippi. Those figures were roughly 50 percentage points or more below the figures for whites. [*Katzenbach*] concluded that "[u]nder the compulsion of these unique circumstances, Congress responded in a permissibly decisive manner." We also noted then and have emphasized since that this extra-ordinary legislation was intended to be temporary, set to expire after five years.

At the time, the coverage formula—the means of linking the exercise of the unprecedented authority with the problem that warranted it—made sense. We found that "Congress chose to limit its attention to the geographic areas where immediate action seemed necessary." *Katzenbach*. . . . Nearly 50 years later, things have changed dramatically. Shelby County contends that the preclearance requirement, even without regard to its disparate coverage, is now unconstitutional. Its arguments have a good deal of force. In the covered jurisdictions, "[v]oter turnout and registration rates now approach parity. Blatantly discriminatory evasions of federal decrees are rare. And minority candidates hold office at unprecedented levels." The tests and devices that blocked access to the ballot have been forbidden nationwide for over 40 years. . . .

The following chart, compiled from the Senate and House Reports, compares voter registration numbers from 1965 to those from 2004 in the six originally covered States. These are the numbers that were before Congress when it reauthorized the Act in 2006:

	1965			2004		
	White	Black	Gap	White	Black	Gap
Alabama	69.2	19.3	49.9	73.8	72.9	0.9
Georgia	62.[6]	27.4	35.2	63.5	64.2	−0.7
Louisiana	80.5	31.6	48.9	75.1	71.1	4.0
Mississippi	69.9	6.7	63.2	72.3	76.1	−3.8
South Carolina	75.7	37.3	38.4	74.4	71.1	3.3
Virginia	61.1	38.3	22.8	68.2	57.4	10.8

... Census Bureau data from the most recent election indicate that African-American voter turnout exceeded white voter turnout in five of the six States originally covered by § 5, with a gap in the sixth State of less than one half of one percent. The preclearance statistics are also illuminating. In the first decade after enactment of § 5, the Attorney General objected to 14.2 percent of proposed voting changes. In the last decade before reenactment, the Attorney General objected to a mere 0.16 percent.

There is no doubt that these improvements are in large part *because of* the Voting Rights Act. The Act has proved immensely successful at redressing racial discrimination and integrating the voting process. During the "Freedom Summer" of 1964, in Philadelphia, Mississippi, three men were murdered while working in the area to register African-American voters. On "Bloody Sunday" in 1965, in Selma, Alabama, police beat and used tear gas against hundreds marching in support of African-American enfranchisement. Today both of those towns are governed by African-American mayors. [O]ur Nation has made great strides.

Yet the Act has not eased the restrictions in § 5 or narrowed the scope of the coverage formula in § 4(b) along the way. Those extraordinary and unprecedented features were reauthorized—as if nothing had changed. In fact, the Act's unusual remedies have grown even stronger. . . .

The provisions of § 5 apply only to those jurisdictions singled out by § 4. We now consider whether that coverage formula is constitutional in light of current conditions. . . .

Coverage today is based on decades-old data and eradicated practices. The formula captures States by reference to literacy tests and low voter registration and turnout in the 1960s and early 1970s. But such tests have been banned nationwide for over 40 years. And voter registration and turnout numbers in the covered States have risen dramatically in the years since Racial disparity in those numbers was compelling evidence justifying the preclearance remedy and the coverage formula. See, *e.g., Katzenbach.* There is no longer such a disparity.

[H]istory did not end in 1965. [A] fundamental problem remains: Congress did not use the record it compiled to shape a coverage formula grounded in current conditions. It instead reenacted a formula based on 40-year-old facts having no logical relation to the present day. . . . There is no valid reason to insulate the coverage formula from review merely because it was previously enacted 40 years ago. If Congress had started from scratch in 2006, it plainly could not have enacted the present coverage formula. It would have been irrational for Congress to distinguish between States in such a fundamental way based on 40-

year-old data, when today's statistics tell an entirely different story. And it would have been irrational to base coverage on the use of voting tests 40 years ago, when such tests have been illegal since that time. But that is exactly what Congress has done. . . .

Our decision in no way affects the permanent, nationwide ban on racial discrimination in voting found in § 2. We issue no holding on § 5 itself, only on the coverage formula. Congress may draft another formula based on current conditions. Such a formula is an initial prerequisite to a determination that exceptional conditions still exist justifying such an "extraordinary departure from the traditional course of relations between the States and the Federal Government." [W]hile any racial discrimination in voting is too much, Congress must ensure that the legislation it passes to remedy that problem speaks to current conditions.

The judgment of the Court of Appeals is reversed. It is so ordered.

JUSTICE GINSBURG, with whom JUSTICE BREYER, JUSTICE SOTOMAYOR, and JUSTICE KAGAN join, dissenting.

[The question] is who decides whether, as currently operative, § 5 remains justifiable,[1] this Court, or a Congress charged with the obligation to enforce the post-Civil War Amendments "by appropriate legislation." With overwhelming support in both Houses, Congress concluded that, for two prime reasons, § 5 should continue in force, unabated. First, continuance would facilitate completion of the impressive gains thus far made; and second, continuance would guard against backsliding. Those assessments were well within Congress' province to make and should elicit this Court's unstinting approbation. . . .

For three reasons, legislation *re*authorizing an existing statute is especially likely to satisfy the minimal requirements of the rational-basis test. First, when reauthorization is at issue, Congress has already assembled a legislative record justifying the initial legislation. . . . Second, the very fact that reauthorization is necessary arises because Congress has built a temporal limitation into the Act. It has pledged to review, after a span of years (first 15, then 25) and in light of contemporary evidence, the continued need for the VRA. Third, a reviewing court should expect the record supporting reauthorization to be less stark than the record originally made. . . . Congress approached the 2006 reauthorization of the

---

[1]   The Court purports to declare unconstitutional only the coverage formula set out in § 4(b). But without that formula, § 5 is immobilized.

VRA with great care and seriousness. The same cannot be said of the Court's opinion today. . . .

[The opinion of THOMAS, J., concurring, is omitted.]

NOTES

During the oral argument, Chief Justice Roberts asked Solicitor General Donald Verrilli, "Do you know which state has the worst ratio of white voter turnout to African American voter turnout?" Mr. Verrilli's response: "I do not." Roberts said, "Massachusetts." Then he asked, "Do you know what has the best, where African American turnout actually exceeds white turnout? Mississippi." Roberts' statistics came from an opinion in the lower court.

6.3 THE THIRTEENTH AMENDMENT

In the next case the Court turned to congressional enforcement powers under the Thirteenth Amendment. Recall that § 1 of this amendment is not limited to state action; it also prohibits private action that constitutes slavery. Should § 2 also reach private action that constitutes the badges or incidents of slavery? The next case says yes.

JONES V. ALFRED H. MAYER CO.
392 U.S. 409, 88 S.Ct. 2186, 20 L.Ed.2d 1189 (1968)

JUSTICE STEWART delivered the opinion of the Court.

In this case we are called upon to determine the scope and the constitutionality of an Act of Congress, 42 U.S.C.A. § 1982, which provides that:

> All citizens of the United States shall have the same right, in every
> State and Territory, as is enjoyed by white citizens thereof to inherit,
> purchase, lease, sell, hold, and convey real and personal property.

On September 2, 1965, the petitioners filed a complaint in the District Court for the Eastern District of Missouri, alleging that the respondents had refused to sell them a home in the Paddock Woods community of St. Louis County for the sole reason that petitioner Joseph Lee Jones is a Negro. Relying in part upon § 1982, the petitioners sought injunctive and other relief. . . . For the reasons that follow, we reverse the judgment of the Court of Appeals. We hold that § 1982 bars *all* racial discrimination, private as well as public, in the sale or rental of property, and that the statute, thus construed, is a valid exercise of the power of Congress to enforce the Thirteenth Amendment.

At the outset, it is important to make clear precisely what this case does *not* involve. Whatever else it may be, 42 U.S.C.A. § 1982 is not a comprehensive open housing law. In sharp contrast to the Fair Housing Title (Title VIII) of the Civil Rights Act of 1968, the statute in this case deals only with racial discrimination and does not address itself to discrimination on grounds of religion or national origin. It does not deal specifically with discrimination in the provision of services or facilities in connection with the sale or rental of a dwelling. It does not prohibit advertising or other representations that indicate discriminatory preferences. It does not refer explicitly to discrimination in financing arrangements or in the provision of brokerage services. It does not empower a federal administrative agency to assist aggrieved parties. It makes no provision for intervention by the Attorney General. . . .

We begin with the language of the statute itself. In plain and unambiguous terms, § 1982 grants to all citizens, without regard to race or color, "the same right" to purchase and lease property "as is enjoyed by white citizens." As the Court of Appeals in this case evidently recognized, that right can be impaired as effectively by "those who place property on the market" as by the State itself. For, even if the State and its agents lend no support to those who wish to exclude persons from their communities on racial grounds, the fact remains that, whenever property "is placed on the market for whites only, whites have a right denied to Negroes." . . . On its face, therefore, § 1982 appears to prohibit *all* discrimination against Negroes in the sale or rental of property—discrimination by private owners as well as discrimination by public authorities. [R]espondents argue that Congress cannot possibly have intended any such result. Our examination of the relevant history, however, persuades us that Congress meant exactly what it said.

In its original form, 42 U.S.C.A. § 1982 was part of § 1 of the Civil Rights Act of 1866. [T]he same Congress that wanted to do away with the Black Codes *also* had before it an imposing body of evidence pointing to the mistreatment of Negroes by private individuals and unofficial groups, mistreatment unrelated to any hostile state legislation. . . . The congressional debates are replete with references to private injustices against the Negroes—references to white employers who refused to pay their Negro workers, white planters who agreed among themselves not to hire freed slaves without the permission of their former masters, white citizens who assaulted Negroes or who combined to drive them out of their communities. . . . President Andrew Johnson vetoed the Act on March 27, and in the brief congressional debate that followed, his supporters characterized its reach in all-embracing terms. One stressed the fact that § 1 would confer "the right . . . to purchase . . . real estate . . . without any qualification and without any restriction whatever. . . ." Another predicted, as a corollary, that the Act would preclude preferential treatment for white persons in the rental of hotel rooms and in the sale of church pews. Those observations elicited no reply. On April 6 the Senate, and on April 9 the House, overrode the President's veto by the requisite majorities, and the Civil Rights Act of 1866 became law. . . .

The remaining question is whether Congress has power under the Constitution to do what § 1982 purports to do: to prohibit all racial discrimination, private and public, in the sale and rental of property. Our starting point is the Thirteenth Amendment, for it was pursuant to that constitutional provision that Congress originally enacted what is now § 1982. . . .

As its text reveals, the Thirteenth Amendment "is not a mere prohibition of State laws establishing or upholding slavery, but an absolute declaration that slavery or involuntary servitude shall not exist in any part of the United States." *Civil Rights Cases.* It has never been doubted, therefore, "that the power vested in Congress to enforce the article by appropriate legislation," ibid., includes the power to enact laws "direct and primary, operating upon the acts of individuals, whether sanctioned by State legislation or not." Id.

. . . Does the authority of Congress to enforce the Thirteenth Amendment "by appropriate legislation" include the power to eliminate all racial barriers to the acquisition of real and personal property? We think the answer to that question is plainly yes. "By its own unaided force and effect," the Thirteenth Amendment "abolished slavery, and established universal freedom." *Civil Rights Cases.* Whether or not the Amendment *itself* did any more than that—a question not involved in this case—it is at least clear that the Enabling Clause of that Amendment empowered Congress to do much more. For that clause clothed "Congress with power to pass *all laws necessary and proper for abolishing all badges and incidents of slavery in the United States.*" Ibid. (Emphasis added.)

. . . Senator Trumbull of Illinois, the Chairman of the Judiciary Committee, had brought the Thirteenth Amendment to the floor of the Senate in 1864. In defending the constitutionality of the 1866 Act, he argued . . .

> I have no doubt that under this provision . . . we may destroy all these discriminations in civil rights against the black man; and if we cannot, our constitutional amendment amounts to nothing. It was for that

purpose that the second clause of that amendment was adopted, which says that Congress shall have authority, by appropriate legislation, to carry into effect the article prohibiting slavery. Who is to decide what that appropriate legislation is to be? The Congress of the United States; and it is for Congress to adopt such appropriate legislation as it may think proper, so that it be a means to accomplish the end.

Surely Senator Trumbull was right. Surely Congress has the power under the Thirteenth Amendment rationally to determine what are the badges and the incidents of slavery, and the authority to translate that determination into effective legislation. Nor can we say that the determination Congress has made is an irrational one. For this Court recognized long ago that, whatever else they may have encompassed, the badges and incidents of slavery—its "burdens and disabilities"—included restraints upon "those fundamental rights which are the essence of civil freedom, namely, the same right . . . to inherit, purchase, lease, sell and convey property, as is enjoyed by white citizens." *Civil Rights Cases.* Just as the Black Codes, enacted after the Civil War to restrict the free exercise of those rights, were substitutes for the slave system, so the exclusion of Negroes from white communities became a substitute for the Black Codes. And when racial discrimination herds men into ghettos and makes their ability to buy property turn on the color of their skin, then it too is a relic of slavery.

Negro citizens, North and South, who saw in the Thirteenth Amendment a promise of freedom—freedom to "go and come at pleasure" and to "buy and sell when they please"—would be left with "a mere paper guarantee" if Congress were powerless to assure that a dollar in the hands of a Negro will purchase the same thing as a dollar in the hands of a white man. At the very least, the freedom that Congress is empowered to secure under the Thirteenth Amendment includes the freedom to buy whatever a white man can buy, the right to live wherever a white man can live. If Congress cannot say that being a free man means at least this much, then the Thirteenth Amendment made a promise the Nation cannot keep.

Justice Harlan, whom Justice White joins, dissenting:

Like the Court, I begin analysis of § 1982 by examining its language. . . . For me, there is an inherent ambiguity in the term "right," as used in § 1982. The "right" referred to may either be a right to equal status under the law, in which case the statute operates only against state-sanctioned discrimination, or it may be an "absolute" right enforceable against private individuals. To me, the words of the statute, taken alone, suggest the former interpretation, not the latter.

[Moreover,] this is one of those rare instances in which an event which occurs after the hearing of argument so diminishes a case's public significance, when viewed in light of the difficulty of the questions presented, as to justify this Court in dismissing the writ as improvidently granted.

The occurrence to which I refer is the recent enactment of the Civil Rights Act of 1968. Title VIII of that Act contains comprehensive "fair housing" provisions, which by the terms of § 803 will become applicable on January 1, 1969, to persons who, like the petitioners, attempt to buy houses from developers. . . . The political process now having taken hold again in this very field, I am at a loss to understand why the Court should have deemed it appropriate or, in the circumstances of this case, necessary to proceed with such precipitate and insecure strides. I am not dissuaded from my view by the circumstance that . . . the 1968 Act apparently will not entitle these petitioners to the relief which they seek. For the certiorari jurisdiction was not conferred upon this Court . . . "for the benefit of the particular litigants," but to decide issues, "the settlement of which is of importance to the public as distinguished from . . . the parties." I deem it far more important that this Court should avoid, if possible, the decision of constitutional and unusually difficult statutory questions than that we fulfill the expectations of every litigant who appears before us. . . .

[The concurring opinion of DOUGLAS, J., is omitted.]

NOTES

1. *Runyon v. McCrary,* 427 U.S. 160, 96 S.Ct. 2586, 49 L.Ed.2d 415 (1976), concerned the application and constitutionality of 42 U.S.C.A. § 1981, which provides:

   > All persons within the jurisdiction of the United States shall have the same right in every State and Territory to make and enforce contracts, to sue, be parties, give evidence, and to the full and equal benefit of all laws and proceedings for the security of persons and property as is enjoyed by white citizens, and shall be subject to like punishment, pains, penalties, taxes, licenses, and exactions of every kind, and to no other.

   The Court, relying on *Jones,* held that section 1981 applied to private contracts and, as interpreted, was constitutional.

   In *Runyon,* various private schools advertised and offered their services to the members of the general public in what was clearly an offering of a contractual relationship. The schools would perform educational services for the plaintiffs and in return would receive payments for the instructions. The findings of fact in the lower court showed that the parents of Michael McCrary and Colin Gonzales tried to enter into contractual relationships with these schools, which refused solely because they were black. The Court found this racial exclusion was a "classic violation" of § 1981. The Court emphasized that what was important was that the private school was open to any white who could pay the fees. The contract was offered to the public at large, except for blacks. One would therefore not expect § 1981 to apply to truly private matters such as marriage contracts or other similar contracts where parties discriminate not merely because of race. No one solicits such contracts from the general public. The Court specifically left open the question of whether § 1981 would apply to a school that discriminated on the basis of race for religious reasons. Unlike pure racial discrimination, which has no constitutional protection, religiously based discrimination finds some protection in the First Amendment.

2. *McDonald v. Santa Fe Trail Transportation Co.,* 427 U.S. 273, 96 S.Ct. 2574, 49 L.Ed.2d 493 (1976), was decided the same day as *Runyon.* The employer discharged two *white* employees, the petitioners, for theft of its property but did not discharge a *black* employee similarly charged. The Court, per Justice Marshall, held that petitioners stated a claim under 42 U.S.C.A. § 1981:

> [O]ur examination of the language and history of § 1981 convinces us that § 1981 is applicable to racial discrimination in private employment against white persons. [W]e cannot accept the view that the terms of § 1981 exclude its application to racial discrimination against white persons. On the contrary, the statute explicitly applies to "*all* persons" (emphasis added) including white persons. [T]he phrase "as is enjoyed by white citizens" . . . simply [emphasizes] "the racial character of the rights being protected."

White, J., joined by Rehnquist, JJ., dissented on that point. White referred to the *McDonald* holding in combination with the *Runyon* holding and argued: "Thus, under the majority's construction of § 1981 in this case, a former slave owner was given a cause of action against his former slave if the former slave refused to work for him on the ground that he was a white man. It is inconceivable that Congress ever intended such a result."

The entire Court agreed that Title VII of the Civil Rights Act of 1964 prohibits racial discrimination in private employment against whites on the same terms as racial discrimination against nonwhites.

3. *McDonald*, in footnote 8, said that it was not considering the permissibility of an affirmative action program, whether judicially prompted or otherwise required. Later, *United Steelworkers of America AFL-CIO-CLC v. Weber*, 443 U.S. 193, 99 S.Ct. 2721, 61 L.Ed.2d 480 (1979), held that Title VII did not forbid private employers and unions from voluntarily agreeing on bona fide affirmative action plans that give racial preferences. "We conclude, therefore, that the adoption of the Kaiser—USWA plan for the Gramercy plant falls within the area of discretion left by Title VII to the private sector voluntarily to adopt affirmative action plans designed to eliminate conspicuous racial imbalance in traditionally segregated job categories."

4. In *General Building Contractors Association v. Pennsylvania*, 458 U.S. 375, 102 S.Ct. 3141, 73 L.Ed.2d 835 (1982), the Court held that proof of intentional discrimination is necessary for liability to be imposed under § 1981. Merely proof of disparate racial impact is not enough; "§ 1981, like the Equal Protection Clause, can be violated only by purposeful discrimination."

Freedom of Speech

7.1 ADVOCACY OF ILLEGAL CONDUCT

SCHENCK V. UNITED STATES

249 U.S. 47, 39 S.Ct. 247, 63 L.Ed. 470 (1919)

MR. JUSTICE HOLMES delivered the opinion of the Court.

[Defendants were convicted of] a conspiracy to violate the Espionage Act of June 15, 1917, by causing and attempting to cause insubordination, & c., in the military and naval forces of the United States, and to obstruct the recruiting and enlistment service of the United States, when the United States was at war with the German Empire, to-wit, that the defendants wilfully conspired to have printed and circulated to men who had been called and accepted for military service under the Act of May 18, 1917, a document set forth and alleged to be calculated to cause such insubordination and obstruction. . . . It denied the power to send our citizens away to foreign shores to shoot up the people of other lands, and added that words could not express the condemnation such cold-blooded ruthlessness deserves, & c., & c., winding up "You must do your share to maintain, support and uphold the rights of the people of this country." Of course the document would not have been sent unless it had been intended to have some effect, and we do not see what effect it could be expected to have upon persons subject to the draft except to influence them to obstruct the carrying of it out. The defendants do not deny that the jury might find against them on this point.

But it is said, suppose that that was the tendency of this circular, it is protected by the First Amendment to the Constitution. Two of the strongest expressions are said to be quoted respectively from well-known public men. It well may be that the prohibition of laws abridging the freedom of speech is not confined to previous restraints, although to prevent them may have been the main purpose, as intimated in *Patterson v. Colorado,* 205 U.S. 454, 462, 27 Sup.Ct. 556, 51 L.Ed. 879. We admit that in many places and in ordinary times the defendants in saying all that was said in the circular would have been within their constitutional rights. But the character of every act depends upon the circumstances in which it is done. The most stringent protection of free speech would not protect a man in falsely shouting fire in a theatre and causing a panic. It does not even protect a man from an injunction against uttering words that may have all the effect of force. *Gompers v. Buck's Stove & Range Co.,* 221 U.S. 418, 439, 31 Sup.Ct. 492, 55 L.Ed. 797, 34 L.R.A.(N.S.) 874. The question in every case is whether the words used are used in such circumstances and are of such a nature as to create a clear and present danger that they will bring about the substantive evils that Congress has a right to prevent. It is a question of proximity and degree. When a nation is at war many things that might be said in time of peace are such a hindrance to its effort that their utterance will not be endured so long as men fight and that no Court could regard them as protected by any constitutional right. It seems to be admitted that if an actual obstruction of the recruiting service were proved, liability for words that produced that effect might be enforced. The statute of 1917 in § 4 punishes conspiracies to obstruct as well as actual obstruction. If the act, (speaking, or circulating a paper,) its tendency and the intent with which it is done are the same, we perceive no ground for saying that success alone warrants making the act a crime. . . .

Judgments affirmed.

ABRAMS V. UNITED STATES
250 U.S. 616, 40 S.Ct. 17, 63 L.Ed. 1173 (1919)

[Defendants were convicted of conspiring to violate the Espionage Act, and the Supreme Court, through Justice Clarke, affirmed. According to the majority opinion, the claim that the Espionage Act conflicts with the First Amendment "is sufficiently discussed and definitely negatived in *Schenck v. U.S.*"]

MR. JUSTICE HOLMES, dissenting.

This indictment is founded wholly upon the publication of two leaflets. . . . The first of these leaflets says that the President's cowardly silence about the intervention in Russia reveals the hypocrisy of the plutocratic gang in Washington. It intimates that "German militarism combined with allied capitalism to crush the Russian revolution"—goes on that the tyrants of the world fight each other until they see a common enemy—working class enlightenment. . . . The other leaflet, headed "Workers—Wake Up," with abusive language says that America together with the Allies will march for Russia to help the Czecko-Slovaks in their struggle against the Bolsheviki, and that this time the hypocrites shall not fool the Russian emigrants and friends of Russia in America. . . .

In this case sentences of twenty years imprisonment have been imposed for the publishing of two leaflets that I believe the defendants had as much right to publish as the Government has to publish the Constitution of the United States now vainly invoked by them. Even if I am technically wrong and enough can be squeezed from these poor and puny anonymities to turn the color of legal litmus paper; I will add, even if what I think the necessary intent were shown; the most nominal punishment seems to me all that possibly could be inflicted, unless the defendants are to be made to suffer not for what the indictment alleges but for the creed that they avow—a creed that I believe to be the creed of ignorance and immaturity when honestly held, as I see no reason to doubt that it was held here, but which, although made the subject of examination at the trial, no one has a right even to consider in dealing with the charges before the Court.

Persecution for the expression of opinions seems to me perfectly logical. If you have no doubt of your premises or your power and want a certain result with all your heart you naturally express your wishes in law and sweep away all opposition. To allow opposition by speech seems to indicate that you think the speech impotent, as when a man says that he has squared the circle, or that you do not care whole-heartedly for the result, or that you doubt either your power or your premises. But when men have realized that time has upset many fighting faiths, they may come to believe even more than they believe the very foundations of their own conduct that the ultimate good desired is better reached by free trade in ideas—that the best test of truth is the power of the thought to get itself accepted in the competition of the market, and that truth is the only ground upon which their wishes safely can be carried out. That at any rate is the theory of our Constitution. It is an experiment, as all life is an experiment. Every year if not every day we have to wager our salvation upon some prophecy based upon imperfect knowledge. While that experiment is part of our system I think that we should be eternally vigilant against attempts to check the expression of opinions that we loathe and believe to be fraught with death, unless they so imminently threaten immediate interference with the lawful and pressing purposes of the law that an immediate check is required to save the country. I wholly disagree with the argument of the Government that the First Amendment left the common law as to seditious libel in force. History seems to me against the notion. I had conceived that the United States through many years had shown its repentance for the Sedition Act of 1798, by repaying fines that it imposed. Only the emergency that makes it immediately dangerous to leave the correction of evil counsels to time warrants making any exception to the sweeping command, "Congress shall make no law . . . abridging the freedom of speech." Of course I am speaking only of expressions of opinion and exhortations, which were all that were uttered here, but I regret that I cannot put into more impressive words my belief that in their conviction upon this indictment the defendants were deprived of their rights under the Constitution of the United States.

MR. JUSTICE BRANDEIS concurs with the foregoing opinion.

GITLOW V. NEW YORK
268 U.S. 652, 45 S.Ct. 625, 69 L.Ed. 1138 (1925)

[New York law made it a felony to advocate "by word of mouth or writing" the doctrine of criminal anarchy, "that organized government should be overthrown by force or violence . . . or by any unlawful means." Defendants were convicted for publishing a radical manifesto that urged revolutionary socialism to use "mass industrial revolts to broaden the strike, make it general and militant, and develop it into mass political strikes and revolutionary mass action for the annihilation of the parliamentary state."]

MR. JUSTICE STANFORD delivered the opinion of the Court.

For present purposes we may and do assume that freedom of speech and of the press—which are protected by the First Amendment from abridgment by Congress—are among the fundamental personal rights and "liberties" protected by the due process clause of the Fourteenth Amendment from impairment by the States. . . .

By enacting the present statute the State has determined, through its legislative body, that utterances advocating the overthrow of organized government by force, violence and unlawful means, are so inimical to the general welfare and involve such danger of substantive evil that they may be penalized in the exercise of its police power. That determination must be given great weight. Every presumption is to be indulged in favor of the validity of the statute. . . . That utterances inciting to the overthrow of organized government by unlawful means, present a sufficient danger of substantive evil to bring their punishment within the range of legislative discretion, is clear. Such utterances, by their very nature, involve danger to the public peace and to the security of the State. They threaten breaches of the peace and ultimate revolution. And the immediate danger is none the less real and substantial, because the effect of a given utterance cannot be accurately foreseen. The State cannot reasonably be required to measure the danger from every such utterance in the nice balance of a jeweler's scale. A single revolutionary spark may kindle a fire that, smoldering for a time, may burst into a sweeping and destructive conflagration. It cannot be said that the State is acting arbitrarily or unreasonably when in the exercise of its judgment as to the measures necessary to protect the public peace and safety, it seeks to extinguish the spark without waiting until it has enkindled the flame or blazed into the conflagration. . . .

It is clear that the question in such cases is entirely different from that involved in those cases where the statute merely prohibits certain acts involving the danger of substantive evil, without any reference to language itself, and it is sought to apply its provisions to language used by the defendant for the purpose of bringing about the prohibited results. [T]he general statement in the *Schenck Case* that the "question in every case is whether the words are used in such circumstances and are of such a nature as to create a clear and present danger that they will bring about the substantive evils,"—upon which great reliance is placed in the defendant's argument—was manifestly intended, as shown by the context, to apply only in cases of this class, and has no application to those like the present, where the legislative body itself has previously determined the danger of substantive evil arising from utterances of a specified character. [T]he judgment of the Court of Appeals is

Affirmed.

JUSTICE HOLMES, dissenting.

Mr. Justice Brandeis and I are of opinion that this judgment should be reversed. . . . I think that the criterion sanctioned by the full Court in *Schenck v. United States,* applies. . . . If what I think the correct test is applied, it is manifest that there was no present danger of an attempt to overthrow the government by force on the part of the admittedly small minority who shared the defendant's views. It is said that this manifesto was more than a theory, that it was an incitement. Every idea is an incitement. It offers itself for belief and if believed it is acted on unless some other belief outweighs it or some failure of energy stifles the movement at its birth. The only difference between the expression of an opinion and an incitement in the narrower sense is the speaker's enthusiasm for the result. Eloquence may set fire to reason. But whatever may be thought of the redundant discourse before us it had no chance of starting a present conflagration. If in the long run the beliefs expressed in proletarian dictatorship are destined to be accepted by the dominant forces of the community, the only meaning of free speech is that they should be given their chance and have their way.

If the publication of this document had been laid as an attempt to induce an uprising against government at once and not at some indefinite time in the future it would have presented a different question. The object would have been one with which the law might deal, subject to the doubt whether there was any danger that the publication could produce any result, or in other words, whether it was not futile and too remote from possible consequences. But the indictment alleges the publication and nothing more.

WHITNEY V. CALIFORNIA
274 U.S. 357, 47 S.Ct. 641, 71 L.Ed. 1095 (1927)

[Whitney was-convicted of violating the California law against criminal syndicalism. Justice Stanford, for the Court, affirmed.]

JUSTICE BRANDEIS, concurring.

Miss Whitney was convicted of the felony of assisting in organizing, in the year 1919, the Communist Labor Party of California, of being a member of it, and of assembling with it. These acts are held to constitute a crime, because the party was formed to teach criminal syndicalism. The statute which made these acts a crime restricted the right of free speech and of assembly theretofore existing. The claim is that the statute, as applied, denied to Miss Whitney the liberty guaranteed by the Fourteenth Amendment.

The felony which the statute created is a crime very unlike the old felony of conspiracy or the old misdemeanor of unlawful assembly. The mere act of assisting in forming a society for teaching syndicalism, of becoming a member of it, or of assembling with others for that purpose is given the dynamic quality of crime. There is guilt although the society may not contemplate immediate promulgation of the doctrine. Thus the accused is to be punished, not for contempt, incitement or conspiracy, but for a step in preparation, which, if it threatens the public order at all, does so only remotely. The novelty in the prohibition introduced is that the statute aims, not at the practice of criminal syndicalism, nor even directly at the preaching of it, but at association with those who propose to preach it.

Despite arguments to the contrary which had seemed to me persuasive, it is settled that the due process clause of the Fourteenth Amendment applies to matters of substantive law as well as to matters of procedure. Thus all fundamental rights comprised within the term liberty are protected by the Federal Constitution from invasion by the States. The right of free speech, the right to teach and the right of assembly are, of course, fundamental rights. These may not be denied or abridged. But, although the rights of free speech and assembly are fundamental, they are not in their nature absolute. Their exercise is subject to restriction, if the particular restriction proposed is required in order to protect the State from destruction or from serious injury, political, economic or moral. That the necessity which is essential to a valid restriction does not exist unless speech would produce, or is intended to produce, a clear and imminent danger of some substantive evil which the State constitutionally may seek to prevent has been settled. See *Schenck v. United States.*

It is said to be the function of the legislature to determine whether at a particular time and under the particular circumstances the formation of, or assembly with, a society organized to advocate criminal syndicalism constitutes a clear and present danger of substantive evil; and that by enacting the law here in question the legislature of California determined that question in the affirmative. Compare *Gitlow v. New York.* But where a statute is valid only in case certain conditions exist, the enactment of the statute cannot alone establish the facts which are essential to its validity. . . .

This Court has not yet fixed the standard by which to determine when a danger shall be deemed clear; how remote the danger may be and yet be deemed present; and what degree of evil shall be deemed sufficiently substantial to justify resort to abridgement of free speech and assembly as the means of protection. To reach sound conclusions on these matters, we must bear in mind why a State is, ordinarily, denied the power to prohibit dissemination of social; economic and political doctrine which a vast majority of its citizens believes to be false and fraught with evil consequence.

Those who won our independence believed that the final end of the State was to make men free to develop their faculties; and that in its government the deliberative forces should prevail over the arbitrary. They valued liberty both as an end and as a means. They believed liberty to be the secret of happiness and courage to be the secret of liberty. They believed that freedom to think as you will and to speak as you think are means indispensable to the discovery and spread of political truth; that without free speech and assembly discussion would be futile; that with them, discussion affords ordinarily adequate protection against the dissemination of noxious doctrine; that the greatest menace to freedom is an inert people; that public discussion is a political duty; and that this should be a fundamental principle of the American government.[3] They recognized the risks to which all human institutions are subject. But they knew that order cannot be secured merely through fear of punishment for its *infra*ction; that it is hazardous to discourage thought, hope and imagination; that fear breeds repression; that repression breeds hate; that hate menaces stable government; that the path of safety lies in the opportunity to discuss freely supposed grievances and proposed remedies; and that the fitting remedy for evil counsels is good ones. Believing in the power of reason as applied through public discussion, they eschewed silence coerced by law—the argument of force in its worst form. Recognizing the occasional tyrannies of governing majorities, they amended the Constitution so that free speech and assembly should be guaranteed.

Fear of serious injury cannot alone justify suppression of free speech and assembly. Men feared witches and burnt women. It is the function of speech to free men from the bondage of irrational fears. To justify suppression of free speech there must be reasonable ground to fear that serious evil will result if free speech is practiced. There must be reasonable ground to believe that the danger apprehended is imminent. There must be reasonable ground to believe that the evil to be prevented is a serious one. Every denunciation of existing law tends in some measure to increase the probability that there will be violation of it. Condonation of a breach enhances the probability. Expressions of approval add to the probability. Propagation of the criminal state of mind by teaching syndicalism increases it. Advocacy of law-breaking heightens it still further. But even advocacy of violation, however reprehensible morally, is not a justification for denying free speech where the advocacy falls short of incitement and there is nothing to indicate that the advocacy would be immediately acted on. The wide difference between advocacy and incitement, between preparation and attempt, between assembling and conspiracy, must be borne in mind. In order to support a finding of clear and present danger it must be shown either that immediate serious violence was to be expected or was advocated, or that the past conduct furnished reason to believe that such advocacy was then contemplated.

. . . If there be time to expose through discussion the falsehood and fallacies, to avert the evil by the processes of education, the remedy to be applied is more speech, not enforced silence. Only an emergency can justify repression. Such must be the rule if authority is to be reconciled with freedom. Such, in my opinion, is the command of the Constitution. It is therefore always open to Americans to

---

[3]   Compare Thomas Jefferson: "We have nothing to fear from the demoralizing reasonings of some, if others are left free to demonstrate their errors and especially when the law stands ready to punish the first criminal act produced by the false reasonings; these are safer corrections than the conscience of the judge." . . .

challenge a law abridging free speech and assembly by showing that there was no emergency justifying it.

Moreover, even imminent danger cannot justify resort to prohibition of these functions essential to effective democracy, unless the evil apprehended is relatively serious. Prohibition of free speech and assembly is a measure so stringent that it would be inappropriate as the means for averting a relatively trivial harm to society. A police measure may be unconstitutional merely because the remedy, although effective as means of protection, is unduly harsh or oppressive. Thus, a State might, in the exercise of its police power, make any trespass upon the land of another a crime, regardless of the results or of the intent or purpose of the trespasser. It might, also, punish an attempt, a conspiracy, or an incitement to commit the trespass. But it is hardly conceivable that this Court would hold constitutional a statute which punished as a felony the mere voluntary assembly with a society formed to teach that pedestrians had the moral right to cross unenclosed, unposted, waste lands and to advocate their doing so, even if there was imminent danger that advocacy would lead to a trespass. The fact that speech is likely to result in some violence or in destruction of property is not enough to justify its suppression. There must be the probability of serious injury to the State. Among free men, the deterrents ordinarily to be applied to prevent crime are education and punishment for violations of the law, not abridgment of the rights of free speech and assembly. . . .

Whether in 1919, when Miss Whitney did the things complained of, there was in California such clear and present danger of serious evil, might have been made the important issue in the case. She might have required that the issue be determined either by the court or the jury. She claimed below that the statute as applied to her violated the Federal Constitution; but she did not claim that it was void because there was no clear and present danger of serious evil, nor did she request that the existence of these conditions of a valid measure thus restricting the rights of free speech and assembly be passed upon by the court or a jury. . . . Under these circumstances the judgment of the state court cannot be disturbed. . . . This is a writ of error to a state court. Because we may not enquire into the errors now alleged, I concur in affirming the judgment of the state court.

MR. JUSTICE HOLMES joins in this opinion.

NOTES

1. Brandeis labeled his opinion "concurring," but it reads like a dissent. Brandeis' technical reason for affirming the conviction (she did not specifically raise the "clear and present danger" test), was probably just a ploy or stratagem. The justices can call their opinions whatever they want. He wanted his opinion to carry more authority for future Justices, and an opinion called "concurring" should carry more weight. Dissents, by definition, are not precedent. Brandeis understood that the Supreme Court had not yet used Holmes' "clear and present danger test" to overturn a free speech conviction. If the Court used it at all, it only did so to affirm a conviction. (Brandeis did not know it yet but the Supreme Court would never use the "clear and present danger" test to overturn a conviction.)

2. *Dennis v. United States*, 341 U.S. 494, 71 S.Ct. 857, 95 L.Ed. 1137 (1951), upheld the defendants' conviction for violation of the Smith Act. As Chief Justice Vinson, who wrote the plurality opinion, explained: "The indictment charged the petitioners with wilfully [sic] and knowingly conspiring to advocate and teach the duty and necessity of overthrowing and destroying the Government of the United States by force and violence." The Court affirmed the convictions. Said Vinson:

    > Obviously, the words ["clear and present danger"] cannot mean that before the Government may act, it must wait until the *putsch* is about to be executed, the plans have been laid and the signal awaited. If Government is aware that a group aiming at its overthrow is attempting to indoctrinate its members and to commit them to a course whereby they will strike when the leaders feel the circumstances permit, action by the Government is required. . . . In the instant case the trial judge charged the jury that they could not convict unless they found that petitioners intended to overthrow the Government "as speedily as circumstances would permit." This does not mean, and could not properly mean, that they would not strike until there was certainty of success. What was meant was that the revolutionists would strike when they thought the time was ripe. We must therefore reject the contention that success or probability of success is the criterion.

    > Any attempt to overthrow the government by force, "even though doomed from the outset because of inadequate numbers or power of the

revolutionists, is a sufficient evil for Congress to prevent." Vinson then adopted the Second Circuit's rephrasing of the clear and present danger test: "Chief Judge Learned Hand, writing for the majority below, interpreted the phrase as follows: 'In each case [courts] must ask whether the gravity of the "evil," discounted by its improbability, justifies such invasion of free speech as is necessary to avoid the danger.' We adopt this statement of the rule."

Vinson agreed that the requisite danger existed. "The mere fact that from the period 1945 to 1948 petitioners' activities did not result in an attempt to overthrow the Government by force and violence is of course no answer to the fact that there was a group that was ready to make the attempt. . . . It is the existence of the conspiracy which creates the danger. If the ingredients to the reaction are present, we cannot bind the Government to wait until the catalyst is added."

Justice Frankfurter, concurring, argued that the ascendancy of the Communist doctrine was a matter of common knowledge that "would amply justify a legislature in concluding that recruitment of additional members for the Party would create a substantial danger to national security." In *Gitlow v. New York, supra,* it would require "excessive tolerance of the legislative judgment to suppose that the *Gitlow* publication in the circumstances could justify serious concern. In contrast, there is ample justification for a legislative judgment that the conspiracy now before us is a substantial threat to national order and security."

3.   *Yates v. United States,* 354 U.S. 298, 77 S.Ct. 1064, 1 L.Ed.2d 1356 (1957), reversed and remanded the convictions of petitioners convicted of conspiring "to advocate and teach the duty and necessity of overthrowing the Government of the United States by force and violence." Justice Harlan, for the majority, stated that the Court was "faced with the question whether the Smith Act prohibits advocacy and teaching of forcible overthrow as an abstract principle, divorced from any effort to instigate action to that end, so long as such advocacy or teaching is engaged in with evil intent. We hold that it does not." The lower courts had misconceived *Dennis*:

> [T]he view of the District Court [was] that mere doctrinal justification of forcible overthrow, if engaged in with the intent to accomplish overthrow, is punishable *per se* under the Smith Act. That sort of advocacy, even though uttered with the hope that it may ultimately lead to violent revolution, is too remote from concrete action to be regarded as the kind of indoctrination

preparatory to action which was condemned in *Dennis.* . . . The essential distinction is that those to whom the advocacy is addressed must be urged to *do* something, now or in the future, rather than merely to *believe* in something.

4.   *Dennis* resulted in a drop in free speech prosecutions. Still, the status of free speech in light of the" clear and present danger test" was unclear. Then came *Brandenburg,* the next major decision.

BRANDENBURG V. OHIO
395 U.S. 444, 89 S.Ct. 1827, 23 L.Ed.2d 430 (1969)

PER CURIAM.

The appellant, a leader of a Ku Klux Klan group, was convicted under the Ohio Criminal Syndicalism statute for "advocating] . . . the duty, necessity, or propriety of crime, sabotage, violence, or unlawful methods of terrorism as a means of accomplishing industrial or political reform" and for "voluntarily assembli[ng] . . . with any society, group, or assemblage of persons formed to teach or advocate the doctrines of criminal syndicalism." He was fined $1,000 and sentenced to one to 10 years' imprisonment. . . . We reverse.

The record shows that a man, identified at trial as the appellant, telephoned an announcer-reporter on the staff of a Cincinnati television station and invited him to come to a Ku Klux. Klan "rally" to be held at a farm in Hamilton County. With the cooperation of the organizers, the reporter and a cameraman attended the meeting and filmed the events. Portions of the films were later broadcast on the local station and on a national network. . . .

One film showed 12 hooded figures, some of whom carried firearms. They were gathered around a large wooden cross, which they burned. No one was present other than the participants and the newsmen who made the film. Most of the words uttered during the scene were incomprehensible when the film was projected, but scattered phrases could be understood that were derogatory of Negroes and, in one instance, of Jews. Another scene on the same film showed the appellant, in Klan regalia, making a speech. The speech, in full, was as follows:

> This is an organizers' meeting. We have had quite a few members here today which are—we have hundreds, hundreds of members throughout the State of Ohio. I can quote from a newspaper clipping from the Columbus, Ohio *Dispatch,* five weeks ago Sunday morning. The Klan has more members in the State of Ohio than does any other

organization. We're not a revengent organization, but if our President, our Congress, our Supreme Court, continues to suppress the white, Caucasian race, it's possible that there might have to be some revengeance taken.

We are marching on Congress July the Fourth, four hundred thousand strong. From there we are dividing into two groups, one group to march on St. Augustine, Florida, the other group to march into Mississippi. Thank you.

The second film showed six hooded figures one of whom, later identified as the appellant, repeated a speech very similar to that recorded on the first film. The reference to the possibility of "revengeance" was omitted, and one sentence was added: "Personally, I believe the nigger should be returned to Africa, the Jew returned to Israel." Though some of the figures in the films carried weapons, the speaker did not.

The Ohio Criminal Syndicalism Statute was enacted in 1919. From 1917 to 1920, identical or quite similar laws were adopted by 20 States and two territories. In 1927, this Court sustained the constitutionality of California's Criminal Syndicalism Act, Cal.Penal Code §§ 11400–11402, the text of which is quite similar to that of the laws of Ohio. *Whitney v. California.* The Court upheld the statute on the ground that, without more, "advocating" violent means to effect political and economic change involves such danger to the security of the State that the State may outlaw it. But *Whitney* has been thoroughly discredited by later decisions. See *Dennis v. United States.* These later decisions have fashioned the principle that the constitutional guarantees of free speech and free press do not permit a State to forbid or proscribe advocacy of the use of force or of law violation except where such advocacy is directed to inciting or producing imminent lawless action and is likely to incite or produce such action.[2] As we said in *Noto v. United States,* 367 U.S. 290, 297–298, 81 S.Ct. 1517,1520–1521, 6 L.Ed.2d 836 (1961), "the mere abstract teaching . . . of the moral propriety or even moral necessity for a resort to force and violence, is not the same as preparing a group for violent action and steeling it to such action." A statute which fails to draw this distinction impermissibly intrudes upon the freedoms guaranteed by the First and

---

[2] It was on the theory that the Smith Act, 54 Stat. 670, 18 U.S.C.A. § 2385, embodied such a principle and that it had been applied only in conformity with it that this Court sustained the Act's constitutionality. *Dennis v. United States.* That this was the basis for *Dennis* was emphasized in *Yates v. United States,* in which the Court overturned convictions for advocacy of the forcible overthrow of the Government under the Smith Act, because the trial judge's instructions had allowed conviction for mere advocacy, unrelated to its tendency to produce forcible action.

Fourteenth Amendments. It sweeps within its condemnation speech which our Constitution has immunized from governmental control.

Measured by this test, Ohio's Criminal Syndicalism Act cannot be sustained. [W]e are here confronted with a statute which, by its own words and as applied, purports to punish mere advocacy and to forbid, on pain of criminal punishment, assembly with others merely to advocate the described type of action. Such a statute falls within the condemnation of the First and Fourteenth Amendments. The contrary teaching of *Whitney v. California, supra,* cannot be supported, and that decision is therefore overruled.

Reversed.

JUSTICE BLACK, concurring.

I agree with the views expressed by Mr. Justice Douglas in his concurring opinion in this case that the "clear and present danger" doctrine should have no place in the interpretation of the First Amendment. I join the Court's opinion, which, as I understand it, simply cites *Dennis v. United States,* but does not indicate any agreement on the Court's part with the "clear and present danger" doctrine on which *Dennis* purported to rely.

[The concurring opinion of DOUGLAS, J., is omitted.]

HESS V. INDIANA

414 U.S. 105, 94 S.Ct. 326, 38 L.Ed.2d 303 (1973)

PER CURIAM.

Gregory Hess appeals from his conviction in the Indiana courts for violating the State's disorderly conduct statute. . . .

The events leading to Hess' conviction began with an antiwar demonstration on the campus of Indiana University. In the course of the demonstration, approximately 100 to 150 of the demonstrators moved onto a public street and blocked the passage of vehicles. When the demonstrators did not respond to verbal directions from the sheriff to clear the street, the sheriff and his deputies began walking up the street, and the demonstrators in their path moved to the curbs on either side, joining a large number of spectators who had gathered. Hess was standing off the street as the sheriff passed him. The sheriff heard Hess utter the word "fuck" in what he later described as a loud voice and immediately arrested him on the disorderly conduct charge. It was later stipulated that what appellant had said was "We'll take the fucking street later," or "We'll take the fucking street again." Two witnesses who were in the immediate vicinity testified, apparently without contradiction, that they heard Hess' words and witnessed his arrest. They indicated that Hess did not appear to be exhorting the crowd to go back into the street, that he was facing the crowd and not the street when he uttered the statement, that his statement did not appear to be addressed to any particular person or group, and that his tone, although loud, was no louder than that of the other people in the area. . . .

The Indiana Supreme Court placed primary reliance on the trial court's finding that Hess' statement "was intended to incite further lawless action on the part of the crowd in the vicinity of appellant and was likely to produce such action." At best, however, the statement could be taken as counsel for present moderation; at worst, it amounted to nothing more than advocacy of illegal action at some indefinite future time. This is not sufficient to permit the State to punish Hess' speech. Under our decisions, "the constitutional guarantees of free speech and free press do not permit a State to forbid or proscribe advocacy of the use of force or of law violation except where such advocacy is directed to inciting or producing *imminent* lawless action and is likely to incite or produce such action." *Brandenburg v. Ohio*, 395 U.S. 444, 447, 89 S.Ct. 1827, 1829, 23 L.Ed.2d 430 (1969). (Emphasis added.) Since the uncontroverted evidence showed that Hess' statement was not directed to any person or group of persons, it cannot be said that he was advocating, in the normal sense, any action. And since there was no evidence, or rational inference from the import of the language, that his words were intended to produce, and likely to produce, *imminent* disorder, those words could not be punished by the State on the ground that they had "a 'tendency to lead to violence.' " [T]he judgment of the Supreme Court of Indiana is reversed.

JUSTICE REHNQUIST, with whom CHIEF JUSTICE BURGER and JUSTICE BLACKMUN join, dissenting.

[C]ertain facts are clearly established. Appellant was arrested during the course of an antiwar demonstration conducted at Indiana University in May 1970. The demonstration was of sufficient size and vigor to require the summoning of police, and both the Sheriff's Department and the Bloomington Police Department were asked to help university officials and police remove demonstrators blocking doorways to a campus building. At the time the sheriff arrived, "approximately 200–300 persons" were assembled at that particular building.

The doorways eventually were cleared of demonstrators, in the process, two students were placed under arrest. This action did not go unnoticed by the demonstrators. As the stipulation notes, "[i]n apparent response to these arrests, about 100–150 of the persons who had gathered as spectators went into Indiana Avenue in front of Bryan Hall and in front of the patrol car in which the two arrestees had been placed." Thus, by contrast to the majority's somewhat antiseptic description of this massing as being "[i]n the course of the demonstration," the demonstrators' presence in the street was not part of the normal "course of the demonstration" but could reasonably be construed as an attempt to intimidate and impede the arresting officers. Furthermore, as the stipulation also notes, the demonstrators "did not respond to verbal directions" from the sheriff to clear the street. Thus, the sheriff and his deputies found it necessary to disperse demonstrators by walking up the street directly into their path. Only at that point did the demonstrators move to the curbs.

[T]he sentence "We'll take the fucking street later (or again)" is susceptible of characterization as an exhortation, particularly when uttered in a loud voice while facing a crowd. The opinions of two defense witnesses cannot be considered *proof* to the contrary, since the trial court was perfectly free to reject this testimony if it so desired. [Instead of] considering the "evidence" in the light most favorable to the appellee and resolving credibility questions against the appellant, as many of our cases have required, the Court has instead fashioned its own version of events from a paper record, some "uncontroverted evidence," and a large measure of conjecture. Since this is not the traditional function of any appellate court, and is surely not a wise or proper use of the authority of this Court, I dissent.

NOTES

1. The Court issued *Brandenburg* on June 9, 1969, just days before Chief Justice Warren resigned from the Court, on June 23, 1969. Some commentators at the time were not sure that *Brandenburg* signaled a major change in the law because it was just a *per curiam opinion* and Warren was leaving the Court. The opinion in *Hess v. Indiana* removed all doubts.

2. *Brandenburg/Hess* adopted a new, four-part test that emphasizes the need for the state to prove incitement. For the state conviction to be valid, the state must prove:

    > (1) the speaker subjectively intended incitement; (2) in context, the words used are "likely to incite or produce" "imminent, lawless action;" and (3) the words used by the speaker objectively encouraged, urged, and (4) the words provoked imminent action.

HOLDER V. HUMANITARIAN LAW PROJECT

561 U.S. 1, 130 S.Ct. 2705, 177 L.Ed.2d 355 (2010)

CHIEF JUSTICE ROBERTS delivered the opinion of the Court.

Congress has prohibited the provision of "material support or resources" to certain foreign organizations that engage in terrorist activity. [P]laintiffs in this litigation seek to provide support to two such organizations. Plaintiffs claim that they seek to facilitate only the lawful, nonviolent purposes of those groups, and that applying the material-support law to prevent them from doing so violates the Constitution. In particular, they claim that the statute is too vague, in violation of the Fifth Amendment, and that it infringes their rights to freedom of speech and association, in violation of the First Amendment. We conclude that the material-support statute is constitutional as applied to the particular activities plaintiffs have told us they wish to pursue. We do not, however, address the resolution of more difficult cases that may arise under the statute in the future.

This litigation concerns 18 U.S.C.A. § 2339B, which makes it a federal crime to "knowingly provid[e] material support or resources to a foreign terrorist organization." [I]t is defined as follows:

> "[T]he term 'material support or resources' means any property, tangible or intangible, or service, including currency or monetary instruments or financial securities, financial services, lodging, training, expert advice or assistance, safehouses, false documentation or identification, communications equipment, facilities, weapons, lethal substances, explosives, personnel (1 or more individuals who may be or include oneself), and transportation, except medicine or religious materials."

The authority to designate an entity a "foreign terrorist organization" rests with the Secretary of State. [Any] entity designated a foreign terrorist organization may seek review of that designation before the D. C. Circuit within 30 days of that designation.

In 1997, the Secretary of State designated 30 groups as foreign terrorist organizations. Two of those groups are the Kurdistan Workers' Party (also known as the Partiya Karkeran Kurdistan, or PKK) and the Liberation Tigers of Tamil Eelam (LTTE). The PKK is an organization founded in 1974 with the aim of establishing an independent Kurdish state in southeastern Turkey. The LTTE is an organization founded in 1976 for the purpose of creating an independent Tamil state in Sri Lanka. The District Court in this action found that the PKK and the LTTE engage in political and humanitarian activities. The Government has presented evidence that both groups have also committed numerous terrorist attacks, some of which have harmed American citizens. The LTTE sought judicial review of its designation as a foreign terrorist organization; the D.C. Circuit upheld that designation. The PKK did not challenge its designation.

Plaintiffs ... claimed that they wished to provide support for the humanitarian and political activities of the PKK and the LTTE in the form of monetary contributions, other tangible aid, legal training, and political advocacy, but that they could not do so for fear of prosecution under § 2339B. ... Plaintiffs challenge § 2339B's prohibition on four types of material support—"training," "expert advice or assistance," "service," and "personnel."

[P]laintiffs claim that § 2339B is invalid to the extent it prohibits them from engaging in certain specified activities. ... (1) "train[ing] members of [the] PKK on how to use humanitarian and international law to peacefully resolve disputes"; (2) "engag[ing] in political advocacy on behalf of Kurds who live in Turkey"; and (3) "teach[ing] PKK members how to petition various representative bodies such as the United Nations for relief." With respect to the other plaintiffs, those activities are: (1) "train[ing] members of [the] LTTE to present claims for tsunami-related aid to mediators and international bodies"; (2) "offer[ing] their legal expertise in negotiating peace agreements between the LTTE and the Sri Lankan government"; and (3) "engag[ing] in political advocacy on behalf of Tamils who live in Sri Lanka." ...

... Section 2339B(a)(1) prohibits "knowingly" providing material support. It then specifically describes the type of knowledge that is required: "To violate this paragraph, a person must have knowledge that the organization is a designated terrorist organization ..., that the organization has engaged or engages in terrorist activity ..., or that the organization has engaged or engages in terrorism. ..." ...

[T]eaching the PKK how to petition for humanitarian relief before the United Nations involves advice derived from, as the statute puts it, "specialized knowledge." ... Providing material support that constitutes "personnel" is defined as knowingly providing a person "to work under that terrorist organization's direction or control or to organize, manage, supervise, or otherwise direct the operation of that organization." § 2339B(h). The statute makes clear that "personnel" does not cover *independent* advocacy: "Individuals who act entirely independently of the foreign terrorist organization to advance its goals or objectives shall not be considered to be working under the foreign terrorist organization's direction and control."

. . . Plaintiffs claim that Congress has banned their "pure political speech." It has not. Under the material-support statute, plaintiffs may say anything they wish on any topic. They may speak and write freely about the PKK and LTTE, the governments of Turkey and Sri Lanka, human rights, and international law. They may advocate before the United Nations. As the Government states: "The statute does not prohibit independent advocacy or expression of any kind." Section 2339B also "does not prevent [plaintiffs] from becoming members of the PKK and LTTE or impose any sanction on them for doing so." Congress has not, therefore, sought to suppress ideas or opinions in the form of "pure political speech." Rather, Congress has prohibited "material support," which most often does not take the form of speech at all. And when it does, the statute is carefully drawn to cover only a narrow category of speech to, under the direction of, or in coordination with foreign groups that the speaker knows to be terrorist organizations.

[Section] 2339B regulates speech on the basis of its content. [The First Amendment issue is] whether the Government may prohibit what plaintiffs want to do—provide material support to the PKK and LTTE in the form of speech. [Congress found:] "[F]oreign organizations that engage in terrorist activity are so tainted by their criminal conduct that *any contribution to such an organization* facilitates that conduct." § 301(a)(7) (emphasis added). . . .

Material support meant to "promot[e] peaceable, lawful conduct," can further terrorism by foreign groups in multiple ways. "Material support" is a valuable resource by definition. Such support frees up other resources within the organization that may be put to violent ends. It also importantly helps lend legitimacy to foreign terrorist groups—legitimacy that makes it easier for those groups to persist, to recruit members, and to raise funds—all of which facilitate more terrorist attacks. "Terrorist organizations do not maintain *organizational* 'firewalls' that would prevent or deter . . . sharing and commingling of support and benefits." McKune Affidavit, App. 135, ¶ 11. "[T]errorist groups systematically conceal their activities behind charitable, social, and political fronts." "Indeed, some designated foreign terrorist organizations use social and political components to recruit personnel to carry out terrorist operations, and to provide support to criminal terrorists and their families in aid of such operations." McKune Affidavit, App. 135, ¶ 11; (". . . Hamas is able to use its overt political and charitable organizations as a financial and logistical support network for its terrorist operations"). . . . The statute reaches only material support coordinated with or under the direction of a designated foreign terrorist organization.

Independent advocacy that might be viewed as promoting the group's legitimacy is not covered.[6]

Providing foreign terrorist groups with material support in any form also furthers terrorism by straining the United States' relationships with its allies and undermining cooperative efforts between nations to prevent terrorist attacks. . . . For example, the Republic of Turkey—a fellow member of NATO—is defending itself against a violent insurgency waged by the PKK. That nation and our other allies would react sharply to Americans furnishing material support to foreign groups like the PKK, and would hardly be mollified by the explanation that the support was meant only to further those groups' "legitimate" activities. . . .

We turn to the particular speech plaintiffs propose to undertake. First, plaintiffs propose to "train members of [the] PKK on how to use humanitarian and international law to peacefully resolve disputes." Congress can, consistent with the First Amendment, prohibit this direct training. It is wholly foreseeable that the PKK could use the "specific skill[s]" that plaintiffs propose to impart, § 2339A(b)(2), as part of a broader strategy to promote terrorism. The PKK could, for example, pursue peaceful negotiation as a means of buying time to recover from short-term setbacks, lulling opponents into complacency, and ultimately preparing for renewed attacks. . . .

Second, plaintiffs propose to "teach PKK members how to petition various representative bodies such as the United Nations for relief." [E]arlier in this litigation, plaintiffs sought to teach the LTTE "to present claims for tsunami-related aid to mediators and international bodies," which naturally included monetary relief. Money is fungible, and Congress logically concluded that money a terrorist group such as the PKK obtains using the techniques plaintiffs propose to teach could be redirected to funding the group's violent activities.

Finally, plaintiffs propose to "engage in political advocacy on behalf of Kurds who live in Turkey," and "engage in political advocacy on behalf of Tamils who live in Sri Lanka." [P]laintiffs do not specify their expected level of coordination with the PKK or LTTE or suggest what exactly their "advocacy" would consist of. Plaintiffs' proposals are phrased at such a high level of generality that they cannot prevail in this preenforcement challenge. . . .

---

[6]   The dissent also contends that the particular sort of material support plaintiffs seek to provide cannot be diverted to terrorist activities, in the same direct way as funds or goods. This contention misses the point. Both common sense and the evidence submitted by the Government make clear that material support of a terrorist group's lawful activities facilitates the group's ability to attract "funds," "financing," and "goods" that will further its terrorist acts.

If only good can come from training our adversaries in international dispute resolution, presumably it would have been unconstitutional to prevent American citizens from training the Japanese Government on using international organizations and mechanisms to resolve disputes during World War II. It would, under the dissent's reasoning, have been contrary to our commitment to resolving disputes through " 'deliberative forces,' " for Congress to conclude that assisting Japan on that front might facilitate its war effort more generally. That view is not one the First Amendment requires us to embrace.

All this is not to say that any future applications of the material-support statute to speech or advocacy will survive First Amendment scrutiny. . . . We also do not suggest that Congress could extend the same prohibition on material support at issue here to domestic organizations. We simply hold that, in prohibiting the particular forms of support that plaintiffs seek to provide to foreign terrorist groups, § 2339B does not violate the freedom of speech.

Plaintiffs' final claim is that the material-support statute violates their freedom of association under the First Amendment . . . "The statute does not prohibit being a member of one of the designated groups or vigorously promoting and supporting the political goals of the group. . . . What [§ 2339B] prohibits is the act of giving material support . . ." Plaintiffs want to do the latter.

It is so ordered.

JUSTICE BREYER, with whom JUSTICES GINSBURG and SOTOMAYOR join, dissenting.

. . . I cannot agree with the Court's conclusion that the Constitution permits the Government to prosecute the plaintiffs criminally for engaging in coordinated teaching and advocacy furthering the designated organizations' lawful political objectives. [P]laintiffs do not propose to solicit a crime. They will not engage in fraud or defamation or circulate obscenity. And the First Amendment protects advocacy even of *unlawful* action so long as that advocacy is not "directed to inciting or producing *imminent lawless action* and . . . *likely to incite or produce* such action." *Brandenburg* v. *Ohio* (1969) *(per curiam)* (emphasis added). Here the plaintiffs seek to advocate peaceful, *lawful* action to secure *political* ends; and they seek to teach others how to do the same. No one contends that the plaintiffs' speech to these organizations can be prohibited as incitement under *Brandenburg*.

. . . Speech, association, and related activities on behalf of a group will often, perhaps always, help to legitimate that group. [If] one accepts this argument, there is no natural stopping place. The argument applies as strongly to "independent" as to "coordinated" advocacy. That fact is reflected in part in the Government's claim that the ban here, so supported, prohibits a lawyer hired by a designated group from filing on behalf of that group an *amicus* brief before the United Nations or even before this Court. . . . Nor can the Government overcome these considerations simply by narrowing the covered activities to those that involve *coordinated*, rather than *independent*, advocacy. . . .

NOTES

1. The Government claimed that § 2339B prohibits a lawyer hired by a designated terrorist group from filing on behalf of that group an *amicus* brief before the Supreme Court. During oral argument, Justice Kennedy asked Solicitor General Kagan, "Do you stick with the argument made below that it's unlawful to file an amicus brief?" Solicitor General Kagan answered, lawyers could "file amicus briefs in a case that might involve the PKK or the LTTE for themselves, but to the extent that a lawyer drafts an amicus brief for the PKK or for the LTTE, that's the amicus party, then that indeed would be prohibited." Justice Stevens retorted, "Then it says to me that your opponent's argument here today is prohibited." Kagan replied, "No, no, no, because Petitioners here are arguing for themselves." The "Petitioners can do all the advocacy they want, can engage in courts in any way they wish. The only thing that's prohibited is if the PKK hired a lawyer to write an amicus brief on its behalf." 2010 WestLaw 621318, *46 (Feb. 23, 2010).

2. The lawyer for Respondents also argued that, under the statute, if the New York *Times* published op-eds by Hamas spokespersons—Hamas is on the terrorist list—"thereby providing a benefit to Hamas, working with the Hamas spokesperson, they are all criminals." Justice Scalia responded, "We can cross that bridge when we come to it. This is an as-applied challenge and we are talking about the kind of advice and assistance that your clients want to give." The lawyer said, "Right."

3. Chief Justice Roberts asked Respondents, if your organization provides "personnel that participate in legal activity on behalf of a terrorist organization, and the organization can then say, well, because you are providing this personnel, we can . . . shift them to bomb making?" The response: "If what is being prohibited is speech, I'm not sure that it would be permissible for the government to say we are going to criminalize your speech, even though it is advocating lawful activities. . . ."

4.   Roberts asked if Congress prohibit offering personnel, such as a nurse, at any
      Hamas hospitals. Respondent replied that this was "an as-applied challenge"
      so "it would not require the Court to decide whether any nonspeech
      assistance could be proscribed." Justice Sotomayor asked, "So what is
      unlawful about teaching people medicine and how to cure people from
      infection?" The response: "if that were what they were doing, Your Honor,
      if it was teaching, then it would be protected by the First Amendment."
      Justice Sotomayor said, "you are not advocating a difference in this case
      between training that could reasonably be used in terrorist activities, because
      teaching people how to care for the ill could be used to teach people how to
      care for the wounded." Respondent said, "Right." How would you answer
      these questions?

7.2 PRIOR RESTRAINT

Near v. Minnesota ex rel. Olson, 283 U.S. 697, 51 S.Ct. 625, 75 L.Ed. 1357 (1931)
is a case that *New York Times Co. v. United States*, below, cited several times. In *Near*,
Chief Justice Hughes spoke for the Court, and invalidated a state law allowing a
state court to abate, as a public nuisance, a "malicious, scandalous and defamatory
newspaper magazine or other periodical."[1] The Court said: "If we cut through
mere details of procedure, the operation and effect of the statute in substance is
that public authorities may bring the owner or publisher of a newspaper or
periodical before a judge upon a charge of conducting a business of publishing
scandalous and defamatory matter—in particular that the matter consists of
charges against public officers of official dereliction—and unless the owner or
publisher is able and disposed to bring competent evidence to satisfy the judge
that the charges are true and published with good motives and for justifiable ends,
his newspaper or periodical is suppressed and further publication is made
punishable as a contempt. This is the essence of censorship. [I]t has generally, if
not universally, considered that it is the chief purpose of the [speech] guaranty to
prevent previous restraints upon publication."

---

[1]   The dissent of Butler, J., joined by Van Devanter, McReynolds, & Sutherland, JJ., included long
excerpts from the newspaper, a brief portion of which follows:

"Practically every vendor of vile hooch, every owner of a moonshine still, every snake-faced gangster
and embryonic yegg in the Twin Cities is a JEW. . . . I simply state a fact when I say that ninety
percent of the crimes committed against society in this city are committed by Jew gangsters. . . . It is
Jew, Jew, Jew. . . . I am launching no attack against the Jewish people AS A RACE. I am merely
calling attention to a FACT. . . . Up to the present we have been merely tapping on the window.
Very soon we shall start smashing glass." 283 U.S. at 724–27 n. 1.

The *Near* Court added, in dictum, that "the protection even as to previous restraint is not absolutely unlimited. But the limitation has been recognized only in exceptional cases ... No one would question but that a government might prevent actual obstruction to its recruiting service or the publication of the sailing dates of transports or the number and location of troops."

NEW YORK TIMES CO. V. UNITED STATES

403 U.S. 713, 91 S.Ct. 2140, 29 L.Ed.2d 822 (1951)

[On June 13, 1971, the Sunday *New York Times* published the first installment of what became popularly known as the Pentagon Papers, based on a forty-seven-volume, top-secret study of American involvement in the Vietnam War. Commissioned by Secretary of Defense Robert S. McNamara in 1967, the documentary history covered the American interest in the Indochinese area from World War II to May 1968, when the Paris peace talks began.* Daniel Ellsberg, a former Pentagon official, had engaged in an unauthorized disclosure—a "leak"—of the documents.

[After the *Times'* third installment, on Tuesday, Attorney General John Mitchell secured a temporary restraining order in the Southern District of New York on the grounds that the massive leak endangered national security. A few days later, on June 18, the *Washington Post* began to publish parts of the secret report, and the government once again sought a restraining order. Both district courts, after a hearing, denied an injunction. The Second Circuit remanded for further proceedings but the D.C. Circuit affirmed its district court. The Supreme Court granted certiorari in both cases, with Justices Black, Douglas, Brennan, and Marshall dissenting. They would have denied certiorari and lifted any restraints imposed on the *Times* and *Post.* Certiorari was granted on June 25, the case was set

---

* The Pentagon's secret history showed:

"That the Kennedy Administration, though ultimately spared from major escalation decisions by the death of its leader, transformed a policy of "limited-risk gamble," which it inherited, into a 'broad commitment' that left President Johnson with a choice between more war and withdrawal.

"That the Johnson Administration, though the President was reluctant and hesitant to take the final decisions, intensified the covert warfare against North Vietnam and began planning in the spring of 1964 to wage overt war, a full year before it publicly revealed the depth of its involvement and its fear of defeat.

"That this campaign of growing clandestine military pressure through 1964 and the expanding program of bombing North Vietnam in 1965 were begun despite the judgment of the Government's intelligence community that the measures would not cause Hanoi to cease its support of the Vietcong insurgency in the South, and that the bombing was deemed militarily ineffective within a few months."

See, The Pentagon Papers, As Published by the New York Times, Based on The Investigative Reporting of Neil Sheehan at xi (Bantam Books, Inc. 1971).

for oral argument on June 26 at 11:00 A.M., and the Supreme Court opinion was issued on June 30.]

PER CURIAM.

We granted certiorari in these cases in which the United States seeks to enjoin the New York Times and the Washington Post from publishing the contents of a classified study entitled "History of U.S. Decision-Making Process on Viet Nam Policy."

"Any system of prior restraints of expression comes to this Court bearing a heavy presumption against its constitutional validity." *Bantam Books, Inc. v. Sullivan,* 372 U.S. 58, 70, 83 S.Ct. 631, 639, 9 L.Ed.2d 584 (1963); see also *Near v. Minnesota ex rel. Olson,* [noted *supra*]. The Government "thus carries a heavy burden of showing justification for the imposition of such a restraint." *Organization for a Better Austin v. Keefe,* 402 U.S. 415, 419, 91 S.Ct. 1575, 1578, 29 L.Ed.2d 1 (1971). The District Court for the Southern District of New York in the *New York Times* case and the District Court for the District of Columbia and the Court of Appeals for the District of Columbia Circuit in the *Washington Post* case held that the Government had not met that burden. We agree.

The judgment of the Court of Appeals for the District of Columbia Circuit is therefore affirmed. The order of the Court of Appeals for the Second Circuit is reversed and the case is remanded with directions to enter a judgment affirming the judgment of the District Court for the Southern District of New York. The stays entered June 25, 1971, by the Court are vacated. The judgments shall issue forthwith.

So ordered.

JUSTICE BLACK, with whom JUSTICE DOUGLAS joins, concurring.

I adhere to the view that the Government's case against the Washington Post should have been dismissed and that the injunction against the New York Times should have been vacated without oral argument when the cases were first presented to this Court. I believe that every moment's continuance of the injunctions against these newspapers amounts to a flagrant, indefensible, and continuing violation of the First Amendment. Furthermore, after oral argument, I agree completely that we must affirm the judgment of the Court of Appeals for the District of Columbia Circuit and reverse the judgment of the Court of Appeals for the Second Circuit for the reasons stated by my Brothers Douglas and Brennan. In my view it is unfortunate that some of my Brethren are apparently willing to hold that the publication of news may sometimes be enjoined. Such a holding would make a shambles of the First Amendment. . . .

In the First Amendment the Founding Fathers gave the free press the protection it must have to fulfill its essential role in our democracy. The press was to serve the governed, not the governors. The Government's power to censor the press was abolished so that the press would remain forever free to censure the Government. The press was protected so that it could bare the secrets of government and inform the people. Only a free and unrestrained press can effectively expose deception in government. And paramount among the responsibilities of a free press is the duty to prevent any part of the government from deceiving the people and sending them off to distant lands to die of foreign fevers and foreign shot and shell. In my view, far from deserving condemnation for their courageous reporting, the New York Times, the Washington Post, and other newspapers should be commended for serving the purpose that the Founding Fathers saw so clearly. In revealing the workings of government that led to the Vietnam war, the newspapers nobly did precisely that which the Founders hoped and trusted they would do.

[W]e are asked to hold that despite the First Amendment's emphatic command, the Executive Branch, the Congress, and the Judiciary can make laws enjoining publication of current news and abridging freedom of the press in the name of "national security." The Government does not even attempt to rely on any act of Congress. Instead it makes the bold and dangerously far-reaching contention that the courts should take it upon themselves to "make" a law abridging freedom of the press in the name of equity, presidential power and national security, even when the representatives of the people in Congress have adhered to the command of the First Amendment and refused to make such a law. To find that the President has "inherent power" to halt the publication of news by resort to the courts would wipe out the First Amendment and destroy the fundamental liberty and security of the very people the Government hopes to make "secure." No one can read the history of the adoption of the First Amendment without being convinced beyond any doubt that it was injunctions like those sought here that Madison and his collaborators intended to outlaw in this Nation for all time.

The word "security" is a broad, vague generality whose contours should not be invoked to abrogate the fundamental law embodied in the First Amendment. The guarding of military and diplomatic secrets at the expense of informed representative government provides no real security for our Republic. The

Framers of the First Amendment, fully aware of both the need to defend a new nation and the abuses of the English and Colonial governments, sought to give this new society strength and security by providing that freedom of speech, press, religion, and assembly should not be abridged.

JUSTICE DOUGLAS, with whom JUSTICE BLACK joins, concurring.

The power to wage war is "the power to wage war successfully." But the war power stems from a declaration of war. The Constitution by Art. I, § 8, gives Congress, not the President, power "[t]o declare War." Nowhere are presidential wars authorized. We need not decide therefore what leveling effect the war power of Congress might have.

These disclosures[3] may have a serious impact. But that is no basis for sanctioning a previous restraint on the press. . . .

The Government says that it has inherent powers to go into court and obtain an injunction to protect the national interest, which in this case is alleged to be national security. *Near v. Minnesota ex rel. Olson* repudiated that expansive doctrine in no uncertain terms. The dominant purpose of the First Amendment was to prohibit the widespread practice of governmental suppression of embarrassing information. It is common knowledge that the First Amendment was adopted against the widespread use of the common law of seditious libel to punish the dissemination of material that is embarrassing to the powers-that-be.

JUSTICE BRENNAN, concurring.

I write separately in these cases only to emphasize what should be apparent: that our judgments in the present cases may not be taken to indicate the propriety, in the future, of issuing temporary stays and restraining orders to block the publication of material sought to be suppressed by the Government. So far as I can determine, never before has the United States sought to enjoin a newspaper from publishing information in its possession. . . .

The error that has pervaded these cases from the outset was the granting of any injunctive relief whatsoever, interim or otherwise. The entire thrust of the Government's claim throughout these cases has been that publication of the material sought to be enjoined "could," or "might," or "may" prejudice the national interest in various ways. But the First Amendment tolerates absolutely no

---

[3]   There are numerous sets of this material in existence and they apparently are not under any controlled custody. Moreover, the President has sent a set to the Congress. We start then with a case where there already is rather wide distribution of the material that is destined for publicity, not secrecy. I have gone over the material listed in the *in camera* brief of the United States. It is all history, not future events. None of it is more recent than 1968.

prior judicial restraints of the press predicated upon surmise or conjecture that untoward consequences may result.* Our cases, it is true, have indicated that there is a single, extremely narrow class of cases in which the First Amendment's ban on prior judicial restraint may be overridden. Our cases have thus far indicated that such cases may arise only when the Nation "is at war," *Schenck v. United States,* during which times "[n]o one would question but that a government might prevent actual obstruction to its recruiting service or the publication of the sailing dates of transports or the number and location of troops." *Near v. Minnesota ex rel. Olson*. . . . "[T]he chief purpose of [the First Amendment's] guaranty [is] to prevent previous restraints upon publication." *Near v. Minnesota ex rel. Olson.* Thus, only governmental allegation and proof that publication must inevitably, directly, and immediately cause the occurrence of an event kindred to imperiling the safety of a transport already at sea can support even the issuance of an interim restraining order. In no event may mere conclusions be sufficient: for if the Executive Branch seeks judicial aid in preventing publication, it must inevitably submit the basis upon which that aid is sought to scrutiny by the judiciary. And therefore, every restraint issued in this case, whatever its form, has violated the First Amendment—and not less so because that restraint was justified as necessary to afford the courts an opportunity to examine the claim more thoroughly. Unless and until the Government has clearly made out its case, the First Amendment commands that no injunction may issue.

JUSTICE STEWART, with whom JUSTICE WHITE joins, concurring.

. . . We are asked, quite simply, to prevent the publication by two newspapers of material that the Executive Branch insists should not, in the national interest, be published. I am convinced that the Executive is correct with respect to some of the documents involved. But I cannot say that disclosure of any of them will surely result in direct, immediate, and irreparable damage to our Nation or its people. That being so, there can under the First Amendment be but one judicial resolution of the issues before us. I join the judgments of the Court.

JUSTICE WHITE, with whom JUSTICE STEWART joins, concurring.

---

* *Freedman v. Maryland,* 380 U.S. 51, 85 S.Ct. 734, 13 L.Ed.2d 649 (1965), and similar cases regarding temporary restraints of allegedly obscene materials are not in point. For those cases rest upon the proposition that "obscenity is not protected by the freedoms of speech and press." *Roth v. United States* [§ 15.10, below]. Here there is no question but that the material sought to be suppressed is within the protection of the First Amendment; the only question is whether, notwithstanding that fact, its publication may be enjoined for a time because of the presence of an overwhelming national interest. Similarly, copyright cases have no pertinence here: the Government is not asserting an interest in the particular form of words chosen in the documents, but is seeking to suppress the ideas expressed therein. And the copyright laws, of course, protect only the form of expression and not the ideas expressed.

I concur in today's judgments, but only because of the concededly extraordinary protection against prior restraints enjoyed by the press under our constitutional system. I do not say that in no circumstances would the First Amendment permit an injunction against publishing information about government plans or operations.[1] Nor, after examining the materials the Government characterizes as the most sensitive and destructive, can I deny that revelation of these documents will do substantial damage to public interests. Indeed, I am confident that their disclosure will have that result. But I nevertheless agree that the United States has not satisfied the very heavy burden that it must meet to warrant an injunction against publication in these cases, at least in the absence of express and appropriately limited congressional authorization for prior restraints in circumstances such as these.

The Government's position is simply stated: The responsibility of the Executive for the conduct of the foreign affairs and for the security of the Nation is so basic that the President is entitled to an injunction against publication of a newspaper story whenever he can convince a court that the information to be revealed threatens "grave and irreparable" injury to the public interest; and the injunction should issue whether or not the material to be published is classified, whether or not publication would be lawful under relevant criminal statutes enacted by Congress, and regardless of the circumstances by which the newspaper came into possession of the information.

. . . If the United States were to have judgment under such a standard in these cases, our decision would be of little guidance to other courts in other cases, for the material at issue here would not be available from the Court's opinion or from public records, nor would it be published by the press. Indeed, even today where we hold that the United States has not met its burden, the material remains sealed in court records and it is properly not discussed in today's opinions. Moreover, because the material poses substantial dangers to national interests and because of the hazards of criminal sanctions, a responsible press may choose never to publish the more sensitive materials. To sustain the Government in these cases would start the courts down a long and hazardous road that I am not willing to travel, at least without congressional guidance and direction.

[H]ere, publication has already begun and a substantial part of the threatened damage has already occurred. The fact of a massive breakdown in security is

---

1   [W]hen the press is enjoined under the copyright laws the complainant is a private copyright holder enforcing a private right. These situations are quite distinct from the Government's request for an injunction against publishing information about the affairs of government, a request admittedly not based on any statute.

known, access to the documents by many unauthorized people is undeniable, and the efficacy of equitable relief against these or other newspapers to avert anticipated damage is doubtful at best.

What is more, terminating the ban on publication of the relatively few sensitive documents the Government now seeks to suppress does not mean that the law either requires or invites newspapers or others to publish them or that they will be immune from criminal action if they do. . . .

The Criminal Code contains numerous provisions potentially relevant to these cases. Section 797 makes it a crime to publish certain photographs or drawings of military installations. Section 798, also in precise language, proscribes knowing and willful publication of any classified information concerning the cryptographic systems or communication intelligence activities of the United States as well as any information obtained from communication intelligence operations. If any of the material here at issue is of this nature, the newspapers are presumably now on full notice of the position of the United States and must face the consequences if they publish. I would have no difficulty in sustaining convictions under these sections on facts that would not justify the intervention of equity and the imposition of a prior restraint.

[I am not] saying that either of these newspapers has yet committed a crime or that either would commit a crime if it published all the material now in its possession. That matter must await resolution in the context of a criminal proceeding if one is instituted by the United States. In that event, the issue of guilt or innocence would be determined by procedures and standards quite different from those that have purported to govern these injunctive proceedings.

JUSTICE MARSHALL, concurring.

. . . The Constitution provides that Congress shall make laws, the President execute laws, and courts interpret laws. *Youngstown Sheet & Tube Co. v. Sawyer,* [section 5.1, *supra*]. It did not provide for government by injunction in which the courts and the Executive Branch can "make law" without regard to the action of Congress. . . .

On at least two occasions Congress has refused to enact legislation that would have made the conduct engaged in here unlawful and given the President the power that he seeks in this case. In 1917 during the debate over the original Espionage Act, still the basic provisions of § 793, Congress rejected a proposal to give the President in time of war or threat of war authority to directly prohibit by proclamation the publication of information relating to national defense that might be useful to the enemy. . . . In 1957 the United States Commission on Government Security found that "[a]irplane journals, scientific periodicals, and even the daily newspaper have featured articles containing information and other data which should have been deleted in whole or in part for security reasons." In response to this problem the Commission proposed that "Congress enact legislation making it a crime for any person willfully to disclose without proper authorization, for any purpose whatever, information classified 'secret' or 'top secret,' knowing, or having reasonable grounds to believe, such information to have been so classified." After substantial floor discussion on the proposal, it was rejected.

CHIEF JUSTICE BURGER, dissenting.

. . . An issue of this importance should be tried and heard in a judicial atmosphere conducive to thoughtful, reflective deliberation, especially when haste, in terms of hours, is unwarranted in light of the long period the Times, by its own choice, deferred publication.[1] [I]t is hardly believable that a newspaper long regarded as a great institution in American life would fail to perform one of the basic and simple duties of every citizen with respect to the discovery or possession of stolen property or secret government documents. That duty, I had thought—perhaps naively—was to report forthwith, to responsible public officers. This duty rests on taxi drivers, Justices, and the New York Times. The course followed by the Times, whether so calculated or not, removed any possibility of orderly litigation of the issues. If the action of the judges up to now has been correct, that result is sheer happenstance. . . . I would direct that the District Court on remand give priority to the *Times* case to the exclusion of all other business of that court but I would not set arbitrary deadlines.

JUSTICE HARLAN, with whom CHIEF JUSTICE BURGER and JUSTICE BLACKMUN join, dissenting.

[T]he Court has been almost irresponsibly feverish in dealing with these cases. Both the Court of Appeals for the Second Circuit and the Court of Appeals for the District of Columbia Circuit rendered judgment on June 23. The New York Times' petition for certiorari, its motion for accelerated consideration thereof, and its application for interim relief were filed in this Court on June 24 at about 11 a.m. The application of the United States for interim relief in the *Post* case was also filed here on June 24 at about 7:15 p.m. This Court's order setting a hearing before us on June 26 at 11 a.m., a course which I joined only to avoid the

---

1   [T]he *Times* conducted its analysis of the 47 volumes of Government documents over a period of several months and did so with a degree of security that a government might envy. . . .

possibility of even more peremptory action by the Court, was issued less than 24 hours before. The record in the *Post* case was filed with the Clerk shortly before 1 p.m. on June 25; the record in the *Times* case did not arrive until 7 or 8 o'clock that same night. The briefs of the parties were received less than two hours before argument on June 26.

This frenzied train of events took place in the name of the presumption against prior restraints created by the First Amendment. Due regard for the extraordinarily important and difficult questions involved in these litigations should have led the Court to shun such a precipitate timetable.

[T]he potential consequences of erroneous decision are enormous. The time which has been available to us, to the lower* and to the parties has been wholly inadequate for giving these cases the kind of consideration they deserve. . . .

Forced as I am to reach the merits of these cases, I dissent from the opinion and judgments of the Court. . . . Even if there is some room for the judiciary to override the executive determination, it is plain that the scope of review must be exceedingly narrow. I can see no indication in the opinions of either the District Court or the Court of Appeals in the *Post* litigation that the conclusions of the Executive were given even the deference owing to an administrative agency, much less that owing to a co-equal branch of the Government operating within the field of its constitutional prerogative.

JUSTICE BLACKMUN, dissenting.

. . . Judge Wilkey, dissenting in the District of Columbia case, after a review of only the affidavits before his court (the basic papers had not then been made available by either party), concluded that there were a number of examples of documents that, if in the possession of the Post, and if published, "could clearly result in great harm to the nation," and he defined "harm" to mean "the death of soldiers, the destruction of alliances, the greatly increased difficulty of negotiation with our enemies, the inability of our diplomats to negotiate. . . ." I, for one, have now been able to give at least some cursory study not only to the affidavits, but to the material itself. I regret to say that from this examination I fear that Judge Wilkey's statements have possible foundation. I therefore share his concern. I hope that damage has not already been done. If, however, damage has been done,

---

* The hearing in the *Post* case before Judge Gesell began at 8 a.m. on June 21, and his decision was rendered, under the hammer of a deadline imposed by the Court of Appeals, shortly before 5 p.m. on the same day. The hearing in the *Times* case before Judge Gurfein was held on June 18, and his decision was rendered on June 19. The government's appeals in the two cases were heard by the Courts of Appeals for the District of Columbia and Second Circuits, each court sitting *en banc*, on June 22. Each court rendered its decision on the following afternoon.

and if, with the Court's action today, these newspapers proceed to publish the critical documents and there results therefrom "the death of soldiers, the destruction of alliances, the greatly increased difficulty of negotiation with our enemies, the inability of our diplomats to negotiate," to which list I might add the factors of prolongation of the war and of further delay in the freeing of United States prisoners, then the Nation's people will know where the responsibility for these sad consequences rests.

NOTES

1. The government never brought criminal charges against any newspaper, but it did prosecute Daniel Ellsberg. In that case the trial judge directed a verdict of acquittal because of various prosecution improprieties. On the question of the constitutionality of a criminal prosecution against a newspaper for publishing secret information leaked to it, see *Landmark Communications, Inc. v. Virginia*, 435 U.S. 829, 98 S.Ct. 1535, 56 L.Ed.2d 1 (1978). Burger, C.J., for the Court, explained that the issue:

    > whether the First Amendment permits the criminal punishment of third persons who are strangers to the inquiry, including the news media, for divulging or publishing truthful information regarding confidential proceedings of the Judicial Inquiry and Review Commission. We are not here concerned with the possible applicability of the statute to one who secures the information by illegal means and thereafter divulges it. We do not have before us any constitutional challenge to a State's power to keep the Commission's proceedings confidential or to punish participants for breach of this mandate. Nor does Landmark argue for any constitutionally compelled right of access for the press to those proceedings.

    Although confidentiality promotes the effectiveness of the judicial inquiry—

    > We conclude that the publication Virginia seeks to punish under its statute lies near the core of the First Amendment, and the Commonwealth's interests advanced by the imposition of criminal sanctions are insufficient to justify the actual and potential encroachments on freedom of speech and of the press which follow therefrom.

There were no dissents, but Stewart, J., concurring in the judgment, noted: "Though government may deny access to information and punish its theft, government may not prohibit or punish the publication of that information once it falls into the hands of the press, unless the need for secrecy is manifestly overwhelming."

2. In *Smith v. Daily Mail Publishing Co.,* 443 U.S. 97, 99 S.Ct. 2667, 61 L.Ed.2d 399 (1979), Burger, C.J., for the Court, invalidated a state statute that made it a crime for a newspaper to publish, without the written approval of the juvenile court, the name of any youth charged as a juvenile offender. The newspaper lawfully secured the information "simply by asking various witnesses, the police and an assistant prosecuting attorney who were at the school." Whether one views the statute "as a prior restraint or as a penal sanction for publishing lawfully obtained, truthful information is not dispositive because even the latter action requires the highest form of state interest to sustain its validity. [S]tate action to punish the publication of truthful information seldom can satisfy constitutional standards." *Cox Broadcasting Corp. v. Cohn,* 420 U.S. 469, 95 S.Ct. 1029, 43 L.Ed.2d 328 (1975) held that a the state, even in a right to privacy action, may not impose sanctions on the accurate publication of the name of a rape victim obtained from public records that are open to public inspection. *Butterworth v. Smith,* 494 U.S. 624, 110 S.Ct. 1376, 108 L.Ed.2d 572 (1990) invalidated a Florida statute that prohibited (with certain limited exceptions) a grand jury witness from disclosing testimony that he gave to the grand jury, even after the grand jury term had ended. A Florida news reporter wanted to publish his experiences in dealing with the grand jury. The unanimous Court found that the state's interest in preserving grand jury secrecy is either not served by, or is insufficient, to warrant prohibiting or enjoining truthful speech on matters of public concern.

7.3 FIGHTING WORDS AND HOSTILE AUDIENCES

In *Chaplinsky v. New Hampshire,* 315 U.S. 568, 62 S.Ct. 766, 86 L.Ed. 1031 (1942), Chaplinsky, encountering the city fire marshal, addressed him as a "God damned racketeer and a damned fascist." The Court upheld his conviction under a narrowly drawn state statute banning face-to-face words "having a direct tendency to cause acts of violence by the person to whom, individually, the remark is addressed." The test, said the Court, "is what men of common intelligence would understand would be words likely to cause an average addressee to fight."

Terminiello v. Chicago, 337 U.S. 1, 69 S.Ct. 894, 93 L.Ed. 1131 (1949), invalidated a breach of the peace conviction of Terminiello for denouncing Jews and others, including the turbulent and angry crowd outside the auditorium where he was speaking. The trial judge had instructed the jury to convict if the speech "stirs the public to anger, invites dispute, brings about a condition of unrest, or creates a disturbance, or if it molests the inhabitants in the enjoyment of peace and quiet by arousing alarm." The Court reversed the conviction without reaching the question of whether the speech constituted "fighting words." The jury instruction was in error. "[A] function of free speech under our system of government is to invite dispute," and to do the other things explicitly forbidden by the jury instruction. A conviction "resting on any of those grounds [relied on in the jury instruction] may not stand."

Feiner v. New York, 340 U.S. 315, 71 S.Ct. 303, 95 L.Ed. 295 (1951), upheld the disorderly conduct conviction of Feiner, who was speaking on a street corner attacking, *e.g.*, President Truman as a "bum" and the American Legion as the "Nazi Gestapo." Some in the crowd were hostile, and others favored Feiner. After he had spoken for about a half hour, urging blacks to "rise up in arms," the police arrested him and led him away in an effort to prevent violent reaction. "It is one thing to say that the police cannot be used as an instrument of suppression of unpopular views, and another to say that, when as here the speaker passed the bounds of argument or persuasion and undertakes incitement to riot, they are powerless to prevent a breach of the peace."

COHEN V. CALIFORNIA
403 U.S. 15, 91 S.Ct. 1780, 29 L.Ed.2d 284 (1971)

JUSTICE HARLAN delivered the opinion of the Court.

This case may seem at first blush too inconsequential to find its way into our books, but the issue it presents is of no small constitutional significance. Appellant Paul Robert Cohen was convicted in the Los Angeles Municipal Court of violating that part of California Penal Code § 415 which prohibits "maliciously and willfully disturbing] the peace or quiet of any neighborhood or person . . . by . . . offensive conduct. . . ." He was given 30 days' imprisonment. The facts upon which his conviction rests are detailed in the opinion of the Court of Appeal of California, Second Appellate District, as follows:

On April 26, 1968, the defendant was observed in the Los Angeles County Courthouse in the corridor outside of division 20 of the municipal court wearing a jacket bearing the words "Fuck the Draft" which were plainly visible. There were women and children present in the corridor. The defendant was arrested. The defendant testified that he wore the jacket knowing that the words were on the jacket as a means of informing the public of the depth of his feelings against the Vietnam War and the draft.

The defendant did not engage in, nor threaten to engage in, nor did anyone as the result of his conduct in fact commit or threaten to commit any act of violence. The defendant did not make any loud or unusual noise, nor was there any evidence that he uttered any sound prior to his arrest.

In affirming the conviction the Court of Appeal held that "offensive conduct" means "behavior which has a tendency to provoke *others* to acts of violence or to in turn disturb the peace," and that the State had proved this element because, on the facts of this case, "[i]t was certainly reasonably foreseeable that such conduct might cause others to rise up to commit a violent act against the person of the defendant or attempt to forceably remove his jacket." . . .

The conviction quite clearly rests upon the asserted offensiveness of the *words* Cohen used to convey his message to the public. The only "conduct" which the State sought to punish is the fact of communication. . . . Further, the State certainly lacks power to punish Cohen for the underlying content of the message the inscription conveyed. At least so long as there is no showing of an intent to incite disobedience to or disruption of the draft, Cohen could not, consistently with the First and Fourteenth Amendments, be punished for asserting the evident position on the inutility or immorality of the draft his jacket reflected.

Appellant's conviction, then, rests squarely upon his exercise of the "freedom of speech" protected from arbitrary governmental interference by the Constitution and can be justified, if at all, only as a valid regulation of the manner in which he exercised that freedom, not as a permissible prohibition on the substantive message it conveys. . . . In this vein, too, however, we think it important to note that several issues typically associated with such problems are not presented here.

In the first place, Cohen was tried under a statute applicable throughout the entire State. Any attempt to support this conviction on the ground that the statute seeks to preserve an appropriately decorous atmosphere in the courthouse where Cohen was arrested must fail. . . .

In the second place, as it comes to us, this case cannot be said to fall within those relatively few categories of instances where prior decisions have established the power of government to deal more comprehensively with certain forms of individual expression simply upon a showing that such a form was employed. This is not, for example, an obscenity case. Whatever else may be necessary to give rise to the States' broader power to prohibit obscene expression, such expression must be, in some significant way, erotic. . . .

This Court has also held that the States are free to ban the simple use, without a demonstration of additional justifying circumstances, of so-called "fighting words," those personally abusive epithets which, when addressed to the ordinary citizen, are, as a matter of common knowledge, inherently likely to provoke violent reaction. *Chaplinsky v. New Hampshire.* While the four-letter word displayed by Cohen in relation to the draft is not uncommonly employed in a personally provocative fashion, in this instance it was clearly not "directed to the person of the hearer." No individual actually or likely to be present could reasonably have regarded the words on appellant's jacket as a direct personal insult. Nor do we have here an instance of the exercise of the State's police power to prevent a speaker from intentionally provoking a given group to hostile reaction. Cf. *Feiner v. New York; Terminiello v. Chicago.* There is, as noted above, no showing that anyone who saw Cohen was in fact violently aroused or that appellant intended such a result.

Finally, in arguments before this Court much has been made of the claim that Cohen's distasteful mode of expression was thrust upon unwilling or unsuspecting viewers, and that the State might therefore legitimately act as it did in order to protect the sensitive from otherwise unavoidable exposure to appellant's crude form of protest. Of course, the mere presumed presence of unwitting listeners or viewers does not serve automatically to justify curtailing all speech capable of giving offense. While this Court has recognized that government may properly act in many situations to prohibit intrusion into the privacy of the home of unwelcome views and ideas which cannot be totally banned from the public dialogue, we have at the same time consistently stressed that "we are often 'captives' outside the sanctuary of the home and subject to objectionable speech." The ability of government, consonant with the Constitution, to shut off discourse solely to protect others from hearing it is, in other words, dependent upon a showing that substantial privacy interests are being invaded in an essentially intolerable manner. Any broader view of this authority would effectively empower a majority to silence dissidents simply as a matter of personal predilections.

In this regard, persons confronted with Cohen's jacket were in a quite different posture than, say, those subjected to the raucous emissions of sound trucks blaring outside their residences. Those in the Los Angeles courthouse could effectively avoid further bombardment of their sensibilities simply by averting their eyes. And, while it may be that one has a more substantial claim to a recognizable privacy interest when walking through a courthouse corridor than, for example, strolling through Central Park, surely it is nothing like the interest in being free from unwanted expression in the confines of one's own home. Given the subtlety and complexity of the factors involved, if Cohen's "speech" was otherwise entitled to constitutional protection, we do not think the fact that some unwilling "listeners" in a public building may have been briefly exposed to it can serve to justify this breach of the peace conviction where, as here, there was no evidence that persons powerless to avoid appellant's conduct did in fact object to it, and where that portion of the statute upon which Cohen's conviction rests evinces no concern, either on its face or as construed by the California courts, with the special plight of the captive auditor, but, instead, indiscriminately sweeps within its prohibitions all "offensive conduct" that disturbs "any neighborhood or person."

Against this background, the issue flushed by this case stands out in bold relief. It is whether California can excise, as "offensive conduct," one particular scurrilous epithet from the public discourse, either upon the theory of the court below that its use is inherently likely to cause violent reaction or upon a more general assertion that the States, acting as guardians of public morality, may properly remove this offensive word from the public vocabulary.

The rationale of the California court is plainly untenable. At most it reflects an "undifferentiated fear or apprehension of disturbance [which] is not enough to overcome the right to freedom of expression." We have been shown no evidence that substantial numbers of citizens are standing ready to strike out physically at whoever may assault their sensibilities with execrations like that uttered by Cohen. There may be some persons about with such lawless and violent proclivities, but that is an insufficient base upon which to erect, consistently with constitutional values, a governmental power to force persons who wish to ventilate their dissident views into avoiding particular forms of expression. The argument amounts to little more than the self-defeating proposition that to avoid physical censorship of one who has not sought to provoke such a response by a hypothetical coterie of the violent and lawless, the States may more appropriately effectuate that censorship themselves.

Admittedly, it is not so obvious that the First and Fourteenth Amendment must be taken to disable the States from punishing public utterance of this unseemly expletive in order to maintain what they regard as a suitable level of discourse within the body politic. . . . To many, the immediate consequence of this freedom may often appear to be only verbal tumult, discord, and even offensive utterance. These are, however, within established limits, in truth necessary side effects of the broader enduring values which the process of open debate permits us to achieve. That the air may at times seem filled with verbal cacophony is, in this sense not a sign of weakness but of strength. We cannot lose sight of the fact that, in what otherwise might seem a trifling and annoying instance of individual distasteful abuse of a privilege, these fundamental societal values are truly implicated.

[T]he principle contended for by the State seems inherently boundless. How is one to distinguish this from any other offensive word? Surely the State has no right to cleanse public debate to the point where it is grammatically palatable to the most squeamish among us. Yet no readily ascertainable general principle exists for stopping short of that result were we to affirm the judgment below. For, while the particular four-letter word being litigated here is perhaps more distasteful than most others of its genre, it is nevertheless often true that one man's vulgarity is another's lyric. Indeed, we think it is largely because governmental officials cannot make principled distinctions in this area that the Constitution leaves matters of taste and style so largely to the individual.

Additionally, we cannot overlook the fact, because it is well illustrated by the episode involved here, that much linguistic expression serves a dual communicative function: it conveys not only ideas capable of relatively precise, detached explication, but otherwise inexpressible emotions as well. In fact, words are often chosen as much for their emotive as their cognitive force. We cannot sanction the view that the Constitution, while solicitous of the cognitive content of individual speech, has little or no regard for that emotive function which, practically speaking, may often be the more important element of the overall message sought to be communicated. . . .

Finally, and in the same vein, we cannot indulge the facile assumption that one can forbid particular words without also running a substantial risk of suppressing ideas in the process. Indeed, governments might soon seize upon the censorship of particular words as a convenient guise for banning the expression of unpopular views. We have been able, as noted above, to discern little social benefit that might result from running the risk of opening the door to such grave results.

It is, in sum, our judgment that, absent a more particularized and compelling reason for its actions, the State may not, consistently with the First and Fourteenth Amendments, make the simple public display here involved of this single four-letter expletive a criminal offense. Because that is the only arguably sustainable rationale for the conviction here at issue, the judgment below must be

Reversed.

[The dissenting opinion of BLACKMUN, joined by BURGER, C.J., and BLACK, J., and joined in part by WHITE, J., is omitted.]

NOTES

1. After *Cohen,* the Court has generally overturned similar convictions on the grounds, often used in First Amendment cases, that the state statute was overbroad or too vague. *Gooding v. Wilson,* 405 U.S. 518, 92 S.Ct. 1103, 31 L.Ed.2d 408 (1972), is an illustrative case. When police officers were attempting to restore order to a public building, Wilson said to one: "White son of a bitch, I'll kill you," and to another: "You son of a bitch, if you ever put your hands on me again, I'll cut you all to pieces." The Georgia statute prohibited "opprobrious or abusive language tending to cause a breach of the peace." The majority found, after examining Georgia law, that the state standard allowed juries to determine guilt as "measured by common understanding and practice," a phrase not necessarily limited to "fighting words."

2. In *Collin v. Smith,* 578 F.2d 1197 (7th Cir.), certiorari denied 439 U.S. 916, 99 S.Ct. 291, 58 L.Ed.2d 264 (1978),[2] members of the National Socialist Party of America, clothed with the swastika and other symbols of the Nazis, planned to march in front of the Village Hall in Skokie, a Chicago suburb with a large Jewish population, including several thousand survivors of the

---

[2]   See also, *Bible Believers v. Wayne County,* 805 F.3d 228 (6th Cir. 2015) (en banc)(10 to 5). The court held that county police violated the constitutional rights of the Christian evangelists when they barred them from continuing to proselytize an angry crowd at the 2012 Arab International Festival. The dissent argued that "threat of violence" at the festival on the streets of Dearborn, Michigan "had grown too great to permit [Christian evangelists] to continue proselytizing." The majority rejected that and quoting, 5 Ronald D. Rotunda & John E. Nowak, Treatise on Constitutional Law: Substance and Procedure § 20.39(a) (5th ed. 2013), that "The authority of *Feiner* has been undercut significantly in subsequent [Supreme Court] cases."

Nazi holocaust. The court invalidated various attempts to forbid the march, including ordinance No. 77–5–N–995 prohibiting the dissemination of any materials promoting and inciting racial hatred. The court said in part:

> It is said that the proposed march is not speech, or even speech plus, but rather an invasion, intensely menacing no matter how peacefully conducted. The Village's expert psychiatric witness, in fact, testified that the effect of the march would be much the same regardless of whether uniforms and swastikas were displayed, due to the intrusion of self-proclaimed Nazis into what he characterized as predominately Jewish turf. There is room under the First Amendment for the government to protect targeted listeners from offensive speech, but only when the speaker intrudes on the privacy of the home, or a captive audience cannot practically avoid exposure. . . .
>
> This case does not involve intrusion into people's homes. There *need be* no captive audience, as Village residents may, if they wish, simply avoid the Village Hall for thirty minutes on a Sunday afternoon, which no doubt would be their normal course of conduct on a day when the Village Hall was not open in the regular course of business. Absent such intrusion or captivity, there is no justifiable substantial privacy interest to save 995 from constitutional infirmity, when it attempts, by fiat, to declare the entire Village, at all times, a privacy zone that may be sanitized from the offensiveness of Nazi ideology and symbols. [T]he ordinance could conceivably be applied to criminalize dissemination of *The Merchant of Venice* or a vigorous discussion of the merits of reverse racial discrimination in Skokie. Although there is reason to think, as the district court concluded, that the ordinance is fatally vague as well, because it turns in part on subjective reactions to prohibited conduct, we do not deem it necessary to rest our decision on that ground.

R.A.V. v. City of St. Paul
505 U.S. 377, 112 S.Ct. 2538, 120 L.Ed.2d 305 (1992)

Justice Scalia delivered the opinion of the Court.

In the predawn hours of June 21, 1990, petitioner and several other teenagers allegedly assembled a crudely-made cross by taping together broken chair legs.

They then allegedly burned the cross inside the fenced yard of a black family that lived across the street from the house where petitioner was staying. Although this conduct could have been punished under any of a number of laws,[1] one of the two provisions under which respondent city of St. Paul chose to charge petitioner (then a juvenile) was the St. Paul Bias-Motivated Crime Ordinance, which provides:

> "Whoever places on public or private property a symbol, object, appellation, characterization or graffiti, including, but not limited to, a burning cross or Nazi swastika, which one knows or has reasonable grounds to know arouses anger, alarm or resentment in others on the basis of race, color, creed, religion or gender commits disorderly conduct and shall be guilty of a misdemeanor."

Petitioner moved to dismiss this count on the ground that the St. Paul ordinance was substantially overbroad and impermissibly content-based and therefore facially invalid under the First Amendment.[2] The [Minnesota Supreme Court] rejected petitioner's overbreadth claim because, as construed in prior Minnesota cases, the modifying phrase "arouses anger, alarm or resentment in others" limited the reach of the ordinance to conduct that amounts to "fighting words," *i.e.*, "conduct that itself inflicts injury or tends to incite immediate violence . . .," *In re Welfare of R.A.V.*, (Minn.1991) (citing *Chaplinsky v. New Hampshire* (1942)), and therefore the ordinance reached only expression "that the first amendment does not protect." The court also concluded that the ordinance was not impermissibly content-based because, in its view, "the ordinance is a narrowly tailored means toward accomplishing the compelling governmental interest in protecting the community against bias-motivated threats to public safety and order." . . .

I.   In construing the St. Paul ordinance, we are bound by the construction given to it by the Minnesota court. Accordingly, we accept the Minnesota Supreme Court's authoritative statement that the ordinance reaches only those expressions that constitute "fighting words" within the meaning of *Chaplinsky*. [Assuming] that all of the expression reached by the ordinance is proscribable under the "fighting

---

[1]   The conduct might have violated Minnesota statutes carrying significant penalties. See, *e.g.*, Minn.Stat. § 609.713(1) (providing for up to five years in prison for terroristic threats); § 609.563 (arson) (providing for up to five years and a $10,000 fine, depending on the value of the property intended to be damaged); § 606.595 (criminal damage to property) (providing for up to one year and a $3,000 fine, depending upon the extent of the damage to the property).

[2]   Petitioner has also been charged, in Count I of the delinquency petition, with a violation of Minn.Stat. § 609.2231(4) (Supp.1990) (racially motivated assaults). Petitioner did not challenge this count.

words" doctrine, we nonetheless conclude that the ordinance is facially unconstitutional in that it prohibits otherwise permitted speech solely on the basis of the subjects the speech addresses. . . .

We have sometimes said that [some] categories of expression are "not within the area of constitutionally protected speech," *Roth v. United States,* 354 U.S. 476, 77 S.Ct. 1304, 1 L.Ed.2d 1498 (1957) [obscenity]; *Chaplinsky, supra,* or that the "protection of the First Amendment does not extend" to them. Such statements must be taken in context, however, and are no more literally true than is the occasionally repeated shorthand characterizing obscenity "as not being speech at all." What they mean is that these areas of speech can, consistently with the First Amendment, be regulated *because of their constitutionally proscribable content* (obscenity, defamation, etc.)—not that they are categories of speech entirely invisible to the Constitution, so that they may be made the vehicles for content discrimination unrelated to their distinctively proscribable content. Thus, the government may proscribe libel; but it may not make the further content discrimination of proscribing only libel critical of the government. We recently acknowledged this distinction in *[New York] v. Ferber,* 458 U.S. 747, 102 S.Ct. 3348, 73 L.Ed.2d 1113 (1982) where, in upholding New York's child pornography law, we expressly recognized that there was no "question here of censoring a particular literary theme. . . ." . . .

Our cases surely do not establish the proposition that the First Amendment imposes no obstacle whatsoever to regulation of particular instances of such proscribable expression, so that the government "may regulate [them] freely," post (White, J., concurring in judgment). That would mean that a city council could enact an ordinance prohibiting only those legally obscene works that contain criticism of the city government or, indeed, that do not include endorsement of the city government. Such a simplistic, all-or-nothing-at-all approach to First Amendment protection is at odds with common sense and with our jurisprudence as well.[4] . . .

The proposition that a particular instance of speech can be proscribable on the basis of one feature (*e.g.,* obscenity) but not on the basis of another (*e.g.,* opposition to the city government) is commonplace, and has found application in

---

[4] . . . Justice Stevens seeks to avoid the point by dismissing the notion of obscene anti-government speech as "fantastical," apparently believing that any reference to politics prevents a finding of obscenity. [T]hat is obviously false. A shockingly hard core pornographic movie that contains a model sporting a political tattoo can be found, "*taken as a whole* [to] lack serious literary, artistic, political, or scientific value," *Miller v. California,* 413 U.S. 15, 24, 93 S.Ct. 2607, 2614–2615, 37 L.Ed.2d 419 (1973) (emphasis added). [T]he concept of racist fighting words is, unfortunately, anything but a "highly speculative hypothetical."

many contexts. We have long held, for example, that nonverbal expressive activity can be banned because of the action it entails, but not because of the ideas it expresses—so that burning a flag in violation of an ordinance against outdoor fires could be punishable, whereas burning a flag in violation of an ordinance against dishonoring the flag is not. *Texas v. Johnson*, 491 U.S. 397, 109 S.Ct. 2533, 105 L.Ed.2d 342 (1989). Similarly, we have upheld reasonable "time, place, or manner" restrictions, but only if they are "justified without reference to the content of the regulated speech." And just as the power to proscribe particular speech on the basis of a noncontent element (*e.g.*, noise) does not entail the power to proscribe the same speech on the basis of a content element; so also, the power to proscribe it on the basis of *one* content element (*e.g.*, obscenity) does not entail the power to proscribe it on the basis of *other* content elements.

. . . Fighting words are thus analogous to a noisy sound truck: [either] can be used to convey an idea; but neither has, in and of itself, a claim upon the First Amendment. As with the sound truck, however, so also with fighting words: The government may not regulate use based on hostility—or favoritism—towards the underlying message expressed.

[T]he First Amendment imposes not an "underinclusiveness" limitation but a "content discrimination" limitation upon a State's prohibition of proscribable speech. There is no problem whatever, for example, with a State's prohibiting obscenity (and other forms of proscribable expression) only in certain media or markets, for although that prohibition would be "underinclusive," it would not discriminate on the basis of content. . . .

When the basis for the content discrimination consists entirely of the very reason the entire class of speech at issue is proscribable, no significant danger of idea or viewpoint discrimination exists. Such a reason, having been adjudged neutral enough to support exclusion of the entire class of speech from First Amendment protection, is also neutral enough to form the basis of distinction within the class. To illustrate: A State might choose to prohibit only that obscenity which is the most patently offensive *in its prurience*—*i.e.*, that which involves the most lascivious displays of sexual activity. But it may not prohibit, for example, only that obscenity which includes offensive *political* messages. And the Federal Government can criminalize only those threats of violence that are directed against the President, see 18 U.S.C. § 871—since the reasons why threats of violence are outside the First Amendment (protecting individuals from the fear of violence, from the disruption that fear engenders, and from the possibility that the threatened violence will occur) have special force when applied to the person of the President. See *Watts v. United States,* 394 U.S. 705, 707, 89 S.Ct. 1399, 1401, 22 L.Ed.2d 664 (1969) (upholding the facial validity of § 871 because of the "overwhelming interest in protecting the safety of [the] Chief Executive and in allowing him to perform his duties without interference from threats of physical violence"). But the Federal Government may not criminalize only those threats against the President that mention his policy on aid to inner cities. And to take a final example (one mentioned by Justice Stevens), a State may choose to regulate price advertising in one industry but not in others, because the risk of fraud (one of the characteristics of commercial speech that justifies depriving it of full First Amendment protection) is in its view greater there. But a State may not prohibit only that commercial advertising that depicts men in a demeaning fashion.

[S]ince words can in some circumstances violate laws directed not against speech but against conduct (a law against treason, for example, is violated by telling the enemy the nation's defense secrets), a particular content-based subcategory of a proscribable class of speech can be swept up incidentally within the reach of a statute directed at conduct rather than speech. Thus, for example, sexually derogatory "fighting words," among other words, may produce a violation of Title VII's general prohibition against sexual discrimination in employment practices, 42 U.S.C. § 2000e–2; 29 CFR § 1604.11 (1991). Where the government does not target conduct on the basis of its expressive content, acts are not shielded from regulation merely because they express a discriminatory idea or philosophy.

[T]o validate [selective restrictions on speech] (where totally proscribable speech is at issue) it may not even be necessary to identify any particular "neutral" basis, so long as the nature of the content discrimination is such that there is no realistic possibility that official suppression of ideas is afoot. (We cannot think of any First Amendment interest that would stand in the way of a State's prohibiting only those obscene motion pictures with blue-eyed actresses.) Save for that limitation, the regulation of "fighting words," like the regulation of noisy speech, may address some offensive instances and leave other, equally offensive, instances alone.

II.   Applying these principles to the St. Paul ordinance, we conclude that, even as narrowly construed by the Minnesota Supreme Court, the ordinance is facially unconstitutional. Although the phrase in the ordinance, "arouses anger, alarm or resentment in others," has been limited by the Minnesota Supreme Court's construction to reach only those symbols or displays that amount to "fighting words," the remaining, unmodified terms make clear that the ordinance applies only to "fighting words" that insult, or provoke violence, "on the basis of race, color, creed, religion or gender." Displays containing abusive invective, no matter how vicious or severe, are permissible unless they are addressed to one of the specified disfavored topics. Those who wish to use "fighting words" in connection with other ideas—to express hostility, for example, on the basis of political affiliation, union membership, or homosexuality—are not covered. The First Amendment does not permit St. Paul to impose special prohibitions on those speakers who express views on disfavored subjects.

In its practical operation, moreover, the ordinance goes even beyond mere content discrimination, to actual viewpoint discrimination. Displays containing some words—odious racial epithets, for example—would be prohibited to proponents of all views. But "fighting words" that do not themselves invoke race, color, creed, religion, or gender—aspersions upon a person's mother, for example—would seemingly be usable *ad libitum* in the placards of those arguing *in favor* of racial, color, etc. tolerance and equality, but could not be used by that speaker's opponents. One could hold up a sign saying, for example, that all "anti-Catholic bigots" are misbegotten; but not that all "papists" are, for that would insult and provoke violence "on the basis of religion." St. Paul has no such authority to license one side of a debate to fight freestyle, while requiring the other to follow Marquis of Queensberry Rules.

What we have here, it must be emphasized, is not a prohibition of fighting words that are directed at certain persons or groups (which would be *facially* valid if it met the requirements of the Equal Protection Clause); but rather, a prohibition of fighting words that contain (as the Minnesota Supreme Court repeatedly emphasized) messages of "bias-motivated" hatred and in particular, as applied to this case, messages "based on virulent notions of racial supremacy." 464 N.W.2d, at 508, 511. . . . St. Paul's brief asserts that a general "fighting words" law would not meet the city's needs because only a content-specific measure can communicate to minority groups that the "group hatred" aspect of such speech "is not condoned by the majority." The point of the First Amendment is that majority preferences must be expressed in some fashion other than silencing speech on the basis of its content.

. . . St. Paul concedes in its brief that the ordinance applies only to "racial, religious, or gender-specific symbols" such as "a burning cross, Nazi swastika or other instrumentality of like import." [T]he reason why fighting words are categorically excluded from the protection of the First Amendment is not that their content communicates any particular idea, but that their content embodies a particularly intolerable (and socially unnecessary) *mode* of expressing *whatever* idea the speaker wishes to convey. St. Paul has not singled out an especially offensive mode of expression—it has not, for example, selected for prohibition only those fighting words that communicate ideas in a threatening (as opposed to a merely obnoxious) manner. Rather, it has proscribed fighting words of whatever manner that communicate messages of racial, gender, or religious intolerance. Selectivity of this sort creates the possibility that the city is seeking to handicap the expression of particular ideas. That possibility would alone be enough to render the ordinance presumptively invalid, but St. Paul's comments and concessions in this case elevate the possibility to a certainty. . . .

Finally, St. Paul and its *amici* . . . assert that the ordinance helps to ensure the basic human rights of members of groups that have historically been subjected to discrimination, including the right of such group members to live in peace where they wish. . . . The dispositive question in this case, therefore, is whether content discrimination is reasonably necessary to achieve St. Paul's compelling interests; it plainly is not. An ordinance not limited to the favored topics, for example, would have precisely the same beneficial effect. In fact the only interest distinctively served by the content limitation is that of displaying the city council's special hostility towards the particular biases thus singled out. That is precisely what the First Amendment forbids. The politicians of St. Paul are entitled to express that hostility—but not through the means of imposing unique limitations upon speakers who (however benightedly) disagree.

Let there be no mistake about our belief that burning a cross in someone's front yard is reprehensible. But St. Paul has sufficient means at its disposal to prevent such behavior without adding the First Amendment to the fire. . . .

JUSTICE WHITE, with whom JUSTICE BLACKMUN and JUSTICE O'CONNOR join, and with whom Justice Stevens joins except as to Part I(A), concurring in the judgment. . . .

I.   (C) . . . Under the general rule the Court applies in this case, Title VII hostile work environment claims would suddenly be unconstitutional. Title VII makes it unlawful to discriminate "because of [an] individual's race, color, religion, sex, or national origin," and the regulations covering hostile workplace claims forbid "sexual harassment," which includes "unwelcome sexual advances, requests for sexual favors, and other verbal or physical conduct of a sexual nature" which creates "an intimidating, hostile, or offensive working environment." The regulation does not prohibit workplace harassment generally; it focuses on what the majority would characterize as the "disfavored topic" of sexual harassment.

In this way, Title VII is similar to the St. Paul ordinance that the majority condemns because it "imposes special prohibitions on those speakers who express views on disfavored subjects." Under the broad principle the Court uses to decide the present case, hostile work environment claims based on sexual harassment should fail First Amendment review; because a general ban on harassment in the workplace would cover the problem of sexual harassment, any attempt to proscribe the subcategory of sexually harassing expression would violate the First Amendment. . . .

JUSTICE STEVENS, with whom JUSTICE WHITE and JUSTICE BLACKMUN join as to Part I, concurring in the judgment. . . .

I. [T]he Court establishes a near-absolute ban on content-based regulations of expression and holds that the First Amendment prohibits the regulation of fighting words by subject matter. Thus, while the Court rejects the "all-or-nothing-at-all" nature of the categorical approach, it promptly embraces an absolutism of its own: within a particular "proscribable" category of expression, the Court holds, a government must either proscribe all speech or no speech at all. . . .

III. . . . The Court writes:

"One could hold up a sign saying, for example, that 'all anti-Catholic bigots' are misbegotten; but not that all 'papists' are, for that would insult and provoke violence 'on the basis of religion.' "

This may be true, but it hardly proves the Court's point. The Court's reasoning is asymmetrical. The response to a sign saying that "all [religious] bigots are misbegotten" is a sign saying that "all advocates of religious tolerance are misbegotten." Assuming such signs could be fighting words (which seems to me extremely unlikely), neither sign would be banned by the ordinance for the attacks were not "based on . . . religion" but rather on one's beliefs about tolerance. Conversely (and again assuming such signs are fighting words), just as the ordinance would prohibit a Muslim from hoisting a sign claiming that all Catholics were misbegotten, so the ordinance would bar a Catholic from hoisting a similar sign attacking Muslims.

The St. Paul ordinance is evenhanded. In a battle between advocates of tolerance and advocates of intolerance, the ordinance does not prevent either side from hurling fighting words at the other on the basis of their conflicting ideas, but it does bar both sides from hurling such words on the basis of the target's "race, color, creed, religion or gender.". . . .

[The Opinion of BLACKMUN, J., concurring in the judgment, is omitted.]

NOTES

1. Justice Stevens, before he answered Scalia's hypothetical, had to change it. He replaced "all anti-Catholic bigots" with "all [religious] bigots." The hypothetical ordinance (before Stevens' change) makes it a crime to state that "all papists are misbegotten," but not a crime to state that "all anti-Catholic bigots are misbegotten."

2. *Wisconsin v. Mitchell*, 508 U.S. 476, 113 S.Ct. 2194, 124 L.Ed.2d 436 (1993), held, unanimously, that a Wisconsin statute that enhanced a criminal defendant's sentence whenever he intentionally selects his victim based on the victim's race did not violate defendant's free speech rights. Mitchell selected and beat up his victim—"a white boy"—on the grounds of color. The First Amendment allows the state to introduce the defendant's previous declarations or statements to establish the elements of a crime or to prove motive or intent, subject to evidentiary rules dealing with relevancy, reliability, and so forth. Nothing in *R.A.V. v. St. Paul*, requires any different result. The St. Paul law was explicitly directed at speech, while the one here is aimed at conduct (assault & battery) unprotected by the First Amendment.

3. *Virginia v. Black*, 538 U.S. 343, 123 S.Ct. 1536, 155 L.Ed.2d 535 (2003), dealt with cross burnings. The divided Court held that the state may ban cross burning carried out with the "intent to intimidate" because the government can ban "true threats." "Intimidation in the constitutionally proscribable sense of the word is a type of true threat, where a speaker directs a threat to a person or group of persons with the intent of placing the victim in fear of bodily harm or death." While "some cross burnings fit within this meaning of intimidating speech," not all do. The plurality said that the Virginia statute treats any cross burning as prima facie evidence of intent to intimidate, and that renders the statute unconstitutional in its current form.

    Thomas, J., dissenting, said:

    > In our culture, cross burning has almost invariably meant lawlessness and understandably instills in its victims well—grounded fear of physical violence. [T]his statute prohibits only conduct, not expression. And, just as one cannot burn down someone's house to make a political point and then seek refuge in the First Amendment, those who hate cannot terrorize and

intimidate to make their point. In light of my conclusion that the statute here addresses only conduct, there is no need to analyze it under any of our First Amendment tests.

4. *Elonis v. United States*, 576 U.S.___, 135 S.Ct. 2001, 192 L. Ed. 2d 1 (2015) dealt with threats on Facebook. Elonis posted rap lyrics on his Facebook page containing graphically violent language and imagery about his ex-wife, coworkers, a kindergarten class, and state and federal law enforcement. His posts included disclaimers stating that the lyrics were fictitious and that he was exercising his First Amendment rights. Many people who knew him viewed his posts as threatening. His boss fired him for threatening co-workers, and his wife obtained a state court protection-from-abuse order against him. The FBI monitored him and eventually arrested him. The jury convicted him of violating 18 U.S.C. § 875(c), which makes it a crime to transmit in interstate commerce "any communication containing any threat" to "injure the person of another." The jury instruction was that Elonis was guilty if a *reasonable person* would interpret his statements as a threat. That instruction did not require the jury to determine the defendant's "mental state." Chief Justice Roberts, for the Court, reversed and held that courts should generally interpret criminal statutes to include a *scienter* requirement and *mens rea* even when the statute does not contain them. Did the speaker act with a *subjective* intent to threaten? A " 'reasonable person' standard is a familiar feature of civil liability in tort law, but is inconsistent with 'the conventional requirement for criminal conduct—*awareness* of some wrongdoing.' " (Emphasis in original). Given the statutory interpretation, "it is not necessary to consider any First Amendment issues."

7.4 THE PUBLIC FORUM

7.4.1 What Is the Public Forum?

Justice Owen Roberts, in his concurring opinion in *Hague v. C.I.O.*, 307 U.S. 496, 59 S.Ct. 954, 83 L.Ed. 1423 (1939), expressed what has become the modern view of the government's limited power to regulate speech in areas that have become a public forum. Said Roberts: "Wherever the title of streets and parks may rest, they have immemorially been held in trust for the use of the public and, time out of mind, have been used for purposes of assembly, communicating thoughts between citizens, and discussing public questions." He rejected Justice Holmes' view, expressed when he sat on the state court: "For the legislature absolutely or conditionally to forbid public speaking in a highway or public park is no more an infringement of rights of a member of the public than for the owner of a private house to forbid it in his house." *Commonwealth v. Davis,* 162 Mass. 510, 511 (1895), affirmed under the name of *Davis v. Massachusetts,* 167 U.S. 43, 17 S.Ct. 731, 42 L.Ed. 71 (1897). As the Supreme Court said many years later: "In places which by long tradition or by government fiat have been devoted to assembly and debate, the rights of the state to limit expressive activity are sharply circumscribed." The Court then quoted Justice Owen Roberts and concluded that the streets and parks are "quintessential public forums [where] the government may not prohibit all communicative activity." *Perry Education Association v. Perry Local Educator's Association,* 460 U.S. 37, 103 S.Ct. 948, 74 L.Ed.2d 794 (1983).

The state cannot simply ban speech in the public forum. Nor does it have much power to ban speech based on its content (*i.e.,* what the speech says). For example, the state can ban loud sound trucks, because they can be a nuisance. However, the state cannot ban sound trucks that blast political messages, because that would ban speech based on its content.

However, the state can place reasonable content-neutral limits on speech to protect public order. For example, public order would be disrupted if two different parades were on the same street at the same time. The Court allows reasonable time, place, or manner restrictions that are content-neutral (that is, do not discriminate on the basis of content) and leave open alternative and ample channels of communication. The first question, then, is whether government property is a public forum. If it is, are the time, place, or manner restrictions reasonable and without regard to content?

Thus, in *Schneider v. Irvington,* 308 U.S. 147, 60 S.Ct. 146, 84 L.Ed. 155 (1939), invalidated various ordinances that imposed flat bans on distributing leaflets in public places. The justification offered—to prevent littering—was insufficient because the city could less drastically prohibit the actual littering. The city had no power to prohibit a person rightfully on a public street from handing out literature to one willing to receive it.

In *Police Department of Chicago v. Mosley,* 408 U.S. 92, 92 S.Ct. 2286, 33 L.Ed.2d 212 (1972), involved a city ordinance prohibited all picketing within 150 feet of a school, *except* it allowed peaceful picketing of any school involved in a labor dispute. The Court held that this ordinance is unconstitutional because it banned a form of speech (peaceful picketing) based on the content of the speech (whether it was peaceful labor picketing or other peaceful picketing. "But, above all else, the First Amendment means that government has no power to restrict expression because of its message, its ideas, its subject matter, or its content."

In the *Perry* decision, referred to above, the Court tried to distinguish between when government property is in the public forum and when it is not. Clearly streets and parks are in the public forum; they have "immemorially been held in trust for the use of the public."

Perry explained that there is second category of public forum—places that the state has opened up for the public to use "as a place for expressive activity." For example, if a state university makes its facilities available for the activities of registered student groups, it cannot close these facilities to a registered student group because of what the group will say at the meeting. *Widmar v. Vincent,* 454 U.S. 263, 102 S.Ct. 269, 70 L.Ed.2d 440 (1981) (registered student group may use the state university room for religious worship or religious teaching).

In the third category, said *Perry,* is public property that is not a public forum. In these cases, "the state may reserve the forum for its intended purposes, communicative or otherwise, as long as the regulation on speech is reasonable and not an effort to suppress expression merely because public officials oppose the speaker's view." Thus, *Greer v. Spock,* 424 U.S. 828, 96 S.Ct. 1211, 47 L.Ed.2d 505 (1976), upheld regulations at Fort Dix because it was a military base: the base prohibited political, partisan speeches and protest marches at the base, although it allows entertainers and other speakers: "The decision of the military authorities that a civilian lecture on drug abuse, a religious service by a visiting preacher at the base chapel, or a rock musical concert would be supportive of the military mission of Fort Dix surely did not leave the authorities powerless thereafter to prevent any civilian from entering Fort Dix to speak on any subject whatever."

The Court recognizes that not all government property is a public forum, but *Perry* gave no bright line test to distinguish category two (public property that the state has opened up for public use) from category three (public property that is not a public forum). For example, not all military forts are in category three. In *Flower v. United States,* 407 U.S. 197, 92 S.Ct. 1842, 32 L.Ed.2d 653 (1972) (*per curiam*), the Court reversed the conviction of a person arrested for distributing peace leaflets on a street within a military post. The Court found that the military commander had not restricted the public from this street; he stationed no guard at the entrance or along the route; and a constant flow of civilian motor and pedestrian traffic occupied this street. Although the street was within the military base, it was treated as a public street.

The next case, decided before *Perry,* is still good law. It illustrates the problem of determining when government property is in the public forum.

ADDERLEY V. FLORIDA

385 U.S. 39, 87 S.Ct. 242, 17 L.Ed.2d 149 (1966)

JUSTICE BLACK delivered the opinion of the Court.

Petitioners, Harriett Louise Adderley and 31 other persons, were convicted by a jury in a joint trial in the County Judge's Court of Leon County, Florida, on a charge of "trespass with a malicious and mischievous intent" upon the premises of the county jail contrary to § 821.18 of the Florida statutes set out below.[1] Petitioners, apparently all students of the Florida A. & M. University in Tallahassee, had gone from the school to the jail about a mile away, along with many other students, to "demonstrate" at the jail their protests of arrests of other protesting students the day before, and perhaps to protest more generally against state and local policies and practices of racial segregation, including segregation of the jail. The county sheriff, legal custodian of the jail and jail grounds, tried to persuade the students to leave the jail grounds. When this did not work, he notified them that they must leave, that if they did not leave he would arrest them for trespassing, and that if they resisted he would charge them with that as well. Some of the students left but others, including petitioners, remained and they were arrested. On appeal the convictions were affirmed. . . .

Petitioners have insisted from the beginning of this case that it is controlled by and must be reversed because of our prior cases of *Edwards v. South Carolina,* 372 U.S. 229, 83 S.Ct. 680, 9 L.Ed. 2d 697, and *Cox v. Louisiana,* 379 U.S. 536, 559, 85 S.Ct. 453, 476, 13 L.Ed.2d 471, 487. We cannot agree.

The *Edwards* case, like this one, did come up when a number of persons demonstrated on public property against their State's segregation policies. They also sang hymns and danced, as did the demonstrators in this case. But here the analogies to this case end. In *Edwards,* the demonstrators went to the South Carolina State Capitol grounds to protest. In this case they went to the jail. Traditionally, state capitol grounds are open to the public. Jails, built for security purposes, are not. The demonstrators at the South Carolina Capitol went in through a public driveway and as they entered they were told by state officials there that they had a right as citizens to go through the State House grounds as long as they were peaceful. Here the demonstrators entered the jail grounds through a driveway used only for jail purposes and without warning to or permission from the sheriff. More importantly, South Carolina sought to

---

[1] "Every trespass upon the property of another, committed with a malicious and mischievous intent, the punishment of which is not specially provided for, shall be punished by imprisonment not exceeding three months, or by fine not exceeding one hundred dollars." Fla. Stat. § 821.18 (1965).

prosecute its State Capitol demonstrators by charging them with the common-law crime of breach of the peace. [T]he South Carolina Supreme Court had itself declared that the "breach of the peace" charge is "not susceptible of exact definition." South Carolina's power to prosecute, it was emphasized, would have been different had the State proceeded under a "precise and narrowly drawn regulatory statute evincing a legislative judgment that certain specific conduct be limited or proscribed" such as, for example, "limiting the periods during which the State House grounds were open to the public" The South Carolina breach-of-the-peace statute was thus struck down as being so broad and all-embracing as to jeopardize speech, press, assembly and petition . . . [I]t was on this same ground of vagueness that in *Cox v. Louisiana,* the Louisiana breach-of-the-peace law used to prosecute Cox was invalidated.

The Florida trespass statute under which these petitioners were charged cannot be challenged on this ground. It is aimed at conduct of one limited kind, that is, for one person or persons to trespass upon the property of another with a malicious and mischievous intent. There is no lack of notice in this law, nothing to entrap or fool the unwary.

Petitioners seem to argue that the Florida trespass law is void for vagueness because it requires a trespass to be "with a malicious and mischievous intent. . . ." But these words do not broaden the scope of trespass so as to make it cover a multitude of types of conduct as does the common-law breach-of-the-peace charge. On the contrary, these words narrow the scope of the offense.

. . . The sheriff, as jail custodian, had power, as the state courts have here held, to direct that this large crowd of people get off the grounds. There is not a shred of evidence in this record that this power was exercised, or that its exercise was sanctioned by the lower courts, because the sheriff objected to what was being sung or said by the demonstrators or because he disagreed with the objectives of their protest. The record reveals that he objected only to their presence on that part of the jail grounds reserved for jail uses. There is no evidence at all that on any other occasion had similarly large groups of the public been permitted to gather on this portion of the jail grounds for any purpose. . . . The State, no less than a private owner of property, has power to preserve the property under its control for the use to which it is lawfully dedicated. . . . The United States Constitution does not forbid a State to control the use of its own property for its own lawful nondiscriminatory purpose.

These judgments are

Affirmed.

JUSTICE DOUGLAS, with whom CHIEF JUSTICE WARREN, JUSTICE BRENNAN, and JUSTICE FORTAS concur, dissenting:

The jailhouse, like an executive mansion, a legislative chamber, a courthouse, or the state-house itself (*Edwards v. South Carolina, supra*) is one of the seats of government, whether it be the Tower of London, the Bastille, or a small county jail. And when it houses political prisoners or those who many think are unjustly held, it is an obvious center for protest. The right to petition for the redress of grievances has an ancient history and is not limited to writing a letter or sending a telegram to a congressman. . . .

There is no question that petitioners had as their purpose a protest against the arrest of Florida A. & M. students for trying to integrate public theatres. The sheriff's testimony indicates that he well understood the purpose of the rally. The petitioners who testified unequivocally stated that the group was protesting the arrests, and state and local policies of segregation, including segregation of the jail. This testimony was not contradicted or even questioned. . . . There was no violence; no threat of violence; no attempted jail break; no storming of a prison; no plan or plot to do anything but protest. The evidence is uncontradicted that the petitioners' conduct did not upset the jailhouse routine; things went on as they normally would. . . .

We do violence to the First Amendment when we permit this "petition for redress of grievances" to be turned into a trespass action. It does not help to analogize this problem to the problem of picketing. Picketing is a form of protest usually directed against private interests. I do not see how rules governing picketing in general are relevant to this express constitutional right to assemble and to petition for redress of grievances. In the first place the jailhouse grounds were not marked with "NO TRESPASSING!" signs, nor does respondent claim that the public was generally excluded from the grounds. Only the sheriff's fiat transformed lawful conduct into an unlawful trespass. To say that a private owner could have done the same if the rally had taken place on private property is to speak of a different case, as an assembly and a petition for redress of grievances run to government, not to private proprietors. . . .

. . . A noisy meeting may be out of keeping with the serenity of the statehouse or the quiet of the courthouse. No one, for example, would suggest that the Senate gallery is the proper place for a vociferous protest rally. And in other cases it may be necessary to adjust the right to petition for redress of grievances to the other interests inhering in the uses to which the public property is normally put. But this is quite different from saying that all public places are off limits to people with grievances. And it is farther yet from saying that the "custodian" of the public property in his discretion can decide when public places shall be used for the communication of ideas, especially the constitutional right to assemble and petition for redress of grievances.

NOTES

1. *United States Postal Service v. Council of Greenburgh Civic Associations,* 453 U.S. 114, 101 S.Ct. 2676, 69 L.Ed.2d 517 (1981), upheld the constitutionality of 18 U.S.C.A. § 1725, prohibiting the deposit of unstamped "mailable matter" in a letter box approved by the U.S. Postal Service. Mailboxes "are not like streets or parks but more like "the jail or prison in *Adderley v. Florida*," so it "is a giant leap from the traditional 'soap box' to the letter box designated as an authorized depository of the United States mails." Because a letterbox is not a traditional public forum, it "is thus unnecessary for us to examine § 1725 in the context of a 'time, place, and manners' restriction on the use of the traditional 'public forums'." In this case § 1725 "does not regulate speech on the basis of content." In exercising its authority to develop and operate a national postal system, Congress may "properly legislate with the generality of cases in mind, and should not be put to the test of defending in one township after another the constitutionality of a statute under the traditional 'time, place, and manner' analysis."

2. Sidewalks surrounding the Supreme Court building were at issue in *United States v. Grace,* 461 U.S. 171, 103 S.Ct. 1702, 75 L.Ed.2d 736 (1983). A federal law prohibits the "display [of] any flag, banner, or device designed or adapted to bring into public notice any party, organization, or movement" in the U.S. Supreme Court building and on its "grounds," which were defined to include the public sidewalks surrounding the Supreme Court building. The Court held that to the extent this law applied to the public sidewalks surrounding the Supreme Court building, it was unconstitutional. These sidewalks "are indistinguishable from any other sidewalks in Washington, D.C., and we can discern no reason why they should be treated any differently." Sidewalks "generally without further inquiry," are "public forum property." These sidewalks are not within a special type of enclave, such as a military base. Nor are these public sidewalks like the actual Supreme Court building and grounds which, although publicly owned, have "not been traditionally held open for the use of the public for expressive activities. [Such] property is not transformed into 'public forum' property merely because the public is

permitted to freely enter and leave the grounds at practically all times and the public is admitted to the building during specified hours."

3. **SCHOOL ASSEMBLIES.** *Bethel School District No. 403 v. Fraser*, 478 U.S. 675, 106 S.Ct. 3159, 92 L.Ed.2d 549 (1986) upheld (7 to 2) a broad power of school authorities to discipline a student for delivering at the school assembly a speech that promoted a student government candidate by using "pervasive sexual innuendo." He described his candidate as "a man who is firm—he's firm in his pants, he's firm in his shirt, his character is firm—but most of all, his belief in you, the students of Bethel, is firm." The school suspended the 17-year-old student for two days. The audience of about 600 students included students 14 years old or older. Some responded to the speech with hooting and yelling; others "by gestures [that] graphically simulated the sexual activities pointedly alluded to in respondent's speech." Burger, C.J., for the Court, said: "Surely it is a highly appropriate function of public school education to prohibit the use of vulgar and offensive terms in public discourse." The penalties imposed in this case "were unrelated to any political viewpoint." Stevens, J., dissented. The speaker was in a better position to determine whether his audience would be offended "than is a group of judges who are at least two generations, and 3,000 miles away from the scene of the crime."

4. **SCHOOL NEWSPAPERS.** *Hazelwood School District v. Kuhlmeier*, 484 U.S. 260, 108 S.Ct. 562, 98 L.Ed.2d 592 (1988) (5 to 3) held that educators may exercise broad editorial control over the contents of a high school newspaper produced as part of the school's journalism curriculum.[3] There was no First Amendment violation when the principal did not allow the school-sponsored newspaper to publish two articles, one dealing with student pregnancy and the other dealing with the impact of divorce on students. The principal was concerned that it might be easy to identify the pregnant students from the story and that the references to sexual activity and birth control were inappropriate for some of the younger students. He also believed that the second article should not be published unless the person criticized had the opportunity to defend himself.

The high school newspaper was not a public forum because the school authorities did not open it for indiscriminate use by the general public: the students publishing the newspaper received grades and academic credit; the

---

[3] In a footnote the Court stated: "We need not now decide whether the same degree of deference is appropriate with respect to school-sponsored expressive activities at the college and university level."

journalism teacher exercised a great deal of authority over the newspaper; the principal reviewed each issue prior to publication; the school subsidized the school newspaper's annual budget. This case concerns "educators' authority over school-sponsored publications, theatrical productions, and other expressive activities that students, parents, and members of the public might reasonably perceive to bear the imprimatur of the school." These activities are part of the school curriculum, even if they do not occur in a traditional classroom setting, "so long as they are supervised by faculty members and designed to impart particular knowledge or skills to student participants and audiences." A school, in its capacity as publisher of a school newspaper or producer of a school play, may "disassociate itself" from speech that is "ungrammatical, poorly written, inadequately researched, biased or prejudiced, vulgar or profane, or unsuitable for immature audiences." Educators may exercise editorial control over the style and content of student speech "in school-sponsored activities so long as their actions are reasonably related to legitimate pedagogical concerns." There is a violation of free speech only when the censorship of the school-sponsored activity "has no valid educational purpose."

5. **PUBLIC SIGNS.** *Reed v. Town of Gilbert*, 576 U.S. ___, 135 S.Ct. 2218, 192 L.Ed.2d 236 (2015). Thomas, J., for the Court, reversed the 9th Circuit, with no dissents. The sign ordinance of the Town of Gilbert is an unconstitutional, content-based regulation of speech. The town has a comprehensive sign code prohibiting the display of outdoor signs without a permit. It includes 23 exemptions, three of which apply to ideological, political, and temporary directional signs. The temporary directional signs have greater restrictions than either ideological or political signs. The Good News Community Church holds services at different facilities because it has no permanent church. It uses temporary directional signs to invite people to services. The law provides that these signs can go up only 12 hours before their Sunday services start, so the church cannot post the signs until late on Saturday night when they are harder. The restrictions "depend entirely on the communicative content of the sign." For example, the Town treats differently a sign informing its reader of the time and place a book club will discuss John Locke's Two Treatises of Government from a sign expressing the view that one should vote for one of Locke's followers in an upcoming election. The "Church's signs inviting people to attend its worship services are treated differently from signs conveying other types of ideas. On its face, the Sign Code is a content-based regulation of speech." Imposing strict limits

on temporary directional signs is hardly necessary to beautify the Town when other signs create the same problem. Nor has the Town shown that temporary directional signs pose a greater threat to public safety than ideological or political signs.

The Town has ample "content-neutral options" available to resolve problems with safety and aesthetics, such as size, building materials, lighting, moving parts, and portability. The Town can also forbid posting signs on public property, so long as it does so in an evenhanded, content-neutral manner.

7.4.2 The Procedural Context

Often the government seeks to exercise its time, place, and manner restrictions on speech in the public forum by the use of licensing schemes. When the state gives an administrator the power to withhold a license, it must do so carefully. A "licensing standard which gives an official authority to censor the content of speech" is very different from a licensing statute that is "limited by its terms, or by nondiscriminatory practice, to considerations of public safety and the like." Justice Frankfurter, concurring, in *Niemotko v. Maryland,* 340 U.S. 268, 71 S.Ct. 325, 95 L.Ed. 267 (1951).

To understand this principle let us briefly review some of the important cases. In *Lovell v. Griffin,* 303 U.S. 444, 58 S.Ct. 666, 82 L.Ed. 949 (1938), a member of the Jehovah's Witnesses was prosecuted for distributing religious tracts, in violation of duly vague city ordinance that forbade distribution of circulars and similar material without a permit from the city manager. The defendant had neither secured a license nor applied for one. The city argued that because the defendant had not applied for the license, she could not complain of being subjected to arbitrary power. A unanimous Supreme Court disagreed. Because the ordinance contained no standards to guide the administrator, it was void on its face as a prior restraint of speech. Therefore, it was not necessary for the defendant to apply for a permit—she was objecting not to a license denial but to the vague licensing procedures. As the Court later stated in *Thornhill v. Alabama,* 310 U.S. 88, 60 S.Ct. 736, 84 L.Ed. 1093 (1940): "One who might have had a license for the asking may therefore call into question the whole scheme of licensing when he is prosecuted for failure to procure it." The defendant then is not objecting to the "sporadic abuse of power by the censor" but to the "pervasive threat inherent" in the entire statutory scheme.

To be distinguished from *Lovell* and its progeny is the line of cases illustrated by *Poulos v. New Hampshire,* 345 U.S. 395, 73 S.Ct. 760, 97 L.Ed. 1105 (1953), another Jehovah's Witness case. In *Poulos* the defendant was convicted for conducting a religious service in a public park without a proper license. Unlike *Lovell,* the defendant did apply for the license. Also, unlike *Lovell,* the licensing scheme was not unduly vague nor overbroad in its application. After he was denied the license, he did not appeal that denial within the state court system; rather, he ignored the denial and held his meeting in the public park anyway. The Supreme Court upheld his conviction. First, the ordinance was valid on its face, for it required uniform, nondiscriminatory, and consistent treatment in the granting of licenses for public meetings on the public streets and in the public parks. Second, the defendant could be convicted for holding his meeting without a license even though the city had wrongfully denied him a license:

> It must be admitted that judicial correction of arbitrary refusal by administrators to perform official duties under valid laws is exulcerating and costly. But to allow applicants to proceed without the required permits to . . . hold public meetings without prior safety arrangements or take other unauthorized action is apt to cause breaches of the peace or create public dangers. . . . Delay is unfortunate, but the expense and annoyance of litigation is a price citizens must pay for life in an orderly society where the rights of the First Amendment have a real and abiding meaning.

There was no suggestion in *Poulos* that the defendant could not have had a prompt judicial determination of the license denial.

The next two cases fall on different sides of the line drawn by *Lovell* and *Poulos.* Both involve the same Birmingham ordinance, which was unconstitutionally vague—so vague that it could not be saved by a narrow state court interpretation. And both cases involve the exact same civil rights march under the leadership of Martin Luther King, Jr. In the first case, city officials persuaded an Alabama state court to enjoin the petitioners from demonstrating without a permit. The petitioners marched in violation of the injunction and were convicted of criminal contempt. The Court upheld the convictions. In the second case the petitioners were convicted of marching without a permit, in violation of the ordinance. The Court overturned these convictions.

WALKER V. CITY OF BIRMINGHAM

388 U.S. 307, 87 S.Ct. 1824, 18 L.Ed.2d 1210 (1967)

JUSTICE STEWART delivered the opinion of the Court.

On Wednesday, April 10, 1963, officials of Birmingham, Alabama, filed a bill of complaint in a state circuit court asking for injunctive relief against 139 individuals and two organizations. . . . The circuit judge granted a temporary injunction as prayed in the bill, enjoining the petitioners from, among other things, participating in or encouraging mass street parades or mass processions without a permit as required by a Birmingham ordinance.[1]

Five of the eight petitioners were served with copies of the writ early the next morning. Several hours later four of them held a press conference. There a statement was distributed, declaring their intention to disobey the injunction because it was "raw tyranny under the guise of maintaining law and order." . . . That night a meeting took place at which one of the petitioners announced that "[i]njunction or no injunction we are going to march tomorrow." The next afternoon, Good Friday, a large crowd gathered. . . . Some of the crowd followed the marchers and spilled out into the street. At least three of the petitioners participated in this march. Meetings sponsored by some of the petitioners were held that night and the following night, where calls for volunteers to "walk" and go to jail were made. On Easter Sunday, April 14, a crowd of between 1,500 and 2,000 people congregated in the midafternoon in the vicinity of Seventh Avenue and Eleventh Street North in Birmingham. One of the petitioners was seen organizing members of the crowd in formation. A group of about 50, headed by three other petitioners, started down the sidewalk two abreast. At least one other petitioner was among the marchers. Some 300 or 400 people from among the onlookers followed in a crowd that occupied the entire width of the street and overflowed onto the sidewalks. Violence occurred. Members of the crowd threw rocks that injured a newspaperman and damaged a police motorcycle.

The next day the city officials who had requested the injunction applied to the state circuit court for an order to show cause why the petitioners should not be held in contempt for violating it. At the ensuing hearing the petitioners sought to attack the constitutionality of the injunction on the ground that it was vague

---

[1]   . . . The Birmingham parade ordinance, § 1159 of the Birmingham City Code, provides that:

It shall be unlawful to organize or hold, or to assist in organizing or holding, or to take part or participate in, any parade or procession or other public demonstration on the streets or other public ways of the city, unless a permit therefor has been secured from the commission. . . . The commission shall grant a written permit . . . unless in its judgment the public welfare, peace, safety, health, decency require that it be refused.

and overbroad, and restrained free speech. They also sought to attack the Birmingham parade ordinance upon similar grounds, and upon the further ground that the ordinance had previously been administered in an arbitrary and discriminatory manner.

The circuit court refused to consider any of the contentions [holding] that the only issues before it were whether it had jurisdiction to issue the temporary injunction, and whether thereafter the petitioners had knowingly violated it. Upon these issues the court found against the petitioners, and imposed upon each of them a sentence of five days in jail and a $50 fine, in accord with an Alabama statute. The Supreme Court of Alabama affirmed. . . .

Without question the state court that issued the injunction had, as a court of equity, jurisdiction over the petitioners and over the subject matter of the controversy. And this is not a case where the injunction was transparently invalid or had only a frivolous pretense to validity. We have consistently recognized the strong interest of state and local governments in regulating the use of their streets and other public places. *Poulos v. State of New Hampshire; Adderley v. State of Florida.* When protest takes the form of mass demonstrations, parades, or picketing on public streets and sidewalks, the free passage of traffic and the prevention of public disorder and violence become important objects of legitimate state concern. . . .

The generality of the language contained in the Birmingham parade ordinance upon which the injunction was based would unquestionably raise substantial constitutional issues concerning some of its provisions. *Schneider v. State of New Jersey [Town of Irvington]*, 308 U.S. 147, 60 S.Ct. 146, 84 L.Ed. 155. The petitioners, however, did not even attempt to apply to the Alabama courts for an authoritative construction of the ordinance. Had they done so, those courts might have given the licensing authority granted in the ordinance a narrow and precise scope, as did the New Hampshire courts in *Poulos v. State of New Hampshire.* Here, just as in . . . *Poulos,* it could not be assumed that this ordinance was void on its face.

The breadth and vagueness of the injunction itself would also unquestionably be subject to substantial constitutional question. But the way to raise that question was to apply to the Alabama courts to have the injunction modified or dissolved. The injunction in all events clearly prohibited mass parading without a permit, and the evidence shows that the petitioners fully understood that prohibition when they violated it.

The petitioners also claim that they were free to disobey the injunction because the parade ordinance on which it was based had been administered in the past in an arbitrary and discriminatory fashion. In support of this claim they sought to introduce evidence that, a few days before the injunction issued, requests for permits to picket had been made to a member of the city commission. One request had been rudely rebuffed.[9] [I]t does not follow that the parade ordinance was void on its face. The petitioners, moreover, did not apply for a permit either to the commission itself or to any commissioner after the injunction issued. Had they done so, and had the permit been refused, it is clear that their claim of arbitrary or discriminatory administration of the ordinance would have been considered by the state circuit court upon a motion to dissolve the injunction.

This case would arise in quite a different constitutional posture if the petitioners, before disobeying the injunction, had challenged it in the Alabama courts, and had been met with delay or frustration of their constitutional claims. But there is no showing that such would have been the fate of a timely motion to modify or dissolve the injunction. There was an interim of two days between the issuance of the injunction and the Good Friday march. The petitioners give absolutely no explanation of why they did not make some application to the state court during that period. The injunction had issued *ex parte;* if the court had been presented with the petitioners' contentions, it might well have dissolved or at least modified its order in some respects. If it had not done so, Alabama procedure would have provided for an expedited process of appellate review. It cannot be presumed that the Alabama courts would have ignored the petitioners' constitutional claims. . . . This is not a case where a procedural requirement has been sprung upon an unwary litigant when prior practice did not give him fair notice of its existence. . . .

These precedents clearly put the petitioners on notice that they could not bypass orderly judicial review of the injunction before disobeying it. Any claim that they were entrapped or misled is wholly unfounded, a conclusion confirmed by evidence in the record showing that when the petitioners deliberately violated the injunction they expected to go to jail.

The rule of law that Alabama followed in this case reflects a belief that in the fair administration of justice no man can be judge in his own case, however exalted

---

[9]   Mrs. Lola Hendricks, *not* a petitioner in this case, testified that on April 3: ". . . I asked Commissioner Connor for the permit, and asked if he could issue the permit, or other persons who would refer me to, persons who would issue a permit. He said, 'No, you will not get a permit in Birmingham, Alabama to picket. I will picket you over to the City Jail,' and he repeated that twice."

his station, however righteous his motives, and irrespective of his race, color, politics, or religion. This Court cannot hold that the petitioners were constitutionally free to ignore all the procedures of the law and carry their battle to the streets. One may sympathize with the petitioners' impatient commitment to their cause. But respect for judicial process is a small price to pay for the civilizing hand of law, which alone can give abiding meaning to constitutional freedom.

Affirmed.

CHIEF JUSTICE WARREN, whom JUSTICE BRENNAN and JUSTICE FORTAS join, dissenting.

Petitioners in this case contend that they were convicted under an ordinance that is unconstitutional on its face because it submits their First and Fourteenth Amendment rights to free speech and peaceful assembly to the unfettered discretion of local officials. They further contend that the ordinance was unconstitutionally applied to them because the local officials used their discretion to prohibit peaceful demonstrations by a group whose political viewpoint the officials opposed. The Court does not dispute these contentions, but holds that petitioners may nonetheless be convicted and sent to jail because the patently unconstitutional ordinance was copied into an injunction—issued *ex parte* without prior notice or hearing on the request of the Commissioner of Public Safety— forbidding all persons having notice of the injunction to violate the ordinance without any limitation of time. I dissent because I do not believe that the fundamental protections of the Constitution were meant to be so easily evaded, or that "the civilizing hand of law" would be hampered in the slightest by enforcing the First Amendment in this case. . . .

These facts lend no support to the court's charges that petitioners were presuming to act as judges in their own case, or that they had a disregard for the judicial process. They did not flee the jurisdiction or refuse to appear in the Alabama courts. Having violated the injunction, they promptly submitted themselves to the courts to test the constitutionality of the injunction and the ordinance it parroted. They were in essentially the same position as persons who challenge the constitutionality of a statute by violating it, and then defend the ensuing criminal prosecution on constitutional grounds. It has never been thought that violation of a statute indicated such a disrespect for the legislature that the violator always must be punished even if the statute was unconstitutional. On the contrary, some cases have required that persons seeking to challenge the constitutionality of a statute first violate it to establish their standing to sue.

Indeed, it shows no disrespect for law to violate a statute on the ground that it is unconstitutional and then to submit one's case to the courts with the willingness to accept the penalty if the statute is held to be valid. . . .

I do not believe that giving this Court's seal of approval to such a gross misuse of the judicial process is likely to lead to greater respect for the law any more than it is likely to lead to greater protection for First Amendment freedoms. The *ex parte* temporary injunction has a long and odious history in this country, and its susceptibility to misuse is all too apparent from the facts of the case. . . .

JUSTICE DOUGLAS, with whom CHIEF JUSTICE WARREN, JUSTICE BRENNAN, and JUSTICE FORTAS concur, dissenting.

The right to defy an unconstitutional statute is basic in our scheme. Even when an ordinance requires a permit to make a speech, to deliver a sermon, to picket, to parade, or to assemble, it need not be honored when it is invalid on its face. *Lovell v. City of Griffin; Thornhill v. State of Alabama.*

[W]here a permit has been arbitrarily denied, one need not pursue the long and expensive route to this Court to obtain a remedy. The reason is the same in both cases. For if a person must pursue his judicial remedy before he may speak, parade, or assemble, the occasion when protest is desired or needed will have become history and any later speech, parade, or assembly will be futile or pointless. . . . An ordinance—unconstitutional on its face or patently unconstitutional as applied—is not made sacred by an unconstitutional injunction that enforces it.

[The dissenting opinion of BRENNAN, J., joined by WARREN, C.J., and DOUGLAS & FORTAS, JJ., is omitted.]

SHUTTLESWORTH V. CITY OF BIRMINGHAM

394 U.S. 147, 89 S.Ct. 935, 22 L.Ed.2d 162 (1969)

JUSTICE STEWART delivered the opinion of the Court.

The petitioner stands convicted for violating an ordinance of Birmingham, Alabama, making it an offense to participate in any "parade or procession or other public demonstration" without first obtaining a permit from the City Commission. The question before us is whether that conviction can be squared with the Constitution of the United States.

On the afternoon of April 12, Good Friday, 1963, 52 people, all Negroes, were led out of a Birmingham church by three Negro ministers, one of whom was the petitioner, Fred L. Shuttlesworth. . . .

At the end of four blocks the marchers were stopped by the Birmingham police, and were arrested for violating § 1159 of the General Code of Birmingham. [This *same* march and the *same* section of the Birmingham Code was the subject of the Court's opinion in *Walker v. City of Birmingham, supra.*] . . .

The petitioner was convicted for violation of § 1159 and was sentenced to 90 days' imprisonment at hard labor and an additional 48 days at hard labor in default of payment of a $75 fine and $24 costs. [The state supreme court], . . . giving the language of § 1159 an extraordinarily narrow construction, reversed the judgment of the Court of Appeals and reinstated the conviction. We granted certiorari to consider the petitioner's constitutional claims.

There can be no doubt that the Birmingham ordinance, as it was written, conferred upon the City Commission virtually unbridled and absolute power to prohibit any "parade," "procession," or "demonstration" on the city's streets or public ways. For in deciding whether or not to withhold a permit, the members of the Commission were to be guided only by their own ideas of "public welfare, peace, safety, health, decency, good order, morals or convenience." This ordinance as it was written, therefore, fell squarely within the ambit of the many decisions of this Court over the last 30 years, holding that a law subjecting the exercise of First Amendment freedoms to the prior restraint of a license, without narrow, objective, and definite standards to guide the licensing authority, is unconstitutional. "It is settled by a long line of recent decisions of this Court that an ordinance which, like this one, makes the peaceful enjoyment of freedoms which the Constitution guarantees contingent upon the uncontrolled will of an official—as by requiring a permit or license which may be granted or withheld in the discretion of such official—is an unconstitutional censorship or prior restraint upon the enjoyment of those freedoms." And our decisions have made clear that a person faced with such an unconstitutional licensing law may ignore it and engage with impunity in the exercise of the right of free expression for which the law purports to require a license. "The Constitution can hardly be thought to deny to one subjected to the restraints of such an ordinance the right to attack its constitutionality, because he has not yielded to its demands."

It is argued, however, that what was involved here was not "pure speech," but the use of public streets and sidewalks, over which a municipality must rightfully exercise a great deal of control in the interest of traffic regulation and public safety. That, of course, is true. We have emphasized before this that "the First and Fourteenth Amendments [do not] afford the same kind of freedom to those who would communicate ideas by conduct such as patrolling, marching, and picketing on streets and highways, as these amendments afford to those who communicate ideas by pure speech." "Governmental authorities have the duty and responsibility to keep their streets open and available for movement."

But our decisions have also made clear that picketing and parading may nonetheless constitute methods of expression, entitled to First Amendment protection. "Wherever the title of streets and parks may rest, they have immemorially been held in trust for the use of the public and, time out of mind, have been used for purposes of assembly, communicating thoughts between citizens, and discussing public questions. Such use of the streets and public places has, from ancient times, been a part of the privileges, immunities, rights, and liberties of citizens. The privilege of a citizen of the United States to use the streets and parks for communication of views on national questions may be regulated in the interest of all; it is not absolute, but relative, and must be exercised in subordination to the general comfort and convenience, and in consonance with peace and good order; but it must not, in the guise of regulation, be abridged or denied." *Hague v. C.I.O.,* (opinion of Mr. Justice Roberts, joined by Mr. Justice Black).

Accordingly, "[a]lthough this Court has recognized that a statute may be enacted which prevents serious interference with normal usage of streets and parks, ... we have consistently condemned licensing systems which vest in an administrative official discretion to grant or withhold a permit upon broad criteria unrelated to proper regulation of public places." Even when the use of its public streets and sidewalks is involved, therefore, a municipality may not empower its licensing officials to roam essentially at will, dispensing or withholding permission to speak, assemble, picket, or parade, according to their own opinions regarding the potential effect of the activity in question on the "welfare," "decency," or "morals" of the community.

Understandably, under these settled principles, the Alabama Court of Appeals was unable to reach any conclusion other than that § 1159 was unconstitutional. The terms of the Birmingham ordinance clearly gave the City Commission extensive authority to issue or refuse to issue parade permits on the basis of broad criteria entirely unrelated to legitimate municipal regulation of the public streets and sidewalks.

It is said, however, that no matter how constitutionally invalid the Birmingham ordinance may have been as it was written, nonetheless the authoritative construction that has now been given it by the Supreme Court of Alabama has so modified and narrowed its terms as to render it constitutionally acceptable. It is true that in affirming the petitioner's conviction in the present case, the Supreme Court of Alabama performed a remarkable job of plastic surgery upon the face of the ordinance. The court stated that when § 1159 provided that the City Commission could withhold a permit whenever "in its judgment the public welfare, peace, safety, health, decency, good order, morals or convenience require," the ordinance really meant something quite different:

> [We hold] that under § 1159 the Commission is without authority to act in an arbitrary manner or with unfettered discretion in regard to the issuance of permits. Its discretion must be exercised with uniformity of method of treatment upon the facts of each application, free from improper or inappropriate considerations and from unfair discrimination. A systematic, consistent and just order of treatment with reference to the convenience of public use of the streets and sidewalks must be followed. Applications for permits to parade must be granted if, after an investigation it is found that the convenience of the public in the use of the streets or sidewalks would not thereby be unduly disturbed.

In transforming § 1159 into an ordinance authorizing no more than the objective and even-handed regulation of traffic on Birmingham's streets and public ways, the Supreme Court of Alabama made a commendable effort to give the legislation "a field of operation within constitutional limits." We may assume that this exercise was successful, and that the ordinance as now authoritatively construed would pass constitutional muster. It does not follow, however, that the severely narrowing construction put upon the ordinance by the Alabama Supreme Court in November of 1967 necessarily serves to restore constitutional validity to a conviction that occurred in 1963 under the ordinance as it was written. . . .

In *Cox* [*v. New Hampshire,* 312 U.S. 569, 61 S.Ct. 762, 85 L.Ed. 1049] the Court found that control of the streets had not been exerted unconstitutionally. There the Court was dealing with a parade-permit statute that was silent as to the criteria governing the granting of permits. In affirming the appellants' convictions for parading without a permit, the New Hampshire Supreme Court had construed the statute to require the issuance of a permit to anybody who applied, subject only to the power of the licensing authority to specify the "time, place and manner" of the parade in order to accommodate competing demands for public use of the streets. . . .

In the present case we are confronted with quite a different situation. In April of 1963 the ordinance that was on the books in Birmingham contained language that affirmatively conferred upon the members of the Commission absolute power to refuse a parade permit whenever they thought "the public welfare, peace, safety, health, decency, good order, morals or convenience require that it be refused." It would have taken extraordinary clairvoyance for anyone to perceive that this language meant what the Supreme Court of Alabama was destined to find that it meant more than four years later; and, with First Amendment rights hanging in the balance, we would hesitate long before assuming that either the members of the Commission or the petitioner possessed any such clairvoyance at the time of the Good Friday march.

But we need not deal in assumptions. For, as the respondent in this case has reminded us, in assessing the constitutional claims of the petitioner, "[i]t is less than realistic to ignore the surrounding relevant circumstances. These include not only facts developed in the Record in this case, but also those shown in the opinions in the related case of *Walker v. City of Birmingham*." The petitioner here was one of the petitioners in the *Walker* case, in which, just two Terms ago, we had before us a record showing many of the "surrounding relevant circumstances" of the Good Friday march. As the respondent suggests, we may properly take judicial notice of the record in that litigation between the same parties who are now before us.

Uncontradicted testimony was offered in *Walker* to show that over a week before the Good Friday march petitioner Shuttlesworth sent a representative to apply for a parade permit. She went to the City Hall and asked "to see the person or persons in charge to issue permits, permits for parading, picketing, and demonstrating." She was directed to Commissioner Connor, who denied her request in no uncertain terms. "He said, 'No, you will not get a permit in Birmingham, Alabama to picket. I will picket you over to the City Jail,' and he repeated that twice." . . .

These "surrounding relevant circumstances" make it indisputably clear, we think that in April of 1963—at least with respect to this petitioner and his organization—the city authorities thought the ordinance meant exactly what it said. . . .

This case, therefore, is a far cry from *Cox v. New Hampshire*, where it could be said that there was nothing to show "that the statute has been administered otherwise than in the . . . manner which the state court has construed it to require." Here, by contrast, it is evident that the ordinance was administered so as in the words of Chief Justice Hughes, "to deny or unwarrantedly abridge the right of assembly and the opportunities for the communication of thought . . . immemorially associated with resort to public places." The judgment is

Reversed.

MR. JUSTICE BLACK concurs in the result.

MR. JUSTICE MARSHALL took no part in the consideration or decision of this case.

[The concurring opinion of HARLAN, J., is omitted.]

7.5 FAIR TRIAL VERSUS FREE PRESS

NEBRASKA PRESS ASSOCIATION V. STUART
427 U.S. 539, 96 S.Ct. 2791, 49 L.Ed.2d 683 (1976)

CHIEF JUSTICE BURGER delivered the opinion of the Court.

The respondent State District Judge entered an order restraining the petitioners from publishing or broadcasting accounts of confessions or admissions made by the accused or facts "strongly implicative" of the accused in a widely reported murder of six persons. We granted certiorari to decide whether the entry of such an order on the showing made before the state court violated the constitutional guarantee of freedom of the press. . . .

In *Sheppard v. Maxwell,* 384 U.S. 333, 86 S.Ct. 1507, 16 L.Ed.2d 600 (1966), the Court focused sharply on the impact of pretrial publicity and a trial court's duty to protect the defendant's constitutional right to a fair trial. [T]he Court ordered a new trial for the petitioner, even though the first trial had occurred 12 years before. Beyond doubt the press had shown no responsible concern for the constitutional guarantee of a fair trial; the community from which the jury was drawn had been inundated by publicity hostile to the defendant. But the trial judge "did not fulfill his duty to protect [the defendant] from the inherently prejudicial publicity which saturated the community and to control disruptive influences in the courtroom." [In *Sheppard*, a] new trial followed, in which the accused was acquitted.

Cases such as these are relatively rare, and we have held in other cases that trials have been fair in spite of widespread publicity. In *Stroble v. California,* 343 U.S. 181, 72 S.Ct. 599, 96 L.Ed. 872 (1952), for example, the Court affirmed a conviction and death sentence challenged on the ground that pretrial news accounts, including the prosecutor's release of the defendant's recorded confession, were allegedly so inflammatory as to amount to a denial of due process. The Court disapproved of the prosecutor's conduct, but noted that the publicity had receded some six weeks before trial, that the defendant had not moved for a change of venue, and that the confession had been found voluntary and admitted in evidence at trial. The Court also noted the thorough examination of jurors on *voir dire* and the careful review of the facts by the state courts, and held that petitioner had failed to demonstrate a denial of due process. . . .

. . . None of our decided cases on prior restraint involved restrictive orders entered to protect a defendant's right to a fair and impartial jury, but the opinions on prior restraint have a common thread relevant to this case. [For example] in *New York Times Co. v. United States*, [§ 7.2, *supra*], the Government sought to enjoin the publication of excerpts from a massive, classified study of this Nation's involvement in the Vietnam conflict "[E]very member of the Court, tacitly or explicitly, accepted the . . . condemnation of prior restraint as presumptively unconstitutional." . . .

The thread running through all these cases is that prior restraints on speech and publication are the most serious and the least tolerable infringement on First Amendment rights. A criminal penalty or a judgment in a defamation case is subject to the whole panoply of protections afforded by deferring the impact of the judgment until all avenues of appellate review have been exhausted. Only after judgment has become final, correct or otherwise, does the law's sanction become fully operative. A prior restraint, by contrast and by definition, has an immediate and irreversible sanction. If it can be said that a threat of criminal or civil sanctions after publication "chills" speech, prior restraint "freezes" it at least for the time. The damage can be particularly great when the prior restraint falls upon the communication of news and commentary on current events. . . .

The authors of the Bill of Rights did not undertake to assign priorities as between First Amendment and Sixth Amendment rights, ranking one as superior to the other. [I]t is not for us to rewrite the Constitution by undertaking what they declined to do. It is unnecessary, after nearly two centuries, to establish a priority applicable in all circumstances. Yet it is nonetheless clear that the barriers to prior restraint remain high unless we are to abandon what the Court has said for nearly a quarter of our national existence and implied throughout all of it.

We turn now to the record in this case to determine . . . (a) the nature and extent of pretrial news coverage; (b) whether other measures would be likely to mitigate the effects of unrestrained pretrial publicity; and (c) how effectively a restraining order would operate to prevent the threatened danger. The precise terms of the restraining order are also important. We must then consider whether the record supports the entry of a prior restraint on publication, one of the most extraordinary remedies known to our jurisprudence.

A.   . . . Our review of the pretrial record persuades us that the trial judge was justified in concluding that there would be intense and pervasive pretrial publicity concerning this case. He could also reasonably conclude, based on common human experience, that publicity might impair the defendant's right to a fair trial.

B.   . . . We have [also] examined this record to determine the probable efficacy of the measures short of prior restraint on the press and speech. There is no finding that alternative measures [discussed in *Sheppard v. Maxwell, supra*] would not have protected Simants' rights, and the Nebraska Supreme Court did no more than imply that such measures might not be adequate. Moreover, the record is lacking in evidence to support such a finding.

C.   We must also assess the probable efficacy of prior restraint on publication as a workable method of protecting Simants' right to a fair trial, and we cannot ignore the reality of the problems of managing and enforcing pretrial restraining orders. [T]he events disclosed by the record took place in a community of 850 people. It is reasonable to assume that, without any news accounts being printed or broadcast, rumors would travel swiftly by word of mouth. One can only speculate on the accuracy of such reports, given the generative propensities of rumors; they could well be more damaging than reasonably accurate news accounts. But plainly a whole community cannot be restrained from discussing a subject intimately affecting life within it. Given these practical problems, it is far from clear that prior restraint on publication would have protected Simants' rights.

D.   Finally, another feature of this case leads us to conclude that the restrictive order entered here is not supportable. At the outset the County Court entered a very broad restrictive order, the terms of which are not before us; it then held a preliminary hearing open to the public and the press. There was testimony concerning at least two incriminating statements made by Simants to private persons; the statement—evidently a confession—that he gave to law enforcement officials was also introduced. The State District Court's later order was entered after this public hearing and, as modified by the Nebraska Supreme Court, enjoined reporting of (1) "[c]onfessions or admissions against interest made by the accused to law enforcement officials"; (2) "[c]onfessions or admissions against interest, oral or written, if any, made by the accused to third parties, excepting any statements, if any, made by the accused to representatives of the news media";

and (3) all "[o]ther information strongly implicative of the accused as the perpetrator of the slayings."

To the extent that his order prohibited the reporting of evidence adduced at the open preliminary hearing, it plainly violated settled principles: "[T]here is nothing that proscribes the press from reporting events that transpire in the courtroom." *Sheppard v. Maxwell.* [O]nce a public hearing had been held, what transpired there could not be subject to prior restraint.

The third prohibition of the order was defective in another respect as well. As part of a final order, entered after plenary review, this prohibition regarding "implicative" information is too vague and too broad to survive the scrutiny we have given to restraints on First Amendment rights. The third phase of the order entered falls outside permissible limits. . . .

Of necessity our holding is confined to the record before us. But our conclusion is not simply a result of assessing the adequacy of the showing made in this case; it results in part from the problems inherent in meeting the heavy burden of demonstrating, in advance of trial, that without prior restraint a fair trial will be denied. The practical problems of managing and enforcing restrictive orders will always be present. In this sense, the record now before us is illustrative rather than exceptional. It is significant that when this Court has reversed a state conviction because of prejudicial publicity, it has carefully noted that some course of action short of prior restraint would have made a critical difference. . . .

JUSTICE WHITE, concurring.

[T]here is grave doubt in my mind whether orders with respect to the press such as were entered in this case would ever be justifiable.

JUSTICE BRENNAN, with whom JUSTICE STEWART and JUSTICE MARSHALL join, concurring in the judgment. . . .

The right to a fair trial by a jury of one's peers is unquestionably one of the most precious and sacred safeguards enshrined in the Bill of Rights. I would hold, however, that resort to prior restraints on the freedom of the press is a constitutionally impermissible method for enforcing that right; judges have at their disposal a broad spectrum of devices for ensuring that fundamental fairness is accorded the accused without necessitating so drastic an incursion on the equally fundamental and salutary constitutional mandate that discussion of public affairs in a free society cannot depend on the preliminary grace of judicial censors.

[The concurring opinion of POWELL, J., and the opinion of STEVENS, J., concurring in the judgment, are omitted.]

RICHMOND NEWSPAPERS, INC. V. VIRGINIA
448 U.S. 555, 100 S.Ct. 2814, 65 L.Ed.2d 973 (1980)

MR. CHIEF JUSTICE BURGER announced the judgment of the Court and delivered an opinion in which JUSTICE WHITE and JUSTICE STEVENS joined.

The narrow question presented in this case is whether the right of the public and press to attend criminal trials is guaranteed under the United States Constitution. . . .

We begin consideration of this case by noting that the precise issue presented here has not previously been before this Court for decision. In *Gannet Co., Inc. v. DePasquale,* 443 U.S. 368, 99 S.Ct. 2898, 61 L.Ed.2d 608 (1979), the Court was not required to decide whether a right of access to *trials,* as distinguished from hearings on *pre*trial motions, was constitutionally guaranteed. The Court held that the Sixth Amendment's guarantee to the accused of a public trial gave neither the public nor the press an enforceable right of access to a *pre* trial suppression hearing. [T]he Court did not decide whether the First and Fourteenth Amendments guarantee a right of the public to attend trials; nor did the dissenting opinion reach this issue. . . . But here for the first time the Court is asked to decide whether a criminal trial itself may be closed to the public upon the unopposed request of a defendant, without any demonstration that closure is required to protect the defendant's superior right to a fair trial, or that some other overriding consideration requires closure. . . .

We have found nothing to suggest that the presumptive openness of the trial, which English courts were later to call "one of the essential qualities of a court of justice," *Daubney v. Cooper,* 10 B. & C. 237, 240, 109 Eng.Rep. 438, 440 (K.B.1829), was not also an attribute of the judicial systems of colonial America. In Virginia, for example, such records as there are of early criminal trials indicate that they were open, and nothing to the contrary has been cited. . . . Both Hale in the 17th century and Blackstone in the 18th saw the importance of openness to the proper functioning of a trial; it gave assurance that the proceedings were conducted fairly to all concerned, and it discouraged perjury, the misconduct of participants, and decisions based on secret bias or partiality. . . . The early history of open trials in part reflects the widespread acknowledgement, long before there were behavioral scientists, that public trials had significant community therapeutic value. Even without such experts to frame the concept in words, people sensed from experience and observation that, especially in the administration of criminal justice, the means used to achieve justice must have the support derived from public acceptance of both the process and its results. . . .

The First Amendment, in conjunction with the Fourteenth, prohibits governments from "abridging the freedom of speech, or of the press; or the right of the people peaceably to assemble, and to petition the Government for a redress of grievances." These expressly guaranteed freedoms share a common core purpose of assuring freedom of communication on matters relating to the functioning of government. Plainly it would be difficult to single out any aspect of government of higher concern and importance to the people than the manner in which criminal trials are conducted; . . . What this means in the context of trials is that the First Amendment guarantees of speech and press, standing alone, prohibit government from summarily closing courtroom doors which had long been open to the public at the time that amendment was adopted. . . .

It is not crucial whether we describe this right to attend criminal trials to hear, see, and communicate observations concerning them as a "right of access," or a "right to gather information," for we have recognized that "without some protection for seeking out the news, freedom of the press could be eviscerated." The explicit, guaranteed rights to speak and to publish concerning what takes place at a trial would lose much meaning if access to observe the trial could, as it was here, be foreclosed arbitrarily.

We hold that the right to attend criminal trials[17] is implicit in the guarantees of the First Amendment; without the freedom to attend such trials, which people have exercised for centuries, important aspects of freedom of speech and "of the press could be eviscerated."

Having concluded there was a guaranteed right of the public under the First and Fourteenth Amendments to attend the trial of Stevenson's case, we return to the closure order challenged by appellants. The Court in *Gannett,* made clear that although the Sixth Amendment guarantees the accused a right to a public trial, it does not give a right to a private trial. Despite the fact that this was the fourth trial of the accused, the trial judge made no findings to support closure; no inquiry was made as to whether alternative solutions would have met the need to ensure fairness; there was no recognition of any right under the Constitution for the public or press to attend the trial. In contrast to the pretrial proceeding dealt with in *Gannett,* there exist in the context of the trial itself various tested alternatives to satisfy the constitutional demands of fairness. See, *e.g., Nebraska Press Association v. Stuart.* There was no suggestion that any problems with witnesses could not have been dealt with by their exclusion from the courtroom or their sequestration

---

[17]   Whether the public has a right to attend trials of civil cases is a question not raised by this case, but we note that historically both civil and criminal trials have been presumptively open.

during the trial. Nor is there anything to indicate that sequestration of the jurors would not have guarded against their being subjected to any improper information. All of the alternatives admittedly present difficulties for trial courts, but none of the factors relied on here was beyond the realm of the manageable. Absent an overriding interest articulated in findings, the trial of a criminal case must be open to the public.[18] Accordingly, the judgment under review is reversed.

Reversed.

MR. JUSTICE POWELL took no part in the consideration or decision of this case.

MR. JUSTICE STEVENS, concurring:

This is a watershed case. Until today the Court has accorded virtually absolute protection to the dissemination of information or ideas, but never before has it squarely held that the acquisition of newsworthy matter is entitled to any constitutional protection whatsoever. An additional word of emphasis is therefore appropriate. [F]or the first time, the Court unequivocally holds that an arbitrary interference with access to important information is an abridgement of the freedoms of speech and of the press protected by the First Amendment.

[The opinion of BRENNAN, J., joined by MARSHALL, JJ., concurring in the judgment; the opinion of BLACKMUN, J., concurring in the judgment; the concurring opinion of WHITE, J., and the dissent of REHNQUIST, J., are omitted.]

NOTES

1.   The Sixth Amendment gives the accused a right to a public trial but not a right to a private trial. In *Richmond Newspapers, Inc. v. Virginia*, 448 U.S. 555, 100 S.Ct. 2814, 65 L.Ed.2d 973 (1980), the Court, with no majority opinion, ruled that under the First Amendment, trials in criminal case must be open to the public. The plurality said, "Absent an overriding interest articulated in findings, the trial of a criminal case must be open to the public." The plurality did not give any examples of what might be an "overriding interest." It did

---

[18]   We have no occasion here to define the circumstances in which all or parts of a criminal trial may be closed to the public, but our holding today does not mean that the First Amendment rights of the public and representatives of the press are absolute. Just as a government may impose reasonable time, place, and manner restrictions upon the use of its streets in the interest of such objectives as the free flow of traffic, so may a trial judge, in the interest of the fair administration of justice, impose reasonable limitations on access to a trial. . . . It is far more important that trials be conducted in a quiet and orderly setting than it is to preserve that atmosphere on city streets. Moreover, since courtrooms have limited capacity, there may be occasions when not every person who wishes to attend can be accommodated. In such situations, reasonable restrictions on general access are traditionally imposed, including preferential seating for media representatives.

say that if there were any problems with the witnesses or jurors, the trial court could sequester them during the trial.

2. *Globe Newspaper Co. v. Superior Court,* 457 U.S. 596, 102 S.Ct. 2613, 73 L.Ed.2d 248 (1982), involved a statute, unique to Massachusetts, that *required* trial judges to exclude the press and general public from the courtroom during the testimony of the victim in cases involving certain specified sexual offenses. The Court invalidated the mandatory state law (which required no particularized determinations in individual cases), but left open the possibility that under appropriate circumstances and in individual cases the trial court could exclude the press and public during the testimony of minor victims of sex crimes. The Court, per Justice Brennan, explained that under *Richmond Newspapers* the First Amendment, as applied to the states, grants to the press and general public "a right of access to *criminal trials*" (emphasis in original). Thus, states may deny access only if denial serves "a compelling governmental interest, and is narrowly tailored to serve that interest." The judge should consider the minor victim's wishes regarding disclosure, as well as the victim's age and maturity, the interests of relatives, the nature of the crime, and so on. In the present case the defendant objected to closure, the state made no motion for closure, and the victims may have been willing to testify without closure.

3. *Seattle Times Co. v. Rhinehart,* 467 U.S. 20, 104 S.Ct. 2199, 81 L.Ed.2d 17 (1984), was a *civil* case. The unanimous Court upheld a state court's protective order that prohibited a newspaper (a defendant in a libel case) from publishing pretrial discovery information in advance of trial regarding the plaintiff's financial affairs and names and addresses of donors, clients, or members of the plaintiff's religious group. The newspaper could not use the information it procured by discovery (because it was a party in that case) in any way except where necessary to prepare for and try the case. The protective order did not apply to information gained by means other than the discovery process. Discovery rules are a matter of "legislative grace," and a "litigant has no First Amendment right of access to information made available only for purposes of trying his suit." A protective order "prohibiting dissemination of discovered information before trial is not the kind of classic prior restraint that requires exacting First Amendment scrutiny." If a court issues a protective order on a showing of good cause, limited to the pretrial civil discovery, and does not restrict the dissemination of information if gained from other sources, it does not offend the First Amendment.

4. In *Press-Enterprise Co. v. Superior Court,* 464 U.S. 501, 104 S.Ct. 819, 78 L.Ed.2d 629 (1984), the Court held that the First Amendment guarantee of open criminal trials also applied to *voir dire* examination of potential jurors. The trial in this case involved the rape and murder of a teenage girl. Generalized interests in protecting the accused's right to a fair trial and the prospective jurors' right to privacy do not without more, overcome the presumption of openness. "The presumption of openness may be overcome only by an overriding interest based on findings that closure is essential to preserve higher values and is narrowly tailored to serve that interest. The interest is to be articulated along with findings specific enough that a reviewing court can determine whether the closure order was properly entered."

5. In *Branzburg v. Hayes,* 408 U.S. 665, 92 S.Ct. 2646, 33 L.Ed.2d 626 (1972), the Court (5 to 4) rejected a news reporter's claim for a constitutional privilege to refuse to reveal confidential sources when questioned by a grand jury. Branzburg had written an article in the *Courier-Journal* describing in detail his observations of two young residents of Jefferson County synthesizing hashish from marihuana, an activity that they claimed earned them about $5,000 in three weeks. The article included a photograph of a pair of hands working above a laboratory table with a substance identified by the caption as hashish. Branzburg promised not to reveal the identity of the two hashish makers. Shortly thereafter, the Jefferson County grand jury subpoenaed Branzburg, who appeared but refused to identify the individuals he had seen possessing marihuana or the persons he had seen making hashish from marihuana. A state trial court judge ordered Branzburg to answer these questions, and a narrow majority of the Supreme Court affirmed, rejecting the argument that if a reporter must breach his confidences, his sources would dry up "all to the detriment of the free flow of information protected by the First Amendment." The majority did say that a grand jury investigation conducted "other than in good faith" would pose "wholly different issues.

Justice Powell, who cast the crucial fifth vote, would apply the *Branzburg* rule more narrowly:

> [I]f the newsman is called upon to give information bearing only a remote and tenuous relationship to the subject of the investigation, or if he has some other reason to believe that his testimony implicates confidential source relationships without a legitimate need of law enforcement, he will have access to the Court on a

motion to quash and an appropriate protective order may be entered.

6. In *Chandler v. Florida,* 449 U.S. 560, 101 S.Ct. 802, 66 L.Ed.2d 740 (1981), Chief Justice Burger, for the Court, held that a state may provide for radio, television, and still photographic coverage of a criminal trial for public broadcast, notwithstanding the objection of the criminal defendant. The Court refused to issue any blanket, *per se* prohibition based on the First Amendment against radio, television, and photographic coverage of the trial.

7.6 COMMERCIAL SPEECH

CENTRAL HUDSON GAS & ELECTRIC CORP. V. PUBLIC SERVICE COMMISSION
447 U.S. 557, 100 S.Ct. 2343, 65 L.Ed.2d 341 (1980)

MR. JUSTICE POWELL delivered the opinion of the Court.

This case presents the question whether a regulation of the Public Service Commission of the State of New York violates the First and Fourteenth Amendments because it completely bans promotional advertising by an electrical utility.

In December 1973, the Commission, appellee here, ordered electric utilities in New York State to cease all advertising that "promot[es] the use of electricity." . . . The Commission declared all promotional advertising contrary to the national policy of conserving energy. [T]he Commission adopted the restriction because it was deemed likely to "result in some dampening of unnecessary growth" in energy consumption. . . .

The Commission's order restricts only commercial speech, that is, expression related solely to the economic interests of the speaker and its audience. The First Amendment, as applied to the States through the Fourteenth Amendment, protects commercial speech from unwarranted governmental regulation. Commercial expression not only serves the economic interest of the speaker, but also assists consumers and furthers the societal interest in the fullest possible dissemination of information. In applying the First Amendment to this area, we have rejected the "highly paternalistic" view that government has complete power to suppress or regulate commercial speech. "[P]eople will perceive their own best interests if only they are well enough informed, and . . . the best means to that end is to open the channels of communication rather than to close them. . . ." Even when advertising communicates only an incomplete version of the relevant facts, the First Amendment presumes that some accurate information is better than no information at all.

Nevertheless, our decisions have recognized "the 'commonsense' distinction between speech proposing a commercial transaction, which occurs in an area traditionally subject to government regulation, and other varieties of speech." The Constitution therefore accords a lesser protection to commercial speech than to other constitutionally guaranteed expression. The protection available for particular commercial expression turns on the nature both of the expression and of the governmental interests served by its regulation.

The First Amendment's concern for commercial speech is based on the informational function of advertising. Consequently, there can be no constitutional objection to the suppression of commercial messages that do not accurately inform the public about lawful activity. The government may ban forms of communication more likely to deceive the public than to inform it, or commercial speech related to illegal activity, *Pittsburgh Press Co. v. Human Relations Comm'n*, 413 U.S. 376, 388, 93 S.Ct. 2553, 2560, 37 L.Ed.2d 669 (1973).[6] If the communication is neither misleading nor related to unlawful activity, the government's power is more circumscribed. . . .[9]

In commercial speech cases, then, a four-part analysis has developed. At the outset, we must determine whether the expression is protected by the First Amendment. For commercial speech to come within that provision, it at least must concern lawful activity and not be misleading. Next, we ask whether the asserted governmental interest is substantial. If both inquiries yield positive answers, we must determine whether the regulation directly advances the governmental interest asserted, and whether it is not more extensive than is necessary to serve that interest.

The Commission does not claim that the expression at issue either is inaccurate or relates to unlawful activity. [Because] appellant holds a monopoly over the sale of electricity in its service area, the state court suggested that the

---

[6]   In most other contexts, the First Amendment prohibits regulation based on the content of the message. Two features of commercial speech permit regulation of its content. First, commercial speakers have extensive knowledge of both the market and their products. Thus, they are well situated to evaluate the accuracy of their messages and the lawfulness of the underlying activity. In addition, commercial speech, the offspring of economic self-interest, is a hardy breed of expression that is not "particularly susceptible to being crushed by overbroad regulation."

[9]   We review with special care regulations that entirely suppress commercial speech in order to pursue a nonspeech-related policy. [A] ban on speech could screen from public view the underlying governmental policy. [I]n recent years this Court has not approved a blanket ban on commercial speech unless the expression itself was flawed in some way, either because it was deceptive or related to unlawful activity.

Commission's order restricts no commercial speech of any worth. . . . Even in monopoly markets, the suppression of advertising reduces the information available for consumer decisions and thereby defeats the purpose of the First Amendment. . . .

The Commission offers two state interests as justifications for the ban on promotional advertising. The first concerns energy conservation. [N]o one can doubt the importance of energy conservation. Plainly, therefore, the state interest asserted is substantial. . . . The State's concern that rates be fair and efficient represents a clear and substantial governmental interest.

Next, we focus on the relationship between the State's interests and the advertising ban. Under this criterion, the Commission's laudable concern over the equity and efficiency of appellant's rates does not provide a constitutionally adequate reason for restricting protected speech. The link between the advertising prohibition and appellant's rate structure is, at most, tenuous. . . .

The Commission also has not demonstrated that its interest in conservation cannot be protected adequately by more limited regulation of appellant's commercial expression. To further its policy of conservation, the Commission could attempt to restrict the format and content of Central Hudson's advertising. It might, for example, require that the advertisements include information about the relative efficiency and expense of the offered service, both under current conditions and for the foreseeable future. In the absence of a showing that more limited speech regulation would be ineffective, we cannot approve the complete suppression of Central Hudson's advertising. . . .

MR. JUSTICE BLACKMUN, with whom MR. JUSTICE BRENNAN joins, concurring in the judgment.

I agree with the Court that the Public Service Commission's ban on promotional advertising of electricity by public utilities is inconsistent with the First and Fourteenth Amendments. I concur only in the Court's judgment, however, because [its test] does not provide adequate protection for truthful, nonmisleading, noncoercive commercial speech.

The Court asserts that "a four-part analysis has developed" from our decisions concerning commercial speech. . . . I agree with the Court that this level of intermediate scrutiny is appropriate for a restraint on commercial speech designed to protect consumers from misleading or coercive speech, or a regulation related to the time, place, or manner of commercial speech. I do not agree, however, that the Court's four-part test is the proper one to be applied when a

State seeks to suppress information about a product in order to manipulate a private economic decision that the State cannot or has not regulated or outlawed directly. . . .

I seriously doubt whether suppression of information concerning the availability and price of a legally offered product is ever a permissible way for the State to "dampen" demand for or use of the product. Even though "commercial" speech is involved, such a regulatory measure strikes at the heart of the First Amendment. [T]t is a covert attempt by the State to manipulate the choices of its citizens, not by persuasion or direct regulation, but by depriving the public of the information needed to make a free choice. As the Court recognizes, the State's policy choices are insulated from the visibility and scrutiny that direct regulation would entail and the conduct of citizens is molded by the information that government chooses to give them. Ante, at n. 9. See Rotunda, *The Commercial Speech Doctrine in the Supreme Court*, 1976 U. of Ill. Law Forum 1080, 1080–1083 (1976). If the First Amendment guarantee means anything, it means that, absent clear and present danger, government has no power to restrict expression because of the effect its message is likely to have on the public. . . .

It appears that the Court would permit the State to ban all direct advertising of air conditioning, assuming that a more limited restriction on such advertising would not effectively deter the public from cooling its homes. In my view, our cases do not support this type of suppression. If a governmental unit believes that use or over-use of air conditioning is a serious problem, it must attack that problem directly, by prohibiting air conditioning or regulating thermostat levels. . . .

MR. JUSTICE STEVENS, with whom MR. JUSTICE BRENNAN joins, concurring in the judgment.

. . . The Court first describes commercial speech as "expression related solely to the economic interests of the speaker and its audience." Although it is not entirely clear whether this definition uses the subject matter of the speech or the motivation of the speaker as the limiting factor, it seems clear to me that it encompasses speech that is entitled to the maximum protection afforded by the First Amendment. Neither a labor leader's exhortation to strike, nor an economist's dissertation on the money supply, should receive any lesser protection because the subject matter concerns only the economic interests of the audience. Nor should the economic motivation of a speaker qualify his constitutional protection; even Shakespeare may have been motivated by the prospect of pecuniary reward. Thus, the Court's first definition of commercial speech is unquestionably too broad.

The Court's second definition refers to "speech proposing a commercial transaction." [This definition] should not include the entire range of communication that is embraced within the term "promotional advertising." [I]f the perceived harm associated with greater electrical usage is not sufficiently serious to justify direct regulation, surely it does not constitute the kind of clear and present danger that can justify the suppression of speech. [I concur] because I do not consider this to be a "commercial speech" case. . . .

[The opinion of BRENNAN, J. concurring in the judgment, and the dissenting opinion of REHNQUIST, J., are omitted.]

NOTES

1. *First National Bank v. Bellotti*, 435 U.S. 765, 98 S.Ct. 1407, 55 L.Ed.2d 707 (1978) invalidated a Massachusetts criminal statute that forbade corporations from spending money to influence the vote on referendums. The banks in this case wanted to publicize their views against a proposed state constitutional amendment that would allow a graduated personal income tax:

    > The inherent worth of the speech in terms of its capacity for informing the public does not depend upon the identity of its source, whether corporation, association, union, or individual . . . A commercial advertisement is constitutionally protected not so much because it pertains to the seller's business as because it furthers the societal interest in the "free flow of commercial information."

2. **OUTDOOR ADVERTISING.** In *Linmark Associates, Inc. v. Township of Willingboro*, 431 U.S. 85, 97 S.Ct. 1614, 52 L.Ed.2d 155 (1977), Justice Marshall, for a unanimous Court, invalidated a township ordinance that prohibited the posting "For Sale" or "Sold" signs. The purpose of the prohibition was to stem the flight of white homeowners from a racially integrated community. The township did not ban all lawn signs; rather, it prohibited particular signs because of their content, "because it fears their 'primary' effect—that they will cause those receiving the information to act on it." In order to promote integrated housing, Willingboro could "create inducements to retain individuals who are considering selling their homes," but it could not ban "for sale" signs because of their content. The First Amendment "disabled

the State from achieving its goal by restricting the free flow of truthful information."

City of Ladue v. Gilleo, 512 U.S. 43, 114 S.Ct. 2038, 129 L.Ed.2d 36 (1994) unanimously invalidated a city ordinance that banned most residential signs. The law allowed small residential signs advertising that the property is for sale, signs for churches and schools, commercial signs in commercially zoned districts, etc. It did not allow Margaret Gilleo to display an 8.5 by 11 inch sign in her window: "For Peace in the Gulf." She opposed the Persian Gulf War. The City justified the ordinance because signs "tarnish the natural beauty of the landscape."

3.   **LAWYERS.** In 1977, the Supreme Court invalidated state regulations forbidding lawyers from advertising the prices at which certain routine services will be performed. *Bates v. State Bar of Arizona,* 433 U.S. 350, 97 S.Ct. 2691, 53 L.Ed.2d 810 (1977).

Shapero v. Kentucky Bar Association, 486 U.S. 466, 108 S.Ct. 1916, 100 L.Ed.2d 475 (1988) (6 to 3) invalidated state prohibitions against lawyers sending truthful, non-deceptive letters to potential clients known to face particular legal problems (targeted, direct-mail advertising). Targeted mailing is merely a more efficient form of mass mailing. Brennan, J., in a plurality opinion, went on to conclude that the letter was not misleading simply because it contained assertions that stated no objective fact ("It may surprise you what I may be able to do for you").

7.7 CAMPAIGN FINANCE

INTRODUCTORY NOTE

Congress enacted the Federal Election Campaign Act in response to the Watergate scandal. Various candidates for federal office and political parties and organizations brought action challenging it constitutionality on First Amendment grounds. *Buckley v. Valeo,* 424 U.S. 1, 96 S. Ct. 612, 46 L. Ed. 2d 659 (1976) (per curiam). Plaintiffs included the American Civil Liberties Union, the American Conservative Union, a U.S. Senator (James L. Buckley, Conservative Party, N.Y.), former Senator Eugene J. McCarthy, a prominent Democratic opponent of the Viet Nam war, Stewart R. Mott, who described himself as "particularly active in the Vietnam protest movement," and others. *Buckley* upheld most of the Federal

Election Campaign Act of 1977. The per curiam opinion and the various separate dissents and concurring opinions totaled 294 pages in the U.S. Reports.

In particular, the Court upheld provisions limiting individual *contributions* to campaigns. The majority said that the speech interests in campaign contributions are marginal, because they convey only an undifferentiated expression of support. "To the extent that large contributions are given to secure a political *quid pro quo* from current and potential office holders, the integrity of our system of representative democracy is undermined." *Buckley* allows the legislature to limit large *contributions* to a candidate because of the perception of undue influence flowing from such contributions. Allowing small contributions allows each contributor to express his or her support, but does not preclude that person from expressing his or her own political views.

In contrast, the majority invalidated the *expenditures* for political campaign activities. "[V]irtually every means of communicating ideas in today's mass society require the expenditure of money." When the government limits expenditures, it is directly limiting communications. The whole purpose of the limit on expenditures is to suppress communication, but the First Amendment forbids that. The Court held that the amount of money an individual could spend to advocate either his or her own candidacy or that of another is a matter within his own discretion. A person cannot corrupt himself by spending his own money on his candidacy or his viewpoint.

Chief Justice Burger, one of the dissenters in *Buckley*, quoted Senator Howard Baker's warning during the debate on this legislation:

> [T]here is something politically incestuous about the Government financing and, I believe, inevitably then regulating, the day-to-day procedures by which the Government is selected. [I]t is extraordinarily important that the Government not control the machinery by which the public expresses the range of its desires, demands, and dissent.

Buckley led to a host of others, all accepting the contribution/expenditure distinction. As *Buckley* said, "The major evil associated with rapidly increasing campaign expenditures is the danger of candidate dependence on large contributions. The interest in alleviating the corrupting influence of large contributions is served by the Act's contribution limitations and disclosure provisions rather than by" the law's "campaign expenditure ceilings."

In McConnell v. Federal Election Commission, 540 U.S. 93, 124 S.Ct. 619, 157 L.Ed.2d 491 (2003) the Court upheld most of the Bipartisan Campaign Reform

Act of 2002 (BCRA). BCRA amended various statutes, including the Federal Election Campaign Act of 1971 (FECA), which was the focus in *Buckley v. Valeo*. A divided Supreme Court issued opinions totaling nearly 300 pages in the U.S. Reporter system, including dissents. BCRA, like the Internal Revenue Code, is complex, and the Supreme Court opinion is not light reading. The divided Court upheld most of the law on its face and said it would deal as-applied challenges if any party brought them.

Davis v. Federal Election Commission, 554 U.S. 724, 128 S.Ct. 2759, 171 L.Ed.2d 737 (2008) (5 to 4), invalidated a portion of BCCR that it did not consider in *McConnell*. The so-called Millionaire's Amendment limited individual contributions to a candidate to $2,300 per campaign. The law also limited coordinated expenditures by political party committees to $40,900. If, however, a candidate is running against a self-financed candidate (an opponent spending $350,000 or more of his or her own money), then the law eased the restrictions, but only for the non-self-financing candidate, by (1) trebling his individual contribution limit and (2) allowing unlimited coordinated party expenditures. The Government justified the Amendment as an attempt to level the playing field for less-wealthy candidates. *Buckley v. Valeo* already rejected a cap on a candidate's expenditure of personal funds to finance his own campaign speech. The interest in preventing the "actual and apparent corruption of the political process" does not justify penalizing a candidate who uses his own money. He cannot corrupt himself. The law imposes discriminatory fundraising limitations on any candidate who "robustly exercise" First Amendment rights. "[I]t is a dangerous business for Congress to use the election laws to influence the voters' choices."

McConnell upheld a portion of BCCRA that primarily prohibits corporations and labor unions from using general treasury funds for *independent* communications that are intended to (or have the effect of) influencing the outcome of federal elections within certain time periods (30 to 60 day period preceding federal primary and general elections). The ban applied even if advertisements did not "expressly" advocate the election or defeat of federal candidates (*i.e.*, did not use so-called "magic words"). For example, the Union could not buy an advertisement that said, "Free trade kills jobs," just as a corporation could not advertise, "We need free trade to s support our export industry. The Court revisited that issue *in Citizens United v. FEC* (2010), which follows these NOTES.

CITIZENS UNITED V. FEDERAL ELECTION COMMISSION

558 U.S. 310, 130 S.Ct. 876, 175 L.Ed.2d 753 (2010)

JUSTICE KENNEDY delivered the opinion of the Court.

Federal law prohibits corporations and unions from using their general treasury funds to make independent expenditures for speech defined as an "electioneering communication" or for speech expressly advocating the election or defeat of a candidate. Limits on electioneering communications were upheld in *McConnell v. Federal Election Comm'n* (2003). [We now hold that] Government may regulate corporate political speech through disclaimer and disclosure requirements, but it may not suppress that speech altogether. We turn to the case now before us.

Citizens United is a nonprofit corporation [and] has an annual budget of about $12 million. Most of its funds are from donations by individuals; but, in addition, it accepts a small portion of its funds from for-profit corporations.

In January 2008, Citizens United released a film entitled *Hillary: The Movie*. We refer to the film as *Hillary*. It is a 90-minute documentary about then-Senator Hillary Clinton, who was a candidate in the Democratic Party's 2008 Presidential primary elections. *Hillary* mentions Senator Clinton by name and depicts interviews with political commentators and other persons, most of them quite critical of Senator Clinton. *Hillary* was released in theaters and on DVD, but Citizens United wanted to increase distribution by making it available through video-on-demand.

To implement the proposal, Citizens United was prepared to pay for the video-on-demand; and to promote the film, it produced two 10-second ads and one 30-second ad for *Hillary*. Each ad includes a short (and, in our view, pejorative) statement about Senator Clinton, followed by the name of the movie and the movie's Website address. Citizens United desired to promote the video-on-demand offering by running advertisements on broadcast and cable television.

[T]he Bipartisan Campaign Reform Act of 2002 (BCRA), [prohibits] any "electioneering communication," [which] is defined as "any broadcast, cable, or satellite communication" that "refers to a clearly identified candidate for Federal office" and is made within 30 days of a primary or 60 days of a general election. The Federal Election Commission's (FEC) regulations further define an electioneering communication as a communication that is "publicly distributed." "In the case of a candidate for nomination for President . . . *publicly distributed* means" that the communication "[c]an be received by 50,000 or more persons in a State where a primary election . . . is being held within 30 days." Corporations and unions are barred from using their general treasury funds* for express advocacy or electioneering communications. They may establish, however, a "separate segregated fund" (known as a political action committee, or PAC) for these purposes. The moneys received by the segregated fund are limited to donations from stockholders and employees of the corporation or, in the case of unions, members of the union.

Citizens United wanted to make *Hillary* available through video-on-demand within 30 days of the 2008 primary elections. It feared, however, that both the film and the ads would be covered by § 441b's ban on corporate-funded independent expenditures, thus subjecting the corporation to civil and criminal penalties under § 437g. [Citizens United] argued that (1) § 441b is unconstitutional as applied to *Hillary;* and (2) BCRA's disclaimer and disclosure requirements, BCRA §§ 201 and 311, are unconstitutional as applied to *Hillary* and to the three ads for the movie. . . .

. . . The First Amendment does not permit laws that force speakers to retain a campaign finance attorney, conduct demographic marketing research, or seek declaratory rulings before discussing the most salient political issues of our day. Prolix laws chill speech for the same reason that vague laws chill speech. . . .

. . . *Hillary* is equivalent to express advocacy [because it is], in essence, is a feature-length negative advertisement that urges viewers to vote against Senator Clinton for President. . . . The narrative may contain more suggestions and arguments than facts, but there is little doubt that the thesis of the film is that she is unfit for the Presidency. . . .

[T]he Government . . . suggests that an as-applied challenge to § 441b's ban on books may be successful, although it would defend § 441b's ban as applied to almost every other form of media including pamphlets. See Tr. of Oral Arg. 65–66 (Sept. 9, 2009). The Government thus, by its own position, contributes to the uncertainty that § 441b causes. . . .

. . . Campaign finance regulations now impose "unique and complex rules" on "71 distinct entities." These entities are subject to separate rules for 33 different types of political speech. The FEC has adopted 568 pages of regulations, 1,278 pages of explanations and justifications for those regulations, and 1,771 advisory opinions since 1975. In fact, after this Court . . . adopted an objective "appeal to

---

* [Ed. Note: "General treasury funds" means assets of an organization used to pay its necessary, usual, incidental expenses. The organization typically does not derive its general treasury funds from a special solicitation, but from its regular, ongoing revenue streams.]

vote" test for determining whether a communication was the functional equivalent of express advocacy, the FEC adopted a two-part, 11-factor balancing test to implement [that] ruling. . . . Government officials pore over each word of a text to see if, in their judgment, it accords with the 11-factor test they have promulgated. This is an unprecedented governmental intervention into the realm of speech. . . .

. . . The law before us is an outright ban, backed by criminal sanctions. Section 441b makes it a felony for all corporations—including nonprofit advocacy corporations—either to expressly advocate the election or defeat of candidates or to broadcast electioneering communications within 30 days of a primary election and 60 days of a general election. Thus, the following acts would all be felonies under § 441b: The Sierra Club runs an ad, within the crucial phase of 60 days before the general election, that exhorts the public to disapprove of a Congressman who favors logging in national forests; the National Rifle Association publishes a book urging the public to vote for the challenger because the incumbent U.S. Senator supports a handgun ban; and the American Civil Liberties Union creates a Web site telling the public to vote for a Presidential candidate in light of that candidate's defense of free speech. These prohibitions are classic examples of censorship.

Section 441b is a ban on corporate speech notwithstanding the fact that a PAC created by a corporation can still speak. . . . PACs are burdensome alternatives; they are expensive to administer and subject to extensive regulations. For example, every PAC must appoint a treasurer, forward donations to the treasurer promptly, keep detailed records of the identities of the persons making donations, preserve receipts for three years, and file an organization statement and report changes to this information within 10 days. . . . PACs must file detailed monthly reports with the FEC, which are due at different times depending on the type of election that is about to occur . . . PACs have to comply with these regulations just to speak. This might explain why fewer than 2,000 of the millions of corporations in this country have PACs. . . .

Section 441b's prohibition on corporate independent expenditures is thus a ban on speech. . . . If § 441b applied to individuals, no one would believe that it is merely a time, place, or manner restriction on speech. Its purpose and effect are to silence entities whose voices the Government deems to be suspect. . . .

For these reasons, political speech must prevail against laws that would suppress it, whether by design or inadvertence. Laws that burden political speech are "subject to strict scrutiny," which requires the Government to prove that the restriction "furthers a compelling interest and is narrowly tailored to achieve that interest." . . . We find no basis for the proposition that, in the context of political speech, the Government may impose restrictions on certain disfavored speakers. Both history and logic lead us to this conclusion.

The Court has recognized that First Amendment protection extends to corporations. *First National Bank v. Bellotti*, 435 U.S. 765, 98 S.Ct. 1407, 55 L.Ed.2d 707 (1978). [P]olitical speech does not lose First Amendment protection "simply because its source is a corporation." *Bellotti, supra*; see *Pacific Gas & Elec. Co. v. Public Util. Comm'n.*, 475 U.S. 1, 8, 106 S.Ct. 903, 89 L.Ed.2d 1 (1986) (plurality opinion) ("The identity of the speaker is not decisive in determining whether speech is protected. Corporations and other associations, like individuals, contribute to the 'discussion, debate, and the dissemination of information and ideas' that the First Amendment seeks to foster" (quoting *Bellotti*)). The Court has thus rejected the argument that political speech of corporations or other associations should be treated differently under the First Amendment simply because such associations are not "natural persons."

At least since the latter part of the 19th century, the laws of some States and of the United States imposed a ban on corporate direct contributions to candidates. Yet not until 1947 did Congress first prohibit independent expenditures by corporations and labor unions in § 304 of the Labor Management Relations Act 1947. In passing this Act Congress overrode the veto of President Truman, who warned that the expenditure ban was a "dangerous intrusion on free speech."

For almost three decades thereafter, the Court did not reach the question whether restrictions on corporate and union expenditures are constitutional. The question was in the background of *United States v. CIO*, 335 U.S. 106, 68 S.Ct. 1349, 92 L.Ed. 1849 (1948). There, a labor union endorsed a congressional candidate in its weekly periodical. The Court stated that "the gravest doubt would arise in our minds as to [the federal expenditure prohibition's] constitutionality" if it were construed to suppress that writing. The Court engaged in statutory interpretation and found the statute did not cover the publication. Four Justices, however, said they would reach the constitutional question and invalidate the Labor Management Relations Act's expenditure ban. *Id.* (Rutledge, J., joined by Black, Douglas, and Murphy, JJ., concurring in result). The concurrence explained that any " 'undue influence' " generated by a speaker's "large expenditures" was outweighed "by the loss for democratic processes resulting from the restrictions upon free and full public discussion." . . .

. . . The expenditure ban invalidated in *Buckley*, applied to corporations and unions and some of the prevailing plaintiffs in *Buckley* were corporations . . . *Buckley* cited with approval the *United States v. Automobile Workers*, 352 U.S. 567, 77 S. Ct. 529, 1 L. Ed. 2d 563 (1957) dissent, which argued that § 610 was unconstitutional. 424 U.S., at 43, 96 S.Ct. 612 (citing 352 U.S., at 595–596, 77 S.Ct. 529 (opinion of Douglas, J.)). . . .

Less than two years after *Buckley, Bellotti* reaffirmed the First Amendment principle that the Government cannot restrict political speech based on the speaker's corporate identity. *Bellotti* could not have been clearer when it struck down a state-law prohibition on corporate independent expenditures related to referenda issues:

> "We thus find no support . . . that speech that otherwise would be within the protection of the First Amendment loses that protection simply because its source is a corporation that cannot prove, to the satisfaction of a court, a material effect on its business or property. [That proposition] amounts to an impermissible legislative prohibition of speech based on the identity of the interests that spokesmen may represent in public debate over controversial issues and a requirement that the speaker have a sufficiently great interest in the subject to justify communication. . . . In the realm of protected speech, the legislature is constitutionally disqualified from dictating the subjects about which persons may speak and the speakers who may address a public issue."

[The Government argues against the "corrosive and distorting effects of immense aggregations of wealth that are accumulated with the help of the corporate form."] If the First Amendment has any force, it prohibits Congress from fining or jailing citizens, or associations of citizens, for simply engaging in political speech. If the antidistortion rationale were to be accepted, however, it would permit Government to ban political speech simply because the speaker is an association that has taken on the corporate form. The Government contends that [it can] ban corporate expenditures for almost all forms of communication stemming from a corporation. [T]he Government could prohibit a corporation from expressing political views in media beyond those presented here, such as by printing books. The Government responds "that the FEC has never applied this statute to a book," and if it did, "there would be [a] quite good as-applied challenge." This troubling assertion of brooding governmental power cannot be reconciled with the confidence and stability in civic discourse that the First Amendment must secure.

Political speech is "indispensable to decisionmaking in a democracy, and this is no less true because the speech comes from a corporation rather than an individual." *Bellotti*; see *ibid.* (the worth of speech "does not depend upon the identity of its source, whether corporation, association, union, or individual"); *Buckley* ("[T]he concept that government may restrict the speech of some elements of our society in order to enhance the relative voice of others is wholly foreign to the First Amendment"); *Automobile Workers* (Douglas, J., dissenting); *CIO,* (Rutledge, J., concurring in result). This protection for speech is inconsistent with [the] antidistortion rationale. . . . *Buckley* rejected the premise that the Government has an interest "in equalizing the relative ability of individuals and groups to influence the outcome of elections." *Buckley* was specific in stating that "the skyrocketing cost of political campaigns" could not sustain the governmental prohibition. The First Amendment's protections do not depend on the speaker's "financial ability to engage in public discussion."

The Court reaffirmed these conclusions when it invalidated the BCRA provision that increased the cap on contributions to one candidate if the opponent made certain expenditures from personal funds. See *Davis v. Federal Election Comm'n*, 554 U.S. 724, 742, 128 S.Ct. 2759, 2774, 171 L.Ed.2d 737 (2008) ("Leveling electoral opportunities means making and implementing judgments about which strengths should be permitted to contribute to the outcome of an election. [I]t is a dangerous business for Congress to use the election laws to influence the voters' choices"). The rule that political speech cannot be limited based on a speaker's wealth is a necessary consequence of the premise that the First Amendment generally prohibits the suppression of political speech based on the speaker's identity.

[The Government seeks] to distinguish wealthy individuals from corporations on the ground that "[s]tate law grants corporations special advantages—such as limited liability, perpetual life, and favorable treatment of the accumulation and distribution of assets." This does not suffice, however, to allow laws prohibiting speech. "It is rudimentary that the State cannot exact as the price of those special advantages the forfeiture of First Amendment rights." . . . All speakers, including individuals and the media, use money amassed from the economic marketplace to fund their speech. The First Amendment protects the resulting speech, even if it was enabled by economic transactions with persons or entities who disagree with the speaker's ideas.

[The] antidistortion rationale would produce the dangerous, and unacceptable, consequence that Congress could ban political speech of media corporations. Media corporations are now exempt [by statute] from § 441b's ban on corporate expenditures. Yet media corporations accumulate wealth with the help of the corporate form, the largest media corporations have "immense aggregations of wealth," and the views expressed by media corporations often "have little or no correlation to the public's support" for those views. Thus, under the Government's reasoning, wealthy media corporations could have their voices diminished to put them on par with other media entities. There is no precedent for permitting this under the First Amendment.

The media exemption discloses further difficulties with the law now under consideration. There is no precedent supporting laws that attempt to distinguish between corporations which are deemed to be exempt as media corporations and those which are not. "We have consistently rejected the proposition that the institutional press has any constitutional privilege beyond that of other speakers." With the advent of the Internet and the decline of print and broadcast media, moreover, the line between the media and others who wish to comment on political and social issues becomes far more blurred.

The law's exception for media corporations is, on its own terms, all but an admission of the invalidity of the antidistortion rationale. [T]he law exempts some corporations but covers others, even though both have the need or the motive to communicate their views. The exemption applies to media corporations owned or controlled by corporations that have diverse and substantial investments and participate in endeavors other than news. So even assuming the most doubtful proposition that a news organization has a right to speak when others do not, the exemption would allow a conglomerate that owns both a media business and an unrelated business to influence or control the media in order to advance its overall business interest. At the same time, some other corporation, with an identical business interest but no media outlet in its ownership structure, would be forbidden to speak or inform the public about the same issue. This differential treatment cannot be squared with the First Amendment. . . . Factions will necessarily form in our Republic, but the remedy of "destroying the liberty" of some factions is "worse than the disease." The Federalist No. 10 (J. Madison). Factions should be checked by permitting them all to speak, and by entrusting the people to judge what is true and what is false. . . .

What we have said also shows the invalidity of other arguments made by the Government. For the most part relinquishing the antidistortion rationale, the Government falls back on the argument that corporate political speech can be banned in order to prevent corruption or its appearance. In *Buckley,* the Court found this interest "sufficiently important" to allow limits on contributions but did not extend that reasoning to expenditure limits. When *Buckley* examined an expenditure ban, it found "that the governmental interest in preventing corruption and the appearance of corruption [was] inadequate to justify [the ban] on independent expenditures." . . . The anticorruption interest is not sufficient to displace the speech here in question. Indeed, 26 States do not restrict independent expenditures by for-profit corporations. The Government does not claim that these expenditures have corrupted the political process in those States.

[W]e now conclude that independent expenditures, including those made by corporations, do not give rise to corruption or the appearance of corruption. . . . Citizens United has not made direct contributions to candidates, and it has not suggested that the Court should reconsider whether contribution limits should be subjected to rigorous First Amendment scrutiny. . . .

The Government contends further that corporate independent expenditures can be limited because of its interest in protecting dissenting shareholders from being compelled to fund corporate political speech. This asserted interest . . . would allow the Government to ban the political speech even of media corporations. Assume, for example, that a shareholder of a corporation that owns a newspaper disagrees with the political views the newspaper expresses. Under the Government's view, that potential disagreement could give the Government authority to restrict the media corporation's political speech. The First Amendment does not allow that power.

[T]he statute is both underinclusive and overinclusive. As to the first, if Congress had been seeking to protect dissenting shareholders, it would not have banned corporate speech in only certain media within 30 or 60 days before an election. A dissenting shareholder's interests would be implicated by speech in any media at any time. As to the second, the statute is overinclusive because it covers all corporations, including nonprofit corporations and for-profit corporations with only single shareholders. As to other corporations, the remedy is not to restrict speech but to consider and explore other regulatory mechanisms. The regulatory mechanism here, based on speech, contravenes the First Amendment.

We need not reach the question whether the Government has a compelling interest in preventing foreign individuals or associations from influencing our Nation's political process. Cf. 2 U.S.C.A. § 441e (contribution and expenditure ban applied to "foreign national[s]"). Section 441b is not limited to corporations or associations that were created in foreign countries or funded predominately by foreign shareholders. Section 441b therefore would be overbroad even if we assumed, *arguendo,* that the Government has a compelling interest in limiting foreign influence over our political process.

. . . We return to the principle established in *Buckley* and *Bellotti* that the Government may not suppress political speech on the basis of the speaker's corporate identity. No sufficient governmental interest justifies limits on the political speech of nonprofit or for-profit corporations. [The] restrictions on corporate independent expenditures are therefore invalid and cannot be applied to *Hillary.* [W]e are further required to overrule the part of *McConnell* that upheld BCRA § 203's extension of § 441b's restrictions on corporate independent expenditures. The *McConnell* Court relied on the antidistortion interest [but] we have found this interest unconvincing and insufficient. This part of *McConnell* is now overruled.

Citizens United next challenges BCRA's disclaimer and disclosure provisions as applied to *Hillary* and the three advertisements for the movie. Under BCRA § 311, televised electioneering communications funded by anyone other than a candidate must include a disclaimer that " '_____ is responsible for the content of this advertising.' " The required statement must be made in a "clearly spoken manner," and displayed on the screen in a "clearly readable manner" for at least four seconds. It must state that the communication "is not authorized by any candidate or candidate's committee"; it must also display the name and address (or Web site address) of the person or group that funded the advertisement. Under BCRA § 201, any person who spends more than $10,000 on electioneering communications within a calendar year must file a disclosure statement with the FEC. That statement must identify the person making the expenditure, the amount of the expenditure, the election to which the communication was directed, and the names of certain contributors.

Disclaimer and disclosure requirements may burden the ability to speak, but they "impose no ceiling on campaign-related activities," *Buckley* and "do not prevent anyone from speaking," *McConnell.* The Court has subjected these requirements to "exacting scrutiny," which requires a "substantial relation" between the disclosure requirement and a "sufficiently important" governmental interest. . . .

Citizens United argues that the disclaimer requirements in § 311 are unconstitutional as applied to its ads. . . . We disagree. . . . Citizens United argues that disclosure requirements can chill donations to an organization by exposing donors to retaliation. Some *amici* point to recent events in which donors to certain causes were blacklisted, threatened, or otherwise targeted for retaliation. . . . § 201 would be unconstitutional as applied to an organization if there were a reasonable probability that the group's members would face threats, harassment, or reprisals if their names were disclosed. The examples cited by *amici* are cause for concern. Citizens United, however, has offered no evidence that its members may face similar threats or reprisals. To the contrary, Citizens United has been disclosing its donors for years and has identified no instance of harassment or retaliation. . . .

When word concerning the plot of the movie *Mr. Smith Goes to Washington* reached the circles of Government, some officials sought, by persuasion, to discourage its distribution. Under [the Government's rationale], though, officials could have done more than discourage its distribution—they could have banned the film. After all, it, like *Hillary,* was speech funded by a corporation that was critical of Members of Congress. *Mr. Smith Goes to Washington* may be fiction and caricature; but fiction and caricature can be a powerful force. . . .

The judgment of the District Court is reversed with respect to the constitutionality of 2 U.S.C.A. § 441b's restrictions on corporate independent expenditures. The judgment is affirmed with respect to BCRA's disclaimer and disclosure requirements. The case is remanded for further proceedings consistent with this opinion.

It is so ordered.

Justice SCALIA, with whom Justice ALITO joins, and with whom Justice THOMAS joins in part, concurring.[1]

I join the opinion of the Court. I write separately to address Justice STEVENS' discussion of "*Original Understandings,*" (opinion concurring in part and dissenting in part) (hereinafter referred to as the dissent). This section of the dissent purports to show that today's decision is not supported by the original understanding of the First Amendment. The dissent attempts this demonstration, however, in splendid isolation from the text of the First Amendment. It never shows why "the freedom of speech" that was the right of Englishmen did not include the freedom to speak in association with other individuals, including association in the corporate form. To be sure, in 1791 (as now) corporations could pursue only the objectives set forth in their charters; but the dissent provides no evidence that their speech in the pursuit of those objectives could be censored.

. . . Though faced with a constitutional text that makes no distinction between types of speakers, the dissent feels no necessity to provide even an isolated statement from the founding era to the effect that corporations are *not*

---

[1]   Justice THOMAS does not join Part IV of the Court's opinion [which is not printed here].

covered, but places the burden on petitioners to bring forward statements showing that they *are* ("there is not a scintilla of evidence to support the notion that anyone believed [the First Amendment] would preclude regulatory distinctions based on the corporate form"). . . .

JUSTICE STEVENS, with whom JUSTICE GINSBURG, JUSTICE BREYER, and JUSTICE SOTOMAYOR join, concurring in part and dissenting in part.

. . . Neither Citizens United's nor any other corporation's speech has been "banned." All that the parties dispute is whether Citizens United had a right to use the funds in its general treasury to pay for broadcasts during the 30-day period. The notion that the First Amendment dictates an affirmative answer to that question is, in my judgment, profoundly misguided. Even more misguided is the notion that the Court must rewrite the law relating to campaign expenditures by *for-profit* corporations and unions to decide this case. . . . The Court invokes "ancient First Amendment principles," and original understandings, [but] there is not a scintilla of evidence to support the notion that anyone believed it would preclude regulatory distinctions based on the corporate form. . . .

In fairness, our campaign finance jurisprudence has never attended very closely to the views of the Framers, whose political universe differed profoundly from that of today. We have long since held that corporations are covered by the First Amendment, and many legal scholars have long since rejected the concession theory of the corporation. [However], corporations have "limited liability" for their owners and managers, "perpetual life," separation of ownership and control, "and favorable treatment of the accumulation and distribution of assets . . . that enhance their ability to attract capital and to deploy their resources in ways that maximize the return on their shareholders' investments." [C]orporations have no consciences, no beliefs, no feelings, no thoughts, no desires. Corporations help structure and facilitate the activities of human beings, to be sure, and their "personhood" often serves as a useful legal fiction. But they are not themselves members of "We the People" by whom and for whom our Constitution was established.

. . . Our colleagues have raised some interesting and difficult questions about Congress' authority to regulate electioneering by the press, and about how to define what constitutes the press. *But that is not the case before us.* Section 203 does not apply to media corporations, and even if it did, Citizens United is not a media corporation. . . .

[The opinion of ROBERTS, C.J., with whom ALITO, J., joins, concurring, and the opinion of THOMAS, J., concurring in part and dissenting in part is omitted.]

NOTES

1.   When the Government first argued this case in the Supreme Court, Chief Justice Roberts asked the Deputy Solicitor General, if a corporation published a "500-page book, and at the end it says, and so vote for X, the government could ban that?" The response was yes: that "would be express advocacy and it would be covered by the pre-existing Federal Election Campaign Act provision." Oral Argument, 2009 WL 760811(March 24, 2009) 2009 WL 760811 *29 (March 24, 2009). Later, Roberts said, if "we accept your constitutional argument, we're establishing a precedent that you yourself say would extend to banning the book," and the Government agreed: "I think the Court has already held [that] in *McConnell*." On reargument, Solicitor General Elena Kagan said that the "government's answer has changed" as to a book, but "a pamphlet would be different. A pamphlet is pretty classic electioneering," 2009 WL 6325467, *64, *65, *66 (September 9, 2009). The Solicitor General did admit § 441b prohibits "full-length books," but that, unlike pamphlets, "there would be [a] quite good as-applied challenge to any attempt to apply 441b in that context."

2.   Before *Citizens United*, 26 states already allowed unlimited corporate spending in elections. Two others allowed limited corporate spending. These states represented over 60% of the nation's population.

3.   *Citizens United* said that it did not "reach the question whether the Government has a compelling interest in preventing foreign individuals or associations from influencing our Nation's political process." Another provision, 2 U.S.C.A. § 441e, prohibits all foreign nationals, "directly or indirectly," from contributing or spending any money in any U.S. election, state or federal. Is that section constitutional? Congress ban independent political expenditures by U.S. corporations if foreigners own 20% of its stock? What about unions with foreign membership? The United Food and Commercial Workers International Union, for example, is a labor union representing approximately 1.3 million workers in the United States and Canada.

4.   What is your reaction to this op-ed on campaign finance? Steve Simpson & Paul Sherman, *Stephen Colbert's Free Speech Problem*, Wall St. Journal, May 19, 2011, at A15:

> Comedy Central funnyman Stephen Colbert [believes that] *Citizens United v. FEC* is, literally, ridiculous. To make his case that the

ruling invites "unlimited corporate money" to dominate politics, Mr. Colbert decided to set up a political action committee (PAC)[4] of his own. [H]e called in Trevor Potter, a former Federal Elections Commission (FEC) chairman [&] high-powered Washington lawyer. Mr. Potter delivered some unfunny news: Mr. Colbert couldn't set up his PAC because his show airs on Comedy Central, which is owned by Viacom, and corporations like Viacom cannot make contributions to PACs that give money to candidates. . . . Mr. Colbert's on-air discussions of the candidates he supports might count as an illegal "in-kind" contribution from Viacom to Mr. Colbert's PAC. [However], the comedian might still be able to set up a "Super PAC," a group that can raise unlimited sums of money as long as it spends it only on independent ads, without donating at all to candidates. Super PACs exist because of another case that proponents of campaign-finance law despise, *SpeechNow.org v. FEC*.[5]

So the newly dubbed "Colbert Super PAC" was off to the races. [But] Mr. Potter returned with more bad news: Viacom didn't like Mr. Colbert's plan because his on-air commentary might still amount to a contribution from Viacom to his Super PAC. . . . "Why does it get so complicated to do this? I mean, this is page after page of legalese," Mr. Colbert lamented. "All I'm trying to do is affect the 2012 election. It's not like I'm trying to install iTunes."
. . .

So what is someone who wants to speak during elections to do? [For] Stephen Colbert, the answer is to instruct high-priced attorneys to plead your case with the FEC [and request] a "media exemption" that would allow him to publicize his Super PAC on air without creating legal headaches for Viacom.

How's that for a punch line? Rich and successful television personality needs powerful corporate lawyers to convince the FEC

---

[4]   Ed. Note: PACs can raise money to run political ads and make contributions to candidates.

[5]   Ed. Note: 599 F.3d 686 (D.C. Cir. 2010), cert. denied, sub nom. *Keating v. FEC*, 562 U.S. 1003, 131 S.Ct. 553, 178 L.Ed.2d 371 (2010). Plaintiffs objected that the federal campaign laws prohibited individuals from giving more than $5,000 to a political committee. So, Donald Trump could spend as much of his money as he wanted on political speech, but could contribute only $5,000 to a group effort. The D.C. Circuit (*en banc* and without dissent) held the law limiting contributions by individuals to political committees that made only *independent* expenditures violated free speech but the law's organizational and reporting provisions are constitutional.

to allow him to continue making fun of the Supreme Court. . . .
Media companies' exemption from campaign-finance laws has
existed for decades. That was part of the Supreme Court's point in
Citizens United: Media corporations are allowed to spend lots of
money on campaign speech, so why not other corporations?

[R]eal people who want to speak out during elections face these
confounding laws all the time. [T]he laws remain byzantine and
often impossible to navigate, even after *Citizens United*. There's a
joke in here somewhere, but it isn't on the Supreme Court.[6]

7.8 SYMBOLIC SPEECH

7.8.1   Introduction

UNITED STATES V. O'BRIEN
391 U.S. 367, 88 S.Ct. 1673, 20 L.Ed.2d 672 (1968)

MR. CHIEF JUSTICE WARREN delivered the opinion of the Court.

On the morning of March 31, 1966, David Paul O'Brien and three
companions burned their Selective Service registration certificates on the steps of
the South Boston Courthouse. . . . For this act, O'Brien was indicted, tried,
convicted, and sentenced in the United States District Court for the District of
Massachusetts. He [told] the jury that he burned the certificate publicly to
influence others to adopt his antiwar beliefs, as he put it, "so that other people
would reevaluate their positions with Selective Service, with the armed forces, and
reevaluate their place in the culture of today, to hopefully consider my position."
. . .

Section 462(b), [which O'Brien was charged with violating] is part of the
Universal Military Training and Service Act of 1948. Section 462(b)(3), one of six
numbered subdivisions of § 462(b), was amended by Congress in 1965, (adding
the words italicized below), so that at the time O'Brien burned his certificate an
offense was committed by any person, "who forges, alters, *knowingly destroys,*
knowingly mutilates, or in any manner changes any such certificate. . . ." (Italics
supplied.) In the District Court, O'Brien argued that the 1965 Amendment
prohibiting the knowing destruction or mutilation of certificates was

---

[6]   Ed. Note: The FEC (5 to 1) approved Colbert's request to form a PAC to take unlimited contributions
from the public to make independent expenditures. The FEC also said that coverage of the PAC by Comedy
Central and Viacom (its parent) would be within the press exemption (and thus not reportable political activity).
However, if Viacom produced ads for the PAC, those are in-kind contributions.

unconstitutional because it was enacted to abridge free speech, and because it served no legitimate legislative purpose. . . . We hold that the 1965 Amendment is constitutional both as enacted and as applied. . . .

O'Brien first argues that the 1965 Amendment is unconstitutional as applied to him because his act of burning his registration certificate was protected "symbolic speech" within the First Amendment. . . .

We cannot accept the view that an apparently limitless variety of conduct can be labeled "speech" whenever the person engaging in the conduct intends thereby to express an idea. However, even on the assumption that the alleged communicative element in O'Brien's conduct is sufficient to bring into play the First Amendment, it does not necessarily follow that the destruction of a registration certificate is constitutionally protected activity. This Court has held that when "speech" and "nonspeech" elements are combined in the same course of conduct, a sufficiently important governmental interest in regulating the nonspeech element can justify incidental limitations on First Amendment freedoms. [A] government regulation is sufficiently justified if it is within the constitutional power of the Government; if it furthers an important or substantial governmental interest; if the governmental interest is unrelated to the suppression of free expression; and if the incidental restriction on alleged First Amendment freedoms is no greater than is essential to the furtherance of that interest. We find that the 1965 Amendment to § 12(b)(3) of the Universal Military Training and Service Act meets all of these requirements, and consequently that O'Brien can be constitutionally convicted for violating it.

The constitutional power of Congress to raise and support armies and to make all laws necessary and proper to that end is broad and sweeping. . . . Congress may establish a system of registration for individuals liable for training and service, and may require such individuals within reason to cooperate in the registration system. The issuance of certificates indicating the registration and eligibility classification of individuals is a legitimate and substantial administrative aid in the functioning of this system. And legislation to insure the continuing availability of issued certificates serves a legitimate and substantial purpose in the system's administration. . . .

The registration certificate serves as proof that the individual described thereon has registered for the draft. The classification certificate shows the eligibility classification of a named but undescribed individual. Voluntarily displaying the two certificates is an easy and painless way for a young man to dispel a question as to whether he might be delinquent in his Selective Service obligations. [S]ince both certificates are in the nature of "receipts" attesting that the registrant has done what the law requires, it is in the interest of the just and efficient administration of the system that they be continually available, in the event, for example, of a mix-up in the registrant's file. . . . The information supplied on the certificates facilitates communication between registrants and local boards, simplifying the system and benefitting all concerned. [E]ach card bears the registrant's Selective Service number, and a registrant who has his number readily available so that he can communicate it to his local board when he supplies or requests information can make simpler the board's task in locating his file. . . . The many functions performed by Selective Service certificates establish beyond doubt that Congress has a legitimate and substantial interest in preventing their wanton and unrestrained destruction and assuring their continuing availability by punishing people who knowingly and willfully destroy or mutilate them. . . .

It is equally clear that the 1965 Amendment specifically protects this substantial governmental interest. We perceive no alternative means that would more precisely and narrowly assure the continuing availability of issued Selective Service certificates than a law which prohibits their willful mutilation or destruction. The 1965 Amendment prohibits such conduct and does nothing more. In other words, both the governmental interest and the operation of the 1965 Amendment are limited to the noncommunicative aspect of O'Brien's conduct. The governmental interest and the scope of the 1965 Amendment are limited to preventing harm to the smooth and efficient functioning of the Selective Service System. When O'Brien deliberately rendered unavailable his registration certificate, he willfully frustrated this governmental interest. For this noncommunicative impact of his conduct, and for nothing else, he was convicted.

The case at bar is therefore unlike one where the alleged governmental interest in regulating conduct arises in some measure because the communication allegedly integral to the conduct is itself thought to be harmful. In *Stromberg v. People of State of California*, 283 U.S. 359, 51 S.Ct. 532, 75 L.Ed. 1117 (1931), for example, this Court struck down a statutory phrase which punished people who expressed their "opposition to organized government" by displaying "any flag, badge, banner, or device." Since the statute there was aimed at suppressing communication it could not be sustained as a regulation of noncommunicative conduct.

In conclusion, we find that because of the Government's substantial interest in assuring the continuing availability of issued Selective Service certificates, because amended § 462(b) is an appropriately narrow means of protecting this interest and condemns only the independent noncommunicative impact of conduct within its reach, and because the noncommunicative impact of O'Brien's act of burning his registration certificate frustrated the Government's interest, a sufficient governmental interest has been shown to justify O'Brien's conviction.

O'Brien finally argues that the 1965 Amendment is unconstitutional as enacted because what he calls the "purpose" of Congress was "to suppress freedom of speech." We reject this argument because under settled principles the purpose of Congress, as O'Brien uses that term, is not a basis for declaring this legislation unconstitutional.

It is a familiar principle of constitutional law that this Court will not strike down an otherwise constitutional statute on the basis of an alleged illicit legislative motive. . . . Inquiries into congressional motives or purposes are a hazardous matter. When the issue is simply the interpretation of legislation, the Court will look to statements by legislators for guidance as to the purpose of the legislature, because the benefit to sound decision-making in this circumstance is thought sufficient to risk the possibility of misreading Congress' purpose. It is entirely a different matter when we are asked to void a statute that is, under well-settled criteria, constitutional on its face, on the basis of what fewer than a handful of Congressmen said about it. What motivates one legislator to make a speech about a statute is not necessarily what motivates scores of others to enact it, and the stakes are sufficiently high for us to eschew guesswork. We decline to void essentially on the ground that it is unwise legislation which Congress had the undoubted power to enact and which could be reenacted in its exact form if the same or another legislator made a "wiser" speech about it.

[Only three Congressmen, in the floor debates, commented on this legislation.] It is principally on the basis of the statements by these three Congressmen that O'Brien makes his congressional-"purpose" argument. [I]f we were to examine legislative purpose in the instant case, we would be obliged to consider not only these statements but also the more authoritative reports of the Senate and House Armed Services Committees. . . . While both reports make clear a concern with the "defiant" destruction of so-called "draft cards" and with "open" encouragement to others to destroy their cards, both reports also indicate that this concern stemmed from an apprehension that unrestrained destruction of cards would disrupt the smooth functioning of the Selective Service System. . . .

[The concurring opinion of HARLAN, J., and the dissenting opinion of DOUGLAS, J., are omitted.]

NOTES

1. *O'Brien* offers a four-part test for when symbolic speech has First Amendment protection:

    "[1] if it is within the constitutional power of the Government; [2] if it furthers an important or substantial governmental interest; [3] if the governmental interest is *unrelated to the suppression of free expression; and* [4] if the incidental restriction on alleged First Amendment freedoms is no greater than is essential to the furtherance of that interest."

2. Part 3 is the crucial portion of the *O'Brien* test: the governmental interest is unrelated to the suppression of free expression. In this case, the government did not ban—

    - *Public* burning of a draft card, or

    - *Contemptuous* burning of a draft care

    Either of those two restrictions is specifically "related to the suppression of free expression." The law at issue in *O'Brien* does not prohibit a person from publicly burning a photocopy of his draft card, or burning something he pretends is his draft care. Thus, that law is unrelated to suppressing speech.

3. Apply the *O'Brien* test to *Tinker,* the case that follows. There, the school banned armbands, but it allowed political campaign buttons and even the Iron Cross. The school ban in *Tinker* failed part three of the *O'Brien* test.

7.8.2   Schools

TINKER V. DES MOINES INDEPENDENT COMMUNITY SCHOOL DISTRICT
393 U.S. 503, 89 S.Ct. 733, 21 L.Ed.2d 731 (1969)

MR. JUSTICE FORTAS delivered the opinion of the Court.

Petitioner John F. Tinker, 15 years old, and petitioner Christopher Eckhardt, 16 years old, attended high schools in Des Moines, Iowa. Petitioner Mary Beth Tinker, John's sister, was a 13-year-old student in junior high school. In December 1965, a group of adults and students in Des Moines held a meeting at the Eckhardt home. The group determined to publicize their objections to the hostilities in Vietnam and their support for a truce by wearing black armbands during the holiday season and by fasting on December 16 and New Year's Eve. Petitioners and their parents had previously engaged in similar activities, and they decided to participate in the program.

The principals of the Des Moines schools became aware of the plan to wear armbands. On December 14, 1965, they met and adopted a policy that any student wearing an armband to school would be asked to remove it, and if he refused he would be suspended until he returned without the armband. Petitioners were aware of the regulation that the school authorities adopted.

On December 16, Mary Beth and Christopher wore black armbands to their schools. John Tinker wore his armband the next day. They were all sent home and suspended from school until they would come back without their armbands. They did not return to school until after the planned period for wearing armbands had expired—that is, until after New Year's Day. . . .

First Amendment rights, applied in light of the special characteristics of the school environment, are available to teachers and students. It can hardly be argued that either students or teachers shed their constitutional rights to freedom of speech or expression at the schoolhouse gate. . . .

The problem posed by the present case does not relate to regulation of the length of skirts or the type of clothing, to hair style, or deportment. It does not concern aggressive, disruptive action or even group demonstrations. Our problem involves direct, primary First Amendment rights akin to "pure speech." The school officials banned and sought to punish petitioners for a silent, passive expression of opinion, unaccompanied by any disorder or disturbance on the part of petitioners. There is here no evidence whatever of petitioners' interference, actual or nascent, with the schools' work or of collision with the rights of other students to be secure and to be let alone. Accordingly, this case does not concern speech or action that intrudes upon the work of the schools or the rights of other students. . . . There is no indication that the work of the schools or any class was disrupted. Outside the classrooms, a few students made hostile remarks to the children wearing armbands, but there were no threats or acts of violence on school premises.

The District Court concluded that the action of the school authorities was reasonable because it was based upon their fear of a disturbance from the wearing of the armbands. But, in our system, undifferentiated fear or apprehension of disturbance is not enough to overcome the right to freedom of expression. Any departure from absolute regimentation may cause trouble. Any variation from the majority's opinion may inspire fear. Any word spoken, in class, in the lunchroom, or on the campus, that deviates from the views of another person may start an argument or cause a disturbance. But our Constitution says we must take this risk; and our history says that it is this sort of hazardous freedom—this kind of openness—that is the basis of our national strength and of the independence and vigor of Americans who grow up and live in this relatively permissive, often disputatious, society.

In order for the State in the person of school officials to justify prohibition of a particular expression of opinion, it must be able to show that its action was caused by something more than a mere desire to avoid the discomfort and unpleasantness that always accompany an unpopular viewpoint. Certainly where there is no finding and no showing that engaging in the forbidden conduct would "materially and substantially interfere with the requirements of appropriate discipline in the operation of the school," the prohibition cannot be sustained.

In the present case, the District Court made no such finding, and our independent examination of the record fails to yield evidence that the school authorities had reason to anticipate that the wearing of the armbands would substantially interfere with the work of the school or impinge upon the rights of other students. . . . On the contrary, the action of the school authorities appears to have been based upon an urgent wish to avoid the controversy which might result from the expression, even by the silent symbol of armbands, of opposition to this Nation's part in the conflagration in Vietnam. . . .

It is also relevant that the school authorities did not purport to prohibit the wearing of all symbols of political or controversial significance. The record shows that students in some of the schools wore buttons relating to national political campaigns, and some even wore the Iron Cross, traditionally a symbol of Nazism. The order prohibiting the wearing of armbands did not extend to these. Instead, a particular symbol—black armbands worn to exhibit opposition to this Nation's involvement in Vietnam—was singled out for prohibition. Clearly, the prohibition of expression of one particular opinion, at least without evidence that it is necessary to avoid material and substantial interference with school work or discipline, is not constitutionally permissible. . . .

If a regulation were adopted by school officials forbidding discussion of the Vietnam conflict, or the expression by any student of opposition to it anywhere on school property except as part of a prescribed classroom exercise, it would be obvious that the regulation would violate the constitutional rights of students, at least if it could not be justified by a showing that the students' activities would materially and substantially disrupt the work and discipline of the school. . . . In the circumstances of the present case, the prohibition of the silent, passive "witness of the armbands," as one of the children called it, is no less offensive to the Constitution's guarantees. . . .

Reversed and remanded.

MR. JUSTICE BLACK, dissenting.

. . . While the absence of obscene remarks or boisterous and loud disorder perhaps justifies the Court's statement that the few armband students did not actually "disrupt" the classwork, I think the record overwhelmingly shows that the armbands did exactly what the elected school officials and principals foresaw they would, that is, took the students' minds off their classwork and diverted them to thoughts about the highly emotional subject of the Vietnam war. [I]f the time has come when pupils of state-supported schools, kindergartens, grammar schools, or high schools, can defy and flout orders of school officials to keep their minds on their own schoolwork, it is the beginning of a new revolutionary era of permissiveness in this country fostered by the judiciary. . . .

[The concurring opinions of STEWART, J., and WHITE, J., and the dissenting opinion of HARLAN, J., are omitted.]

NOTES

Consider this hypothetical. The school says that no one in the school band, while performing as a band member, can wear any symbols on the band uniform. That ban should pass the *O'Brien* test. The purpose of that ban is to make sure that the band uniform (the clothes that the members wear) is, in fact, uniform. Uniforms are supposed to be uniform, *i.e.*, identical.

MORSE V. FREDERICK
551 U.S. 393, 127 S.Ct. 2618, 168 L.Ed.2d 290 (2007)

CHIEF JUSTICE ROBERTS delivered the opinion of the Court.

At a school-sanctioned and school-supervised event, a high school principal saw some of her students unfurl a large banner conveying a message she reasonably regarded as promoting illegal drug use. Consistent with established school policy prohibiting such messages at school events, the principal directed the students to take down the banner. One student—among those who had brought the banner to the event—refused to do so. The principal confiscated the banner and later suspended the student. The Ninth Circuit held that the principal's actions violated the First Amendment, and that the student could sue the principal for damages.

Our cases make clear that students do not "shed their constitutional rights to freedom of speech or expression at the schoolhouse gate." *Tinker v. Des Moines Independent Community School Dist.* (1960). At the same time, we have held that "the constitutional rights of students in public school are not automatically coextensive with the rights of adults in other settings," *Bethel School Dist. No. 403 v. Fraser* (1986) [§ 7.4], and that the rights of students "must be 'applied in light of the special characteristics of the school environment.' " *Hazelwood School Dist. v. Kuhlmeier*, 484 U.S. 260, 108 S.Ct. 562, 98 L.Ed.2d 592 (1988) [§ 7.4] (quoting *Tinker*). Consistent with these principles, we hold that schools may take steps to safeguard those entrusted to their care from speech that can reasonably be regarded as encouraging illegal drug use. We conclude that the school officials in this case did not violate the First Amendment by confiscating the pro-drug banner and suspending the student responsible for it.

On January 24, 2002, the Olympic Torch Relay passed through Juneau, Alaska, on its way to the winter games in Salt Lake City, Utah. The torchbearers were to proceed along a street in front of Juneau-Douglas High School (JDHS) while school was in session. Petitioner Deborah Morse, the school principal, decided to permit staff and students to participate in the Torch Relay as an approved social event or class trip. Students were allowed to leave class to observe the relay from either side of the street. Teachers and administrative officials monitored the students' actions.

Respondent Joseph Frederick, a JDHS senior, was late to school that day. When he arrived, he joined his friends (all but one of whom were JDHS students) across the street from the school to watch the event. . . . As the torchbearers and camera crews passed by, Frederick and his friends unfurled a 14-foot banner bearing the phrase: "BONG HiTS 4 **JESUS**." The large banner was easily readable by the students on the other side of the street.

Principal Morse immediately crossed the street and demanded that the banner be taken down. Everyone but Frederick complied. Morse confiscated the banner and told Frederick to report to her office, where she suspended him for 10 days. Morse later explained that she told Frederick to take the banner down because she thought it encouraged illegal drug use, in violation of established school policy. . . .

Frederick administratively appealed his suspension, but the Juneau School District Superintendent upheld it, limiting it to time served (8 days). In a memorandum setting forth his reasons, the superintendent determined that Frederick had displayed his banner "in the midst of his fellow students, during school hours, at a school-sanctioned activity." He further explained that Frederick "was not disciplined because the principal of the school 'disagreed' with his message, but because his speech appeared to advocate the use of illegal drugs." . . .

The superintendent continued: "The common-sense understanding of the phrase 'bong hits' is that it is a reference to a means of smoking marijuana. Given [Frederick's] inability or unwillingness to express any other credible meaning for the phrase, I can only agree with the principal and countless others who saw the banner as advocating the use of illegal drugs. [His] speech was not political. [Frederick's] speech was potentially disruptive to the event and clearly disruptive of and inconsistent with the school's educational mission to educate students about the dangers of illegal drugs and to discourage their use." . . .

Frederick then [sued seeking] declaratory and injunctive relief, unspecified compensatory damages, punitive damages, and attorney's fees. The [Ninth Circuit] found a violation of Frederick's First Amendment rights because the school punished Frederick without demonstrating that his speech gave rise to a "risk of substantial disruption." [The issue,] whether Frederick had a First Amendment right to wield his banner, [we resolve against Frederick].

At the outset, we reject Frederick's argument that this is not a school speech case—as has every other authority to address the question. The event occurred during normal school hours. It was sanctioned by Principal Morse "as an approved social event or class trip," and the school district's rules expressly provide that pupils in "approved social events and class trips are subject to district rules for student conduct." Teachers and administrators were interspersed among the students and charged with supervising them. The high school band and cheerleaders performed. Frederick, standing among other JDHS students across the street from the school, directed his banner toward the school, making it plainly visible to most students. Under these circumstances, we agree with the superintendent that Frederick cannot "stand in the midst of his fellow students, during school hours, at a school-sanctioned activity and claim he is not at school." There is some uncertainty at the outer boundaries as to when courts should apply school-speech precedents, but not on these facts.

The message on Frederick's banner is cryptic. . . . Frederick himself claimed "that the words were just nonsense meant to attract television cameras." But

Principal Morse thought the banner would be interpreted by those viewing it as promoting illegal drug use, and that interpretation is plainly a reasonable one. . . .

The dissent mentions Frederick's "credible and uncontradicted explanation for the message—he just wanted to get on television." But that is a description of Frederick's *motive* for displaying the banner; it is not an interpretation of what the banner says. The *way* Frederick was going to fulfill his ambition of appearing on television was by unfurling a pro-drug banner at a school event, in the presence of teachers and fellow students.

[T]he dissent emphasizes the importance of political speech and the need to foster "national debate about a serious issue," as if to suggest that the banner is political speech. But not even Frederick argues that the banner conveys any sort of political or religious message. Contrary to the dissent's suggestion, this is plainly not a case about political debate over the criminalization of drug use or possession.

The question thus becomes whether a principal may, consistent with the First Amendment, restrict student speech at a school event, when that speech is reasonably viewed as promoting illegal drug use. We hold that she may. . . .

Tinker held that student expression may not be suppressed unless school officials reasonably conclude that it will "materially and substantially disrupt the work and discipline of the school." The essential facts of *Tinker* are quite stark, implicating concerns at the heart of the First Amendment. The students sought to engage in political speech, [opposing the Vietnam War].

This Court's next student speech case was [*Bethel School District No. 403 v.*] *Fraser*, 478 U.S. 675, 106 S.Ct. 3159, 92 L.Ed.2d 549 (1986) [§ 7.4]. Matthew Fraser was suspended for delivering a speech before a high school assembly in which he employed what this Court called "an elaborate, graphic, and explicit sexual metaphor." Analyzing the case under *Tinker,* the District Court and Court of Appeals found no disruption, and therefore no basis for disciplining Fraser. This Court reversed, holding that the "School District acted entirely within its permissible authority in imposing sanctions upon Fraser in response to his offensively lewd and indecent speech."

The mode of analysis employed in *Fraser* is not entirely clear. [T]he Court also reasoned that school boards have the authority to determine "what manner of speech in the classroom or in school assembly is inappropriate." [I]t is enough to distill from *Fraser* two basic principles. First, *Fraser's* holding demonstrates that "the constitutional rights of students in public school are not automatically coextensive with the rights of adults in other settings." Had Fraser delivered the same speech in a public forum outside the school context, it would have been protected. In school, however, Fraser's First Amendment rights were circumscribed "in light of the special characteristics of the school environment." *Tinker, supra.* Second, *Fraser* established that the mode of analysis set forth in *Tinker* is not absolute. Whatever approach *Fraser* employed, it certainly did not conduct the "substantial disruption" analysis prescribed by *Tinker*.

Our most recent student speech case, [*Hazelwood School District v. Kuhlmeier* (1988)], concerned "expressive activities that students, parents, and members of the public might reasonably perceive to bear the imprimatur of the school." Staff members of a high school newspaper sued their school when it chose not to publish two of their articles. The Court of Appeals analyzed the case under *Tinker,* ruling in favor of the students because it found no evidence of material disruption to classwork or school discipline. This Court reversed, holding that "educators do not offend the First Amendment by exercising editorial control over the style and content of student speech in school-sponsored expressive activities so long as their actions are reasonably related to legitimate pedagogical concerns." *Kuhlmeier.*

Kuhlmeier does not control this case because no one would reasonably believe that Frederick's banner bore the school's imprimatur. [But] *Kuhlmeier* acknowledged that schools may regulate some speech "even though the government could not censor similar speech outside the school." And, like *Fraser,* it confirms that the rule of *Tinker* is not the only basis for restricting student speech. . . .

The "special characteristics of the school environment," *Tinker,* and the governmental interest in stopping student drug abuse—reflected in the policies of Congress and myriad school boards, including JDHS—allow schools to restrict student expression that they reasonably regard as promoting illegal drug use. *Tinker* warned that schools may not prohibit student speech because of "undifferentiated fear or apprehension of disturbance" or "a mere desire to avoid the discomfort and unpleasantness that always accompany an unpopular viewpoint." The danger here is far more serious and palpable. The particular concern to prevent student drug abuse at issue here, embodied in established school policy, extends well beyond an abstract desire to avoid controversy.

Petitioners urge us to adopt the broader rule that Frederick's speech is proscribable because it is plainly "offensive" as that term is used in *Fraser*. We think this stretches *Fraser* too far. [M]uch political and religious speech might be perceived as offensive to some. The concern here is not that Frederick's speech was offensive, but that it was reasonably viewed as promoting illegal drug use. . . .

JUSTICE ALITO, with whom JUSTICE KENNEDY, concurring.

I join the opinion of the Court on the understanding that (a) it goes no further than to hold that a public school may restrict speech that a reasonable observer would interpret as advocating illegal drug use and (b) it provides no support for any restriction of speech that can plausibly be interpreted as commenting on any political or social issue, including speech on issues such as "the wisdom of the war on drugs or of legalizing marijuana for medicinal use." [P]ublic schools may ban speech advocating illegal drug use. But I regard such regulation as standing at the far reaches of what the First Amendment permits. I join the opinion of the Court with the understanding that the opinion does not endorse any further extension.

JUSTICE STEVENS, with whom JUSTICE SOUTER and JUSTICE GINSBURG join, dissenting.

[T]he school's interest in protecting its students from exposure to speech "reasonably regarded as promoting illegal drug use," cannot justify disciplining Frederick for his attempt to make an ambiguous statement to a television audience simply because it contained an oblique reference to drugs. [T]he protects student speech if the message itself neither violates a permissible rule nor expressly advocates conduct that is illegal and harmful to students. This nonsense banner does neither, and the Court does serious violence to the First Amendment in upholding—indeed, lauding—a school's decision to punish Frederick for expressing a view with which it disagreed. [T]he Court's holding in this case strikes at "the heart of the First Amendment" because it upholds a punishment meted out on the basis of a listener's disagreement with her understanding (or, more likely, misunderstanding) of the speaker's viewpoint.

[W]hile conventional speech may be restricted only when likely to "incit[e] imminent lawless action," *Brandenburg* [§ 15–1], it is possible that our rigid imminence requirement ought to be relaxed at schools. But it is one thing to restrict speech that *advocates* drug use. It is another thing entirely to prohibit an obscure message with a drug theme that a third party subjectively—and not very reasonably—thinks is tantamount to express advocacy. [J]ust as we insisted in *Tinker* that the school establish some likely connection between the armbands and their feared consequences, so too JDHS must show that Frederick's supposed advocacy stands a meaningful chance of making otherwise-abstemious students try marijuana. . . .

[T]he school district's interest in deterring teenage alcohol use is at least comparable to its interest in preventing marijuana use. Under the Court's reasoning, must the First Amendment give way whenever a school seeks to punish a student for any speech mentioning beer, or indeed anything else that might be deemed risky to teenagers? While I find it hard to believe the Court would support punishing Frederick for flying a "WINE SiPS 4 **JESUS**" banner—which could quite reasonably be construed either as a protected religious message or as a pro-alcohol message—the breathtaking sweep of its opinion suggests it would. . . .

[The opinion of THOMAS, J., concurring, and the opinion of BREYER, J., concurring in the judgment in part and dissenting in part is omitted.]

NOTES

1. Does it violate the free speech clause if a public school allows students to wear t-shirts with a Mexican flag design but bans students from wearing t-shirts with an American flag design? That was the issue in *Dariano v. Morgan Hill Unified School District*, 767 F.3d 764 (9th Cir. 2014). *Tinker* made clear that the students wearing armbands—let us call them the doves—were not interfering with anything. Some of the students opposed to the doves—let us call them the hawks—were upset. A "few students [the hawks] made hostile remarks to the children wearing armbands," but that did not justify the school punishing the doves. If the school were going to punish anyone, it should punish the hawks. The Supreme Court has never approved of a "heckler's veto"—If the heckler is disturbing the speaker, the law interferes to protect the speaker, not the heckler. *Texas v. Johnson* (the flag burning case), the next case, makes that point.

2. The *Morgan Hill Unified School District* claimed that if some students wore the American Flag colors on Cinco de Mayo, the 5th of May, celebrating Mexican heritage and pride, other students—"Mexican students" (the term the court used)—might turn to violence. The school ban on the students wearing American flag colors, the court argued, was "in order to protect their own safety." The *Dariano* trial court said, to support its restriction of free speech, a male student "shoved a Mexican flag at [a student with an American flag symbol] and said something in Spanish expressing anger at Plaintiffs' clothing." The remedy that the *Dariano* court chose was not to punish the student who "shoved a Mexican flag" at the other student, but to restrict the free speech rights of that other student. Do you think that makes sense? For example, in *Tinker*, if the hawks engaged in violence against the doves, would

that mean that the school district could ban the armbands "in order to protect [the doves'] own safety"?

If the students in mathematics class insisted on talking about the Vietnam War, one could see that would be a case (in the words of *Tinker*) were there was "interference, actual or nascent, with the schools' work." Is *Morse* a case where the student's banner interfered with schoolwork?

7.8.3   Flag Burning

TEXAS V. JOHNSON

491 U.S. 397, 109 S.Ct. 2533, 105 L.Ed.2d 342 (1989)

JUSTICE BRENNAN delivered the opinion of the Court.

After publicly burning an American flag as a means of political protest, Gregory Lee Johnson was convicted of desecrating a flag in violation of Texas law. This case presents the question whether his conviction is consistent with the First Amendment. We hold that it is not.

While the Republican National Convention was taking place in Dallas in 1984, respondent Johnson participated in a political demonstration dubbed the "Republican War Chest Tour." [T]he purpose of this event was to protest the policies of the Reagan administration and of certain Dallas-based corporations. [Johnson accepted] an American flag handed to him by a fellow protestor who had taken it from a flag pole outside one of the targeted buildings.

The demonstration ended in front of Dallas City Hall, where Johnson unfurled the American flag, doused it with kerosene, and set it on fire. While the flag burned, the protestors chanted, "America, the red, white, and blue, we spit on you." After the demonstrators dispersed, a witness to the flag-burning collected the flag's remains and buried them in his backyard. No one was physically injured or threatened with injury, though several witnesses testified that they had been seriously offended by the flag-burning.

Of the approximately 100 demonstrators, Johnson alone was charged with a crime. The only criminal offense with which he was charged was the desecration of a venerated object in violation of Tex.Penal Code Ann. § 42.09(a)(3) (1989).[1]

---

[1]   Tex.Penal Code Ann. § 42.09 (1989) provides in full:

"§ 42.09. Desecration of Venerated Object

"(a) A person commits an offense if he intentionally or knowingly desecrates:

"(1) a public monument;

(2) a place of worship or burial; or

After a trial, he was convicted, sentenced to one year in prison, and fined $2,000. [T]he Texas Court of Criminal Appeals reversed, holding that the State could not, consistent with the First Amendment, punish Johnson for burning the flag in these circumstances. . . .

Johnson was convicted of flag desecration for burning the flag rather than for uttering insulting words. . . . Texas conceded for purposes of its oral argument in this case that Johnson's conduct was expressive conduct, and this concession seems to us [to be] prudent. . . . Johnson burned an American flag as part—indeed, as the culmination—of a political demonstration that coincided with the convening of the Republican Party and its renomination of Ronald Reagan for President. The expressive, overtly political nature of this conduct was both intentional and overwhelmingly apparent. At his trial, Johnson explained his reasons for burning the flag as follows: "The American Flag was burned as Ronald Reagan was being renominated as President. And a more powerful statement of symbolic speech, whether you agree with it or not, couldn't have been made at that time. It's quite a just position [juxtaposition]. We had new patriotism and no patriotism." In these circumstances, Johnson's burning of the flag was conduct "sufficiently imbued with elements of communication," to implicate the First Amendment.

The Government generally has a freer hand in restricting expressive conduct than it has in restricting the written or spoken word. See *O'Brien*. It may not, however, proscribe particular conduct *because* it has expressive elements. [W]e have limited the applicability of *O'Brien*'s relatively lenient standard to those cases in which "the governmental interest is unrelated to the suppression of free expression." [T]he governmental interest in question be unconnected to expression in order to come under *O'Brien*'s less demanding rule.

. . . The State offers two separate interests to justify this conviction: preventing breaches of the peace, and preserving the flag as a symbol of nationhood and national unity. We hold that the first interest is not implicated on this record and that the second is related to the suppression of expression.

Texas claims that its interest in preventing breaches of the peace justifies Johnson's conviction for flag desecration. . . . The State's position, therefore,

---

(3) a state or national flag.

"(b) For purposes of this section, 'desecrate' means deface, damage, or otherwise physically mistreat in a way that the actor knows will seriously offend one or more persons likely to observe or discover his action.

"(c) An offense under this section is a Class A misdemeanor."

amounts to a claim that an audience that takes serious offense at particular expression is necessarily likely to disturb the peace and that the expression may be prohibited on this basis. Our precedents do not countenance such a presumption. [W]e have . . . required careful consideration of the actual circumstances surrounding such expression, asking whether the expression "is directed to inciting or producing imminent lawless action and is likely to incite or produce such action." *Brandenburg v. Ohio.* . . .

Nor does Johnson's expressive conduct fall within that small class of "fighting words" that are "likely to provoke the average person to retaliation, and thereby cause a breach of the peace." No reasonable onlooker would have regarded Johnson's generalized expression of dissatisfaction with the policies of the Federal Government as a direct personal insult or an invitation to exchange fisticuffs. . . . Texas already has a statute specifically prohibiting breaches of the peace, which tends to confirm that Texas need not punish this flag desecration in order to keep the peace.

The State also asserts an interest in preserving the flag as a symbol of nationhood and national unity. [T]his interest is related to expression in the case of Johnson's burning of the flag. . . . We are thus outside of *O'Brien*'s test altogether.

It remains to consider whether the State's interest in preserving the flag as a symbol of nationhood and national unity justifies Johnson's conviction. . . . Johnson was prosecuted because he knew that his politically charged expression would cause "serious offense." If he had burned the flag as a means of disposing of it because it was dirty or torn, he would not have been convicted of flag desecration under this Texas law: federal law designates burning as the preferred means of disposing of a flag "when it is in such condition that it is no longer a fitting emblem for display." 36 U.S.C. § 176(k), and Texas has no quarrel with this means of disposal. Brief for Petitioner 45. The Texas law is thus not aimed at protecting the physical integrity of the flag in all circumstances, but is designed instead to protect it only against impairments that would cause serious offense to others. . . .

Whether Johnson's treatment of the flag violated Texas law thus depended on the likely communicative impact of his expressive conduct. [T]his restriction on Johnson's expression is content-based. . . . We must therefore subject the

State's asserted interest in preserving the special symbolic character of the flag to "the most exacting scrutiny."[8]

Texas argues that its interest in preserving the flag as a symbol of nationhood and national unity survives this close analysis. [T]he State emphasizes the " 'special place' reserved for the flag in our Nation. . . ." If there is a bedrock principle underlying the First Amendment, it is that the Government may not prohibit the expression of an idea simply because society finds the idea itself offensive or disagreeable. . . . We have not recognized an exception to this principle even where our flag has been involved. In *Street v. New York*, 394 U.S. 576, 89 S.Ct. 1354, 22 L.Ed.2d 572 (1969), we held that a State may not criminally punish a person for uttering words critical of the flag. [N]othing in our precedents suggests that a state may foster its own view of the flag by prohibiting expressive conduct relating to it.[10]

Texas' focus on the precise nature of Johnson's expression, moreover, misses the point of our prior decisions: their enduring lesson, that the Government may not prohibit expression simply because it disagrees with its message, is not dependent on the particular mode in which one chooses to express an idea.[11] If we were to hold that a State may forbid flag-burning wherever it is likely to endanger the flag's symbolic role, but allow it whenever burning a flag promotes that role—as where, for example, a person ceremoniously burns a dirty flag—we would be saying that when it comes to impairing the flag's physical integrity, the flag itself may be used as a symbol—as a substitute for the written or spoken word or a "short cut from mind to mind"—only in one direction. . . .

We never before have held that the Government may ensure that a symbol be used to express only one view of that symbol or its referents. Indeed, in *Schacht v. United States*, [398 U.S. 58, 90 S.Ct. 1555, 26 L.Ed.2d 44 (1970)] we invalidated a federal statute permitting an actor portraying a member of one of our armed

---

[8]   . . . There was no evidence that Johnson himself stole the flag he burned, nor did the prosecution or the arguments urged in support of it depend on the theory that the flag was stolen. . . . Johnson was prosecuted *only* for flag desecration—not for trespass, disorderly conduct, or arson.

[10]   Our decision in *Halter v. Nebraska*, 205 U.S. 34, 27 S.Ct. 419, 51 L.Ed. 696 (1907), addressing the validity of a state law prohibiting certain commercial uses of the flag, is not to the contrary. [T]hat case involved purely commercial rather than political speech. . . .

[11]   The Chief Justice's dissent appears to believe that Johnson's conduct may be [criminalized] because "this act . . . conveyed nothing that could not have been conveyed and was not conveyed just as forcefully in a dozen different ways." Not only does this assertion sit uneasily next to the dissent's quite correct reminder that the flag occupies a unique position in our society—which demonstrates that messages conveyed without use of the flag are not "just as forcefu[l]" as those conveyed with it—but it also ignores the fact that, in *Spence v. Washington*, 418 U.S. 405, 411 n. 4, 94 S.Ct. 2727, 2731 n. 4, 41 L.Ed.2d 842 (1974), we "rejected summarily" this very claim.

forces to " 'wear the uniform of that armed force if the portrayal does not tend to discredit that armed force.' " This proviso, we held, "which leaves Americans free to praise the war in Vietnam but can send persons like Schacht to prison for opposing it, cannot survive in a country which has the First Amendment."

We perceive no basis on which to hold that the principle underlying our decision in *Schacht* does not apply to this case. To conclude that the Government may permit designated symbols to be used to communicate only a limited set of messages would be to enter territory having no discernible or defensible boundaries. Could the Government, on this theory, prohibit the burning of state flags? Of copies of the Presidential seal? Of the Constitution? In evaluating these choices under the First Amendment, how would we decide which symbols were sufficiently special to warrant this unique status? To do so, we would be forced to consult our own political preferences, and impose them on the citizenry, in the very way that the First Amendment forbids us to do. There is, moreover, no indication—either in the text of the Constitution or in our cases interpreting it— that a separate juridical category exists for the American flag alone. . . .

[O]ur toleration of criticism such as Johnson's is a sign and source of our strength. Indeed, one of the proudest images of our flag, the one immortalized in our own national anthem, is of the bombardment it survived at Fort McHenry. It is the Nation's resilience, not its rigidity, that Texas sees reflected in the flag—and it is that resilience that we reassert today.

The way to preserve the flag's special role is not to punish those who feel differently about these matters. It is to persuade them that they are wrong. [P]recisely because it is our flag that is involved, one's response to the flag-burner may exploit the uniquely persuasive power of the flag itself. We can imagine no more appropriate response to burning a flag than waving one's own, no better way to counter a flag-burner's message than by saluting the flag that burns, no surer means of preserving the dignity even of the flag that burned than by—as one witness here did—according its remains a respectful burial. We do not consecrate the flag by punishing its desecration, for in doing so we dilute the freedom that this cherished emblem represents.

Johnson was convicted for engaging in expressive conduct. The State's interest in preventing breaches of the peace does not support his conviction because Johnson's conduct did not threaten to disturb the peace. Nor does the State's interest in preserving the flag as a symbol of nationhood and national unity justify his criminal conviction for engaging in political expression. The judgment of the Texas Court of Criminal Appeals is therefore affirmed.

JUSTICE KENNEDY, concurring.

[S]ometimes we must make decisions we do not like. [T]the flag protects those who hold it in contempt. . . .

CHIEF JUSTICE REHNQUIST, with whom JUSTICE WHITE and JUSTICE O'CONNOR, join, dissenting.

In holding this Texas statute unconstitutional, the Court ignores Justice Holmes' familiar aphorism that "a page of history is worth a volume of logic." For more than 200 years, the American flag has occupied a unique position as the symbol of our Nation, a uniqueness that justifies a governmental prohibition against flag burning in the way respondent Johnson did here. [Chief Justice Rehnquist then followed with a thorough discussion of the history of the American flag, and quoted references to the flag in "The Star Spangled Banner" and Ralph Waldo Emerson's "Concord Hymn". He also reprinted John Greenleaf Whittier's poem, "Barbara Frietchie" (including the famous lines: " 'Shoot if you must, this old grey head,/But spare your country's flag,' she said.")]

[T]he public burning of the American flag by Johnson was no essential part of any exposition of ideas, and at the same time it had a tendency to incite a breach of the peace. Johnson was free to make any verbal denunciation of the flag that he wished; indeed, he was free to burn the flag in private. He could publicly burn other symbols of the Government or effigies of political leaders. [F]lag burning is the equivalent of an inarticulate grunt or roar that, it seems fair to say, is most likely to be indulged in not to express any particular idea, but to antagonize others. . . . It was Johnson's use of this particular symbol, and not the idea that he sought to convey by it or by his many other expressions, for which he was punished.

Our prior cases dealing with flag desecration statutes have left open the question that the Court resolves today. In *Street v. New York,* the defendant burned a flag in the street, shouting "We don't need no damned flag" . . . The Court ruled that since the defendant might have been convicted solely on the basis of his words, the conviction could not stand, but it expressly reserved the question of whether a defendant could constitutionally be convicted for burning the flag.

Chief Justice Warren, in dissent, stated: "I believe that the States and Federal Government do have the power to protect the flag from acts of desecration and disgrace. . . ." Justices Black and Fortas also expressed their personal view that a prohibition on flag burning did not violate the Constitution. See *id.,* (Black, J., dissenting) ("It passes my belief that anything in the Federal Constitution bars a

State from making the deliberate burning of the American Flag an offense"); *id.* (Fortas, J., dissenting) ("[T]he States and the Federal Government have the power to protect the flag from acts of desecration committed in public. . . . A person may 'own' a flag, but ownership is subject to special burdens and responsibilities. A flag may be property, in a sense; but it is property burdened with peculiar obligations and restrictions. . . ."). [O]ne of the high purposes of a democratic society is to legislate against conduct that is regarded as evil and profoundly offensive to the majority of people—whether it be murder, embezzlement, pollution, or flag burning. . . .

[The opinion of STEVENS, J., dissenting, is omitted.]

NOTES

1.   On April 8, 1989, the Presidium of the USSR Supreme Soviet adopted legislation making it a criminal offense to "discredit" a public official. Soviet reformers immediately attacked this legislation. In defense of the legislation, the Soviet old guard published an article in *Nedelya*, the Sunday supplement to *Izvestia*, with a circulation of millions. (*Nedelya*, 1989, No. 15, p. 19). This article listed dozens of foreign laws punishing disrespect for public officials or public symbols. In particular it listed 18 U.S.C.A. § 700, punishing "Desecration of the Flag of the United States." and 24 Penn. Code § 1104, punishing desecration of state and local flags.

Andrei Sakharov, speaking to the Congress of People's Deputies (*Izvestia*, May 29, 1989, p. 6) attacked the April 8, 1989 legislation as limiting free speech:

The Edict of the Presidium of the Supreme Soviet of the USSR [was] adopted on April 8. [It] contradicts the principles of democracy. There is a most important principle, which is formulated in the Universal Declaration of Human Rights, adopted in 1948, and by such an international organization as "Amnesty International." This is the principle that no actions connected with persuasion, unless they are connected with violence or with a call to violence, can be the subject of criminal prosecution. This is a key principle lying at the base of a democratic political system. And this key word "violence" is lacking in the language of the Edict of April 8. . . .

On June 8, 1989, the Supreme Soviet responded to the criticism by Sakharov and other Soviet reformers by repealing the edict.

2.   When this flag burning case was publicly announced, Justice Brennan took the uncommon step of reading excerpts for more than 10 minutes, rather than giving the more usual two minute summaries. Justice Stevens also read lengthy portions of his dissent. Public opinion polls indicated that the flag decision was very unpopular. Congress enacted a new statute prohibiting flag burning, and two lower federal courts promptly invalidated it. The Supreme Court also invalidated it, in the following case:

UNITED STATES V. EICHMAN

496 U.S. 310, 110 S.Ct. 2404, 110 L.Ed.2d 287 (1990)

JUSTICE BRENNAN delivered the opinion of the Court. . . .

After our decision in *Johnson,* Congress passed the Flag Protection Act of 1989. The Act provides in relevant part:

"(a)(1) Whoever knowingly mutilates, defaces, physically defiles, burns, maintains on the floor or ground, or tramples upon any flag of the United States shall be fined under this title or imprisoned for not more than one year, or both.

"(2) This subsection does not prohibit any conduct consisting of the disposal of a flag when it has become worn or soiled.

"(b) As used in this section, the term 'flag of the United States' means any flag of the United States, or any part thereof, made of any substance, of any size, in a form that is commonly displayed." 18 U.S.C.A. § 700.

[We decline the Government's invitation to reconsider *Johnson*].[4] The only remaining question is whether the Flag Protection Act is sufficiently distinct from the Texas statute that it may constitutionally be applied to proscribe appellees' expressive conduct.

The Government contends that the Flag Protection Act is constitutional because, unlike the statute addressed in *Johnson,* the Act does not target expressive conduct on the basis of the content of its message. [However,] the Government's asserted *interest* is . . . concerned with the content of such expression. . . . The Act criminalizes the conduct of anyone who "knowingly mutilates, defaces, physically defiles, burns, maintains on the floor or ground, or tramples upon any flag." Each

---

[4]   We deal here with concededly political speech and have no occasion to pass on the validity of laws regulating commercial exploitation of the image of the United States flag. See *Texas v. Johnson,* 491 U.S. 397, 415–416, n. 10 (1989); cf. *Halter v. Nebraska,* 205 U.S. 34 (1907).

of the specified terms—with the possible exception of "burns"—unmistakably connotes disrespectful treatment of the flag and suggests a focus on those acts likely to damage the flag's symbolic value. And the explicit exemption in § 700(a)(2) for disposal of "worn or soiled" flags protects certain acts traditionally associated with patriotic respect for the flag. . . .

Affirmed.

[The dissenting opinion of STEVENS, J., joined by REHNQUIST, C.J., and WHILE and O'CONNOR, JJ. Is omitted.]

NOTES

1. In *Halter v. Nebraska,* 205 U.S. 34, 27 S.Ct. 419, 51 L.Ed. 696 (1907), cited in *Eichman* at note 4, Harlan, J., for the Court, upheld a Nebraska statute that made it a misdemeanor to sell merchandise that had printed, for purposes of advertisement, a representation of the flag of the United States. The state law expressly excluded any newspaper, periodical, or book on which there was a representation of a flag "disconnected from any advertisement." The defendants offered for sale a bottle of beer and on the label there was printed a representation of the American flag. Only Peckham, J., dissented, without opinion.

2. After *Eichman,* a proposed constitutional amendment to prohibit flag-burning again failed to achieve the necessary votes in Congress. If *Eichman* had gone the other way, would it be legal to explode fireworks depicting the flag, or to place the flag design on a birthday cake that is then cut and eaten, or to burn a newspaper that included a photograph of the flag, or to make a movie where actors, portraying war protestors, burn the flag?

7.9 OBSCENITY

ROTH V. UNITED STATES
354 U.S. 476, 77 S.Ct. 1304, 1 L.Ed.2d 1498 (1957)*

MR. JUSTICE BRENNAN delivered the opinion of the Court.

The constitutionality of a criminal obscenity statute is the question in each of these cases. In *Roth,* the primary constitutional question is whether the federal obscenity statute violates the provision of the First Amendment that "Congress

---

* Together with *Alberts v. California.*

shall make no law . . . abridging the freedom of speech, or of the press. . . ." In *Alberts,* the primary constitutional question is whether the obscenity provisions of the California Penal Code invade the freedoms of speech and press as they may be incorporated in the liberty protected from state action by the Due Process Clause of the Fourteenth Amendment. . . .

The dispositive question is whether obscenity is utterance within the area of protected speech and press.[8] Although this is the first time the question has been squarely presented to this Court, either under the First Amendment or under the Fourteenth Amendment, expressions found in numerous opinions indicate that this Court has always assumed that obscenity is not protected by the freedoms of speech and press. The guaranties of freedom of expression in effect in 10 of the 14 States which by 1792 had ratified the Constitution, gave no absolute protection for every utterance. Thirteen of the 14 States provided for the prosecution of libel, and all of those States made either blasphemy or profanity, or both, statutory crimes. . . .

All ideas having even the slightest redeeming social importance— unorthodox ideas, controversial ideas, even ideas hateful to the prevailing climate of opinion—have the full protection of the guaranties, unless excludable because they encroach upon the limited area of more important interests. But implicit in the history of the First Amendment is the rejection of obscenity as utterly without redeeming social importance. This rejection for that reason is mirrored in the universal judgment that obscenity should be restrained, reflected in the international agreement of over 50 nations, in the obscenity laws of all of the 48 States, and in the 20 obscenity laws enacted by the Congress from 1842 to 1956. . . . We hold that obscenity is not within the area of constitutionally protected speech or press.

It is strenuously urged that these obscenity statutes offend the constitutional guaranties because they punish incitation to impure sexual *thoughts,* not shown to be related to any overt antisocial conduct which is or may be incited in the persons stimulated to such *thoughts.* . . . It is insisted that the constitutional guaranties are violated because convictions may be had without proof either that obscene material will perceptibly create a clear and present danger of antisocial conduct, or will probably induce its recipients to such conduct. But, in light of our holding that obscenity is not protected speech, [it is unnecessary to consider such issues.]

---

[8] No issue is presented in either case concerning the obscenity of the material involved.

However, sex and obscenity are not synonymous. Obscene material is material which deals with sex in a manner appealing to prurient interest.[20] The portrayal of sex, *e.g.*, in art, literature and scientific works, is not itself sufficient reason to deny material the constitutional protection of freedom of speech and press. Sex, a great and mysterious motive force in human life, has indisputably been a subject of absorbing interest to mankind through the ages; it is one of the vital problems of human interest and public concern. . . . It is therefore vital that the standards for judging obscenity safeguard the protection of freedom of speech and press for material which does not treat sex in a manner appealing to prurient interest.

The early leading standard of obscenity allowed material to be judged merely by the effect of an isolated excerpt upon particularly susceptible persons. *Regina v. Hicklin,* [1868] L.R. 3 Q.B. 360. Some American courts adopted this standard but later decisions have rejected it and substituted this test: whether to the average person, applying contemporary community standards, the dominant theme of the material taken as a whole appeals to prurient interest. The *Hicklin* test, judging obscenity by the effect of isolated passages upon the most susceptible persons, might well encompass material legitimately treating with sex, and so it must be rejected as unconstitutionally restrictive of the freedoms of speech and press. On the other hand, the substituted standard provides safeguards adequate to withstand the charge of constitutional infirmity. Both trial courts below sufficiently followed the proper standard. . . .

It is argued that the statutes do not provide reasonably ascertainable standards of guilt and therefore violate the constitutional requirements of due process. . . . The thrust of the argument is that these words ["obscene," "lewd," "filthy," "lascivious," "indecent"] are not sufficiently precise because they do not mean the same thing to all people, all the time, everywhere.

[L]ack of precision is not itself offensive to the requirements of due process. [A]ll that is required is that the language "conveys sufficiently definite warning as to the proscribed conduct when measured by common understanding and practices. . . ." These words, applied according to the proper standard for judging obscenity, already discussed, give adequate warning of the conduct proscribed and

---

[20] I.e., material having a tendency to excite lustful thoughts. . . . We perceive no significant difference between the meaning of obscenity developed in the case law and the definition of the A.L.I., Model Penal Code, § 207.10(2) (Tent.Draft No. 6, 1957), viz.:

> A thing is obscene if, considered as a whole, its predominant appeal is to prurient interest, *i.e.*, a shameful or morbid interest in nudity, sex, or excretion, and if it goes substantially beyond customary limits of candor in description or representation of such matters.

mark ". . . boundaries sufficiently distinct for judges and juries fairly to administer the law. . . . That there may be marginal cases in which it is difficult to determine the side of the line on which a particular fact situation falls is no sufficient reason to hold the language too ambiguous to define a criminal offense. . . ."

In summary, then, we hold that these statutes, applied according to the proper standard for judging obscenity, do not offend constitutional safeguards against convictions based upon protected material, or fail to give men in acting adequate notice of what is prohibited.

MR. CHIEF JUSTICE WARREN, concurring in the result.

. . . The history of the application of laws designed to suppress the obscene demonstrates convincingly that the power of government can be invoked under them against great art or literature, scientific treatises, or works exciting social controversy. Mistakes of the past prove that there is a strong countervailing interest to be considered in the freedoms guaranteed by the First and Fourteenth Amendments. . . .

The personal element in these cases is seen most strongly in the requirement of *scienter*. Under the California law, the prohibited activity must be done "wilfully and lewdly." The federal statute limits the crime to acts done "knowingly." In his charge to the jury, the district judge stated that the matter must be "calculated" to corrupt or debauch. The defendants in both these cases were engaged in the business of purveying textual or graphic matter openly advertised to appeal to the erotic interest of their customers. They were plainly engaged in the commercial exploitation of the morbid and shameful craving for materials with prurient effect. I believe that the State and Federal Governments can constitutionally punish such conduct. That is all that these cases present to us, and that is all we need to decide. . . .

MR. JUSTICE HARLAN, concurring in the result in No. 61 and dissenting in No. 582:

I do not think that reviewing courts can escape [their] responsibility by saying that the trier of the facts, be it a jury or a judge, has labeled the questioned matter as "obscene," for, if "obscenity" is to be suppressed, the question whether a particular work is of that character involves not really an issue of fact but a question of constitutional *judgment* of the most sensitive and delicate kind. Many juries might find that Joyce's "Ulysses" or Boccaccio's "Decameron" was obscene, and yet the conviction of a defendant for selling either book would raise, for me, the gravest constitutional problems, for no such verdict could convince me, without more, that these books are "utterly without redeeming social importance." In short, I do not understand how the Court can resolve the constitutional problems now before it without making its own independent judgment upon the character of the material upon which these convictions were based. . . .

I concur in the judgment of the Court in No. 61, *Alberts v. California.* . . . In judging the constitutionality of this conviction, we should remember that our function in reviewing state judgments under the Fourteenth Amendment is a narrow one. [T]he state legislature has made the judgment that printed words *can* "deprave or corrupt" the reader—that words can incite to antisocial or immoral action. The assumption seems to be that the distribution of certain types of literature will induce criminal or immoral sexual conduct. It is well known, of course, that the validity of this assumption is a matter of dispute among critics, sociologists, psychiatrists, and penologists. [I]t is not irrational, in our present state of knowledge, to consider that pornography can induce a type of sexual conduct which a State may deem obnoxious to the moral fabric of society. In fact the very division of opinion on the subject counsels us to respect the choice made by the State.

[I]n the final analysis, I concur in the judgment because, upon an independent perusal of the material involved, and in light of the considerations discussed above, I cannot say that its suppression would so interfere with the communication of "ideas" in any proper sense of that term that it would offend the Due Process Clause. I therefore agree with the Court that appellant's conviction must be affirmed.

I dissent in No. 582, *Roth v. United States.* . . . I do not think it follows that state and federal powers in this area are the same, and that just because the State may suppress a particular utterance, it is automatically permissible for the Federal Government to do the same. [T]he interests which obscenity statutes purportedly protect are primarily entrusted to the care, not of the Federal Government, but of the States. Congress has no substantive power over sexual morality. Such powers as the Federal Government has in this field are but incidental to its other powers, here the postal power, and are not of the same nature as those possessed by the States, which bear direct responsibility for the protection of the local moral fabric. . . .

MR. JUSTICE DOUGLAS, with whom MR. JUSTICE BLACK concurs, dissenting. . . .

The tests by which these convictions were obtained require only the arousing of sexual thoughts. Yet the arousing of sexual thoughts and desires happens every day in normal life in dozens of ways. Nearly 30 years ago a questionnaire sent to college and normal school women graduates asked what things were most stimulating sexually. Of 409 replies, 9 said "music"; 18 said "pictures"; 29 said "dancing"; 40 said "drama"; 95 said "books"; and 218 said "man." . . .

Any test that turns on what is offensive to the community's standards is too loose, too capricious, too destructive of freedom of expression to be squared with the First Amendment. Under that test, juries can censor, suppress, and punish what they don't like, provided the matter relates to "sexual impurity" or has a tendency "to excite lustful thoughts." [I]n the battle between the literati and the Philistines, the Philistines are certain to win. If experience in this field teaches anything, it is that "censorship of obscenity has almost always been both irrational and indiscriminate." The test adopted here accentuates that trend.

[T]here is no special historical evidence that literature dealing with sex was intended to be treated in a special manner by those who drafted the First Amendment. In fact, the first reported court decision in this country involving obscene literature was in 1821. I reject too the implication that problems of freedom of speech and of the press are to be resolved by weighing against the values of free expression, the judgment of the Court that a particular form of that expression has "no redeeming social importance." The First Amendment, its prohibition in terms absolute, was designed to preclude courts as well as legislatures from weighing the values of speech against silence. The First Amendment puts free speech in the preferred position.

Freedom of expression can be suppressed if, and to the extent that, it is so closely brigaded with illegal action as to be an inseparable part of it. As a people, we cannot afford to relax that standard. For the test that suppresses a cheap tract today can suppress a literary gem tomorrow. All it need do is to incite a lascivious thought or arouse a lustful desire. The list of books that judges or juries can place in that category is endless. . . .

NOTES

1. Following *Roth,* the Court made further efforts to define what is "obscene." E.g., *Jacobellis v. Ohio,* 378 U.S. 184, 84 S.Ct. 1676, 12 L.Ed.2d 793 (1964). Justice Brennan's plurality opinion, joined by Justice Goldberg, emphasized that the Court in obscenity cases must make "an independent constitutional judgment on the facts of the case as to whether the material involved is constitutionally protected." The standard of review is not that of "sufficient

evidence." Rather, the Court must exercise *de novo* review of the work. Also, the reference in *Roth* to "contemporary community standards" was not to state or local communities but to "society at large," "the public or people in general." This national standard meant that the definition of obscenity might vary because of the passage of time, but not because of a change in location. Warren, C.J., joined by Clark, J., dissenting, argued that local community standards should govern.

Justice Stewart's concurrence stated simply:

It is possible to read the Court's opinion in *Roth v. United States* and *Alberts v. California,* in a variety of ways. In saying this, I imply no criticism of the Court, which in those cases was faced with the task of trying to define what may be indefinable. I have reached the conclusion, which I think is confirmed at least by negative implication in the Court's decisions since *Roth* and *Alberts,* that under the First and Fourteenth Amendments criminal laws in this area are constitutionally limited to hard-core pornography. I shall not today attempt further to define the kinds of material I understand to be embraced within that shorthand description; and perhaps I could never succeed in intelligibly doing so. But I know it when I see it, and the motion picture involved in this case is not that.

2.   In *A Book Named "John Cleland's Memoirs of a Woman of Pleasure" v. Attorney Gen. of Massachusetts,* 383 U.S. 413, 86 S.Ct. 975, 16 L.Ed.2d 1 (1966), the Court, again with no majority opinion, reversed a decision that a book, *Memoirs of a Woman of Pleasure,* was obscene. The book, commonly called *Fanny Hill,* was written about 1750. A Massachusetts law allowed the Attorney General to put the book itself on trial rather than its publisher or distributor, and to seek a declaration of obscenity. Justice Brennan's plurality opinion argued that to be "obscene"—

three elements must coalesce: it must be established that (a) the dominant theme of the material taken as a whole appeals to a prurient interest in sex; (b) the material is patently offensive because it affronts contemporary community standards relating to the description or representation of sexual matters; and (c) the material is utterly without redeeming social value. . . .

The Supreme Judicial Court erred in holding that a book need not be "unqualifiedly worthless before it can be deemed obscene." A book cannot be proscribed unless it is found to be *utterly* without redeeming social value. This is so even though the book is found to possess the requisite prurient appeal and to be patently offensive. Each of the three federal constitutional criteria is to be applied independently; the social value of the book can neither be weighed against nor canceled by its prurient appeal or patent offensiveness.

Later, Brennan, reacting to the Court's inability to muster an opinion of the Court, summarized what was happening: "In the face of this divergence of opinion the Court began the practice in *Redrup v. New York,* 386 U.S. 767, 87 S.Ct. 1414, 18 L.Ed.2d 515 (1967), of per curiam reversals of convictions for the dissemination of material that at least five members of the Court, applying their separate tests, deemed not to be obscene." He added, "No fewer than 31 cases have been disposed of in this fashion."[7]

3. **PANDERING.** Justice Brennan's majority opinion in *Ginzburg v. U.S.,* 383 U.S. 463, 86 S.Ct. 942, 16 L.Ed.2d 31 (1966) assumed that the three publications involved in that case, standing alone, might not be obscene, but nonetheless upheld the conviction because of their pandering—a "background of commercial exploitation of erotica solely for the sake of their prurient appeal." The trial court found that the publisher, because of the salacious appeal of such names, sought mailing privileges from Intercourse and Blue Ball, Pennsylvania, and eventually settled on Middlesex, New Jersey. The advertising circulars emphasized the sexual candor of the materials and guaranteed full refunds if they "failed to reach you because of U.S. Post Office censorship interference."

Brennan argued: "The deliberate representation of petitioners' publications as erotically arousing, for example, stimulated the reader to accept them as prurient; he looks for titillation, not for saving intellectual content." Also "the brazenness of such an appeal heightens the offensiveness of the publication to those who are offended by such material." "Where the purveyor's sole emphasis is on the sexually provocative aspects of his publications, that fact may be decisive in the determination of obscenity."

Later, *Splawn v. California,* 431 U.S. 595, 97 S.Ct. 1987, 52 L.Ed.2d 606 (1977) said: "There is no doubt that as a matter of First Amendment obscenity law, evidence of pandering to prurient interests in the creation, promotion, or dissemination of material is relevant to determining whether

---

[7]   *Paris Adult Theatre I v. Slaton,* 413 U.S. 49, 82 & n.8, 93 S.Ct. 2628, 2646 & n.8, 37 L.Ed.2d 446 (1973) (Brennan, J., dissenting).

the material is obscene." Stevens, J., dissented, joined Stewart, and Marshall and also Brennan (who wrote the Court's opinion in *Ginzburg*). The dissent argued, that "if they were not otherwise obscene, I cannot understand how these films lost their protected status by being truthfully described." Moreover, "there is a definite social interest in permitting them to be accurately described. Only an accurate description can enable a potential viewer to decide whether or not he wants to see them."

4. **PROTECTION OF JUVENILES.** Justice Brennan also wrote the majority opinion in *Ginsberg v. New York,* 390 U.S. 629, 88 S.Ct. 1274, 20 L.Ed.2d 195 (1968). The issue was the constitutionality of a New York criminal obscenity statute that prohibits the sale to minors (under 17 years old) of material defined to be obscene on the basis of its appeal to them whether or not it would be obscene to adults." The Court upheld the law even though the " 'girlie' picture magazines involved in the sales are not obscene for adults." This variable obscenity is within the power of the state, the Court said, because the state's power over children is broader than its power over adults. First, the law supports the parents' claim of authority to direct the rearing of their children. If the parents want their children to see such materials, nothing in the law prohibits such parents from purchasing the magazines for their children. Second, the "State has an independent interest in the well-being of its youth." Justice Stewart concurred on the basis that "in some precisely delineated areas, a child—like someone in a captive audience—is not possessed of that full capacity for individual choice which is the presupposition of First Amendment guarantees."

5. **OBSCENITY IN THE HOME.** *Stanley v. Georgia,* 394 U.S. 557, 89 S.Ct. 1243, 22 L.Ed.2d 542 (1969), reversed an obscenity conviction because "the mere private possession of obscene matter cannot constitutionally be made a crime." The Court reasoned that the right of speech protects also the right to receive. The defendant had a right "to satisfy his intellectual and emotional needs in the privacy of his own home." While the state contended that viewing such obscenity could lead to deviant criminal behavior, there "appears to be little empirical basis for that assertion."

Some lower courts and commentators thought that *Stanley* impaired the holding in *Roth.* Their predictions did not bear fruit. *United States v. Reidel,* 402 U.S. 351, 91 S.Ct. 1410, 28 L.Ed.2d 813 (1971), held that a federal obscenity statute was constitutional as applied to the distribution of obscene materials to willing adult recipients. The focus of *Stanley* "was on freedom of mind and thought and on the privacy of one's home. It does not require that we fashion or recognize a constitutional right in people like Reidel to distribute or sell obscene materials." Thus, the state may also prohibit an individual from transporting obscene materials for private use. *United States v. Orito,* 413 U.S. 139, 93 S.Ct. 2674, 37 L.Ed.2d 513 (1973).

MILLER V. CALIFORNIA

413 U.S. 15, 93 S.Ct. 2607, 37 L.Ed.2d 419 (1973)

MR. CHIEF JUSTICE BURGER delivered the opinion of the Court.

. . . This case involves the application of a State's criminal obscenity statute to a situation in which sexually explicit materials have been thrust by aggressive sales action upon unwilling recipients who had in no way indicated any desire to receive such materials. . . .

Apart from the initial formulation in the *Roth* case, no majority of the Court has at any given time been able to agree on a standard to determine what constitutes obscene, pornographic material subject to regulation under the States' police power. We have seen "a variety of views among the members of the Court unmatched in any other course of constitutional adjudication." . . .

The case we now review was tried on the theory that the California Penal Code § 311 approximately incorporates the three-stage *Memoirs* test, *supra*. But now the *Memoirs* test has been abandoned as unworkable by its author,[4] and no Member of the Court today supports the *Memoirs* formulation.

This much has been categorically settled by the Court, that obscene material is unprotected by the First Amendment. . . . We acknowledge, however, the inherent dangers of undertaking to regulate any form of expression. State statutes designed to regulate obscene materials must be carefully limited. As a result, we now confine the permissible scope of such regulation to works which depict or describe sexual conduct. . . .

The basic guidelines for the trier of fact must be: (a) whether "the average person, applying contemporary community standards" would find that the work, taken as a whole, appeals to the prurient interest; (b) whether the work depicts or describes, in a patently offensive way, sexual conduct specifically defined by the applicable state law; and (c) whether the work, taken as a whole, lacks serious literary, artistic, political, or scientific value. We do not adopt as a constitutional standard the *"utterly* without redeeming social value" test of *Memoirs v.*

---

[4]   See the dissenting opinion of Justice Brennan in *Paris Adult Theatre 1 v. Slaton.*

Massachusetts, that concept has never commanded the adherence of more than three Justices at one time. If a state law that regulates obscene material is thus limited, as written or construed, the First Amendment values applicable to the States through the Fourteenth Amendment are adequately protected by the ultimate power of appellate courts to conduct an independent review of constitutional claims when necessary.

[A] few plain examples of what a state statute could define [under] the standard announced in this opinion:

(a) Patently offensive representations or descriptions of ultimate sexual acts, normal or perverted, actual or simulated.

(b) Patently offensive representations or descriptions of masturbation, excretory functions, and lewd exhibition of the genitals.

Sex and nudity may not be exploited without limit by films or pictures exhibited or sold in places of public accommodation any more than live sex and nudity can be exhibited or sold without limit in such public places. At a minimum, prurient, patently offensive depiction or description of sexual conduct must have serious literary, artistic, political, or scientific value to merit First Amendment protection. For example, medical books for the education of physicians and related personnel necessarily use graphic illustrations and descriptions of human anatomy. In resolving the inevitably sensitive questions of fact and law, we must continue to rely on the jury system, accompanied by the safeguards that judges, rules of evidence, presumption of innocence, and other protective features provide, as we do with rape, murder, and a host of other offenses against society and its individual members.

Mr. Justice Brennan, author of the opinions of the Court, or the plurality opinions [in many previous obscenity cases], has abandoned his former position and now maintains that no formulation of this Court, the Congress, or the States can adequately distinguish obscene material unprotected by the First Amendment from protected expression, *Paris Adult Theatre I v. Slaton,* (Brennan, J., dissenting). Paradoxically, Mr. Justice Brennan indicates that suppression of unprotected obscene material is permissible to avoid exposure to unconsenting adults, as in this case, and to juveniles, although he gives no indication of how the division between protected and nonprotected materials may be drawn with greater precision for these purposes than for regulation of commercial exposure to consenting adults only. Nor does he indicate where in the Constitution he finds the authority to distinguish between a willing "adult" one month past the state law age of majority and a willing "juvenile" one month younger.

Under the holdings announced today, no one will be subject to prosecution for the sale of exposure of obscene materials unless these materials depict or describe patently offensive "hard core" sexual conduct specifically defined by the regulating state law, as written or construed. We are satisfied that these specific prerequisites will provide fair notice to a dealer in such materials that his public and commercial activities may bring prosecution. . . .

[T]oday, for the first time since *Roth* was decided in 1957, a majority of this Court has agreed on concrete guidelines to isolate "hard core" pornography from expression protected by the First Amendment. . . .

Under a National Constitution, fundamental First Amendment limitations on the powers of the States do not vary from community to community, but this does not mean that there are, or should or can be, fixed, uniform national standards of precisely what appeals to the "prurient interest" or is "patently offensive." These are essentially questions of fact, and our Nation is simply too big and too diverse for this Court to reasonably expect that such standards could be articulated for all 50 States in a single formulation, even assuming the prerequisite consensus exists. When triers of fact are asked to decide whether "the average person, applying contemporary community standards" would consider certain materials "prurient," it would be unrealistic to require that the answer be based on some abstract formulation. The adversary system, with lay jurors as the usual ultimate factfinders in criminal prosecutions, has historically permitted triers of fact to draw on the standards of their community, guided always by limiting instructions on the law. To require a State to structure obscenity proceedings around evidence of a *national* "community standard" would be an exercise in futility.

[N]either the State's alleged failure to offer evidence of "national standards," nor the trial court's charge that the jury consider state community standards, were constitutional errors. . . . It is neither realistic nor constitutionally sound to read the First Amendment as requiring that the people of Maine or Mississippi accept public depiction of conduct found tolerable in Las Vegas, or New York City.

[W]e (a) reaffirm the *Roth* holding that obscene material is not protected by the First Amendment; (b) hold that such material can be regulated by the States, subject to the specific safeguards enunciated above, without a showing that the material is "*utterly* without redeeming social value"; and (c) hold that obscenity is to be determined by applying "contemporary community standards," not "national standards.". . . . Vacated and remanded.

[The dissenting opinion of DOUGLAS, J. and the dissenting opinion of BRENNAN, J., joined by STEWART and MARSHALL, JJ., are omitted.]

PARIS ADULT THEATRE I V. SLATON
413 U.S. 49, 93 S.Ct. 2628, 37 L.Ed.2d 446 (1973)

MR. CHIEF JUSTICE BURGER delivered the opinion of the Court.

[W]e hold that there are legitimate state interests at stake in stemming the tide of commercialized obscenity, even assuming it is feasible to enforce effective safeguards against exposure to juveniles and to passersby. Rights and interests "other than those of the advocates are involved." These include the interest of the public in the quality of life and the total community environment, the tone of commerce in the great city centers, and, possibly, the public safety itself. The Hill-Link Minority Report of the Commission on Obscenity and Pornography indicates that there is at least an arguable correlation between obscene material and crime. . . . It is not for us to resolve empirical uncertainties underlying state legislation, save in the exceptional case where that legislation plainly impinges upon rights protected by the Constitution itself. . . .

Finally, petitioners argue that conduct which directly involves "consenting adults" only has, for that sole reason, a special claim to constitutional protection. Our Constitution establishes a broad range of conditions on the exercise of power by the States, but for us to say that our Constitution incorporates the proposition that conduct involving consenting adults only is always beyond state regulation, is a step we are unable to take.[15]. . .

MR. JUSTICE BRENNAN, with whom MR. JUSTICE STEWART and MR. JUSTICE MARSHALL join, dissenting . . .

Our experience with the *Roth* approach has certainly taught us that the outright suppression of obscenity cannot be reconciled with the fundamental principles of the First and Fourteenth Amendments. [N]o one definition, no matter how precisely or narrowly drawn, can possibly suffice for all situations, or carve out fully suppressible expression from all media without also creating a

---

[15]   The state statute books are replete with constitutionally unchallenged laws against prostitution, suicide, voluntary self-mutilation, brutalizing "bare fist" prize fights, and duels, although these crimes may only directly involve "consenting adults." Statutes making bigamy a crime surely cut into an individual's freedom to associate, but few today seriously claim such statutes violate the First Amendment or any other constitutional provision. . . . As Professor Irving Kristol has observed: "Bearbaiting and cockfighting are prohibited only in part out of compassion for the suffering animals; the main reason they were abolished was because it was felt that they debased and brutalized the citizenry who flocked to witness such spectacles." On the Democratic Idea in America 33 (1972).

substantial risk of encroachment upon the guarantees of the Due Process Clause and the First Amendment. . . .

Our experience since *Roth* requires us not only to abandon the effort to pick out obscene materials on a case-by-case basis, but also to reconsider a fundamental postulate of *Roth:* that there exists a definable class of sexually oriented expression that may be totally suppressed by the Federal and State Governments. [T]he concept of "obscenity" cannot be defined with sufficient specificity and clarity to provide fair notice to persons who create and distribute sexually oriented materials, to prevent substantial erosion of protected speech as a byproduct of the attempt to suppress unprotected speech, and to avoid very costly institutional harms.

[T]he state interests in protecting children and in protecting unconsenting adults may stand on a different footing from the other asserted state interests. [I]f children are "not possessed of that full capacity for individual choice which is the presupposition of the First Amendment guarantees," then the State may have a substantial interest in precluding the flow of obscene materials even to consenting juveniles. [W]hatever the strength of the state interests in protecting juveniles and unconsenting adults from exposure to sexually oriented materials, those interests cannot be asserted in defense of the holding of the Georgia Supreme Court in this case. That court assumed for the purposes of its decision that the films in issue were exhibited only to persons over the age of 21 who viewed them willingly and with prior knowledge of the nature of their contents. And on that assumption the state court held that the films could still be suppressed. The justification for the suppression must be found, therefore, in some independent interest in regulating the reading and viewing habits of consenting adults.

[W]hile I cannot say that the interests of the State—apart from the question of juveniles and unconsenting adults—are trivial or nonexistent, I am compelled to conclude that these interests cannot justify the substantial damage to constitutional rights and to this Nation's judicial machinery that inevitably results from state efforts to bar the distribution even of unprotected material to consenting adults. I would hold, therefore, that at least in the absence of distribution to juveniles or obtrusive exposure to unconsenting adults, the First and Fourteenth Amendments prohibit the State and Federal Governments from attempting wholly to suppress sexually oriented materials on the basis of their allegedly "obscene" contents. Nothing in this approach precludes those governments from taking action to serve what may be strong and legitimate interests through regulation of the manner of distribution of sexually oriented material.

[The dissenting opinion of DOUGLAS, J. is omitted.]

NOTES

1. *Hamling v. United States,* 418 U.S. 87, 94 S.Ct. 2887, 41 L.Ed.2d 590 (1974), affirmed obscenity convictions and elaborated on the community standards test. The federal obscenity statute should not be interpreted as requiring proof of uniform national standards. The federal law permits the juror to draw on the knowledge of the community or vicinage, from which he comes. The fact that "distributors of allegedly obscene materials may be subjected to varying community standards in the various federal districts into which they transmit the materials does not render a federal statute unconstitutional because of the failure of application of uniform national standards of obscenity." The government must show *scienter, i.e.,* "that a defendant had knowledge of the contents of the materials he distributed and that he knew the character and nature of the materials." However, the government need not show that the defendant knew of the legal status of the materials. To require such proof "would permit the defendant to avoid prosecution by simply claiming that he had not brushed up on the law."

    That same day the Court decided *Jenkins v. Georgia,* 418 U.S. 153, 94 S.Ct. 2750, 41 L.Ed.2d 642 (1974), which Court reversed the obscenity conviction of defendant charged with showing the film "Carnal Knowledge" in a theatre. The movie (released in 1971) appeared on several "Ten Best" lists for the year. The Court turned to the film itself. "Our own viewing of the film satisfies us that 'Carnal Knowledge' could not be found under the Miller standard to depict sexual conduct in a patently offensive way." The nudity alone did not make the film obscene, and "it would be a serious misreading of Miller to conclude that the juries have unbridled discretion in determining what is 'patently offensive.' " Justice Brennan, joined by Justices Stewart and Marshall, concurred in the result: "After the Court's decision today, there can be no doubt that *Miller* requires appellate courts—including this Court—to review independently the constitutional fact of obscenity." Thus "one cannot say with certainty that material is obscene until at least five members of this Court, applying inevitably obscure standards, have pronounced it so."

2. **CHILD PORNOGRAPHY.** *New York v. Ferber*, 458 U.S. 747, 102 S.Ct. 3348, 73 L.Ed.2d 1113 (1982), upheld, without dissent, a state statute that made it a crime for a person knowingly to promote sexual performances by children under the age of 16 by distributing material that depicts such performances even though the materials themselves were not necessarily "obscene" in a constitutional sense. The purpose of the prohibition is to protect the children; in contract, the purpose of obscenity laws is to protect the consenting adult. *Ferber* articulated five basic premises. First, the state's interests in protecting the physical and psychological well-being of minors was compelling. Second, prohibiting the distribution of films and photos depicting such activities is closely related to this compelling interest in two ways: the permanent record of the child's activity and its circulation exacerbates the harm to the minor, and also the distribution feeds the demand, which encourages the sexual exploitation of the children and the production of the material. Third, advertising and selling of the material encourages the evil by supplying an economic motive. Fourth, any value of allowing live performances and photographic reproduction of children engaged in lewd sexual conduct is de minimis. The Court noted, for example, that the person who put together the material depicting the sexual performance could always use an adult model who looked younger. And, fifth, the classification of child pornography as outside of First Amendment protection is consistent with precedent and justified by the need to protect the welfare of the children.

    Ferber adjusted the *Miller* formulation as follows: the trier of fact need not find that the material appeals to the prurient interest of the average person; sexual conduct need not be portrayed in a patently offensive manner; and the material at issue need not be considered as a whole. "We note that the distribution of descriptions or other depictions of sexual conduct, not otherwise obscene, which do not involve live performance or photographic or other visual reproduction of live performances, retains First Amendment protection. As with obscenity laws, criminal responsibility may not be imposed without some element of scienter on the part of the defendant."

3. *Osborne v. Ohio*, 495 U.S. 103, 110 S.Ct. 1691, 109 L.Ed.2d 98 (1990), held that the state may constitutionally prohibit the possession and viewing of child pornography at home. The distinction with *Stanley v. Georgia*, is "obvious: the State does not rely on a paternalistic interest in regulating Osborne's mind." Rather, the purpose of the law is "to protect the victims of child pornography; it hopes to destroy a market for the exploitative use of

children." The statute prohibited any person from possessing or viewing any material showing a minor (not his child or ward) in a state of nudity unless (a) the material or performance is presented for a bona fide purpose by or to a person having a proper interest, or (b) the possessor knows that the minor's parents or guardian has consented in writing to such photographing of the minor. The law required scienter and is limited to depictions of nudity that involve lewd exhibition or involve graphic focus of the minor's genitals. Brennan, J., joined by Marshall & Stevens, JJ., dissented: "*Stanley v. Georgia* prevents the State from criminalizing appellant's possession of the photographs at issue in this case."

4.   **DEPICTIONS OF VIOLENCE.** *United States v. Stevens*, 559 U.S. 460, 130 S.Ct. 1577, 176 L.Ed.2d 435 (2010). Defendant was convicted of violating 18 U.S.C.A. § 48, prohibiting depictions of animal cruelty. He sold videos of dogs fighting. Roberts, C.J., for the Court (8 to 1) held that the federal statute criminalizing the commercial creation, sale, or possession of depictions of animal cruelty was substantially overbroad, and thus, facially invalid under the First Amendment.

Because § 48 bans expression based on content—"visual or auditory depiction 'in which a living animal is intentionally maimed, mutilated, tortured, wounded, or killed,'"—it is presumptively invalid under the First Amendment. It applies only to "*portrayals* of harmful acts, not the underlying conduct." Second, *Ferber* does not establish a "freewheeling authority to declare new categories of speech outside the scope of the First Amendment." If there are other "categories of speech" that are like *Ferber* and historically unprotected, "there is no evidence that 'depictions of animal cruelty'" would be included.

Congress enacted § 48 to prohibit "crush videos" but its language goes much farther. "Crush videos often depict women slowly crushing animals to death 'with their bare feet or while wearing high heeled shoes,' sometimes while 'talking to the animals in a kind of dominatrix patter' over '[t]he cries and squeals of the animals, obviously in great pain.'" However, § 48's definition of "depiction of animal cruelty" does not require that the conduct be cruel. Its prohibition includes any depiction if a living animal is intentionally "wounded, or killed." This law "draws no distinction based on the reason the intentional killing of an animal is made illegal, and includes, for example, the humane slaughter of a stolen cow." Depicting entirely lawful conduct violates § 48 if that depiction later finds its way into another jurisdiction where the same conduct is unlawful. President Clinton, when he signed the law, said the Government would only apply the law to depictions of "wanton cruelty," but no one "suggests that the videos in this case fit that description."

The Court did not decide if a law limited to crush videos or other depictions of extreme animal cruelty would be constitutional. "We hold only that § 48 is not so limited but is instead substantially overbroad," and thus invalid. Only Justice Alito dissented. He objected to the overbreadth analysis used to invalidate a law that "was enacted not to suppress speech, but to prevent horrific acts of animal cruelty—in particular, the creation and commercial exploitation of 'crush videos,' a form of depraved entertainment that has no social value." He would interpret the statute very narrowly and only allow "as applied" challenges.

Brown v. Entertainment Merchants Association, 564 U.S. 786, 131 S.Ct. 2729, 180 L.Ed.2d 708 (2011). Video game and software litigants sued to enjoin a California law that imposed a civil fine of $1,000 on anyone who rents or sells violent video games to minors (under 18). These games are indeed violent: "Victims are dismembered, decapitated, disemboweled, set on fire, and chopped into little pieces. . . . Blood gushes, splatters, and pools." The Supreme Court (7 to 2), held the law violated free speech. Scalia, J., spoke for the majority.

Even crudely "violent video games, tawdry TV shows, and cheap novels and magazines" are a form of speech. Technology is ever-changing, but the First Amendment's command, does not vary "when a new and different medium for communication appears." Like movies, video games communicate ideas "through many familiar literary devices (such as characters, dialogue, plot, and music) and through features distinctive to the medium (such as the player's interaction with the virtual world)."

There are a few categories of historically unprotected speech—obscenity, incitement, and fighting words—but "new categories of unprotected speech may not be added to the list by a legislature that concludes certain speech is too harmful to be tolerated." The obscenity exception does not include "whatever a legislature finds shocking, but only depictions of 'sexual conduct.' " Unlike obscenity, there is no "longstanding tradition" in this country of restricting children's access to depictions of violence:

Certainly the books we gave children to read—or read to them when they are younger—contain no shortage of gore. Grimm's Fairy Tales, for example, are grim indeed. As her just deserts for trying to poison Snow White, the wicked queen is made to dance in red hot slippers "till she fell dead on the floor, a sad example of envy and jealousy." Cinderella's evil stepsisters have their eyes pecked out by doves. And Hansel and Gretel (children!) kill their captor by baking her in an oven. High-school reading lists are full of similar fare. Homer's Odysseus blinds Polyphemus the Cyclops by grinding out his eye with a heated stake. The Odyssey of Homer, Book IX, p. 125 ("Even so did we seize the fiery-pointed brand and whirled it round in his eye, and the blood flowed about the heated bar. And the breath of the flame singed his eyelids and brows all about, as the ball of the eye burnt away, and the roots thereof crackled in the flame"). In the Inferno, Dante and Virgil watch corrupt politicians struggle to stay submerged beneath a lake of boiling pitch, lest they be skewered by devils above the surface. And Golding's Lord of the Flies recounts how a schoolboy called Piggy is savagely murdered by *other children* while marooned on an island.

Before video games, there were dime novels, comic books, and graphic movie lyrics. "Reading Dante is unquestionably more cultured and intellectually edifying than playing Mortal Kombat. But these cultural and intellectual differences are not *constitutional* ones."

Video games are "interactive," because "the player participates in the violent action on screen and determines its outcome." But interactive fiction also not new. There is little new under the sun. "Since at least the publication of *The Adventures of You: Sugarcane Island* in 1969, young readers of choose-your-own-adventure stories have been able to make decisions that determine the plot by following instructions about which page to turn to."

Because video games, like books, plays, cartoons, and movies, qualify for First Amendment protections, content-based restrictions are invalid unless they pass strict scrutiny. California failed to demonstrate that a compelling government interest justified this law. It conceded that it "cannot show a direct causal link between violent video games and harm to minors." A few studies show "at best some correlation between exposure to violent entertainment and minuscule real-world effects, such as children's feeling more aggressive or making louder noises in the few minutes after playing a violent game than after playing a nonviolent game." Even these studies do not prove "that violent video games *cause* minors to act aggressively . . ." The state's expert admitted that "the *same* effects" of playing violent video games "when children watch cartoons starring Bugs Bunny or the Road Runner, or when they play video games like Sonic the Hedgehog" (rated "E" [appropriate for all ages]), or even when they view "a picture of a gun."

Parents, if they choose to do so, can limit their children's access because the video-game industry has a voluntary rating system that informs consumers about the content of games. Justice Thomas' dissent argued that parents traditionally have the power to control what their children read and hear. However, the Court questioned whether punishing third parties for conveying protected speech to "children *just in case* their parents disapprove of that speech is a proper governmental means of aiding parental authority." Such laws do not "enforce *parental* authority over children's speech and religion; they impose *governmental* authority, subject only to a parental veto." If California has power to prevent children from hearing or viewing anything "without their *parents' prior consent*," it could make it criminal "to admit persons under 18 to a political rally without their parents' prior written consent—even a political rally in support of laws against corporal punishment of children, or laws in favor of greater rights for minors."

The Court concluded that this law is both over-and under-inclusive when judged against its asserted justification. The law assumes a causal connection between violent entertainment and violent action, but it does not restrict children viewing violent Saturday morning cartoons. It does not forbid parents or uncles and aunts from giving violent video games (this supposedly "dangerous, mind-altering material") to children. California singled out video games but not movies for disfavored treatment and does not explain why. Underinclusiveness raises serious doubts the law is really about preventing violence or disfavoring a particular idea, "whether it be violence, or gore, or racism."

Alito, J., (joined by Roberts, C.J.) concurred in the judgment because the law was too vague. Thomas, J., and Breyer, J., filed separate dissents, Thomas argued that the original meaning of the First Amendment does not allow minors to receive any speech their parents do not want them to receive. Breyer analogized the California law to child pornography.

7.10 LIES

UNITED STATES V. ALVAREZ

567 U.S. ___, 132 S.Ct. 2537, 183 L.Ed.2d 574 (2012)

JUSTICE KENNEDY announced the judgment of the Court and delivered an opinion, in which THE CHIEF JUSTICE, JUSTICE GINSBURG, and JUSTICE SOTOMAYOR join.

Lying was his habit. Xavier Alvarez, the respondent here, lied when he said that he played hockey for the Detroit Red Wings and that he once married a starlet from Mexico. But when he lied in announcing he held the Congressional Medal of Honor, respondent ventured onto new ground; for that lie violates a federal criminal statute, the Stolen Valor Act of 2005. 18 U.S.C. § 704.

In 2007, respondent attended his first public meeting as a board member of the Three Valley Water District Board. The board is a governmental entity with headquarters in Claremont, California. He introduced himself as follows: "I'm a retired marine of 25 years. I retired in the year 2001. Back in 1987, I was awarded the Congressional Medal of Honor. I got wounded many times by the same guy." None of this was true. [These] statements do not seem to have been made to secure employment or financial benefits or admission to privileges reserved for those who had earned the Medal.

Respondent was indicted under the Stolen Valor Act for lying about the Congressional Medal of Honor at the meeting. [He] pleaded guilty to one count, reserving the right to appeal on his First Amendment claim. [T]he Ninth Circuit, in a decision by a divided panel, found the Act invalid under the First Amendment and reversed the conviction. . . .

The Government contends the criminal prohibition is a proper means to further its purpose in creating and awarding the Medal. When content-based speech regulation is in question, however, exacting scrutiny is required. [T]he statutory provisions under which respondent was convicted must be held invalid, and his conviction must be set aside.

[R]espondent violated § 704(b); and, because the lie concerned the Congressional Medal of Honor, he was subject to an enhanced penalty under subsection (c). Those statutory provisions are as follows:

"(b) FALSE CLAIMS ABOUT RECEIPT OF MILITARY DECORATIONS OR MEDALS.—Whoever falsely represents himself or herself, verbally or in writing, to have been awarded any decoration or medal authorized by Congress for the Armed Forces of the United States . . . shall be fined under this title, imprisoned not more than six months, or both.

"(c) ENHANCED PENALTY FOR OFFENSES INVOLVING CONGRESSIONAL MEDAL OF HONOR.—

"(1) IN GENERAL.—If a decoration or medal involved in an offense under subsection (a) or (b) is a Congressional Medal of Honor, in lieu of the punishment provided in that subsection, the offender shall be fined under this title, imprisoned not more than 1 year, or both."

. . . The Government defends the statute as necessary to preserve the integrity and purpose of the Medal, an integrity and purpose it contends are compromised and frustrated by the false statements the statute prohibits. It argues that false statements "have no First Amendment value in themselves," and thus "are protected only to the extent needed to avoid chilling fully protected speech." [T]he Constitution "demands that content-based restrictions on speech be presumed invalid . . . and that the Government bear the burden of showing their constitutionality."

In light of the substantial and expansive threats to free expression posed by content-based restrictions, this Court has rejected as "startling and dangerous" a "free-floating test for First Amendment coverage . . . [based on] an ad hoc balancing of relative social costs and benefits." *United States v. Stevens*, 559 U.S. 460, 470, 130 S.Ct. 1577, 1585, 176 L.Ed.2d 435 (2010). Instead, content-based restrictions on speech have been permitted, as a general matter, only when confined to the few " 'historic and traditional categories [of expression] long familiar to the bar.' " *Id.* Among these categories are advocacy intended, and likely, to incite imminent lawless action, see *Brandenburg v. Ohio* (1969) (per curiam); obscenity, *see, e.g., Miller v. California* (1973); defamation, *see, e.g., New York Times Co. v. Sullivan* (1964) (providing substantial protection for speech about public figures); *Gertz v. Robert Welch, Inc.* (1974) (imposing some limits on liability for defaming a private figure); speech integral to criminal conduct, *see, e.g., Giboney v. Empire Storage & Ice Co.*, 336 U.S. 490, 69 S.Ct. 684, 93 L.Ed. 834 (1949); so-called "fighting words," *see Chaplinsky v. New Hampshire* (1942); child pornography, *see New York v. Ferber* (1982); fraud, *see Virginia Bd. of Pharmacy v. Virginia Citizens Consumer Council, Inc.*, 425 U.S. 748, 771, 96 S.Ct. 1817, 48 L.Ed.2d 346 (1976); true threats, *see Watts v. United States*, 394 U.S. 705, 89 S.Ct. 1399, 22 L.Ed.2d 664 (1969) (per curiam); and speech presenting some grave and imminent threat the government has the power to prevent, *see Near v. Minnesota ex rel. Olson*, 283 U.S.

697, 716, 51 S.Ct. 625, 75 L.Ed. 1357 (1931), although a restriction under the last category is most difficult to sustain, *see New York Times Co. v. United States* (1971) (per curiam). These categories have a historical foundation in the Court's free speech tradition. The vast realm of free speech and thought always protected in our tradition can still thrive, and even be furthered, by adherence to those categories and rules.

Absent from those few categories where the law allows content-based regulation of speech is any general exception to the First Amendment for false statements. This comports with the common understanding that some false statements are inevitable if there is to be an open and vigorous expression of views in public and private conversation, expression the First Amendment seeks to guarantee. ("Th[e] erroneous statement is inevitable in free debate").

The Government disagrees with this proposition. It cites language from some of this Court's precedents to support its contention that false statements have no value and hence no First Amendment protection. These isolated statements in some earlier decisions do not support the Government's submission that false statements, as a general rule, are beyond constitutional protection. That conclusion would take the quoted language far from its proper context. For instance, the Court has stated "[f]alse statements of fact are particularly valueless [because] they interfere with the truth-seeking function of the marketplace of ideas," . . .

These quotations all derive from cases discussing defamation, fraud, or some other legally cognizable harm associated with a false statement, such as an invasion of privacy or the costs of vexatious litigation. In those decisions the falsity of the speech at issue was not irrelevant to our analysis, but neither was it determinative. The Court has never endorsed the categorical rule the Government advances: that false statements receive no First Amendment protection. Our prior decisions have not confronted a measure, like the Stolen Valor Act, that targets falsity and nothing more. . . . The requirements of a knowing falsehood or reckless disregard for the truth as the condition for recovery in certain defamation cases exists to allow more speech, not less. A rule designed to tolerate certain speech ought not blossom to become a rationale for a rule restricting it.

The Government then gives three examples of regulations on false speech that courts generally have found permissible: first, the criminal prohibition of a false statement made to a Government official, 18 U.S.C. § 1001; second, laws punishing perjury; and third, prohibitions on the false representation that one is speaking as a Government official or on behalf of the Government, see, *e.g.*, § 912;

§ 709. These restrictions, however, do not establish a principle that all proscriptions of false statements are exempt from exacting First Amendment scrutiny.

The federal statute prohibiting false statements to Government officials punishes "whoever, in any matter within the jurisdiction of the executive, legislative, or judicial branch of the Government . . . makes any materially false, fictitious, or fraudulent statement or representation." § 1001. Section 1001's prohibition on false statements made to Government officials, in communications concerning official matters, does not lead to the broader proposition that false statements are unprotected when made to any person, at any time, in any context.

The same point can be made about what the Court has confirmed is the "unquestioned constitutionality of perjury statutes," both the federal statute, § 1623, and its state-law equivalents. *United States v. Grayson*, 438 U.S. 41, 54, 98 S.Ct. 2610, 57 L.Ed.2d 582 (1978). See also *Konigsberg v. State Bar of Cal.*, 366 U.S. 36, 51, n. 10, 81 S.Ct. 997, 6 L.Ed.2d 105 (1961). It is not simply because perjured statements are false that they lack First Amendment protection. Perjured testimony "is at war with justice" because it can cause a court to render a "judgment not resting on truth." Perjury undermines the function and province of the law and threatens the integrity of judgments that are the basis of the legal system. *See United States v. Dunnigan*, 507 U.S. 87, 97, 113 S.Ct. 1111, 122 L.Ed.2d 445 (1993) ("To uphold the integrity of our trial system . . . the constitutionality of perjury statutes is unquestioned"). Unlike speech in other contexts, testimony under oath has the formality and gravity necessary to remind the witness that his or her statements will be the basis for official governmental action, action that often affects the rights and liberties of others. Sworn testimony is quite distinct from lies not spoken under oath and simply intended to puff up oneself.

Statutes that prohibit falsely representing that one is speaking on behalf of the Government, or that prohibit impersonating a Government officer, also protect the integrity of Government processes, quite apart from merely restricting false speech. Title 18 U.S.C. § 912, for example, prohibits impersonating an officer or employee of the United States. Even if that statute may not require proving an "actual financial or property loss" resulting from the deception, the statute is itself confined to "maintain[ing] the general good repute and dignity of . . . government . . . service itself." *United States v. Lepowitch*, 318 U.S. 702, 704, 63 S.Ct. 914, 87 L.Ed. 1091 (1943) (internal quotation marks omitted). The same can be said for prohibitions on the unauthorized use of the names of federal agencies such as the Federal Bureau of Investigation in a manner calculated to convey that the communication is approved, see § 709, or using words such as "Federal" or "United States" in the collection of private debts in order to convey that the communication has official authorization, see § 712. These examples, to the extent that they implicate fraud or speech integral to criminal conduct, are inapplicable here. . . .

Although the First Amendment stands against any "freewheeling authority to declare new categories of speech outside the scope of the First Amendment," *United States v. Stevens*, 559 U.S. 460, 130 S.Ct. 1577, 176 L.Ed.2d 435 (2010) [§ 7.10], the Court has acknowledged that perhaps there exist "some categories of speech that have been historically unprotected . . . but have not yet been specifically identified or discussed . . . in our case law." Before exempting a category of speech from the normal prohibition on content-based restrictions, however, the Court must be presented with "persuasive evidence that a novel restriction on content is part of a long (if heretofore unrecognized) tradition of proscription," *Brown v. Entertainment Merchants Assn.*, 564 U.S. ___, ___, 131 S.Ct. 2729, 2734, 180 L.Ed.2d 708 (2011)[§ 7.10]. The Government has not demonstrated that false statements generally should constitute a new category of unprotected speech on this basis. . . .

The Act by its plain terms applies to a false statement made at any time, in any place, to any person. It can be assumed that it would not apply to, say, a theatrical performance. Still, the sweeping, quite unprecedented reach of the statute puts it in conflict with the First Amendment. Here the lie was made in a public meeting, but the statute would apply with equal force to personal, whispered conversations within a home. The statute seeks to control and suppress all false statements on this one subject in almost limitless times and settings. And it does so entirely without regard to whether the lie was made for the purpose of material gain. *See San Francisco Arts & Athletics, Inc. v. United States Olympic Comm.*, 483 U.S. 522, 539–540, 107 S.Ct. 2971, 97 L.Ed.2d 427 (1987) (prohibiting a nonprofit corporation from exploiting the "commercial magnetism" of the word "Olympic" when organizing an athletic competition (internal quotation marks omitted)).

. . . Where false claims are made to effect a fraud or secure moneys or other valuable considerations, say offers of employment, it is well established that the Government may restrict speech without affronting the First Amendment. But the Stolen Valor Act is not so limited in its reach. Were the Court to hold that the interest in truthful discourse alone is sufficient to sustain a ban on speech, absent any evidence that the speech was used to gain a material advantage, it would give government a broad censorial power unprecedented in this Court's cases or in our constitutional tradition. The mere potential for the exercise of that power casts a chill, a chill the First Amendment cannot permit if free speech, thought, and discourse are to remain a foundation of our freedom.

. . . Although the objectives the Government seeks to further by the statute are not without significance, the Court must, and now does, find the Act does not satisfy exacting scrutiny. [M]ilitary medals "serve the important public function of recognizing and expressing gratitude for acts of heroism and sacrifice in military service," and also " 'foste[r] morale, mission accomplishment and esprit de corps' among service members." [Such] interests are related to the integrity of the military honors system in general, and the Congressional Medal of Honor in particular. Although millions have served with brave resolve, the Medal, which is the highest military award for valor against an enemy force, has been given just 3,476 times. Established in 1861, the Medal is reserved for those who have distinguished themselves "conspicuously by gallantry and intrepidity at the risk of his life above and beyond the call of duty." The stories of those who earned the Medal inspire and fascinate, from Dakota Meyer who in 2009 drove five times into the midst of a Taliban ambush to save 36 lives; to Desmond Doss who served as an army medic on Okinawa and on June 5, 1945, rescued 75 fellow soldiers, and who, after being wounded, gave up his own place on a stretcher so others could be taken to safety. . . .

But to recite the Government's compelling interests is not to end the matter. The First Amendment requires that the Government's chosen restriction on the speech at issue be "actually necessary" to achieve its interest. There must be a direct causal link between the restriction imposed and the injury to be prevented. [W]hen a pretender claims the Medal to be his own, the lie might harm the Government by demeaning the high purpose of the award, diminishing the honor it confirms, and creating the appearance that the Medal is awarded more often than is true. Furthermore, the lie may offend the true holders of the Medal. From one perspective it insults their bravery and high principles when falsehood puts them in the unworthy company of a pretender. [T]hese interests do not satisfy the Government's heavy burden when it seeks to regulate protected speech. The Government points to no evidence to support its claim that the public's general perception of military awards is diluted by false claims such as those made by Alvarez. . . .

The lack of a causal link between the Government's stated interest and the Act is not the only way in which the Act is not actually necessary to achieve the

Government's stated interest. The Government has not shown, and cannot show, why counterspeech would not suffice to achieve its interest. The facts of this case indicate that the dynamics of free speech, of counterspeech, of refutation, can overcome the lie. Respondent lied at a public meeting. Even before the FBI began investigating him for his false statements "Alvarez was perceived as a phony." Once the lie was made public, he was ridiculed online, his actions were reported in the press, and a fellow board member called for his resignation. There is good reason to believe that a similar fate would befall other false claimants. Indeed, the outrage and contempt expressed for respondent's lies can serve to reawaken and reinforce the public's respect for the Medal, its recipients, and its high purpose. The acclaim that recipients of the Congressional Medal of Honor receive also casts doubt on the proposition that the public will be misled by the claims of charlatans or become cynical of those whose heroic deeds earned them the Medal by right.

The remedy for speech that is false is speech that is true. . . . *See Whitney v. California* (1927) (Brandeis, J., concurring) ("If there be time to expose through discussion the falsehood and fallacies, to avert the evil by the processes of education, the remedy to be applied is more speech, not enforced silence"). The theory of our Constitution is "that the best test of truth is the power of the thought to get itself accepted in the competition of the market," *Abrams v. United States* (1919) (Holmes, J., dissenting). [S]uppression of speech by the government can make exposure of falsity more difficult, not less so. Society has the right and civic duty to engage in open, dynamic, rational discourse. These ends are not well served when the government seeks to orchestrate public discussion through content-based mandates.

[T]he Government responds that because "some military records have been lost . . . some claims [are] unverifiable." This proves little, however; for without verifiable records, successful criminal prosecution under the Act would be more difficult in any event. So, in cases where public refutation will not serve the Government's interest, the Act will not either.

[W]hen the Government seeks to regulate protected speech, the restriction must be the "least restrictive means among available, effective alternatives." There is, however, at least one less speech-restrictive means by which the Government could likely protect the integrity of the military awards system. A Government-created database could list Congressional Medal of Honor winners. Were a database accessible through the Internet, it would be easy to verify and expose false claims. It appears some private individuals have already created databases similar to this, and at least one database of past winners is online and fully searchable. The Solicitor General responds that although Congress and the Department of Defense investigated the feasibility of establishing a database in 2008, the Government "concluded that such a database would be impracticable and insufficiently comprehensive." Without more explanation, it is difficult to assess the Government's claim, especially when at least one database of Congressional Medal of Honor winners already exists.

. . . The Stolen Valor Act infringes upon speech protected by the First Amendment. The judgment of the Court of Appeals is affirmed. It is so ordered.

JUSTICE BREYER, with whom JUSTICE KAGAN joins, concurring in the judgment.

I agree with the plurality that the Stolen Valor Act of 2005 violates the First Amendment. But I do not rest my conclusion upon a strict categorical analysis. [T]he Government can achieve its legitimate objectives in less restrictive ways. [I]n some contexts, particularly political contexts, such a narrowing will not always be easy to achieve. In the political arena a false statement is more likely to make a behavioral difference (say, by leading the listeners to vote for the speaker) but at the same time criminal prosecution is particularly dangerous (say, by radically changing a potential election result) and consequently can more easily result in censorship of speakers and their ideas. Thus, the statute may have to be significantly narrowed in its applications. [I]t is likely that a more narrowly tailored statute combined with such information-disseminating devices will effectively serve Congress' end. . . .

JUSTICE ALITO, with whom JUSTICE SCALIA and JUSTICE THOMAS join, dissenting.

. . . Properly construed, [the Stolen Valor Act] is limited in five significant respects. First, the Act applies to only a narrow category of false representations about objective facts that can almost always be proved or disproved with near certainty. Second, the Act concerns facts that are squarely within the speaker's personal knowledge. Third, as the Government maintains, and both the plurality, and the concurrence, seemingly accept, a conviction under the Act requires proof beyond a reasonable doubt that the speaker actually knew that the representation was false. Fourth, the Act applies only to statements that could reasonably be interpreted as communicating actual facts; it does not reach dramatic performances, satire, parody, hyperbole, or the like. Finally, the Act is strictly viewpoint neutral. The false statements proscribed by the Act are highly unlikely to be tied to any particular political or ideological message. In the rare cases where that is not so, the Act applies equally to all false statements, whether they tend to disparage or commend the Government, the military, or the system of military honors. . . .

Congress passed the Stolen Valor Act in response to a proliferation of false claims concerning the receipt of military awards. For example, in a single year, more than 600 Virginia residents falsely claimed to have won the Medal of Honor. An investigation of the 333 people listed in the online edition of Who's Who as having received a top military award revealed that fully a third of the claims could not be substantiated. . . .

It is well recognized in trademark law that the proliferation of cheap imitations of luxury goods blurs the " 'signal' given out by the purchasers of the originals." In much the same way, the proliferation of false claims about military awards blurs the signal given out by the actual awards by making them seem more common than they really are . . . The plurality recommends a law that would apply only to lies that are intended to "secure moneys or other valuable considerations." . . . Unless even a small financial loss—say, a dollar given to a homeless man falsely claiming to be a decorated veteran—is more important in the eyes of the First Amendment than the damage caused to the very integrity of the military awards system, there is no basis for distinguishing between the Stolen Valor Act and the alternative statutes that the plurality and concurrence appear willing to sustain. . . .

. . . Respondent's brief features a veritable paean to lying. . . . "Everyone lies," he says. Brief for Respondent 10. . . . An academic amicus tells us that the First Amendment protects the right to construct "self-aggrandizing fabrications such as having been awarded a military decoration." Brief for Jonathan D. Varat as Amicus Curiae 5.

[T]here are broad areas in which any attempt by the state to penalize purportedly false speech would present a grave and unacceptable danger of suppressing truthful speech. Laws restricting false statements about philosophy, religion, history, the social sciences, the arts, and other matters of public concern would present such a threat. [However,] the Stolen Valor Act presents no risk at all that valuable speech will be suppressed. [F]alsely claiming to have won the Medal of Honor is qualitatively different from even the most prestigious civilian awards and that the misappropriation of that honor warrants criminal sanction. . . .

NOTES

1. One of the judges in the Ninth Circuit argued, "that (non-satirical and non-theatrical) knowingly false statements of fact are *always* unprotected." *United States v. Alvarez*, 617 F.3d 1198, 1224 (9th Cir.2010) (Bybee, J., dissenting)).

2. Kozinski, J., in the same Ninth Circuit case, rejected that view: " 'Always' is a deliciously dangerous word, often eaten with a side of crow." He added, "If false factual statements are unprotected, then the government can prosecute not only the man who tells tall tales of winning the Congressional Medal of Honor, but also the JDater who falsely claims he's Jewish or the dentist who assures you it won't hurt a bit. Phrases such as 'I'm working late tonight, hunny,' 'I got stuck in traffic' and 'I didn't inhale' could all be made into crimes. Without the robust protections of the First Amendment, the white lies, exaggerations and deceptions that are an integral part of human intercourse would become targets of censorship, subject only to the rubber stamp known as 'rational basis review.' " 638 F.3d 666, 673 (9th Cir. 2011) (concurring in the denial of rehearing en banc).

Freedom of Religion

8.1 FINANCIAL ASSISTANCE TO RELIGIOUS SCHOOLS AND INSTITUTIONS

ZORACH V. CLAUSON

343 U.S. 306, 72 S.Ct. 679, 96 L.Ed. 954 (1952)

MR. JUSTICE DOUGLAS delivered the opinion of the Court.

New York City has a program which permits its public schools to release students during the school day so that they may leave the school buildings and school grounds and go to religious centers for religious instruction or devotional exercises. A student is released on written request of his parents. Those not released stay in the classrooms. The churches make weekly reports to the schools, sending a list of children who have been released from public school but who have not reported for religious instruction.

This "released time" program involves neither religious instruction in public school classrooms nor the expenditure of public funds. All costs, including the application blanks are paid by the religious organizations. The case is therefore unlike *McCollum v. Board of Education,* 333 U.S. 203, 68 S.Ct. 461, 92 L.Ed. 648, which involved a "released time" program from Illinois. In that case the [public school] classrooms were turned over to religious instructors. We accordingly held that the program violated the First Amendment which (by reason of the Fourteenth Amendment) prohibits the states from establishing religion or prohibiting its free exercise.

Appellants, who are taxpayers and residents of New York City and whose children attend its public schools, challenge the present law, contending it is in essence not different from the one involved in the *McCollum* case. Their argument, stated elaborately in various ways, reduces itself to this: the weight and influence of the school is put behind a program for religious instruction; public school teachers police it, keeping tab on students who are released; the classroom activities come to a halt while the students who are released for religious instruction are on leave; the school is a crutch on which the churches are leaning for support in their religious training; without the cooperation of the schools this "released time" program, like the one in the *McCollum* case, would be futile and ineffective. . . .

It takes obtuse reasoning to inject any issue of the "free exercise" of religion into the present case. No one is forced to go to the religious classroom and no religious exercise or instruction is brought to the classrooms of the public schools. . . . If in fact coercion were used, if it were established that any one or more teachers were using their office to persuade or force students to take the religious instruction, a wholly different case would be presented. Hence we put aside that claim of coercion both as respects the "free exercise" of religion and "an establishment of religion" within the meaning of the First Amendment.

Moreover, apart from that claim of coercion, we do not see how New York by this type of "released time" program has made a law respecting an establishment of religion within the meaning of the First Amendment. There is much talk of the separation of Church and State in the history of the Bill of Rights and in the decisions clustering around the First Amendment. There cannot be the slightest doubt that the First Amendment reflects the philosophy that Church and State should be separated. And so far as interference with the "free exercise" of religion and an "establishment" of religion are concerned, the separation must be complete and unequivocal. The First Amendment within the scope of its coverage permits no exception; the prohibition is absolute. The First Amendment, however, does not say that in every and all respects there shall be a separation of Church and State. Rather, it studiously defines the manner, the specific ways, in which there shall be no concert or union or dependency one on the other. That is the common sense of the matter. Otherwise the state and religion would be aliens to each other—hostile, suspicious, and even unfriendly. Churches could not be required to pay even property taxes. Municipalities would not be permitted to render police or fire protection to religious groups. Policemen who help parishioners into their places of worship would violate the Constitution. Prayers in our legislative halls; the appeals to the Almighty in the messages of the Chief Executive; the proclamations making Thanksgiving Day a holiday; "so help me God" in our courtroom oaths—these and all other references to the Almighty that run through our laws, or public rituals, our ceremonies would be flouting the First Amendment. A fastidious atheist or agnostic could even object to the supplication with which the Court opens each session: "God save the United States and this Honorable Court."

We would have to press the concept of separation of Church and State to these extremes to condemn the present law on constitutional grounds. The nullification of this law would have wide and profound effects. A Catholic student applies to his teacher for permission to leave the school during hours on a Holy Day of Obligation to attend a mass. A Jewish student asks his teacher for permission to be excused for Yom Kippur. A Protestant wants the afternoon off for a family baptismal ceremony. In each case the teacher requires parental consent in writing. In each case the teacher, in order to make sure the student is not a truant, goes further and requires a report from the priest, the rabbi, or the minister. The teacher in other words cooperates in a religious program to the extent of making it possible for her students to participate in it. . . .

We are a religious people whose institutions presuppose a Supreme Being. We guarantee the freedom to worship as one chooses. We make room for as wide a variety of beliefs and creeds as the spiritual needs of man deem necessary. We sponsor an attitude on the part of government that shows no partiality to any one group and that lets each flourish according to the zeal of its adherents and the appeal of its dogma. When the state encourages religious instruction or cooperates with religious authorities by adjusting the schedule of public events to sectarian needs, it follows the best of our traditions. For it then respects the religious nature of our people and accommodates the public service to their spiritual needs. To hold that it may not would be to find in the Constitution a requirement that the government show a callous indifference to religious groups. That would be preferring those who believe in no religion over those who do believe. Government may not finance religious groups nor undertake religious instruction nor blend secular and sectarian education nor use secular institutions to force one or some religion on any person. But we find no constitutional requirement which makes it necessary for government to be hostile to religion and to throw its weight against efforts to widen the effective scope of religious influence. The government must be neutral when it comes to competition between sects. It may not thrust any sect on any person. It may not make a religious observance compulsory. It may not coerce anyone to attend church, to observe a religious holiday, or to take religious instruction. But it can close its doors or suspend its operations as to those who want to repair to their religious sanctuary for worship or instruction. No more than that is undertaken here. . . .

In the *McCollum* case the classrooms were used for religious instruction and the force of the public school was used to promote that instruction. Here, as we have said, the public schools do no more than accommodate their schedules to a program of outside religious instruction. We follow the *McCollum* case. But we cannot expand it to cover the present released time program unless separation of Church and State means that public institutions can make no adjustments of their schedules to accommodate the religious needs of the people. We cannot read into the Bill of Rights such a philosophy of hostility to religion.

Affirmed.

MR. JUSTICE BLACK, dissenting.

Illinois ex rel. McCollum v. Board of Education, 333 U.S. 203, 68 S.Ct. 461, 92 L.Ed. 648, held invalid as an "establishment of religion" an Illinois system under which school children, compelled by law to go to public schools, were freed from some hours of required school work on condition that they attend special religious classes held in the school buildings. . . . I see no significant difference between the invalid Illinois system and that of New York here sustained. Except for the use of the school buildings in Illinois, there is no difference between the systems which I consider even worthy of mention. In the New York program, as in that of Illinois, the school authorities release some of the children on the condition that they attend the religious classes, get reports on whether they attend, and hold the other children in the school building until the religious hour is over. . . . Difficulty of decision in the hypothetical situations mentioned by the Court, but not now before us, should not confuse the issues in this case. Here the sole question is whether New York can use its compulsory education laws to help religious sects get attendants presumably too unenthusiastic to go unless moved to do so by the pressure of this state machinery.

MR. JUSTICE JACKSON, dissenting.

[S]chooling is more or less suspended during the "released time" so the nonreligious attendants will not forge ahead of the churchgoing absentees. But it serves as a temporary jail for a pupil who will not go to Church. It takes more subtlety of mind than I possess to deny that this is governmental constraint in support of religion. It is as unconstitutional, in my view, when exerted by indirection as when exercised forthrightly. As one whose children, as a matter of free choice, have been sent to privately supported Church schools, I may challenge the Court's suggestion that opposition to this plan can only be antireligious, atheistic, or agnostic. My evangelistic brethren confuse an objection to compulsion with an objection to religion. It is possible to hold a faith with enough confidence to believe that what should be rendered to God does not need to be decided and collected by Caesar. . . .

[The dissenting opinion of FRANKFURTER, J., is omitted.]

8.2 FINANCIAL AID TO RELIGIOUS SCHOOLS AND INSTITUTIONS

THE *LEMON* TEST. To what extent may a state or the federal government give financial aid to a student or a private school system if the student attends a religiously-affiliated school? This question has concerned the Court for years, and for many years the answers it gave were inconsistent. In *Lemon v. Kurtzman,* 403 U.S. 602, 91 S.Ct. 2105, 29 L.Ed.2d 745 (1971), Burger, C.J., for the Court, laid out a three-part test.

> First, the statute must have a secular legislative purpose; second, its principal or primary effect must be one that neither advances nor inhibits religion, finally, the statute must not foster "an excessive government entanglement with religion."

Later decisions have sometimes used (and often criticized) the *Lemon* test. In *Lamb's Chapel v. Center Moriches Union Free School District,* 508 U.S. 384, 113 S.Ct. 2141, 124 L.Ed.2d 352 (1993), a state law authorized a public school to permit after-hours use of school facilities for social, civic and recreational meetings. With no dissents, White, J., for the Court held (citing *Lemon*) that a school district violated the free speech clause when it denied access to school premises to a church because it wanted to show religiously oriented films: "the First Amendment forbids the government to regulate speech in ways that favor some viewpoints or ideas at the expense of others." Scalia, J., concurred in the judgment:

> As to the Court's invocation of the *Lemon* test: Like some ghoul in a late-night horror movie that repeatedly sits up in its grave and shuffles abroad, after being repeatedly killed and buried, *Lemon* stalks our Establishment Clause jurisprudence once again, frightening the little children and school attorneys of Center Moriches Union Free School District. Its most recent burial, only last Term, was, to be sure, not fully six feet under: Our decision in *Lee v. Weisman,* 505 U.S. 577, 586–587, 112 S.Ct. 2649, 2654, 120 L.Ed.2d 467 (1992), conspicuously avoided using the supposed "test" but also declined the invitation to repudiate it. Over the years, however, no fewer than five of the currently sitting Justices have, in their own opinions, personally driven pencils through

the creature's heart (the author of today's opinion repeatedly), and a sixth has joined an opinion doing so.

In cases involving financial aid to private schools, including religiously-affiliated schools, the Justices readily agree that aid to schools meets the first part of the *Lemon* test. Helping to educate the nation's youth is an obvious secular purpose. Once the Court moves beyond this phase, however, members of the Court dispute how this test should be applied and even its relevance (some cases call the *Lemon* test merely a "guideline").

HIGHER EDUCATION. In the case of financial aid to higher education, the Court has generally approved the aid because of the justices have repeatedly concluded that that religion does not so permeate colleges and universities and it does in K through 12th grade. They conclude that for higher education, religious and secular functions are separable.[1]

Thus, in *Tilton v. Richardson,* 403 U.S. 672, 91 S.Ct. 2091, 29 L.Ed.2d 790 (1971), the Court upheld federal grants for the construction of academic facilities at private colleges (some of which were church related) with the restriction that the facilities could not be used for any sectarian purposes. *Hunt v. McNair,* 413 U.S. 734, 93 S.Ct. 2868, 37 L.Ed.2d 923 (1973), upheld a state plan to finance the construction of secular college facilities by revenue bonds. The college in *Hunt* was subject to substantial control by the Baptist Church, but it was not "pervasively sectarian." The colleges repaid the bonds but benefited from the tax-free status of the interest payments. *Roemer v. Board of Public Works,* 426 U.S. 736, 96 S.Ct. 2337, 49 L.Ed.2d 179 (1976), upheld a state grant program that provided subsidies for each full-time student, excluding students enrolled in seminarian or theological academic programs. The college recipient could use the funds for any purposes except sectarian ones. The Court upheld the aid and accepted the lower court finding that the colleges involved in that case were "not 'pervasively sectarian'" even though they had mandatory religion or theology courses and some classes were begun with a prayer.

In *Witters v. Washington Department of Services for the Blind,* 474 U.S. 481, 106 S.Ct. 748, 88 L.Ed.2d 846 (1986), Justice Marshall for the Court held that nothing in the First Amendment prevented a state from extending financial assistance under a state vocational rehabilitation assistance program to a blind person who chose to attend a private Christian college and studying to become a pastor, or

---

[1] This conclusion is not a new one. Compare *Bradfield v. Roberts,* 175 U.S. 291, 20 S.Ct. 121, 44 L.Ed. 168 (1899) (upholding public aid to corporation composed entirely of Roman Catholic nuns; the corporate charter limited itself to the secular purpose of operating a charitable hospital).

missionary. "Any aid provided under Washington's program that ultimately flows to religious institutions does so only as a result of the genuinely independent and private choices of aid recipients." The program "creates no financial incentive for students to undertake sectarian education," and the "mere circumstance that petitioner has chosen to use neutrally available state aid to help pay for his religious education [does not] confer any message of state endorsement of religion." There were no dissents.

K THROUGH 12TH GRADE. In the case of financial aid to grade schools and secondary schools, the Court has often been less predictable, and the lines it has drawn have been far from clear. In his dissent in *Wallace v. Jaffree,* 472 U.S. 38, 105 S.Ct. 2479, 86 L.Ed.2d 29 (1985), Justice Rehnquist summarized a few of the cases to illustrate the difficulty the Court has had in finding principled results:

> For example, a State may lend to parochial school children geography textbooks [*Board of Education v. Allen,* 392 U.S. 236, 88 S.Ct. 1923, 20 L.Ed.2d 1060 (1968)] that contain maps of the United States, but the State may not lend maps of the United States for use in geography class. [*Meek v. Pittenger,* 421 U.S., at 362–366, 95 S.Ct., at 1761–1763 (1975)]. A science book is permissible, a science kit is not. See *Wolman v. Walter,* 433 U.S., at 249, 97 S.Ct., at 2606 (1977). A State may lend textbooks on American colonial history, but it may not lend a film on George Washington, or a film projector to show it in history class. A State may lend classroom workbooks, but may not lend workbooks in which the parochial school children write, thus rendering them non-reusable. A State may pay for bus transportation to religious schools [*Everson v. Board of Education,* 330 U.S. 1, 67 S.Ct. 504, 91 L.Ed. 711 (1947)] but may not pay for bus transportation from the parochial school to the public zoo or natural history museum for a field trip. [*Wolman, supra.*] A State may pay for diagnostic services conducted in the parochial school, but therapeutic services must be given in a different building; speech and hearing "services" conducted by the State inside the sectarian school are forbidden, *Meek v. Pittenger,* 421 U.S. 349, 367, 371, 95 S.Ct. 1753, 1764, 1766, 49 L.Ed.2d 179 (1975), but the State may conduct speech and hearing diagnostic testing inside the sectarian school. *Wolman,* 433, U.S. at 241, 97 S.Ct., at 2602. Exceptional parochial school students may receive counseling, but it must take place outside of the parochial school [*Wolman, supra; Meek, supra*], such as in a trailer parked down the street. A State may give cash to a parochial school to pay for the administration of State-written tests and state-ordered reporting services [*Committee for*

Public Education v. Reagan, 444 U.S., at 648, 657–659, 100 S.Ct., at 844, 848–849], but it may not provide funds for teacher-prepared tests on secular subjects. [*Levitt v. Committee for Public Education,* 413 U.S., at 479–482, 93 S.Ct., at 2818–2820.] Religious instruction may not be given in public school [*Illinois ex rel. McCollum v. Board of Education,* 333 U.S. 203, 68 S.Ct. 461, 92 L.Ed. 649 (1948)], but the public school may release students during the day for religion classes elsewhere, and may enforce attendance at those classes with its truancy laws [*Zorach v. Clauson,* 343 U.S. 306, 72 S.Ct. 679, 96 L.Ed. 954 (1952)].

These cases and others set the stage for *Zelman v. Simmons-Harris* (2002), where the Court approved a financial aid for parents who send their children to private schools.

ZELMAN V. SIMMONS-HARRIS

536 U.S. 639, 122 S.Ct. 2460, 153 L.Ed.2d 604 (2002)

CHIEF JUSTICE REHNQUIST delivered the opinion of the Court.

The State of Ohio has established a pilot program designed to provide educational choices to families with children who reside in the Cleveland City School District. The question presented is whether this program offends the Establishment Clause of the United States Constitution. We hold that it does not.

There are more than 75,000 children enrolled in the Cleveland City School District. The majority of these children are from low-income and minority families [who do not] enjoy the means to send their children to any school other than an inner-city public school. For more than a generation, however, Cleveland's public schools have been among the worst performing public schools in the Nation. In 1995, a Federal District Court declared a "crisis of magnitude" and placed the entire Cleveland school district under state control. . . . Only 1 in 10 ninth graders could pass a basic proficiency examination, and students at all levels performed at a dismal rate compared with students in other Ohio public schools. More than two-thirds of high school students either dropped or failed out before graduation. Of those students who managed to reach their senior year, one of every four still failed to graduate. Of those students who did graduate, few could read, write, or compute at levels comparable to their counterparts in other cities.

It is against this backdrop that Ohio enacted, among other initiatives, its Pilot Project Scholarship Program. The program provides financial assistance to families in any Ohio school district that is or has been "under federal court order requiring supervision and operational management of the district by the state superintendent." Cleveland is the only Ohio school district to fall within that category.

The program provides two basic kinds of assistance to parents of children in a covered district. First, the program provides tuition aid for students in kindergarten through third grade, expanding each year through eighth grade, to attend a participating public or private school of their parent's choosing. Second, the program provides tutorial aid for students who choose to remain enrolled in public school.

The tuition aid portion of the program is designed to provide educational choices to parents who reside in a covered district. Any private school, whether religious or nonreligious, may participate in the program and accept program students so long as the school is located within the boundaries of a covered district and meets statewide educational standards. Participating private schools must agree not to discriminate on the basis of race, religion, or ethnic background, or to "advocate or foster unlawful behavior or teach hatred of any person or group on the basis of race, ethnicity, national origin, or religion." Any public school located in a school district adjacent to the covered district may also participate in the program. Adjacent public schools are eligible to receive a $2,250 tuition grant for each program student accepted in addition to the full amount of per-pupil state funding attributable to each additional student. All participating schools, whether public or private, are required to accept students in accordance with rules and procedures established by the state superintendent.

Tuition aid is distributed to parents according to financial need. Families with incomes below 200% of the poverty line are given priority and are eligible to receive 90% of private school tuition up to $2,250. For these lowest-income families, participating private schools may not charge a parental co-payment greater than $250. For all other families, the program pays 75% of tuition costs, up to $1,875, with no co-payment cap. These families receive tuition aid only if the number of available scholarships exceeds the number of low-income children who choose to participate. Where tuition aid is spent depends solely upon where parents who receive tuition aid choose to enroll their child. If parents choose a private school, checks are made payable to the parents who then endorse the checks over to the chosen school. . . .

The program has been in operation within the Cleveland City School District since the 1996–1997 school year. In the 1999–2000 school year, 56 private schools participated in the program, 46 (or 82%) of which had a religious affiliation. None of the public schools in districts adjacent to Cleveland have elected to participate.

More than 3,700 students participated in the scholarship program, most of whom (96%) enrolled in religiously affiliated schools. Sixty percent of these students were from families at or below the poverty line. In the 1998–1999 school year, approximately 1,400 Cleveland public school students received tutorial aid. This number was expected to double during the 1999–2000 school year. . . .

The Establishment Clause of the First Amendment, applied to the States through the Fourteenth Amendment, prevents a State from enacting laws that have the "purpose" or "effect" of advancing or inhibiting religion. There is no dispute that the program challenged here was enacted for the valid secular purpose of providing educational assistance to poor children in a demonstrably failing public school system. Thus, the question presented is whether the Ohio program nonetheless has the forbidden "effect" of advancing or inhibiting religion.

To answer that question, our decisions have drawn a consistent distinction between government programs that provide aid directly to religious schools, and programs of true private choice, in which government aid reaches religious schools only as a result of the genuine and independent choices of private individuals, *Witters v. Washington Dept. of Services for Blind* (1986). While our jurisprudence with respect to the constitutionality of direct aid programs has "changed significantly" over the past two decades, our jurisprudence with respect to true private choice programs has remained consistent and unbroken. Three times we have confronted Establishment Clause challenges to neutral government programs that provide aid directly to a broad class of individuals, who, in turn, direct the aid to religious schools or institutions of their own choosing. Three times we have rejected such challenges.

In *Mueller* [*v. Allen*, 463 U.S. 388, 103 S.Ct. 3062, 77 L.Ed.2d 721 (1983)], we rejected an Establishment Clause challenge to a Minnesota program authorizing tax deductions for various educational expenses, including private school tuition costs, even though the great majority of the program's beneficiaries (96%) were parents of children in religious schools. [W]e emphasized the principle of private choice, noting that public funds were made available to religious schools "only as a result of numerous, private choices of individual parents of school-age children." . . . In *Witters,* we used identical reasoning to reject an Establishment Clause challenge to a vocational scholarship program that provided tuition aid to a student studying at a religious institution to become a pastor. [*Mueller*] rested not on whether few or many recipients chose to expend government aid at a religious school but, rather, on whether recipients generally were empowered to direct the aid to schools or institutions of their own choosing. Finally, in *Zobrest* [*v. Catalina*

Foothills School Dist., 509 U.S. 1, 113 S.Ct. 2462, 125 L.Ed.2d 1 (1993)], we applied *Mueller* and *Witters* to reject an Establishment Clause challenge to a federal program that permitted sign-language interpreters to assist deaf children enrolled in religious schools. . . .

Mueller, Witters, and *Zobrest* thus make clear that where a government aid program is neutral with respect to religion, and provides assistance directly to a broad class of citizens who, in turn, direct government aid to religious schools wholly as a result of their own genuine and independent private choice, the program is not readily subject to challenge under the Establishment Clause. A program that shares these features permits government aid to reach religious institutions only by way of the deliberate choices of numerous individual recipients. The incidental advancement of a religious mission, or the perceived endorsement of a religious message, is reasonably attributable to the individual recipient, not to the government, whose role ends with the disbursement of benefits. . . .

[T]he program challenged here is a program of true private choice, consistent with *Mueller, Witters,* and *Zobrest,* and thus constitutional. [T]he Ohio program is neutral in all respects toward religion. It is part of a general and multifaceted undertaking by the State of Ohio to provide educational opportunities to the children of a failed school district. It confers educational assistance directly to a broad class of individuals defined without reference to religion, *i.e.,* any parent of a school-age child who resides in the Cleveland City School District. The program permits the participation of *all* schools within the district, religious or nonreligious. Adjacent public schools also may participate and have a financial incentive to do so. Program benefits are available to participating families on neutral terms, with no reference to religion. The only preference stated anywhere in the program is a preference for low-income families, who receive greater assistance and are given priority for admission at participating schools.

[No financial incentives skew the program toward religious schools because] "the aid is allocated on the basis of neutral, secular criteria that neither favor nor disfavor religion, and is made available to both religious and secular beneficiaries on a nondiscriminatory basis." The program here in fact creates financial *dis*incentives for religious schools, with private schools receiving only half the government assistance given to community schools and one-third the assistance given to magnet schools. Adjacent public schools, should any choose to accept program students, are also eligible to receive two to three times the state funding of a private religious school. Families too have a financial disincentive to choose a private religious school over other schools. Parents that choose to participate in the scholarship program and then to enroll their children in a private school (religious or nonreligious) must copay a portion of the school's tuition. Families that choose a community school, magnet school, or traditional public school pay nothing. Although such features of the program are not necessary to its constitutionality, they clearly dispel the claim that the program "creates ... financial incentive[s] for parents to choose a sectarian school." *Zobrest*.[3]

Respondents suggest that even without a financial incentive for parents to choose a religious school, the program creates a "public perception that the State is endorsing religious practices and beliefs." But we have repeatedly recognized that no reasonable observer would think a neutral program of private choice, where state aid reaches religious schools solely as a result of the numerous independent decisions of private individuals, carries with it the *imprimatur* of government endorsement. Any objective observer familiar with the full history and context of the Ohio program would reasonably view it as one aspect of a broader undertaking to assist poor children in failed schools, not as an endorsement of religious schooling in general.

... That 46 of the 56 private schools now participating in the program are religious schools does not condemn it as a violation of the Establishment Clause. The Establishment Clause question is whether Ohio is coercing parents into sending their children to religious schools, and that question must be answered by evaluating *all* options Ohio provides Cleveland schoolchildren, only one of which is to obtain a program scholarship and then choose a religious school.

... 82% of Cleveland's participating private schools are religious schools, but it is also true that 81% of private schools in Ohio are religious schools. To attribute constitutional significance to this figure, moreover, would lead to the absurd result that a neutral school-choice program might be permissible in some parts of Ohio, such as Columbus, where a lower percentage of private schools are religious schools, but not in inner-city Cleveland, where Ohio has deemed such programs most sorely needed, but where the preponderance of religious schools happens to be greater. Cf. Brief for State of Florida et al. as *Amici Curiae* 17 ("[T]he

---

[3] Justice Souter suggests the program is not "neutral" because program students cannot spend scholarship vouchers at traditional public schools. *Post*, (dissenting opinion). This objection is mistaken: Public schools in Cleveland already receive $7,097 in public funding per pupil—$4,167 of which is attributable to the State. Program students who receive tutoring aid and remain enrolled in traditional public schools therefore direct almost twice as much state funding to their chosen school as do program students who receive a scholarship and attend a private school. Justice Souter does not seriously claim that the program differentiates based on the religious status of beneficiaries or providers of services, the touchstone of neutrality under the Establishment Clause.

percentages of sectarian to nonsectarian private schools within Florida's 67 school districts . . . vary from zero to 100 percent"). . . .

Respondents and Justice Souter claim that even if we do not focus on the number of participating schools that are religious schools, we should attach constitutional significance to the fact that 96% of scholarship recipients have enrolled in religious schools. [That] 96% figure upon which respondents and Justice Souter rely discounts entirely (1) the more than 1,900 Cleveland children enrolled in alternative community schools, (2) the more than 13,000 children enrolled in alternative magnet schools, and (3) the more than 1,400 children enrolled in traditional public schools with tutorial assistance. Including some or all of these children in the denominator of children enrolled in nontraditional schools during the 1999–2000 school year drops the percentage enrolled in religious schools from 96% to under 20%. The 96% figure also represents but a snapshot of one particular school year. In the 1997–1998 school year, by contrast, only 78% of scholarship recipients attended religious schools. . . .[7]

In sum, the Ohio program is entirely neutral with respect to religion. It provides benefits directly to a wide spectrum of individuals, defined only by financial need and residence in a particular school district. It permits such individuals to exercise genuine choice among options public and private, secular and religious. The program is therefore a program of true private choice. In keeping with an unbroken line of decisions rejecting challenges to similar programs, we hold that the program does not offend the Establishment Clause. The judgment of the Court of Appeals is reversed.

It is so ordered.

Justice O'Connor, concurring.

. . . Medicare and Medicaid provide federal funds to pay for the healthcare of the elderly and the poor, respectively; the Pell Grant program and the G.I. Bill subsidize higher education of low-income individuals and veterans; and the CCDBG program finances child care for low-income parents. [R]eligious hospitals, which account for 18 percent of all hospital beds nationwide, rely on Medicare funds for 36 percent of their revenue. . . .

---

[7] Justice Breyer would raise the invisible specters of "divisiveness" and "religious strife" to find the program unconstitutional. (dissenting opinion). It is unclear exactly what sort of principle Justice Breyer has in mind, considering that the program has ignited no "divisiveness" or "strife" other than this litigation. . . .

JUSTICE THOMAS, concurring.

. . . Religious schools, like other private schools, achieve far better educational results than their public counterparts. For example, the students at Cleveland's Catholic schools score significantly higher on Ohio proficiency tests than students at Cleveland public schools. Of Cleveland eighth graders taking the 1999 Ohio proficiency test, 95 percent in Catholic schools passed the reading test, whereas only 57 percent in public schools passed. And 75 percent of Catholic school students passed the math proficiency test, compared to only 22 percent of public school students. [T]he State has a constitutional right to experiment with a variety of different programs to promote educational opportunity. That Ohio's program includes successful schools simply indicates that such reform can in fact provide improved education to underprivileged urban children. . . . As Frederick Douglass poignantly noted "no greater benefit can be bestowed upon a long benighted people, than giving to them, as we are here earnestly this day endeavoring to do, the means of an education."

JUSTICE STEVENS, dissenting.

[T]he voluntary character of the private choice to prefer a parochial education over an education in the public school system seems to me quite irrelevant to the question whether the government's choice to pay for religious indoctrination is constitutionally permissible. . . .

JUSTICE SOUTER, with whom JUSTICE STEVENS, JUSTICE GINSBURG, and JUSTICE BREYER join, dissenting.

[A]lmost two out of three families using vouchers to send their children to religious schools did not embrace the religion of those schools. The families made it clear they had not chosen the schools because they wished their children to be proselytized in a religion not their own, or in any religion, but because of educational opportunity.[12] . . .

[The dissenting opinion of BREYER, J., joined by STEVENS & SOUTER, JJ., is omitted.]

---

[12] When parents were surveyed as to their motives for enrolling their children in the voucher program, 96.4% cited a better education than available in the public schools, and 95% said their children's safety. When asked specifically in one study to identify the most important factor in selecting among participating private schools, 60% of parents mentioned academic quality, teacher quality, or the substance of what is taught (presumably secular); only 15% mentioned the religious affiliation of the school as even a consideration.

8.3 NON-FINANCIAL ASSISTANCE TO RELIGIOUS SCHOOLS AND INSTITUTIONS

SCHOOL DISTRICT OF ABINGTON TOWNSHIP V. SCHEMPP

374 U.S. 203, 83 S.Ct. 1560, 10 L.Ed.2d 844 (1963)

MR. JUSTICE CLARK delivered the opinion of the Court.

The Facts in Each Case: No. 142. The Commonwealth of Pennsylvania by law, requires that "At least ten verses from the Holy Bible shall be read, without comment, at the opening of each public school on each school day. Any child shall be excused from such Bible reading, or attending such Bible reading, upon the written request of his parent or guardian." The Schempp family, husband and wife and two of the three children, brought suit to enjoin enforcement of the statute. . . .

No. 119. In 1905 the Board of School Commissioners of Baltimore City adopted a rule [providing] for the holding of opening exercises in the schools of the city, consisting primarily of the "reading, without comment, of a chapter in the Holy Bible and/or the use of the Lord's Prayer." The petitioners, Mrs. Madalyn Murray and her son, William J. Murray III, are both professed atheists. Following unsuccessful attempts to have the respondent school board rescind the rule, this suit was filed for mandamus to compel its rescission and cancellation. It was alleged that William was a student in a public school of the city and Mrs. Murray, his mother, was a taxpayer therein. . . .

First, this Court has decisively settled that the First Amendment's mandate that "Congress shall make no law respecting an establishment of religion, or prohibiting the free exercise thereof" has been made wholly applicable to the States by the Fourteenth Amendment. Second, this Court has rejected unequivocally the contention that the Establishment Clause forbids only governmental preference of one religion over another. Almost 20 years ago in *Everson [v. Board of Educ.,* 330 U.S. 1, 15, 67 S.Ct. 504, 91 L.Ed. 711 (1947)], the Court said that "[n]either a state nor the Federal Government can set up a church. Neither can pass laws which aid one religion, aid all religions, or prefer one religion over another." . . .

The interrelationship of the Establishment and the Free Exercise Clauses was first touched upon by Mr. Justice Roberts for the Court in *Cantwell v. Connecticut,* 310 U.S. 296 [1940], at 303–304, where it was said that their "inhibition of legislation" had a double aspect. On the one hand, it forestalls compulsion by law of the acceptance of any creed or the practice of any form of worship. Freedom of conscience and freedom to adhere to such religious organization or form of worship as the individual may choose cannot be restricted by law. On the other hand, it safeguards the free exercise of the chosen form of religion. Thus the Amendment embraces two concepts,—freedom to believe and freedom to act. The first is absolute but, in the nature of things, the second cannot be.

[I]n *Engel v. Vitale* [370 U.S. 421, 32 S.Ct. 1261, 8 L.Ed.2d 601 (1962)], only last year, these principles were so universally recognized that the Court, without the citation of a single case and over the sole dissent of Mr. Justice Stewart, reaffirmed them. The Court found the 22-word prayer used in "New York's program of daily classroom invocation of God's blessings as prescribed in the Regents' prayer [to be] a religious activity." It held that "it is no part of the business of government to compose official prayers for any group of the American people to recite as a part of a religious program carried on by government."

[T]o withstand the strictures of the Establishment Clause there must be a secular legislative purpose and a primary effect that neither advances nor inhibits religion. The Free Exercise Clause, likewise considered many times here, withdraws from legislative power, state and federal, the exertion of any restraint on the free exercise of religion. Its purpose is to secure religious liberty in the individual by prohibiting any invasions thereof by civil authority. Hence it is necessary in a free exercise case for one to show the coercive effect of the enactment as it operates against him in the practice of his religion. The distinction between the two clauses is apparent—a violation of the Free Exercise Clause is predicated on coercion while the Establishment Clause violation need not be so attended.

Applying the Establishment Clause principles to the cases at bar we find that the States are requiring the selection and reading at the opening of the school day of verses from the Holy Bible and the recitation of the Lord's Prayer by the students in unison. These exercises are prescribed as part of the curricular activities of students who are required by law to attend school. They are held in the school buildings under the supervision and with the participation of teachers employed in those schools. None of these factors, other than compulsory school attendance, was present in the program upheld in *Zorach v. Clauson.* The trial court in No. 142 has found that such an opening exercise is a religious ceremony and was intended by the State to be so. We agree with the trial court's finding as to the religious character of the exercises. Given that finding, the exercises and the law requiring them are in violation of the Establishment Clause.

There is no such specific finding as to the religious character of the exercises in No. 119, and the State contends (as does the State in No. 142) that the program is an effort to extend its benefits to all public school children without regard to their religious belief. Included within its secular purposes, it says, are the promotion of moral values, the contradiction to the materialistic trends of our times, the perpetuation of our institutions and the teaching of literature. The case came up on demurrer, of course, to a petition which alleged that the uniform practice under the rule had been to read from the King James version of the Bible and that the exercise was sectarian. The short answer, therefore, is that the religious character of the exercise was admitted by the State. But even if its purpose is not strictly religious, it is sought to be accomplished through readings, without comment, from the Bible. Surely the place of the Bible as an instrument of religion cannot be gainsaid, and the State's recognition of the pervading religious character of the ceremony is evident from the rule's specific permission of the alternative use of the Catholic Douay version as well as the recent amendment permitting nonattendance at the exercises. None of these factors is consistent with the contention that the Bible is here used either as an instrument for nonreligious moral inspiration or as a reference for the teaching of secular subjects.

The conclusion follows that in both cases the laws require religious exercises and such exercises are being conducted in direct violation of the rights of the appellees and petitioners. Nor are these required exercises mitigated by the fact that individual students may absent themselves upon parental request, for that fact furnishes no defense to a claim of unconstitutionality under the Establishment Clause. Further, it is no defense to urge that the religious practices here may be relatively minor encroachments on the First Amendment. The breach of neutrality that is today a trickling stream may all too soon become a raging torrent and, in the words of Madison, "it is proper to take alarm at the first experiment on our liberties."

It is insisted that unless these religious exercises are permitted a "religion of secularism" is established in the schools. We agree of course that the State may not establish a "religion of secularism" in the sense of affirmatively opposing or showing hostility to religion, thus "preferring those who believe in no religion over those who do believe." *Zorach v. Clauson, supra*. We do not agree, however, that this decision in any sense has that effect. In addition, it might well be said that one's education is not complete without a study of comparative religion or the history of religion and its relationship to the advancement of civilization. It certainly may be said that the Bible is worthy of study for its literary and historic qualities. Nothing we have said here indicates that such study of the Bible or of religion, when presented objectively as part of a secular program of education, may not be effected consistently with the First Amendment. But the exercises here do not fall into those categories. They are religious exercises, required by the States in violation of the command of the First Amendment that the Government maintain strict neutrality, neither aiding nor opposing religion.

Finally, we cannot accept that the concept of neutrality, which does not permit a State to require a religious exercise even with the consent of the majority of those affected, collides with the majority's right to free exercise of religion.[10] While the Free Exercise Clause clearly prohibits the use of state action to deny the rights of free exercise to *anyone,* it has never meant that a majority could use the machinery of the State to practice its beliefs. . . .

MR. JUSTICE BRENNAN, concurring.

[A]n awareness of history and an appreciation of the aims of the Founding Fathers do not always resolve concrete problems. . . . It may be that Jefferson and Madison would have held such exercises to be permissible. . . . But I doubt that their view, even if perfectly clear one way or the other, would supply a dispositive answer to the question presented by these cases. A more fruitful inquiry, it seems to me, is whether the practices here challenged threaten those consequences which the Framers deeply feared; whether, in short, they tend to promote that type of interdependence between religion and state which the First Amendment was designed to prevent. [N]ot every involvement in public life violates the Establishment Clause . . .

The saying of invocational prayers in legislative chambers, state or federal, and the appointment of legislative chaplains, might well represent no involvements of the kind prohibited by the Establishment Clause. Legislators, federal and state, are mature adults who may presumably absent themselves from such public and ceremonial exercises without incurring any penalty, direct or indirect. It may also be significant that, at least in the case of the Congress, Art. I, § 5, of the Constitution makes each House the monitor of the "Rules of its

---

[10] We are not of course presented with and therefore do not pass upon a situation such as military service, where the Government regulates the temporal and geographic environment of individuals to a point that, unless it permits voluntary religious services to be conducted with the use of government facilities, military personnel would be unable to engage in the practice of their faiths.

Proceedings" so that it is at least arguable whether such matters present "political questions" the resolution of which is exclusively confided to Congress. . . .

The holding of the Court today plainly does not foreclose teaching *about* the Holy Scriptures or about the differences between religious sects in classes in literature or history. Indeed, whether or not the Bible is involved, it would be impossible to teach meaningfully many subjects in the social sciences or the humanities without some mention of religion.

[T]he use of the motto "In God We Trust" on currency, or documents and public buildings and the like may not offend the clause. It is not that the use of those four words can be dismissed as "de minimis"—for I suspect there would be intense opposition to the abandonment of that motto. The truth is that we have simply interwoven the motto so deeply into the fabric of our civil polity that its present use may well not present that type of involvement which the First Amendment prohibits.

This general principle might also serve to insulate the various patriotic exercises and activities used in the public schools and elsewhere which, whatever may have been their origins, no longer have a religious purpose or meaning. The reference to divinity in the revised pledge of allegiance, for example, may merely recognize the historical fact that our Nation was believed to have been founded "under God." Thus reciting the pledge may be no more of a religious exercise than the reading aloud of Lincoln's Gettysburg Address, which contains an allusion to the same historical fact.

MR. JUSTICE STEWART, dissenting.

[I]t seems to me clear that certain types of exercises would present situations in which no possibility of coercion on the part of secular officials could be claimed to exist. Thus, if such exercises were held either before or after the official school day, or if the school schedule were such that participation were merely one among a number of desirable alternatives, it could hardly be contended that the exercises did anything more than to provide an opportunity for the voluntary expression of religious belief.

[The concurring opinion of DOUGLAS, J., and of GOLDBERG, J., joined by HARLAN, J., are omitted.

NOTES

1. **FLAG SALUTES.** In *Minersville School District v. Gobitis,* 310 U.S. 586, 60 S.Ct. 1010, 84 L.Ed. 1375 (1940), the Court, speaking through Justice Frankfurter, upheld a Pennsylvania regulation requiring school children and their teachers to salute the national flag as part of a daily school exercise. The Gobitis children, members of the Jehovah's Witnesses, refused on the grounds that showing such respect for the flag is forbidden by the scriptural prohibition against worshiping false gods and making graven images. Because the children refused to salute the flag, the school authorities expelled them, and they entered private school. The *Gobitis* decision received widespread publicity, and appeared to endorse the salute and rebuke the Witnesses.

    In June, 1940, several hundred incidents occurred in which force was directed against Jehovah's Witnesses; violent incidents continued at a rate of almost a hundred a month through most of 1940, all following a fixed pattern. Hundreds of street fights broke out. A Jehovah's Witness, distributing tracts on a street corner, was approached by several toughs carrying an American flag. When he refused their command to salute the flag, they beat him and destroyed his literature. Where the approach was made to a group of Witnesses, the affair turned into a full-scale brawl.

    Often the violence transcended mere street-fighting, especially in the period immediately following the *Gobitis* decision. On June 9, 1940, an angry mob sacked and burned a Witness "Kingdom Hall" at Kennebunk, Maine. On June 22, a Witness was tarred and feathered in Parco, Wyoming. On June 27, a mob of veterans forcibly deported a large number of Witnesses from Jackson, Mississippi, eventually dropping them off at Dallas, Texas. In August a Nebraska Witness was abducted from his home and partially castrated. While the frequency of violent incidents tapered off after 1940, nasty cases continued to occur.[2]

2. In *West Virginia State Board of Education v. Barnette,* 319 U.S. 624, 63 S.Ct. 1178, 87 L.Ed. 1628 (1943), the Court, speaking through Justice Jackson, overruled *Gobitis.* While Justice Stone was the sole dissent in *Gobitis,* Justice Frankfurter was the sole dissent in *Barnette.*[3]

---

[2]   David R. Manwarning, The Flag-Salute Case, at 27–28, in The Third Branch of Government: 8 Cases in Constitutional Politics (C. Herman Pritchett & Alan F. Westin, eds. 1963).

[3]   Frankfurter's dissent said: "One who belongs to the most vilified and persecuted minority in history is not likely to be insensible to the freedoms guaranteed in our Constitution. Were my purely personal attitude relevant, I should wholeheartedly associate myself with the general libertarian views in the Court's opinion,

Jackson explained that the issue before the Court did not really "turn on one's possession of particular religious views or the sincerity with which they are held. While religion supplies appellees' motive for enduring the discomforts of making the issue in this case, many citizens who do not share these religious views hold such a compulsory rite to infringe constitutional liberty of the individual. It is not necessary to inquire whether non-conformist beliefs will exempt from the duty to salute unless we first find power to make the salute a legal duty." The *Barnette* Court noted that *Gobitis* had assumed the existence of the power and then rejected a claim of immunity based on religious beliefs. The *Barnette* Court found no such power.

If there is any fixed star in our constitutional constellation, it is that no official, high or petty, can prescribe what shall be orthodox in politics, nationalism, religion, or other matters of opinion or force citizens to confess by word or act their faith therein. . . . We think the action of the local authorities in compelling the flag salute and pledge transcends constitutional limitations on their power and invades the sphere of intellect and spirit which it is the purpose of the First Amendment of our Constitution to reserve from all official control.

Barnette then affirmed the lower court judgment enjoining enforcement of the flag salute law against Jehovah's Witnesses.

Note that *Barnette*,—unlike *Schempp* and other school prayer cases—did not strike down the flag salute all together, but only required the school to excuse all those objecting. *Schempp*, at the end of the majority opinion, cited and quoted *Barnette* with approval. The two cases are consistent because *Barnette* is really a free speech case, and the flag salute is a pledge (a secular act), not a prayer.

3. **THE TEN COMMANDMENTS AND NATIVITY SCENES.** In *Stone v. Graham*, 449 U.S. 39, 101 S.Ct. 192, 66 L.Ed.2d 199 (1980) (*per curiam*), the Court invalidated a Kentucky statute that required a copy of the Ten Commandments (purchased with private funds) to be posted on the wall of each public classroom in the state. At the bottom of each display was the

---

[but] I cannot bring my mind to believe that the 'liberty' secured by the Due Process Clause gives this Court authority to deny to the State of West Virginia the attainment of that which we all recognize as a legitimate legislative end, namely, the promotion of good citizenship, by employment of the means here chosen."

following notation: "The secular application of the Ten Commandments is clearly seen in its adoption as the fundamental legal code of Western Civilization and the Common Law of the United States." The U.S. Supreme Court said, "The pre-eminent purpose for posting the Ten Commandments on schoolroom walls is plainly religious in nature." The Commandments are a "sacred text," do not confine themselves "to arguably secular matters, such as honoring one's parents, killing or murder," and concern religious duties such as avoiding idolatry. "This is not a case in which the Ten Commandments are integrated into the school curriculum, where the Bible may constitutionally be used in an appropriate study of history, civilization, ethics, comparative religion, or the like." Because the statute has no secular legislative purpose, it violates the establishment clause.

Two cases, both decided in 2005, involved display of the ten commandments in a courthouse, *McCreary County v. ACLU*, 545 U.S. 844, 125 S.Ct. 2722, 162 L.Ed.2d 729 (2005), and in the outdoors, on public grounds, *Van Orden v. Perry*, 545 U.S. 677, 125 S.Ct. 2854, 162 L.Ed.2d 607 (2005) (a 6-foot granite monument of the Ten Commandments on the grounds of the Texas capitol, along with other monuments). In two cases totaling nearly 150 pages in the U.S. Reports, a fragmented Supreme Court upheld the constitutionality of displaying the Ten Commandments in *Van Orden* (no majority opinion), but prohibited such displays in *McCreary* (5 to 4 opinion, with a court majority), based on the special facts of each case. Differing alignments of justices said that displays of the Ten Commandments are not *per se* unconstitutional but the courts will have to resolve the issue on a case-by-case basis.

When the *Van Orden* Court issued its various opinions, Rehnquist wisecracked before the packed courtroom: "I didn't know we had that many people on our court." The Texas display of the Ten Commandments was a 6-foot high monolith situated among 21 historical markers and 17 monuments surrounding the Texas State Capitol.

The Rehnquist plurality acknowledged that the Court's "cases, Januslike, point in two directions in applying the Establishment Clause." "Our institutions presuppose a Supreme Being, yet these institutions must not press religious observances upon their citizens." He argued that the *Lemon* test, whatever its fate in Establishment Clause jurisprudence, is "not useful in dealing with the sort of passive monument that Texas has erected on its

Capitol grounds." Instead, the Court will look to history and the nature of the monument.

> We need only look within our own Courtroom. Since 1935, Moses has stood, holding two tablets that reveal portions of the Ten Commandments written in Hebrew, among other lawgivers in the south frieze. Representations of the Ten Commandments adorn the metal gates lining the north and south sides of the Courtroom as well as the doors leading into the Courtroom. Moses also sits on the exterior east facade of the building holding the Ten Commandments tablets. [A] large statue of Moses holding the Ten Commandments, alongside a statue of the Apostle Paul, has overlooked the rotunda of the Library of Congress' Jefferson Building since 1897. And the Jefferson Building's Great Reading Room contains a sculpture of a woman beside the Ten Commandments with a quote above her from the Old Testament (Micah 6:8). A medallion with two tablets depicting the Ten Commandments decorates the floor of the National Archives. Inside the Department of Justice, a statue entitled "The Spirit of Law" has two tablets representing the Ten Commandments lying at its feet. In front of the Ronald Reagan Building is another sculpture that includes a depiction of the Ten Commandments. So too a 24-foot-tall sculpture, depicting, among other things, the Ten Commandments and a cross, stands outside the federal courthouse that houses both the Court of Appeals and the District Court for the District of Columbia. Moses is also prominently featured in the Chamber of the United States House of Representatives.

The list goes on. E.g., the apex of the Washington Monument is inscribed "Laus Deo" (*i.e.*, "Praise be to God"), and multiple memorial stones in that monument contain Biblical citations. The Texas statute, unlike the Kentucky statute in *Stone v. Graham*, did not have "an improper and plainly religious purpose." Instead, in context of various monuments, "The inclusion of the Ten Commandments monument in this group has a dual significance, partaking of both religion and government." Breyer, J., concurring in the judgment, agreed. This case is unlike *McCreary*, where the history of its display "demonstrates the substantially religious objectives" and motives of the proponents of the display.

The Court has treated nativity scenes or other Christmas decorations, which some cities erect in December of each year, the same way—if the city crèche, in context, is part of larger display that includes secular items and celebrates the season, the Court will approve it. In, *Lynch v. Donnelly*, 465 U.S. 668, 104 S.Ct. 1355, 79 L.Ed.2d 604 (1984), the display included "a Santa Claus house, reindeer pulling Santa's sleigh, candy-striped poles, a Christmas tree, carolers, cutout figures representing such characters as a clown, an elephant, and a teddy bear, hundreds of colored lights, a large banner that reads 'SEASONS GREETINGS,' and the crèche at issue here." The Court upheld it (5 to 4).

4.   **LEGISLATIVE PRAYER.** *Marsh v. Chambers,* 463 U.S. 783, 103 S.Ct. 3330, 77 L.Ed.2d 1019 (1983), held that there is no violation of the establishment clause when the Nebraska legislature begins each of its sessions with a prayer, in the Judeo-Christian tradition, by a chaplain paid by the state with the legislature's approval. A Presbyterian minister served as chaplain since 1965, receiving nearly $320 per month for each month while the legislature was in session. The Court upheld the Nebraska practice, because of the historical background:

> The opening of sessions of legislative and other deliberative public bodies with prayer is deeply embedded in the history and tradition of this country. From colonial times through the founding of the Republic and ever since, the practice of legislative prayer has coexisted with the principles of disestablishment and religious freedom. In the very courtrooms in which the United States District Judge and later three Circuit Judges heard and decided this case, the proceedings opened with an announcement that concluded, "God save the United States and this Honorable Court." The same invocation occurs at all sessions of this Court.

> [T]he First Congress, as one of its early items of business, adopted the policy of selecting a chaplain to open each session with prayer. [The] delegates [to the first Congress] did not consider opening prayers as a proselytizing activity or as symbolically placing the government's "official seal of approval on one religious view." [Moreover, here] the individual claiming injury [a state legislator] by the practice is an adult, presumably not readily susceptible to "religious indoctrination," or peer pressure.

In light of the unambiguous and unbroken history of more than 200 years, there can be no doubt that the practice of opening legislative sessions with prayer has become part of the fabric of our society. To invoke Divine guidance on a public body entrusted with making the laws is not, in these circumstances, an "establishment" of religion or a step toward establishment; it is simply a tolerable acknowledgment of beliefs widely held among the people of this country. . . . The content of the prayer is not of concern to judges where, as here, there is no indication that the prayer opportunity has been exploited to proselytize or advance any one, or to disparage any other, faith or belief. That being so, it is not for us to embark on a sensitive evaluation or to parse the content of a particular prayer.

Justice Brennan, joined by Justice Marshall, dissented. Brennan recalled his concurring opinion in *Schempp,* but stated, but, "after much reflection, I have come to the conclusion that I was wrong then and that the Court is wrong today. I now believe that the practice of official invocational prayer, as it exists in Nebraska and most other State Legislatures, is unconstitutional."

Town of Greece v. Galloway, 572 U.S. ___, 134 S.Ct. 1811, 188 L. Ed. 2d 835 (2014), held (5 to 4) that a town's board meetings may begin its sessions with a ceremonial prayer. Plaintiffs did not object to the prayers but argued they must be nonsectarian, not identifiable with any one religion. The Court rejected that argument. "An insistence on nonsectarian or ecumenical prayer as a single, fixed standard is not consistent with the tradition of legislative prayer outlined in the Court's cases." The town board selected clergy from the listing in a local directory. While the prayer program is open to all creeds, nearly all of the local congregations are Christian, so nearly all of the participating prayers have been Christian. The Court did not think it was the state's place to edit the prayer of the speaker. Breyer's dissent conceded that the plaintiffs "do not argue that the town intentionally discriminated against non-Christians when choosing whom to invite."

Outside the these ceremonial prayers that open up legislative sessions, the Court has not allowed other the state school to invite ministers for the purpose of giving, for example, (1) a benediction at graduation, *Lee v. Weisman*, 505 U.S. 577, 112 S.Ct. 2649, 120 L.Ed.2d 467 (1992) held (5 to 4), or (2) a prayer at football games. *Santa Fe Independent School District v. Doe,* 530 U.S. 290, 120 S.Ct. 2266, 147 L.Ed.2d 295 (2000) (6 to 3).

8.4 RELIGIOUS EXCEPTIONS TO STATE DUTIES

McGowan v. Maryland, 366 U.S. 420, 81 S.Ct. 1101, 6 L.Ed.2d 393 (1961), upheld the constitutionality of a state law that prohibited the Sunday sale of all merchandise except the retail sale of tobacco products, confectioneries, milk, bread, fruits, gasoline, oils, greases, drugs and medicines, and newspapers and periodicals. The appellants in this case were indicted for the Sunday sale of a three-ring, loose-leaf binder, a can of floor wax, a stapler and staples, and a toy submarine. They argued that the law violated the guarantee of separation of church and state in that the statutes are laws respecting an establishment of religion. The Court readily agreed that the laws originally were motivated by religious forces (in fact, one of the sections was entitled "Sabbath Breaking"), but the Court upheld the law because of its secular purpose to set aside a uniform day of "rest, repose, recreation and tranquility—a day which all members of the family and community have the opportunity to spend and enjoy together, a day on which there exists relative quiet and disassociation from the everyday intensity of commercial activities, a day on which people may visit friends and relatives who are not available during working days." The Court basically says that the state, if it wishes, can set aside, by law, day a week that is a little less hectic than the other six. If the state picks a day, it can pick any day and it is not surprising that it picks a day that coincides with the preferences of the majority of the voters. Only Justice Douglas dissented.

That same day, in *Braunfeld v. Brown,* 366 U.S. 599, 81 S.Ct. 1144, 6 L.Ed.2d 563 (1961), a divided Court, with no majority opinion, upheld a Pennsylvania Sunday closing statute as applied to Orthodox Jewish merchants who complained that the enforcement against them of the Pennsylvania statute prohibited the free exercise of their religion. Because the statute compelled them to close on Sunday, they suffered substantial economic loss, to the benefit of their non-Sabbatarian competitors, when they also continued their Sabbath observance by closing their business on Saturday.

Chief Justice Warren's opinion reasoned: "To strike down, without the most critical scrutiny, legislation which imposes only an indirect burden on the exercise of religion, *i.e.,* legislation which does not make unlawful the religious practice itself, would radically restrict the operating latitude of the legislature." Warren relied on *Reynolds v. United States,* 98 U.S. 145, 25 L.Ed. 244 (1879), which "upheld the polygamy conviction of a member of the Mormon faith despite the fact that an accepted doctrine of his church then imposed upon its male members the *duty* to practice polygamy. And in *Prince v. Massachusetts,* 321 U.S. 158, 64 S.Ct. 438, 88 L.Ed. 645 (1944), [the Supreme] Court upheld a statute making it a crime for a girl under eighteen years of age to sell any newspapers, periodicals, or merchandise in public places despite the fact that a child of the Jehovah's Witnesses faith believed that it was her religious *duty* to perform this work." (emphasis in original.)

The Sunday closing law did not interfere as much as the laws in *Reynolds* or *Prince* because no merchant embraced a religious belief that required him to stay open on Sunday. However, Warren noted: "If the purpose or effect of a law is to impede the observance of one or all religions or is to discriminate invidiously between religions, that law is constitutionally invalid even though the burden may be characterized as being only indirect. But if the State regulates conduct by enacting a general law within its power, the purpose and effect of which is to advance the State's secular goals, the statute is valid despite its indirect burden on religious observance unless the State may accomplish its purpose by means which do not impose such a burden." In this case Warren believed that a state *may* exempt Saturday observers from the Sunday closing law. Some states do that, as it "may well be the wiser solution." But the state could conclude that such an exemption could dilute the goal of setting aside one day free "of commercial noise." In addition, to exempt Saturday observers could provide them with a competitive advantage over Sunday observers, who would then complain about being discriminated against. Moreover, it would be difficult to police because people could easily claim they were not Sunday adherents in order to obtain a competitive advantage.

In *Sherbert v. Verner,* 374 U.S. 398, 83 S.Ct. 1790, 10 L.Ed.2d 965 (1963), the Court invalidated a state law that denied unemployment compensation benefits to a Seventh Day Adventist who was discharged by her employer because she would not work on Saturday, her Sabbath.

Justice Brennan for the Court noted that, FIRST, the effect of the law is to impose a heavy burden on appellant, even if only "indirect." (Granted, "direct" versus "indirect" distinction are hard to fathom because the Court never really defines what makes a burden direct or indirect.) SECOND, and more significantly, no countervailing interest justifies the state's position. South Carolina already allowed Sunday worshipers to refuse to work on Sunday without forfeiting unemployment benefits. If the state will give unemployment compensation to worshippers who refuse to work on Sunday, it should treat Saturday worshippers the same way. The state can hardly object to possible fraudulent claims if it allowed the exemption for Saturday worshippers when it already decided it would investigate possible fraud for Sunday worshippers. If one is going to investigate all Sunday worshippers (to make sure they do not feign religious objection), there is no extra administrative burden to investigate what day the person claims when the state allows only one day. The law discriminated among religions—only Saturday worshippers are the ones ineligible for unemployment benefits.

However, *Estate of Thornton v. Caldor, Inc.,* 472 U.S. 703, 105 S.Ct. 2914, 86 L.Ed.2d 557 (1985), invalidated a state statute that gave employees an absolute and unqualified right not to work on their chosen Sabbath. This statute violated the establishment clause. The "statute takes no account of the convenience or interests of the employer or those of other employees who do not observe a Sabbath." The law allowed no exception for special circumstances, "such as the Friday Sabbath observer employed in an occupation with a Monday through Friday schedule—a school teacher, for example."

Gillette v. United States, 401 U.S. 437, 91 S.Ct. 828, 28 L.Ed.2d 168 (1971), upheld the constitutionality of a federal law exempting from military service those who conscientiously object to all wars but not those who conscientiously object only to unjust wars. The statute "does not discriminate on the basis of religious affiliation or belief, apart of course from beliefs concerning war." Although the objection must be grounded in religious training and belief, the statute does not require any particular sectarian affiliation or theological position. The Court concluded: "it is supportable for Congress to have decided that the objector to all war—to all killing in war—has a claim that is distinct enough and intense enough to justify special status, while the objector to a particular war does not. Of course, we do not suggest that Congress would have acted irrationally or unreasonably had it decided to exempt those who object to particular wars."

WISCONSIN V. YODER
406 U.S. 205, 92 S.Ct. 1526, 32 L.Ed.2d 15 (1972)

CHIEF JUSTICE BURGER delivered the opinion of the Court.

Respondents Jonas Yoder and Wallace Miller are members of the Old Order Amish religion, and respondent Adin Yutzy is a member of the Conservative Amish Mennonite Church. They and their families are residents of Green County, Wisconsin. Wisconsin's compulsory school-attendance law required them to cause their children to attend public or private school until reaching age 16 but the respondents declined to send their children, ages 14 and 15, to public school after they completed the eighth grade. . . .

On complaint of the school district administrator for the public schools, respondents were charged, tried, and convicted of violating the compulsory-attendance law in Green County Court and were fined the sum of $5 each. Respondents defended on the ground that the application of the compulsory-attendance law violated their rights under the First and Fourteenth Amendments. The trial testimony showed that respondents believed, in accordance with the tenets of Old Order Amish communities generally, that their children's attendance at high school, public or private, was contrary to the Amish religion and way of life. They believe that by sending their children to high school, they would not only expose themselves to the danger of the censure of the church community, but, as found by the county court, also endanger their own salvation and that of their children. The State stipulated that respondents' religious beliefs were sincere.

. . . Old Order Amish communities today are characterized by a fundamental belief that salvation requires life in a church community separate and apart from the world and worldly influence. This concept of life aloof from the world and its values its central to their faith. . . . Formal high school education beyond the eighth grade is contrary to Amish beliefs, not only because it places Amish children in an environment hostile to Amish beliefs with increasing emphasis on competition in class work and sports and with pressure to conform to the styles, manners, and ways of the peer group, but also because it takes them away from their community, physically and emotionally, during the crucial and formative adolescent period of life.

[I]n order for Wisconsin to compel school attendance beyond the eighth grade against a claim that such attendance interferes with the practice of a legitimate religious belief, it must appear either that the State does not deny the free exercise of religious belief by its requirement, or that there is a state interest of sufficient magnitude to override the interest claiming protection under the Free Exercise Clause.

. . . A way of life, however virtuous and admirable, may not be interposed as a barrier to reasonable state regulation of education if it is based on purely secular considerations; to have the protection of the Religion Clauses, the claims must be rooted in religious belief. . . . Thus, if the Amish asserted their claims because of their subjective evaluation and rejection of the contemporary secular values accepted by the majority, much as Thoreau rejected the social values of his time and isolated himself at Walden Pond, their claims would not rest on a religious basis. Thoreau's choice was philosophical and personal rather than religious, and such belief does not rise to the demands of the Religion Clauses. Giving no weight to such secular considerations, however, we see that the record in this case abundantly supports the claim that the traditional way of life of the Amish is not merely a matter of personal preference, but one of deep religious conviction, shared by an organized group, and intimately related to daily living. . . .

The impact of the compulsory-attendance law on respondents' practice of the Amish religion is not only severe, but inescapable, for the Wisconsin law affirmatively compels them, under threat of criminal sanction, to perform acts undeniably at odds with fundamental tenets of their religious beliefs. See *Braunfeld v. Brown.* [T]he State's broader contention [is] that its interest in its system of compulsory education is so compelling that even the established religious practices of the Amish must give way. . . .

The State advances two primary arguments in support of its system of compulsory education. It notes, as Thomas Jefferson pointed out early in our history, that some degree of education is necessary to prepare citizens to participate effectively and intelligently in our open political system if we are to preserve freedom and independence. Further, education prepares individuals to be self-reliant and self-sufficient participants in society. We accept these propositions. However, the evidence adduced by the Amish in this case is persuasively to the effect that an additional one or two years of formal high school for Amish children in place of their long-established program of informal vocational education would do little to serve those interests. . . . It is one thing to say that compulsory education for a year or two beyond the eighth grade may be necessary when its goal is the preparation of the child for life in modern society as the majority live, but it is quite another if the goal of education be viewed as the preparation of the child for life in the separated agrarian community that is the keystone of the Amish faith.

The State attacks respondents' position as one fostering "ignorance" from which the child must be protected by the State. No one can question the State's duty to protect children from ignorance but this argument does not square with the facts disclosed in the record. Whatever their idiosyncrasies as seen by the majority, this record strongly shows that the Amish community has been a highly successful social unit within our society, even if apart from the conventional "mainstream." Its members are productive and very law-abiding members of society; they reject public welfare in any of its usual modern forms. The Congress itself recognized their self-sufficiency by authorizing exemption of such groups as the Amish from the obligation to pay social security taxes. . . .

The State, however, supports its interest in providing an additional one or two years of compulsory high school education to Amish children because of the possibility that some such children will choose to leave the Amish community, and that if this occurs they will be ill-equipped for life. . . . There is nothing in this record to suggest that the Amish qualities of reliability, self-reliance, and dedication to work would fail to find ready markets in today's society. . . .

Contrary to the suggestion of the dissenting opinion of Mr. Justice Douglas, our holding today in no degree depends on the assertion of the religious interest of the child as contrasted with that of the parents. It is the parents who are subject to prosecution here for failing to cause their children to attend school, and it is their right of free exercise, not that of their children, that must determine Wisconsin's power to impose criminal penalties on the parent. The dissent argues that a child who expresses a desire to attend public high school in conflict with the wishes of his parents should not be prevented from doing so. There is no reason for the Court to consider that point since it is not an issue in the case. . . .

For the reasons stated we hold, with the Supreme Court of Wisconsin, that the First and Fourteenth Amendments prevent the State from compelling respondents to cause their children to attend formal high school to age 16. Our disposition of this case, however, in no way alters our recognition of the obvious fact that courts are not school boards or legislatures, and are ill-equipped to determine the "necessity" of discrete aspects of a State's program of compulsory education. This should suggest that courts must move with great circumspection in performing the sensitive and delicate task of weighing a State's legitimate social concern when faced with religious claims for exemption from generally applicable educational requirements. It cannot be overemphasized that we are not dealing with a way of life and mode of education by a group claiming to have recently discovered some "progressive" or more enlightened process for rearing children for modern life.

JUSTICE DOUGLAS, dissenting in part.

. . . If the parents in this case are allowed a religious exemption, the inevitable effect is to impose the parents' notions of religious duty upon their children. Where the child is mature enough to express potentially conflicting desires, it would be an invasion of the child's rights to permit such an imposition without canvassing his views. [I]t is an imposition resulting from this very litigation As the child has no other effective forum, it is in this litigation that his rights should be considered. And, if an Amish child desires to attend high school, and is mature enough to have that desire respected, the State may well be able to override the parents' religiously motivated objections. [The child] may want to be a pianist or an astronaut or an oceanographer. To do so he will have to break from the Amish tradition. It is the future of the student, not the future of the parents, that is imperiled by today's decision. If a parent keeps his child out of school beyond the grade school, then the child will be forever barred from entry into the new and amazing world of diversity that we have today. . . .

I think the emphasis of the Court on the "law and order" record of this Amish group of people is quite irrelevant. A religion is a religion irrespective of what the misdemeanor or felony records of its members might be. I am not at all sure how the Catholics, Episcopalians, the Baptists, Jehovah's Witnesses, the Unitarians, and my own Presbyterians would make out if subjected to such a test. . . .

[The concurring opinion of STEWART, joined by BRENNAN, J., and the concurring opinion of WHITE, J., joined by BRENNAN & STEWART, JJ., are omitted. POWELL & REHNQUIST, JJ., took no part in the consideration or decision of this case.]

NOTES

1. *Thomas v. Review Board,* 450 U.S. 707, 101 S.Ct. 1425, 67 L.Ed.2d 624 (1981), held that under *Sherbert v. Verner,* Indiana could not constitutionally deny unemployment benefits to a Jehovah's Witness who quit his job when he was transferred to a department that produced turrets for military tanks. His religious beliefs forbade participation in the production of armaments. The Court noted:

   > The Indiana court also appears to have given significant weight to the fact that another Jehovah's Witness had no scruples about working on tank turrets; for that other Witness, at least, such work was "scripturally" acceptable. Intrafaith differences of that kind are not uncommon among followers of a particular creed, and the judicial process is singularly ill equipped to resolve such differences in relation to the Religion Clauses. One can, of course, imagine an asserted claim so bizarre, so clearly nonreligious in motivation, as not to be entitled to protection under the Free Exercise Clause; but that is not limited to beliefs which are shared by all of the members

of a religious sect. Particularly in this sensitive area, it is not within the judicial function and judicial competence to inquire whether the petitioner or his fellow worker more correctly perceived the commands of their common faith. Courts are not arbiters of scriptural interpretation. The narrow function of a reviewing court in this context is to determine whether there was an appropriate finding that petitioner terminated his work because of an honest conviction that such work was forbidden by his religion.

2. *United States v. Lee,* 455 U.S. 252, 102 S.Ct. 1051, 71 L.Ed.2d 127 (1982), upheld the imposition of social security taxes as applied to persons who object on religious grounds to public insurance benefits and to payment of taxes to support public insurance funds. The Court stated, "Not all burdens on religion are unconstitutional. The state may justify a limitation on religious liberty by showing that it is essential to accomplish an overriding governmental interest." The Court therefore ruled against Lee, a member of the Old Order Amish:

> Unlike the situation presented in *Wisconsin v. Yoder* it would be difficult to accommodate the comprehensive social security system with myriad exceptions flowing from a wide variety of religious beliefs. The obligation to pay the social security tax initially is not fundamentally different from the obligation to pay income taxes; the difference—in theory at least—is that the social security tax revenues are segregated for use only in furtherance of the statutory program. There is no principled way, however, for purposes of this case, to distinguish between general taxes and those imposed under the Social Security Act. If, for example, a religious adherent believes war is a sin, and if a certain percentage of the federal budget can be identified as devoted to war-related activities, such individuals would have a similarly valid claim to be exempt from paying that percentage of the income tax. The tax system could not function if denominations were allowed to challenge the tax system because tax payments were spent in a manner that violates their religious belief. Because the broad public interest in maintaining a sound tax system is of such a high order, religious belief in conflict with the payment of taxes affords no basis for resisting the tax.

Bob Jones University v. United States, 461 U.S. 574, 103 S.Ct. 2017, 76 L.Ed.2d 157 (1983), upheld the statutory authority of the Internal Revenue

Service to deny tax-exempt status to religious, charitable, and educational institutions that engage in racial discrimination. Bob Jones University permits unmarried blacks to enroll but denies admission to applicants in an interracial marriage or who "espouse" interracial marriage or dating. The other petitioner, Goldsboro Christian Schools, Inc., has a racially discriminatory admissions policy and normally accepts only whites, but it has, on occasion, accepted children from racially mixed marriages in which one of the parents is white. Both schools base their policy on their interpretations of the Bible.

The I.R.S. position did not violate the free exercise rights of these schools because of the overriding governmental interest:

> Denial of tax benefits will inevitably have a substantial impact on the operation of private religious schools, but will not prevent those schools from observing their religious tenets. The governmental interest at stake here is compelling. [It] has a fundamental, overriding interest in eradicating racial discrimination in education—discrimination that prevailed, with official approval, for the first 165 years of this Nation's history. That governmental interest substantially outweighs whatever burden denial of tax benefits places on petitioners' exercise of their religious beliefs. The interests asserted by petitioners cannot be accommodated with that compelling governmental interest, and no "less restrictive means" are available to achieve the governmental-interest.

EMPLOYMENT DIVISION, DEPARTMENT OF HUMAN RESOURCES V. SMITH

494 U.S. 872, 110 S.Ct. 1595, 108 L.Ed.2d 876 (1990)

JUSTICE SCALIA delivered the opinion of the Court.

This case requires us to decide whether the Free Exercise Clause of the First Amendment permits the State of Oregon to include religiously inspired peyote use within the reach of its general criminal prohibition on use of that drug, and thus permits the State to deny unemployment benefits to persons dismissed from their jobs because of such religiously inspired use. . . .

Respondents, Alfred Smith and Galen Black were fired from their jobs with a private drug rehabilitation organization because they ingested peyote for sacramental purposes at a ceremony of the Native American Church, of which both are members. When respondents applied to petitioner Employment Division for unemployment compensation, they were determined to be ineligible for benefits because they had been discharged for work-related "misconduct". The Oregon Court of Appeals reversed that determination, holding that the denial of benefits violated respondents' free exercise rights under the First Amendment. . . .

Respondents' claim for relief rests on our decisions in *Sherbert v. Verner,* [and] *Thomas v. Review Board*, in which we held that a State could not condition the availability of unemployment insurance on an individual's willingness to forgo conduct required by his religion. [H]owever, the conduct at issue in those cases was not prohibited by law.

[Respondents assert] that their religious motivation for using peyote places them beyond the reach of a criminal law that is not specifically directed at their religious practice, and that is concededly constitutional as applied to those who use the drug for other reasons. . . . It is no more necessary to regard the collection of a general tax, for example, as "prohibiting the free exercise [of religion]" by those citizens who believe support of organized government to be sinful, than it is to regard the same tax as "abridging the freedom . . . of the press" of those publishing companies that must pay the tax as a condition of staying in business. [I]f prohibiting the exercise of religion (or burdening the activity of printing) is not the object of the tax but merely the incidental effect of a generally applicable and otherwise valid provision, the First Amendment has not been offended. Compare *Citizen Publishing Co. v. United States,* 394 U.S. 131, 139, 89 S.Ct. 927, 931–32, 22 L.Ed.2d 148 (1969) (upholding application of antitrust laws to press), with *Grosjean v. American Press Co.,* 297 U.S. 233, 250–251, 56 S.Ct. 444, 449, 80 L.Ed. 660 (1936) (striking down license tax applied only to newspapers with weekly circulation above a specified level).

. . . We have never held that an individual's religious beliefs excuse him from compliance with an otherwise valid law prohibiting conduct that the State is free to regulate. . . . We first had occasion to assert that principle in *Reynolds v. United States,* 98 U.S. 145, 25 L.Ed. 244 (1879), where we rejected the claim that criminal laws against polygamy could not be constitutionally applied to those whose religion commanded the practice. "Laws," we said, "are made for the government of actions, and while they cannot interfere with mere religious belief and opinions, they may with practices. . . . Can a man excuse his practices to the contrary because of his religious belief? To permit this would be to make the professed doctrines of religious belief superior to the law of the land, and in effect to permit every citizen to become a law unto himself." . . .

The only decisions in which we have held that the First Amendment bars application of a neutral, generally applicable law to religiously motivated action have involved not the Free Exercise Clause alone, but the Free Exercise Clause in conjunction with other constitutional protections, such as freedom of speech and of the press, see *Cantwell v. Connecticut,* 310 U.S., at 304–307, 60 S.Ct., at 903–905 (invalidating a licensing system for religious and charitable solicitations under which the administrator had discretion to deny a license to any cause he deemed nonreligious); *Murdock v. Pennsylvania,* 319 U.S. 105, 63 S.Ct. 870, 87 L.Ed. 1292 (1943) (invalidating a flat tax on solicitation as applied to the dissemination of religious ideas); or the right of parents, acknowledged in *Pierce v. Society of Sisters,* 268 U.S. 510, 45 S.Ct. 571, 69 L.Ed. 1070 (1925), to direct the education of their children, see *Wisconsin v. Yoder* (1972) (invalidating compulsory school-attendance laws as applied to Amish parents who refused on religious grounds to send their children to school). . . .

The present case does not present such a hybrid situation, but a free exercise claim unconnected with any communicative activity or parental right. Respondents urge us to hold, quite simply, that when otherwise prohibitable conduct is accompanied by religious convictions, not only the convictions but the conduct itself must be free from governmental regulation. We have never held that, and decline to do so now. . . .

Even if we were inclined to breathe into *Sherbert* some life beyond the unemployment compensation field, we would not apply it to require exemptions from a generally applicable criminal law. The *Sherbert* test, it must be recalled, was developed in a context that lent itself to individualized governmental assessment of the reasons for the relevant conduct. [O]ur decisions in the unemployment cases stand for the proposition that where the State has in place a system of individual exemptions, it may not refuse to extend that system to cases of "religious hardship" without compelling reason.

[T]he sounder approach, and the approach in accord with the vast majority of our precedents, is to hold the test inapplicable to such challenges. The government's ability to enforce generally applicable prohibitions of socially harmful conduct, like its ability to carry out other aspects of public policy, "cannot depend on measuring the effects of a governmental action on a religious objector's spiritual development." To make an individual's obligation to obey such a law contingent upon the law's coincidence with his religious beliefs, except where the State's interest is "compelling"—permitting him, by virtue of his beliefs, "to become a law unto himself," *Reynolds v. United States,*—contradicts both constitutional tradition and common sense.

The "compelling government interest" requirement seems benign, because it is familiar from other fields. But using it as the standard that must be met before the government may accord different treatment on the basis of race, or before the government may regulate the content of speech, is not remotely comparable to using it for the purpose asserted here. What it produces in those other fields—equality of treatment, and an unrestricted flow of contending speech—are constitutional norms; what it would produce here—a private right to ignore generally applicable laws—is a constitutional anomaly.[3] . . .

[I]f "compelling interest" really means what it says (and watering it down here would subvert its rigor in the other fields where it is applied), many laws will not meet the test. Any society adopting such a system would be courting anarchy, but that danger increases in direct proportion to the society's diversity of religious beliefs, and its determination to coerce or suppress none of them. [P]recisely because we value and protect that religious divergence, we cannot afford the luxury of deeming *presumptively invalid,* as applied to the religious objector, every regulation of conduct that does not protect an interest of the highest order. . . .

[A] number of States have made an exception to their drug laws for sacramental peyote use. But to say that a nondiscriminatory religious-practice exemption is permitted, or even that it is desirable, is not to say that it is constitutionally required, and that the appropriate occasions for its creation can be discerned by the courts. It may fairly be said that leaving accommodation to the political process will place at a relative disadvantage those religious practices that are not widely engaged in; but that unavoidable consequence of democratic government must be preferred to a system in which each conscience is a law unto itself or in which judges weigh the social importance of all laws against the centrality of all religious beliefs.

---

[3]   Justice O'Connor suggests that "[t]here is nothing talismanic about neutral laws of general applicability," and that all laws burdening religious practices should be subject to compelling-interest scrutiny because "the First Amendment unequivocally makes freedom of religion, like freedom from race discrimination and freedom of speech, a 'constitutional norm,' not an 'anomaly.' " (O'Connor, J., concurring). But this comparison with other fields supports, rather than undermines, the conclusion we draw today. Just as we subject to the most exacting scrutiny laws that make classifications based on race, or on the content of speech, so too we strictly scrutinize governmental classifications based on religion. But we have held that race-neutral laws that have the *effect* of disproportionately disadvantaging a particular racial group do not thereby become subject to compelling-interest analysis under the Equal Protection Clause, see *Washington v. Davis,* [§ 13.2.3] (police employment examination); and we have held that generally applicable laws unconcerned with regulating speech that have the *effect* of interfering with speech do not thereby become subject to compelling-interest analysis under the First Amendment, see *Citizen Publishing Co. v. United States,* 394 U.S. 131, 139, 89 S.Ct. 927, 22 L.Ed.2d 148 (1969) (antitrust laws). Our conclusion that generally applicable, religion-neutral laws that have the effect of burdening a particular religious practice need not be justified by a compelling governmental interest is the only approach compatible with these precedents.

Because respondents' ingestion of peyote was prohibited under Oregon law, and because that prohibition is constitutional, Oregon may, consistent with the Free Exercise Clause, deny respondents unemployment compensation when their dismissal results from use of the drug. The decision of the Oregon Supreme Court is accordingly reversed.

It is so ordered.

JUSTICE O'CONNOR, with whom JUSTICE BRENNAN, JUSTICE MARSHALL, and JUSTICE BLACKMUN join as to Parts I and II, concurring in the judgment.* . . .

I.   [T]he constitutional question upon which we granted review—whether the Free Exercise Clause protects a person's religiously motivated use of peyote from the reach of a State's general criminal law prohibition—is properly presented in this case. . . .

II.   [T]he freedom to act, unlike the freedom to believe, cannot be absolute. [T]he Government [must] justify any substantial burden on religiously motivated conduct by a compelling state interest and by means narrowly tailored to achieve that interest. [I]f, as an empirical matter, a government's criminal laws might usually serve a compelling interest in health, safety, or public order, the First Amendment at least requires a case-by-case determination of the question, sensitive to the facts of each particular claim. [W]e cannot assume, merely because a law carries criminal sanctions and is generally applicable, that the First Amendment never requires the State to grant a limited exemption for religiously motivated conduct. . . .

III.   [R]espondents do not seriously dispute that Oregon has a compelling interest in prohibiting the possession of peyote by its citizens. [T]he critical question in this case is whether exempting respondents from the State's general criminal prohibition "will unduly interfere with fulfillment of the governmental interest." . . . Because the health effects caused by the use of controlled substances exist regardless of the motivation of the user, the use of such substances, even for religious purposes, violates the very purpose of the laws that prohibit them. Cf. *State v. Massey,* 229 N.C. 734, 51 S.E.2d 179 (denying religious exemption to municipal ordinance prohibiting handling of poisonous reptiles), *appeal dism'd sub nom. Bunn v. North Carolina,* 336 U.S. 942, 69 S.Ct. 813, 93 L.Ed. 1099 (1949). Moreover, in view of the societal interest in preventing trafficking in controlled substances, uniform application of the criminal prohibition at issue is essential to

---

*   Although Justice Brennan, Justice Marshall, and Justice Blackmun join Parts I and II of this opinion, they do not concur in the judgment.

the effectiveness of Oregon's stated interest in preventing any possession of peyote.

[G]ranting a selective exemption in this case would seriously impair Oregon's compelling interest in prohibiting possession of peyote by its citizens. Under such circumstances, the Free Exercise Clause does not require the State to accommodate respondents' religiously motivated conduct. . . .

JUSTICE BLACKMUN, with whom JUSTICE BRENNAN and JUSTICE MARSHALL join, dissenting.

[I]t is important to articulate in precise terms the state interest involved. It is not the State's broad interest in fighting the critical "war on drugs" that must be weighed against respondents' claim, but the State's narrow interest in refusing to make an exception for the religious, ceremonial use of peyote. . . . It offers, however, no evidence that the religious use of peyote has ever harmed anyone. The factual findings of other courts cast doubt on the State's assumption that religious use of peyote is harmful. . . .

The State's apprehension of a flood of other religious claims is purely speculative. Almost half the States, and the Federal Government, have maintained an exemption for religious peyote use for many years, and apparently have not found themselves overwhelmed by claims to other religious exemptions. Allowing an exemption for religious peyote use would not necessarily oblige the State to grant a similar exemption to other religious groups. The unusual circumstances that make the religious use of peyote compatible with the State's interests in health and safety and in preventing drug trafficking would not apply to other religious claims. Some religions, for example, might not restrict drug use to a limited ceremonial context, as does the Native American Church. See, *e.g., Olsen,* 279 U.S.App.D.C., at 7, 878 F.2d, at 1464 ("the Ethiopian Zion Coptic Church . . . teaches that marijuana is properly smoked 'continually all day' "). Some religious claims, involve drugs such as marijuana and heroin, in which there is significant illegal traffic, with its attendant greed and violence, so that it would be difficult to grant a religious exemption without seriously compromising law enforcement efforts. That the State might grant an exemption for religious peyote use, but deny other religious claims arising in different circumstances, would not violate the Establishment Clause. [T]he State must treat all religions equally, and not favor one over another, this obligation is fulfilled by the uniform application of the "compelling interest" *test* to all free exercise claims, not by reaching uniform *results* as to all claims. A showing that religious peyote use does not unduly interfere with the State's interests is "one that probably few other religious groups or sects could make." *Yoder*. . . .

NOTES

1.   *Church of Lukumi Babalu Aye, Inc. v. City of Hialeah,* 508 U.S. 520, 113 S.Ct. 2217, 124 L.Ed.2d 472 (1993). Santeria is a combination of tradition African religion and Roman Catholicism. Adherents include thousands of people, typically Cuban-Americans, who live in South Florida. A principal form of devotion is ritual sacrifice of animals such as goats, doves, and sheep. The animals are killed by cutting their carotid arteries in their necks, after which the congregation usually (but not always) eats the cooked remains. When a Santeria church planned to establish a house of worship in the city of Hialeah, the city council passed several ordinances specifically designed to forbid animal sacrifice. One law made it illegal to "sacrifice" any animal in the city limits, and defined "sacrifice" as the "unnecessary" killing of an animal in a public or private ritual "not for the primary purpose of food consumption." The law created an exception for slaughtering by "licensed establishments" and for "small numbers of hogs and/or cattle per week in accordance with an exemption provided by state law."

Kennedy, J., for the Court, invalidated the various ordinances. *Smith*'s requirements that the law be neutral and of general applicability are "interrelated," and thus failure to satisfy one requirement is "a likely indication that the other has not been satisfied." These ordinances did not meet either requirement. Under *Smith,* if the object of a law is to restrict practices because of their religious motivation, then "the law is not neutral." The object of the Hialeah ordinances was to infringe on Santeria practices. Additional evidence of "religious gerrymandering" is that the law defines "sacrifice" to exclude almost all killing of animals *except* for killing for religious reasons. The law even exempted Kosher slaughter of animals. Under *Smith,* if the state grants individualized exemptions from general requirements, the state "may not refuse to extend that system of cases of 'religious hardship' without compelling reason."

If the city is concerned about improper disposal of animal remains, it could impose general rules governing disposal of organic garbage. If the city is concerned about how animals are treated while in confinement, it could regulate that, regardless of the motivation for confining the animal. Instead, the city chose to prohibit possession of animals only if the purpose is sacrifice. The city stated that it wanted to prevent cruelty to animals, but it allowed many types of animal deaths for nonreligious reasons, such as fishing, extermination of mice in the home, and the infliction of pain "in the interest of medical science." The law even allowed the use of live rabbits to train greyhounds.

2. Congress responded to *Smith* by enacting the Religious Freedom Restoration Act of 1993 (RFRA), 42 U.S.C.A. §§ 2000bb, et seq. Section 2000bb–1 provides: "Government shall not substantially burden a person's exercise of religion even if the burden results from a rule of general applicability," unless the Government shows that the burden is "in furtherance of a compelling governmental interest," and is "the least restrictive means of furthering" that interest.

    City of Boerne v. Flores, 521 U.S. 507, 117 S.Ct. 2157, 138 L.Ed.2d 624 (1997) (5 to 4), [excerpted in § 6.1], invalidated RFRA, as not within Congressional power to impose on the *states* under § 5 of the Fourteenth Amendment. (Zoning authorities denied the Catholic Archbishop a building permit to enlarge a church that had become too small for its worshipers because it was in an historic preservation district. RFRA, however, is constitutional as applied to the federal government.

3. The Court applied RFRA to a federal law in *Gonzales v. O Centro Espirita Beneficente Uniao do Vegetal* (UDV), 546 U.S. 418, 126 S.Ct. 1211, 163 L.Ed.2d 1017 (2006). UDV is a religious sect that participates in communion by drinking hoasca, a tea that contains hallucinogenic plants from the Amazon Rainforest. UDV sought to enjoin the Federal Government from enforcing the Controlled Substances Act to ban the sect's use of hoasca. UDV relied on RFRA, which prohibits the Federal Government from substantially burdening a person's exercise of religion, "even if the burden results from a rule of general applicability," unless the Government can show that the burden (1) furthers a compelling government interest and is (2) the least restrictive means of furthering that interest. Roberts, C.J., for a unanimous Court, held that the Government had not met its burden. In 1994, Congress created an exception under the Controlled Substances Act to allow all recognized Indian tribes to use peyote. Everything the Government says about hoasca applies in equal measure to peyote. Given the peyote exemption, it is difficult to deny a "similar exception for the 130 or so American members of the UDV who want to practice" their religion. "The well-established peyote exception also fatally undermines the Government's

broader contention that the Controlled Substances Act establishes a closed regulatory system that admits of no exceptions under RFRA."

4.   *Hosanna-Tabor Evangelical Lutheran Church and School v. E.E.O.C.*, 565 U.S. ___, 132 S.Ct. 694, 181 L.Ed.2d 650 (2012). The Lutheran Church-Missouri Synod divides its schoolteachers into two categories: "called" and "lay." It regards "called" teachers as called to their vocation by God. They must complete certain academic requirements, including theological study. If called, the teacher receives the formal title "Minister of Religion, Commissioned." In contrast, "lay" teachers do not have to be Lutheran and there is no requirement that the Synod train them. Lay and called teachers at Hosanna-Tabor "generally performed the same duties," but the school hires lay teachers only if called teachers are unavailable. The Equal Employment Opportunity Commission (EEOC) sued the Lutheran congregation, alleging that the school fired a "called" teacher in retaliation for her threatening to file an Americans with Disabilities Act (ADA) lawsuit.

Roberts, C.J., for the unanimous Court, held that both the Establishment and Free Exercise Clauses bar this action when the employer is a religious group and the employee is one of the group's ministers. The government cannot interfere "with the decision of a religious group to fire one of its ministers." The Court rejected the EEOC's argument that the First Amendment analysis is the same, whether the association "is the Lutheran Church, a labor union, or a social club."

Employment Division, Department of Human Resources v. Smith (1990) does not prevent recognizing a ministerial exception. Although the ADA's prohibition on retaliation is a valid and neutral law of general applicability, "a church's selection of its ministers is unlike an individual's ingestion of peyote." *Smith* involved the government regulating only outward physical acts. In this case, the EEOC is interfering with "an internal church division that affects the faith and the mission of the church itself." *Smith* distinguished between the government regulating "physical acts" from the government lending "its power to one or the other side in controversies over religious authority or dogma."

The EEOC argued that the church school's reason for firing the teacher (she did not commit to internal dispute resolution) was only a pretext, but that "misses the point." The purpose of the ministerial exception "is not to safeguard a church's decision to fire a minister only when it is made for a religious reason. The exception instead ensures that the authority to select and control who will minister to the faithful—a matter 'strictly ecclesiastical'—is the church's alone."

5. In 2011, San Francisco considered enacting a city ordinance that would criminalize the circumcision of males under age 18. However, it has no problem with parents who pierce the ears of their baby girls so they can wear earrings. Doctors often say that circumcision is healthy because it makes it harder to contract certain diseases, which is why Christians often circumcise their baby boys. Jews circumcise for religious reasons, a sign of the Covenant between God and man. This proposed city law would forbid all circumcision, grant no religious waiver, impose a year in jail, and a $1,000 fine per violation.

A state law prevented this ordinance from being enacted, so it was not tested in litigation. If it were enacted, would it be a "generally applicable law," and thus constitutional, under *Employment Division v. Smith*, or is it not a neutral law of general applicability, because it allows parents to pierce the ears of baby girls?

Glossary

A

Advisory Opinion. A nonbinding statement by a court that interprets a statute or advises on the meaning of a constitutional provision in response to the request of a party for a legal answer. The Constitution prohibits federal courts from issuing advisory opinions, because Article III limits federal jurisdiction to a case or controversy. Some state constitutions allow their courts to issue advisory opinions

Alternative Holding. *See also* Holding. In a decision, alternative holdings all count as holdings. For example, if a court invalidates a state law as violating both equal protection and due process (the law violates equal protection and the law violates due process), both holdings are precedent. Courts often say that each alternative holding is binding and the court will not treat the holdings as dictum. Courts and litigants argue whether a statement of the law is an alternative holding or dictum.

Amicus Curiae. *Amicus Curiae* (Latin for "friend of the court") is someone who is not a party to a lawsuit but files a brief before the court (or someone the court invites to file a brief) because that person or entity has in interest in the legal question before the Court. Often this phrase is shortened to "*amicus*"

Anti-Federalists. The name for the group of people who opposed the creation of a stronger U.S. federal government; they later opposed the ratification of the Constitution of 1787. Anti-federalists included Patrick Henry, Samuel Adams, George Mason, and James Monroe.

Appeal. To seek to have a higher court review the decision of the lower court is to appeal the decision. The party that makes the appeal is the appellant. An "appeal as of right" is an appeal to a higher court when the appellant does not first need to obtain permission from the higher court.

Apportionment. Also called, one person, one vote. The Equal Protection Clause requires legislative voting districts to have about the same population. *Reynolds v. Sims*, 377 U.S. 533 (1964).

Articles of Confederation. The Continental Congress adopted the Articles of Confederation on November 15, 1777. It was the first Constitution of the United States and was effective from March 1, 1781, until 1789 when the present Constitution was ratified.

Attainder, Bill of. A Bill of Attainder is a bill that the legislature enacts to directs that a person suffer punishment (often, the death sentence) without a trial. The U.S. Constitution prohibits bills of attainder, Art. I, § 9, cl. 3 (banning Congress from enacting bills of attainder) and Art. I, § 10, clause 1 (banning states from enacting bills of attainder).

B

Bench Opinion. A court's oral opinion, which the judge delivers in open court

Bill of Rights. The first ten amendments to the US Constitution. The states ratified them in 1791. Sometimes the Bill of Rights refers to the first eight amendments.

C

***Certiorari*, Writ of.** *Certiorari* is from the Law Latin, meaning "to be more fully informed."

> "The discretionary writ of certiorari has come to control access to almost all branches of Supreme Court jurisdiction. Appeal jurisdiction has been narrowly limited, and certification of questions from federal courts of appeals has fallen into almost complete desuetude. Certiorari control over the cases that come before the Court enables the Court to define its own institutional role." CHARLES ALAN WRIGHT ET AL., FEDERAL PRACTICE AND PROCEDURE § 4004, vol. 16B (3d ed. updated as of 2016).

Certiorari is often abbreviated as "*cert.*" A "Petition for *Certiorari*" is the paper the petitioner files before the U.S. Supreme Court to seek review of the lower federal court or the state court. The party that seeks review is the petitioner.

Concurring in the Result. An opinion by a justice (that the justices may join) that agrees with the result of the majority but offers different reasoning.

Concurring Opinion. An opinion by a justice (that other justices may joint) that agrees with the majority but adds other reasoning or offers limiting principles or makes distinctions that the majority does not embrace.

Confederation. *See also* Federation. A confederation is a union of states where the central government has less power than it would have in a federation.

> "A confederation is a stronger form of association than an alliance . . . , but is weaker than a federation. The individual member units retain their status as sovereign States, and are separately recognized as members of the international community. This distinguishes a confederation from a federation in which the constituent States surrender their sovereignty to a central authority retaining only internal constitutional autonomy."

Fred L. Morrison, *Confederations of States*, in 2 THE MAX PLANCK ENCYCLOPEDIA OF PUBLIC INTERNATIONAL LAW 601, 602 (Rüdiger Wolfrum ed., 2012).

Constitutional Convention of 1787. This convention drafted the Constitution, which the states adopted in 1789.

D

Dictum. *See also* Holding; *Stare Decisis*; Precedent; *Res Judicata*. A case is only authority (precedent) for what it actually decides. *Dictum* or *Obiter Dictum* [Latin meaning, "something said in passing"] is statement of opinion or belief within a case that is not necessary to the decision of the case. *Dictum*, unlike precedent, does not bind the Court when deciding another case. The plural of *dictum* is *dicta*.

Dissenting Opinion. An opinion by a justice (that other justices may join) that disagrees with the reasoning and result of the majority opinion.

Diversity Jurisdiction. Article III allows federal court jurisdiction to extend to cases between citizens of different states are often called "diversity jurisdiction."

In general, federal courts have jurisdiction because of the nature of the question (often called, federal question jurisdiction—all cases arising under the Constitution, U.S. laws, and treaties, admiralty and maritime jurisdiction) or because of the nature the parties (ambassadors, other public ministers, and consuls; cases to which the United States is a party, controversies between two or more states, between a state and citizens of another state, citizens of different states, citizens of the same state claiming lands under the grants of different states, and between a state or citizens thereof and foreign states, citizens or subjects). Article III, § 2, clause 1.

Due Process. There is a due process clause in the U.S. Constitution, 5th Amendment, which applies to the Federal Government. The due process clause in the 14th Amendment applies to the states. In addition, the Court has incorporated (applied to the states under the incorporation doctrine) the 5th Amendment's due process clause.

E

Eminent Domain. The power of a government (state, local, or federal) to take private property for public use and paying just compensation. In the United Kingdom, this power is called "compulsory purchase."

Exclusionary Rule. The Exclusionary Rule excludes or suppresses evidence obtained in violation of an accused person's constitutional rights.

> "The deterrence of unreasonable searches and seizures is a major purpose of the exclusionary rule [but it] serves other purposes as well. [C]ourts [should] not become 'accomplices in willful disobedience of a Constitution they are sworn to uphold.' . . . A third purpose of the exclusionary rule [is to assure] 'the people—all potential victims of unlawful government conduct—that the government would not profit from its lawless behavior, thus minimizing the risk of seriously undermining popular trust in the government.'"

Wayne R. LaFave, Jerold H. Israel, Nancy J. King, & Orin S. Kerr, Criminal Procedure § 3.1(b) (4th ed. updated as of 2015).

Executive Privilege. Executive privilege is the claim that the President should be exempt from disclosing to Congress or to the courts certain information because it involves matters that should be kept secret, such as sensitive foreign policy or national security matters. The leading case on Executive Privilege is *United States v. Nixon*, 418 U.S. 683, 706, 94 S. Ct. 3090, 3106–07, 41 L. Ed. 2d 1039 (1974), which said—

> "neither the doctrine of separation of powers, nor the need for confidentiality of high-level communications, without more, can sustain an absolute, unqualified Presidential privilege of immunity from judicial process under all circumstances. The President's need for complete candor and objectivity from advisers calls for great deference from the courts. However, when the privilege depends solely on the broad, undifferentiated claim of public interest in the confidentiality of such conversations, a confrontation with other values arises. Absent a claim of need to protect military, diplomatic, or sensitive national security

secrets, we find it difficult to accept the argument that even the very important interest in confidentiality of Presidential communications is significantly diminished by production of such material for in camera inspection with all the protection that a district court will be obliged to provide."

***Ex Post Facto* Clause.** The U.S. Constitution forbidding Congress (Art. I, § 9, cl. 3) and the states (Art. I, § 10, cl. 1) from enacting *ex post facto* (having retroactive force or effect) laws. These clauses limit Congress and state legislatures when enacting penal laws that have a retrospective effect. An *ex post facto* law is a measure that imposes criminal liability on past transactions. Early in its history, the Supreme Court determined that the *ex post facto* clauses only prohibited the states and the federal government from passing *criminal or penal* measures that had a retroactive effect. 2 RONALD D. ROTUNDA & JOHN E. NOWAK, TREATISE ON CONSTITUTIONAL LAW: SUBSTANCE AND PROCEDURE § 15.9(b)(i) (Thomson Reuters, 5th ed. 2012).

F

Federal Question Jurisdiction. Article III allows federal court jurisdiction to extend to cases involving federal questions, often called "federal question jurisdiction."

In general, federal courts have jurisdiction because of the nature of the question (often called, federal question jurisdiction—all cases arising under the Constitution, U.S. laws, and treaties, admiralty and maritime jurisdiction) or because of the nature the parties (ambassadors, other public ministers, and consuls; cases to which the United States is a party, controversies between two or more states, between a state and citizens of another state, citizens of different states, citizens of the same state claiming lands under the grants of different states, and between a state or citizens thereof and foreign states, citizens or subjects). Article III, § 2, clause 1.

Federation. *See also* Confederation. A federation is a union of states united under a strong central authority but the individual states also retain limited local sovereignty over local affairs.

Fruit-of-the-Poisonous-Tree Doctrine. The Fruit-of-the-Poisonous-Tree Doctrine bars introducing evidence derived from an illegal search, arrest, or interrogation because the evidence (the "fruit") was tainted by the illegality (the "poisonous tree").

G

Gerrymandering. Even if an electoral district has the same number of voters as another electoral district, the district may be drawn in such a way as to give one political party an advantage over the other. For example, if both districts contain 100,000 people and the 60% of the people are Republican, those two districts may not elect two Republican legislators. A Democratic majority in the state legislature may draw the two districts so that one district is overwhelming Republican (90% while the other is majority Democrat, so that there will be one Democratic legislator although the Republicans have, over all, 60% of the voters.

The practice of manipulating a geographical area into electoral districts, often of highly irregular shape, to advantage one political party is called gerrymandering. The Boston Gazette on 26 March 1812 may have been the first to use the term, "gerrymandering." The portmanteau derives from Massachusetts Governor Elbridge Gerry, who signed the bill that altered the state Senate's voting districts to favor his party, the Democratic-Republican Party. One newly created district resembled a salamander, inspiring a critic to coin the word *gerrymander* by combining the governor's name, *Gerry*, with the ending of *salamander*. Gerry later was elected as Vice President under James Madison.

H

Harmless Error. The Court will not reverse the lower court's error (*e.g.*, its refusal to admit evidence or its admission of evidence that it should have excluded) if the error is "harmless," that is, an error that did not affect the result. If the lower court error is constitutional, the higher court will reverse unless there is no reasonable possibility that the error might have contributed to the conviction (harmless beyond a reasonable doubt). If the error is statutory, the higher court will reverse if there is a significant possibility that the jury would have acquitted but for the error.

Federal Rules of Criminal Procedure, Rule 52 provides:

> **(a) Harmless Error.** Any error, defect, irregularity, or variance that does not affect substantial rights must be disregarded.
>
> **(b) Plain Error.** A plain error that affects substantial rights may be considered even though it was not brought to the court's attention.

Holding. *See also* Alternative Holding. The holding is the part of the opinion of the court that announces the rule of law (the precedent) that the court is applying to the particular facts of the case.

See Bravo v. United States, 532 F.3d 1154, 1162 (11th Cir. 2008): "[I]n this circuit additional or alternative holdings are not dicta, but instead are as binding as solitary holdings."

Courts and commentators often argue whether the court's statement of a rule is holding, alternative holding, or *dictum*.

I

Incorporation Doctrine. Over the years, the Court interpreted the 14th Amendment's due process clause to incorporate most of the provisions in the Bill of Rights to apply those rights to the states

In Forma Pauperis. *In forma pauperis* comes from Latin, meaning "in the manner of a pauper." Paupers or indigents are typically excused from paying filing fees and court costs when suing. See 28 U.S.C.A. § 1915, Proceedings *in forma pauperis*.

Issue preclusion. Issue preclusion means:

> "When an issue of fact or law is actually litigated and determined by a valid and final judgment, and the determination is essential to the judgment, the determination is conclusive in a subsequent action between the parties, whether on the same or a different claim." American Law Institute, Restatement (Second) of the Law of Judgments § 27 (ALI 1982).

J

Judicial Restraint versus Judicial Activism. Judicial Restraint of Judicial Self-Restraint refers to the principle that some Justices have advocated (notably Justice Felix Frankfurter) that the Court should be reluctant to invalidate statutes unless their constitutionality is relatively clear and within specific prohibitions of the Constitution (such as free speech, search and seizure).

In contrast, Judicial Activism refers to the principle that the Court should be more active in invalidating legislation, even when there is no textual connection between the Constitution and the right in question, *e.g.*, abortion.

Judicial Review. Judicial review refers to the power of any state or federal court to review and invalidate legislative and executive actions as being unconstitutional.

In the United States, all courts have this power, while in Europe constitutional issues are often limited to the Constitutional Court.

L

Law of the Case. Law of the case is a principle that provides that a decision in a former appeal of a case is binding on the parties in a later appeal of that case.

M

Mandamus. *Mandamus* comes from Latin, meaning "we command." A court issues a writ of mandamus to compel the lower court (or a governmental body or government official) to perform a particular act or to correct a prior act or failure to act.

N

Natural Law. "Natural law" refers to a set of universal principles and rules that properly govern moral human conduct.

In contrast, "positive law" refers statutes and regulations, that is, law enacted by a duly authorized legislature or other body authorized to enact law. Positive law means law that human authority has established. Statutory law may codify natural law (*e.g.*, the law against murder is a natural law), but the prohibition against murder is preexisting in the law of nature and human beings can discover this prohibition through rational analysis.

Murder, rape, theft are all *malum in se* (Latin, meaning "wrong in itself"), while the prohibition against driving on the wrong side of the state is *malum prohibitum* (from the Latin, "wrong [because] prohibited"), illegal only because the statute or regulation makes it illegal.

> "An offense *malum in se* is properly defined as one which is naturally evil as adjudged by the sense of a civilized community, whereas an act *malum prohibitum* is wrong only because made so by statute. For the reason that acts malum in se have, as a rule, become criminal offenses by the course and development of the common law, an impression has sometimes obtained that only acts can be so classified which the common law makes criminal; but this is not at all the test. An act can be, and frequently is, *malum in se*, when it amounts only to a civil trespass, provided it has a malicious element or manifests an evil nature or wrongful disposition to harm or injure another in his person or property. The distinction between the two classes of acts is well stated in 19 Am. & Eng. Enc. (2d Ed.), at page 705: 'An offense *malum in se* is

one which is naturally evil, as murder, theft, and the like. Offenses at common law are generally *malum in se*. An offense *malum prohibitum*, on the contrary, is not naturally an evil, but becomes so in consequence of being forbidden.' " *State v. Horton*, 51 S.E. 945, 946 (N.C. 1905) (internal citation omitted).

Necessary and Proper Clause. Article I, § 8, clause 18, which is also called the Sweeping Clause:

> "To make all Laws which shall be necessary and proper for carrying into Execution the foregoing Powers, and all other Powers vested by this Constitution in the Government of the United States, or any Department or Office thereof."

O

Obiter Dictum. *See also Dictum. Obiter Dictum* is Latin meaning, "something said in passing." *Obiter dictum* is another term meaning dictum.

One Person, One Vote. Also called, one man, one vote. The Equal Protection Clause requires legislative voting districts to have about the same population. *Reynolds v. Sims*, 377 U.S. 533 (1964).

P

Parallel Citations. Sometimes more than one reporter system will reprint a case. These additional publications of a case are called parallel citations. For example, the Supreme Court decision in *Miranda v. Arizona*, is found at 384 U.S. 436, 86 S. Ct. 1602, 16 L. Ed. 2d 694 (1966). That means it is found at volume 384 of the U.S. Reports (beginning at p. 436); volume 86 of the Supreme Court Reporter System (beginning at p. 1602); volume 16 of Lawyer's Edition 2d (beginning at p. 694.

Notice that the citation is to 16 L.Ed.2d. There is also 16 L.Ed., which refers to the first series of Lawyer's Edition. If you turn to 16 L.Ed. 694, you will find a different decision, *Tate v. Carney*, 65 U.S. (24 How.) 357, 16 L. Ed. 693 (1860). There was no Supreme Court Reporter going back that far. The reference to "24 How." means that it is volume 24 of the Reporter System when Benjamin Chew Howard was the official reporter. He was the official reporter from 1843 to 1860). Volumes 42–65 of the U.S Reporter System refers to volumes 1 to 24 of the Howard Reporter System, abbreviated "How."

Per Curiam. An opinion that the court as a whole signs instead of an individual judge signing as the author

Peremptory Challenge. When the lawyers review the prospective jurors in either a civil or criminal case, the law typically allows the lawyer for each party to excuse a juror "for cause," that is, a reason why the juror cannot serve. (The prospective juror, for example, knows one of the defendants.) The law typically gives each party a certain number of peremptory challenges, that is, the lawyer can excuse a prospective juror without cause.

Plurality Opinion. An opinion that does not attract the votes of enough justices to constitute a majority, but receiving more votes than any other opinion.

Political Question. A "political question" is a question that is non-judiciable. A political question is a question that federal courts will not decide.

> Prominent on the surface of any case held to involve a political question is found a textually demonstrable constitutional commitment of the issue to a coordinate political department; or a lack of judicially discoverable and manageable standards for resolving it; or the impossibility of deciding without an initial policy determination of a kind clearly for nonjudicial discretion; or the impossibility of a court's undertaking independent resolution without expressing lack of the respect due coordinate branches of government or an unusual need for unquestioning adherence to a political decision already made; or the potentiality of embarrassment from multifarious pronouncements by various departments on one question.

Baker v. Carr, 309 U.S. 186, 217, 82 S.Ct. 691, 710 (1962).

Positive Law. "Positive law" refers statutes and regulations, that is, law enacted by a duly authorized legislature or other body authorized to enact law. Positive law means law that human authority has established.

Positive law should be contrasted with "natural law," which refers to a set of universal principles and rules that properly govern moral human conduct. Statutory law may codify natural law (*e.g.*, the law against murder), but the prohibition against murder is preexisting in the law of nature and human beings discover this prohibition through rational analysis.

Murder is *malum in se*, while the prohibition against driving on the wrong side of the state is *malum prohibitum* (from the Latin, "wrong [because] prohibited"), illegal only because the statute or regulation makes it illegal.

> "An offense *malum in se* is properly defined as one which is naturally evil as adjudged by the sense of a civilized community, whereas an act *malum prohibitum* is wrong only because made so by statute. For the reason that

acts *malum in se* have, as a rule, become criminal offenses by the course and development of the common law, an impression has sometimes obtained that only acts can be so classified which the common law makes criminal; but this is not at all the test. An act can be, and frequently is, *malum in se*, when it amounts only to a civil trespass, provided it has a malicious element or manifests an evil nature or wrongful disposition to harm or injure another in his person or property. The distinction between the two classes of acts is well stated in 19 Am. & Eng. Enc. (2d Ed.), at page 705: 'An offense *malum in se* is one which is naturally evil, as murder, theft, and the like. Offenses at common law are generally *malum in se*. An offense *malum prohibitum*, on the contrary, is not naturally an evil, but becomes so in consequence of being forbidden.' " *State v. Horton*, 51 S.E. 945, 946 (N.C. 1905)(internal citation omitted).

Precedent. *See also Stare Decisis; Dictum; Obiter Dictum; Res Judicata.* If a case is precedent, the Court must follow its prior ruling when deciding the case before it. Similar cases are subject to the same rule of law, unless the Court overrules its prior precedent or distinguishes it.

Preemption. Federal preemption means that a federal statute or regulation overrides (preempts) a state statute, regulation, or state constitution. The concept of federal preemption derives from the Supremacy Clause, Art. VI, clause 2. The federal statute may provide for preemption explicitly, or the Court may conclude that the statute impliedly preempts the state law.

Prior Restraint. In cases involving free speech, a governmental restriction on speech or publication *before* its actual expression is a "prior restraint." The Licensing of the Press Act of 1662, an Act of Parliament (14 Car. II. c. 33) prohibited anyone from printing any material unless the appropriate state or clerical functionary first licensed it. No one could import or sell a book without a license. The government required registration of all printing presses and limited the number of master printers to twenty, all of whom had to secure a license and furnish a bond. The First Amendment rejects all that. In modern times, the Court seldom allows any prior restraint.

In contrast to prior restraint is subsequent punishment, which imposes sanctions only after a person has published the offending material. Courts consider prior restraint as a more serious infringement on free speech because it prevents the offending material from ever seeing the light of day. *Nebraska Press Association v.*

Stuart, 427 U.S. 539, 559–60, 96 S. Ct. 2791, 2803, 49 L. Ed. 2d 683 (1976) (most internal citations omitted) explains—

> "prior restraints on speech and publication are the most serious and the least tolerable infringement on First Amendment rights. A criminal penalty or a judgment in a defamation case is subject to the whole panoply of protections afforded by deferring the impact of the judgment until all avenues of appellate review have been exhausted. Only after judgment has become final, correct or otherwise, does the law's sanction become fully operative.

> "A prior restraint, by contrast and by definition, has an immediate and irreversible sanction. If it can be said that a threat of criminal or civil sanctions after publication "chills" speech, prior restraint "freezes" it at least for the time.

> "The damage can be particularly great when the prior restraint falls upon the communication of news and commentary on current events. Truthful reports of public judicial proceedings have been afforded special protection against subsequent punishment. For the same reasons the protection against prior restraint should have particular force as applied to reporting of criminal proceedings, whether the crime in question is a single isolated act or a pattern of criminal conduct.

>> 'A responsible press has always been regarded as the handmaiden of effective judicial administration, especially in the criminal field. Its function in this regard is documented by an impressive record of service over several centuries. The press does not simply publish information about trials but guards against the miscarriage of justice by subjecting the police, prosecutors, and judicial processes to extensive public scrutiny and criticism.' *Sheppard v. Maxwell,* 384 U.S., at 350, 86 S.Ct., at 1515."

Pro Se and ***Pro Per.*** *Pro se* is Latin meaning, "for oneself; on one's own behalf." A *pro se* litigant is a party who appears in court without a lawyer. The litigant represents himself (*pro se*).

Propria persona is Latin meaning, "in his own person." It means the same as "*pro se.*" "*Pro Se*" is typically used in federal court, while the term, "*pro per*" is more typically used in state court.

R

Res Judicata. *Res Judicata* is Latin meaning, "a thing adjudicated." Precedent creates a rule of law and that law (the court's holding) binds others who are similarly situated. *Res judicata* creates a decision that binds the parties to the case; it means that the judicial decision has definitively settled that issue as to the same parties. *Res judicata* is a general term referring two different effects of judgments.—

> " 'The first is the effect of foreclosing any litigation of matters that never have been litigated, because of the determination that they should have been advanced in an earlier suit. The second is the effect of foreclosing relitigation of matters that have once been litigated and decided. The first of these, preclusion of matters that were never litigated, has gone under the name, *'true res judicata,'* or the names, 'merger' and 'bar.' The second doctrine, preclusion of matters that have once been decided, has usually been called *'collateral estoppel.'* "

Charles Alan Wright, The Law of Federal Courts § 100A (5th ed. 1994) (Emphasis added).

S

Separation of Powers. The powers of each of the three branches of the Federal Government serve to check the power of the other branches. This is sometimes called "horizontal federalism."

In addition, the power of the states serve to provide a limited check on the powers of the Federal Government. This is sometimes called, "vertical federalism."

Seriatim Opinions. A series of opinions, each written individually by a different judge, as contrasted to a single opinion of one judge speaking for the court as a whole. Before Chief Justice John Marshall joined the Court, the tradition was for the justices to write seriatim opinions

Slip Opinion. Before the various opinions are collected and published together (*e.g.*, the opinions of a term of court), each is published as a slip opinion, and individual opinion that one can cite as authority even though the court reporter has not published it in final form.

Solicitor General.

> "By law, only the Solicitor General or his designee can conduct and argue before the Supreme Court cases 'in which the United States is interested.' Thus, if a trial court appoints a special, independent prosecutor in order to prosecute a criminal contempt of court, that

court-appointed special prosecutor cannot represent the United States in seeking Supreme Court review of any lower court decision unless the Solicitor General authorizes the filing of such a petition. Because the court-appointed independent prosecutor is really seeking to further the government's unique sovereign interest in vindicating the authority of its judiciary, the case is one in which the United States is 'interested.'

"[The Solicitor General] also has a special relation with the Supreme Court. In fact, the Solicitor General has often been referred to as the "tenth justice." [T]he Court relies on the Solicitor General to confess error if, in the Solicitor General's opinion, there has been error below. It is then up to the Supreme Court to decide whether to accept this confession of error. [L]ower court judges do not necessarily approve of the Solicitor General refusing to support their decisions. Thus, Judge Learned Hand is supposed to have complained: 'It's bad enough to have the Supreme Court reverse you, but I will be damned if I will be reversed by some Solicitor General.'

"Although the Solicitor General serves at the pleasure of the President, by tradition the Solicitor General also acts with some independence. Thus, if the Solicitor General does not believe in the legal validity of the arguments that the government wants presented, he will refuse to sign the brief. In close cases, the Solicitor General will sign the brief but tag on a disclaimer that has become known as 'tying a tin can.' The disclaimer would state, for example, 'The foregoing is presented as the position of the Internal Revenue Service.' The justices would then know that the Solicitor General, although not withholding a legal argument, was not personally sponsoring or adopting the particular legal position."

1 RONALD D. ROTUNDA AND JOHN E. NOWAK, TREATISE ON CONSTITUTIONAL LAW: SUBSTANCE & PROCEDURE § 2.2(b)(Thomson Reuters, 5th ed. 2012).

Standing. In federal court, a party must have "standing" to sue, that is, standing to complain about an alleged injury. In general, the party claiming injury must show (1) that the challenged conduct has caused this alleged injury, and (2) that the interest the litigant seeks to protect is arguably within the zone of interests meant to be regulated by the statutory or constitutional guarantee in question. See, *Association of Data Processing Serv. Organizations, Inc. v. Camp*, 397 U.S. 150, 153–55, 90 S. Ct. 827, 830–31, 25 L. Ed. 2d 184 (1970).

Stare Decisis. *Stare Decisis* is Latin for, "to stand by things decided." *Stare Decisis* means that the Court must follow its precedent.

State Action. The U.S. Constitution generally places restrictions on the state (the Federal Government or the State Government, or their instrumentalities, such as cities, counties, state or federal agencies, or those acting "under color of law," such as the local police, the FBI, and so forth. Hence, in order to find a constitutional violation, the Court must first find "state action." State action can exist even if the person is acting contrary to state law but is still acting under color of state law (*e.g.*, the policeman who breaks into your home without a warrant when state law, and the Constitution, both forbid that).

The only way a private person can violate the Constitution is by holding a slave. That is because the Thirteenth Amendment prohibits all slavery, even if the person holding the slave does not in opposition to state or federal law.

Subpoena. A *subpoena*, from Latin, meaning "under penalty," is a writ or order commanding a person to appear before a court or other tribunal, subject to a penalty for failing to comply.

> ***Subpoena ad Testificandum.*** A *subpoena ad testificandum* ordering a witness to appear and give testimony.

> ***Subpoena Duces Tecum.*** A *subpoena duces tecum* orders the witness to appear in court and to bring specified documents, records, or things.

Supremacy Clause. Article VI, clause 2 of the Constitution provides:

> "This Constitution, and the Laws of the United States which shall be made in Pursuance thereof; and all Treaties made, or which shall be made, under the Authority of the United States, shall be the supreme Law of the Land; and the Judges in every State shall be bound thereby, any Thing in the Constitution or Laws of any State to the Contrary notwithstanding."

Sweeping Clause. Article I, § 8, clause 18, which is also called the Necessary and Proper Clause:

> "To make all Laws which shall be necessary and proper for carrying into Execution the foregoing Powers, and all other Powers vested by this Constitution in the Government of the United States, or any Department or Office thereof."

T

Tenth Amendment. The federal government only has those powers that the Constitution expressly (or impliedly) delegates to it. The Tenth Amendment (as the Court now interprets it) reserves all other powers to the people. Under the modern case law, the Tenth Amendment is a truism—the people have retained all that they have not surrendered. In each state, the people may choose to delegate as much of that power as they wish to their state except where the Constitution explicitly places restraints on the states. Thus, the federal government has the limited powers delegated to it: it can exercise these powers—as well as implied powers necessary and proper to the exercise of those powers—unless that power violates a specific restraint on the federal government embodied in the Constitution.

U

United States Code. When Congress enacts a law, it is part of the U.S. Statutes at Large. Typically, these individual laws are codified in the United States Code (often abbreviated as U.S.C.), which is the official compilation and codification of the general and permanent federal statutes of the United States.

Thomson Reuters Westlaw (a legal publisher) publishes its own version of the U.S. Code called the United State Code Annotated (often-abbreviated U.S.C.A.). This version includes research aids, summaries of cases interpreting the particular section, a summary and citations to the legislative history and commentators for each section.

V

Veto Power. Article I, § 7 of the Constitution grants the President the authority to veto legislation passed by Congress. The President has 10 days (excluding Sundays) to act on legislation or the legislation automatically becomes law. There are two types of vetoes: the "regular veto" and the "pocket veto."

The regular veto is a qualified negative veto. The President returns the unsigned legislation to the originating house of Congress within a 10-day period, often accompanied by a "veto message." Congress can override the President's veto if two-thirds vote of each house votes to override. President George Washington issued the first regular veto on April 5, 1792. The first successful congressional override occurred on March 3, 1845, when Congress overrode President John Tyler's veto of S. 66.

Congress cannot override a pocket veto. It becomes effective when the President fails to sign a bill after Congress has adjourned and is unable to override the veto. Article I, § 7, provides: "the Congress by their adjournment prevent its return, in which case, it shall not be law." Over time, Congress and the President have clashed over the use of the pocket veto, debating the term "adjournment." The President has attempted to use the pocket veto during intra- and inter-session adjournments and Congress has denied this use of the veto. The Legislative Branch, backed by modern court rulings, asserts that the Executive Branch may only pocket veto legislation when Congress has adjourned *sine die* from a session. President James Madison was the first President to use the pocket veto in 1812. See, http://history.house.gov/Institution/Presidential-Vetoes/Presidential-Vetoes/

Voir Dire. *Voir dire* comes from the Law French, meaning "to speak the truth." It refers to jury selection, where a judge or lawyer asks questions of a prospective juror to determine whether the person is qualified and suitable to serve as a juror.

Index